THE WORLD'S GREAT DAILIES
Profiles of Fifty Newspapers

THE WORLD'S GREAT DAILIES

Profiles of Fifty Newspapers

by

JOHN C. MERRILL

University of Maryland

and

HAROLD A. FISHER

Bowling Green (Ohio) State University

COMMUNICATION ARTS BOOKS

HASTINGS HOUSE, PUBLISHERS
New York 10016

Library of Congress Cataloging in Publication Data

Merrill, John Calhoun, 1924–
    The world's great dailies.

    (Communication arts books)
    Bibliography: p.
    Includes index.
    1. Newspapers.   I. Fisher, Harold A., joint author.

II. Title.
PN4731.M446   070   79-19075
ISBN 0-8038-8095-2
ISBN 0-8038-8096-0 pbk.

Published simultaneously in Canada by Copp Clark Ltd., Toronto

Designed by Al Lichtenberg
Printed in the United States of America

*To all those journalists
everywhere who want greatness
for their newspapers and who
work diligently to bring
it about . . .*

Contents

Acknowledgements

INNUMERABLE PERSONS in many parts of the world have contributed significantly to this book. It is as impossible to name them all as it is to forget their help. Some of them, connected with journalism or with university teaching and research, are named in various footnotes throughout the pages which follow. Many others, as staff members of the dailies profiled here, were extremely kind to us as we visited their newspapers and talked with them and their colleagues. (Between us, we have visited about 50 nations, where we have taught, lectured, conducted seminars and workshops, and researched aspects of their media systems.)

Also our sincere gratitude goes to many persons connected with the newspapers who sent use descriptive materials, wrote personal letters, and completed questionnaires for us in these profiles. To all of these—mentioned in notes or in the profiles themselves—we offer our profoundest thanks.

—JCM and HAF, 1979

Preface

It has been over a decade since John Merrill's *Elite Press* was published, for the first time providing an extended discussion of the world's quality daily journalism and forty profiles of representative daily newspapers from all parts of the world. A "gap-filling" and successful book, albeit quite controversial in many quarters, *The Elite Press* struck a responsive chord internationally and was soon out of print. The book's publisher, Pitman Publishing Corp. of New York and London, merged with Fearon Publishers, Inc. of Belmont, California, ceased publication of books of this type, and in 1977 relinquished rights to the book.

Since about 1974 large numbers of journalists and journalism professors around the world have suggested that a revision of *The Elite Press,* or another such book, be written. This obvious interest in a book of this type has led the present authors to develop this volume, which we consider a new book and not simply a revision of *The Elite Press.* Although somewhat similar, it is different in two main ways: (1) it makes no attempt to rank newspapers as to quality as did the 1968 volume, and (2) it provides fifty newspaper profiles instead of forty which appeared in the 1968 book.

In this book, which we are calling *The World's Great Dailies,* there are no "top ten" or "top twenty" papers so designated, and there is no "elite press pyramid" provided with its list of primary, secondary, and tertiary elite. Merrill's 1968 book received its greatest criticism from those who were unhappy with such lists and rankings. In the present volume we are not determining the fifty profiles which are included by survey responses; rather we are arbitrarily selecting the newspapers ourselves for inclusion. We make no pretense of a "scientific selection," and want to emphasize that these are our own choices as representatives of the "great" or best dailies in the world. They are newspapers which we believe (and we have not taken such selection lightly) represent the very best in the world's journalism, regardless of how differently this journalism may manifest itself in different cultures and ideological contexts.

In the General Introduction which follows, we have tried to provide the reader with our extended definition of "great" daily newspapers, and we hope that this will help explain why we have included the journals which we have in this volume. The reader will quickly note that the majority of dailies profiled in this book are from the so-called "Free World"—or the Western capitalistic countries. Since the authors are naturally biased in favor of privately owned papers of the capitalistic and pluralistic press systems, it should come as no surprise that outstanding dailies of these systems get more exposure. This does not mean, of course, that the authors would exclude certain newspapers from countries not preferred ideologically from our category of "great" newspapers. So the reader will find among those newspapers profiled here such dailies as *L'Osservatore Romano, Pravda, Al Ahram, People's Daily,* and *Ha'aretz*—all operating under considerable governmental restriction, pressure, and control.

In spite of the fact that we have eliminated qualitative rankings of newspapers from this book, there will still be many who will criticize us for our audacity in the act of choosing fifty dailies as "great" or "elite" newspapers. Many persons will ask how we can think a certain daily is great—for instance, *Svenska Dagbladet*—if we do not know the Swedish language. Our answer: We have talked with many people we respect, people who do read Swedish and are familiar with the newspapers of Sweden; also we have considered the many serious articles we have read about *Svenska Dagbladet,* and we have based our opinion on the widespread and general reputation which the newspaper has developed. We do not believe that it is necessary for us to actually *read* all the papers included in this volume to pass judgment on them.

Neither of the authors has actually attended Harvard, Oxford, or Heidelberg universities; we do not know them first-hand, but we have no reluctance in designating them as "great universities." And, the authors feel that it is not necessary for us to have personally read Milton's *Paradise Lost* in order to list it among the "great" literary works of all time; likewise, it is not necessary that we have known personally such men as Thomas Jefferson, Winston Churchill, or Franklin D. Roosevelt (or even such men as Francisco Franco, Joseph Stalin, or Mao Tse-tung) to name them as "great" political leaders.

At any rate, we are willing to accept any criticism which comes our way, and we have no hesitation in standing by our newspaper selections, however unpopular some of them may be for certain of our readers. All we can say is that we have been conscientious in our selections, have studied in depth and visited many of these dailies, and are convinced that these profiles are good representatives of the world's "great newspapers."

We regret that many other "great" and "near-great" dailies could not have been included in this volume. For certainly there are many other significant ones which could have been profiled here also. We believe that the fifty found here are all outstanding dailies, illustrating what is meant by quality or "great" newspapers; certainly many others are highly significant dailies also and their absence from this volume does not indicate an inferior status. The fifty here represent the authors' preferences, for the most part, among the newspapers of the world which serve as role-models of quality journalism. A few dailies which we desired originally to profile never responded to our queries;

others responded but were tardy in completing our questionnaire—or they failed to complete it at all.

Some of the newspapers included in this volume did not appear in the 1968 *Elite Press*. For example, several new American dailies have made their way into the profiles of this book—e.g., *The Washington Post*, the Louisville *Courier-Journal*, *The Miami Herald*, *The Wall Street Journal*, and *The Atlanta Constitution*. In addition, *The Times of India* and *The Statesman* (of India) are now profiled, as are Brazil's *Jornal do Brasil* and South Africa's *Rand Daily Mail*. Also we have seen fit to add the excellent *El Pais* (not even in existence in 1968) of Madrid, and *La Vanguardia Española* of Barcelona, *The Straits Times* of Singapore, and the *Süddeutsche Zeitung* of Munich. We feel these are all important additions and should make the present book even more useful than was *The Elite Press*.

*   *   *

Many other important dailies of the world could have been included in this volume, as we have said. And at this point we would like to give the names of some of these we consider especially important:

In the U.S.A.—*The Boston Globe; The Philadelphia Inquirer, The Milwaukee Journal, The Des Moines Register, The* (Memphis) *Commercial Appeal, The* (Portland) *Oregonian, The Washington* (D.C.) *Star, Newsday, Chicago Tribune,* the *Albuquerque Journal,*and *The St. Petersburg Times.*

In Europe—*Dagens Nyheter* (Sweden), *Het Laatste Nieuws* (Belgium), *Voix du Nord* and *Progrès de Lyon* (France); *Il Messaggero* and *Il Giorno* (Italy); *Information* (Denmark); *Nieuwe Rotterdamse Courant* and *Het Vrije Volk* (Holland); *Rheinische Post* (West Germany); *Neues Deutschland* (East Germany); *Journal de Genève* (Switzerland); *Kathimerini* (Greece); *Komsomolskaya Pravda* (USSR); *Rude Pravo* (Czechoslovakia); *Trybuna Ludu* (Poland), and *Politika* (Yugoslavia).

In Asia—*Central Daily News* and *United Daily News* (Republic of China—Taiwan); *Ananda Bazar Patrika* (India); *Manila Times* (Philippines); *Mainichi Shimbun* and *Nihon Keizai* (Japan).

In Latin America—*La Prensa* and *La Nación* (Argentina); *Excélsior* and *Novedades* (Mexico); *Granma* (Cuba); *Correio da Manhã* and *Diario de Noticias* (Brazil); *El Mercurio* (Chile), *El Tiempo* (Colombia), and *El Comercio* (Peru).

In other countries— *East African Standard* (Kenya), *Toronto Daily Star* (Canada), and *The Australian* (Australia).

Of course, we realize that many readers will not like some of our choices, and there will undoubtedly be those who would like to add other dailies to our proposed list. Nevertheless, we stand by our choices of "great" or "elite" daily newspapers and believe that they will be shared by most persons who attempt to keep up with the serious journalism of the world.

We have been struck, during the course of gathering information for this book, with the frequency with which we come across the names of the rather small number of daily "elite" newspapers of the world; their names come up time and time again in conversations with editors, professors, librarians, and government officials—and also in the press itself, and in specialized publications like *Atlas: World Press Review* which presents "news and views from the foreign press" for English-language readers. And, by and large, these names correspond closely to those dealt with in this volume.

So, in spite of common difficulties in presenting the "great" among all man-made products or institutions, we hope that this book of profiles will prove interesting and useful to those desiring to know more about the international press.

J.C.M.
University of Maryland

H.A.F.
Bowling Green (Ohio) State University

1

A GENERAL INTRODUCTION:
The International Scene

"GREAT" NEWSPAPERS –
Striving for Quality and Prestige

IN SPITE OF THE rather bleak and disheartening aspects of the world's press today, it should be made clear at once that this is basically an optimistic book. It sees on the horizon of international journalism a small, but growing, number of serious, responsible newspapers which are generally striving to allay world misunderstanding and to bring mankind into a community of reason. Although this group of serious newspapers is not large at present, it is a very important nucleus around which a more refined and cosmopolitan world press can be built. And there are signs that more and more editors and publishers in many parts of the world are desirous of improving their products, of shattering bonds of provincialism and nationalism, and of emphasizing serious information and interpretation.

This optimistic approach will be scoffed at by many critics of the press who see bad publications tending to drive out good ones by a kind of journalistic Gresham's Law. And these critics can point to numerous cases where, indeed, poor newspapers have lived on where good ones have died. Regardless of these cases, however, increasing quality of the press can be noted around the world: at least during the twentieth century more dailies (and weeklies to a lesser degree) have taken their places as serious, intellectually oriented journals with cosmopolitan outlooks. It appears to these writers that increasing numbers of publishers are finding it can be quite profitable, and much more satisfying, to deal with serious discussion, to value truth and balance, and to present news interpreted in a responsible way. As the international newspaper readers become better educated, raise their level of taste, and seek a higher standard of press performance, there will be a wide assortment of quality newspapers ready to take them on as readers.

Without a doubt these elite papers are among us, getting better all the while, and expanding their numbers with every passing year. It is unfortunate that so many Americans feel that beyond a few United States journals such as *The New York Times, The Washington Post,* and *The Christian Science Monitor* there is only journalistic mediocrity throughout the world. Little do they realize that newspapers of just as high standards, serious purpose, and international significance exist in many nations, and that daily journals such as West Germany's *Frankfurter Allgemeine Zeitung,* Britain's *Guardian,* France's *Le Monde,* Switzerland's *Neue Zürcher Zeitung,* Japan's *Asahi Shimbun,* and Brazil's *O Estado de S. Paulo* take a journalistic back seat to no paper in the United States. It is ignorance, provincialism, or blind nationalism that keeps more of the American people from recognizing the tremendous and notable strides that have taken place in recent years throughout the world. It is cause for hope, for optimism, that such journals exist and, even more, that they appear to be getting better and their number is increasing.

From this optimistic position which sets the tone of the book, let us note briefly the more discouraging aspect of the world press situation—the aspect that is the loudest, the gaudiest, the biggest; the aspect that tends to overshadow the encouraging dimension to such an extent that many citizens tend to lose all hope for the press playing a significant part in cementing international fellowship and in stimulating a rational society.

The pessimistic picture that the average person gets of the world press does not stem from a deficiency in the amount of journalism crossing national borders. Certainly, the person exposing himself to the printed media of communication recognizes that he has no shortage of information. Quantitatively, the world press is far advanced. But, in spite of the fact that the mass media are pouring out a glut of material over vast audiences, distrust and misunderstanding among peoples everywhere reach alarming proportions. This situation may well result from the fact that this verbal glut is still largely tenuous and superficial and not very helpful in overcoming international frustration, animosity, and irrationality.

Alan Simpson, former president of Britain's Institute of Journalists, has echoed a growing chorus of concerned journalists throughout the world in commenting that "we are living in difficult and dangerous days" and that "it is vital that the public be provided with the fullest and most objective coverage of the news."[1] Certainly the world's press has the potential to provide this full and objective news coverage, to help ease tensions and erase unrealistic stereotypes that exist; but in the main it is not living up to this potential. Instead, it either lulls its readers into an unthinking and dangerous complacency or frenetically stretches international animosities and worsens the world's psychic crisis.

An informed public opinion must be forthcoming throughout the world if judicious decisions are to be made; a free-flowing and intelligent supply of news and views must nourish this public opinion. Irrational acts by national groups or nations can have dire consequences in our close-knit world, where, as Barbara Ward has said, "We are all neighbors, sitting on each other's doorsteps."[2]

Lester Markel, when Sunday editor of *The New York Times,* stressed that we "cannot have understanding—and thus peace—among the peoples of the world unless they come to know one another better, unless they have better,

[1] *Journal of the Institute of Journalists,* London, 50:492 (July–August, 1962), p. 89.
[2] Lecture, April, 1961, at School of Journalism, University of Iowa.

truer, information about one another."[3] And he said that the main avenue for
this information is the newspaper. Unfortunately, however, there are far too few
newspapers like the one for which Markel worked; in general the world's press
is a heterogeneous hodgepodge of triviality, too busy entertaining and flashing
atypical and distorted images before its readers to pay much attention to presenting a sane, dignified, and balanced world view. With few exceptions, the
world's press is more concerned with the "gamelike" aspects of its operation, of
helping the reader to forget the deadly seriousness of national and international
affairs and to enjoy himself in the "play" of newsreading.

In other words, the vast majority of the world's newspapers are entertain-
ment/play-oriented and cater in varying degrees to the superficial whims of
"mass" audiences. Perhaps this press orientation is psychologically refreshing to
the readers who would like to escape from the efforts of thinking and concern,
but it does seem sad that so many newspapers fill their columns with shallow,
often inconsequential and incoherent stories when world conditions call for a
more thoughtful world citizenry and more responsible journalism. Even if news
(the accounts of world happenings) is simply a playful exercise at which the
multitudes enjoy themselves, it is discomforting that the real events behind the
verbal images are pragmatically significant and need to be confronted and dealt
with realistically and intelligently.

A mere chronicling of negative aspects of reality, a steady diet of sensation
(war, crime, sex, rioting, etc.) may satiate the mass appetite for vicarious and ef-
fortless "adventure," but it does little to create a homogeneity of thought or
thoughtful people. Most editors and publishers, no doubt, would agree with this
premise, but unfortunately few of them manage to follow it on the pages of their
newspapers.

The popular press—the "hodgepodge press"—calls the people of the world
to play. It does not call them to think, to assess, to become concerned, involved,
or empathic. Its journalism is splashy, superficial, thoughtless, and tenuous. It
is complacent journalism that appeals to self and to *status quo,* to mere verbal
frolicking about the surface of vital issues. It is "supermarket" journalism—a
little of everything for everybody. It shows no thoughtful selection, assessment
of editorial matter, meaning or interpretation. It is vulgar in the truest sense of
the word—speaking to the masses of semiliterates who feel they need to read
something called a "newspaper" but who have no desire to understand the vital
issues of the day, and even less desire to concern themselves with these issues.

When one glances about at the reading fare offered by the world's press
generally and at the disjointed manner in which it is presented, he can understand why astute press critics indict newspapers for being mainly inane sheets
of gossip or instruments of national propaganda seeking to create barriers to understanding by presenting without interpretation "unreal" and "alarmist" news
without a context of meaning and often without follow-up. Many see the press
as perpetuating psychological war among nations and peoples, or as purveying
images of personalities which would imply that eccentric and dangerous persons are the only significant newsmakers.

---

[3] Quoted in Robert U. Brown, "Shop Talk at Thirty," *Editor & Publisher* (April 30, 1960), p. 112.

Envy, resentment, suspicion, and hatred are leaving their marks every-where and one wonders if there is a chance for humanity to survive intact and in a civilized way. The press generally gives little help. Instead of being con-veyors of enlightenment, the national press systems tend too often to be press agents for individual nations or special groups. This nationalistic and conflict-oriented tone is very evident in most of the world's press.[4]

The serious observer of the world press sees contradictions in the news col-umns, discrepancies in reporting among world news agencies, slantings, exag-gerations and exclusions, and opinion in news columns that is shallow and uninformed. Is it any wonder that the world press is doing so little to supplant ignorance with knowledge, bewilderment with understanding, and irrationalism with reason?

But now we should get back to the original thesis: In spite of the dismal picture just painted, there is hope. For there is, in the midst of this desert of journalistic anonymity and mediocrity that is the popular and middle-level press, a small group of newspapers in many nations striving constantly to rise above the hodgepodge journalistic formula. These are the serious newspapers whose standards of editorial practice are conditioned more by an intellectual orientation than by a desire for mammoth circulation or impressive profits. They are serious in tone and lacking in flippancy.

These few notable newspapers found in some fifteen to twenty of the world's nations, often struggling against great odds, comprise the cream of the *elite press* of the world. They are the concerned papers, the knowledgeable papers, the serious papers. And they are the papers which serious people and opinion leaders in all countries take seriously. They are interested in interna-tional undercurrents of similarity, not differences; they appeal to thought and logic, not to prejudices and emotion. They are interested in solidifying the world, not in further splintering it. They are interested in ideas and issues, not in mere facts. They are all relatives of one another, regardless of place of publi-cation or language. They have the same concerns, and they are stubborn and outspoken—no matter what their circulations may be.

While it is true to a degree that "the press rightly holds up a mirror to soci-ety," as a noted British journalist has remarked,[5] a "great" paper must do more.

---

[4] Journalistic ideological "war" had broken out in force during the late 1970s—between the Marxist and the Capitalist press systems, and also between the Western "advanced" press systems and the "underdeveloped" or Third World press systems. Journalists and politicians in one "camp" were—of-ten in *UNESCO* forums—criticizing press systems in another "camp." Typical of such criticisms: Gustav Smid of the Press Department of the Czechoslovak Foreign Ministry in 1978 contended that American journalists deliberately present a distorted view of his nation and that there was really no "free press" in the West. See, "Journalists and World Peace," *The New Republic* (Jan. 21, 1978), p. 21. In addition, Third World nations are persistent in their condemnation of the developed "Western" national press systems for fostering world news "disequilibrium," providing negative and unfair images of the underdeveloped world, impeding the free flow of news, and indulging in "cultural im-perialism." This ideological warfare is being waged even in the world's great newspapers as well as in various international forums such as UNESCO, the International Organization of Journalists, and the IPI.

[5] H. H. Hayman in *Journal of the Institute of Journalists* London, 51:501 (Sept.–Oct., 1963), p. 103. Another British journalist and author, Malcolm Muggeridge, would not quite agree with Hayman; in fact, Muggeridge sees the press generally (but television especially) as a crass distorter of reality and

It must judge events and not simply report them, and have definite opinions and express them courageously. This paper, even if it believed it could do so, would not be satisfied to merely "reflect" society; its mission is far greater than that. It sees itself as a leader, an interpreter, a pioneer into the frontiers of human and international relations. More than attempting simply to reflect society in all of its imperfections, the truly great newspaper hopes to present such news and views as to reform society, or portions of it. The aim of the elite press, then, is directing in a reasonable way instead of reflecting in a fragmented and distorted way.

The great papers continually sort and coordinate the endless stream of news reports, attempting to arrange them so as to give meaning to the news, for these papers realize that news items out of context are only confusing to the reader. As the editors of Switzerland's first-rate *Neue Zürcher Zeitung* have put it, a newspaper should offer "a picture of events, not a blurred mosaic, and to the extent that a newspaper is able to make events clearer and easier to understand, to that extent does it fulfill its mission."[6] *The New York Times'* James Reston echoes this important point when he says that "the news we have to report and explain these days . . . is more intricate and many-sided." He continues, "It does not fit easily into the short news story with the punch lead. It often defies accurate definition in very short space. Very often it rebels against our passion for what is bright and brief."[7]

Looking a little further at the elite press, still rather generally, we will note that this small group of dailies (and some few weeklies) will not appeal to the typical reader looking over a wide assortment of journals at a newsstand. First of all, the makeup or physical appearance of these elite papers will not attract him. For example, the *Neue Zürcher Zeitung,* without a doubt one of the two or three best papers in the world, has a rather dull, ultraserious tone to its page makeup. Headlines are small, pictures are few, and there are no comics, no entertainment (or very little), no crossword puzzles, no women's page. Another top-ranking daily, *Le Monde* of Paris, also is in staid typographical dress and is top-heavy with analytical writing.

Not all elite papers are as typographically and editorially conservative in tone as these two tabloids of Switzerland and France; the few quality dailies of Scandinavia (*Berlingske Tidende* of Copenhagen, for instance) are much more sprightly, both in dress and in editorial character. It can definitely be said, however, that there is little in any of the great papers of the general levity, splash, crackle, and pop that characterizes the general press of the world. The elite press actually attempts to do what the Commission on Freedom of the Press said the press should do for society in its 1947 report—"to present a truthful, comprehensive, and intelligent account of the day's events in a context which gives them meaning."[8] With intelligent realism, editors of the elite papers realize,

a conveyer of nonproductive and largely negative ("harmful") aspects of society. (Public lecture at California State University, Long Beach, Feb. 6, 1978).

[6] Dr. Fred Luchsinger, former foreign editor and later editor of the NZZ.

[7] *The Press in Perspective,* ed. by Ralph Casey (Baton Rouge: Louisiana State University Press, 1963), p. 35.

[8] *A Free and Responsible Press* (Chicago: University of Chicago Press, 1947), p. 20. Such an objective is, of course, impossible, but the great newspapers strive (within their ideologies) to attain it. In the

however, that the most difficult standard to meet is that of "comprehensiveness." The realities of publishing—time, space, money, staff—predicate against comprehensive coverage by any one newspaper, even the massive *New York Times*. But the elite paper, through intelligent editing, tries to compensate for this intrinsic shortcoming.

It should be stressed at this point that prior to this century the serious voices speaking to mass audiences were virtually nonexistent. Isolated intellectual spoke to isolated intellectual usually in an intranational or intracultural context. No truly international newspapers were to be found, and when excellent ones did exist within countries, there was slight chance of their being read abroad except in a few academic centers.

Today, on the other hand, a larger slice of the world's population is literate, even well-educated. And of this educated group more and more persons are able to read foreign languages or have access to serious journals—like *Atlas* of the United States—which give them a rich diet of informed world news and views in translation. In addition, each year more general magazines and newspapers quote in part or in whole from foreign journals. In other words, serious journalism is crossing national borders in an ever-increasing flow and more and more people are being exposed to it directly, through translation, or through opinion leaders in their respective countries. One elite paper quotes another, and a "quality journalism" spreads across nations and across languages and develops a common denominator, not of popular *event/reportorial* journalism, but of *idea/interpretation* journalism that is a catalyst to world reason.

This cooperation of the press of the world in an effort to achieve understanding and international stability should not be simply idealistic theorizing; it should be expected of more and more newspapers as literacy increases and education expands, and as editors and publishers see the good that quality journalism can do. Clarence K. Streit, an American journalist with an outstanding career, has asked if it is too much to expect for the press to help in giving publicity to "reasonable men" who are trying to avoid "the twin dangers of war and endless tension . . . by appeal to sober common sense"?[9] From most of the great newspapers of the world would come a resounding "No, it is not too much to expect!"

This book is designed to show something of the nature of a quality press— what makes it great, how it has developed, and its present-day journalistic philosophy. It aspires to serve not only as an introduction to the world's great newspapers but as an encouragement to those who would like to see the press a powerful agent for social stability and progressive leadership, and to be an inspiration to those publishers and editors who would like to raise their sights, their standards, and their quality.

non-Communist world today one of the main stumbling blocks is the growing number of newspaper strikes which has cut readers of, e.g. *The New York Times*, *The Washington Post*, *The Times*, of London, and *Le Monde*, off completely from their readers for varying periods of time.

[9] "The Press, Atlantic Union and World Peace," *Montana Journalism Review* (Spring, 1962), p. 9.

GREATNESS:

A Matter of Context

"GREAT" NEWSPAPERS which have grown up throughout the world are read by the elite of the country where they are published as well as by the elite in other countries and express a significant segment of international elite opinion. This press is aimed at a rather cohesive audience, and in general its readers are better educated and have a greater interest in public affairs than the average readers of the mass (or popular) press. It is aimed at the educated citizen who is aware of, and concerned about, the central issues of his time, and undoubtedly it is read by more opinion leaders than are other types of newspapers.

In one of its forms, this press has built a reputation for being well informed and expressing serious, well-seasoned opinion of the nation concerned. In a less commendable sense (from a Western viewpoint) it is considered the voice or one of the principal voices of the particular government that permits it to exist. In any sense, it is this press that people who desire to be informed, or indoctrinated with the "line," will want to read regularly.

Through the elite press is disseminated either the thoughtful, pluralistic, and sophisticated dialogue of a free society, or the necessary social and political guidance of the closed society. The free man reads the "great" press (the name it is given in this book) heuristically; the person in an authoritarian society reads it pragmatically. In the first case, the elite paper offers ideas which the reader wants to consider; in the other, it gives the reader what he *must* know to be a well-integrated member of his society. In one case, the reader of the elite newspaper is stimulated to free individual thought and action; in the other, he is indoctrinated for concerted activity. In one case, the paper is a catalyst to democratic self-determination; in the other it is an instrument with which to control the social system.

In one case, pride in the principles of free journalism and in the particular newspaper motivates staff members to high standards; in the other, journalism has become a deadly serious business in which mistakes—typographical or otherwise—are not tolerated. In other words, on the one hand the high standards

9

and serious tone are maintained freely from within; and on the other they are enforced from without. For example, Yugoslavia's *Borba and Politika* are elite in the sense of being serious, influential, typographically immaculate, and carefully written. So are Czechoslovakia's *Rude Pravo,* Rumania's *Scinteia,* and any of the other Communist Party organs that set the tone, policy, and standards for the newspaper press of the Communist societies. So, also, are well-edited and literate journals like Egypt's *Al Ahram,* the Manila *Times* of the Philippines,[10] and Taiwan's *Central Daily News.* These are serious, carefully edited papers with considerable prestige in certain circles, but they lack one important ingredient—freedom.

It is this absence of freedom, perhaps as much as any other thing, that places a large group of the world's influential papers in a separate category of eliteness—and a lower, less desired one, from the Western democratic viewpoint. In a very real sense, then, there are actually two main classes of elite papers: (1) the free paper of the open society, and (2) the restricted or managed paper of the closed society.

Across the spectrum of serious world journalism are many elite papers juxtapositioned in extremely paradoxical ways, illustrating the validity of placing such papers into the two main classes just mentioned: A Cuban *Granma* and a Brazilian *O Estado de S. Paulo;* an Egyptian *Al Ahram* and an Italian *Corriere della Sera;* a Japanese *Mainichi* and a Chinese *Renmin Ribao;* a West German *Frankfurter Allgemeine* and an East German *Neues Deutschland.*

In every major country one newspaper, and often two or three, stands out as a journal of elite opinion, catering to the intelligentsia and the opinion leaders, however variously defined. Well informed on government matters, they achieve a reputation for reliability, for expert knowledge, and even for presenting the most accurate image of governmental thinking. Although their circulations are seldom larger than 300,000, their influence is tremendous, for they are read regularly by public officials, scholars, journalists, theologians, lawyers and judges, and business leaders. And what is more, they are read in other countries by those persons whose business it is to keep up with world affairs. Even papers like *Pravda* and *Izvestia* are read seriously by persons in the free world who consider these journals as accurately reflecting official viewpoints of the Soviet Union. And, no doubt, Soviet officials, regardless of their feelings about Western journalistic bias and capitalistic exploitation of the press, peruse *The New York Times* and the London *Times* regularly for their picture of the United States and Britain.

As is true with so many really important institutions and concepts, the elite press is difficult to define. Its nature is rather tenuous, ephemeral, temporary and, most of all, relative. Part of it speaks coldly, with detached scientific precision; another part involves itself with the reader in a warm and personal manner. While one part snarls, another purrs. One part, trying for quantity as well as quality, submerges the reader in a flood of facts; another carefully sifts

---

[10] See Artemio R. Guillermo, "Decline and Fall of the Freest Press in Asia," *The Quill* (April 1975), pp. 21–23, for an account of how the press of the Philippines lost its freedom in 1972.

through the news and thoughtfully offers the reader a coherent and rich diet of significance. But regardless of the differences among the elite newspapers, they are all serious, concerned, intelligent, and articulate.

However true it may be that these papers "are a distinct species," it is quite obvious that there are types or natures of quality and of prestige among the world's papers, and these distinctions make categorizing and defining extremely difficult. Some papers, quite qualitative in one sense, are so vastly different from other papers (also qualitative) that it is difficult to talk of them in the same context, or to judge them against the same set of criteria. First of all, elite papers fall into the two main types or contexts already mentioned: (1) libertarian, or those published in a free or open society, and (2) authoritarian, or those published in a restricted or closed society.[11] Certainly it is unwise, or at least disconcerting, to try to compare meaningfully the elite paper of Context 1 with the elite paper of Context 2.

Then, in each of these two basic contexts there are other (or "sub") contexts into which elite papers might fall, and one paper is found in more than one context at one time: (3) daily, (4) weekly, (5) specialized, and (6) general. Of course, there are other contexts, for example, a semiweekly in a quasi-authoritarian country; but these six contexts are quite useful in talking about elite newspapers.

Obviously a daily and a weekly newspaper would be of different quality types, even if their basic context (Nos 1 or 2) was the same. This might be due to differing directions in editorial emphasis or ideological orientation, or simply to the differentiating factor of daily and weekly deadlines.

Two elite daily papers, moreover, may be of very distinct natures, perhaps with Contexts 5 and 6 different, or perhaps, 1 and 2. For example, the daily *The Wall Street Journal* and the daily Baltimore *Sun* little resemble one another because one is a specialized, and the other is a general, journal. Nor would the *Berlingske Tidende* of Denmark (published for the serious general reader in an open society) be of the same nature as the very prestigious *Komsomolskaya Pravda* of Russia (published for the Young Communists in a closed society). Wilbur Schramm when at Stanford University, pointed out that great differences exist among free society elite papers and gave the examples of (1) the "analytical" types such as *Le Monde* and the *Frankfurter Allgemeine,* and (2) the "news-oriented" types such as *The New York Times.*[12]

All sorts of combination games could be played by shuffling papers around in the major and minor contexts for comparative purposes. Consider the specialized (Context 5), daily (Context 3), semifree (Contexts, 1, 2) *Osservatore Ro-*

---

[11] See J. C. Merrill, *The Imperative of Freedom: A Philosophy of Journalistic Autonomy* (New York: Hastings House, 1974) for a discussion of the libertarian and the authoritarian press systems and the drift, which the author sees, toward authoritarianism the world over. Long-time British journalist, Malcolm Muggeridge, in 1978 agreed completely with Merrill's contention; individualism is being all but wiped out, said Muggeridge, by a drift toward collectivism of all types, institutionalization, and professionalism. Freedom in journalism, as much as in other areas, is fast disappearing, said the well-known author and former journalist. (Muggeridge, public lecture "The True Crisis of Our Time" at California State University, Long Beach, Feb. 6, 1978).

[12] Wilbur Schramm, *One Day in the World's Press* (Palo Alto: Stanford University Press, 1959), p. 5.

mano of Vatican City; actually it is difficult to consider it in the same class with either China's *People's Daily* (Contexts 2, 3, 6) or with England's *Times* (Contexts 1, 3, 6). One should recognize, of course, that the *Osservatore Romano* is different from *The Times* for reasons other than the fact that it is published in a more closed society, has a more restricted editorial policy, or is the reflection of a quite different kind of institution. These differences, however, are significant and many press observers would feel that the Church paper is closer to the *People's Daily* than to *The Times*. This, too, is quite misleading and unfair, for beyond the fact that both the Chinese and the Vatican paper lack the libertarian publishing context, considerable and important differences exist between them. They are both restricted, it is true, but we must always be aware of the fact that Restricted Paper "A" can be, and often is, quite different from Restricted Paper "B." Without belaboring this point, we should add that considering only one of these contexts for comparative purposes is not enough. The distinctiveness of *Osservatore Romano* comes more from other factors, such as its specialized religious orientation and its failure to present much factual news, than from the *freedom* (or lack of it) with which it is published.

In comparing elite papers it is obviously advantageous (really indispensable) to use the context method. Correlation of several contexts places newspapers of relative similitude before us. For example, if we are considering general daily papers of a conservative leaning we must include in the list *Svenska Dagbladet* of Stockholm, the *Chicago Tribune*, *The Times* of London, *The Scotsman* of Edinburgh, the *Corriere della Sera* of Milan, and the *Frankfurter Allgemeine* of Frankfurt am Main. Their free-world counterparts among the liberal dailies would include *The Guardian* of Manchester and London, *Dagens Nyheter* of Stockholm, the *Post-Dispatch* of St. Louis, *Le Monde* of Paris, *Neue Zürcher Zeitung* of Zurich, and *Süddeutsche Zeitung* of Munich.

The word "prestige" is likely to be used synonymously with "quality" when referring to an admired newspaper, and there is perhaps no reason to quibble with this. However, it might be helpful to make a distinction between a quality and a prestige paper for the sake of discussion. A very simple distinction might be this:

QUALITY: a good, influential, *free* newspaper.
PRESTIGE: a good, influential, *restricted* newspaper.

Prestige papers, in the above sense, would include official government organs such as *Pravda* in the U.S.S.R. or *El Nacional* in Mexico, or perhaps *Osservatore Romano* of Vatican City. These are good papers, to be sure, but they are "kept" organs operating in the strict confines of some official policy. They are influential, but their appeal to the intellectual elite is a narrow, specialized, ideological appeal. Their basic nature is quite different from that of a free elite journal (or quality paper) such as Switzerland's *Neue Zürcher Zeitung,* Sweden's *Dagens Nyheter,* or West Germany's *Die Welt.* It seems that some confusion could be removed if one would talk of the free elite as the quality paper and the authoritarian elite as the prestige paper.

This book largely deals with quality papers (*e.g., Le Monde*) which have prestige, not prestige papers (*e.g., Pravda*) which have quality. In other words, the emphasis here is with the elite press in the Westernized, libertarian sense. It might be well to reiterate this distinction between what we are calling the quality paper and the prestige paper:

QUALITY PAPER: a courageous, independent, news-views-oriented journal, published in an open society.

PRESTIGE PAPER: a serious journal of some power elite, concerned with dogma or policy dissemination, spokesman or propagandist for some person or group, and published in a closed society.

A prestige paper, then, is well known primarily (or solely) because it is the voice of some authoritarian institution and as such wields influence among the audience submissive to that institution. It is more concerned with being a "bulletin board" for the power elite than with reporting and discussing current events. In spite of its influence, it is closed to but one viewpoint—usually the government's—and is wary of those persons or groups with deviant ideologies. These papers, without a doubt, are tremendously important today as instruments of agitation, indoctrination, and social control.

But it is chiefly with the quality or free-press "great" newspapers that this book concerns itself. These are the papers that open minds and stimulate discussion and intelligent reflection. These are the papers—whether they be dailies or weeklies, specialized or general, large or small—that offer hope to the world. They are the reasonable journals, freely and courageously speaking out calmly above the din of party politics and nationalistic drum-beating. They are urging peoples to work together for the good of all, to consider all sides of complex issues, to refrain from emotional decisions, to cherish that which has proved good and discard that which has been detrimental, to consider seriously the basic issues and problems that confront mankind.

Whether they are called "conservative" or "liberal" in their own societies is of no consequence. These labels have little or nothing to do with quality journalism or with the elite press; they are simply tags, having some vague meaning within their societal fabric but little or none elsewhere. The quality of the liberal *Guardian* is no better than the quality of the conservative *Times,* and both the conservative *Frankfurter Allgemeine* and the more liberal *Süddeutsche Zeitung* of West Germany are quality dailies. Many persons in the United States equate all quality papers and all intellectuals with liberalism. This is unfortunate and quite erroneous and simply shows an illiberalism of thought. This sort of thing is unheard of in Europe where liberalism is more along classic lines, closely connected with an open mind and a progressive spirit and a sense of tolerance than with one's purported position on a Left-Right continuum.

Conservative or liberal, the *quality* dailies of the world fight mental and emotional rigidity; they try to break down irrational biases; they try to present a wealth of reliable information and thoughtful interpretation, and they constantly attempt to narrow the "credibility gap." This is why they are great. But it should be remembered also, however, that the *prestige* dailies of the world, while not subscribing to the same objectives and policy as the *quality* dailies described above, are part of of the world's serious and influential press—and as such must also be counted among the "great" daily newspapers of the world.

Marks of Greatness
for International Dailies

ALTHOUGH THE EFFORT has just been made to explain the distinctions among the various types of "great" newspapers, it should be re-emphasized that this book is primarily concerned with the serious dailies of the libertarian nations—the "free" dailies—which, as has been pointed out, may be distinguished rather easily from the elite of the authoritarian nations by considering their political and social setting. However, most writers do not make such a distinction and it is quite common to find the leading serious papers of the world (regardless of where they are) referred to by an assortment of terms used interchangeably.

The British call these papers "quality" or "class" papers, distinguishing them from popular or mass papers. The French often refer to them as *journaux de prestige,* while Germans frequently allude to them as *Weltblätter,* stressing their international reputation. In the United States there seems to be no standard name—serious, quality, and prestige being adjectives usually applied to them. Here and there they are also referred to as great, intellectual, cosmopolitan, international, and elite.

Quite obviously these terms can reasonably be used synonymously to talk about this type of newspaper, but it would seem useful to differentiate, at least, among those of a free ("open") and those of an authoritarian ("closed") society. This is the reason an elite paper in Paraguay or in the Soviet Union is called a prestige paper, while one in a country like Britain, Japan or the United States is referred to as a quality paper. Both types can be considered as part of the elite or "great" press although they are certainly of distinct natures.

Even though the prestige papers of the closed society are quite different from the quality papers of the open society, they would still appear to have a considerable amount of reasonableness and national and international concern; for this reason a paper like *Pravda,* appealing to opinion leaders with a serious turn of mind, can be accommodated under the label "elite" as well as can a

14

paper like *The Times* of London.[13] Many persons will, if they are of the Western world, disagree with this premise, saying that *Pravda* and its ilk, because of their doctrinaire orientation and attachment to one party, cannot contribute to reason. From a capitalistic perspective, this is quite true, but a Communist might just as well say that since the Western capitalistic newspaper is tied to the vested interests of "big business," it is not really free and cannot present news and views without considerable bias, subjectivity, prejudice, and selfish motivation.

Both viewpoints are to some degree valid and invalid. At any rate, there is no cause for rejecting the premise that within the serious, influential press of any political system there is a certain respect and concern with seriousness, humanity, and social progress. And this is the basic premise of this book. Of course, the emphasis here is on the free elite press, since the writers are convinced that these papers are the ones which offer the greatest hope for personal, national, and international discourse and liberalizing "mind-opening." Nevertheless, however superior we may think the libertarian elite to be, this seems little justification for dismissing the entire government-controlled press of the world as no more than propaganda and unreasonable journalism. This is the reason we have a substantial number of profiles of dailies from such countries included in this book.

While this book is mainly concerned with the free elite newspaper, it recognizes the importance, leadership, seriousness, and considerable reasonableness of the authoritarian elite. The purpose here is to highlight the free elite and to discuss the characteristics or criteria by which it is judged. Marks of the statist elite, touched on lightly earlier, will receive little further attention. These prestige papers of the closed societies are intentionally de-emphasized for two main reasons: (1) they are not felt to be as intellectually potent as the free elite and thus not as significant in creating a world community of reason, and (2) very little of a reliable nature is known about these papers, much of their operations and policies being wrapped in secrecy.

Therefore, let us proceed with a discussion of the free elite of the world and attempt to determine the characteristics which define them. These papers will generally be referred to as quality papers except where they are given some alternate name by other writers.

Even though it is obvious that quality newspapers have many natures, there is a certain character which they all have in common. The over-all tone and style, plus the interest and emphasis which the quality papers share with one another, make them a recognizable segment of the total press system.

If a reader looks through several copies of a few of the quality papers, he will find an obvious emphasis on idea-oriented news—stories that bear a significance beyond the straight facts (or bits of information) which they carry. They

---

[13] Many knowledgeable observers would, of course, contest this statement. Lev Navrozov, for instance, would not even call *Pravda* a "real newspaper." He writes: "What is translated in the West by the word "newspaper" (such as *Pravda*) is not a newspaper. Only the upper castes are to read real newspapers like the *Blue Tass*, each successive higher caste reading its own, more complete, and more secret newspaper." See "Notes American Innocence," *Commentary*, 58:2, August, 1974, p. 37.

are stories which present the news "as a piece," relating the varying stories in a subtle (not always immediately recognizable) fashion. The economic stories relate to the political, the political to the cultural and social, and so on. Even the so-called human interest item (when it appears) puts the spotlight briefly on an important social (in a broad sense) point of contention, and taken together with the edition's total editorial focus, helps set the tone of the national and international events.

A quality paper's popularity is not built on voyeurism, sensationalism, or prurience. It offers its readers facts (in a meaningful context), ideas, interpretation; in short, it presents a continuing education. It gives its reader the feeling that he is getting a synthesized look at the most significant happenings and thinking of the day. The reader of the quality paper does not feel like a news-scrap collector; rather he has at hand carefully selected and written stories that mean something, that present background and point out trends, that give insights into personalities who run the world or who might step into such positions tomorrow.

The respected publisher of Buenos Aires' *La Prensa*, the late Dr. Gainza Paz, in a speech in New York in 1965, had the following comments to make about a quality paper's relation to its readers:

> We know the responsibility of all good editors: to stimulate reader interest in the progress and development of their country. We also know that we ought to find ways of awakening that interest, despite the fact that sometimes uninformed readers appear to be indifferent.
>
> We also know that newspapers should interpret the news without bias, and without fear of giving conflicting viewpoints. And most importantly . . . a paper should express its own view clearly and without concern for the consequences.
>
> But even beyond its duty to inform, beyond its editorial policy, no matter how courageous that may be, the true journalist must somehow create a bond of confidence between the readers and the newspaper. Only then can he expect to have their support in defense of a press freedom that guarantees the people's right to know.[14]

Although the quality paper reflects a serious and intellectual orientation, its editors and chief writers seek a minimum of specialized jargon and strive always for clarity of expression. The editors realize, however (unlike their counterparts on many mass papers), that technical, specialized, and scientific words are often better than lay terms, and if they are to educate, they must use these more difficult (but more precise) expressions.

The late French writer and journalist, Albert Camus, perhaps has given as clear a view of the philosophy of quality journalism as has been given. With several others he founded in Paris the newspaper *Combat* in 1944, and made it in many ways the prototype of what he meant by an elite or quality journal. He attacked most newspapers as being too popularized, commercial, insincere, unconcerned, and careless with the truth. The press generally, he believed, was seeking to please rather than to enlighten.

---

[14] Alberto Gainza Paz, making the presentation of the 1965 World Press Achievement Award of the American Newspaper Publishers Association Foundation to the editor of the small provincial *Yeni Adana* of Adana, Turkey (New York City, April 21, 1965).

Camus defined a good journalist in this way: "One who, first of all, is supposed to have ideas. Next, his task is to inform the public on events which have just taken place. He is a sort of day-to-day historian whose prime concern is the truth." He elaborated on this, however, by saying that the "first news" is not always the best news and that "it is better to come in second and report the truth than to be first and false." He reprimanded the popular papers for their gaudy makeup and sensational content, saying that they are overly concerned with colorful details and eye-catching layout. Taking issue with those who said that this is the kind of journalism the public wants, he said: "No, this is what the public has been taught to want over a period of twenty years, which isn't at all the same thing. . . . But if a score of newspapers spew forth the same mediocrity and distortion every day, the public will breathe in this poisoned air and be unable to get along without it."[15]

Camus recommended that serious and responsible newspapers make some sacrifices in profits and in readership in order to provide daily reflection and the scrupulous reporting necessary to keep high-level journalistic standards. What he advocated, he illustrated in *Combat*—makeup and content which were serious but not academic, dignified but lively. Virtue, to Camus, was by no means boring, and he demanded conciseness of expression, a feeling for form, a nonrigidity in style, incisive interpretation, and a piercing wit. He had several little catchwords to illustrate his journalistic principles. To define an editorial, he would say, "One idea, two examples, three pages," and to report a news item, "Facts, local color, juxtapositions."

In 1955, long after the *Combat* period, Camus renewed his ties with journalism by writing regularly for the weekly serious paper of Paris, *L'Express* (now a magazine). What Camus left behind him for the world of quality journalism is a legacy of values which, in a way, might serve to guide the free elite papers of the world. Jean Daniel, writing about Camus, noted that his main contribution was critical reporting, which Daniel defined in this way: "A passionately dedicated effort to eliminate passion from reporting; in other words, complete candor as to the limitations of the observer in his understanding of the phenomenon observed. It is an attitude of respect toward those to whom one is responsible for communicating the journalistic fact, once that fact has been defined."[16]

One of the chief concerns of the free elite—and Camus would have considered it so—is the editorial page or section. Editorials, essays, cartoons, columns, and letters to the editor are not bland "stay-out-of-trouble" types; rather they are strong, vital, outspoken, knowledgeable, thoughtful, and thought-provoking. They are often critical of government, regardless of what government or party is in power. The free elite takes very seriously its place as critic of government and of excesses in other institutions of society.

[15] Jean Daniel, "Camus as Journalist," *New Republic* (June 13, 1964), p. 19. The American journalist, H. L. Mencken, dealt vividly with the "mediocrity and distortion" of the general press; see a collection of his essays in *A Gang of Pecksniffs*, edited by Theo Lippman, Jr. (New Rochelle, N.Y.: Arlington House, 1975). Cf. for more on Camus as a journalist: J. C. Merrill, *Existential Journalism* (New York: Hastings House, 1977).

[16] Daniel, *op. cit.*

Great newspapers, of all the many types, seem most concerned about the future, about the implications of current events in days to come. They are insightful and predictive because of their concern and knowledge. Andrew Sharf, in a book written in 1964 analyzing the behavior of the British press during the rise of Hitler, repeatedly praised the three quality papers—*The Times, The Guardian,* and *The Daily Telegraph*—for their general coverage of the news from Germany during the 1930's. Although he singled out *The Guardian* as the most astute and the only one which consistently saw clearly what was happening in Germany and pointed to the direct connection between antisemitism and the Nazis' other policies, Sharf noted that the accuracy and completeness of German coverage was outstanding in all three papers.[17]

In one sense, the elite press serves as the true conscience of a nation, and even, to a large degree, as the conscience of the world. Even many papers which are not very well known internationally like to consider themselves part of their national conscience. This concern is important and indicates that such papers are progressing up the elite pyramid, or they are at least contemplating the invigorating climb. Undoubtedly key staff members, especially policy-making editors (such as John W. Dafoe of the *Winnipeg Free Press* in Canada) largely forge the quality of a paper and see to it that there is a continuity of editorial policy and hire men who can be counted on to contribute further to the paper's prestige.

What exactly is meant by "editorial policy"? Although it is broad and complex, there are certain things which can be said about it which might be helpful to an understanding of it. It has to do with consistency in outlook and in publishing practices; it is the course a newspaper chooses to follow as it answers the two all-important questions: What shall we print? How shall we print it? Editorial policy is composed of the practices, rules, and principles which the paper sets as a guide and standard for itself. As such, it really governs every phase of the newspaper from the type of staff sought, the kind of news dealt with, the ideological orientation embraced, and even the size of type used in printing.

Seldom are the most important phases of a paper's editorial policy expressed in writing; they are simply understood. The staff member (as does the reader) comes to know through experience the editorial policy of the paper. Usually the policy of a paper is established when the paper is founded; there is a certain permanence and stability about it, although it would be wrong to think that it does not change over the years. So far as a quality paper is concerned, an inflexible editorial policy is no sign of excellence. (Even the traditional *Times* of London cleared its front page of advertising for news in the spring of 1966.)

In countries which have several or many national dailies, one would expect to find a larger quality press—at least in the sense of dealing largely with national and international topics. In Britain, for example, the national serious dailies have almost completely taken over the job of informing the public on major topics, leaving most of the provincial press with the responsibility of

[17]*The British Press and Jews Under Nazi Rule* (London: Oxford University Press, 1964).

dealing with provincial matters. In the United States where there is really no national press, every paper (with the exception of many grass-roots weeklies) feels it must be something to everybody.

On the other hand, the international elite or great paper must evidence a *cosmopolitanism* quite alien to mass papers and only occasionally approached in middle-area general appeal papers. Concern for news and views of other countries is a definite characteristic of the elite paper; thus the emphasis on international trade, political relations, cross-cultural economic, social, scientific, and educational affairs. The elite paper not only takes its serious national affairs seriously, but also deems it important to inform its readers of the salient international affairs and the concerns of other nations. The elite paper is able to see the world as a piece, not simply as a hodgepodge of nationalistic states isolated and unimportant to one another.

An aura of dignity and stability is also a characteristic of the great paper. This manifests itself not only in a conservative, soft-sell makeup but also in a rather heavy, semiacademic writing style that approaches the type one finds in such journals as London's *Economist*. In the elite paper there is an overriding tone of seriousness, of respect for the reader's intelligence and store of knowledge; there is an absence of sensation or hysteria that tends to dominate the general newspaper press of the world. The elite paper has a clearer conception of what is really significant and vital than do other types of papers. It has a serious-minded and moral approach to news that keeps it digging and interested in the news at any cost. All of this, of course, makes the quality press *reliable*.

The elite paper is *courageous*. The mere fact that it has foregone the temptation to popularize, to sensationalize, to build up a large readership shows that it has courage. It dares to give the readers a serious and heavy portion of news and views; it constantly attempts to lead, not follow, public opinion. This, in itself, takes courage. It has a reputation for speaking out on issues when it is not popular to do so; is forward-looking, progressive, and eager to change when the change is in accord with society's best interests, regardless of whether it is considered (or considers itself) liberal or conservative (or something else).

The elite paper is *responsible*: responsible to its leaders. In a free society, of course, this makes it also responsible to its government and to people everywhere. Its main job is to get all the facts the people need to reach correct judgments. (Communist prestige papers like *Pravda* or *Renmin Ribao* are also responsible, but their responsibility is of a different nature, being directed toward the system and emphasizing the solidarity of the state rather than considering the individual citizen as the object of its responsibility. In a sense, the communist elite paper's responsibility is one of Party-Government-People consensus, a sort of responsibility for conformity and harmony, not a responsibility which enthrones honesty and pluralistic discourse.)

If, then, the free elite press should be reliable; the readers should be able to trust it. It must be adequate to a free people's needs. One thing remains certain: the free elite papers try to provide their readers with adequate and trustworthy information. When a quality paper fails in some such basic responsibility, the probability is great that the reason is without, not within, the newspaper. The problem, in other words, is most often external to the quality newspaper and has developed in spite of the determination of the paper that it not develop.

Before surveying some specific studies of criteria of the quality press, it should be re-emphasized that elite papers are written and edited for the discerning reader, the inquisitive reader, the knowledgeable reader, the thoughtful reader, the issue-oriented (not the fact-oriented) reader. The quality paper, in short, is designed for the person who takes serious things seriously and is conscientiously seeking the truth.

Many persons, most, in fact, do not take serious things seriously, and they have their press. The person who reads the American *National Enquirer* or the British *News of the World* (a Sunday paper) may want or need these trivial forays into a crazy-quilt world of gaudiness and news anarchy. Thus, the popular press has its place, serves its purpose, but it should be recognized for what it is. Admittedly, the reader of the *National Enquirer* may also be a reader of an elite paper in his more serious moments, but the point is that he knows the difference. His journalistic habits are consciously schizophrenic. But he probably is not a typical newspaper reader, for there is reason to believe that serious persons, opinion leaders, intellectuals would not be comfortable reading the *National Enquirer*. However, if a single person does read both types of papers, he knows they are of quite different characters, speak different languages, have different goals, and address different audiences, or at least appeal to the different tastes or sensibilities of an individual.

Let us turn now to several studies (since 1960) which have dealt with the marks of the free elite. Many other articles and books have approached quality journalism and its characteristics from a variety of perspectives during this same period, and even before, but the four studies which follow reflect the thinking of scholars and practicing journalists of many nations relative to the marks or characteristics of the quality, or free elite, newspapers.

In 1961 the United States magazine, *Saturday Review*, undertook a mail-questionnaire survey of all deans, full professors, and associate professors in the 46 schools accredited by the American Council on Education for Journalism.[18] Object: to discover which of the 119 American dailies with circulations of 100,000 or more were most highly regarded by these journalism educators and what criteria were used in rating a daily paper. Selecting from the responses of ther 125 respondents, here are the 10 main criteria used to adjudge an American daily as superior:

1. Completeness of coverage in foreign and international affairs, business, the arts, science, and education.
2. Concern with interpretive pieces, backgrounding articles, and depth news articles.

---

[18] "Rating the American Newspaper," *Saturday Review* (May 13, 1961), pp. 59–62. There have been a few other attempts by magazines (such as *Time*) to present lists of "the best" American newspapers during the 1970's, but none of these stories has dealt with criteria for evaluation as did the *Saturday Review* in 1961.

3. Typographical and general editorial dignity.
4. Lack of sensationalism.
5. Depth and analytical perception of stories.
6. Absence of hysteria and cultural tone.
7. Thorough and impartial news coverage and serious-minded, moral approach to news.
8. Imagination, decency, interest in democratic problems and humanity.
9. Excellent editorial page.
10. Orientation that rises above provincialism and sensationalism.

In the summer of 1964 a survey of a panel of 26 professors of international communication in the United States was conducted to help determine criteria used, in this case, to rate a newspaper in the top twenty quality papers of the world.[19] The most important criterion in the panel's view was an emphasis on political, economic, and cultural news and views. A long tradition of freedom and editorial courage was considered second most important. This, of course, would eliminate highly controlled newspapers of the authoritarian nations from a roster of quality papers. The third criterion of political and economic independence was closely related to the second.

A strong editorial page and/or section given over to opinion and interpretive essays was named as fourth most important for a quality paper, followed by staff enterprise in obtaining and writing news and commentary.

Other criteria thought by the panel very important for determining a quality paper:

Large proportion of space given to world affairs; lack of provincialism; consistently good writing in all sections of the paper; high regard by opinion leaders and by other serious publications; large, well-educated staff; typographical and printing excellence and general makeup dignity; de-emphasis of sensational news and pictures; high overall quality of coverage on world, national, and local levels; active integrity; consistent opposition to intolerance and unfairness; active community leadership, and comprehensive news coverage in its pre-empted area, and influence wtih the decision-makers and policy-makers at home and in other countries.

It is rather obvious from the above criteria that this American panel of journalism professors, at least, thinks about an international quality daily in a rather special or restricted way. First, the panelists see it as a general newspaper, not as one which specializes in a certain type of material (*e.g., The Wall Street Journal,* as good as it may be) nor as one which represents some organization or institution and largely is concerned with policy-dissemination (*e.g.,* the Vatican's *Osservatore Romano*), however qualitative and prestigious it may be in a limited context. Secondly, they mainly see the international quality newspaper as a free (libertarian) journal, unattached to, and uncensored by, government. This

[19] J. C. Merrill, "U.S. Panel Names World's Ten 'Quality' Dailies," *Journalism Quarterly,* 41:4 (Autumn, 1964), pp. 568–572. Cf. Merrill, "What Are the World's Best Dailies? *Gazette,* Leiden, 10:3 (1964), pp. 259–260, and "Los 20 Mejores Diarios del Mundo," *La Prensa,* Buenos Aires (August 22, 1964).

would, of course, eliminate such papers as *Pravda* of the U.S.S.R., however prestigious it may be in the Communist system.

Thirdly, the panel's criteria indicate that its members felt a quality paper must stress politics, economics, and culture, and that this emphasis must extend to the international scene and not simply to the country where it is published. Cosmopolitanism, then, was considered to be very important, along with editorial courage and an impact on the opinion leaders of its own nation and of other nations. A dignity of page makeup as well as a large, enterprising, well-educated staff round out the basic image of a quality paper as seen by the 1964 American panel. Underlying implications here are that the quality paper must be supranational in circulation and scope, literate, courageous, forceful, free, knowledgeable, stimulating, credible, serious, socially concerned, world-conscious, and dignified. It is little wonder that the group of international quality newspapers is small.

One other survey should be mentioned. Merrill, in late 1965, sent a brief questionnaire to 185 editors in the United States, Britain, West Germany, Denmark, Switzerland, Italy, Japan, Mexico, Australia, and India.[20] The purpose of this survey was to follow up his 1964 survey and to get some comment from an international panel relative to the world's leading elite newspapers—this time from newspaper editors instead of journalism professors. Questionnaires were sent to editors of newspapers (with more than 50,000 circulation) chosen at random from the 1965 *Editor & Publisher International Yearbook*. Ninety-two were returned (a very high response) and after an additional group of forms was mailed to other editors and the total return numbered exactly one hundred, the seeking of completed questionnaires stopped, although response from Indian and Australian editors was disproportionately small.

The returns from various countries follow:

United States (18); West Germany (14); Britain (12); Japan (12); Switzerland (11); Italy (10); Mexico (9); Denmark (8); Australia (4), and India (2).

Admittedly, this is a small sample, but the intent was not to take a statistically reliable survey (and claim any scientific validity for it), but to elicit some comments (hopefully representative) from respondents in ten free-world countries. This, it is felt, was accomplished with some comments more incisive and more frank than had been anticipated.

The questionnaires had only two brief parts: (1) the editors were asked to name five dailies of the world (no more than one from a single country) which they considered good examples of leading quality, influential, or elite newspa-

[20] "International 'Elite Press' Survey, 1965." (Sponsored in part by the Research Council, University of Missouri–Columbia.) Merrill has not conducted further international surveys of this nature since, but on the basis of his continued study of newspapers around the world he believes that editors and professors would list approximately the same papers as "great" as they did in 1965. A few—e.g. *Excélsior* of Mexico, *La Prensa* of Argentina, the *St. Louis Post-Dispatch* of the U.S., and *The Guardian* of Britain—would probably get lower marks than in 1965, while others—e.g. *Boston Globe, Philadelphia Inquirer,* and the *St. Petersburg Times* of the U.S., *Süddeutsche Zeitung* of West Germany, *Politika* of Yugoslavia, and *El Mercurio* of Chile—would likely find, in 1979, their places in higher ranks of the world's great dailies.

pers,[21] and (2) they were asked to give at least five main determinants or characteristics which they used in deciding on the five dailies.

Instead of summarizing in detail the criteria deemed important in classifying a quality newspaper by the international panel of editors, it will suffice here to say that their standards of evaluation included all those mentioned by the *Saturday Review* survey (1961), and the Merrill survey of United States professors teaching international communications (1964). This, of course, did not come as a surprise, but did reinforce the previous surveys, or said another way, it extended or projected these criteria into an international context. It showed that newsmen in diverse countries (nonauthoritarian) tend to have a common set of standards which they use in determining the leading newspapers of the world. It should be noted here that the present authors have talked with dozens of world's editors since 1964—in fact, well into the late 1970's—and have found that these evaluative criteria are still quite valid.

What were these main themes or criteria considered most important by international respondents for determining a leading quality paper? They have been grouped in five rather large categories, and although they reiterate in large part what has already been said, their presentation should serve well to summarize and conclude this chapter. Marks of the free elite are these:

1. Independence; financial stability; integrity; social concern; good writing and editing.
2. Strong opinion and interpretive emphasis; world consciousness; nonsensationalism in articles and markeup.
3. Emphasis on politics, international relations, economics, social welfare, cultural endeavors, education, and science.
4. Concern with getting, developing, and keeping a large, intelligent, well-educated, articulate, and technically proficient staff.
5. Determination to serve and help expand a well-educated, intellectual readership at home and abroad; desire to appeal to, and influence, opinion leaders everywhere.

---

[21] For the actual newspapers named and ranked in response to this questionnaire, see Chapter 4 in Merrill, *The Elite Press* (New York: Pitman Pub. Corp., 1968), pp. 32–43.

Global Patterns
of the Great Dailies

ALTHOUGH THE GREAT DAILIES of the world may be referred to as belonging to a "community," it is clearly an uneven, multifaceted one. A seriousness of tone and purpose and a high readership among influential persons are about the only common denominators of this elite press. The membership of the elite, because of differences in language, economic stability, freedom from government control, and basic philosophy, is splintered and fragmented and suffers from too little rapport and theoretical consensus. Thus, the world's great press is heterogeneous and pluralistic in spite of its commonalities of seriousness, general civility, and influence. Struggling against great obstacles everywhere but with renewed hope and vigor, it is developing unevenly throughout the world. It falls roughly into at least three major patterns.

The first pattern is primarily *political or ideological*. Elite papers tend toward separation from government or they tend toward integration with government. While the free elite see themselves as independent agents, standing aloof from, and unaffected by, government, the authoritarian elite envision themselves as partners in government, cooperative agents of their government bent on carrying forth the sociopolitical system of their people.

Both groups of elite papers are dedicated to their philosophies and take their responsibilities, as they see them, quite seriously. It should be noted, however, that such a binary classification of the world's elite is too simple in reality and that all papers everywhere are free to varying degrees and restricted to varying degrees, although the character of the freedom and the restraint may differ significantly.

Many students of the press place considerable emphasis on social responsibility in determining the elite status of a newspaper. To what degree is the paper socially responsible? The answer to this question, to many, will largely determine the quality or eliteness of a newspaper. In the United States and other Western democracies social responsibility is thought of generally in terms of nonauthoritarianism or freedom from government control. In other words, social

24

responsbility is the press utopia into which only libertarian-oriented papers may pass. This, however, seems much too simple a theory and is unsatisfactory in the modern world of fragmented and pluralistic serious journalism.

Why cannot the authoritarian press or the Communistic press claim to be socially responsible also? In fact, in certain respects, a newspaper would be more "responsible" if some type of governmental supervision existed; indeed, reporters could be kept from nosing about in critical areas during critical times. And, as the Russians are quick to point out, the amount of sensational material could be controlled in the press, or eliminated altogether. Government activities could always be supported and public policy could be pushed on all occasions. The press could be more educational in the sense that more news of art exhibits, concerts, national progress, and the like could be stressed. In short, the press would eliminate the negative and stress the positive. Then, with one voice the press of the nation would be responsible to its society; and the definition of responsible would be functional—defined and carried out in the context of the existing government and social structure.

So it seems realistic to believe that all newspapers (of any political system) which reflect the philosophy of their governmental system and try to present serious, educational reading fare are not only responsible to their society but are members of the elite press, or they are climbing into that select fraternity.

Assuming that a nation's sociopolitical philosophy determines its press system, and undoubtedly it does, then it follows that the nation's leading and most prestigious papers are socially responsible and form the elite. For example, the Marxist or Communist press system considers itself socially responsible, and certainly it is responsible to its own social system. A capitalistic press, operating in a pluralistic context, would be socially irresponsible if suddenly transplanted into the Communist country.

The same thing might be said of the so-called authoritarian press system, exemplified in most African nations. A critical press such as found in the United States, a press which by its pluralistic nature would tend to undermine national policy and disrupt national harmony, would be anathema in a nation like Uganda. It would be considered anything but responsible in that context. In other words, the elite press of a nation, even one under considerable governmental control, will still prove its eliteness through its subtleties, skillful restraint, and capacity to make the most of the situation in which it finds itself. In many ways, of course, it takes much more journalistic ability and acumen, as well as courage, to be an elite newspaper in a country such as Uganda than in a country like Britain or Sweden.

A second important pattern among the world's elite, and one that is even more ragged than the political one just mentioned, is that of *economic diversity*. This pattern, of course, is related to the political context, but actually it is quite different. For example, one elite paper in a libertarian nation can run into dire financial difficulties while another in the same country prospers and grows. An elite paper is not determined by how much property it owns or the profit it makes. Elite papers throughout the world exemplify a wide range of economic development and prosperity, but their overriding concern with serious news and views manifests itself quite apart from such differences in economic health.

Naturally, there is a point below which an elite paper (or any paper) may not fall and keep up its desired level of quality. Certainly, it must have the facilities to do good printing. It must be able to pay enough to get conscientious, well-educated staff members. It must be able to receive a variety of services from news agencies, as well as to collect much national and world news with its own correspondents. It must, therefore, either have a rather sizable circulation, or it must develop a special elite readership which will offset a small circulation. Although some elite papers like *Asahi Shimbun* of Japan and *Pravda* of the Soviet Union have tremendous circulations, most of the world's elite have only modest ones. The elite newspaper (especially in a libertarian nation) runs the risk of lowering its quality when it makes a bid for larger readership, at least unless it does it very slowly. For it is the popular or mass press that is after the big circulations; the elite press is after readers of discernment and seriousness.

Unfortunately for international rationality, the public, as Leo Rosten has said, "chooses the frivolous as against the serious, the lurid as against the tragic, the trivial as against fact, the diverting as against the significant." Rosten points out that very few people in any society "have reasonably good taste or care deeply about ideas" and that even fewer appear to be "equipped—by temperament and capacity, rather than education—to handle ideas with both skill and pleasure."[22] The elite press is unwilling to sacrifice its high purpose for a larger circulation which it might obtain by being more lively and readable in the sense of the popular press. Great newspapers recognize that their readership will probably be small, but they know that it is unusually potent, sapient, and prestigious. It should be mentioned, however, that there are some few of these elite papers—in nations such as Sweden where the whole public is literate and uncommonly serious—which manage to be rational and serious and at the same time furnish all types of reading material.

The third pattern of the elite press is *geographical*. And this, of course, is closely related to national development. Most of the elite are published in developed or modern countries, although there are a few that represent the developing (modernizing) or transitional nations. Europe and North America are the principal homes of the elite newspapers. This is not surprising since these two continents are the most industrialized, the most technological, and the most literate of all the continents. As the economic bases become stabilized and literate and well-educated populations of other continents grow, the evenness of dispersion of the elite press throughout the world should improve significantly. Presently, however, elite newspapers are scattered about the earth in a very uneven fashion. This pattern of clusters and vast gaps greatly hinders the total impact of serious, concerned journalism in the world as a whole. It might be well to look more closely at this geographical pattern of the world's elite press.

Asia, with the exception of China, Japan, and India, is virtually without an elite press.[23] Of the three, Japan stands out for its great progress in quality jour-

---

[22] Leo Rosten, "The Intellectual and the Mass Media," *Daedalus* (Spring, 1960), pp. 333–46.
[23] There are, certainly, exceptions, such as *The Straits Times* of Singapore, and the well-edited *Nation* of Bangkok, Thailand. But we believe that it is true that, outside Japan, India and China, few Asian dailies evidence considerable dignity and sophistication.

nalism, and popular journalism too, for that matter. *Asahi Shimbun* is without a doubt the best quality daily in Japan and shows that an elite paper can, with editorial flexibility and sagacity, develop a large circulation within a free-market press. *Pravda* and its counterpart in Peking, *Renmin Ribao,* of course, have fewer problems building circulation since Communist Party members and many others find that they need to have these daily journals of guidance and news. In India, the problems of the elite papers are much more acute than in either the U.S.S.R, China, or Japan. There are many reasons for this, but the chief one is probably the problem of too many languages. At present the major elite papers of India are published in English, understood only by the educated found mainly in a few of the large cities. And, even within the English-reading public, the circulation of the English elite is segmented since there are three very important elite dailies in the country—*The Statesman* of Calcutta, *The Hindu* of Madras, and the *Times of India* of Bombay. The vernacular languages of India, of which Hindi is the official one, have not caught on as press languages. Although there are a few well-written and edited papers in some of these dialects, they have little or no national or international prestige. To the language problem facing the development of the Indian elite press must be added these (generally applicable throughout Southeast Asia): low literacy rate, underdeveloped educational system, scarcity of training facilities and trained journalists, and old and inadequate printing equipment.

In Africa, with the exception of Egypt in the extreme northeast and the Republic of South Africa in the far south, there is no significant elite press; and even in these two republics considerable governmental sensitivity has hindered development of a truly quality press. Egypt, with its nationalized newspapers, would, from a Western viewpoint, have to take second place to South Africa as a libertarian press nation with elite papers of a pluralistic nature. In South Africa, for example, in spite of government sensitivity to what it feels are press "excesses," the papers, especially those in English, show considerable freedom and critical ability. Without a doubt, South Africa has the freest newspapers on the continent, and within the English-language press are papers which are the equal in quality and tone to the elite of most nations of the world.

Johannesburg's morning *Rand Daily Mail* is a good example. It has consistently presented facts and opinion which have irritated the government, and has given its readers healthy portions of national and foreign news. Although most Afrikaans-language papers present a rather narrow pro-government picture, an important exception is *Die Burger* of Cape Town, committed generally to the policies of the Nationalist Party but often refreshingly independent and unconventional. It is also interesting that in South Africa the freest papers, generally the English-language papers, have the largest circulations. For instance, the Johannesburg *Star* has a circulation of almost double the combined circulations of the city's two Afrikaans papers, the *Transvaler* and the *Vaderland.*

The Egyptian press (which might better be considered part of the Middle Eastern press), has slowly but increasingly become a government-controlled press. In 1956 came the biggest blow to press freedom: President Nasser transferred the ownership of all papers to the National Union (the Government party) in order to assure popular support for his regime. And in 1960 the Egyptian papers were placed in groups or units, each having an administrative council appointed by the government. In spite of this nationalization (or "people's press") of the newspapers with accompanying restrictions, a few of the highly regarded old dailies of Cairo still provide their Arab readership with substantial amounts of serious journalism. For example, *Al Ahram* gives a good selection of news and features, and uses UPI and Reuters and other foreign agencies (and many interpretive articles on international affairs) to keep its cosmopolitan tone. Probably the most influential papers of the Arab world are still found in Egypt in spite of the fact that free, vigorous, and critical journalism has declined.

In the neighboring Middle East the press systems are mainly transitional, caught between the severe problems of many parts of Asia on one side and of Africa on the other. One hindrance to elite press development in this area is that these nations cannot decide whether to have their press systems (and governments) veer toward libertarianism or toward authoritarianism. Governments through the region are generally suspicious of the press and sensitive to its criticism. The press of Israel is probably the most internationally minded in the Middle East. For instance, *Ma'ariv* of Tel Aviv, subscribes to Reuters, UPI, AP, and the London *Daily Telegraph* services and has several correspondents and their families in foreign capitals. And this paper, although the country's largest, is not as serious as others such as the staid *Ha'aretz*.

Latin America, in spite of awesome economic and literacy problems, has somehow managed to develop a rather sizable group of elite newspapers. Without a doubt, this region of the world has a far more advanced press in all respects than is generally found in Asia and Africa. One obvious explanation for this is the fact that Spanish is the almost common language of the press in Latin America, whereas in both Asia and Africa the polyglot of languages and dialects makes the development of newspapers of substantial influence and circulation extremely difficult, if not impossible.

Many Latin American dailies meet the demands of serious readers for percipient journalism; most every major nation south of the United States has at least one journal which is in, or aspires to, the elite press. Brazil has its *O Estado de S. Paulo* and *O Jornal;* Argentina its *La Nación* and *La Prensa,* Chile its *Mercurio,* Peru its *Comercio,* Colombia its *Tiempo,* and Mexico its *Excélsior,*[24] *Novedades,* and *El Universal.* These and many other serious dailies of Latin America do an outstanding job of providing large proportions of scientific and humanistic news and views, with much emphasis on foreign affairs. Perhaps the Latin American serious press, like its ancestral press of Iberia, places undue stress on philosophical, theological, and literary discussion; but this is simply an intellectual Latin proclivity and the elite press does well to serve it.

In Oceania, Australia alone has a press which includes newspapers of the elite type. Barriers to press growth in this sprawling island region are mainly (1)

[24] In 1976 the prestigious *Excélsior* of Mexico City lost much of its freedom, its outstanding director, Julio Scherer García, and also much of its prestige. For a good account of what happened to the daily, see Octavio Paz, "Mexico: Freedom as Fiction/A Newspaper is Muzzled; an Image Dies," *Atlas: World Press Review* (October, 1976), p. 44. Cf., on Mexican press freedom, Miguel Aleman Velasco, "Mexico and the Right to Information," *Intermedia* (London), Vol. 6, No. 6, Nov., 1978, pp. 14–19.

small populations, (2) technological underdevelopment, (3) scarcity of trained journalists, and (4) geographical isolation from the mainstream of international concerns. In Australia several papers might be included among the elite and several others are aspirants. *The Age* of Melbourne is usually considered the most serious and influential with the country's press elite. Even a paper like the same city's *Herald,* an afternoon journal with some appeal to all classes, furnishes its readers a substantial diet of serious material. Its economic coverage and its weekly book page are especially laudable. And *The Australian,* begun in 1964, has become an excellent national daily with offices in several cities.

In North America (above the Mexican border) the elite press thrives. Whereas Canadian elite tend to cluster in that country's South, especially in Toronto and Montreal, the elite of the United States are rather well dispersed throughout the country. *The Globe and Mail* of Toronto is Canada's only truly national daily. The same city's *Daily Star* is the country's largest (about 340,000) and contains much serious material, although it displays it in a rather sensational manner. Canadian newspaper makeup is much closer to that typically found in the United States than it is to that of Britain. Montreal's evening *La Presse,* a comprehensive afternoon daily with an exceptionally fine weekend edition, is the largest French-language daily in the Western Hemisphere. In Winnipeg, Manitoba, the *Free Press* provides excellent international coverage and national coverage of the central and western portions of Canada.

Although there are elite and near-elite papers in every major section of the United States, most of them are concentrated along the East Coast and in the Middle West and around the fringes of the South. In the East are such sophisticated dailies as *The New York Times, The Washington Post, The Philadelphia Inquirer, The Christian Science Monitor, The* (Baltimore) *Sun,* and *The Miami Herald.* In the Middle West a few of the leaders among the elite are the *St. Louis Post-Dispatch,* the *Minneapolis Tribune, The Des Moines Register, The Milwaukee Journal,* and *The Kansas City Star.* In Kentucky, there is *The Courier-Journal* of Louisville; in Georgia, *The Atlanta Constitution;* in Texas, *The Dallas Morning News* and the *Houston Post.* Quality papers of national and international prestige tend to fade out in the plains and mountain area of the West, with *The Denver Post* ruling a vast empire from its strategic position. Along the West Coast, there are several good dailies but the *Los Angeles Times* and *The Oregonian* of Portland are probably the best.

If the press of North America is well developed and the elite papers numerous, the press of Europe (western Europe) might be said to be overdeveloped and the elite papers very numerous. From Scandinavia to Spain, and from Britain to Russia, elite dailies (and weeklies) spread their serious journalism into every corner of the continent and, increasingly, into distant lands. The great dailies of Europe are probably the most erudite and knowledgeable in the world, providing insights available nowhere else.

All types of quality papers are to be found in Europe. There are the great dailies of most of western Europe, led by the superserious *Neue Zürcher Zeitung* of Switzerland, *Le Monde* of France, *The Times* and *The Guardian* of Britain, and *Frankfurter Allgemeine* of West Germany. There are the elite of

Spain such as *ABC, La Vanguardia Española,* and *El País,*[25] and the Communist elite such as *Pravda* and *Izvestia* of Russia and *Borba* and *Politika* of Yugoslavia. There are the dailies of Scandinavia such as Oslo's *Aftenposten,* Copenhagen's *Berlingske Tidende,* and Stockholm's *Dagens Nyheter* that combine a rather flashy typographical dress with a heavy diet of serious news and views. There are also such dailies as *Die Welt* of Bonn and *Corriere della Sera* of Milan which are able to combine a modern demeanor with a solid seriousness. And, of course, there is the stolid drabness of ultraseriousness to be found in the daily of Vatican City, *Osservatore Romano.* The European elite press offers the reader a wide selection of packaging and political orientation; there is a paper whose journalistic style and philosophy, as well as size, layout, and typographical tone, appeal to any kind of serious newspaper reader.

It is interesting to note that in the areas of the world where daily journalism is most advanced and there are many elite newspapers, there are also the largest numbers of journalism schools, press institutes, and training programs of one type or another. This concern with, or emphasis on, journalism education is coupled with a high development of education generally. In the developing nations, such as are common in Asia and Africa, what little emphasis on journalistic training has been begun is still concerned chiefly with the technical aspects of journalism: typesetting, printing, newsprint acquisition, and the overcoming of basic economic handicaps. On the other hand, in the more advanced nations where the elite press is strongest, these elemental problems are secondary in journalism education and a concern with editorial quality, ethical standards, and social responsibility come in for more consideration. This nontechnical and noneconomic emphasis or approach inevitably results in a higher quality journalism.

* * *

The purpose of the fifty profiles which follow in the main part of this book is to provide a closer look at some of the great daily papers of the world. We do not contend that these fifty exhaust the ranks of the great or elite world dailies; they are merely what we believe to be a good representative sample of such newspapers. As such, they should provide the reader with some insights into what makes a newspaper great.

Profiles of great dailies which follow are not exhaustive histories or analyses; rather, they offer a brief view of typical elite papers in an attempt to highlight their common and differentiating characteristics and to provide some historical perspective. An underlying purpose, and perhaps the most important one, is to show that among the thousands of daily papers in the world, there are conscientious and intelligent journals dedicated to serious discourse and bound together by invisible cords into a fraternity of prestige and excellence.

[25] This daily of Madrid has been one of the fastest rising stars in the skies of Europe's great newspapers. It is a well-edited and well-written, tough-minded, thorough and intelligent paper. Founded after Franco died in November, 1975, it was called even by 1977 "one of the most informative and accurate in Europe." Stanley Meisler in the *Los Angeles Times* (Part II, p. 9), Sept. 30, 1977.

2

FIFTY PROFILES:
Examples of Greatness

MADRID, MIERCOLES 22 DE FEBRERO DE 1978

El presidente y los ministros, a pie

HUELGA EN EL PARQUE MOVIL DE MINISTERIOS

La mayoría de los empleados del Parque Móvil de Ministerios de Madrid se declaró ayer en huelga en apoyo de diversas reivindicaciones laborales. El paro se extendió inmediatamente a otras ocho provincias y se cree que hoy será secundado por otras cuatro más. El presidente del Gobierno y sus ministros y los presidentes de las Cortes y del Tribunal de Cuentas del Reino se vieron directamente afectados, ya que sus conductores se encontraban en huelga.

ABC

(SPAIN)

ONE OF SPAIN'S MOST prestigious dailies, *ABC* claims the highest circulation of all newspapers in the country. Its format, that of a small tabloid, combines the contents of a picture paper and a daily with thorough news coverage and excellent features.

Despite Spain's unrest and inflation, *ABC*'s circulation has been rising steadily in recent years—a mark of its popularity and credibility. In 1968, its circulation was near the 200,000 mark, with its Sunday edition just passing the 240,000 total. Present circulation of the weekday editions hovers around 240,000 daily, while that of its Sunday paper is around 375,000 (*La Vanguardia* of Barcelona claims a circulation of 280,000.) Some 75 percent of the issues are sold in street sales, the remaining 25 percent by subscription.[1] Ever since 1929, an edition of *ABC* has been published in Seville, where it circulates over 70,000 copies. In recent years, this edition's editor has been Joaquin Carlos López Lozano, one of Spain's most distinguished journalists.

ABC, while maintaining its position as Spain's top circulation daily, faces stiff competition. Three-fourths of the nation's dailies are morning newspapers, all offering competition with *ABC*'s morning publication. In recent years, other quality newspapers such as *El País* have been vying for *ABC*'s prestige as a national daily and its circulation leadership. But, to date, *ABC*'s appealing format, thorough news coverage and excellent presentation of educational, cultural and religious developments and features have kept it Spain's top circulation daily.

ABC was founded as a weekly in 1903 by Torcuato Luca de Tena y Alvarez-Ossorio. Just two years later, on June 1, 1905, it was converted to a daily with a three-column format and solid news on the front page. Thus, its history is rather brief when compared with many of Europe's elite newspapers. The first daily issue of *ABC* declared that it would be a newspaper of general information, but that the use of pictures would be stressed. The paper has taken that approach ever since.

[1] Carlos Mendo, Sub-director of *ABC*, in response to questionnaire and letter to H. Fisher, January, 18, 1978.

Torcuato Luca de Tena y Alvarez-Ossorio had brought the idea of an illustrated news magazine from Berlin. Born in Seville in 1861 as the son of an industrialist, he had studied law and had travelled widely throughout Europe.
There he developed a love for journalism as he observed the great progress in
the graphic arts in France and Germany. When he returned, he launched
Blanco y Negro in May, 1891, and it was an immediate success. His 1903 exper-
iment in tabloid-sized journalism, the *ABC*, also caught on at once. He was
honored for his visionary work in small-format journals when King Alfonso XIII
conferred on him the title of "Marques de Luca de Tena" on January 23, 1929.[2]
Without a doubt, he ranks in Spanish journalism history as one of the two or
three greatest journalists.

The paper's founder directed its activities until he died in 1929. Then, for a
decade, his son Ignacio took charge of the paper's directorial duties. Across the
conflict years of World War II, from 1939 to 1947 José Losada de la Torre
served as *ABC*'s director. He was succeeded by Ramón Pastor y Medívil, who
quit as director in 1952 in favor of the founder's grandson, Torcuato Luca de
Tena y Brunet. The latter remained at the helm just two years. Then, in 1954,
Luis Calvo Andaluz took over *ABC*'s directorship, a position he held until 1962,
when Torcuato de Luca de Tena y Brunet returned to head the paper. He continued in that position until 1975, when he became publisher of the newspaper.
Meantime, Mr. Cebrian Bone succeeded to the position of editor-in-chief in
March, 1975, and assumed those duties until mid-September, 1977. The
present editor of *ABC* and president of the private company Prensa Española,
which owns the *ABC*, is Señor Guillermo Luca de Tena y Brunet.[3]

ABC's history has not been without vicissitudes. Its founders represented
the Bourbon Monarchist views. Ever since, to varying degrees, it has always
aligned itself with the Monarchy, and sometimes has come under attack for that
allegiance. For example, for speaking out strongly in favor of the Monarchy, it
was taken over by the Republican Government in May, 1931. It was long tolerated as the big opposition paper, but was watched very closely by the Republican Government when it was in power. In the end, the paper proved to be a
maverick. In August, 1932, it was suspended for nearly four months for urging
less censorship. Again, in June, 1936, the Government stepped in, this time actually taking over the building of "Prensa Española, S.A.," the publishing company that was printing *ABC* and other publications. The entire editorial and
printing organization of *ABC* was held under tight control by the Republicans
until Madrid was "liberated" by Franco's forces in March, 1939.

During the time of Franco and the restoration of the Monarchy in Spain,
ABC backed the regime. But that stance did not imply for the paper that it
should not be critical or that it would escape trouble. In June, 1972, for example, the paper published a cartoon which implied that Spain's fundamental
laws were present but not functioning effectively. For this action, the nation's
Information Ministry opened proceedings against Torcuato Luca de Tena, then

[2] For early history of *ABC* and its editors, see Arturo Mori, *La Prensa Española de Nuestro Tiempo*
(Mexico: Ediciones Mensaje, 1943), pp. 61–64.
[3] Mendo letter and questionnaire.

editor of *ABC*.[4] This action was part of a two-year period (1972–1973) when penalties were imposed on 133 Spanish journals. During this time, the daily *Madrid* was first suspended, then closed down early in 1973. Several foreign newspapers were also seized by a hyper-sensitive Information Ministry.

As this period of restrictions progressed, newspapers began to resist more aggressively. Article Two of Spain's Law on the Press was seen as a measure which would permit the Government to tighten up controls and bring back strict censorship on political or social issues. At the same time, the press had certain liberties, for the Government was opening up and seeking acceptance in the European Economic Community. Radio and television were granted a certain autonomy. As a result, the papers began to consider ways to retain and perhaps expand their restricted freedoms.[5] The suspensions, seizures and restrictions picked up their pace as the newspapers tried to publish their own views more openly. The Barcelona paper *Noticiero Universal* was charged for writing an article in favor of a general political amnesty. The news magazine *Cambio 16* was fined and suspended for urging political reform. During February and March, 1975, about a dozen newsmen were indicted or tried before the Public Order Court, the political arm of Spain's judiciary system. Because it contained an interview with Count Juan of Barcelona, governmental officials ordered *ABC* to remove an entire section of its February 23, 1975, edition. Official ambivalence about suppression was reflected, however, when on the next day it allowed the *ABC* publisher to run the interview after all.[6]

The democratization of Spain and the subsequent relaxation of political restrictions in 1977 were accompanied by violence between right and left which caught Spain's media in the crossfire. At the same time, police and the bureaucracy found it hard to shake off the restrictive customs they had exercised for a generation. A *Diario 16* reporter was arrested and held for 20 days and the editor of *El País* was jailed and fined for an article on contraception. Some newspapers were bombed and several foreign journalists were assaulted during this period. *ABC* rode out the storm as the media's rights and freedoms gradually gained credence and official support.[7]

The first eight to sixteen pages of *ABC* comprise a picture magazine section in rotogravure, complete with full page advertisements. The entire front page usually consists of a single action photograph, but sometimes there are several related pictures. All of *ABC*'s photographs are clear, well-composed and graphic. The picture magazine section will contain photo essays in the style made famous by *Life* magazine or will be features accompanied by photographs. Then a news and feature section numbering anywhere from 35 to 65 pages follows. On Wednesdays, when advertising is especially heavy and may cover a total of 45 to 50 pages, the paper may extend to 120 or more pages. In general, the quantity of advertising is heavy.

The paper's nameplate appears at the beginning of its news-feature section.

[4] "Spain," *IPI Report*, 21:9 (September, 1972), pp. 6–7.
[5] "Europe: Spain," *IPI Report*, 23:1 (January, 1974), p. 9.
[6] "The Press Under Pressure: Spain," *IPI Report*, 24:4/5 (April/May, 1975), p. 13.
[7] "World Press Freedom Review of 1977," *IPI Report*, 27:1 (January, 1978), p. 10.

The first page typically includes a top international, national or local story or two for the day. The second page is reserved for editorials and page three, opposite, for reader opinions. A "National Information" section, often extending eight pages and including a page of news on Parliament follows. There is then a seven- or eight-page spread of international news, representing the nation's best foreign news coverage. This part of the paper also regularly features a consistently good page of educational news and another on the church, plus pages given to Madrid news. Near the end of this section, there are two pages worthy of note: a page of the latest information entitled "Ultima Hora En ABC," and a feature page entitled "Tribuna Pública."

One of ABC's greatest strengths is its emphasis on culture. Its cultural features of many types—on the arts, drama, music, literature, films, and so on—are particularly noteworthy. Its literary critiques are considered extremely good. The ABC learned to develop high quality in the non-controversial cultural areas during the authoritative days when it had to temper its one-time fiery political pieces. Between its emphases on numerous and varied news features and on culture and the arts, ABC has achieved an aura of intellectualism and quality that compensates to a large degree for its deficiencies in "hard news" and in certain production techniques.

In recent years, the ABC's news coverage has improved as it has added to its editorial staff. In 1968, it had a total editorial staff of about 120, including 51 writers and editors, 60 reporters stationed throughout Spain and 9 foreign correspondents. Today, the editorial staff numbers 166, with 61 reporters in Madrid to cover national and local governmental news.

Perhaps ABC's greatest strength in news coverage is its presentation of foreign events and information. It keeps nine full-time correspondents in the world's key cities: New York, Bonn, Brussels, Moscow, Lisbon, Rome, Paris and Buenos Aires. Part-time correspondents also report from Oslo and Tel Aviv. Other overseas material comes from the seven news wire agencies the paper receives: UPI, AP, Reuters, AFP, Europa Press, EFE (the Spanish News Agency) and Logos (a domestic, regional agency). The paper's frequently excellent overseas news photos come either from its own correspondents or from UPI and Cifragrafica Wirephoto. ABC can point with pride to several distinguished foreign correspondents, among them Luis Calvo, Jacinto Miquelarena and José Maria Massip.[8]

Probably ABC's top asset is its large group of famous contributors who write stimulating pieces on a wide variety of subjects for its pages. This group of critical writers on books, the theater, the cinema, art, music and bull-fighting are the best in Spanish journalism. There are also several talented, versatile collaborators, such as Cézar González Ruano, who is able to write on almost any subject with power and charm. ABC's intense and precise language has always set the tone for high quality for all of Spanish journalistic writing. Its vigorous journalistic style, which to a large extent has been accepted as a sort of "formula" in Spanish journalism, was basically established by José Cuartero (1869–1946).

[8] Mendo questionnaire.

Cuartero never wasted a word, and his articles were forceful and expressive—especially his political editorials. Others of *ABC*'s staff, such as Alfonso Rodriquez Santa Maria, who has been considered the most forceful and versatile writer in Spain in recent years, have carried on the newspaper's concern for quality writing.

Today, *ABC* is thought of as a Spanish institution. It is designed to appeal primarily to Spain's middle-class readers and it is read widely by them all over the nation. But its readership extends beyond Spain and its airmail edition, launched in 1950, has grown steadily in popularity.

ABC continues to stand for "the unity of Spain, the defense of the Monarchy as form of State and the free-enterprise system."[9] During the days when it was unable to express it political views pungently and critically and had to compensate by upgrading its non-political pieces and pictures in non-controversial areas, *ABC* was already considered an elite newspaper, among the best that Spain could offer. Now that restrictions have relaxed and the paper can be completely independent and now that it is upgrading its factual reporting to add to the continuing excellence of its writing and the vigor of its literary and cultural emphases, *ABC* promises to become an even higher quality newspaper. In fact, the product of Serrano 61 in Madrid—*ABC*—appears to have the potential to rate one day as one of the world's very best dailies.

Aftenposten

(NORWAY)

Aftenposten calls itself "Norway's leading newspaper," and there are numerous justifications to substantiate its claim. There are equally good reasons to rank this Oslo daily among the world's quality, elite newspapers.

The *Aftenposten* (Evening Post) undoubtedly rates as Norway's most prestigious paper and as one of the four or five best in all Scandinavia. It claims Norway's largest circulation, with some 215,000 copies of the morning edition and 187,000 of its evening issue. It, incidentally, is the only Norwegian paper with two separate editions each day. About 87 percent of the sales are subscriptions; the remainder come from street kiosks. In keeping with Norwegian law, no Sunday edition is published, but the big weekend edition put out on Saturday circulates some 250,000 copies.[1] If any Norwegian paper might be considered a

---

[9] Mendo questionnaire.

[1] Trygve Ramberg and Hans Vatne, Managing Editors, *Aftenposten*, in reply to questionnaire, May 8, 1978.

national daily, it is the *Aftenposten,* for at least 60,000 copies circulate outside Oslo on weekdays and as many as 80,000 on Saturdays. In addition to its two daily editions, *Aftenposten* publishes the weekly color magazine *A-Magasinet,* a weekly Radio and TV magazine and the monthly *Today* magazine.

Like most Norwegian newspapers, *Aftenposten* has no formal party affiliation, but it does favor the Conservative Party. It rates its own political point-of-view midway on a seven-point "conservative-liberal" scale. Its major ideological competitor is the 60,000-circulation *Arbeiderbladet,* Norway's leading social democratic newspaper and the official organ of the Labor Party. The other competitor is the liberal afternoon *Dagbladet,* with a circulation of about 90,000. Judged by circulation figures, Norway's Conservative-leaning dailies are the strongest, though only slightly more so than the more liberal or center-of-the-road papers. But, with 40 papers belonging to the Labor Party, the left is not to be scorned and is stronger than in most other Scandinavian countries. For several years now, there has been a loosening of newspaper-party ties, especially of the conservative-liberal variety such as *Aftenposten.*[2]

Aftenposten springs from a strong, vigorous freedom-seeking press tradition. The roots of the Norwegian press extend back to the fourteenth century handwritten sheets describing political events, battles and catastrophes. Norway was ruled by Denmark until 1814, and history reveals a long public struggle for greater freedoms, including the freedom of the press. Consequently, it is not surprising that, with the coming of Norwegian independence from Denmark, power was placed in a people's parliament and Section 100 of the Constitution read: "There shall be liberty of the press. Everyone shall be at liberty to speak his mind freely regarding the administration of the state or any other subject whatsoever."[3] Then a long fight ensued to overcome the dominance of the Swedish king, who originally had helped Norway recover from economic depression. During that period, the press grew rapidly and several of today's leading dailies were born, among them the *Aftenposten,* founded in 1860 by Christian Schibsted.

Schibsted headed a new direction in Norwegian newspapers. Until his day, the main emphasis had been on politically-oriented articles. Schibsted sensed that his readers were hungry for news, and he began emphasizing local coverage of events, a strength of the *Aftenposten* ever since. When Schibsted's main competitor, the *Morgenbladet* came out with an afternoon edition to take trade away from *Aftenposten,* Schibsted countered by furnishing his afternoon edition at no additional cost to what customers were paying for his morning paper. Schibsted quickly built up his paper's reputation for excellent coverage not only of local events but also of national government and of many cities in Norway and abroad. As a result, *Aftenposten*'s circulation rose rapidly to 14,500 daily, ahead of its rival. In 1889, Schibsted's son Amandus became editor of *Aftenposten.*[4]

[2] "Norway," *IPI Report,* 26:4 (April, 1977), p. 5.
[3] Kenneth E. Olson, *The History Makers: The Press of Europe from Its Beginnings through 1965* (Baton, Rouge, Louisiana State University Press, 1966), p. 68.
[4] *Ibid.,* p. 68f.

Aftenposten

Morgenutgave. Onsdag 22. februar 1978. Nr. 89. 119. årgang. Kr. 2,50. Flysendt Nord-Norge kr. 2,75.

Kongen i Syden

Utvalgte elitenavdelinger i stram giv akt hilste kong Olav ved ankomsten til Lisboa igår.
(Foto: John Myhre.)

Militære elitenavdelinger og klingende musikk hilste kong Olav velkommen på Lisboas flyplass da han igår innledet sitt offisielle besøk i Portugal. Langs veien inn til Quelusslottet som er Kongens residens under oppholdet, ventet barn med hjemmelagede norske flagg og håndtegnede plakater med teksten «Takk, Norge». Senere på dagen åpnet Kongen en stor Munch-utstilling.
Side 44.

Slutt på arabisk boikott av Aker

De arabiske land er blitt enige om å oppheve boikotten av Akergruppen som handelspartner. Akergruppen ble, etter det Aftenposten erfarer, strøket av de arabiske lands uoffisielle svartelister ved årsskiftet.

Boikotten av den norske verkstedgruppen ble innledet etter at Akergruppen i 1960-årene leverte flere fruktskip til Israel, skip som det ble hevdet letti kunne utrustes til bruk i krig. Opphevelsen av boikotten førte til at Bergens Mekaniske Verksteder kom inn i bildet ved bygging av to hotellskip til Egypt. Etter det Aftenposten erfarer, har Akergruppen selv søkt om å bli strøket av listen.
(s. 23)

«Dødsattest til bokmål»

Det er på tide å utstede dødsattest over 1938-rettskrivningen for bokmålet når den ikke har klart å slå igjennom på førti år, sier Lars Roar Langslet til Aftenposten om dagens språksituasjon i vårt land. Det er absurd å ha en rettskrivning som er så fjern fra det folk eller sier på trykk i aviser og bøker. Langslet legger til at NRK bør legge større vekt på å kvalitativt godt nynorsk enn å ha blikket ensidig festet på prosentandelen og tallmagi.
Side 3.

Norsk hurra for VM-ener

Han har skrevet skihistorie den 22 år gamle Josef Luszczek fra Zakopane i Polen. Han gikk til topps i en meget hard sekundstrid på tirsdagens 15 km, foran Sovjets Beljajev og finnen Mieto. Dermed skaffet ungguten Polen det første VM i langrenn og når man vet at han var den eneste polske løperen i tirsdagens 15 km, så ble det 100 prosent uttbytte. Denne polakken som til nå er VM's største i sporet kommer til Holmenkollen. Sporten.

Det var norske som fikk se Josef Luszczek i aksjon i Lahtis og som jublet med ham på polakkens største dag
(Foto: Erik Berglund.)

Hun blir i rasbygden

Minuttet før sneskavlen løsnet i Oldervik, kalvet Elsa Jensens Litago. Jeg flykter ikke fra dyrene, sier hun. – Tvinges jeg herfra, anmelder jeg øvrigheten til dyrebeskyttelsen! Rasfaren er fortsatt stor mange steder på kysten i nord. I Breivikeidet fire mil fra Tromsø er 80 mennesker bedt om å forlate sine hjem. Side 4.

Elsa Jensens kalv kom til verden like før raset gikk i Oldervik. – Folk fra øvrigheten kom og ba oss flytte til byen, men skulle vi flykte fra kua, kalven og sauene? spør hun. Rundt henne ligger plankebiter. Over henne henger sneskavlen.
(Foto: Alf G. Andersen.)

Kronglet vei ut av uføret for bedriftene

– Pyntejusteringer og utsettelse av reformer og pålegg kan ikke på lengre sikt redde norske bedrifter. Den smale og kronglete vei ut av uføret er tilpasning til markedet og konkurransen og mer varige rammevilkår fra Statens side, skriver sivil-

økonom Per Gundhus i dagens gjestespalte på næringslivssiden. Han oppfordrer dyktige bedriftsledere til å om-unngått grunnsetning av samøringsøkonomiens skjær til i større grad å tre frem og dele sine erfaringer.
Side 25.

Grieghallen i rute

Efter en usammenhengende byggeperiode på ti år, nærmer nå Grieghallen seg klargjøring. Det arbeides på spreng for å få huset ferdig til Festspillene i Bergen åpner, og innvielsesdatoen er satt til 23. mai. I første omgang vil huset bare benyttes som konsertlokale.
1. side 4. seksjon (s. 35).

Aktuell debatt
Side 22

Rubrikkannonsenes plassering
Vi henviser til oversikten med sidehenvisning på siste side, 1. seksjon.

When the Norwegians finally freed themselves from Swedish control in 1905, the press exercised its freedom well and played a critical role in national progress, and *Aftenposten*'s part in this process was not insignificant. It was particularly instrumental in keeping the nation informed about labor controversies and social welfare legislation.

During World War II, however, press freedom was effectively curbed by the Nazi Party machine. *Aftenposten* had patriotically warned Norwegians of the dangers of German expansionism. When the Nazis struck in April, 1940, the editor of *Aftenposten* was awakened, marched to his office, where he was confronted by his former elevator operator, a Quisling supporter, dressed in a German officer's uniform and telling him the paper was now in German hands. During the remainder of the war, *Aftenposten* and the rest of Norway's newspapers were forced to fill their columns with Nazi propaganda. By 1941, *Aftenposten* was a dull and monotonous voice of Hitler's "new order." Many Norwegian editors found devious ways to inform people of some of the facts between the lines or by adroit wording of ads. Others went underground. In all, 69 were executed and some 3,000 others sent to concentration camps.

Today's *Aftenposten,* a standard-format, eight-column, well-edited and attractive paper, averages 44 pages for its morning issues and 16 for its evening editions. Morning and afternoon issues are edited in one continuous run; morning news material that appeared in the afternoon is not repeated and afternoon stories continue from where they finished when the morning *Aftenposten* was "put to bed." Advertising accounts for some 65 percent of the morning edition's space and about 45 percent of that of evening issues, or, according to the editors, about 56 percent on the average. Ads are attractively done, sometimes in four colors. A few small ads appear on the lower portion of the front page. Three colors are often used on the front page—red, blue, and green most frequently—to mark off in boxes and call attention to certain news items and features. Lately, there is considerable use of color photographs. Color registration is clean and colors are vivid. Makeup is neat. Excellent use of white space, particularly around headlines, adds to the layout appearance. Like many Scandinavian papers, *Aftenposten* combines the best of German-style makeup with the most attractive appearances of American papers, and the results are very pleasing. Like other Scandinavian papers, too, its pages are agglutinated at the fold.

The contents of *Aftenposten* are well organized. A typical morning issue will have four sections, the first contining news and commentary; the second, sports news; the third, business and financial items; and the last, a special section featuring reports, political news and the like. Normally, the leading national and international news can be found on the front page of the first section. Page three features foreign news and is accompanied by several well-selected photographs. Editorial commentary by the paper's editors and guest writers appears on page four. Culture and family pages follow. There is also a page for reader feedback and some for entertainment features (comics, chess, entertainment). Numerous clear, well-composed photographs, many of them of large size, are used effectively throughout the paper.

Of all the Norwegian papers, *Aftenposten* has the best coverage of foreign news, as regards number and amount of sources and amount of copy printed. The paper draws from seven full-time foreign correspondents and seven stringers of its own.[5] It counts among its correspondents overseas the well-known Per Egil Hegge, who has served in Moscow and is currently assigned to Washington, D.C. It receives its principal wire input from Norsk Telegrambrya (NTB), the national news agency which subscribes to Reuters and Agence France-Presse. But it also receives Associated Press, the New York *Times* News Service and the London *Daily Telegraph* News Service. Syndicated services from New York *Times* columnists and several Norwegian sources plus photowires from AP and NTB complete the paper's foreign input. The editors note that "the material from our own correspondents and from New York *Times* make up a very important part of our foreign coverage."[6] In general, the paper takes a more critical view of Communism and a more favorable view of the United States than do the other major Scandinavian dailies.

Aftenposten's national and local news coverage is also outstanding. The paper keeps a corps of 11 correspondents at the National Assembly and at Oslo City Hall. Forty-one reporters cover local news and the cities and towns of Norway. One indicator of the paper's nation-mindedness is the page of news briefs about other parts of Norway it carries daily. Its economic news is considered superior and this observation of the editors explains why:

> In recent years *Aftenposten* has developed a growing business section devoted to the coverage of national and also to some degree international economy. The economic pages include not only business material, but also labor relations and industrial developments. We also include economic journalism directed more to the specific interest and need of the families and single readers.[7]

Aftenposten is particularly strong in the areas of art, music, literary and other cultural material. The paper has developed its cultural pages well. Films, dramas, television, books, music and philosophy are all given fair, extensive and serious treatment. Equally noteworthy is its coverage of educational problems, science and medical news. There is even a page for debates. It carries more book reviews than any other newspaper in Norway. Special book review pages are run in the fall season when the majority of new books appear on the Norwegian market. A full-time staff of 17 prepares material for the cultural pages.

In presenting cultural materials, other features and news, the *Aftenposten* has never catered to crime, sex or other lurid materials. True, it covers crime and sex, but it avoids their sensational aspects. When it does report on an important trial of a sensational nature, it often does not give the names of the defendants, even though radio, television and other papers have done so. While all Norwegian papers seldom report suicides, *Aftenposten* never does.

A total staff of 1,504 members combines efforts to make *Aftenposten* the attractive quality product it is. Of that number, 407 have technical jobs, 887 man-

---

[5] Full-time correspondents are located in New York, Washington, D.C., Moscow, London, Brussels, Bonn and Stockholm. Part-timers are spotted in Copenhagen, Madrid, New Delhi, Rome, Torshavn, Tokyo and Paris.

[6] Ramberg and Vatne questionnaire.

[7] Ramberg and Vatne questionnaire.

agerial and administrative tasks and there are 190 on the writing and editorial staff. Within the last, there are two chief editors, five subordinate editors and two in charge of editorial administration. Besides the general and political reporters and cultural staff already mentioned, ten staffers serve the business and financial section; four, the family pages; 13, the sports desk; another 13 (besides foreign correspondents), the foreign desk; seven, local news; three, the debate pages; and ten, the magazine and Saturday special pages. In addition, there are court and police reporters, entertainment writers, an obituary writer, a dozen photographers and 25 central desk copy editors and rewrite personnel.[8]

In general, the *Aftenposten* staff is committed, well trained and contented. The paper seeks staff members with the highest possible general knowledge and journalistic experience and training. It singles out for staff membership those with special knowledge or academic training in fields such as politics, international relations, economics, arts, language, sports, teaching and education.[9] Morale of staff members is high. In addition to the pride felt in writing for so influential a paper, the *Aftenposten* employee can expect many fringe benefits. There is a good sick pay plan. On the average, *Aftenposten* employees are paid better than those of any other newspaper in Norway.

As of this writing, the *Aftenposten*, like all Norwegian papers, has not been able to modernize to the point of using video display terminals for its editorial work because the Labor Courts have granted composition employees a monopoly on VDT operation. Negotiations between the management and unions to overcome this technicality are under way, however. For its composition work, *Aftenposten* uses cold, computer-controlled equipment, two electronic perforator inputs and two autologic photo type setters. After pasteup in the newsroom in downtown Oslo, the paper then utilizes Eocom wireless lasers scanner transmission to film in the pressroom in the new printing plant located outside the city. The paper is then printed on five Goss Metro presses.

Schibsted Publishing, a private family company owned by six members,[10] publishes *Aftenposten* and another Oslo paper, *VG*, an independent liberal daily. Because it is a high circulation daily, *Aftenposten's* advertising revenues are good. Consequently, it is financially sound and not in need of the government subsidies received by about two-thirds of Norway's papers. The country's population is sparse and widely scattered; therefore, many newspapers are small and risky financial ventures. At the request of the press, the Norwegian Government decided in 1969 to provide "survival" subsidies to the weaker papers, usually those with circulation under 10,000. Subsidies are based on the consumption of newsprint for the editorial portion of the paper. Eligible papers receive assistance through reduced rates for postal distribution, exemption from value added taxes, loans and government advertising. So far, fears that government assistance might affect press freedom have not been substantiated, partly because of the mutual high respect and cooperation that exist between government and the

[8] Ramberg and Vatne questionnaire.
[9] *Ibid.*
[10] The paper's six owners are Helle Bennett, Henrik J. S. Huitfeldt, Catherine Riddervold, Hans Riddervold, Tini Nagell-Erichsen and Einer Fr. Nagell-Erichsen. The last is also Director.

press.[11] Since *Aftenposten* receives no subsidies, there is no immediate threat to the freedom of its advocacy role. However, its editors remain cautious; since the introduction of subsidies, they are saying, "it is important to draw a sharp line between the allocation of subsidies . . . and any public influence on the management or control of newspapers."[12]

The Norwegian press is one of the world's freest and *Aftenposten* editors wish to preserve that freedom. Besides the potential danger subsidies could bring, there have been other recent inroads to threaten full press freedom. Alcohol and tobacco advertising have been banned and a new law designed to protect consumer interests regulates how products and services are to be presented in advertising columns. Some critics are now pressing for publicly appointed members on all newspaper boards.

But *Aftenposten* editors perceive their mandate to be more than mere preservation of a free press, important though that may be. They want that their paper should represent the values that build the responsible society with well-protected individual freedoms:

> *Aftenposten* wishes to stand for freedom, for a free, open society with individuals free to make their own choices. Therefore, it opposes oppression regardless of political color. It tries to advocate social responsibility and equal opportunities, but without unnecessary government control. It believes in the freedom of initiative and opposes socialism. It advocates the basic humanistic Christian values. The paper believes that in our complex age society must take on large responsibility for the common good. But also the individual still must be encouraged to take responsibility for himself.[13]

Aftenposten editors take their newspaper's burden of championing the open, free society composed of free, responsible individuals seriously. The paper's editorial policy aims at publishing fair and correct news unless such reporting violates privacy, press ethics or libel or national security laws. It tries to present all sides in its news coverage and debate pages. It does investigative reporting on topics of importance and interest to its readers. It seeks to be reliable and serious in reporting facts. It bases its editorial decisions on the factual bases of a story, its news value and importance to the public, its fairness to the source and projected reader interest. Its editors hold that ". . . the most important guideline for *Aftenposten* is *not* to please its readers, but to *serve* them— even if it includes the risk of displeasing some of them by bringing material that is controversial."[14] To achieve those ends, the paper often presents opposing or minority views in its news and debate columns.

Because of its policies, *Aftenposten* appeals to a wide range of readers. It aims at all parts of the public, but it leans slightly to the broad middle and upper income groups. Readership also includes a large number of trade union mem-

---

[11] "Subsidy Principle Accepted But . . . ," *IPI Report*, 24:11 (November, 1975, pp. 8–10. See also "Effects of Growing Dependence on Government Aid," *IPI Report*, 25:4 (April, 1976), pp. 18–19; and "Norway," *IPI Report, op. cit.*, pp. 4–5.

[12] Ramberg and Vatne questionnaire.

[13] *Ibid.*

[14] Ramberg and Vatne questionnaire.

bers. There are thought-provoking materials for intellectuals. *Aftenposten,* in fact, considers one of its primary purposes to be education of the people. To that end, although it does not neglect human interest and general entertainment, it provides a steady diet of serious information features and news stories. One of the characteristic serious articles in the paper is the *kronikk* (chronicle), an essay with serious, intellectual content, usually dealing with some national or international problem. The editorial, locally written, also contains serious material, although it is somewhat more informal than the editorials of many quality papers. In culture and the arts, too, there is much informative material to broaden the understanding and appreciation of the reader.

There are, then, numerous reasons to rank *Aftenposten* among the best or elite newspapers, with quality that is protective of freedom and the best in journalistic tradition and with a prestige that reflects influence in high places. Its wide, balanced and serious journalistic coverage, independence on important issues and openness to expression of views and opinions other than its own ensure its role as a quality paper. And it is a serious, intellectually-oriented daily, although not exclusively so. That gives it prestige: one press observer has noted that *Aftenposten* is "a unique paper read by top people throughout the country."[15] At the same time, the paper presents a wholesome, well-rounded diet for the entire Norwegian family. Were Norwegian an international language, no doubt *Aftenposten* would make a significant impact on the thinking of the entire world.

The Age

(AUSTRALIA)

IN SPACIOUS AUSTRALIA, with its sparsely settled interior regions, dailies are concentrated in the state capital coastal cities. The sedate but lively city of Melbourne's candidate for world newspaper reknown is *The Age.* Certainly *The Age* is the state of Victoria's, if not Australia's, most prestigious and respected daily. And it commands an important place among the world's elite newspapers. Authorities have repeatedly classified *The Age* and the *Sydney Morning Herald* as Australia's two leading serious, responsible quality papers.

The similarities between *The Age* and the *Herald* are numerous. Both are morning dailies. Both represent Australia's best in authoritative reporting, penetrating analyses and interesting features. Both seek to appeal to young intellec-

[15] S. Fiorentini, "Serious, Well-Written and Reliable," *World Press News and Advertisers' Review,* London (August 27, 1965), p. 25.

Cabinet to study task force report on levies

Health costs review

Mr. Miller   Mr. Lucock

Opposition scores a tactical victory

From MICHELLE GRATTAN

CANBERRA. — The Labor Opposition scored a tactical triumph on Parliament's opening day yesterday when 17 Government MPs voted with it in a secret ballot.

The defection revolted against the Government's nominee for chairman of committees in the House of Representatives, Mr. P. C. Millar (NCP, Qld.).

They voted instead for the former veteran chairman of committees, Mr. Philip Lucock, also from the National Country Party, whom the Opposition had nominated.

Changes unlikely before July

From MICHELLE GRATTAN

CANBERRA. — The Federal Government yesterday gave notice of a major shake-up in health insurance arrangements to curb costs.

The Governor-General, Sir Zelman Cowen, said in his opening of Parliament speech that health insurance was under scrutiny.

He said the Government was considering ways the health scheme "might be further improved to provide a prompt and effective health insurance scheme which restrains increases in the cost of health care".

The Governor-General, Sir Zelman Cowen opens the 31st Parliament.

PARLIAMENT'S DULL, BUT THE CHANGING OF THE GUARDS IS REALLY WORTH SEEING.

Law practice

Death duties

Jordanians wooing Bob Hawke

AMMAN, Feb. 21. — The Jordanians are out to win ACTU president Bob Hawke.

What Sir Zelman said — 12
Hayden attacks Snedden — 15

Kennedy's killer 'had access to top secrets'

Oswald: a spy for Russians?

NEW YORK, Feb. 21. — Lee Harvey Oswald, the assassin of President Kennedy, had access to top military secrets and may have passed them to the Russians.

This claim is made in the first section of an intensive study of Oswald released today by the Readers' Digest.

Cover story

Budget not enough, say police

By LINDSAY MURDOCH

The Victoria Police Force could not increase its strength on its $118 million a year budget, the Chief Police Commissioner, Mr. Miller, said yesterday.

We have important names, in imported garments.   dominex

Dominex House
75-77 Bourke Street, Melbourne.
Phone 63.6395

Dominex Toorak
533A Toorak Road, Toorak.
Phone: 24.7988

NTG 3558

Appeal row threatens CES

By JOHN RENTSCH

Four Sydney Commonwealth Employment Service officers were stood down yesterday for refusing to process applications from outsiders for jobs in the service.

tuals. And both circulate primarily in their respective states. Although neither strives for national circulation—only the *Australian*,[1] founded in 1964, does—both are read widely throughout the nation. Yet each has a distinctive personality and has made significant qualitative contributions to Australian journalism.

The Age, with its present-day staff of 1,450 working in a modern five-story building on Spencer Street completed in 1969,[2] has come a long way from the days when it was established with a capital of just seven thousand English pounds as an eight-page independent liberal sheet selling for sixpence. But in many ways, among them a high respect for accuracy, a seeking after the truth, a liberal orientation in politics and a serious tone, the paper remains little changed. And all the while, as a "newspaper of record," it has significantly shaped Australian history.

Two brothers, John and Henry Cooke, founded *The Age* during gold rush days in 1854, just three years after Victoria colony had won a separate status from New South Wales. The founders chartered *The Age* as "a journal of politics, commerce and philanthropy." A printer's cooperative took it over in 1855 and after a year it was purchased in June, 1856, by Ebenezer Syme. Later the same year, Ebenezer's brother David became a partner.[3] Until 1908, the story of *The Age* was largely that of David Syme, whose vision, enterprise, fearlessness and liberal personality made a heavy impact both on *The Age* and on the political life of Victoria and the entire nation. Under Syme's leadership, *The Age* championed the high protective tariffs which did much to promote Australia's young industries. Under Syme, the paper's circulation grew from a mere 2,000 in 1860 to about 130,000 at the time of his death in 1908.

David Syme left *The Age* as a trust to his five sons, and his descendants have held financial interests in the paper ever since. Members of the family and their trustees held ownership until 1948, when a private ownership company, David Syme and Company, Ltd. was formed. David's son, Oswald, became Chairman of the directors and another Syme, H. R., General Manager. Today, the Syme family continues to exercise influence on *The Age* through a partnership between the Syme Trust and the John Fairfax and Sons, Ltd. newspaper group. The partnership, set up in 1966, now controls about three-fourths of the corporation's shares and three of the six members of the Board of Directors are direct descendants of David Syme, including *The Age*'s Managing Director, Ranald Macdonald.[4]

In recent years, daily circulation of *The Age* has increased dramatically to a present total of 236,000 copies. During the eight-year 1968–1976 period its daily sales soared over 24 percent; during the same time span the average growth of

[1] *The Australian* was established in Canberra, the capital, in July, 1964, the first new daily in twenty years. The paper is made up in Canberra, and printed in Sydney and Melbourne. It is a modern paper, using video terminals and computerized typesetting techniques. It has built up an outstanding network of correspondents all over Australia. It has become distinguished as a high quality, serious paper.

[2] Letter and questionnaire from P. J. Furze, Assistant to the Managing Director, *The Age,* January 12, 1978.

[3] W. Sprague Holden, *Australia Goes to Press* (Detroit, Wayne State University Press, 1961), p. 238.

[4] Furze questionnaire.

Australian daily circulation was four and one-half percent and *The Age*'s chief Victorian rivals, the *Sun* and the evening *Herald* were losing ground. Since Victoria contains over 27 percent of the nation's population and since 18 of Australia's largest corporations headquarter in Melbourne, prospects for increased circulation appear bright.[5]

The readers of *The Age* tend to be young, better-educated intellectuals fairly high on the economic ladder with a serious interest in news and societal activity. *The Age* considers its readers to be primarily academicians, politicians, government officials, businessmen and big-spending consumers who are active, inquisitive and interested participants in numerous cultural and business activities. It claims it has a much greater proportion of readers in the top socio-economic group, professional and managerial occupations than any other Victorian newspaper. In education and in income, *Age* readers are in the top quartile of the community and its editors consider it the best-read newspaper among the country's opinion-leaders. On-going readership research by *The Age* gives the following demographic profile: 43 percent of its readers (versus 21 percent for the total population) have at least some post-secondary education; 48 percent (v. 32 percent) have an annual income of over $10,000.; 43 percent (v. 37 percent) are aged 18–34 years; 41 percent (v. 22 percent) fall into the top socio-economic class; 21 percent (v. 12 percent) are employed in professional or managerial occupations; and 65 percent (v. 48 percent for total population) are light commercial television viewers watching less than 12 hours per week. *Age* readers tend to be influential in their respective occupations. In every category, *The Age* overshadows the percentages of its rivals.[6]

The readership surveys have also produced the following psychographic profile of readers of *The Age:* liberal attitudes towards social and economic issues, consumerist conscious, critical as consumers and with a strong concern for the environment. The profile also shows readers are cosmopolitan, permissive and tolerant, adventurous, experience seekers who desire the "good life," interested in the arts and financial matters. Few *Age* readers have a consuming sympathy for traditional values.[7] In general, *The Age* successfully maintains the tension between serious, worthwhile journalistic content and the brighter appeals which make it attractive to an alert readership.

At home, *The Age* is widely read and quoted in government circles. In spite of the paper's frequent attacks on his conservatism, it was Prime Minister Robert Menzies' favorite paper. *The Age,* the first paper to publish verbatim stories of a Prime Minister's press conference, has helped to break down the superciliousness with which the government traditionally treats the press. During its 125 years, the paper's involvement in controversial issues with outspoken editorial policies and its political liberal (with a small "l") stance have provided valuable advice to the thoughtful voter. It is concerned that there should be more middle ground in Australian politics. It is highly informative about the political

[5] Brochure, *The Age,* published by *The Age,* 1977, Appendixes b and e.
[6] Brochure, *The Age,* pp. 5 and 8 and Appendix d.
[7] *Ibid.,* pp. 10–11.

arena, and leaders in academic and government circles consider it the most valuable press source for information on Australia and its thinking.

While *The Age* is politically liberal, its social attitudes are somewhat more conservative, though less so now than in its early history. It continues to uphold its early traditions of aggressive, independent and outspoken editorship, authoritative reporting and penetrating analyses of overseas, national and local news. To encourage high-quality standards, it allocates its best-skilled journalists to a highly-respected "Insight" investigative reporting team.[8] For the past ten years, it has followed an editorial policy whereby the reporter responsible for the "straight" reporting of a news event also writes a sidebar "comment" column which is clearly separate from the factual report contained in the news story, and is clearly identified as the opinion of the reporter, whose name is given.[9] This policy has the advantage of allowing editorial commentary by the journalist perhaps best qualified to make such observations, yet it keeps the reporting of the event objective.

The Age claims to provide the best all-round news coverage of the country. It has led its newspaper competitors in sustained and well-researched analyses of many problems facing Australians and has definitely influenced corrective governmental actions. The numerous individual awards the paper's journalists and photographers (Australia has no publication awards) have received provide one form of evidence of the paper's high quality reporting and coverage.

Although *The Age* covers the entire range of news as comprehensively as any other Australian paper, it appears to be at its best with politics and economics. What Professor Henry Mayer of Melbourne University wrote over ten years ago tends to be true today—that the person who wants the best "over-all news content" would read *The Age*.[10] The principal criteria for determining what to cover are "newsworthiness, general public interest and the significance and potential impact of the issue on the community."[11]

The paper's writing and editorial staff totals about 180, with a support staff of another 70 persons. A small but effective staff of six foreign correspondents supplemented by seven stringers provides a steady stream of world news (usually found on pages six and seven) for *The Age*.[12] In addition, the paper takes the overseas wire services of the Australian Associated Press, which, in addition to its own overseas staff, draws from Reuters, the Associated Press and United Press International. And it takes syndicated services from three London sources—the *Observer,* the *Spectator* and *Sunday Times,* plus two from the United States, the New York *Times* and *Newsweek.* Its list of distinguished foreign correspondents in the past ten years includes Creighton Burns, Michael Richardson, Peter Cole-Adams and Bruce Grant.

[8] Furze questionnaire.
[9] *Ibid.*
[10] Henry Mayer, *The Press in Australia* (Melbourne, Melbourne University Press, 1968), p. 221.
[11] Furze questionnaire, *loc. cit.*
[12] As of this writing, full-time correspondents are located in Singapore, Port Moresby, San Francisco, Washington, London and Amman; part-timers in Johannesburg, Nairobi, Tel Aviv, Tokyo, Peking, Wellington and Rome. The evening Melbourne *Herald* has more foreign correspondents—about 24—but some authorities say Perth's *West Australian* has Australia's best foreign coverage.

49

The Age (Australia)

Although *The Age* does not claim to be a national paper, it gets excellent coverage for its front and inside pages from its eight correspondents in Canberra. The most important state and local news items are found on the front page; for full coverage of these fields, there are "Home News" pages (usually pages two through five). The editorial page carries incisive syndicated and local editorial commentary and space for feedback letters (usually pages eight and nine) from readers is extensive.

The second section of the paper is called "Business Age" and gives especial attention to Victoria's business world. These financial pages would be the envy of any daily in the world. Three or four "Sports Age" pages—the best in Australia—make up the back pages of this section.

All materials are well written—Australia's best writing is found in *The Age* and its leading serious daily competitor, the *Sydney Morning Herald*. On the average, the allocation of news space is as follows: international, nine percent; national, 15 percent; state and local, 18 percent; sports, 11 percent; news analysis and commentary, seven; arts, literary and crafts, seven; business and finance, eight and the remainder falls into several smaller percentage categories.[13]

While *The Age* is dignified, more serious than any other Australian paper and thorough in its coverage, it keeps in touch with the wide interests of its readers. Consequently, it provides high-quality entertainment as well, in the form of good syndicate features, comics, and cartoons. There are also many feature stories. A feature story of some leading personality with an accompanying picture regularly occupies a front-page slot. On balance, the paper sets a tone which is more serious than any other Australian daily.

The Age can afford to be intent on quality rather than on sensational popular appeals because of its secure financial condition. The late editor of the paper, Graham Perkin, noted in 1966 that his paper had the fourth highest volume of classified "small" ads in the world. About 1,600,000 classified advertisements are published each year, an average of over 30,000 each week. Space makeup for the average week is now about 340 pages per week as follows: editorial, 120 pages (35 percent); display advertising (some in color), 60 pages (18 percent) and classified ads, 160 pages (47 percent). Because of its solvency, *The Age* has been able in recent years to concentrate major expenditures on improvements in staff, foreign news coverage, plant modernization, sophisticated communications facilities and research. At this writing, video display terminals are being installed to modernize the newsroom.

The cultural pieces and feature articles found in *The Age* are probably without equal in Australia.[14] In addition to daily "service" features on shipping, weather and postal news, it carries a wide selection of interpretive articles and features catering to the entire family. Each week on given days, *The Age* includes significant and helpful regular features: Mondays, "Monday Job Market;" Tuesdays, "Epicure;" Thursdays, a 12-page lift-out Green Guide to entertainment; and Fridays, "Weekender" pages. In its large Saturday edition, which

[13] Furze questionnaire.
[14] Mayer, *op. cit.*

sometimes runs as many as 160 pages, it publishes a Literary Review which is considered by many to be one of the best of its type in the world. Color is sometimes used to set off these special feature pages.

Despite its comprehensiveness and general seriousness, the appearance of *The Age* is lively and attractive. A broadsheet, it exercises flexibility in column width from issue to issue and story to story. Consequently, a half dozen column widths may appear on a page. Good use is made of white space. Nearly all stories are complete on the same page. The front page typically carries a "Today—Tomorrow" announcement box at the top right, with a brief "News Summary" column just below it, followed by the weather and an index to the materials inside. A cartoon enlivens the left hand columns. Inside, the paper is orderly and easy to follow.

Although in the past university graduates have comprised only about 25 percent of *The Age*'s editorial staff, under the Cadet system prerequisites to employment are being stiffened. Now, the beginning reporter must have attained university-level standing. During the first year, the Cadet, as he is called, takes special courses in shorthand to achieve a required proficiency level. He is enrolled in the Royal Melbourne Institute of Technology, where, upon the successful completion of a four-year part-time course, he receives a Bachelor of Arts in Journalism degree.[15] During his Cadetship, the fledgling journalist receives salary raises each year plus other increases depending on the importance of his reporting assignments. Thus, the Cadet program (a similar pattern is used by most Australian newspapers) seeks to blend academic training with practical experience in preparing the young journalist for his professional career.

Although many forces have contributed to *The Age*'s excellence, across its history four people have been particularly influential in shaping it into a leader among Australia's serious, comprehensive quality dailies. To David Syme (and his descendants) must go the credit for setting the stage for its editorial boldness, liberal views, intellectual appeal, strong challenge to government and financial soundness. To J. S. Stephens, chief sub-editor for the paper for 50 years (1885–1935) goes the honor of being "An Inspiration to His Staff" for successfully upholding the paper's highest values all those years.[16] And the present managing director, C. Ranald Macdonald has, in the past decade, both helped to make *The Age* into what is perhaps Australia's most exciting and stimulating quality paper and achieved distinction for himself as chairman of the International Press Institute.

However, it was the late Graham Perkin who made the most significant impact on *The Age*'s development since 1966. As editor for the paper for the last nine years (1966–1975) before his premature death at 45, Perkin was the key figure in *The Age*'s transformation into a modern, attractive, comprehensive yet serious journal. Perkin was an advocate of excellence in investigative reporting and writing. An insatiable desire for truth fired him. His colleague, managing director C. R. Macdonald called Perkin's nine-year editorship a period of inspi-

[15] Furze questionnaire.
[16] Mayer, *op. cit.*, p. 44.

ration and leadership for *The Age*. At the time of Perkin's death, John Hamilton, a writer for *The Age*'s competing evening paper, the Melbourne *Herald*, wrote of Perkin's record after he had become *The Age*'s editor: "Then followed a most marvelous period in journalism as Perkin took hold of a staid, conversative, old newspaper, shook it, rattled it and turned it into what the *Times* of London has twice described as among the ten best newspapers in the world."[17] In a remarkably short time, Perkin had become recognized not only as a great Australian newspaperman but also as a figure of world stature in the field of journalism. In its recent history; no one has done as much as Perkin to help *The Age* live up to the goals to which its founders had dedicated it: ". . . to be the Record of Great Movements, the Advocacy of Free Institutions, the Diffusion of Truth and the Advancement of Man."

Al Ahram

(EGYPT)

THE MODEL OF ELITE JOURNALISM for the press in the remainder of the Arab world is Egypt's authoritative daily, *Al Ahram*. For over 100 years, through marked changes in government and press regulation, this newspaper's coverage of foreign and national news, its attention to social issues and the arts, its insightful editorial commentary and its production quality have made *Al Ahram* a household name in world journalism. Thus, it enjoys a long tradition as "the newspaper of the Arab world."

Although it is not Egypt's largest newspaper—Cairo's *Al Akhbar* has larger circulation—*Al Ahram* tends to be more a "newspaper of record" than other Egyptian dailies. At the same time, it is often considered Egypt's "semi-official" daily, with a capacity to speak for the government while at the same time remaining its critic. Its contents make it particularly appealing to the educated, the intellectuals and those interested in governmental affairs; it has considerably less appeal and information for the interests of the Egyptian villager than its competitor, *Al Gumhuria*.

Al Ahram, which means "The Pyramids," appears seven days a week. Along with *Al Akhbar* and *Al Gumhuria*, it is one of Egypt's highest circulation dailies Although its readership is down somewhat from the late 1960's, early in 1976 it had an impressive daily circulation record of 772,732 copies, with circulation on Fridays (the official Moslem holiday) at 1,104,142. Subscribers composed about

---

[17] John Hamilton, "Graham Perkin—One of the Greatest," Melbourne *Herald*, October 16, 1975.

six percent of the circulation; the remainder were street sales, the usual means of newspaper distribution in the Middle East.[1] In the governmental, diplomatic and educated circles of Egypt, it is *the* paper to read if one is to be fully informed.

Al Ahram's circulation figures for the Middle East and elsewhere reflect its widespread influence and prestige. Its circulation is the widest of any Arabic language newspaper in the world. Over 10,000 copies circulate daily—twice that on Fridays—each to Kuwait, Saudi Arabia, Libya, the Sudan, Syria and the United Arab Emirates. In other Arab nations, even those whose official policies oppose those of Egypt, the paper is widely circulated, particularly among the intellectuals and those in leadership positions. A surprising number of copies also go daily to readers of Arabic in Europe (about 6,500), the United States and Canada (4,650), Australia (about 2,500) and over 36,000 to other countries, especially in South America.[2]

Bishara and Salim Takla, two Lebanese Christians who had come to Egypt to seek more freedom, founded *Al Ahram*. The paper first appeared as a four-page weekly tabloid in Alexandria on August 5th, 1875. In its earliest days, it was dependent largely on the maritime affairs of Egyptian ports. It was published weekly, on either Friday or Saturday, until it became a daily in 1881. In 1890, it appeared in the broadsheet form it still has today. At the turn of the century, it moved to Cairo and on November 3, 1900, began publishing the main edition in the capital. An Alexandria issue was also published for a few years, but later dropped.[3]

Soon after its establishment, Al Ahram became an outstanding example of independent journalism, a purveyor of objective news reports instead of the political harangues common to most Egyptian papers of the time, and a lively and stimulating intellectual journal. Well into the present century, it led the parade of a great diversity of publications in many languages representing every conceivable point of view in Egypt.

As one of Egypt's independent newspapers, *Al Ahram* was subject to restrictions and censorship of the British occupation government, and during this period it was not the strong advocate of the Egyptian cause it might have been. The independents fought such limitations by whatever means they could command, and one of their chief weapons was the political cartoon. In fact, one could say the press was responsible during the 1930's and 1940's for the mobilization of public opinion which led to the 1952 Revolution and independence. During the heavy censorship days of the 1940's, two Egyptian weeklies, *Rose El-Youssef* and *Akher Saa* claimed the attention of Egyptian readers. The former's circulation soared to 70,000, well beyond that of *Al Ahram* and that of all other leading Cairo dailies at the time. By the time of independence, *Al Ahram* was a pale reflection of its colorful youth, and was called by some a "dying newspaper."[4]

[1] Brochure, "*Al Ahram* Newspaper: 100 Years," *Al Ahram* (Cairo, Egypt, 1976).
[2] *Ibid.*
[3] *Ibid.*
[4] Munir K. Nasser, "*Al-Ahram:* Elite Newspaper of the Arab World," PhD. Dissertation, University of Missouri, Columbia, 1977, p. 1.

الأهرام
Al-Ahram
رئيس مجلس الإدارة ورئيس التحرير
يوسف السباعي
رئيس التحرير: علي حمدي الجمال

الأربعاء
22 FEV. 1978

١٢ صفحة

٢٠ مليما

السنة ١٠٢ ربيع الأول ـ العدد ٣٣٣١١

الصاعقة كانت مستعدة لتنفيذ المهمة في أية عاصمة تهبط فيها الطائرة

السادات يشترك اليوم في تشييع الشهداء الأبطال حتى نصب الجندي المجهول

قائد قوات الصاعقة المصرية يعلن في مؤتمر صحفي:

- مفاجأة الاقتحام شلت الإرهابيين ودفعتهم للاستسلام
- القوات القبرصية تطلق النار على ظهورنا خلال عملية الاقتحام
- ٦٠ فردا واجهوا ببسالة المدرعات والحرس الوطني القبرصي

البطولة المتجددة

بقلم: علي حمدي الجمال

    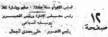 

مشروع أمريكي للتحكم الآلي في القناة

١١ محطة فنية على الشاطئين للمعونة العاجلة للسفن

أسماء شهداء الصاعقة يتم إعلانها اليوم

القوات المسلحة تنعي شهداء عملية قبرص الأبطال

مبارك يبدأ محادثاته مع الحسن

بدء افتتاح الصواريخ والهليكوبتر

١٣٠ مليون جنيه لتنفيذ قانون استصلاح الأرض والقطاع العام

أثرتون يصل اليوم إلى القاهرة بعد أن بحث مع ديان أمس إعلان المبادئ

تنفيذ قرار سحب بعثتنا في قبرص وإبلاغ بريطانيا شكر مصر على دورها

الرئيس يحضر جنازة شهداء الصاعقة

إقامة الجنازة على الهواء مباشرة

كيريانو يعلن استعداد حكومته لبذل كل الجهود لإعادة العلاقات

تعليق للأهرام
موقف غير مفهوم وتصريحات غير مفهومة

In 1957, five years after he came to power in Egypt, President Gamal Abdel Nasser made his long-standing and close friend, Mohammed Hussanein Heikal editor of *Al Ahram*. Long an outstanding journalist, Heikal quickly introduced innovations and began rebuilding the paper's prestige and circulation. "It was under Heikal that *Al Ahram* became one of the most authoritative and dependable sources for understanding what was happening in the Middle East."[5] Among the early changes he introduced, Heikal stressed the front page and emphasized significant news in big headlines. Foreign news was given a special portion of the second page, and a full "op-ed" page, including letters to the editor, commentary and articles of opinion was introduced. Because of his privileged position, Heikal felt free to criticize the ills of the Egyptian society without inhibition in *Al Ahram*.

When Nasser nationalized the press in 1960, Heikal had even more freedom to shape *Al Ahram*. He started a Friday supplement featuring his own regular weekly commentary called "Frankly Speaking." It often filled an entire page and became regarded by world diplomats and ordinary readers alike as the best public reflection of Nasser's thoughts, aspirations and plans. The supplement also featured news analyses and culture, with especial attention to foreign affairs, art, literature, science and sports. Within five years, Heikal made *Al Ahram* a leader in the world press. During his 17-year editorship, circulation arose phenomenally from 68,000 to 650,000 copies on weekdays and to nearly a million copies on Fridays.

Heikal's contribution to *Al Ahram* must not be under-emphasized. With his fluent pen, eloquent style and strong sense of news values, he personally made significant contributions to the development of his paper as the elite daily of the Arab world. As editor-in-chief, he stressed objective news and tried to avoid the emotionalism and sensationalism characteristic of the Egyptian press at the time. Some observers feel Heikal could be objective because of his closeness to Nasser and his access to all secrets of the state; others have criticized his total monopoly over the state news and believe his friendship with Nasser may have handicapped his objectivity.

Heikal made other significant contributions to *Al Ahram*. Because President Nasser relied heavily on radio and television for announcements and brief news of the state and to get his message across to the Egyptian people, Heikal made *Al Ahram* a counterpart which provided in-depth news coverage and commentary. He made it a "newspaper of record," usually publishing all or most of Nasser's long speeches. In the process, he selected and trained young university graduates at *Al Ahram* to become investigative reporters. He also developed the "Al Ahram Strategic Studies Center," which even today is Egypt's leading "think tank." Heikal first set up three separate centers at *Al Ahram* for journalistic, historical and political and economic studies. Later, he fused these three into his joint center for strategic studies and recruited for it a team of researchers to handle complex subjects such as conflict analysis and conflict resolution. As he created the center, Heikal had two quality-improvement purposes in mind—to build a dependable and accurate source of materials for story back-

5 *Ibid.*, p. 2f.

ground and news analysis and to prepare reporters for better control of editorial and opinion pages.[6] Today, professional scholars at the center who conduct research in a serious fashion contribute a full page in *Al Ahram* approximately once a week on a topic of current interest.

After Nasser's death in 1970, Heikal remained as editor of *Al Ahram* until 1974. But President Anwar Sadat increasingly challenged privileged journalistic autonomy and the semi-official spokesman-for-government role Heikal had enjoyed under Nasser. A series of developments increased the widening gulf of differences between them. Heikal had become increasingly outspoken and open in his criticism in *Al Ahram* of Sadat's policies. Heikal also felt Sadat was doing little to stop conservatives' attacks on Nasserism. He criticized Sadat for depending on America to help settle the Arab-Israeli conflict. Meantime, under Sadat, the government began releasing information from the ministries, further undermining Heikal's privileged personal contacts with the administration. President Sadat finally relieved Heikal of his post as chief editor and chairman of the board of *Al Ahram* early in February, 1974. Sadat offered to make Heikal his presidential advisor, a position Heikal declined. Since he left *Al Ahram,* Heikal has devoted his attention to writing books published outside Egypt and to writing articles for non-Egyptian publications.

Sadat's choice of a successor was Ali Amin who, with his brother Mustafa, had published the rival *Al Akhbar*. The new editor-in-chief came directly from a nine-year self-imposed exile in London, where he had gone in protest to Nasser's imprisonment of Mustafa on charges of handing over state secrets to the CIA. Amin replaced Heikal's "Frankly Speaking" Friday column with one of his own entitled "An Idea," in which he has discussed Egypt's internal problems and crusaded for greater personal freedoms, less governmental formalities and the release of all political prisoners. In one such column, he wrote:

> I believe that freedom is not limited to people expressing their views. It also means a press free to draw attention and criticize waste. Billions of pounds have been lost through inefficiency . . . money that could have built thousands of homes and many factories. . . . I'm fed up with government committees and sub-committees. . . . Change won't come all at once, it must come bit by bit and not wait until everything is studied and restudied.[7]

On February 9, 1974, President Sadat lifted all press censorship except on military information vital to the nation's security. Shortly thereafter, most restrictions on foreign correspondents and journals were removed. Instead, the President encouraged the press to give its attention to positive aspects which would aid Egypt's national development.

However, *Al Ahram* began to encounter problems; numerous turnovers in its administration affected its performance, prestige and circulation negatively. Ali Amin remained as editor only a few months before he was transferred to *Al Akhbar*. In all, a succession of five editors-in-chief held the post for brief periods, among them the well-known journalists Ahmed Baha Al-Din and Ihsan Abdel Kudous. But the best-known and loved was Youssef Mohammed Sebai.

[6] Nasser, *op. cit.,* p. 4.
[7] "Cairo Crusader," Associated Press, February 18, 1974.

One of Egypt's leading contemporary writers, Sebai was attending a meeting of the Afro-Asian Peoples' Solidarity Organization, of which he was the Secretary-General, when he was murdered by terrorists' bullets in Cyprus early in 1978. Sebai, called "the godfather of all novelists in Egypt," had produced 15 novels, 21 collections of short stories, four plays and a number of other works and had been Egypt's Minister of Culture before becoming *Al Ahram*'s editor. He was a champion of greater press freedom and better journalistic writing. During the days of the Presidency of Gamal Abdel Nasser, he had interceded with the President whenever journalists or writers were arrested. At the time of his death, the *Al Ahram* staff was stunned at the loss of their editor and President Sadat conferred on Sebai Egypt's highest civilian award posthumously.[8]

Today's editor and chairman of the *Al Ahram* board, Ali Hamdi El-Gammal stresses high-quality journalistic techniques and indicates the paper's high standards and circulation are now restored. He attributes the Friday edition's earlier decline to loss of Heikal's weekly article and to Sadat's new press freedom which allows competition for news among the media.[9] He is determined that *Al Ahram* should print verified news items and avoid publication of false news or rumors. He is seeking to make his paper a voice for human rights, freedom, peace and the problems of the Third World.[10]

When Nasser nationalized the press in 1960, the Arab Socialist Union (ASU) became sole owner of the country's papers. Then, in March, 1975, President Sadat provided for the establishment of a Supreme Press Council and decreed that the ASU could own no more than 50 percent of a newspaper's stock, with editors and employees holding the remaining 50 percent. The Supreme Press Council was to be headed by the Secretary General of the ASU. Further, the Supreme Council was to have direct liaison with the editors-in-chief of newspapers on all publication matters and the ASU would no longer interfere in newspaper work. In 1976, the Arab Press Organization appointed ten years earlier to supervise *Al Ahram*, *Al Akhbar* and other leading newspapers was dissolved. This divestiture of part of the ownership of the press by governmental party was another step taken towards reestablishment of press freedom in Egypt.

Later, as President Sadat and the People's Assemby took measures to allow for a multiple party system, similar action was taken to guarantee the parties the right to publish newspapers as long as those parties observed other provisions of publication law. Party papers are now to be regulated according to the laws which regulate political parties, thus keeping *Al Ahram*, as the representative of Egypt's established party, in a special semi-official role. This law also stipulates for the first time that the press shall be "a national fourth estate" with independence and precise tasks.

Al Ahram is published by the Al-Ahram Organization, which is part of the

---

[8] Christopher Wren, "Egypt May Seek Extradition of Editor's Killers," St. Louis *Post-Dispatch*, February 19, 1978, p. 20A.

[9] Nasser, *op. cit.*, p. 6.

[10] Ali Hamdi El-Gammal, Editor-in-Chief, *Al Ahram*, Cairo, in response to questionnaire, dated May 15, 1978.

Dar Al Hilal Publishing House complex developed primarily by Mohammed Heikal. In addition to *Al Ahram*, three specialized journals are published: *Ahram Iktisaadi* (an economic weekly), *Al-Taliaa* (a monthly), and *Al-Siassa Al-Dawliya* (a political science quarterly). The organization also undertakes numerous private commercial printing contracts. A staff of about 5,000 serves the publishing house.

The newspaper is housed in a large, modern air-conditioned 14-story building in Cairo's busy Al-Galaa Street. Modern, up-to-date techniques and technical equipment are used for writing and editing. Computers store data and feed and control the photo typesetting and hot metal printing processes. *Al Ahram* was the first newspaper in the Middle East to use a computerized photo-composing system, photopolymer plates, and facsimile radio and telephone transmission and reception of text and photos from all over the world. AMAC, the *Al Ahram* Management and Computer Center, has two IBM computers in Cairo and one in Alexandria to aid in data gathering and storage for the paper and to provide commercial research services for those companies desiring them. The Center participates in major Arab world informational projects and cooperates with private interests in specialized fields. *Al Ahram*'s excellent microfilm department records all issues of the paper and offers microfilmed versions on sale to the public. It also provides commercial services for various companies and government institutions.

In appearance, the typical 16 or 18-page *Al Ahram* weekday paper is serious and businesslike. Its makeup and technical qualities are excellent. The front page contains mostly national news of import or a mix of leading national and international items. Main front-page stories are two or three columns wide and usually topped by a bold headline and a smaller sub-heading. Two or three pictures typically adorn the lead page, and numerous pictures are run on the inside pages. Circles, squares, check marks and heavy type are employed to call the reader's attention to important facts.

Until recently, page two featured international news items; now, however, this page contains entertainment schedules and feature articles. The third page carries more feature materials and on Fridays, the editorial commentary, "Al Ahram's Opinion." The fourth page is now devoted to international news plus one column for "News of the Arab World." Page five gives its attention to features, interviews and news on different subject areas each day, with special prominence one day of each week to science, politics, economics, youth, quotations from international newspapers and "Governnotes." Page six is the research page filled by staff or other experts; on Fridays, the Strategic Research Center reports a study that fills this page. *Al Ahram*'s seventh page presents political and other opinions of its staff and guest writers, and the paper's own editorial column, "*Al Ahram's* Opinion" appears on this page every day except Fridays. Page eight typically carries state news; page nine, more news features and analyses of specific fields; page ten, sports; page eleven, further studies and features; page twelve, local news and events; and page thirteen, letters to the editor and "The Women's Page" (on Fridays, the last fills page seven). Two pages (14 and 15) are devoted to death notices. (Among Egyptians, there is the humorous expression in Arabic which translates: "Those who did not die in *Al Ahram*, did not really die!"). Al Ahram's final page presents lighter social news and pictorial features.[11]

From its inception, *Al Ahram* has always carried advertisements. The first issue contained an advertisement on the services of a translation office. Text and a hand-drawn picture appeared together in a syrup advertisement in 1879. Later, the bulk of advertising was carried on page four. Early in the twentieth century, advertising was increased and the entire back page was devoted exclusively to advertisements. In 1933, *Al Ahram* formed its own advertising department, and the first color advertising began appearing as early as 1940. Then, in 1963, an independent Pyramid Advertising Agency was formed by a group of companies of the United Arab Press. It is managed by *Al Ahram* and handles the paper's advertising today. The agency is comprised of four divisions, one each for its own public relations department, for media representation, for production of outdoor ads and for consultancy. Today, four-color advertisements are possible in *Al Ahram*. About half of the paper's total space is devoted to personal, classified and retail advertisements, the highest ad-to-editorial materials ratio of all Egyptian newspapers.

Al Ahram pioneered among Egyptian newspapers in the building up of good international news coverage and very early stationed its own correspondents abroad. It continues its tradition of excellence in foreign coverage today. Presently, it has nine full-time overseas correspondents, stationed in New York, Moscow, Rome, Paris, Bonn, London, Kuwait, Saudi Arabia and the United Arab Emirates. Another six part-time staffers report from Frankfort, Athens, Tokyo, Hong Kong, Beirut and Washington, D.C. The paper supplements the reports of this strong overseas staff with the services of six press wire agencies: Middle East News Agency (MENA), UPI, AP, AFP, TASS and Novosti, plus the syndicated news services of two British and two American newspapers.[12]

The paper was also one of Egypt's first dailies to emphasize local and national news of a non-political nature. Its features are varied and well written. Its cartoons have been particularly noteworthy, and their cleverness and incisiveness have sometimes drawn criticism from the officials or institutions they have featured. For many years, the most popular figure in *Al Ahram*, after editor Heikal, was probably the cartoonist Salah Jaheen. Its news analyses are among the best in the Arab world. Editorially, the paper seeks to present all sides of issues, but it does not hesitate to take strong stands on social and political questions.

Some of the greatest living personalities of Arabic literature are on *Al Ahram*'s regular staff. One such member is Tawfik Al Hakim, the Arab world's leading playwright and the person generally regarded as the creator of the modern literary Arab theater. Another is Naguib Mahfouz, regarded by many as the outstanding novelist in the Arabic-speaking countries. Still another is Youssef

---

[11] The authors are grateful to Egyptian graduate student, Farag ElKamel, University of Chicago, for his assistance in describing *Al Ahram* contents and for other helpful advice in letter to H. Fisher, dated October 16, 1978.

[12] El-Gammal questionnaire.

Idris, one of Egypt's leading writers of plays and short stories. And, of course, Youssef Sebai was yet another outstanding writer-novelist on the staff until his untimely death.

Although *Al Ahram* has been too much an official spokesman to attain the independence ideal for quality journalism, one must conclude that it deserves a place among the world's elite newspapers. A bold independent in its earliest days, under the editorship of Mohammed Heikal it became "must" reading for all who wished to be informed of the state's thinking and development. Today, as greater press freedom is returning to Egypt, it is turning again to the role of a gentle critic of officialdom. Throughout its history, it has maintained excellent coverage and interpretation of international and national affairs. Its treatment of the arts, culture and social activities remains the best in the Arab world. Its editorials, commentary, features and general production continue to rank among the Middle East's best. Thus, *Al Ahram* remains—as it has always been— Egypt's most prestigious and authoritative newspaper, a model to which the rest of print journalism in the Middle East must aspire and what one media scholar has called "The New York *Times* of the Arab world" to the outside world.[13]

Asahi Shimbun

(JAPAN)

EVERY DAY JAPAN'S foremost newspaper, *Asahi Shimbun*[1] produces over 12 million copies, making it one of the largest dailies in the world. Each morning seven and one-half million Japanese buy copies of *Asahi*. Because subscriptions are usually made both to the morning and evening editions of the paper as a "set," each evening the same readers get more than another four and a half million copies.[2] Since studies show that an average of nearly three people read each copy, it can be conservatively estimated that *Asahi* has a readership of nearly 25 million persons each day—almost a quarter of the total population of the country.

In Japan, where door-to-door delivery of newspapers is highly developed, over 97 percent of *Asahi* circulation is delivered by hand to subscribers. That service alone requires the efforts of over six thousand newspaper agents, a fleet of 860 delivery trucks and an army of about 70 thousand newsboys. In the pro-

---

[13] Wilbur Schramm, *One Day in the World's Press* (Palo Alto: Stanford University Press, 1952), p. 81.
[1] *Asahi* means "morning sun" or "dawn sun" and *Shimbun* means "newspaper."
[2] Completed questionnaire from Masateru Shiga, Assistant to the President, *Asahi Shimbun*, January 27, 1978.

cess, they handle enough newsprint impregnated with about twenty metric tons of printer's ink to fill nearly 200 six-ton trucks.[3]

A highly professional, well trained staff of over 9,000, the bulk of them engaged in writing and editorial tasks, prepares the *Asahi* for its mass circulation. The typical 24-page morning editions and 12-page evening editions are printed on the paper's 172 rotary and 30 offset presses. The news-gathering operation is supported by a fleet of three twin-engined air-craft, four helicopters, 125 passenger cars, 82 motorcycles, 53 radio-equipped jeeps, 13 special vehicles for transmitting on-the-spot photos by radio and 13 computers.[4]

Asahi, along with its two main daily competitors—*Mainichi* and *Yomiuri*—commands mass sales without stooping to the sensationalism found in the popular mass circulation dailies of other nations. Of the three, *Yomiuri* is the most entertainment-oriented, *Asahi* the most seriously information-oriented, with *Mainichi* between them. *Asahi* especially seeks to be the newspaper of the "mass elite"—the growing body of intellectuals in a country where nearly 30 percent of the 110-million-plus population is university-educated. Consequently, *Asahi* can provide readers with serious, intelligent journalism and be the best informed, most consistent and most intelligent of Japan's Big Three while still maintaining mass circulation leadership. The *Asahi* does appeal to a wide range of interests, but it makes certain it doesn't coddle its readers. Because it has a reputation for excellence, maintains highest quality journalistic standards and takes leadership in technical developments and news feature innovations, *Asahi* stands out as the most prestigious of all Japanese newspapers.

Actually, the *Asahi Shimbun* has found a formula which allows it to offer quality materials to the intellectuals and high-class entertainment to the average Japanese reader in the same issue. One writer has compared its offerings to the best among Tokyo department stores where "an exclusive boutique linked to a Paris couturier is set amid a vast range of sound quality ware and where there is no bargain counter."[5]

To maintain its reputation for being a high quality serious daily, the *Asahi* covers stories in depth. A large, methodically-organized staff of reporters—*Asahi* has close to 300 bureaus in Japan—meticulously covers every angle of a newsworthy event. When a tense issue arises, the paper may assign as many as 40 reporters to "watchdog" each leading politician involved. It excels in fair, unbiased and prompt reporting as well as complete coverage. As it demonstrated in reporting the Lockheed and South Korean-Japanese business relations scandals, it is fearless in its investigations. But it is also careful to be eminently fair to all parties and to take a positive rather than a destructive approach to those involved. Politicians and administrators find the paper's up-to-date news mandatory reading. Its analyses of issues is exhaustive, but illuminating; however, the reader is usually left to draw his own conclusions. While it takes definite editorial stands, it invites opposing views from readers and outside writers. Its emphasis on reporting facts and wrestling with issues tends to result in sombre

[3] Brochure, "*Asahi Shimbun:* Facts and Figures," The *Asahi Evening News,* 1977.
[4] *Ibid.*
[5] "Newspapers of the World–IV," London *Times,* February 26, 1965.

朝日新聞

顧客保護と雇用を重視

永大倒産で政府が協議

金融支援を指導へ

混乱の拡大防止に全力

債務総額千九百億円（ローン）

英市場でドル暴落

東北・関東に広域地震

宮城沖 M6.8、三十人が負傷

震源

日中交渉 首相、再開方針を明示

「段取りを詰めよ」

佐藤大使に新訓令

野党が修正案を提示

予算の与野党折衝　財源は三案を併記

ソ連側、警戒示す

官房長官、駐日大使と会談

国技館に「シルバーシート」

rather than lively writing. Clearly, the *Asahi* reflects the principles set down in its credo shortly after World War II:

—To be impartial and unbiased; to safeguard freedom of speech and thereby help to perfect a democratic nation and ensure world peace.

—To devote itself, in the name of justice and humanity, to the welfare of the nation and to fight all wrong-doing, violence and corruption.

—To report the truth fairly and promptly; to keep editorial comment liberal and impartial.

—To cherish tolerance at all times; to preserve a sense of responsibility and dignity without sacrificing vitality and freshness.[6]

That *Asahi* has found the successful combination for mass appeal while maintaining a serious high-quality approach becomes apparent when one studies circulation statistics. Sales of the morning edition have risen steadily from under four million copies daily in 1960 to nearly double that in 1978; likewise, circulation of the evening edition has nearly doubled. Half of *Asahi*'s income comes from subscriptions and only about 40 percent from advertisements, just the reverse of most newspaper revenues, and yet another indicator of the paper's popularity and financial soundness.

Even the *Asahi* advertisements reflect the paper's editorial interests in presenting the intellectual elite with a trustworthy, serious, yet interesting paper. A study of the ads in *Asahi* for a typical week indicates a high percentage represent publishers' offerings of books and cultural activities. In reply to a 1972 survey, 52.6 percent of those polled said they thought *Asahi* carried "the most reliable ads" of all Japan's leading dailies.

The 100-year-old *Asahi Shimbun* is more than a newspaper. Although newspapering is its main line of business, *Asahi* is also associated in broadcasting with 48 radio and television stations, a network and CATV affiliates in Tokyo, Osaka and Kyoto. It owns other newspapers and publishes about 200 books annually. It also holds interests in real estate firms, publishing companies and cultural centers. As of March, 1977, *Asahi* held financial interests in some 60 companies apart from radio and television firms; it owned over 51 percent of the stock in 15 of those companies. Among its numerous newspaper ownerships are the *Asahi Evening News*, an English-language paper published since 1954 and circulating about 50,000 copies daily; *Asahi Towns*, a weekly published for the Tokyo suburbs; *Asahi Family*, a surburban newspaper for the outskirts of Osaka; and *Yu Yu*, a color weekly Tokyo community paper. Besides newspapers and books, the company publishes other weeklies, monthly magazines, quarterly journals and annuals.[7]

Despite its size and conglomerate interests, *Asahi* is not a dangerous monopoly endangering other enterprises or restricting the public's capacity to receive diverse news and views. Japan has a pluralism of communication voices which would be difficult to match in any other country. Nor does *Asahi* gobble

[6] Shiga questionnaire.
[7] "*Asahi Shimbun:* Facts and Figures," pp. 26–7.

up local newspapers; there are some 100 Japanese papers that are strong and vigorous, enjoy high prestige among the daily press and have great reader loyalty.

Asahi is published from plants in five cities—Tokyo (started 1888), Osaka (1879), Kitakyushu (1935), Nagoya (1935) and Sapporo(1959). The first four of these rank as "main" offices, with Sapporo (capital of Hokkaido, the northern island) considered a "branch" office. Well over a hundred different editions are published throughout the country each day. In Tokyo alone, there are six main editions in the morning and three in the evening. Sub-editions, printed in many locations throughout Japan, reinforce the printing potential of the main *Asahi* plants in the five cities named above.

As of 1978, Miss Michiko Murayama and Mr. Jun-ichi Ueno were co-owners of the paper, with Tomoo Hirooka, a scholarly and articulate professional newspaperman, serving as president of the corporation and Shoryu Hata as editor. The Murayama and Ueno families have been associated with *Asahi* since its early beginnings. In January, 1879, Ryohei Murayama and Noboru Kimura formed a partnership to found the paper in Osaka. Kimura withdrew from the management shortly after the first issue. In 1881, Murayama was joined by Riichi Ueno and they and their descendents have co-owned *Asahi* ever since. Murayama and Ueno worked well together; it is said they were almost as brothers, and complemented one another. Murayama, enterprising and enthusiastic, was the idea man," while Ueno, steadfast and prudent, added strength and stability to the partnership. A recent rift between the two families has been healed and there is full cooperation again.

Like all Japanese papers, *Asahi* had to be licensed in its early days. In those authoritarian times, the paper's application for permission to publish put forth its intended objectives in courageous terms: "The newspaper will be edited . . . for the guidance of the common people, both men and women, young and old, in order to teach them social justice."[8] Japanese papers at the time were little more than political sheets serving some leader or some cause; they were all extremely biased. However, the *Asahi* made clear its desire to be something different when it published its "Aims" in July, 1882. The article emphasized that, as a newspaper for the masses, it would adhere to a neutral and impartial policy.[9]

In 1888, Murayama and Ueno bought a small Tokyo paper and converted it into the *Tokyo Asahi Shimbun*. This paper was subordinated to the main edition in Osaka until the former moved into a modern eight-story building in central Tokyo in 1927. In 1894, *Asahi* correspondents covered the Sino-Japanese War. During the Boxer Rebellion in China, *Asahi*'s correspondent, Keitaro Murai was the only Japanese newsman among the foreign press beseiged in Peking for two months. His stories written after his release were read throughout the world. In 1904, *Asahi* sent many reporters to the battlefronts in Manchuria to cover the Russo-Japanese War. The full, detailed news coverage provided did much to establish *Asahi* as Japan's leading newspaper. It also gave editors opportunity to

[8] *The Asahi Story* (Tokyo: Asahi Shimbun, 1965), p. 13.
[9] *Asahi Shimbun: The Foremost Newspaper in Japan* (Tokyo: Asahi Shimbun, 1973) p. 30.

make use of improved communications techniques, among them the use of the first news photographs.[10]

Although *Asahi* was usually on the side of moderation, it earned a name for attacking the Government in the early 1900's. In the second decade of the present century, its reporters, and even Murayama himself were beaten up by right-wing extremists. It courageously opposed the remnants of feudalism and often its views offended traditionalists still in power. At a time when Japan was in a ferment of change under the impact of foreign ideas, *Asahi* persistently tried to present the best and most provocative ideas in a form easily understandable to the ordinary reader. It was clearly the most notable liberal voice among the Japanese daily newspapers.

During the period between 1918 and the beginning of World War II the history of *Asahi* was dominated by a ceaseless fight against governmental and militarist efforts to limit freedom of expression. But depression hit Japan in the 1930's and the pressure of militarism grew rapidly. In 1935, three years before its surrender to the militarists who had seized power, the newspaper company had established other editions of *Asahi* on the southern island of Kyushu and at Nagoya. Murayama died in 1933 at the age of 83, and his adopted son and son-in-law, Nagataka Murayama, who had joined *Asahi* in 1920, became the chairman of the board. In 1936, when young military extremists revolted in Tokyo, one of their first targets was *Asahi,* the people's champion for freedom and moderation.[11] In that same year, 1936, the University of Missouri School of Journalism awarded one of its Honor Medals for distinguished journalistic achievement to *Asahi.*

In 1937 the war in China began and the government of Japan maintained a tight grip on newspaper policy through a device that has since become familiar: the control of newsprint. The militarists tried to force the papers to publish only official handouts and, although this did not fully succeed, the government eventually enforced the joint distribution of all newspapers, thus ending the free competition for circulation which had begun with the Japanese press itself in the previous century. Freedom of the press ended abruptly with Japan's entry into World War II.

During the war, newsprint was controlled and carefully rationed. Censorship was extreme and every effort was made to turn the press into a single spokesman for the government. Even so, some papers made at least feeble attempts to maintain free expression of editorial opinion. In 1943, at the height of the war, *Asahi* still had the courage to criticize the Prime Minister, General Hideki Tojo. An article on "The Wartime Prime Minister" kindled General Tojo's anger and he suspended publication. The writer, Seigo Nakano, was arrested and later committed hara-kiri. To get fully coverage, many of *Asahi*'s reporters and photographers suffered and died alongside the soldiers and sailors. In spite of a few rather mildly critical pieces, *Asahi* offered little editorial opposition to

---

[10] Masanori Ito, "History of the Japanese Press," in *The Japanese Press: Past and Present* (Tokyo, *Nihon Shimbun,* Kyokai, 1949), p. 7.
[11] *The Asahi Story,* p. 13.

the militarists during the war, and it was only after cessation of hostilities that a spirit of liberalism was again released.

In a sense, with the defeat of Japan in World War II, one "dark age" of Japanese journalism was substituted for another. *Asahi* ended the war with a depleted staff, a lack of supplies and a run-down plant. The paper was even suspended for a time by General Douglas MacArthur for violating press control regulations during the occupation period. The paper had criticized the United States for breaking international law in using the A-bombs on Hiroshima and Nagasaki.[12]

Between 1935 and the end of the Occupation, *Asahi* was consistent in criticizing the successive governments and in sustaining its editorial policy of championing democracy with vigorous attacks on the evils of militarism and nationalism. The paper even attacked Prime Minister Nobusha Kishi, who had pushed the ratification of the United States-Japan Security Treaty through the Diet. Then, when street demonstrations demanding the resignation of his cabinet got out of hand, *Asahi* and six other newspapers published a joint statement denouncing violence and defending parliamentarianism and appealing to the nation to restore social order.

During the United States-Vietnam War, *Asahi* once more took an antimilitarist peace stance by strongly criticizing American bombing of civilian targets. That action drew charges from the United States State Department that the paper was dominated by Communists.

Because of its juxtaposition between East and West, *Asahi* is especially interested in international news. To provide full coverage, the paper keeps 32 full-time foreign correspondents and three stringers in 23 overseas bureaus. Its stringers are located in Honolulu, San Francisco and Los Angeles, where there are concentrations of Japanese. In addition, *Asahi* takes the services of a dozen international press wires, eight news syndicates and three wirephoto agencies.[13] *Asahi* has a foreign desk of about thirty, each of whom specializes in at least one other language.

As a newsgathering organization, *Asahi* has few peers in the quality of its staff. Applicants for jobs must be university graduates with thorough knowledge of the society, full grasp of the social and cultural role played by a newspaper, sound news judgment and the ability to express ideas clearly. Only one in eighty university graduates applying for jobs with *Asahi* passes the entrance examination, probably the most difficult such test in the world.

The first test round includes a graduate-level translation into Japanese from

---

[12] Lafe Allen, "Effect of Allied Occupation on the Press of Japan," *Journalism Quarterly*, 24:4 (December, 1947), pp. 323–331.

[13] As of January, 1978, the 23 foreign bureaus were located in New York, Washington, D.C., Rio-de-Janeiro, London, Paris, Bonn, Geneva, Rome, Vienna, Moscow, Cairo, Beirut, Dar-es-Salaam, Singapore, Peking, Hong Kong, Bangkok, Manila, Jakarta, New Delhi, Sydney, Seoul and Teheran. Wire agencies received were Associated Press, Reuter, Tass, Samachal, Kyodo, Jiji, Radio Press, Soviet News, China News Service, Nihon Denpa News, Choson News Service (North Korea) and Sin-A-News Service (South Korea). Syndicated services taken came from the New York *Times*, *Le Monde*, The London *Times*, *The Sunday Times*, *Observer*, *Neue Zürcher Zeitung*, *Jeune Afrique* and *Newsweek*. Wirephotos came from AP Photo, UPI-Sun Photo and NANA.

one of five languages (English, French, German, Chinese or Russian), a long essay, a digest of a complicated speech and a comprehensive test on current events, national and world history, geography and politics. The candidate must also show he understands the meaning of important scientific terms.

Those who survive the first round of tests then "undergo an oral session with *Asahi* editors on a variety of news subjects to determine their general comprehension and special interests."[14] Physical examinations follow. The survivors become apprentice journalists in *Asahi's* bureaus, working alongside experienced journalists for a year or two before returning to Tokyo or one of the other main offices as full-fledged reporters. There, competition to get a story published is stiff; in the main offices, nearly 1,200 journalists bring saturation coverage to any news event.

One mark of the success of its training program is the significant number of individual *Asahi* journalists who have distinguished themselves. In 1975, Yukio Matsuyama received special recognition for his coverage of the Watergate and Lockheed scandals. Katsuichi Honda received the 1968 Miles Vaughn prize for reports on North and South Vietnam. Other distinguished correspondents since World War II include Shintaro Ryu, Kyozo Mori and Kiyoshi Ebata.

To accomplish full coverage of any story, many journalists actually "live" in the main headquarters. In the Tokyo plant, for instance, an average of about 300 men sleep in a dormitory every night so as to be available whenever a story breaks. Although salaries are not high for its army of eager journalists, *Asahi* pays better than most, plus providing numerous bonuses, incentive prizes and special rewards.

Asahi is a well-edited and systematic newspaper. The same basic layout is followed from day to day. Thus, its readers can predict where certain types of materials may be found. Basically, the most important domestic and international news consistently will be found on the front page. Page two covers domestic political news and debates in parliament; page three the important news not covered on the front page; four, national and international political news; pages five and six, editorials, reader letters, political commentary by outside writers and a cartoon; and page seven, foreign news. The next four pages feature books, the arts, economics and social commentary. Pages 12 through 17 are primarily advertisements, often of books, with special features and cultural and entertainment information. Sports news is printed on pages 18 and 19. Local news are found on page 21, city news is located on pages 22 and 23 and the back page carries a radio and TV program guide. Like most Japanese newspapers, the *Asahi* is gray and sombre in its makeup, running only a few small photographs.

On Sundays, however, the content pattern varies, due to the cessation of economic activities, to the addition of a four-page color Sunday supplement and to the fact that no Sunday evening edition is published. There is also more coverage of the increased sports activity which marks Japan's weekends. The Sunday edition, therefore, has more advertising and an increased number of book reviews.

14 "Job-Seeking in Japan," *Time*, July 17, 1972, p. 41.

The complexity of the Japanese alphabet limits the size of *Asahi* to 24 pages and produces immense production problems. "Simplified" Japanese is still written with a total of 2,304 characters, plus the numerals. Consequently, few reporters have mastered the necessarily complex Japanese typewriter and copy is filled in longhand. Partially to overcome this problem, *Asahi* pioneered in telephoto transmission of handwritten copy, the introduction in 1960 of *Kanji* character teletype machines and even the facsimile radiophoto transmission of newspapers.

In fact, *Asahi* was the first paper to use facsimile transmissions successfully on a regular basis. The transmissions were first put into use between Tokyo and Sapporo in 1959. Up to 14 pages of a paper are radioed by microwave as full-size photos from Tokyo to Sapporo in Hoikaido, a distance of about 500 miles, where high-speed rotary offset presses print the edition from the negatives. The same system of facsimile transmission has been extended from Tokyo to other cities and towns: to Nagoya in 1970, to Hino, a suburb of Tokyo also in 1970, to Hirosaki on Honshu Island and Setagaya, a borough of Tokyo in 1975. At present the Tokyo plant transmits about 170 pages by the facsimile transmission process to all these branch offices.

Today, *Asahi* uses 38 video display terminals, 25 of them for full page composition, six for editing and correction and seven for the control consoles. It has several other advanced technical innovations, such as thermo-plastic letterpress plates which allow production of printing plates in 15 seconds, a fully automatic developing and etching machine and a laser platemaking system. As of early February, 1978, half of the total composition was by the traditional hot-type system and the other half by computer-controlled full-page compositon.[15]

One of the major changes which has taken place in *Asahi Shimbun* in the past ten years has been the development of computer-controlled page editing. The paper uses a system called the NELSON Project (NELSON being an acronym for "New Editing and Layout System Of Newspapers"). It was installed to save labor, improve working conditions and decrease environmental pollution.[16] It provides for rapid page makeup by coupling two high-speed machines—a processing computer and a full-page photoprinter. NELSON operators give orders to the computer through a terminal console. In Japanese, the script runs vertically and columns are horizontal. But newspapers use a jig-saw puzzle variety of horizontal and vertical headlines and advertisements, resulting in complex makeup patterns. Because the system automatically measures and justifies, it saves much makeup editorial time and effort. The first pages made up by the system were introduced in 1972; by 1977, it was possible to produce 70 pages a day, about half those needed for the various Tokyo editions.

Asahi's other main project is the construction of a modern 16-story main building in Tokyo, overlooking Tokyo Bay and at the edge of the city's central market. When *Asahi* moves into it in 1980, the editors hope to discontinue completely the conventional hot type system and make up all 150 pages daily using

---

[15] Shiga questionnaire.
[16] Letter, Masateru Shiga, Assistant to the President, *Asahi Shimbun* to H. Fisher, dated February 20, 1978.

the NELSON system.[17] In the new building, the press room will be below ground level. Photo engraving and composing floors will be directly above, with two floors of editorial rooms above them. The business section will occupy the top floors.

Yet another mark of *Asahi*'s interests in the qualitative side of life is the active role it takes in cultural and social welfare activities. Throughout its history, *Asahi* has sponsored numerous projects in such fields as exploration and science, aviation, art, music, photography, amateur sports, public health and welfare. Between 1911 and 1962, it backed explorations of Anartica. It sponsored the first airplane flight ever made in Japan. The Asahi Welfare Organization staffs and operates a fully-equipped mobile clinic. In 1958, *Asahi Shimbum* founded the Japan Cancer Society. The Asahi Award, recognizing achievements in science, art, sports and social work, is the largest non-government award given in Japan. There is an Education Equipment Aid Association to help schools in remote areas. Each year, the paper gives Healthy Children Awards to primary children and schools. It sponsors the annual All-Japan High School Baseball Championships and the International Marathon Championship Race. The paper has brought to Japan a wide selection of the world's finest artists, dramatists, musicians and lecturers, the best symphony orchestras and art treasures ranging from a Tutankhamen exhibit to ancient cultural items excavated in China.

Viewed from an overall perspective, *Asahi Shimbun* is a truly remarkable publication. Representing a highly westernized Oriental nation, it manages to bridge the gap between cultures and combine the best of both worlds. Its equipment is among the world's most modern. Its spirit of service is unexcelled. It has a world concern without shedding pride in its own nation. It speaks as the conscience of Japan with thorough reporting and analysis without dictating. It constantly seeks to lift its readers rather than lowering its journalistic standards. By its contents, it consistently raises the nation's entertainment and cultural standards. Not only has it earned its title as "the newspaper of the 'mass elite'," for Japan; it also ranks at or near the pinnacle of the world's great newspapers—and it has managed to keep both its excellent quality and mass appeal in the process.

The Atlanta Constitution

(UNITED STATES)

THE ATLANTA CONSTITUTION, one of the southern United States' most distinguished dailies, publishes its 220,000 copies every day (540,000 Sundays) from

[17] *Ibid.*

They Let Bodies Do The Talking

Story, Page 1-B

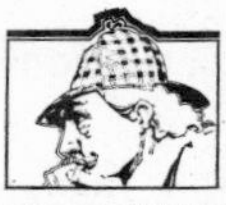

Next Silver Dollar Might Cost 2 Cents

Story, Page 3-A

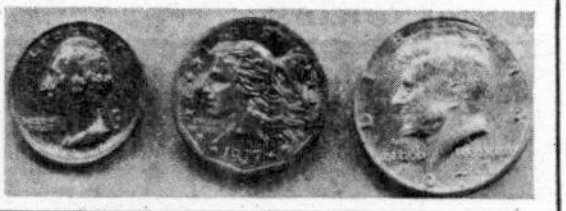

MORNING STREET EDITION

THE ATLANTA CONSTITUTION

For 109 Years the South's Standard Newspaper

MORNING STREET EDITION

FIFTEEN CENTS

Price May Be Higher Outside Retail Trading Zone

VOL. 110, NO. 175 ★★★★ P.O. BOX 4689 ATLANTA, GA. 30302, WEDNESDAY, FEBRUARY 22, 1978 52 PAGES, 4 SECTIONS

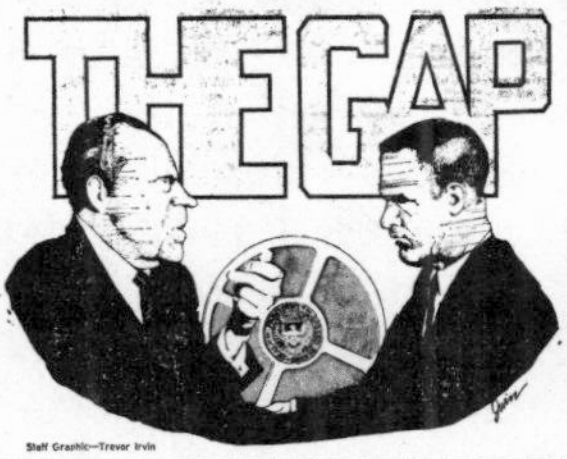

Staff Graphic—Trevor Irvin

The Haldeman Book

Part III: Erased Tape Tied Nixon To Watergate

By H.R. Haldeman
and Joseph DiMona

Three days after the Watergate break-in, President Nixon and H.R. Haldeman had an Oval Office talk about the burglary. The tape-recording equipment was running and 18½ minutes were subsequently erased from that tape. Who did the erasing and why? What was said during those missing minutes? H.R. Haldeman thinks he knows, and he tells in this excerpt, the third of five, from his book "The Ends of Power." The series will continue Thursday in The Atlanta Constitution.

June 17, 1972, a Saturday afternoon in Key Biscayne, Florida, I stretched and yawned. Across the terrace of our villa at the Key Biscayne Hotel, Larry Higby, my young deputy, read a book.

Two weeks before, I had returned with President Richard Nixon from Moscow, where he had worked out the beginnings of the first meaningful disarmament agreement with the Soviets in this century and had begun a new policy — which was being described as "detente" — that could reverse 27 years of cold war.

The President needed a rest, and he flew south on June 16.

Air Force One had dropped him off in the Bahamas, where he went to Walker's Cay, owned by one of his friends, Robert Abplanalp, the aerosol-valve millionaire.

At 2:30 a.m., June 17, 1972, while Nixon slept in his friend's luxurious house in the Caribbean, three Cubans, one Italian-American, and a man named James McCord were arrested in the Democratic National Committee Headquarters in the Watergate complex in Washington. They were carrying electronic wiretapping equipment.

Higby saw a familiar figure in bathing trunks walking toward us on the beach, trailing a long white paper in one hand. "Hey, look," said Higby, "Old Whaleboat." It was Ron Ziegler, the President's Press Secretary, whose Signal Corps name was "Whaleboat."

Ziegler handed me the sheet of paper. It was wire service copy. The news bulletin said that five men had been caught breaking into the Democratic National Committee Headquarters in Washington.

See HALDEMAN, Page 8-A

Jackson Holds Back On Eaves

By Ken Willis
and Jay Lawrence
Constitution Staff Writers

White police officers of the 1960's were "taken aside and tutored" for promotion examinations, Atlanta Mayor Maynard Jackson charged Tuesday in his first meeting with reporters since the bombshell investigative report on the current police cheating scandal was released.

That allegation, which was disputed later Tuesday by the city's police chief of the time, "is a disturbing historical reality and it is a matter that is on the street that is talked about in the black community," the mayor said at a press conference.

Jackson also told reporters he has not finished reading the special investigative report on the current Atlanta police cheating scandal and will decide whether to accept its conclusions and recommendations "by the weekend or Monday or Tuesday maybe."

That report, released Monday night, accused Public Safety Commissioner Reginald Eaves of personally ordering a plan to distribute advance copies of the 1975 promotion exams for captain and sergeant to a select group of persons.

It also accused him of obstructing the investigation by refusing to cooperate with them in his own interrogation.

It strongly suggested that Eaves should be fired because his own reputation and the morale of the bureau had been severely damaged by the scandal.

The mayor praised the investigators, Atlanta attorneys Randolph Thrower and Felker Ward, as two of the "best and most able," but added that the "question now is whether their conclusions are the right ones."

A few minutes later into the press conference, Jackson paused and said, "I must tell you that my job is greatly complicated by a most disturbing fact the importance of which I'll have to consider. I know and everybody else knows we live in a city where for years white examinees were taken aside and tutored."

See JACKSON, Page 10-A

Delay Deepens Impact On Atlanta's Policemen

By Barry Henderson
and Barry King
Constitution Staff Writers

A cloud of apprehension descended over the Atlanta Bureau of Police Services Tuesday in the aftermath of the initial shockwaves generated by Monday night's release of recommendations that firings, demotions and suspensions result from cheating on promotion tests.

High-ranking insiders said the cloud thickened when Mayor Maynard Jackson asked the public for time to consider the report and recommendations of attorneys Randolph Thrower and Felker Ward on their 16-week probe of the cheating scandal.

Although the report made no specific recommendation concerning Public Safety Commissioner Reginald Eaves, it left little doubt that the investigators felt Eaves should be removed from the administration of police matters. In addition, the report singled out 23 other officers, sergeants, lieutenants, captains, a major and a deputy police director for possible disciplinary action. Criminal prosecutions may be warranted for two sergeants and a captain, it said.

"People here are hoping something will happen soon, before the patrolmen on the street just rebel, revolt, lie down on the job," said one source in the police com-

See POLICE, Page 10-A

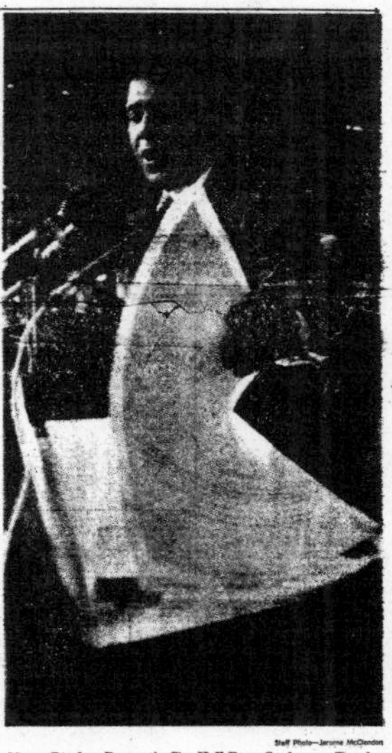

Staff Photo—Jerome McClendon

Mayor Displays Report At City Hall Press Conference Tuesday

Mine Owners Ask Binding Arbitration

From Press Dispatches

WASHINGTON — The Bituminous Coal Operators Association rejected an independent operator's tentative contract with the United Mine Workers as a model for an industry-wide agreement to end the [illegible]-day coal strike, then late Tuesday night proposed binding arbitration with the miners.

The coal operators association dropped collective bargaining and demanded arbitration with the union miners following discussions by Secretary of Labor Ray Marshall with both sides.

The proposal was not expected to be well received by the union since it would deal with the contract offerred by BCOA and rejected by the union bargaining council last week.

The industry proposed that workers immediately end their strike, that each side appoint one arbitrator and the labor secretary another, that the arbitrators be appointed by Friday and that their hearings begin no later than March 6 with a decision due in 15 days.

The BCOA proposal was a hard-line response to efforts by union and federal mediation officials to present the more liberal, one-company Pittsburg & Midway settlement Monday as a model for an industry-wide agreement.

President Carter, facing the first domestic crisis of his administration, laid the groundwork Tuesday morning with Republican and Democratic congressmen to take more drastic measures to halt the strike if the drawn-out negotiations between BCOA and the union remain deadlocked.

The congressional leaders concurred that a voluntary settlement is preferable to any government compulsion to end the strike, but Carter won support for "whatever he needs to do," declared Senate Republican leader Howard Baker of Tennessee.

Carter has refused to intervene directly thus far, instead relying on bluff and counter-bluff in an attempt to force the BCOA and the UMW—both fraught with internal disputes over terms of a settlement—to end the strike themselves.

Marshall presented the industry and union negotiators a government-backed contract proposal before Carter takes any of the three "final" options to force a settlement.

Marshall's proposals probably fall somewhere between the "final" BCOA offer that the UMW rejected on Saturday and a tentative contract agreement by the UMW and Pittsburg & Midway Coal Mining Co.

See COAL, Page 9-A

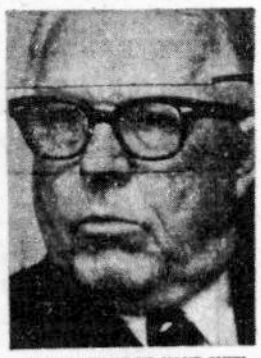

'TIME TO HANG UP YOUR SUIT'
6th District Rep. John Flynt

John Flynt Won't Seek Re-Election

By Jim Merriner
and David Morrison
Constitution Staff Writers

U.S. Rep. John J. Flynt Jr., a Griffin Democrat who has represented Georgia's 6th District for 24 years and gained national prominence recently as chairman of the House Ethics Committee, surprisingly announced his retirement Tuesday.

"There is a time to achieve and a time to hang up your suit," Flynt said in a brief interview at the Atlanta airport Tuesday afternoon before he caught a plane back to Washington.

Several politicians immediately expressed an interest in seeking Flynt's seat in the 1978 elections, including state Sens. Virginia Shapard, D-Griffin, and Peter Banks, D-Barnesville, and state Rep. Nathan Knight, D-Newnan.

Previously announced Republican contenders include Carrollton college teacher Newt Gingrich, narrowly beaten by Flynt in the past two elections, and College Park businessman Mike Esther.

It was learned that a November survey by Robert Teeter, former pollster for President Ford, showed Flynt to be in political trouble in the district.

Voters surveyed in the poll, financed by the national Republican party, gave Flynt 40 percent and Gingrich 35 percent, with the rest either undecided or refusing to answer. It was considered an exceptionally strong showing by a challenger a full year before the election.

Flynt's departure will mean the fifth new face in Georgia's 10-member U.S. House delegation in the last two years.

See FLYNT, Page 9-A

U.S. To Lease Oil Land Off Georgia's Coast

From Staff and Press Dispatches

The U.S. Interior Department announced Tuesday it will lease 1.2 million acres of land off the shores of Georgia, North Carolina, South Carolina and Florida for oil and gas exploration.

Nine petroleum firms have indicated they are interested in bidding on 4.4 million acres in the area, but the department cut down the available land on the basis of fishing activities and in light of other considerations.

Georgia Gov. George Busbee hailed Interior Secretary Cecil Andrus' decision as "an opportunity for Georgia (in whose waters about half of the acreage lies) to make a more positive contribution to the nation's critical energy needs."

Announcement of the sale came the same day the Supreme Court cleared the way for exploratory drilling off New Jersey, Delaware and Maryland. Work on those rigs should begin within a few months, although actual production will not begin for eight years.

A federal court has held up sale of additional Atlantic coast tracts off the New England Coast.

Despite his praise of the leasing plan, Gov. Busbee warned that "the development of those resources must be managed so as to preserve the natural and cultural resources of our coastal environments."

Busbee has been concerned that offshore oil and gas drilling operations might adversely affect the ecology of

See OIL, Page 9-A

Air Force Tightens Security At Nuclear Arms Stockpiles

Constitution Washington Bureau

WASHINGTON — The Air Force said Tuesday it has adopted new security procedures to keep imposters from entering nuclear weapons storage sites as a result of a Cox Newspapers series last month which highlighted the risk of terrorist attacks.

Air Force spokesman Col. Robert Hermann said also that "where feasible," the construction of anti-terrorist barriers at nuclear weapons sites is being accelerated because of disclosures in the articles.

These changes resulted fom a five-week investigation by the Strategic Air Command into how Cox Newspapers reporter Joseph Albright was able to talk his way past the guards of two SAC hydrogen bomb storage sites last December by posing as a fencing contractor.

Hermann said an Air Force investigation into those incidents has led to the following actions:

• Bidding procedures have been revised to make sure that only bona fide contractors and suppliers can obtain blueprints of nuclear

See SECURITY, Page 9-A

Inside

Torrijos

GOOD MORNING. Wednesday in Georgia will be sunny, windy and cold. Highs will range form the 30s in the north to the 40s in the south. Details on Page 2-A.

Torrijos Evidence Called Inconclusive

Page 12-A

an ultra-modern nine-story building at 72 Marietta St. NW in downtown Atlanta. This is the sixth location for the newspaper since its founding by Col. Carey Wentworth Styles on June 16, 1868.

A visitor entering the main lobby off the small plaza of trees, shrubs and flowers, finds himself in a colorful expanse where modular display units house historical items and memorabilia of exciting personalities—past and present—of both the *Constitution* and its sister paper, *The Atlanta Journal*. At key spots throughout the building are portraits of *Constitution* editor Henry W. Grady, who was undoubtedly the paper's best-known editor and one who became a principal spokesman for the "New South." Other portraits prominently displayed are of Joel Chandler Harris, creator of the "Uncle Remus Tales," founder Carey Styles, and former *Constitution* publishers William Hemphill, Clark Howell and Ralph McGill.

Owner of *The Atlanta Constitution* today is Cox Enterprises, Inc. Publisher is Jack Tarver, a native Georgian who joined the editorial staff in 1943. Before becoming an executive (assistant to the president of Atlanta Newspapers, then general manager, then vice president, and then in 1969, president of Atlanta Newspapers), Tarver wrote a daily *Constitution* column, syndicated in 34 newspapers, which was noted for its sharp, satiric wit. Other top administrative officers of the Atlanta Newspapers are James Cox Kennedy, executive vice president and general manager; Thomas H. Wood, president, and William H. Fields, vice president and executive editor.

Hal Gulliver, another Georgia native, Yale graduate and a former student at Berlin's Free University, is the present editor of the *Constitution,* having succeeded Reg Murphy in 1975 when Murphy became editor and publisher of the San Francisco *Examiner.* Gulliver joined the *Constitution* staff in 1962 as reporter and later served as education editor, columnist for the editorial pages, and associate editor. With Reg Murphy he is co-author of *The Southern Strategy,* a book published in 1971. He is also the author of a mystery novel, *Kill With Style,* in 1974.[1]

Associate editor of the *Constitution* is William Shipp, who first came to the paper in 1956 after serving with the U.S. Army in Germany for two years. Edward M. Sears is managing editor of the paper. A Virginian and graduate of the University of Florida College of Journalism and Communication, he worked for several Florida newspapers before joining the *Constitution* in 1970. Assistant managing editor is Calvin Cox, a Mississippian, who has been a staff member of the newspaper since 1945; during his years at the paper he has served as telegraph editor, city editor, night news editor, and editorial associate. Two other editorial staffers who should be mentioned are Jesse Outlar, sports editor and nationally renowned sports columnist, and Lewis Grizzard, who writes with an intriguing style and sophistication a front page column for the paper's City/State section.

The *Constitution* receives news from the Associated Press, the United

---

[1] "A History of *The Atlanta Journal* and *The Atlanta Constitution* . . . Past to Present . . ." (a 9-page article sent the authors by Hal Gulliver, August 24, 1978.

Press International, New York Times News Service, and Dow Jones (economic news). It also gets AP Wirephoto service, and New York Times Pictures. Following are its editorial syndicated columnists: Arthur Hoppe, Carl Rowan, Bill Mauldin, Joseph Kraft, Hugh Hanie, Ernest Furguson, Jesse Jackson, John Osborne, Jack Anderson, James Kilpatrick, Mary McGrory, Don Wright, Eliot Janeway, James Reston, and Tom Wicker. The paper also runs a wealth of other syndicated material such as Dear Abby, Billy Graham, Erma Bombeck, Jules Feiffer, Doonesbury, Bob Greene, and Jimmy the Greek.

At least 80 percent of the *Constitution*'s 220,000 daily circulation goes to subscribers, with the remainder being sold on the street. Advertising's proportion of the total space of a typical issue of the paper ranges from 30 percent to 70 percent. Of the space allotted to news-editorial material, some 10 percent goes for international news; 20 percent for national news; 30 percent for local/state news. Further classification would find some 20 percent sports, 10 percent travel/leisure, 15 percent business, 5 percent editorial and columns, and 25 percent features/entertainment.[2] The newspaper publishes many photographs and daily uses color printing for many of its news and feature pictures.

Investigative reporting is encouraged by the newspaper; in fact, two reporters are employed full-time as investigative reporters. In addition, many reporters have investigative stories in the works at all times. The *Constitution* has some 125 editors and writers on its staff, five of whom work exclusively for the editorial page. Most of the editorial staff are college graduates, but Editor Gulliver stresses that what the paper wants are young people who are quick, alert, accurate, and who write well. Also, the newspaper prefers to get employees who have several years experience on daily newspapers before seeking work there.

The *Constitution* considers itself a "liberal" newspaper, usually supporting Democrats for political office, and having the concept of "fairness" as a central plank in its editorial philosophy. Hal Gulliver puts the paper's policy in these words:[3]

> The philosophy of *The Atlanta Constitution* is not perhaps a new one in the newspapers but I think it is common to some great newspapers. We believe that a good newspaper should speak the truth, adequately cover the interests of its greater community, take tough stands on occasion on issues that are of importance whether local or national or international. Beyond that, a good newspaper ought to be guided by that old thesis of striving to afflict the comfortable and comfort the afflicted. That is still a pretty good theme.

Born in 1868 during the grim Reconstruction Era following the Civil War, *The Atlanta Constitution* had its name suggested by President Andrew Johnson as fitting for a Democrat newspaper espousing the restoration of constitutional government in the South. Its first location was on Alabama Street "Next door to the Ladies' Entrance of the United States Hotel, first floor." The paper began as a lively, four-pager of seven columns edited by Col. Carey W. Styles. After six

---

[2] Questionnaire sent authors by Hal Gulliver, editor, August 24, 1978. Much of the descriptive data about the newspaper today which is found in this profile comes from this Questionnaire.
[3] Letter from H. S. Gulliver to J. Merrill, dated August 22, 1978.

months the direction of the paper fell into the hands of William Arnold Hemphill, business manager, who was principal owner and publisher until 1902.

In 1873 the *Constitution* built the first building, a four-story edifice at 36 Broad St. Following Styles, editors were James Barrick, Isaac W. Avery and Edward Clarke. In 1876 Clarke sold his interest to Evan P. Howell, who became president and editor-in-chief and served in those positions until 1897. It was Howell who in 1876 who hired Henry W. Grady as a political writer who was later to become famed as spokesman for an industrialized proud "New South." Grady, Joel Chandler Harris, and poet Frank L. Stanton formed the *Constitution*'s most famous trimvirate of writers.[4]

Grady rose to managing editor, had an illustrious career, and when he died in December, 1889, was succeeded by Clark Howell, the son of Evan P. Howell. In 1897 Clark Howell took over as editor-in-chief of the *Constitution* on his father's retirement, and became one of the truly outstanding editors (and a successful politician) of the country. On his death he was followed as editor in 1938 by his son, Clark Howell, Jr.

In April, 1929, a young man from Tennessee came to the newspaper as sports writer, and after two years was sports editor. And, in 1938, Ralph McGill became executive editor. Then in 1942 McGill became the eighth editor of the *Constitution*. He is known for many innovations at the newspaper, one of them being a new literary form—the newspaper essay—which he introduced in order to fight for many kinds of reform (economic, social, racial) in his native Southland. One of his hard-hitting columns ("A Church, A School," about the hate-bombing of the Jewish Temple in Atlanta and a Clinton, Tennessee school) won the Pulitzer Prize in 1959 for distinguished editorial writing. McGill became publisher of the *Constitution* in 1960 and served in this position until his death in 1969. During his time at the newspaper he probably received as many honors and awards as any editor in American history.[5]

Three other Pulitzer Prizes have been won by the *Constitution*. One, in 1931, was for reporting excellence in city hall corruption coverage. In 1960 it was for Jack Nelson's exposé of conditions at a state mental hospital, and in 1966 Eugene Patterson, editor at the time, got the Prize for editorial comment. Patterson, an experienced journalist and a fine writer, served as editor from 1960–68. He was succeeded by Reg Murphy,[6] who served as editor until 1975 when he moved to California. The present editor of the Constitution is Hal Gulliver. It is under his editorial direction that the paper is presently expanding and seeking new ways to further improve its facilities, its staff, and its general quality. A 52-page issue of the newspaper is rather typical. Usually there are four main sections—A through D on weekdays. Taking a copy (Monday, Feb. 20, 1978) at random, there was the first section of 18 pages, mainly containing foreign news and some leading national stories, as well as the editorial page and Op-Ed page. Also, in this particular issue, the *Constitution* ran Part I of H. R.

---

[4] *Ibid.*
[5] *Ibid.*
[6] Murphy made headlines himself around the world in 1974 as a victim of a kidnapping. After two days of captivity the editor was freed on payment of $700,000 ransom, later recovered when his kidnapper was arrested.

Haldeman's book, *The Ends of Power,* the story of the Nixon White House. In Section B ("People, etc."), running 8 pages, there were several columns and feature stories, a few TV and movie reviews, and at least a full page of movie advertising.

In the 18-page Section C ("City/State") there were more columns (e.g., one by Jim Merriner, political editor), ten state and local news stories, a page of funeral notices, and several pages of classified advertising. And, in Section D ("Sports"), there were the usual sports news stories; a column by Jesse Outlar, sports editor; a page of "Business News" and a page of comics, interspersed with about two pages of display advertising in this 8-page section.

The Sunday paper, of course, is much fatter and contains a wealth of national and foreign news in addition to a greatly expanded presentation of state and city news and features. The newspaper's own *Magazine* is also included in the Sunday edition, a publication which ranks among the very best of such magazines in the United States.

The Atlanta Constitution is reflective of its city of publication—vigorous, forward-looking experimental, socially concerned, cosmopolitan, and diversified. It has an enthusiastic, intelligent and creative staff with high morale; it has good leadership, also, that is determined to make the paper ever better.

The (Baltimore) *Sun*

(UNITED STATES)

THE BALTIMORE SUN's first issue in 1837 promised to be "free, firm and temperate." In its more than 140-year lifespan, the paper has conscientiously lived up to that initial word. Thanks to its unbroken history of benevolent private ownership, *The Sun* continues determinedly on the course of independence it has always followed. Like a responsible father, it has always held tenaciously to the best principles of serious journalism as it has guided and directed its readers to thoughtful, informed decisions. Always moderate, it maintains an image of respectability, aristocracy and objectivity.

The Sun's beginnings were solid, but not auspicious. When Rhode Islander Arunah S. Abell founded his paper on May 17, 1837, he was seeking to produce a successful penny paper for the common folk. Baltimoreans, with six dailies already from which to choose, were unimpressed when Abell's four-page, four-column tabloid first appeared.[1] Despite the materials Abell put in his paper to

[1] Gerald Johnson, Frank Kent, H. L. Mencken and Hamilton Owens, *The Sunpapers of Baltimore* (New York: Alfred A. Knopf, 1937), pp. 1–2.

appeal to the "non-intellectual" readers, his primary concern was for providing news, "whether or not that news conforms to the editor's own prejudices and opinions."[2] Circulation-wise, *The Sun* soon caught up with and out-ran its rivals. Within a year, it could claim about 12,000 subscribers. But large circulation of penny papers was not Abell's priority. From the beginning, he earnestly tried to supply his readers with accurate and adequate information. Part of the paper's success stemmed from Abell's interest in reporting on the life of the city, which was thriving, vibrant and growing at the time.[3]

Abell, who served both as *The Sun*'s editor and publisher, took an unusual position for the times—that his paper should supply news rather than support a political party. In the first issue of his paper, Abell firmly declared his political and religious independence: "We shall give no place to religious controversy, nor to political discussions of purely partisan character."[4] Instead, he pioneered in news gathering, spending great sums of money on any project which promised to get his paper the news ahead of his rivals. *The Sun* was the first paper to send news by railroad, and Abell developed horsemen to speed news to Baltimore long before the famed pony express was used in the West. In keeping with Abell's drive to get news events first, *The Sun* became one of the nation's first newspapers to use the telegraph.

Before the paper was a month old, it had received its first story (by mail) from a Washington correspondent. This was the beginning of a Washington bureau which has steadily grown and which has brought the paper much attention and many awards. During the Mexican War, *The Sun* provided some of the most notable war reportage; it even informed the President on April 10, 1847, that the United States had captured the fortress at Vera Cruz, not only beating the mails with the news but also the official War Department couriers.

The paper had soon outgrown its original offices on Light Street and, after two years, had moved into a larger building in the center of town. Then in 1851, it was to move into the famous Sun Iron Building at Baltimore and South, where it would remain for the next half century.

During the Civil War, Baltimore was "occupied" by Federal troops and there was a soldier at the elbow of every editor. It is said that *The Sun* "conformed to the necessities of the situation" and "behaved so well that, of all the local newspapers, it was the only one which managed to come through the war without once being suppressed."[5] Just what that means is open to interpretation, but the fact is that *The Sun* did come through the war and difficult times intact. Since the paper was for the South but was against secession, it had problems getting and keeping readers during the war period.

Prior to his death in 1888, Abell gave control of the paper to his three sons, George, Edwin and Walter. By that time it had come out of its war slump and was growing rapidly. In the period after the Civil War, mainly under the leadership of George Abell, The Sun fought vigorously against corruption of all types,

[2] Brochure, "The Baltimore Sunpapers," A. S. Abell Company, 1966.
[3] Johnson et al, *op. cit.*, p. 7ff.
[4] *Ibid.*, p. 29.
[5] Paul Banker, Managing Editor, *The Sun,* in letter and response to questionnaire, October 18, 1966.

The Weather
Mostly sunny but colder today, fair and cold tonight. High, 34; low, 17. Yesterday's high, 40; low, 27.
(Details and Map, Page C2)

Vol. 282—No. 83—F

THE SUN

FINAL

BALTIMORE, WEDNESDAY, FEBRUARY 22, 1978

••• 15 Cents

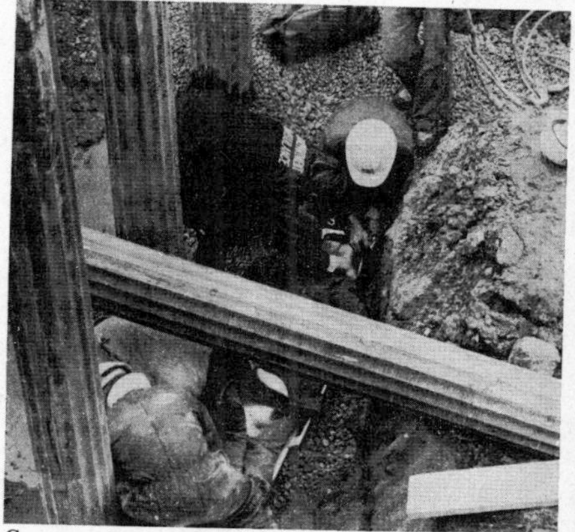

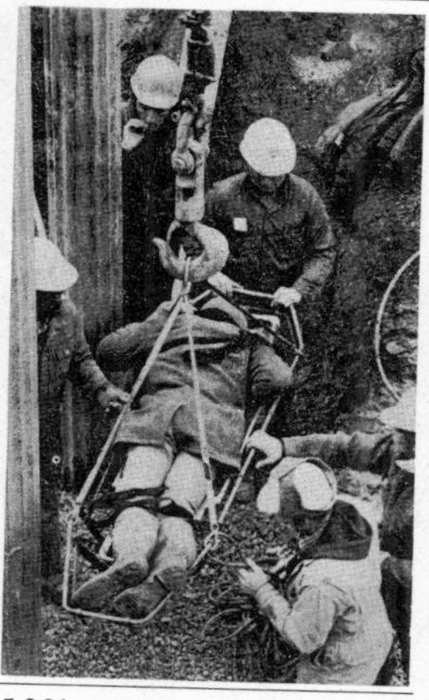

Sunpapers photos—J. Pal Carter

Construction accident

A worker on the tunnel being built to drain off rainfall from the Patterson Park area was injured yesterday when a hollow piling fell into a 75-foot-deep ditch on him. City firefighters had to remove the piling before getting the man, James Brody, 22, of the 2000 block West Lanvale street, into a basket so he could be hauled up. He was treated at City Hospitals for a neck injury and cuts.

Coal firms and union renew talks

Industry proposes use of voluntary binding arbitration

Washington (AP)—Coal industry and United Mine Workers bargainers resumed negotiations yesterday in an attempt to end the 78-day coal strike before the government imposes a settlement.

The Labor Secretary, Ray Marshall, shuttled between meetings of the Bituminous Coal Operators Association and the union to work out a compromise agreement.

The resumption of meetings, although they were not face to face, was termed "somewhat encouraging" by Jody Powell, the White House press secretary. But he added that "whether it's possible through these discussions to make progress remains to be seen."

Late last night, the coal association's president, Joseph Brennan, urged the union to agree to voluntary binding arbitration, saying such a move was "the fairest approach to settling" the strike.

Mr. Brennan said, "Voluntary binding arbitration can return the mines to production, our employees to work and coal to the nation."

A UMW spokesman said it was not likely the union would accept the suggestion.

Meantime an administration official said a proposed settlement reached by the union and an independent coal operator Monday "does figure in a major way" in the new talks.

As government pressure mounted yesterday for a settlement, officials of the coal operators association, which represents 130 companies, had announced they were agreeable to new talks. However, they criticized aspects of the independent settlement.

The coal association's chairman, E. B. Leisenring, said the union's settlement with the independent producer, P. & M. Coal Company, on Monday did not adequately deal with several major issues in dispute. However, he added, "We plan to vigorously present our case to the union bargainers so that true collective bargaining in good faith can be accomplished in the interest of all concerned."

It was the first comment from the industry since talks with the union broke off Saturday after the UMW rejected what was termed the coal operators' final offer.

Arnold R. Miller, president of the United Mine Workers, followed by saying that he, too, was willing to return to bargaining despite what he called "the negative tone of the BCOA announcement."

Mr. Marshall met with industry officials for two hours during the day and then with UMW leaders to hear their positions. No other formal meetings were planned during the evening hours.

Meanwhile, President Carter won bipartisan congressional support to take strong steps to end the walkout. But the administration continued to play a waiting game in hopes the two parties would settle the dispute themselves.

The House speaker, Representative Thomas P. O'Neill, Jr. (D., Mass.), said after meeting with the President that he felt it would be at least 25 days before the coal strike could tie up the nation economically. The strike already has led to power

See MINERS, A6, Col. 4

Ethiopia assures Carter it won't enter Somalia

By HENRY L. TREWHITT
Washington Bureau of The Sun

Washington—Ethiopian leaders assured President Carter yesterday that Ethiopia will not violate the Somali border or interfere in the affairs of other neighbors.

The promise was passed to the President by an aide just back from conferences in Addis Ababa. In another gesture, each country indicated its willingness to fill an ambassadorial vacancy created in the other's capital by current tensions.

In effect, the pledge from Addis Ababa committed Ethiopian forces, backed by Soviet advisers and Cuban troops, not to cross the Somali border if, as expected, they drive Somali invaders from the contested Ogaden region. The prospect that Moscow might control the whole horn of Africa—comprising Ethiopia and Somalia—has caused growing concern here.

At the same time, the United States Navy announced that a task group of four warships has entered the Indian Ocean, approaching the volatile horn. The Navy described it as a "routine deployment," similar to occasional naval visits to the area earlier.

But the task group—a guided missile cruiser, two frigates and an oiler—bringing the number of Navy ships in the Indian Ocean to seven, inevitably was seen as a counterpart to Soviet naval presence. As many as 30 Soviet ships, including many transport vessels, are in the area of the horn, either supplying Ethiopia or patrolling.

There was no indication that the warships from the two superpowers would be in the same local area. The four dispatched from the U.S. Pacific Fleet were still far to the east of the horn yesterday.

In fact political developments yesterday ran counter to fears of growing superpower competition over the horn, at least momentarily. As one American explained it, they at least emphasized a standard against which Ethiopian conduct in the future can be measured.

Less than a year ago, the Soviet Union was a patron of Somalia, the U.S. of Ethiopia. But in a rapid sequence of political maneuvers, the Soviet Union switched to Ethiopia. The U.S. decided against support for Somalia when Somali troops entered Ethiopia in a fight for the contested Ogaden region.

Now an estimated total of 1,000 Soviet

See HORN, A2, Col. 1

Senators hear of Torrijos, drug links

By GILBERT A. LEWTHWAITE
Washington Bureau of The Sun

Washington—United States senators, in secret session, yesterday learned of unsubstantiated intelligence reports linking Brig. Gen. Omar Torrijos Herrera of Panama with drug trafficking.

But the reports were mainly "secondhand and of varying reliability," leading the Select Committee on Intelligence, which originally looked into them, to conclude: "Our investigation has turned up no conclusive evidence that could be used in a court of law."

At the same time the Justice Department released the text of a grand jury indictment of General Torrijos's brother, Moises, and four others in May, 1972. The indictment accused the five of possessing 155 pounds of heroin and conspiring to smuggle it in to the United States when they arrived at New York's John F. Kennedy International Airport July 8, 1971.

According to the information given to the Senate yesterday, a State Department official, under apparent White House instruction, tipped off General Torrijos that his brother was about to be arrested in De-

See CANAL, A4, Col. 1

10% power cutback is set for Western Md. firms

By JAMES GUTMAN

Officials of Maryland, Virginia and West Virginia agreed yesterday to order a mandatory 10 per cent cutback in electricity usage by commercial and industrial customers of the Potomac Edison Company, effective at 12.01 A.M. tomorrow.

Representatives of the three states also agreed to order a 30 per cent power reduction by those Potomac Edison customers March 2.

Acting Governor Lee, however, said last night that the order he will issue today and send to a General Assembly committee this afternoon will call for only a 20 per cent cut in commercial and governmental power use on that date and a 30 per cent cut in industrial power consumption.

A spokesman for Mr. Lee explained that there was nothing in yesterday's agreement preventing the Maryland Governor from issuing whatever order he feels is in the best interests of the state. It was not clear, however, last night how officials of the two other states, which would order the cutbacks through their regulatory commissions, will react to Maryland's change.

The tri-state agreement also called for reducing power to industrial and commercial customers of Potomac Edison to "plant protection levels" about March 15, if that measure becomes necessary. The next step would be rotating blackouts for all utility customers. Potomac Edison supplies power to Western Maryland.

The plan to deal with the effects of the continuing coal strike came after a seven-hour, closed-door meeting in Richmond, called at the request of Gov. John N. Dalton of Virginia to coordinate planning among the states served by coal-short Potomac Edison.

Maryland was represented by Simon F. McHugh, Jr., energy adviser to Mr. Lee, and by Thomas J. Hatem, chairman of the state Public Service Commission.

Mr. Lee's executive order on the mandatory cutbacks will need the approval of the General Assembly's Joint Administrative, Legislative and Executive Review Committee.

The order is likely to cause significant production cutbacks and layoffs among many of Potomac Edison's 1,200 industrial customers in Western Maryland.

It nevertheless falls short of the immediate 30 per cent cutback of power supplies to industrial customers recommend-

See MARYLAND, A6, Col. 5

Dangerous insulation irks FTC

By LYNNE OLSON
Washington Bureau of The Sun

Washington—Because of the skyrocketing demand for home insulation, hundreds of inexperienced persons have entered the insulation business and may be selling dangerous and ineffective materials, the chairman of the Federal Trade Commission said yesterday.

Federal quality standards for home insulation are urgently needed because "as many as eight million additional homes may be insulated this year with materials of questionable safety and quality," Michael Pertschuk, the FTC chairman, added.

Mr. Pertschuk reported that the past two severe winters, soaring fuel bills and President Carter's stress on energy-saving insulation have led to a demand of "phenomenal magnitude" that has far outstripped manufacturing capacity.

As a result, he said, new manufacturers joining the industry are offering cellulose insulation and urea-formaldehyde foams that are made from readily available materials but which are the most potentially dangerous.

Mr. Pertschuk testified at the first in a series of hearings by the House subcommittee on oversight and investigations on home insulation.

Representative John E. Moss (D., Calif.), subcommittee chairman, noted that the House-Senate energy conference committee is considering Mr. Carter's proposal to give tax credits to consumers who insulate their homes.

"Before granting a tax break, or spending government funds to weatherize the homes of the elderly and poor, we must assure ourselves that we are not doing more harm than good," Mr. Moss said.

Noting that an estimated six million homes were insulated last year and eight million more may be insulated in 1978, the congressman said the use of hazardous materials in even a small percentage of the homes could result in a "near-catastrophic level of property damage and personal injury."

Recently, he said, the government unknowingly financed the installation of highly flammable cellulose insulation in nearly 100 Colorado homes—and ultimately had to finance its removal. Although most forms of insulation are poten-

See INSULATION, A6, Col. 3

Insurance on LNG facilities not enough for major disaster, GAO tells Congress

By PETER BEHR
Washington Bureau of The Sun

Washington—The amount of insurance on present and planned liquefied natural gas facilities is probably too small to cover the injuries and damage that could be expected from a major LNG accident, the General Accounting Office said yesterday.

Monte Canfield, Jr., a GAO official, reported on this and other preliminary criticisms by the agency directed at the federal regulation of LNG development. Mr. Canfield testified before a House of Representatives subcommittee yesterday on proposed legislation to tighten federal supervision of LNG development.

Mr. Canfield said that the liability coverage for present and planned LNG import terminals ranged from $50 million to $190 million an incident. "It is unlikely that injured parties could be fully compensated under existing arrangements," he said.

"If the accident resulted from an act of sabotage, or from an 'act of God' such as an earthquake, flood or tornado, the company may not be liable at all," continued Mr. Canfield, director of the energy and minerals division of GAO, a congressional investigatory agency.

An attempt to collect damages from an LNG terminal or tanker owner would be "long, complex and expensive," he added, suggesting that it may be desirable to establish a special compensation fund to meet this problem.

A complete GAO report on LNG development is not due until April, but already drafts of the report have provoked a clash between the agency and natural gas producers, who complain that the GAO's preliminary analysis is biased.

The American Gas Association, for instance, says that liability coverage is adequate to meet "any events that could be creditably postulated." The association contends that the GAO cannot justify its assumptions of the possibility of an extensive LNG accident.

Mr. Canfield's statement did not discuss specific conclusions about particular LNG operations.

The first deliveries of liquefied natural gas from Algeria are expected to arrive at the new Cove Point (Md.) terminal about March 10, according to a spokesman for Columbia Gas System, co-owner of the Maryland terminal with Consolidated Gas Supply Corporation.

One relatively small LNG terminal is

See GAS, A6, Col. 2

Index

3 sections

The disability game—IV

Red tape, poor staffing, delays plague compensation program

By STEPHEN E. NORDLINGER
Washington Bureau of The Sun

Washington—To an elderly woman confined to a wheelchair at a nursing home in Towson, the situation looked desperate. For some reason, the regional federal workers' compensation officer four months ago had suddenly stopped paying for her disability, and she was running out of funds.

Her plight was magnified by the treatment accorded the nursing-home staff when it tried to investigate.

The woman wrote Representative Clarence D. Long (D., 2d) recently seeking help:

"The administrator [at the nursing home] has made repeated person-to-person telephone calls . . . and has been subjected to rudeness and discourtesy, such as being told the telephone is temporarily disconnected, telephone messages left not being delivered, and, worse, having the conversation terminated by an abrupt slamming down of the receiver in her ear," she stated.

"One of the deputies told an assistant administrator [of the nursing home] that the Department of Labor, Office of Workers Compensation Program, is 'in complete disorder.' "

No sooner did the letter reach Mr. Long than the regional office—perhaps by coincidence—straightened out the confusion and resumed payments. But for the woman, who declined to be interviewed, it was another jarring episode in a long battle for compensation for a 1971 spinal injury from a fall.

All through 1975, the regional compensation office ignored six letters she wrote seeking additional compensation payments. When the office finally replied to one letter, it sought information she had already supplied months earlier.

She entered a nursing home two years ago, but even with Mr. Long's help, it took months for her to obtain her regular compensation payments.

"There has been some improvement in the office, but it has a long way to go to where it should be," said Mr. Long. "When a congressman gets involved to help a constituent, he may get action but what about all the others? They get put at the bottom of the pile."

Officials from federal agencies, union leaders and congressional aides handling compensation cases report hardship cases by the thousands caused by a system apparently so entangled in red tape and so poorly staffed that it is failing to meet its obligation of compensating seriously disabled government workers in a timely fashion.

The long delays prompted Congress three years ago to change the law to keep workers on the payroll for a maximum of 45 days while their compensation claims were being processed.

But the new liberal terms simply generated more claims and paper work, and many officials said the delays have grown worse. In most cases, no processing of the serious cases entitled to long-term compensation even begins until the 45 days is over, leaving these workers without an income.

Visitors to regional offices of the workers compensation program said they found stacks of disability files piled in hallways and loaded on top of desks in unused offices.

Examiners reviewing the cases were said in many instances to be so ill-trained and inexperienced that they either automatically approve claims once they reach the top of the pile, even though this action might be unwarranted, or they send them along to a higher authority, causing further delays.

"All the delays are causing more claims to be filed" said John F. Meese, national coordinator for the federal employees Department of the International Association of Machinists and Aerospace Workers.

"A fellow sees a guy make a claim and there the claim sits without a decision. So he decides he might as well file a claim too. He hasn't lost anything. It's damn easy to do. But if they decided the case sooner and more carefully, they might discourage claims that were not really justified."

There was a nationwide backlog of 103,000 unprocessed cases last year, four times the 1975 level and more than three times the level expected a little more than a year ago by a Labor Department task force set up to examine the program.

"As it is now, the situation would make you cry," said Mr. Meese. "There is no feeling for people. They [compensation officials] act as if it is un-American, unpatriotic and unreasonable to complain when you have to wait months to get money to pay bills. We've had to pass the hat so families would not be thrown out of their homes or lose their belongings."

Congress is besieged by complaints from constituents who have been thwarted not only in their repeated attempts to obtain compensation payments, but also to get answers to letters and phone calls about the status of their cases. Dealing with the bureaucracy has been a bitter experience for many of them.

"Of course, we'd like our claims settled for us," said one worker. "But that isn't the whole problem. It is the uncer-

See DISABILITY, A5, Col. 1

but particularly against political machines and corrupt judges who had been appointed by them. The paper's campaigns during the last three decades of the nineteenth century did much to enhance its reputation.

Politically, *The Sun* has always been independent. In strongly Democratic Maryland, the paper (in 1895) supported a Republican gubernatorial candidate, and he won. Since that time, although the paper has usually sided with the Democrats, it has felt free to support Republicans. In fact, it supported Republicans for President from 1940 through 1960.

In 1904, the Sun Iron Building was destroyed by fire, but continuous publication continued with *The Sun* being printed in Washington by *The Star*. After two months, production was moved back to Baltimore and temporary quarters. Two years later the staff moved into a new building at Charles and Baltimore. But it was not long before *The Sun* was cramped and needed a new buiulding. The old Calvert Railway Station was purchased in 1949, demolished, and the cornerstone for the new Sunpapers Building at Calvert and Centre streets was laid. On the edge of the main business district today, it is a perfect site for the paper's ultramodern plant.

During World War II *The Sun* greatly increased its staff and its coverage. In 1966, there were 160 journalists on the editorial staff, all of whom had at least a college education. Foreign coverage was given a big boost during World War II and a *Sun* staffer was the only newspaper correspondent present when the German Army surrendered. Three *Sun* correspondents watched the Japanese sign the surrender papers aboard the *U.S.S. Missouri*.

The Sun introduced its *Sunday Sun* in 1901, selling it for just two cents. At the time, Baltimore had only two Sunday papers, the *American* and the *Herald*. Five years later, in 1906, H. L. Mencken was hired as its Sunday editor and he immediately increased the size of the Sunday edition to 24 pages. A few years later, in 1910, *The Sun*'s owners, A. S. Abell Company acquired the *Baltimore World* for $63,000. and renamed it the *Evening Sun*. Thus, the family of papers, a group known since as the *Sunpapers*, was born. The *Evening Sun* was purchased primarily to keep it out of the hands of William Hearst and to keep alive the *World*'s United Press franchise. In recent decades, the *Evening Sun* and its Hearst Corporation competitor, the *News American* have been locked in combat for Baltimore's evening circulation leadership. The morning *Sunday Sun* is associated more closely with *The Sun* and together they provide readers with seven-day-per-week news and information.

The venerable A. S. Abell Company which operates all of the *Sunpapers* is really a diversified communications concern today. Besides the newspapers, it controls WMAR-TV in Baltimore, WBDC-TV in Salisbury, WMAR-FM radio in Baltimore, two other radio stations, a publishing firm and an industrial park.[6] Despite the size of this complex, the owners "have demonstrated a fierce loyalty to the idea of maintaining the *Sunpapers* as an independent newspaper publishing company."[7] Overall, the Abell Company employs about 2,000 persons and has an annual income estimated at $50 million.

[6] Louis Peddicord, "Who 'Manages' the Daily News You Read?" *Baltimore Magazine*, (August, 1977), pp. 29–30.

[7] William Jones, "Finally, In Baltimore, *The Sun* Also Rises," *The Sun* (August 1, 1977), p. D1.

Although all of the *Sunpapers* are under a unified management, with single accounting, sales and circulation staffs and the same production facilities for all, their editorial products are the work of separate, intensely competitive staffs. Donald H. Patterson, the general manager and senior vice president of the Abell Company says of the news staffs of the two *Sun* papers, "They compete with one another and they occasionally speak to one another."[8] The morning *Sun* has maintained its standards as a high-quality, more formal and serious paper, designed to appeal to the better educated, more affluent and influential readers, while the *Evening Sun*, partly to meet the competition of the unorthodox, sensation-minded *News American*, remains news-minded, but dresses its stories in more popular terms. Of late, the morning *Sun* has been broadening its appeal by adding some features and local news without sacrificing quality or reducing its traditional emphasis on news.

There has always been stiff three-way competition between the *Sun*, the *Evening Sun* and the *News American* for subscribers. Usually the morning *Sun* has been last in the race, due mainly to reader preference for an evening paper. As is the case with most American dailies, circulation of all of Baltimore's newspapers has declined in recent decades. Evening papers have been hardest hit for several reasons: the competition of television, more working wives, less time to read are among the causes cited. Consequently, in recent months, the morning *Sun*'s distribution has caught up with, in some cases, even exceeded that of its sister papers.

The two daily *Sunpapers* hit their all-time highs in 1960, when the morning *Sun* counted a circulation of 201,197 and the *Evening Sun* 220,272. The circulation decline is illustrated by the early 1978 figures: 174,799 for the morning *Sun* and just over 175,000 for its evening counterpart. Both are now ahead of the *News American* in the circulation battle. The *Sunday Sun*, meantime, reached a record peak on March 31, 1977, with 361,380 copies sold. In the 1960's, because the *Sunpapers* offered an attractive monetary incentive to anyone subscribing to all three papers, the circulation figures reflected considerable subscriber duplication. When that offer was removed, the duplication of subscribers to both dailies fell to only six percent. Thus, while combined circulation is down 17 percent from the 1960's, the total number of individual subscribers was actually down just ten percent in the period, and most of the loss has been with the *Evening Sun*.[9] About 75 percent of *The Sun*'s sales are by subscription.

One of *The Sun*'s strengths lies in its international coverage. Although it was active in overseas reporting during World War II, it is really only since 1955, when its London man was its only overseas correspondent, that its foreign emphasis has become truly remarkable. Perhaps the person most responsible for stimulating foreign expansion of *The Sun*'s coverage was Charles Dorsey, Jr., the managing editor in the sixties who once said, "We try to send abroad literate people able to think for themselves, and we leave them alone."[10]

[8] *Ibid.*, p. D11.

[9] Donald Patterson, Publisher, *The Baltimore Sun*, in letter to H. Fisher and response to questionnaire, January 26, 1978.

[10] "Sun Shine," *Time* (May 6, 1963), p. 88.

Today, *The Sun* has as many full-time correspondents as any American paper its size. Eight full-timers cover London, Paris, Bonn, Cairo, Moscow, Hong Kong, New Delhi and Tokyo, with a part-timer in Ottawa. The paper's reports direct from these correspondents are supplemented by input from five wire services and several syndicated services.[11] *The Sun* jealously guards its claim to excellence in foreign correspondence. The *Evening Sun* is not allowed to carry reports from *The Sun's* overseas staff and the latter has repeatedly turned down bids to syndicate its overseas reports. *The Sun* can point with pride to an impressive list of distinguished foreign correspondents, including Paul Ward, Price Day, Philip Potter, Michael Parks, Henry Truitt, Ernest B. Furgurson, Charles Corddry, Louis Rukeyser, David Culhane and Mark Watson.

The Sun's national coverage is equally remarkable. It was "a pioneer in Washington reporting, placing correspondents in the capital during its first year of business."[12] With 14 reporters in Washington today, the paper provides its readers with insightful pieces of scope and depth rarely found in United States' newspapers. Among the earlier distinguished staffers who gave the paper its good name in national reportage were H. L. Mencken, Gerald W. Johnson and Frank Kent. Later, there were reporters like Price Day, Mark Watson and Paul Ward, cartoonists like Edmund Duffy and "Moco" Yardley, and editorial writers like John Owens. Today, the reports from *The Sun's* Washington bureau on energy, the economy and on governmental agencies are among the nation's best.

Although coverage of local news has been *The Sun's* weakest area, it is still considered Maryland's newspaper of record. Since, by tradition, national and international news have always been regarded more important than local stories, the latter have had to be events of marked importance before *The Sun's* editors even gave them a second glance. But recently the inroads of television and the public's preference for upbeat news have influenced *The Sun* to include more local news and feature materials. Two reporters are now assigned specifically to investigative work on the local level and others are encouraged to develop in-depth stories on their local beats. But *The Sun's* local news output still remains considerably smaller than that of its evening sister paper.

Although *The Sun* frequently endorses political candidates, it studiously maintains political independence, both in the news department and on its editorial pages. Its vice president and managing editor, Paul Banker gives the paper's position succinctly: "We judge politicians on their merit regardless of party and then judge their performance on merit, regardless of whether we endorsed or opposed their election."[13] While *The Sun* is fairly conservative on economic matters, it takes a liberal position in its promotion of individual and civil rights. It is unafraid to take strong editorial stands on issues, and, while the editors strive to be fair, they "do not pretend to be objective" when editorializing.[14] However,

[11] Wire services taken are: *AP, Reuters, NYT, Dow Jones* and *Knight.*
[12] Jones, *op. cit.*, p. D11.
[13] Paul A. Banker, Vice President and Managing Editor, *The Sun* and *Sunday Sun,* in response to questionnaire, dated January 12, 1978.
[14] *Ibid.*

news is printed as objectively as possible regardless of the paper's editorial stance, and *The Sun*'s Opinion-Commentary page is always open to all viewpoints.

The Sun's consistent high quality springs partly from its demanding staff standards and its team approach. William Schmick, Jr., publisher of the *Sunpapers* says, "Our basic concept is that you put a good man on his beat and then trust his judgment and competence. If he doesn't do the job, we'll replace him."[15] As for those who prove themselves, the traditional rule in *The Sun* office is "to promote men on the staff to higher positions whenever it is possible to do so."[16] The result is loyalty and esprit-de-corps. Ever since the Abells, *The Sun* has been one of the few newspapers that actively encourages high standards of staff behavior.

Another long-standing rule of *The Sun*'s office is that editors must engage "only in purely journalistic enterprises."[17] Reporters are "actively discouraged from taking any part in politics, community affairs, or anything else that might encourage reporting or editing with an ulterior purpose or promoting—or debunking—something or someone."[18] Paid press junkets, complimentary tickets, other "freebies" and "fringe benefits" are strictly forbidden; everything possible is done to discourage personal journalism and favoritism in stories. Even reporter "analysis" in stories or special columns is discouraged. Reporters know where they stand and that their stories and columns must not crusade. These special staff codes and practices, rather than being repressive, appear to encourage team loyalty. Editorial page editor R. L. Sterne says, "It's not me writing. It's not me speaking. It's not this or that editor writing or speaking. It's the institution speaking."[19] Or, as city editor John Woodruff observes, "You judge the story in terms of what you know your paper is as an institution, as well as in terms of some intrinsic, arbitrary scale of values."[20] As a result, staff members respect and trust one another, a spirit that carries over into the paper's appearance and contents.

Under its banner, on which is inscribed "Light for All," is a serious, aristocratic, high-quality product designed to appeal to the intelligent and the influential. The daily *Sun* is usually 40–44 pages in length and divided into three sections, the first carrying international and national news, business pages, the editorial and op-ed pages, and sometimes a page of local news. The second section is the feature section, containing pages on the arts and entertainment, travel and the comics. The last section typically presents several pages of local news and sports, plus a number of classified advertisement pages. The *Sunday Sun* often runs to 200 or more pages, plus special magazine sections. The front page normally carries about two or three pictures, and several—or none—may appear on the inside pages. But, as *Time* magazine once wrote, "Stories are writ-

[15] Quoted in Peddicord, *op. cit.*, p. 30.
[16] Johnson et al, *op. cit.*, p. 420.
[17] *Ibid.*, p. 422.
[18] Peddicord, *op. cit.*, p. 32.
[19] *Ibid.*, p. 30.
[20] *Ibid.*, p. 32.

ten not to entertain, but to inform; text is never displaced for purely cosmetic considerations—by a picture, say, to break up a formidable-looking front page."[21]

The total content of *The Sun* roughly divides into the following percentages of the paper's total editorial space: national and international news, 10 percent each; state and local news, 16 percent; business, 17; sports, 15; editorials, 14; features and entertainment, 12; travel, 4; home, 3; analysis, 1 percent. Advertising takes up about 55 percent of the paper's total space, somewhat less than most American newspapers. *The Sun,* as a paper which emphasizes objectivity and quality, never has trouble filling its advertising columns, a fact which bears out the paper's philosophy as expounded by Paul Patterson, a former publisher of the *Sunpapers:* "If you put out a good enough paper, people will read it. If enough people read it, advertisers will support it."[22]

In 1974, the A. S. Abell Company achieved two technical breakthroughs that have put the *Sunpapers* in the vanguard of newspaper production techniques. First, the Baltimore Typographical Union adopted a contract agreeing to the operation and maintenance of both optical character readers and video display terminal units. Then the Company contracted with the Harris Corporation to install one of the nation's largest electronic newsroom systems. The paper installed a total of five integrated editing and composition systems, three in the newsroom, one for typesetter processing and the fifth for ad storage. A total of 76 "video typewriters" (VDTs) are part of the re-designed and fully integrated electronic newsroom. Reporters write their materials and place them in computer storage for editing. Wire news transmissions and news from the paper's bureaus are recorded so staff can call them up on the VDTs for display, selection and editing. The typesetter processing and display advertising systems allow call-up of data for video layout on other VDTs in preparation for the paper's photo-typesetters. Editorial personnel prepared a training manual and taught 290 staff members the skills necessary to operate the new system.

In 1976, the *Sunpapers* installed the new electronic advertising storage and processing system which now makes them an all-electronic operation. The processor-storage unit for advertising is capable of storing 66 million characters on each disk. All classified advertisement copy was converted from hot metal to cold type the same year. Several "payoffs" have come since the entire system has become operative: time is saved and deadlines are more easily met; there are fewer errors; fewer workers are required; overtime has virtually been eliminated; and there has been little "down time."

The Sun and its staff have won numerous awards which recognize the paper's writing, reporting, photographic, content, production, advertising and management excellence. In all, nine Pulitzer Prizes have been received, plus many other significant national and local awards. In all, nine awards were received in 1976 and thirteen in 1977.

Today, *The Baltimore Sun,* following Arunah Abell's traditions of supplying

[21] "The Top U.S. Dailies: *The Sun," Time* (January 10, 1964), p. 58.
[22] Jones, *op. cit.,* p. D1.

objective news rapidly, continues to believe its primary responsibility is "to report the news and reflect the concerns of our city, state and nation as we perceive these interests."[23] It demonstrates regularly its willingness to spend what is necessary to provide quality coverage. It still serves its public today with the air of respectability, reserve and aristocracy typical of Abell. It is also vitally interested in providing its public what it needs for informed decision-making. In meeting these aims, *The Sun* offers it readers each morning "one of the best daily products produced in the journalism business."[24] *The Sun* is, in the truest sense of the word, a *news*paper, with the emphasis on "news." And that emphasis, all things considered, must be the primary aim of any newspaper worthy of the appellation "elite."

Berlingske Tidende

(DENMARK)

SOME 230 YEARS AGO, an immigrant German printer who had come to Copenhagen set his mark indelibly upon Denmark's newspaper publishing industry. Ernst Heinrich Berling acquired the royal newspaper privilege held by Joachim Wielandt, publisher of Denmark's first paper, *Ekstraordinaire Relationer* until the latter's death. Berling immediately began publishing the *Kobenhavnske Danske Post Tidender* (Copenhagen Danish Postal News), the forerunner of today's *Berlingske Tidende*.

Berling's first issue was a semi-weekly 16-page pamphlet. For some 150 years, Berling's paper acted as a special voice of government, but it gradually furnished more and more foreign and local news. Ever since 1765, the paper has been housed on Copenhagen's narrow Pilestraede, at first in a small three-story building, but today in a modern, spacious city-block sized edifice. All through the ensuing years, Berling and eight generations of his descendants have owned and have molded Denmark's oldest paper into one of Europe's best serious, responsible, interesting and relevant elite newpapers.[1]

Danish newspapers have a charm and personality all their own and perhaps *Berlinske Tidende* offers the best example of these special press traits. Like the other Danish papers, the *Tidende* is friendly yet reserved, bright yet serious, intriguing yet distant. The charms of the Danish people and their history seem to

---

[23] Banker questionnaire.

[24] Jones, *op. cit.*, p. D1.

[1] Kenneth E. Olson, *The History Makers: The Press of Europe from Its Beginnings through 1965* (Baton Rouge, Louisiana State University Press, 1966), pp. 52 and 64.

exude from the newspapers. Despite some impact from its British and German neighbors, the Danish press has developed its own popular, yet serious national character.

Because Denmark is a small, basically pastoral country, not heavily populated, no newspaper can cater to one select segment of the population. Therefore, newspapers must serve two purposes: to give people what they *want* to read while at the same time giving them what they *ought* to read. So the Danish papers present something for everybody in the family, always in good taste and with emphasis on the family. The result is a healthy, wholesome press devoid of the sensationalism of British and French popular papers. Danish papers do entertain, but the overriding tone is one of responsibility, seriousness, open-mindedness and tolerance. The provincial papers have retained the traditional political interests to a far greater degree than have the Copenhagen papers, leading some to call the latter "journals of news" and the former "journals of views." This characterization is an oversimplification, since all Danish newspapers combine both news and views and the content is often rather heavily tinged with politics.

The Danish press has a long, well-preserved history of freedom. It gained momentary freedom when, in 1770, the King's physician, Johann Struensee, taking over for the incompetent King, ended government censorship of all publications. The monarchy again gained control until the revolution brought freedom once more in the 1830's. In the atmosphere of this second period of freedom, Berling's paper changed to daily publication with an emphasis on news and political controversy. In the same period, Denmark's first liberal paper, *Faedrelandet* (Fatherland) was born. These early roots of Danish press freedom have withstood the acid tests of depression and World War II oppression and remain healthy to this day.[2]

At least partly because of this tradition of freedom, the history of the Danish press is replete with the names of great newspapers, among them *Faedrelandet* and *Dagbladet, Nationaltidende* and *Aftenposten, Dagens Nyheder* and *Morgenbladet, Politiken, Jyllands Posten* and *Aktuelt.* The names of famous journalists such as Carl Ploug, Carl Bille, Christen Nielsen, Christian Ferslew, Herman Bang, Chresten Berg, and Viggo Hørup lighted up the nineteenth-century scene with their intellects and personalities. In this century, journalism has made further imprints upon the nation through such newspaper stalwarts as Henrik Cavling, Frejlif Olsen, Emil Wiinblad, and Vilhelm Lassen, to name only a few. Among all these proud names, the *Berlingske Tidende* stands out as a pacesetter for the entire Danish press. And, of course, the name of its founder, E. H. Berling, stands high among the leading pioneers of Danish journalism.

When Berling's *Post-Tidender* first appeared in 1749, it used the Royal Mail for free distribution of some of its 800 copies. Berling also obtained from the King monopoly privileges on news and advertising. Foreign news consisted mainly of translations from German sources in Hamburg. But, to Berling's credit, news of Copenhagen was stressed and news of the city's birth, mar-

[2] Olson, *op. cit.,* pp. 52–55.

BERLINGSKE ✦ TIDENDE

230. årgang nr. 53 . 2 sektioner, 32 sider . Kr. 2,25   GRUNDLAGT 1749   AF E. H. BERLING   Onsdag 22. februar . 8. uge 1978

Ny parole:

HK gør op med „flip- og slips-prole-tarer"

Af
Claus Kallerup

HK har ifølge forbundsformand Max Harvøe foretaget et endeligt opgør med »flip- og slipsproletarerne, der tror, de er finere end end andre fagforeninger.

»På vores kongres i januar 1977 blev der lagt en ny linie, som vi har fulgt siden, gående ud på mere faglig bevidsthed. HK er og bliver en fagforening, og det vil vi markere mere tydeligt i fremtiden, siger Max Harvøe.

Det kommer som en kommentar til en udtalelse fra direktøren for Butiks- og Kontorfagenes Arbejdsgiverforening, Friis Bredøe, der har konstateret, at HK har indtaget en mere

militant fagpolitisk holdning.

»Det vil blive understreget af det apparat, der både af os og af de andre LO-fagforbund vil blive sat bag fremtidige, væsentlige aktioner. Et samarbejde mellem flere forbund er et voordentlig stærkt våben overfor den enkelte arbejdsgiver, og vi vil bruge det.«

HK-formanden understreger den ny linie i at forsvar for en forbundsudvidelse til medlemmerne om deltagelse i et tillidsmandskursus, hvis mål er at sikre deres kendskab til den socialistiske ideologi.

Han mener ikke, at det strider mod medlemskarenes brede politiske sammensætning, der ifølge en observatørundersøgelse svarer nøje til befolkningens politiske sammensætning.

SIDE 12

Værnepligtige hævder:

Dansk u-båd ved at ruste op

Den 30 mand store besætning om bord på u-båden Tumleren, ville sandsynligvis være omkommet, hvis u-båden under sit togt i slutningen af 1977 var gået ned på den tilladte dybde.

Den u-båden i januar kom i dok, opdagede man nem-

lig en ært alvorlig tæring på to gange to meter i bådens ene side, skriver »Soldaten«, landsblad for værnepligtige. Under togtet bevægede Tumleren sig kun i en dybde af 30 meter. Bladet mener, det er trivliosnt, om den tærede båd kunne have klaret

vandpresset, hvis den var dykket ned i normal dybde, 100 meter.

Chefen for Søværnets Materiel Kommando, admiral Jørgen Petersen, oplyser, at tæringen gav anledning til værnpligtige, at kontrollen skal tages op til revision. Fore-

løbig afventer Søværnet en rapport fra Korrosionscentralen, der har undersøgt tæringen nærmere, samt resultater fra KLV, hvor Tumleren i øjeblikket gennemgår en række prøver.

De værnepligtige ønsker de sikkerhedsmæssige for-

hold undersøgt af Skibstilsynet. Bl.a. mener de værnepligtige, at dele af Søværnets korvetter er lavet af så tyndt materiale, at der er fare for alvorlige skader selv ved mindre kollisioner.

Bo.

[MC-07] INTENT: Morning LaBossiere, Feb. 21—MEETS WITH CARTER—Danish Prime Minister Anker Joergensen (Left) meets with President Carter at the White House Tuesday in their first official meeting since Joergensen (Law AP Wire photo) (tail) (fskc)

Anker J. hos Carter

På en af den amerikanske præsidents mest travle dage med alvorlige indenrigspolitiske problemer, af Jimmy Carter i går udviddet tid til samtaler med den danske statsminister umiddelbart efter Anker Jørgensen i går indledte sit officielle besøg i Washington.

Det er det første officielle statsministerbesøg i USA i otte år, og Anker Jørgensen blev modtaget med alt, hvad der hører til et sådant officielt besøg.

BAGSIDEN

Hvis De vender avisen en kvart, vil De af den indsugende tekst til dette telefonbillede fra Washington kunne se, at statsminister Anker Jørgensen før at møde med præsident Carter har ændret sit navn til Mogens Ladegaard... Forklaringen er simpel den, at en lille landsstore mand ikke er kendt af alle og altså heller ikke af Associated Press. Mogens Ladegaard er forøvrigt navnet på Berlingske fotograf, der får statsministeren på rejsen.

SIDE 12

Boligudgifterne og inflationen:

Alt andet steg ligeså meget som huse

I de sidste fire år er der ikke blevet sværere for en gennemsnitsfamilie at flytte ind i ny nybygget parcelhus. Boligudgiften — efter skattebesparelse — i et nyopført, typisk parcelhus, er steget med 50 pct. gennem de sidste fire år, men da al mindelige leveomkostninger er steget nøjagtig lige så meget, og lønninger og indkommer er samtidig steget endnu mere.

SIDE 6

Erhvervs-debat om den toldfrie butik

SIDE 12

Ubevæbnet politimand fangede pistolrøver

Af
Poul Hørdum

»Jeg var flet en nogle bedre fortællse for bank- og sparekasseperonalets situation. Det fastslog kriminalassistent Knud Sørensen, Køge, da han i går ubevæbnet overmandede en maskeret og bevæbnet ung røver i Sparekassen SDS's filial i Borup.

Selv om røveren, en 21årig studerende fra Amager, havde planlagt røveriet til mindst detalje, var alle odds imod ham, da han i går kl. 11,00 trådte ind i sparekassen.

Et kvarter forinden var kriminalassistent Knud Sørensen 36 år og den 34årige politiassistent Rudi Kold på efterforskningsbesøg i sparekassen. De to politifolk var i færd med at tage personalet fotos af mulige gerningsmand til et røveri i samme filial den 23. december. Udbyttet blev dengang ca. 14.000 kroner.

Lidt paralyseret

»Han sagde straks. Det er røveri. Alle pengene hurtigt. Han gav kasserersken en medbragt plasticpose og forlangte penge fra både kassen og pengeskabet. Vi forholdt os rolige, måske lidt paralyseret af situationen. Men jeg forsøgte dog at indrette mig et signalement, at vur-

dere kaliberen på hans våben og tænkte lidt på faren for at overmande hams, fortæller Knud Sørensen.

Da røveren imens havde flaet 59.660 kroner i plasticposen, vendte han sig og begorordede politifolkene og de to ansatte i et tilstødende rum.

»Jeg gik selv. Jeg længe-de først, greb jeg fat i den, netop som røveren skulle lukke efter os. Jeg fik slået døren med hans våben og sprang på ham. Jeg fik et kraftigt slag i hovedet af pistolskæftet, men holdt fast. Sekunder senere fik jeg hjælp af min kollega.

Mens de to politifolk holdt røveren fast, alarmerede sparekassepersonalet politiet, som telefonisk blev orienteret om, at røveren var anholdt.

Under den efterfølgende afhøring forklarede gerningsmanden, der havde maskeret sig med en gummimaske og var bevæbnet med luftpistol og spejderdolk, at røveriet var planlagt.

Han havde lejet en bil i Kastrup lufthavn mandag og var kørt til Roskilde. Her skal han en cykel og transporterede den til Borup, da flugten først skulle ske med cyklen, derefter i toget. Men måtte var at skaffe penge til røveriet i nærmeste færtørt sjokat. Han fremstilles i dag i grundlovsforhør.

Kriminalassistent Knud Sørensen — fangede røveren
Foto: John E. Jacobsen

Røveren bar denne gummimaske og truede personalet med den kraftige luftpistol.

Kjeld Olesen på retræte

Af
Ejvind Olesen

Trafikminister Kjeld Olesen vil tiltræde den højeste grad af offentlighed omkring afgørelsen af, hvem der skal have bevillingen til en vis flybenhavna Lufthavn i Kastrup fra 1. maj. Ministeren er også indstillet på, at de syv ansøgere tilbud skal offentliggøres snarest, hvis der er juridisk daskning for en sådan disposition. Afg-

reisen af, hvem der skal have bevillingen vil ministeren træffe inden kommunalvalget tirsdag den 7. marts. I øvrigt har Kjeld Olesen besluttet ikke at lade Rigsrevisionen se på de indkomne licitations-tilbud.

»Jeg ønsker ikke på nogen måde at stikke noget under stolen,« siger Kjeld Olesen. »Der kan dog være visse hensyn at tage, hvis en tilbudsgiver har bedt mig om tilbuddet må blive betragtet som fortroligt, og man skal huske på, at en licitation, der er tale om, ikke fungé-

rer på samme måde, som når et firma giver tilbud på en skole eller et nyt rådhus. Juridisk er der ikke krittisere, at jeg annullerede den første licitation, fordi det er tilbudsgivning, som ikke falder ind under licitationsloven.

Jeg vil også gerne slå fast, at afgørelsen af den ny licitation vil ske inden kommunalvalget. Vi er i fuld gang med at gennemgå det materiale, vi i går modtog fra Københavns Lufthavnsvæsen.« slutter ministeren.

Hvis offentligheden skal

rer de samme tilbud, som Kjeld Olesen højeste embedsmand, departementschef Jørgen Halck, er medlem af SAS-styrelsen, som repræsentant for staten interesseret i det skandinaviske luftfartsselskab.

Charterselskaber truer også

De danske charterselskaber, Conair, Maersk Air

have kendskab til de fornyede tilbud, må det blive fra ministeren. De tallene kom frem under den første licitation, skete det i forbindelse med et repræsentantskabsmøde i KLV, hvor både den danske SAS-direktør Frede Ahlgreen Eriksen og direktør Anders Helgstrand fra Sterling Airways har mødte. Den kilde kan ingen mere se. I KLV har man besluttet ikke at orientere om tilbuddene i dette forum i anden omgang.

SAS har gode muligheder for at erfare størrelsen af de

øvrige seks tilbud, idet

1) Fortsættes på
I. sektions bagside

Risø-direktør:

Svenskerne holder oplysninger om atomkraft tilbage

Af
Claus Kallerup

»Danske myndigheder og institutter med interesse i svenske atomenergiforhold må alene på grund af den geografiske nærhed mellem de to lande have krav på at blive holdt orienteret om

rapporter, f. eks. om Barsebæck. Men det har på det seneste vist sig umuligt at få svar på direkte henvendelser,« siger direktør Niels E. Busch, Atomforsøgsanlæget Risø.

Han har gennem længere tid forsøgt at få at vide, hvordan den svenske energikommission har anvendt

nogle kommentarer om Barsebäck-værket, som kommissionen selv havde bedt Risø om at udarbejde i tilknytning til en forelagt rapport, der bl. a. handle om strålingsfarer og ulykkesrisici i forbindelse

2) Fortsættes på
I. sektions bagside

Fiat erklærer Ford priskrig

Fiat erklærer nu Ford Taunus åben priskrig med en modelserie i prisklassen fra 57.000 til 76.000 kr. Ved præsentationen i Italien i går udtalte den danske Fiat-

direktør rent ud, at han vil holde sine stilalenske Taunus'ere 6 procent under Fords priser. Samtidig lancerer den italienske bilfabrik n usine vogne med ud-

styrslister som i svenske biler. Blandt andet er sikkerhedsseler og nakkestøtter, også på bagsædet, nu standard.

BILEN 2. SEKTION SIDE 7

---

riages, deaths, ship movements and financial items appeared regularly in his paper. When Berling died in 1750, he left his business to his two sons. Under them, the paper grew rapidly and moved to its present site in Pilestraede.

For about 150 years, Berling's journal remained State-privileged. Although this guaranteed the *Tidende* financial security, at times it led to government interference in the paper's policies. In 1799, a government decree heavily restrained political and economic discussion. Consequently, throughout the first half of the nineteenth century the *Post-Tidender* and other papers had to fill their pages with non-political materials—entertainment, literature and news of the theater. In the 1820's *Tidender* was published four times each week and in 1831 it generally came out daily. In 1841, it began to appear regularly every weekday and in 1844 it began regular morning and evening daily issues. During this period, in 1838, a new Press Act reintroduced press freedom, but it emphasized press "responsibility" and required that each paper have a "legally responsible person," usually the editor, who would answer for all the contents of the paper.

In 1849, as a result of revolution against the monarchy, power was given to a bicameral *Rigsdag* and Clause 91 of the new Danish Constitution clearly stated, "Everyone has a right to publish his ideas in print but with responsibility before the law. Censorship and other preventive measures may never be introduced again."[3] Two years later, a new Press Act irrevocably introduced full-blown press freedom.

Despite this separation of press and state, the *Berlingske Tidende* maintained its governmental connections until 1901. This was due partly to the fact that the Conservative Party, composed largely of large landowners, substantial burghers and the professional gentry, was in power and the *Tidende* was its strongest voice. Outstanding editors arose during this period to contribute to the paper's excellence. Among them was Mendel Levin Nathanson, who started the literary *feuilleton* and dramatic reviews in Danish journalism with contributions from such leading literary figures as Hans Christian Anderson. During this period also, the founder's great grandson, Carl Berling managed *Tidende* from 1838 to 1858, during which time circulation rose from 1,400 to nearly 10,000, double that of any Copenhagen paper. During this time, *Tidende* was conservative, and as one historian has said, its semiofficial status made for "cautious, level-headed and reliable journalism."[4]

In 1901, *Berlingske Tidende* broke all its government connections. By this time, its total circulation was some 24,000 copies daily and it was drawing sufficient advertising to give it a full independent status. The next significant year was 1913, when the *Tidende* began a Sunday edition complete with a wide range of interesting material and a colored magazine section of size and quality previously unknown in the Danish press. The same year, the paper acquired a new editor-in-chief, Christian Gulman, who did much to upgrade *Tidende*'s journalistic quality. He instituted the interview story, published the first photo-

[3] *Ibid.*, p. 54.
[4] Svend Thorsen, *Newspapers in Denmark* (Copenhagen, Det Danske Selskab, 1953), p. 13.

graph, strengthened the morning edition, built up the paper's foreign coverage and enlarged the staff, including the addition of poets and authors. Gulman's desire to give *Tidende* the reliability of the London *Times*, the literary quality of *Le Journal* of Paris and the wide appeal of London's *Daily Express* had largely been achieved when he died in 1934. Without doubt, Gulman was one of *Tidende*'s greatest editors and one of the most versatile of all Danish journalists of all time.[5]

In the early 1900's *Tidende*'s circulation was about 20,000 and by the end of World War I, it had climbed to 50,000. Circulation growth continued steadily, so that by the beginning of World War II about 125,000 copies were published daily. In the 1930's, one of *Tidende*'s greatest writers on international affairs, Nicalai Blaedel, became well known. He had started his career as a writer for *Politiken*, *Tidende*'s Liberal Party rival. But, in 1927, Blaedel had shifted his position, joined the Conservative Party and begun work for *Dagens Nyheter*. At a time when the Nazis were gaining the ascendancy in Germany, Blaedel constantly tried to inform the Danish public of Hitler's aims. His pieces were the most insightful and predictive of what was happening in Germany and of what tragic events would subsequently occur in Denmark of those published anywhere in the European press.

In 1940, Germany invaded Denmark to "protect her from England," and Blaedel's prophecies came true. The Danish Government was able to spare the press from direct German censorship, but there were blatant attempts to silence the Danish media. The Germans blew up some newspaper plants, blaming Danish saboteurs for the destruction. When *Berlingske Tidende* leaders heard their plant was marked for sabotage, they fortified it with sandbags and armed guards, thinking if they could call for help the German troops would have to come to protect them against the so-called saboteurs. The plan worked. Later, many Danish newspapers went underground. *Berlingske Tidende* staffers continued to put out its regular edition under censorship; then they would disappear to publish an underground paper. Their resistance to the Germans remained united and strong. *Tidende* later discovered that, though one of its staff had been a Nazi collaborator, even he had not informed on his paper.

Danish newspapers recovered from the effects of the war quickly. Strong party-line loyalties began to fade. During the post-war prosperity, the larger papers developed their advertising support. But the prosperity also led to inflation and by the mid-sixties many of the smaller papers found themselves in financial difficulties. Some were even forced to close; in fact, during the 30 post-war years between 1945 and 1975, the number of newspapers published in Denmark decreased from 122 to just 49.[6] As a result, there has been considerable discussion by press and government of the need for subsidies, at least to the smaller papers in order to keep them alive. However, to date little action has been taken. Because of *Berlingske Tidende*'s large circulation, well-developed advertising policies and stable finances, it is not touched by these discussions.

[5] *Ibid.*, p. 72.
[6] "Subsidy Principle Accepted, But . . . ," *IPI Report,* 24:11 (November, 1975), pp. 9–10.

A far more serious problem plagued the *Berlingske Tidende* in 1977.[7] A typographers' union strike closed the paper down completely for 141 days from January 31st until June 21st, when sporadic publication was again resumed. The strikers continued slowdowns, delays and other disruptive devices which prevented full production until the end of September, when accord was finally reached between *Tidende* management and the union.

The conflict arose because, during the prosperity years of the late 1950's and early 1960's, *Berlingske* had to hire additional technical staff to put out its growing paper. This staff stayed on, developed a network of "featherbedding" or making of special agreements for worker benefits, such as full pay for fictitious overtime. When steeply rising production and newsprint costs, coupled with losses of circulation and advertising, led to leaner times in the early 1970's, *Berlingske* was saddled with a 50 percent overstaffing problem in the technical department. For three years, the paper tried to negotiate to no avail. Management offered handsome severance pay for redundant workers. Litigation in the Labor Court backed management, but the labor union refused to comply.

The result was a costly strike for everyone involved. Danish readers were without papers to read, especially during a three-week period in April when sympathy strikers shut down the entire Danish press. The typesetters gained little, since they lost pay during the long strike and, in the end, extra workers were declared redundant and all overtime benefits were lost. All the *Berlingske* publications were struck and suffered loss of circulation: *Tidende* (daily circulation, 150,000; Sundays, 250,000); the tabloid *B.T.* (235,000); *Weekendavisen* (an evening political journal, 50,000); two weekly family magazines, *Billed-Bladet* (400,000) and *Soendags-B.T.* (220,000); and a monthly *Radio-TV* magazine (375,000). During the long struggle, these *Berlingske* publications spent millions of kroner on the strike, court litigation and compensation of the editorial and administrative staff, all of whom were kept on at full pay despite the shutdown. All the while, of course, the publications lost most of their advertising and circulation income.

Although the strike was expensive for *Berlingske Tidende,* recovery has been rapid and advertising circulation and reader goodwill have returned to normal. One side benefit of the strike is that it called considerable public attention to *Berlingske Tidende* and its other publications.

The Danes are among Europe's most avid newspaper readers, with an average of less than three persons per copy. *Berlingske Tidende,* its tabloid-sized companion *B.T.,* together with the leading competitor, *Politiken* hold a lion's share of the readership market, both in Copenhagen and throughout the country. Early in 1977, *Berlingske Tidende* and *B.T.* accounted for 40 percent of newspaper circulation in Copenhagen and 25 percent nationwide.[8] About 65

---

[7] For a more complete discussion of the strike, see the following three articles by Niels Nørlund, editor-in-chief of *Berlingske Tidende:* "Why Papers are Scarce in Copenhagen," *IPI Report,* 26:3 (March, 1977), p. 9; "The *Berlingske Tidende* Dispute," FIEJ *Bulletin,* No. 112 (April, 1977), pp. 13–14; and "Review of the Conflict and its Aftermath," FIEJ *Bulletin,* No. 114 (October, 1977), pp. 9–10.

[8] Niels Nørlund, "The *Berlingske Tidende* Dispute," pp. 13–14.

percent of *Tidende*'s circulation is by subscription, with the remainder coming from street sales.

Berlingske Tidende's readership is distributed among all sectors of the Danish public. Because the country's population is too small (some four million) to support specialized newspapers, the *Tidende,* like all Danish dailies, tries to embrace all readers. But its primary appeal is the middle- and upper-class reader and it offers something for every member of the family in typical Scandinavian style. Its varied assortment of serious and entertainment materials sets it apart from ultraserious dailies like Switzerland's *Neue Zürcher Zeitung.*

Today, *Berlingske Tidende* is an attractive, regular-size-format paper eight columns wide. Weekday editions usually run two or three sections totalling some 40–44 pages. Sunday editions have four sections—news, entertainment, a magazine and a family section—and typically total a hundred pages or more. Each section contains a complete unit of advertisements. A color band is used to set off the masthead. Good use of white space contrasted to bold black headlines gives an attractive appearance. Two or three photographs, often large-sized, are used on the front page. Numerous pictures of all sizes, maps and cartoons enhance the paper's inner pages. Color is frequently used in the advertisements. The pages, like those of most Scandinavian dailies, are glued at the fold. The second section of many weekday issues, called "Dagens Magasin," contains pages on television, film, radio and theater entertainment, music, art, culture, books, comics, weddings, obituaries, travel and special features. Throughout the paper, advertisements and news-information materials share space fifty-fifty.

The editors of *Tidende* give important emphasis to foreign news. The paper maintains a staff of full-time foreign correspondents in London, Paris, Brussels, Bonn, Oslo, Stockholm, Moscow and Washington, D.C. Overseas wire services are taken from the Associated Press and Ritzau, a Danish service which has exchange arrangements with Reuters and the Norwegian, Swedish, Finnish, Dutch, Belgian and Swiss agencies for swapping national and international news. It also takes the New York *Times* and the London *Times* syndicated news services. Coverage of foreign news is regarded outstanding considering the size of the country and the newspaper. About ten percent of the "news hole" is normally given to international news.

The *Tidende* also covers the national and local news well. Several pages are allocated each day for Danish and Scandinavian news. One page is devoted to news briefs from local Danish towns. There are daily finance and business pages which focus on local commerce. Each day, *Tidende* carries a political debate in which all ten Danish political parties, including the Communists and the left-wing Socialists, take part. The editorial pages contain local and guest commentary, letters to the editor and interpretive articles. Pictures and humorous cartoons of special interest to Danes are interspersed with the reader letters and editorial columns.

The paper has a staff of 2,800, including some 650 technical personnel and about 250 writer-editor types. Most reporters have gone through a mandatory four years' journalists training course at Aarhus University, followed by 18 months of on-the-job training. There are also a number of special writers with university education in their fields, such as arts, science or economics.[9] A managing director responsible for the overall economic administration of *Berlingske*'s three dailies, two weeklies and the monthly magazine heads the entire operation. The editors-in-chief are responsible for the editorial side of all papers and periodicals, but each publication has its own editor who accounts for the contents of his own paper or periodical. Two highly-trained and experienced journalists, Aage Deleuran and Niels Nørlund presently serve in these two posts. Each *Berlingske* paper and periodical has its own editorial staff.

Berlingske Tidende's excellence has gained recognition outside Denmark. The University of Missouri School of Journalism awarded the paper one of its Honor Medals in 1961 for its "vigorous international fight for basic freedoms . . . continued defense of freedom of speech and the printed word . . . fairness in its editorial comments . . . and its reliable Danish and world news presentation." In 1965, Niels Nørlund received the University of California at Los Angeles Award for Distinguished Achievement in Journalism.

Although many persist in linking *Berlingske Tidende* to the Conservative Party, the paper in fact takes a Liberal-Conservative stance. Perhaps it is closest to the Conservative Party in its basic editorial position, but this does not mean it opposes the program of Social-Democratic governments which have established themselves in Denmark. Actually, it has adapted well to the general governmental drift to the left without forsaking its basically conservative leanings. It has, for example, criticized the economic policies pursued by the Social-Democrats, but has agreed with the government's foreign views, especially those which have advocated support for NATO and the United Nations and Danish membership in the European Economic Community. This ability to adapt does not mean the paper is opportunist, picking only the best from others and lacking its own platform. As the editors indicate, *Berlingske Tidende* has a broad but clear set of principles: "We support Danish society as established, with Constitutional Monarchy, Parliamentary Democracy, Christianity and strong guarantees for all personal freedoms."[10]

Without question, *Berlingske Tidende*'s claim to be one of Europe's most influential and responsible newspapers is well substantiated. Its long 230-year tradition of quality cannot be denied. Its ownership by eight generations of a single family, coupled with sound advertising policies and wide circulation give it financial stability. Its thorough and reliable news coverage of a wide range of subjects, its accessibility to governmental affairs, its interest in culture and the arts and its attractive and responsible appearance all support its claim to quality and influence. Its strong conservative stance on the best of traditional Danish principles while remaining flexible to all views further upholds this claim. Its combination of serious, quality journalism coupled with appeals to all readers still further vindicates its claim. Perhaps the "clincher" to the claim lies in the fact that readers and advertisers alike made great sacrifices to receive and to support *Berlingske* during its recent strike crisis and quickly welcomed the return of "their" paper.

[9] Niels Nørlund, editor-in-chief, *Berlingske Tidende,* in response to questionnaire, May 23, 1978.
[10] Nørlund questionnaire.

But, in the final analysis, *Berlingske Tidende* is a proud and confident journal which never rests on its historic traditions and laurels or its current press leadership. Rather, it pushes on each day into new journalistic frontiers with dignity and a reasoned self-assurance, speaking in a friendly but reserved, yet healthy voice to its numerous intelligent and faithful readers.

Borba

(YUGOSLAVIA)

YUGOSLAVIA STANDS geographically and politically on a bridge between East and West, a champion of the non-aligned countries' causes. At the same time, it is multi-cultural, representing a coalition of five main ethnic groupings plus numerous minorities, and multi-lingual, with four official languages and at least 16 others spoken within its borders. Those factors, among others, combine to make Yugoslavia's press, including the two dailies that might be called "national"— Belgrade's *Borba* and *Politika*—unique and remarkable. Although this treatment will feature *Borba*, *Politika* must also be considered because both are quality dailies, each in its own right, one complementing the other as they tower over the remainder of the Yugoslav press.

Borba, as the organ of the Socialist Alliance of Yugoslavia, is strongly nationalistic and excels in supplying political news and party views, while *Politika* provides Yugoslavs with a more culturally-oriented and diversified content. *Borba* ("Struggle") is no longer a principal organ of the Communist Party, as it once was.[1] Because of Yugoslavia's ethnic make-up, the two together do "not dominate the opinions of the rest of the country."[2] One evidence of this phenomenon lies in their combined circulation figures, which in 1970 reached only 301,000 or less than 22 percent of the total for the entire nation.

Of the two newspapers, *Politika* is the older. Founded in 1904, it is Yugoslavia's oldest continuing daily. By the beginning of World War II, it had a circulation of about 46,000 copies daily. *Borba* began publication nearly two decades later on February 19, 1922, as an organ of the then outlawed Communist Party of Yugoslavia. It was first published in Zagreb as an independent paper. Its first seven years were activist and difficult: it urged disobedience to the country's ruling monarchy. From its earliest beginnings, it advocated a press independent of political controls and waged a strong editorial war against censorship. These actions earned for it recognition as a champion of press freedom

---

[1] Stevan Marjanovic, Nemanjina, Yugoslavia, in letter to H. Fisher, dated March 10, 1978.
[2] Gertrude Joch Robinson, *Tito's Maverick Media* (Urbana: University of Illinois Press, 1977), p. 47.

and as a government critic. After seven years, *Borba* was banned. Most of its staff, young Communists from Zagreb, were imprisoned for crimes against the state. Among those given sentences was Ognjen Prica, one of the paper's first editors and one who did much to give *Borba* a fighting spirit.

During World War II, fascist armies conquered Yugoslavia and divided it between Germany, Italy, Hungary and Bulgaria. Marshal Tito led the national struggle for liberation against the fascist occupiers and their Quisling governments. Tito was aided effectively by the Communist Party press, which had organized for the continuing publication of newspapers and other literature after most papers were closed down. In 1941, *Borba,* one of the dailies closed down, began publishing in the hills, moving from one place to another with Tito's partisan fighters. Then, when the territory around Uzice (Serbia) was liberated, *Borba* began to come out regularly under the editorship of Edvard Kardelj, a member of the highest political and military leadership of the Communist-led resistance.[3] When the Germans left Belgrade in 1944, *Borba* became the official Communist Party paper and, as such, was the most privileged and authoritative of all the Yugoslav papers.

Since World War II, the Yugoslav press has expanded and changed significantly. Immediately after the country's liberation, many publishing houses, severely damaged or destroyed during the conflict, began rebuilding and acquiring new equipment. The number of newspapers of all types jumped from 97 in 1945 to 217 in 1947 to 367 by 1950. Circulation of all papers increased by an average of 50 million copies annually during this five-year period. *Borba's* circulation rise was particularly phenomenal during this period, quadrupling to 625,000 copies daily. *Politika,* meantime, sponsored by the Popular Front, reached only 280,000. During the 30-year period 1945–1975, the number of dailies doubled from 13 to 26 and average daily circulation climbed from 672,000 to 1,881,000.[4]

Today, there are 16 morning papers, 7 evening dailies, 2 sports and one economic paper. Whereas most publications were formerly published by economic, social or political organizations, today 84 percent are put out by independent news publishing firms.

Six of Yugoslavia's dailies are now published in Belgrade, among them *Borba* and *Politika*. Both are morning papers, *Borba* publishing daily except Thursdays and *Politika* daily and Sundays. *Politika's* influence and circulation have steadily increased to the point where it is now "a very serious socio-political newspaper with a very good national and international reputation,"[5] and also may be considered one of Yugoslavia's largest dailies. Meantime, as *Borba* has moved from being the principal mouthpiece of the Communist Party to becoming the organ of the Socialist Alliance of Yugoslavia, its circulation has suffered considerably, especially from the vigorous decentralization policies of Yugoslavia in recent years. According to official Federation of Yugoslav Journalists' statis-

[3] Zdravko Lekovic and Mihalo Bjelica, *Communication Policies in Yugoslavia* (Paris: UNESCO, 1976), p. 16.
[4] *Ibid.,* p. 20.
[5] Marjanovic letter, *loc. cit.*

ПРОЛЕТЕРИ СВИХ ЗЕМАЉА УЈЕДИНИТЕ СЕ

ГОДИНА LVII   БЕОГРАД   БРОЈ 51
Среда, 22. фебруар 1978.

Директор Светозар Тањић
Главни и одговорни уредник
Никола Вучков
Уређује редакцијска колегија

ЦЕНА 3 ДИНАРА — РУКОПИСИ СЕ НЕ ВРАЋАЈУ

БОРБА

ОРГАН СОЦИЈАЛИСТИЧКОГ САВЕЗА РАДНОГ НАРОДА ЈУГОСЛАВИЈЕ

Први број „Борба" орган Комунистичке партије
Југославије изишао је у Загребу 19. фебруара 1922.
13. августа 1929. забрањено је излажење „Борбе"
а члановима редакције суђено на робији.
У народноослободилачком рату „Борба" поново
излази и то у Ужицу од 23. септембра до 27. новембра 1941. и у Драинчу од 1. октобра 1941. до
27. новембра 1941.
Од 15. новембра 1944. „Борба" наставља излажe-
ње у ослобођеном Београду, а од 22. марта 1948.
у Загребу.
Од 5. јуна 1954. „Борба" је орган Социјалистичког савеза радног народа Југославије.

ПРЕДСЕДНИК АВГАНИСТАНА У ПОСЕТИ НАШОЈ ЗЕМЉИ

Неопходност јединства несврстаног покрета

Председник Тито поздравио госта из пријатељске земље на платоу ис-
пред хотела „Галеб". — Почели званични разговори. — Двојица председ-
ника сагласна да треба активирати снаге несврстаних за решавање ак-
туелних међународних проблема.

У СРДАЧНОЈ И ПРИЈАТЕЉСКОЈ АТМОСФЕРИ: Председници Тито и Дауд за време
љубазљивог разговора

ПОСЛЕ ДРАМАТИЧНИХ ДОГАЂАЈА НА АЕРОДРОМУ У ЛАРНАКИ

Каиро покушава да правда акцију

Видан напор да се дејство египатских командоса оцени као успешно. —
Оштре оптужбе упућене Кипру и указивање на „завeру ширих размера".

(Од сталног дописника „Борбе")

ДОЧЕК НА АЕРОДРОМУ: Египатски кожен доси у Каиро по повратку са Кипра

СК ХРВАТСКЕ

Осми конгрес 24 — 26. априла

Реферат о задацима Саве-
за комуниста Хрватске ће
поднети Милка Планинц.

(Загреб, 21. фебруар)

КОНФЕРЕНЦИЈА ЗА ШТАМПУ КИПАРСКОГ ПРЕДСЕДНИКА

Апел за смиривање ситуације

Наводећи да је његова влада изнела целу истину о догађању у Ларнаки
да учини све на очувању традиционално добрих односа између двеју земаља

(Никозија, 21. фебруар)

ЗАВРШЕНА ПРЕРАДА РЕПЕ

Први пут шећер и за резерве

Произведено 721.000 тона
шећера

КОНФЕРЕНЦИЈА ЗА ШТАМПУ У БЕОГРАДУ СА СТРАНИМ НОВИНАРИМА

Савез комуниста и даље остаје јединствена, револуционарна, водећа идејно-политичка снага југословенског друштва

Са страним новинарима разговарали Стане Доланц
и Тодо Куртовић

Почела градња ауто-пута Бањалука — Окучани

(Бањалука, 21. фебруар)

tics, in 1977 *Politika* was enjoying a circulation of 277,639 while *Borba*'s had fallen to 55,713.[6] *Borba*'s present editor-in-chief, Nicola Burzan attributes this lowered circulation to two factors: "the decentralization and the commercialization of our society, which means that the large majority of readers are choosing the local paper or the one with light features, strips or fiction."[7] Despite the decline, *Borba*'s influence remains substantial.

Borba published its first anti-Russian articles during the 1948 expulsion of the Cominform. For the next six years, it waged a campaign against Stalin's hard-line brand of socialism. During this period, it gained an international reputation as a Communist paper to be taken seriously. This was due both to a group of fine editors and contributors (such as Vladimir Dedijer and Milovan Djilas) and to the events which brought Yugoslavia to the attention of the world press.

In the decade of the fifties, Yugoslavia's leadership pressed for adaptation of Marxism to the country's needs and conditions. Marshal Tito moved to greater Yugoslav self-dependence. One such step was the development of the Socialist Alliance of the Working People of Yugoslavia for which *Borba* became the official organ in 1954. The cultural, social, economic and political changes introduced, among them self-management, decentralization and greater journalistic freedom, impacted the development and structure of the media. The Newspaper Publishing Act of 1956 allowed publishers to organize and control their own affairs and democratically elected workers' councils and management boards to make final decisions about content, selection and layout. The Publishing Council Act of 1957 created supervisory bodies to handle divergent reporting, but forbade any direct censorship. Meantime, Milovan Djilas in the Central Committee and "modernist" writers were pressing for greater freedom of expression in cultural and informational matters. The ultimate result was increased freedom in handling of political news. All of these steps negatively affected *Borba* circulation. As the Socialist Alliance paper responsible for publishing official texts, it could not adapt as quickly to the changes as some rivals, such as the more independent *Politika*.

With the decade of the 1960's came still greater press independence. The 1960 Law of the Press and Other Media of Information explicitly guaranteed press freedom and outlawed pre-censorship. Even negative political commentary was allowed. Media access to sources was liberalized even further by the new 1963 Constitution which guarantees the Yugoslav's right to be informed (Article 34) and freedom of the press and commissions the press, radio and television to "truthfully and objectively inform the public. . . ." (Article 40).[8] The media have adapted to these new freedoms and responsibilities by adopting organizational, content and news filtering process changes. Whereas *Borba*'s director of the 1950's had been Party-appointed Vakasun Micunovíc, the new worker's council elected a journalist, Slobodan Glumac, to replace him in the early 1960's. Like many other papers, *Borba* moved to more hard news and edi-

[6] Statistical Index, *NASA STAMPA*, Publication of Federation of Yugoslav Journalists, Belgrade, (February, 1978).
[7] Nicola Burzan, editor-in-chief, *Borba*, in letter to H. Fisher dated March 8, 1978.
[8] *The Constitution of the Socialist Federal Republic of Yugoslavia*, Belgrade, pp. 24–5.

torial commentary covering a wider range of subjects and to greater emphasis on regional news. Finally, as with all the media, it became more self-dependent and accepted greater responsibility in deciding what information should be made public.

In the 1970's, decentralization has slowed because of the Croatian crisis. The Socialist Alliance has increased its supervision over media policies and personnel. *Borba* itself spelled out the relation of the press to the state by indicating the media must not take over the sole responsibility for information, but must share with political and legislative organs, and the press must work in behalf of the welfare of the working people. Social considerations are to be primary for journalists. More "positive" writing supportive of the state is now demanded. However, at the same time, the courts, which now have the authority to regulate instead of the politicians, have become increasingly reluctant to censor the press. The exception is the political arena, where there have been some new controls.[9]

Despite its decreased circulation in recent years, *Borba* has been able to survive financially because of its associations with a large publishing firm, Borba Newspaper Publishing Enterprise. Since 1973, the firm has been putting out Yugoslavia's largest circulation daily, the evening *Vecernje Novosti*. The Workers' Council which controls the firm has taken on the editing, publishing, printing and sales of other Yugoslav publications, among them the daily *Sport*, the weeklies *Ekonomska Politika, TV Novosti, Nedeljne Novosti, Kekec, Mali Kekec* and *Poletarac* and a magazine for women called *Nada*. As of the end of 1978, Borba Enterprise was employing 2,168 workers, of whom 14 percent were university-trained, 26 percent skilled craftsmen and an additional 32 percent secondary school graduates. Of the total employees serving Borba Enterprise, 210 work directly for *Borba* in the following capacities: writing and editorial staff, 120; technical staff, 60; managerial personnel, 30.[10] For editorial positions, the paper prefers to take young people coming from universities and train them for the journalistic qualifications and standards it desires. *Borba* salaries compare very favorably with those of other Yugoslav workers. In 1970, a *Borba* editor received an income well over twice that of the industrial average.[11]

Borba is published on rotary presses from a five-building complex in the heart of Belgrade and a printing plant at nearby Ada Huja. It is a self-managed newspaper, controlled by the workers and "not managed by the State or anybody else."[12] Under the editorship of Nicola Burzan, the staff keeps the paper's political commentary critical and intellectually lively. But, at the same time, as an organ of the Socialist Alliance, *Borba* is careful to engage only in supportive criticism of Tito and socialism.

Both *Borba* and *Politika* provide good international coverage. Their interest in the world scene at least partly reflects Yugoslavia's championing of the non-

[9] Robinson, *op. cit.*, pp. 56–64.
[10] Nicola Burzan, Editor-in-chief, *Borba* in response to questionnaire and in accompanying brochure materials, March 8, 1978.
[11] Robinson, *op. cit.*, p. 103.
[12] Burzan letter.

aligned world's causes and its efforts to encourage progress and peace. *Borba* has full-time correspondents scattered in eight key posts: Paris, Rome, New York, Moscow, Mexico, Cairo, Nairobi and Warsaw. *Politika* has a similar sized and located foreign staff. Tanjug, Yugoslavia's governmental news agency, greatly extends the coverage of both papers. Tanjug keeps a staff of about 35 correspondents located in strategic news areas of the world. Tanjug provides individualized services for its customers, so that if a paper such as *Borba* wishes an item repeated or more background or coverage of that item, the Tanjug shift editor takes steps to satisfy the request. Thus, the agency's staff of correspondents can serve as an extension of *Borba*'s own resources in coverage of events or situations. In addition, *Borba* particularly benefits, as an official paper, from the services of nearly every major world press agency, among them AFP, Reuter, TASS, Hsinhua, AP and UPI.

Both *Politika* and *Borba* have large staffs to report on Yugoslavian governmental and civic affairs. *Borba* has a staff of 80 reporters to cover national and local events. Editor-in-chief Burzan says, "We seek to write on anything of general interest to our society."[13] *Borba* is particularly interested in the young and in the intellectual readers.

In appearance, *Borba* is serious, somewhat gray, but attractive. The heading, set in red ink, is flanked by a few brief *Borba* historical highlights on the right and the date and chief officers of the paper on the left. Size-wise, *Borba* falls between a tabloid and a broadsheet with its 38 by 56 centimeter (15 by 22 inches) proportions. Headlines are set in heavy black type and are well-spaced, but are not large in size. Some stories are spread horizontally across two or three of the paper's seven columns. There is a tendency to complete stories on the same page on which they begin. A typical issue runs only 12 to 16 pages in length, but since advertising occupies just 5 percent of *Borba*'s total space, there is room for more news and commentary than in many papers double the size. Only a few pictures are used in *Borba;* the average is about two per page. With the exception of the sports pages, few of *Borba*'s photographs are action shots; most are posed pictures of a small group or an individual. Cartoons and maps, though used sparingly, are employed effectively.

The front page contains a mix of national and international stories. Page two carries the editorial commentary. International stories occupy several inside pages with, as might be expected, heavy emphasis on the non-aligned nations. These pages are followed by others on national and local events. Features and sports appear in the back pages. The back page carries the daily radio, television and cinema schedules, as well as a listing of the addresses and telephone numbers of services important to the public, such as pharmacies, travel agencies and the like. Editor-in-chief Burzan breaks down the contents of his paper into these approximate percentages on a typical day: international news, 20 percent; national, 30; local and state, 5; analysis, 10; editorials, 5; features and entertainment, 5; sports, 5; travel/leisure, 5; public service, 5; culture, 5; and advertising, 5 percent.[14]

[13] Burzan questionnaire.
[14] Burzan questionnaire.

Borba's editorials are clear and direct. It engages, as Burzan notes, "in all kinds of ideological discussion (domestic and international, since we follow the policy of pluralism.)"[15] Even in the realm of political criticism, where freedom of expression is much more free than in other Eastern European states but still limited, papers like *Borba* and *Politika* find ways to report and make commentary. Robinson cites an example of how *Borba* handled a car accident involving the son of a Presidium member. The youth had struck and seriously injured a pedestrian while driving at high speed. Yet he was released almost immediately. In an article entitled "Why Mr. Prosecutor?" *Borba* pointed out that the release order was actually telephoned by the public prosecutor.[16]

New York Times foreign correspondent Richard Eder indicates the range of controversy and criticism in which *Borba* and *Politika* engage:

> Criticism of official policies and agencies, revelations of mismanagement and corruption, and the airing of radically varying views on the desirable extent of economic reform and democratization appear regularly.
>
> There are limits. President Tito is not criticized, although ideas he is known to favor are not necessarily immune. Foreign policy questions are treated with some caution. Important government and party figures are not attacked by name, although it sometimes is apparent that criticism of a policy has a particular official as a target.[17]

In the 1970's, *Borba* and *Politika* have extended their coverage, analysis and commentary into the effects of new election procedures, political in-fighting and deals made on candidates' lists.

However, *Borba*'s loyalty to Yugoslavia and the best of socialism cannot be questioned. Editorially, it strives to be a serious political information daily. It stands for brotherhood, equality and unity of all Yugoslav peoples and nationalities. It encourages the development and confirmation of Socialist self-management. It backs the cause of non-aligned countries and presses for peaceful cooperation among all the peoples and nations of the world. Under the directorship of Svetozar Tadic, a journalist, it continually urges for everything progressive at home and abroad. Representation of such policies, editor Burzan is convinced, contribute significantly to *Borba*'s strength:

> We are influential . . . because we stand by strong and just causes—domestically and internationally. We are always ready to engage in controversy and we are always defending the rights of oppressed or menaced. That means we are very strongly engaged for the cause of freedom, democracy (rank-and-file democracy), humanism and progress.[18]

In conclusion, both *Borba* and *Politika* deserve recognition among the world's elite dailies. As prestige papers, they represent excellence in high quality, serious journalism among the non-aligned Third World nations. Together, they serve well both the national needs and international interests of their Yugoslav readers.

[15] Burzan letter.
[16] Robinson, *op. cit.*, p. 122.
[17] Richard Eder, "Mikajlov Given New 4½-Year Term by Belgrade Court," *New York Times*, April 20, 1967.
[18] Burzan letter.

The Christian Science Monitor

(UNITED STATES)

"THE CHRISTIAN SCIENCE MONITOR is the most unusual major newspaper in the United States" was one of the conclusions reached by the New England Daily Newspaper Survey in 1974 after it had evaluated 109 leading American dailies. Without question, *The Monitor* is also one of the States' best quality journals.

The paper's uniqueness derives, at least in part, from its interest in the story behind the event, the excellence of its journalistic reporting and writing and the detachment of its interpretations. While most papers report what happened and some investigate why the event occurred, *The Monitor* goes a step further to seek solutions to the problems related to the event. Tightly organized and well edited, it stresses the significant, the serious, and the lasting aspects of the world's news and issues. In contrast to many newspapers which indulge in abrasive criticism, it manages, without pulling its punches, to be reflective and uncontentious. As one of the few dailies owned by a church, it is designed to appeal to the literate, concerned and moral citizen. It is more interested in presenting in depth a selection of the significant news which shape its readers' lives than in providing a daily surface-depth record of events which will merely attract reader attention. Thus, it is both professionally excellent and a respected moral force.

The Monitor was founded in November, 1908, after the originator of Christian Science, Mary Baker Eddy, had called for the development of a daily newspaper to counteract the sensationalism rampant in the press at that time. Within a remarkably short time—107 days, to be exact—the publishing society of her church issued the first *Monitor*. It is still owned by the First Church of Christ, Scientist, and is published by the Christian Science Publishing Society, both with headquarters in Boston, Massachusetts. Words from Mrs. Eddy's lead editorial in that initial issue have expressed the paper's purpose ever since: "to injure no man, but to bless all mankind." The paper transcended the religious movement which Mrs. Eddy began and became a general paper which has appealed to all readers who desire a rational, nonsensational approach to journalism. Through the years, *The Monitor* has been a great moral force to journalism, but its morality has not been ostentatious.

The Monitor's religious rootage provides much of its uniqueness. Because of its morals, it downplays gory crime, personality conflicts and sexy items unless such news has a socially redeeming value. Its editors are reluctant to print profanity except in a direct quotation or to portray smoking and drinking.

THE CHRISTIAN SCIENCE MONITOR

COPYRIGHT © 1978 THE CHRISTIAN SCIENCE PUBLISHING SOCIETY, VOL. 70, NO. 61. All rights reserved Wednesday, February 22, 1978   25¢

Midwest vs. the fuel crunch

States sharing power — industries join in effort

By Richard J. Cattani
Staff correspondent of
The Christian Science Monitor

Chicago

With conservation appeals, power sharing, and other steps, states in the industrial Midwest are attempting to stave off energy shortages threatened by the United Mine Workers coal strike.

"We're looking an energy emergency in the face and trying to stare it down," says James Woodruff, Michigan Public Service Commission official. "We're stretching out the time before the crunch comes."

Michigan has succeeded in extending its power-generating resources. Switching from coal to oil and gas for firing utility generators, and other steps, have postponed by another 10 days the triggering of mandatory power cuts. The crunch — forced power cuts and possible plant closings — has been pushed back to mid-March.

A Michigan concern: that federal arm-twisting to share "surplus" power with other states could frustrate its own carefully worked out coal-contingency plan. "Michigan is not interested in closing plants so people can go to work in other states," says Michigan Gov. William Milliken.

A similar reluctance to share large blocks of available power is voiced by Illinois's biggest utility, Commonwealth Edison. "We're in the middle of a winter overhaul now," says Commonwealth Edison spokesman William Harrah. "We're already giving power to Northern Indiana Public Service Company."

Steps have been taken to move northward excess power from Mississippi, Arkansas, Texas, and Louisiana, through the Tennessee Valley power grid. President Carter can order power shifts from the South to the Midwest industrial belt, but links to carry the extra power are limited.

The Canton, Ohio-based American Electric Power Company, which controls generating stations in seven states, is stretching its system's coal reserve by buying electricity from other systems, running its coal-fired plants at half capacity, and operating noncoal plants near peak load.

✴Please turn to Page 11

Empty coalscars here; power curbs around bend

By R. Norman Matheny, staff photographer

Middle East reverberates after shoot-out

Egypt and Israel share ire over guerrillas

By John K. Cooley
Staff correspondent of The Christian Science Monitor

Cairo

The growing international row over Egypt's costly military operation to rescue Arab hostages and its failure to seize the two murderers of Egyptian editor Youssef al-Sebai at Larnaca Airport is spreading shock waves in the Mediterranean and Arab worlds.

• Egypt has welcomed home as heroes the 45 Egyptian commandos who survived the Larnaca battle with the Cyprus National Guard.

• President Sadat, from his headquarters at Ismailia on the Suez Canal, has ordered Egyptian diplomats withdrawn from Cyprus and Cypriot diplomats out of Egypt.

• Egyptian commentators began raising questions about behavior of some other Arab leaders.

• Ironically, some of the most wholehearted support for the Egyptian action has come from Israel — at least from Israeli public opinion.

• A wave of Egyptian nationalism and anti-Palestinian feeling, unprecedented since President Sadat began peace talks with Israel in December, is sweeping this capital.

• Cyprus President Spiros Kyprianou is firmly rejecting Egyptian demands for extradition of the two gunmen.

The two men, facing murder charges in a Nicosia, Cyprus, court, identified themselves as Palestinians, but the Palestine Liberation Organization (PLO) denounced them. (One of their hostages, subsequently freed, was PLO spokesman Abu Maizar.)

"Palestinians killed Youssef al-Sebai, and Palestinians are trying to ruin our relations with the rest of the Arab world," said one Egyptian editor bitterly.

✴Please turn to Page 11

Carter planning campaign flurry in off-year races

By Godfrey Sperling Jr.
Staff correspondent of
The Christian Science Monitor

Washington

Even while national urgencies press down on him — inflation, unemployment, energy, and now the coal strike — President Carter is shaping a plan for heavy personal and administration involvement in this year's political campaign.

• Mr. Carter himself will be making an average of two appearances a month in behalf of Democratic candidates across the nation for the next several months.

The President has already started on his campaign schedule, with a recent political trip to New England and a shorter jaunt to Delaware.

By late summer his political traveling and speaking will be accelerated greatly if he can find time away from Congress-related priorities.

A White House source says he expects

✴Please turn to Page 11

Inside today...

Spring fashion special

"The mood is happy. The clothes unstructured," reports Nan Trent, Monitor fashion editor. Although menswear touches abound, dresses are back looking soft and feminine. Page B1

Writers tell why their craft is not easy	24
Breakthrough in glass: artists try new tacks	22
Charlie Criss's assets don't include height	14
Expanding population presses 'have not' nations	15

U.S. Panama drug probe points at Torrijos kin

By James Nelson Goodsell
Latin America correspondent of
The Christian Science Monitor

Panama City

The name of Moisés Torrijos Herrera keeps cropping up in reports of illegal drug traffic between Panama and the United States.

Currently Panama's Ambassador to Spain, he is one of several dozen Panamanians who face arrest if they step onto U.S. soil for alleged drug violations.

What makes the name of Moisés Torrijos of particular interest, of course, is that he is the brother of Panama's strong man, Gen. Omar Torrijos Herrera.

It is this fact that in part lies behind the current U.S. Senate look at the drug smuggling charges in connection with the coming ratification vote on the Panama Canal treaties. Senate opponents of the treaties believe there is political capital to be gained by pressing the investigation.

At the same time, while the charges of drug activities come close to General Torrijos himself, there is no allegation of his own personal

✴Please turn to Page 11

UPI photo

Torrijos brother faces drug charge

Where possible, it avoids criticism of personalities and harsh language. This moral stance leads directly to downplay of the sensational story and selective interpretation of the news. However, except for the daily publication of a religious page and a downplay of news about medicine and health and a reluctance to speak directly of death (Christian Science believes in spiritual healing and eternal life), the religious convictions of *The Monitor*'s founder and owners have little direct effect on editorial policies.[1] Neither its morals nor its religious heritage make its reportage and commentary unrealistic or euphoric. The paper's policies and analyses of Watergate and the Vietnam War were clear and critical and there is no suppression of hard reporting of social problems.

Politically, this paper is independent and non-partisan. Within the limits of its modest news space, it publishes whatever political news it deems to be of national or international significance. Its present policy is to refrain from endorsing individuals or referenda; however, it did endorse Dwight Eisenhower's candidacy for President.

The Monitor may be called "great" partly because of its convictions: to face problems squarely, but calmly; to trace events back to causes; to demonstrate concern for others; to uncover falsity, maintain integrity; and to be wholesome, but not naive. Not only does the paper delineate and state its beliefs more clearly than most newspapers; it also earnestly seeks to carry out these aims in its everyday activity.

The Monitor is particularly upbeat about its resolution to find solutions to personal and worldwide problems. Editor and manager John Hughes believes the role of journalism, and especially of his paper increasingly must be that of "problem-solver":

> Today, they (our readers) not only want to understand the problems of our world, nation and local community, they want them solved. They are not content with a newspaper that tells them that's the way things are, and leaves them with a sense of hopelessness. They want a better world than they inherited and they are, I think, responsive to newspapers that will help them get it. . . .
>
> Today a newspaper must offer its readers the information which will help them decide how to stop it from happening again. Today a newspaper cannot simply relate to its readers the extent of the narcotics problem, nor even the manner in which illicit drugs reach addicts. These days a newspaper must come up with the facts, the ideas, the alternatives, on which solutions to the problem can be based.[2]

Hughes' views are reflected in *The Monitor*'s daily practice of pointing the reader to solutions already practiced or those evidencing promise. As Hughes says, "We edit the paper so that when the reader is through reading it, he is not in a pit of despair. We're not rosy. But we study, we describe solutions." This policy makes life much more difficult for both reporters and editors, since *"Monitor* correspondents not only aim to identify problems, but to seek out specialists

[1] Printed brochure material sent by *The Monitor* to H. Fisher, January 29, 1978.
[2] John Hughes, "Journalism's Next Phase: Problem-Solving," ASNE *Bulletin*, 1971, p. 8.

to learn what they propose as the best ways to attack these problems."[3] This approach means hard digging and painstaking research to discover both the pertinent problems and the plausible solutions which will assist the readers and give them hope and confidence.

As a result of its convictions and policies, *The Monitor* sifts and selects news much more carefully and thoughtfully then most of its competitors. It sorts out the significant news and eliminates the trivia for the reader because it believes, as one of its leading columnists, Joseph Harsch, has put it, "In the news business, facts are a dime a dozen. What is important is the weight of the facts—the balance and the perspective."[4] It seeks to help the reader understand what is really going on in the world in a way that is "clear, complete, concise, and above all, constructive." Erwin Canham, now editor emeritus of *The Monitor,* put this policy succinctly in a 1966 television interview when he said his paper "tries to present the nature of reality . . . to make a meaningful pattern out of a complex world."

The Monitor's attention to international news of significance is particularly noteworthy. It devotes special attention to the developing countries and to problems of international scope, such as hunger, overpopulation and cross-national tensions and agreements. A staff of about 50 seasoned correspondents provides the bulk of the paper's perspectives on the world. Eight full-time correspondents work out of London, Bonn, Johannesburg, Hong Kong, Moscow, Athens, Tokyo and Boston, the last making frequent trips to Latin American. Another 40 part-time correspondents, 15 of them reporting on a frequent basis, are located in all parts of the world. Although it depends primarily on the input from its overseas correspondents, *The Monitor* also takes wire news services from UPI and Reuters, plus syndicated materials from the *Financial Times, Ltd.* of London, the Toronto *Globe and Mail* and the China News Service. A long list of distinguished foreign correspondents, among them Takashi Oka in London, David Willis in Moscow, James Goodsell on Latin America and John Cooley in the Middle East, attests further to the high quality of *The Monitor*'s international coverage.[5]

At the same time, *The Monitor* does not neglect selective coverage of significant trends and events in national government. Ten writer-reporters and one photographer keep a watchful eye on developments in Washington, D.C. Rather than seeking to cover all of national government's activity, it selects and details those stories it deems to be of special relevance and import to its readers. It leaves most of the coverage of local incidents and all sensational materials to other papers. In many ways, *The Monitor* is more like the quality European newspaper than an American one; it evidences the typical European careful selection in the editing process as well as the ability to give its articles a sense of permanent value. It puts all its news in perspective and analyzes information so well that the reader is not lost in a thicket of unrelated items.

[3] Robert P. Hey, Assistant Managing Editor, *The Christian Science Monitor,* in response to questionnaire and in letter to H. Fisher, January 27, 1978.
[4] Brochure, "News: The Way You Need It," *Christian Science Monitor,* 1977.
[5] Hey questionnaire.

Perhaps *The Monitor*'s greatest strengths lie in its interpretive background pieces and its feature articles. It regularly carries several pages of feature articles on a host of subjects: books, home, garden, people, education, children, family, financial, food, style, sports, travel, science, real estate, consumer needs and arts/entertainment. There are revealing, but not gossipy, interviews with people prominent in their fields. The interpretive articles on world affairs, sometimes seemingly longish for a newspaper, are written in magazine style with emphasis on analysis and consequences. There is a regular two-page middle spread which provides documentary background on a country or culture or a subject of significance. And frequently—at least once a week—there is a special pull-out section that treats one or a few cultural, political, educational or art/entertainment subjects in depth. These interpretive articles and features are always timely and relate pertinently to significant developments or segments of life; they provide the reader with a sense of history and a framework for interpreting the world.

The Monitor is a compact, tabloid-sized, 24-to-28 page newspaper, with some editions double that length. It began as a traditional eight-column broadsheet newspaper, a format with which it repeatedly won national awards which recognized its make-up and typography. Then, in 1965, it became the first major American newspaper to go to a five-column layout for editorial matter throughout the paper. Type size was increased 20 percent to make for better readability and a more liberal use of photographs and artwork was instituted.

Then, in April, 1975, the paper went to a new format again, this time with pages half the former size and more than double the number of pages. The paper is now printed in the new format in four North American editions in plants in Los Angeles, Chicago, New Jersey and Beverly, Massachusetts. "Edited and made up in Boston, *The Monitor* is sent, page by page, via facsimile transmission over telephone lines to each plant from Beverly (to which pages are sent by truck)."[6] A weekly international edition is published outside London, pages being flown from Boston to the plant.

The paper is neat, attractive and well-organized throughout. Typically, four or five articles related to significant national or international news developments appear on the front page, along with an "Inside Today" index to the paper's internal contents. Although the paper is published in five wide columns, the arrangement of stories gives it a horizontal appearance. Page two regularly carries a columnist's commentary on some development in the news under the title "Focus," plus a dozen encapsulated briefs of the day's leading news stories—the paper's nearest approach to comprehensive coverage. Several pages of background articles follow; sometimes an entire page or more is given to an area or a series of events or a developmental trend. Pages seldom carry more than three or four articles. After the pages of feature material already alluded to, there is a page on religion, containing a daily religious essay, poetry and other spiritual uplift material. Near the back are two pages entitled "Opinion and Commentary" made up of three or four editorials, mostly from syndicated columnists and

[6] Robert P. Hey, Assistant Managing Editor, *The Christian Science Monitor*, in letter to H. Fisher, dated January 29, 1978.

readers' letters. The final back page is reserved for the paper's own editorials, an editorial cartoon and, frequently, brief syndicated commentary from other newspapers.

Only a few pictures are used throughout *The Monitor,* but they are "pictures with a purpose," relating to and illuminating stories and enlarging the reader's grasp of the story. *The Monitor*'s maps and drawings are especially noteworthy; they are clear and so placed that they assist the reader's understanding of printed materials. Advertising comprises only about one-fourth of the paper's contents and is located so as to be both related to contents and yet to be unobtrusive to the reader. In keeping with the paper's editorial policies, all advertising copy is screened to eliminate references to tobacco, alcohol, pharmaceuticals and X-rated movies, and to examine carefully plugs for racy literature, questionable investments and franchise businesses.

The Monitor is well known for the quality of its writing. As in the past, today's staff includes numerous outstanding writers. Probably the best known now on staff are Richard Strout, Godfrey Sperling, Jr., Harry Ellis, Joseph Harsch, Roscoe Drummond, Robert Cowen, David Willis and Takashi Oka. Its editors include some of the most highly respected journalists in the United States. Writers and editors must be highly professional when they join *The Monitor*'s staff; their qualifications must include a college education and strong journalistic abilities. Some writers bring considerable experience in the field they cover, others advanced academic knowledge.[7]

John Hughes has been editor of *The Monitor* since 1970 and presently serves as its manager and editor. Prior to his appointment as editor, he served for 15 years as one of his paper's foreign correspondents (Africa, 1955–1961; the Far East, 1964–1970) and in other capacities as assistant overseas news editor and managing editor. Hughes, of British extraction, has distinguished himself with an impressive string of awards, including a Nieman Fellowship at Harvard and the Pulitzer Prize for International Reporting. A former United Nations correspondent, Earl Foell became the paper's managing editor in 1970. His assistant is Robert Hey, who served as assistant chief in the Washington bureau covering Congress before coming to his present post. Another Briton, Geoffrey Godsell is the paper's overseas editor. The American news editor, Curtis Sitomer came to Boston from California, where he was *The Monitor*'s Los Angeles bureau chief. Like his fellow administrators, Sitomer holds special honors for his writing and reportage. The paper's chief editorial writer, Charlotte Saikowski recently received recognition from the New England Women's Press Association for her series on permissiveness. The present leadership follows in a tradition of outstanding editorial leaders. For example, its editor emeritus, Erwin Dain Canham, held honorary degrees from 21 colleges and universities and was considered one of the world's outstanding editors.

The Monitor and its staff have received an impressive list of awards and special recognitions. Four of its series have drawn Pulitzer Prize awards. In 1977, two Overseas Press Club awards were received, one for "the best interna-

[7] Hey questionnaire.

tional reporting that demonstrates a concern for humanity," and a second for "the best reporting from abroad requiring exceptional courage and initiative." In 1976, the Overseas Press Club award went to Joseph Harsch, *The Monitor*'s roving columnist, for "the best newspaper interpretation of foreign affairs." Staff members also won Overseas Press Club awards in 1974 and 1975. Twice, in 1973 and again in 1975, the paper has won G. M. Loeb Awards, the "Pulitzer of financial journalism." The award was given in 1975 to business and financial editor David Francis for his fourpart series on multi-national corporations. In all, the paper has captured the Loeb Award six times. Richard Strout was the third American (after Walter Cronkite and James Reston) to take the coveted National Press Club Fourth Estate award. In recent years, the paper has taken numerous other citations and awards for its journalistic work in business and finance, science, the home and general public service. After repeatedly winning the Edmund C. Arnold award for make-up and typography, *The Monitor* now has permanent possession of its trophy cup.[8]

For the past 12 years, *The Monitor* has engaged in an activity that has gained it unique recognition. The paper's Washington bureau chief, Godfrey Sperling founded and regularly hosts breakfasts at which top Washington reporters grill leading news figures. On the occasion of the tenth anniversary of the group's meetings, then President of the United States Gerald Ford spoke and formally recognized Chairman Sperling's leadership of this group.

Recognition of *The Monitor*'s outstanding journalistic quality and service has come from another quarter—fellow media professionals. Public relations and public affairs expert Edward Bernays notes from five surveys his organization has made that *The Monitor* ranks among the nation's top ten newspapers in three areas: "impartial presentation of the news, journalistic independence, and crusading for the public good." Ben Bagdikian, national correspondent from the *Columbia Journalism Review* and a team of 12 leading journalists termed the paper "unique" in the care and thoughtfulness that goes into its news selection and in the detachment of its interpretations. And Walter Cronkite of CBS News declares he has come to depend on *The Monitor* "as a major source of information about what is most important and significant in the nation and in the world."

Perhaps *The Monitor*'s highest plaudits come from its 200,000 readers and subscribers. The latter, comprising about 90 percent of the paper's circulation, are responsive, well-educated, thoughtful, higher-income people who seek the selective in-depth treatment and objective interpretation the paper gives. Three-fourths (five times the national percentage) of the readers have attended college. About two-thirds of the subscriber household heads are in business, the professions or government. Subscriber median income is over $17,000 annually. Most subscribers are homeowners. *The Monitor* holds disproportionate influence in high places of government, as evidenced by the fact that multiple copies go to the White House, as well as to most cabinet officers, virtually all 525 members

---

[8] Information sent to H. Fisher by *The Christian Science Monitor*, January 29, 1978.

of Congress and 90 embassies in Washington, D.C. World leaders in London, the Kremlin, China, the Middle East and elsewhere receive it. The educational world acclaims it: over 30,000 schools, colleges and individulal educators and some 11,000 libraries regularly find it a useful resource. Over 14,000 editors or publishers also take it.[9]

The Monitor provides two syndication services that extend its high quality influence widely. In 1972, a print syndication service was started which carried news articles, columns, features, cartoons, photographs and editorials from the daily *Monitor*. The service is distributed by the Des Moines *Register and Tribune*. As of early 1978, some 159 U.S. newspapers with a combined circulation of nearly ten million and 30 foreign papers with a total circulation of about five million were subscribing to the service.

The second syndication, distribution of 20 top *Monitor* stories on audio tape each week, now goes to 175 radio stations across the United States and Canada. Three writer-announcers prepare *The Monitor* tapes: David Dunbar, editor of the radio syndication service and a former award-winning news director from California; Fay Waldman, an actress with extensive experience in Broadway films; and Paul Cunningham, a veteran news writer and broadcaster from Massachusetts. Stations throughout the country testify to the value of *The Monitor*'s timely and topical feature story tapes to supplement their news services.

In one sense, *The Monitor* is the only true national paper in the United States. The New York *Times* is larger and more influential throughout the country, but *The Monitor* outsells it in 35 states. The *Wall Street Journal* gets into more states, but is usually considered a specialized paper. However, *The Monitor* likes to think of itself as an international paper, and it has good basis on which to make that claim. Its weekly international edition is specially tailored to the needs of readers outside North America. Between North American editions sent abroad and this international edition, *The Monitor* circulates in some 120 countries around the world. As already indicated, its syndicated print services serve 30 foreign papers. Its international staff produces excellent coverage of other countries. And its background articles on overseas situations and its editorials on the international scene may be considered among the world's best. In *The Monitor*, the reader gets an unbiased "seen through their eyes" view of the world for the aim of the paper, as news editor Geoffrey Godsell points out is "to enable *Monitor* readers to see and understand other people of the world as those people understand and see themselves."[10]

In its philosophy of the news publication which seeks not only good global and national coverage and detached interpretation, but also solutions; in its thorough, thoughtful background articles and feature materials; in its clear editorials; in its provision for the total needs of the informed reader; in its careful, highly professional organization and production; and in the excellence of its writing, *The Christian Science Monitor* has few peers anywhere in the world.

[9] Brochure, "Facts about *The Christian Science Monitor*, (Boston: The Christian Science Publishing Society, 1977).
[10] Brochure, "News: The Way You Need It," *op. cit.*

This fine newspaper—the "Cadillac" of American dailies—must be judged, as the New England Daily Newspaper Survey concluded, "one of the leading newspapers of the English-speaking world."[11]

Corriere della Sera

(ITALY)

THE BULK OF ITALY'S newspapers are political journals, attached in some way to a political party and slanting their comments to fit some ideology. Papers not owned by political parties belong to what is called the *stampa d'informazione* (the information press) and they are considered independent. To a degree, independence is a relative quality in all countries, but in Italy the term is even more elastic. This has been particularly true in recent years as socialism and the Communist ideology have gained credence. Italy's largest circulation daily, *Corriere della Sera* (523,000 copies on weekdays, more on Sundays) has provided a prime example of the looseness of the term as it has moved in the past decade from being the nation's most independent newspaper further and further to the Left.

Independent papers in Italy are usually owned by leading industrialists to whom the newspaper is a subordinate interest, and often their integrity is influenced by the owner's commercial considerations or his desire to retain the good will of government. During the economic crises and social upheavals through which Italy has been passing in recent years, the tendency by owner companies to give their prevailing industrial and financial interests priority over press freedom and objectivity has been growing. Consequently, as Piero Ottone, editor of *Corriere della Sera* pointed out at the 1976 International Press Institute convention, the effects of state ownership and meddling by large financial groups on press freedom are becoming more and more similiar in Italy as financial problems mount.[1]

Until recently, *Corriere della Sera* has been the most notable exception to the rule of owner interference. When it was acquired in 1885 by the rich and socially prominent Crespi textile manufacturing family, it was given generous funds so it could be politically independent and provide exceptional news coverage. The Crespis never interfered with editorial freedom, even when the paper expressed opinions contrary to their industrial interests. Apparently *Corriere* has

[11] Brochure, *"The Christian Science Monitor,"* (Boston: The Christian Science Publishing Society).
[1] "Does the West Have a Monopoly in Press Freedom?" *IPI Report,* 25:6 (June, 1976), p. 10.

Anno 103 - N. 44 - L. 200   (Arretrato L. 400)   Edizione romana   Mercoledì 22 febbraio 1978 - L. 200

CORRIERE DELLA SERA

* PREZZI D'ABBONAMENTO QUOTIDIANO — PREZZI D'ABBONAMENTO ANNUALE PERIODICI — PREZZI DI VENDITA ALL'ESTERO — TARIFFE DELLE INSERZIONI PER L'ITALIA (più IVA 14%)
20100 MILANO — 00100 ROMA

IL PROCESSO DI TORINO ALLE BRIGATE ROSSE

INVITO AL CORAGGIO

Il 9 marzo deve aprirsi a Torino, in Corte d'assise, il processo a Curcio e ad altri brigatisti rossi, accusati di gravissimi reati. Sono state convocate cinquanta persone che dovrebbero essere disponibili per il sorteggio della giuria. Solo sette su cinquanta hanno accettato.

Si sono cercate tante spiegazioni dei rinvenii e degli scopi dei terroristi. La più ovvia scaturisce dai fatti. Con le accuse si giudica gli avvocati, i terroristi sono riusciti a far paura a parecchi di coloro che dovrebbero giudicarli e, comunque, prendere parte alle udienze. E chiaro che questo era, sin da principio, l'intento dei assassini: dimostrare che possono uccidere come vogliono, quando vogliono, che lo Stato, che dovrebbe difenderli, è incapace di farlo. In altre parole, e anche ribelle, insufficiente, e finirà col rivelare la propria impotenza nei confronti di chi si schiacciati. Al contrario, de rigettare, prima, durante e dopo i processi, le proprie leggi. Finchè trovare dei candidati alle giurie che si lasciano intimidire dai complici in libertà degli assassini, tale disegno non si può perseguire, con la differenza che i suoi assassini coprono reati comuni, commessi per lucro, mentre quelli dei terroristi hanno un movente politico: l'abbattimento dei sistema democratico che qui si vive. I terroristi di professione sono oggi d'aspretare indulgenza a chi li compito di difendere la democrazia, dovrebbe togliere maggiore fermezza e rigore. Ciò vale per gli organi dello Stato e vale anche per i semplici cittadini che, per esempio, quando il loro concorso è chiesto per formazione d'una giuria.

Naturalmente, vale in primo luogo per i tre poteri dello Stato: il legislativo, l'esecutivo e il giudiziario. Tocca ad essi dare coraggio ai cittadini, che non sono tenuti a dare più coraggio di quanto ne vengono essi a chiedere. E allora che lo Stato dimostri d'essere infallantemente intimidato e tale giudizio della Repubblica: la quale è tenuta a rinconcliare la delinquenza, politica o comune. Il cittadino richde la oscillare fra il ragionamento da Zorro e quelle turba; quelle turbate face le severe vista lui, e la nessuna eccesiva del peliccolai di Torino e dell'eserito di Roma, che ne aborre con quando si sono registrati o un ventre deposta.

Ricava alla sede dei partiti, i Ressembiciment pasci la Repubblica e una TV desta la raffinatamento merita un lungo di plazare le macchine, un giornalista care, montre l'ulti lesti misanti, soldtati teasti morti spritalegici.

Ho constatato Alexander, il mettre te unigione in contre risuflo. Vidi due visito "Lider Kennedy", pronunciate ambi-abbantoni omani. Wili- ly Brandt no flas contre chi cinedeva un invil, anchor Chirac ni muatoto le lui fu riuconta. Se nomono

A PAGINA 17
I commenti di Carli al programma di Andreotti

Leo Valiani

UN'ALTRA CITTÀ COINVOLTA NELLA SPIRALE DEL TERRORISMO

Bomba a un giornale di Venezia: un morto

La vittima è una guardia giurata in servizio al «Gazzettino» - Ha dato un calcio all'ordigno che era stato collocato davanti al portone del quotidiano - L'attentato rivendicato e poi disconosciuto dai neofascisti di «Ordine nuovo» - Un'altra telefonata chiamava in causa le Brigate rosse

DAL NOSTRO INVIATO SPECIALE

VENEZIA — Un'altra vita stroncata dal terrorismo folle. E quella di Franco Battaglierin, 32 anni, tre figli — l'ultima ha diciotto mesi — guardia giurata: l'ha ridotta in pezzi ieri l'altro, verso le 21, una carica di esplosivo che gli aveva fatto collocare davanti al portone del «Gazzettino» di Venezia, il quotidiano della città.

VENEZIA — Il portone davanti al quale è scoppiato l'ordigno, provocando la morte della guardia giurata.

Mino Durand

IL GIALLO DELL'OSPIZIO IN BELGIO

Sarebbero 30 le vittime della «suora omicidi»

La donna avrebbe ucciso i vecchietti per rubare soldi e oggetti d'oro necessari all'acquisto della droga - Conferenza stampa del medico dell'ospedale

DAL NOSTRO INVIATO SPECIALE

WETTEREN (Gand) — Al di là delle ipotesi più pessimistiche, ci di là delle previsioni più macabre, ecco quella che la quarantaquattrenne suora Godfrida avrebbe ucciso trenta vecchietti e non tre o sei di cui finora si era parlato.

Arturo Guatelli

Un ceffone al consigliere di Carter che molesta le ragazze

DAL NOSTRO CORRISPONDENTE

NUOVA YORK — Le vicende di un accorso che si svolge...

Ugo Stille

Forte tensione per la violenza nelle scuole della laguna

No agli insegnanti con la pistola nel cassetto

Romeo, Asor Rosa, Lombardo Radice, Ferrarotti e Colletti giudicano l'autodifesa dei professori veneziani

DAL NOSTRO INVIATO SPECIALE

VENEZIA — Liceo occupato. Niente di strano, se non che, questa volta, ad occuparlo sono i professori. E quanto è primo atto di questa autodifesa nella cui mano sta la vista e il dramma...

Andrea Bonanni

Ricordate Pietro Trimarchi? Fu il primo processare sequenze e opinionata (11 marzo 1966), quando la commissione Marcy Caparosa più potente. Adesso Trimarchi non vuol più parlare. Quelli i-vano i...

Walter Tobagi

CONTINUA IN SECONDA PAGINA

Chirac il duro promette alla Francia una resurrezione senza scosse

DAL NOSTRO INVIATO SPECIALE

PARIGI — Qualcuno ha affermato che «per ogni persona che incontri, qualcosa lo fa cuore e qualcosa lo fa soffrire». Nove su dieci vero: con Jacques Chirac, invece. Non è mai dimostri d'essere infallantemente intimidato e quello della Repubblica: la quale...

Jacques Chirac

Quinta Repubblica ha permesso al Paese uno svolgimento della spettacolare, che la ha fatto superare con coraggio...

Enzo Biagi

CONTINUA IN SECONDA PAGINA

experienced problems with owner interference only after the majority of the Crespi family holdings were transferred to other ownership in 1973 and the paper began its swing to the Left.

Although it is a morning daily today, *Il Corriere della Sera* was established March 5, 1876, six years after Italy's unification, as an evening paper in Milan. Later, when it changed to morning publication, it retained its old name, which means "The Evening Courier." The *Corriere* is one of Italy's oldest extant newspapers; it celebrated its centenary in 1976. It is one of a few Italian papers which has survived several social and political upheavals and two world wars. In the process, it became the country's largest, most important and only truly national newspaper, with the possible exception of *La Stampa*. Beyond that, it has built an international reputation for itself and has become one of the most influential newspapers in Europe.

Eugenio Torelli-Viollier, the paper's founder and first editor, was a Neapolitan publicist who learned journalism from the great French novelist, Alexandre Dumas. The paper began modestly, with a capital of about 30,000 lire provided by several upper middle class Milanese. Its editorial offices were located near the famous La Scala in a single room in the Galleria di Milano, now the historical center of the city. The paper was printed on a crude press located in the Galleria basement.

In its earliest years, the *Corriere* belonged politically to the ranks of the liberal right and it fought courageously to preserve its freedom of opinion. After its purchase by the Crespis, Torelli-Viollier, as editor, was always free in editorial matters, even when he disagreed with his owners. Shortly after he purchased *Corriere*, Benigno Crespi, a cotton manufacturer, acquired new, modern offices for the paper in the center of the city, furnished it with new printing machinery and expanded the staff. As a result, the paper grew rapidly from its initial circulation of 3,000 copies to 50,000 two years later in 1887 and to 100,000 in 1898. By the end of the nineteenth century, when Torelli-Viollier died, the *Corriere* was regarded in Europe's main cities as a reflection both of Italy's leading economic center and of Italian public opinion in general.

Luigi Albertini, known as a person of excellent character and demanding in his journalistic expectations, became editor upon Torelli-Viollier's death. During his editorship, the famous architect and writer Luca Beltrami designed a new building for *Corriere* in the Via Solferino. That building still houses *Corriere* and its evening companion, *Corriere d'Informazione*. Albertini desired to turn the paper into a truly national newspaper and to expand its circulation.[2] He achieved his wish. Under his editorship, *Corriere*'s circulation rose to 400,000 by 1920. Because of his strong opposition to the politics of Mussolini and his party's new laws restricting press freedom, Albertini constantly clashed with the Fascists. He persistently refused to sign a Fascist card, and was eased out of the editorship in 1921, to be replaced by his brother, Alberto. For a period of three months, *Corriere* was shut down; then it re-opened with a Fascist staff. During his editorship, Luigi Albertini had founded two weeklies which have formed part

---

[2] Francesco Fattorello, "A Short Survey of the Italian Press," *Gazette*, Leiden, 11:1 (1965), p. 6.

of the "Corriere della Sera" group. The first, *Domenica del Corriere,* founded in 1899, became successful immediately, partly because of its excellent photographs. It has remained until recently Italy's leading weekly magazine. The second, started in 1909, was *Corriere del Piccoli,* Italy's oldest and biggest children's paper today.

In 1929, Alberto Albertini was followed in the paper's editorship by A. Borelli (until 1943) and then by A. Amicucci (until 1945 and Italy's total defeat in World War II). Between 1925 and 1944, the *Corriere* followed the Fascist line and lost much of its former appeal, losing out to Mussolini's own paper *Popolo d'Italia. Corriere's* circulation dropped during the period from close to 600,000 to about 300,000. In 1947, when Mussolini was ousted, *Corriere della Sera* joined other newspapers striking for full freedom by bannering, "Mussolini is Gone!"

In 1945, when Italy was finally freed from the Germans, the press once again published in freedom, and new journals sprang up to replace the Fascist papers. The old independent papers like *Corriere della Sera* and *La Stampa* were restored to their former owners, and within a year *Corriere's* circulation was back up to 450,000. During this period, a former staff member, Mario Borsa was editor. He was succeeded in 1946 by Guglielmo Emanuel, who served until 1952. Then M. Missiroli held the position until 1961, when Alfio Russo took over. During this post-war period, the paper added "New" to its name—*Nuovo Corriere della Sera*—to distinguish it from its Fascist days. The paper's successful rebuilding of its circulation came partly from the good foreign and national news coverage it provided.

In the decade of the sixties, *Corriere* flourished under the able editorship of Russo. He restored the paper to its pre-war quality, and the paper's reputation grew at home and abroad. Russo had worked as a special Paris correspondent for *Corriere* from 1947 to 1952, then had spent nine years as editor of Florence's *La Nazione.* Russo, a scholarly gentleman, frequently wrote on political subjects. He displayed a personal interest in the entire editorial production of the paper. He had a special affinity for good writing and at the same time did much to improve the level of journalism in all sections of the paper. He once said, "We want beautiful writing, beautiful and precise words, and good grammar. In addition, we demand typographical excellence."[3] Russo believed the best journalist was one well trained in the humanities; preparation in the journalistic skills were of less interest to him. During his editorship, Russo enjoyed complete editorial freedom; he had no obligations to the Crespi family other than to submit brief periodic reports on the general condition of the paper.

The past decade of unrest and change in Italy has seen a procession of editors at *Corriere della Sera.* From 1968 to March, 1972, Giovanni Spadolini served as editor. He continued the paper's excellence in national and international coverage and followed its traditional liberal-conservative policies. His unannounced dismissal and replacement without explanation triggered a unique one-day protest strike by *Corriere's* editorial staff. Spadolini was subsequently elected a Senator in the May elections. But the exact motives of the proprietors in dismissing Spadolini and appointing Piero Ottone to replace him were never made clear to the public.[4] Today's chief editor is F. Di Bella.

Corriere della Sera has long been noted for the excellence of its foreign dispatches. Largely because of its thorough, accurate international coverage, it has long held a tradition of being "A faithful mirror of the world."[5] To gather overseas information, *Corriere* has had 26 correspondents in 20 important foreign cities. Three reporters each covered four newsmaker centers: London, Paris, New York and Bonn. Among its list of notable overseas correspondents are Vero Roberti, who covered Russia, Giorgio Sansa in Paris and Egisto Corrati, whose work in Vietnam brought him special recognition. *Corriere* also has about 25 travelling correspondents called *inviati speciali* (special envoys), who rank among Italy's best writers and reporters. One of the best of these *inviati* was Luigi Barzini (1874–1947), whose travel stories and war dispatches gained him an international reputation. In addition to getting its foreign news from its own full-time correspondents and *inviati speciali,* the *Corriere* receives input from the Italian news agency ANSA (Agenzia Nazionale Stampa Associata), which also transmits Reuters and Agence France-Presse services, and from the news services of the United States.

Since most of Italy's newspapers are regional, *Corriere della Sera* is one of few dailies that could be considered a national paper. Its news coverage of the country has come from its staff of over 600 correspondents reporting throughout Italy. It has kept two large local staffs, one in its home city, Milan, and another in Rome, the nation's capital. In February, 1976, it began fascimile printing of a Rome edition. Although about 85 percent of its readers are in northern Italy, *Corriere* is distributed to the entire nation, even to the offshore islands. About half of the copies go to Italy's larger cities. Most of its readers are from the middle or upper economic classes; about half of the readers consider themselves middle class and another one-fifth upper class.

Corriere della Sera still reflects the literary interests which characterized the better Italian papers before Italian unification. Along with *La Stampa,* it pioneered in a special Italian journalistic institution called *terza pagina* ("third page"), a cultural department carrying essays, analyses, reviews and interpretive pieces. The articles for this page are contributed by Italy's best authors, specialists in various fields and university professors. *Corriere's* "third page" is one of the best in the Italian press, and people who represent important segments of Italian society have been eager to contribute to its columns. The main feature of the "third page" is the opening article, named the *elzeviro* from the typeface in which it is traditionally printed. The article usually runs two full columns down the left side of the page. These *elzeviri* are the country's best light literary articles with serious overtones and are often included in literary anthologies.

The *Corriere* prints a special foreign airmail edition which finds its way in same-day deliveries to the world's leading cities. This edition usually runs 16 pages in length and is widely read wherever Italian is spoken. Its influence has helped establish *Corriere*'s international reputation.

The paper's front page employment of a mix of typefaces, nine columns, few pictures (usually one or two), bold headlines and little white space combine to give it a serious, gray appearance. Presentation of five to seven of the leading national and international stories, fewer than most papers, adds to its business-like countenance. Subscription and single issue price listings in European and overseas countries accompany the nameplate at the top of the page. There is a tendency to place stories into several column wide horizontal boxes and to give reporters by-lines. The lower left-hand corner carries a single "teaser" for a featured inside page story. The editorial, in typical Italian fashion, is placed on the left-hand side of the front page.

Inside the typical 18–20 page edition, there is good coverage of Milanese and Italian news. Since Milan and its environs are heavily industrial, business and financial news receive considerable emphasis. Every day, *Corriere* prints a special page: a woman's page, a young people's page, or a page on motoring, agriculture or literature. Major space is given to sports, especially soccer, which is Italy's national sport, and on Mondays the section for sports is especially large. As is the case with most Italian newspapers, the percentage of space utilized for advertising is not high; advertisements cover some 30 to 35 percent of the total space.

Corriere della Sera has not escaped unscathed from this past decade of Italian unrest. During the years 1972–1975, the paper was struck repeatedly. General industrial conflicts interfered with publication and delivery and affected sales. In 1972, *Corriere* editorial staff struck in protest against a *fait accompli* change of editors. A change in the majority share holdings of *Corriere* and the majority transfer of shares of Rome's *Messaggero* and Genoa's *Il Secolo IXX* led to a protest strike by journalists against the concentration of the press in the country.[6]

In the first such move against the press since the end of the Fascist regime, 30 police searched the editorial offices of *Corriere* and the home of its court reporter, George Zicari, in May, 1972. The search followed an exclusive *Corriere* report shedding light on the recent murder of police superintendent Luigi Calabresi. The paper and Zicari were charged with publishing secret information, a charge based on legal remnants from Fascist days under which an Italian journalist could still be prosecuted for publishing or expressing his opinion on such matters as "secret police investigations." The paper's editor, Piero Ottone, and Zicari argued they had committed no breach of official secrecy. (Actually, the police were miffed by the fact that the paper had turned up and published key evidence they had missed.) The fact that the search was perpetrated on a responsible "bourgeoise" paper raised a storm of protest from the International Press Institute and the Italian National Press Federation.[7]

In a move that appears in keeping with increasing strength of Italy's Com-

[6] "Press Freedom Report," *IPI Report*, 23:1 (January, 1974), p. 10.
[7] Ferrier, *op. cit.*, pp. 1 and 4. See also: "News of the World Press," *IPI Report*, 21:9 (September, 1972), p. 2 and "Italy," *IPI Report* 22:1 (January, 1973), p. 4

munist Party and social leftists in the country and which has never been precisely explained to outsiders, *Corriere della Sera* moved sharply to the Left early in this decade. As a result, one of the paper's editorial staff members, Indro Montanelli led a group of 40 leading editors and writers in a break from *Corriere*. Montanelli became editor-in-chief of *Corriere*'s rival Milan *Il Giornale Nuovo* and was largely responsible for its recent success. His efforts through *Il Giornale* probably kept the Communist Party from winning a majority in the 1976 elections and reportedly led to Red Brigade attacks on his life and that of other journalists in a period of unchecked terror on anti-Communist journalists.[8]

Whether out of intimidation by terrorists or genuine sympathy with the extreme Left or of anger against continuing Rightist and Fascist tendencies or for some other reason or combination of reasons, *Corriere* has found itself on the side of Communist and Leftists causes in recent years. Objective straight news reporting by Conservatives over Telemontecarlo was silenced when terrorists dynamited the antennas, but *Corriere della Sera*'s news on Radio Montecarlo were undisturbed. And when *Corriere* published an excerpt from William Stevenson's *Ninety Minutes at Entebbe*, it carried a long apology which sided with the Italian Communist Party's (PCI) denouncement of the incident as a gross violation of the Ugandan sovereignty and suggesting the Israelis had instigated the entire affair. "The *Corriere* even claimed that the raid was a failure because it failed to prevent subsequent outbreaks of terrorism."[9] In fairness, it must be pointed out that the *Corriere*'s accessions to the Left are not as extreme as some, "but when even the finest come to adopt attitudes so close to those of the PCI (and which the *Corriere* would have dismissed out of hand just a few years earlier), it demonstrates the kind of voluntary censorship that now characterizes Italian political debate."[10]

Despite its recent moves that place in question its political independence, *Corriere della Sera* can point to its long history of independence and struggle for basic freedoms. During the years, it has moved from a "conservative" to more liberal positions, at first gradually to "liberal," then to a distinct "left of center," and, apparently, in recent years, to the extreme Left. But regardless of what label might be given it, one can say the *Corriere* is a serious, progressive and well-informed daily. It has been—and continues to be—authoritative, intelligent and elevated in style. It continues to be staffed by some of Italy's most responsible journalists. As Italy's largest newspaper and one of the country's leading national dailies, it still holds wide influence at home, in Europe and elsewhere and still ranks as one of the world's quality dailies.

[8] Michael Ledeen, "Cultural Terrorism," *Harper's* (September, 1977), p. 99.
[9] *Ibid.*, p. 100.
[10] *Ibid.*

The Daily Telegraph

(ENGLAND)

IN THIS DAY OF CIRCULATION battles for survival, one authority declares that *The Daily Telegraph* is one of only three quality London dailies in which "anything survives of the daily battle for the minds of men which . . . was once a prime function ⁚f the daily newspaper."[1] Alongside London's best elite general dailies, *The Times* and *The Guardian,* and another which appeals to a narrower spectrum of interests, the *Financial Times, The Telegraph* claims this distinction. Among its distinctive contributions to British elite journalism have been *The Telegraph*'s long history of defense of the conservative point-of-view, its respectable blend of serious news with the "popular" items, its concern for the individual and free enterprise, its comprehensive news coverage, its willingness to examine even itself, its desire to offer quality at less cost to the readers and its appeal to the middle economic classes.

Politically, *The Telegraph* has always classified itself as "right of centre" and conservative. Correspondent Louis Heren of the rival *Times* of London says, "Politically, *The Telegraph* is on the right and is locked in combat with creeping socialism."[2] Throughout its career, the paper has tended to align itself with the Conservative Party. But very early, already in the 1870's, it moved away from direct party associations to a conservative (with a small "c") stance based on principles rather than on politics and a desire to reach a literate, middle-class readership. Because its first, broader commitments are decency, law and order with a minimum of interference and free enterprise, "The Conservative Party, in or out of government, has never been able to count *The Daily Telegraph* automatically among its assets."[3]

In its conservative role, *The Telegraph* provides opposite-end-of-the-spectrum balance with the liberal, moralistic-leftist views of *The Guardian.* At the same time, it upholds conservative values while *The Times* debates intellectual issues with the Establishment and the *Financial Times* stresses the economic aspects of the news. One might describe *The Telegraph*'s conservatism as dignified and determined, upholding solid middle class values.

The Daily Telegraph was born in 1855 out of an obscure personal quarrel between its founder, Colonel Arthur Burroughes Sleigh and the Duke of Cambridge. The paper survived the argument and became Britain's first Penny Press

[1] Anthony Smith, *The British Press Since the War* (Plymouth, England, Latimer Trend & Company, Ltd., 1974), pp. 16–17.
[2] Louis Heren, "Fleet Street and the Free Press," *Saturday Review,* June 11, 1977, p. 24.
[3] Michael Green, *The Daily Telegraph* (London: *The Daily Telegraph,* February 6, 1978), p. 1.

daily. At that time, there were ten newspapers in London, all alive and growing, thanks to the recent abolition of the Stamp Tax. "*The Times* cost sevenpence, the rest fivepence—and *The Telegraph* twopence."[4] In 1858, *The Telegraph*'s publisher, printer Joseph Levy, who had promised to produce London's "largest, best and cheapest newspaper," reduced his paper's price to a penny, and circulation quickly rose to 27,000.

The paper's tradition of financial security began at the same time when Levy took as his business partner his brother Lionel, whose interests ranged from investments in South African diamond mines to London theaters.

Levy made another wise decision for his paper. He sensed his 22-year-old son Edward's remarkable flair for journalism and made him responsible for *The Telegraph*'s contents. Edward, who took as his last name "Lawson," "really made the paper by widening its interests, giving it a more human appeal, enlisting brilliant men for its staff, and breaking tradition by providing better headline display."[5]

The combination of these editorial improvements and cheap price soon made *The Daily Telegraph* London's favorite middle class paper. Levy had said his paper would be designed to be read by the working man in his hamlet and the aristocrat in his palace; actually, its primary appeal hit down the center to a wide range of middle class readers. By 1875, its daily circulation, chiefly to these middle class readers, had reached 190,000. Many of its early readers—as today—were London's commuters. One early commentator called it "the newspaper of the man on the knifeboard of the omnibus (commuter train)." Throughout the years, *The Telegraph* has kept its price well below that of its rivals; it still costs only 9 pence compared with 15 pence for other competing quality dailies.

From the start, *The Daily Telegraph* was interested in comprehensive coverage of the news. During Victorian days, special correspondents were sent to cover the American Civil War, the Maori War in New Zealand and trouble spots as widely separated as Italy, South Africa and the Sudan. The paper's reportage of national events was fully as complete. During this period, Edward Lawson evolved the formula that *The Telegraph* should tell the story of the world as it is, not just the nice details, but the unpleasant ones, too. With that approach of "telling things as they are," Lawson sometimes ran the risk of being accused of sensationalism, as for example, when he exposed the evils of prostitution in Victorian London.

By 1877, *The Daily Telegraph*'s circulation had risen to over 242,000 and Edward Lawson had turned most of his editorial duties over to his son, who gave the bulk of his attention to politics. This marked the beginning of a period in which the contents of the paper became duller reading, a time about which one historian observed: "The paper which was founded on sensationalism nearly died of respectability." *The Telegraph* had indeed emphasized politics and heavy industry and de-emphasized human interests. And, as a result, circulation had

[4] *Ibid.* Much of this discussion of *The Telegraph*'s history is taken from Green's article.
[5] Kenneth E. Olson, *The History Makers: The Press of Europe from Its Beginnings through 1965* (Baton Rouge, Louisiana State University Press, 1966), p. 14.

LONGINES
World's Most Honoured Watch

The Daily Telegraph

FINAL
No. 38172. LONDON, WEDNESDAY, FEBRUARY 22, 1978. Printed in LONDON and MANCHESTER 9p

IDC design & build
Cost-effective developments for industry and commerce
IDC Limited Stratford-upon-Avon Tel: 0789 4288

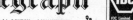

ARMY JOINS BLIZZARD RESCUE

West Country now fears floods

By BRENDA PARRY

A MASSIVE rescue operation with the Army helping to clear blocked roads swung into action in the West Country yesterday after the most devastating blizzards in living memory. With the first signs of a thaw setting in, there are prospects of severe flooding to follow.

The RAF continued helicopter rescue operations in spite of thick fog, and engineers were brought in from all parts of the country in an attempt to restore electricity and water supplies to isolated villages.

While snowploughs have now cleared many roads, police have urged motorists not to drive in the area unless on essential business. Some drivers are believed to be still stranded in mountainous snowdrifts.

Devon and Cornwall police have appealed to relatives in other parts of the country to stop inundating them with requests for information.

"If there is any cause for concern we will contact them," said a spokesman.

Police, firemen, ambulancemen, council workmen, A A and R A C patrolmen and hundreds of civilian volunteers are involved in the emergency operations.

Many villages, as well as isolated farms and houses are still cut off. With the thaw setting in floods have already been reported in Kingsbridge and Totnes in South Devon.

Poor visibility

Meanwhile the search continues in the snow for stranded motorists. With snowdrifts up to 30ft deep in some areas, "it's like looking for a needle in a haystack," said a police spokesman.

Mr Howell, Minister responsible for co-ordinating emergency operations, continued his tour of the region, but poor visibility prevented him from using a helicopter as planned. Many of the rescue helicopters were also grounded because of weather conditions.

A 67-year-old man was found dead in a snowdrift near Midsomer Norton, Somerset. But another tense situation had a happy ending with the birth of a baby boy in an isolated farmhouse in Piddlehinton, near Dorchester.

When Mrs Angela Grist, a veterinary surgeon's wife, went into labour, there seemed to be serious complications. Snowdrifts made it impossible to get her to hospital.

In the end a retired G P who had tramped six miles through the snow delivered the baby just five minutes before a consultant obstetrician arrived from the maternity unit at Dorchester County Hospital in a farm Land Rover.

Grave danger

Mr Colin Grist, the husband, said: "I have delivered many baby animals in my job as a vet, but this was far more harrowing. There was a grave danger at one stage because of the length of labour."

Three young people emerged from an icy prison to find that they had been trapped in their vehicle less than 200 yards away from the warmth and safety of the Countryman's Inn, North Tawton, Devon.

Stewart Bailey, 20, a land surveyor from Byfleet, Surrey, was travelling to a job in North Cornwall on Saturday when he picked up two hitchhikers on their way to Falmouth Art College.

Just before darkness fell on Saturday they hit a 30 ft snowdrift. Unable to open the doors of the vehicle, they shivered and lived on a packet of biscuits for three days.

Delivering drugs to sick people has been a major problem. In Okehampton, two skiers battled through snowdrifts to deliver insulin to a sick girl.

Yesterday Mr Howell congratulated the emergency rescue teams on their "marvellous work" and reassured local councils that they would not have to worry about the eventual cost of the operation.

Farmers would only have to pay the cost of fodder dropped to their animals. They would not be expected to pay the cost of the emergency helicopter deliveries.

Editorial Comment—P18

U.S. PLEDGE TO DEFEND OILFIELDS

By STEPHEN BARBER in Washington

THE CARTER administration yesterday served notice for the first time that it intends to guard the oilfields of the Middle East for America and its allies.

Dr Harold Brown, Defence Secretary, said in a Los Angeles speech that because of the importance of oil, peace and security in the Middle East was essential to the West.

"We intend to safeguard the production of oil and its transportation to consumer nations without interference by hostile powers" he declared.

His remarks were of special relevance to the dangerous situation in the Horn of Africa.

But they were mainly directed to reassuring America's Asian allies that Washington has not forgotten them owing to its preoccupation with the defence of Western Europe against possible Warsaw Pact attack.

Ethiopian promise to Carter—P4

BREZHNEV AND ASSAD ATTACK SADAT

By RICHARD BEESTON in Moscow

Mr Brezhnev and President Assad of Syria denounced President Sadat's Middle-East peace initiative as "futile and insolvent" yesterday, and agreed to establish closer Moscow-Damascus relations.

The presence at these Kremlin talks of the Soviet Defence Minister, Marshal Dmitri Ustinov, indicated discussion of further Russian arms supplies for Syria.

The importance given to the Soviet-Syrian talks suggests that Moscow is now going all out to reassert its influence in the Middle East. Soviet arms shipments, under a deal financed by Libya, reported to be worth £500 million, are already arriving in Syria.

Begin's hard line—P4

PLANE SALES TO LIBYA HALTED

By Our Washington Staff

America yesterday cancelled the sale of two Boeing jet airliners to Libya and ordered a halt to maintenance of cargo planes belonging to the Libyan air force.

The move was made because of the continued support offered by Col Gaddafi's regime to international terrorists.

RUSSIA ARRESTS 18th HELSINKI WATCHER

By RICHARD BEESTON in Moscow

Pyotr Vims, 22, has become the 18th member of the "Helsinki group" of Russian dissidents, formed to monitor human rights in the Soviet Union, to be arrested, Dr Andrei Sakharov, the leading Soviet dissident, said yesterday.

Mr Vims is the son of the dissident Baptist leader, Georgy Vims, in jail for "inciting citizens to illegal acts." Pyotr Vims was arrested in Kiev for refusing to find work.

Russia rejects human rights—P7

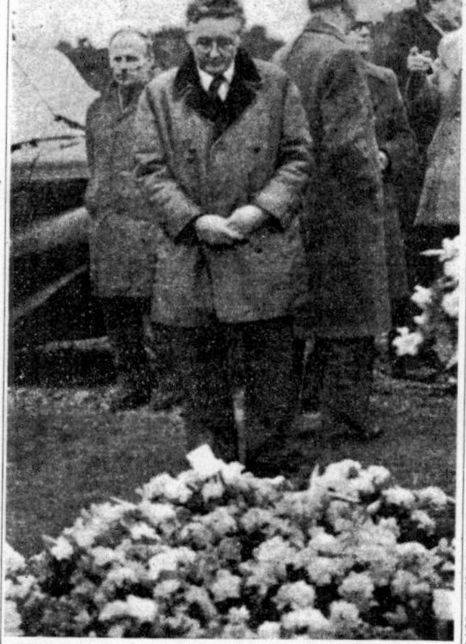

Mr Wesley Huddleston, proprietor of La Mon House, the restaurant near Belfast where 12 people died in the terrorist bomb outrage, looking over the many wreaths at yesterday's funeral at Bangor, Co. Down, for two of the victims, Mr Ian McCracken and his wife Elizabeth. Report—P2.

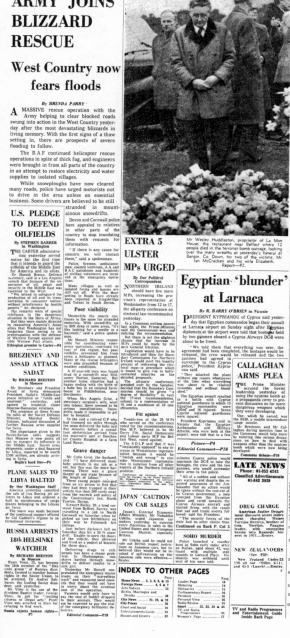

EXTRA 5 ULSTER MPs URGED

By Our Political Correspondent

NORTHERN IRELAND should have five more MPs, increasing the province's representation at Westminster from 12 to 17, the all-party conference on electoral law recommended yesterday.

In a Commons written answer last night, the Prime Minister said the Government was considering the recommendation.

But there is not the slightest chance that the increase in MPs could be made by the next General Election.

Legislation would have to be introduced and then the Boundary Commission for Northern Ireland would start the lengthy process of redrawing the electoral map—a procedure which is bound to give rise to hotly-contested inquiries on the detailed proposals.

The all-party conference, presided over by the Speaker, decided that the Boundary Commission should be given "a degree of flexibility" to vary the 17-seat recommendation, subject to a representation of 16 and a maximum of 18 constituencies.

Fitt against

Twenty-two of the 29 MPs who served on the conference voted for the recommendations. One MP, believed to be Mr Gerry Fitt, Social Democratic and Labour party MP for Belfast West, voted against.

The S D L P said that it was "implacably opposed" to any increase in Westminster representation because it would be "foolish and wrong" to consider Westminster representation in isolation from all other aspects of the Northern Ireland problem."

Conference on electoral law—letter from Mr Speaker to the Prime Minister. Mr Speaker's Conference on Electoral Law—Papers submitted to the conference. Stationery Office. 15p and 75p respectively.

JAPAN 'CAUTION' ON CAR SALES

Japan's External Economic Affairs Minister, Mr Nobuhiko Ushiba, urged Japanese car makers yesterday to exercise every discretion in sales to the United States and the European Common Market, especially Britain.

Mr Ushiba said he could not rule out British import restrictions on Japanese cars, but he believed they would not be invoked if self-restraint on the Japanese side were effective.—Reuter.

Egyptian 'blunder' at Larnaca

By R. BARRY O'BRIEN in Nicosia

PRESIDENT KYPRIANOU of Cyprus said yesterday that Egyptian commandos began their assault at Larnaca airport on Sunday night after Egyptian diplomats at the airport were told that hostages held by two gunmen aboard a Cyprus Airways DC-8 were about to be freed.

"We told them that everything was over, the agreement had been completed, the hostages would be released, the crew would be released and the two gunmen had agreed to surrender to the Cyprus police," President Kyprianou said.

"They attacked the plane without any reason whatsoever at the time when everything was about to be resolved smoothly and without bloodshed."

The Egyptian assault resulted in a battle with Cypriot national guardsmen in which 15 Egyptian commandos were killed and 16 injured. Seven Cypriot national guardsmen were injured.

President Kyprianou said in Nicosia that the Egyptian Ambassador and Military Attaché, who were both at the airport, were told that in a few minutes Cyprus police would approach the DC-8 to take the hostages, the crew and the two gunmen, who would surrender their arms to the police.

Picture—P4
Editorial Comment—P18

"All of a sudden and without any warning and despite the repeated assurances of the Ambassador that no action would be taken without the consent of the Cyprus government, a jeep emerged from the Egyptian plane and raced towards the Cyprus Airways aircraft and started firing, with the result that sad and tragic events followed" said the President.

"The security forces of the state had no other choice than

Continued on Back P, Col 3

SOHO MURDER

Police launched a murder hunt in Soho early today after an Italian, aged about 42, was found with multiple stab wounds in Gerrard Place. His identity was withheld until next of kin were told.

CALLAGHAN ARMS PLEA

THE Prime Minister accused the Soviet leadership yesterday of using the neutron bomb as a propaganda cover to prevent discussion on far more dangerous weapons which they were developing.

One, which he named, was the SS20, a mobile intermediate range missile.

Mr Brezhnev, said Mr Callaghan during question time in the Commons, would help more by entering into serious discussions on how to deal with weapons other than the neutron bomb which were now being developed.

Commons debate—P10

LATE NEWS

Phone: 01-353 4242
Classified Advertisements 01-583 3939

DRUG CHARGE

American Justice Department disclosed secret indictment charging Moises Torrijos Herrera, brother of Gen. Torrijos, Panama leader, with smuggling heroin into Kennedy Airport in 1971.—Reuter.

NEW ZEALANDERS

(See P32)

New Zealand Under-23 139 all out (Miller 6-71), and 45-3 (Lunch).—Reuter.

C

INDEX TO OTHER PAGES

	Page		Page
Home News	2, 3, 8, 9, & 19	Leader Page	18
Foreign News	4, 6 & 7	Motoring	14
Arts Notices	15	Obituaries	16
Births, Marriages and Deaths	36	Parliamentary Report	10
City News	21, 22, & 23	Personal	16
City Prices	20	Personal View	16
Court and Social	16	Radio Review	15
Entertainments Guide	35	**Sport**	32, 33, 34 & 35
Houses and Estates	13	TV and Radio Programmes	35
		Woman's Page	17

TV and Radio Programmes and Entertainment Guide Inside Back Page

ECONOMY FEAR BY PREMIER

By PETER GILL Political Staff

AWAY from the party political fray, the Prime Minister is finding it increasingly difficult to conceal his concern and dismay over the country's economic prospects for the run-up to a General Election.

In the Commons and at a private meeting of senior party colleagues and trades unionists yesterday, Mr Callaghan made it plain that he did not share the optimism of Mr Healey, his own Chancellor, and others in assessing current domestic and international trends.

On the international front, he said he was so fearful of protectionist measures being adopted in Europe and in the United States that he was already in contact with President Carter on the subject.

Any European scramble for protectionism would be led by France, Mr Callaghan feels. He told a meeting of the TUC-Labour party policy liaison committee that the French would be "at the head of the queue."

Bland paper

Discussion at the committee, attended, among others, by Mr Healey, Mr Foot, Leader of the Commons, Mr Jack Jones, retiring Transport Workers' leader, and Mr Len Murray, TUC general secretary, centred on a bland paper on the employment situation presented by Mr Booth, Employment Secretary.

One of Mr Booth's few original points was to express Government disapproval of work-sharing or early retirement to ease unemployment. At the same time he thought there was a strong case for reducing overtime to open up jobs.

Mr Healey sought to look on the bright side. He reminded the committee that there were more people in employment than ever before and more job vacancies than at any other time in the past three years.

He was hard at work on our partners in the Common Market, to improve their own growth rates and thus help towards an expansion of world trade.

Callaghan intervenes

When the Chancellor was asked for our own growth target for next year, the Prime Minister intervened to say this amounted to a Budget secret, and should not be discussed. He was more gloomy about the world economic outlook than Mr Healey, he said.

In the Commons, Mr Callaghan soon found himself locked in a verbal duel with Mrs Thatcher on the slight improvement recorded in the unemployment figures.

His pessimism was soon betrayed when he responded to the Opposition leader's taunt on the unemployment record by claiming that it was "not totally true" to say that it was worse than that of all our major competitors.

Tory barracking nudged him into a declaration that unemployment could get worse this year unless there was a faster growth rate.

SLIGHT FALL IN JOBLESS

By Our Industrial Correspondent

Unemployment in the United Kingdom fell this month by 39,870 to 1,508,674 on Feb. 9, a slight improvement. But although this was borne out by seasonally adjusted figures, there was no inclination in Whitehall to be over-optimistic.

Details—P9
Parliament—P10

'PARAFFIN' WARNING

Police in Kent last night warned householders against buying cut price paraffin following the theft of 2,000 gallons of highly-inflamable aviation-fuel from a Thanet depot. The fuel looks and smells like blue paraffin. If used in a heater it would explode.

Today's Weather

Midnight forecast

GENERAL SITUATION: S.E. flow over most parts with troughs of low pressure approaching from S.W.

LONDON, S.E. & CENT. S. ENGLAND, E. ANGLIA, MIDLANDS, WALES: Fog at first, rain, heavy in places, spreading from S.W. Winds S.E., mod., freshening. Max. 45F (7C).

E. ENGLAND: Fog at first, bright intervals, rain later. Sleet or snow on higher ground. Winds S.E., light or mod. 39F (4C).

S.W. ENGLAND: Rain, heavy in places. Hill and coastal fog. Winds S.E. fresh or strong. 50F (10C), rapid thawing.

S. NORTH SEA, STRAIT OF DOVER: Winds S., Force 3-4, backing E., 6-7. Sea slight becoming rough.

ENG. CH. (E.): S. 4-5, backing E., 6-8, later veering S again. Moderate becoming rough.

OUTLOOK: Rain at times, sleet or snow in N., becoming temporarily milder in S., still cold in N.

Weather Maps—P34

Mrs Thatcher hits back at 'bullies'

By DAVID HARRIS, Political Correspondent

IN WHAT COULD be the trailer of a bitter General Election campaign, the Prime Minister and Mrs Thatcher took their inter-party battle on immigration from the Commons to the Ilford North by-election yesterday.

Mrs Thatcher, on a visit to the constituency which goes to the polls a week today, said she would stick to her views even though she was being bullied, intimidated, vilified and treated to malicious attacks.

Mr Callaghan, in a message to Mrs Tessa Jowell, the Labour candidate, said: "Now some of the Tory leaders are preaching a doctrine that will result in conflict and confrontation. I ask the people of Ilford North to show that they do not want this."

The Prime Minister's comment will be taken as confirmation that he fully backs the attack made on the Conservative leader the previous night by Mr Rees, Home Secretary,

Cartoon—P2
Personal view—P16

who accused Mrs Thatcher not only of making racial hatred respectable, but of inciting the threats to public order now being seen in some cities.

Following up Mrs Thatcher's own repudiation of the Home Secretary's allegation, Mr Whitelaw, deputy leader of the party and the Conservatives' spokesman on home affairs, went to Ilford last night to accuse Mr Rees of committing "a grave error in lending the authority of his great office to make respectable the chorus of misleading abuse."

He said: "Like all other Conservatives, I deeply resent his manufactured, artificial and thoroughly unjustified charge."

He pointed out that last April, in East Flint, Mr Rees had urged Mrs Thatcher to speak out on the issue of immigration because silence would be harmful to race relations.

"Now," added Mr Whitelaw,

Continued on Back P, Col 4

BRITAIN IMPORTS STEEL

By ROLAND GRIBBEN Business Correspondent

BRITISH Steel is carrying out its threat to import products to meet orders in danger of being lost through disputes.

About 20,000 tons of hot rolled coil for tinplate processing has been bought from European steelmakers after disputes at Port Talbot and Llanwern, South Wales, cut production. The order is worth £3 million.

Union leaders at Ebbw Vale, where production is at a standstill because of a "dirty money" dispute involving nearly 800 fitters, want a Government inquiry into the order and into the management of the whole Welsh steel division.

A union official at the plant said yesterday: "British Steel is losing money hand over fist and yet it now has to go abroad to competitors to buy the steel it should be producing itself."

Pay talks resume

Meanwhile pay negotiations between British Steel and its biggest union, the Iron and Steel Trades Confederation, resume today on the steel corporation's "strings" offer of a $9\frac{1}{2}$ per cent. increase if the unions accept plans for an estimated 25,000 redundancies, or $6\frac{1}{2}$ per cent without the "strings."

Both the confederation and craftsmen's unions have hinted they are prepared to settle for the higher figure, but with no commitment to the major run-down programme.

TEXACO DRIVERS ACCEPT DEAL

By Our Industrial Correspondent

Shop stewards representing 720 Texaco petrol and oil tanker drivers, the last to hold out with their go-slow in the recent pay dispute, voted yesterday by 19 to four to accept a revised wages deal and resume normal working.

Supplies are returning to normal slowly after an end to the overtime ban by 8,000 other drivers on Monday.

Petrol confusion—P9

£17m MORE BUSES

London Transport is to buy 350 more new-generation double-deck buses, it was announced yesterday. Options for 200 Leyland "Titans" and 150 Metro-Cammell Weymann "Metrobuses" are being taken up at a cost of £17 million.

Hop across to France this summer.

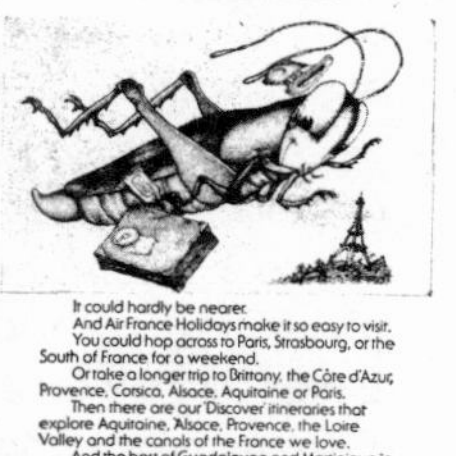

It could hardly be nearer.
And Air France Holidays make it so easy to visit.
You could hop across to Paris, Strasbourg, or the South of France for a weekend.
Or take a longer trip to Brittany, the Côte d'Azur, Provence, Corsica, Alsace, Aquitaine or Paris.
Then there are our 'Discover' itineraries that explore Aquitaine, Alsace, Provence, the Loire Valley and the canals of the France we love.
And the best of Guadeloupe and Martinique in the French Caribbean.
Clip the coupon or ask your Travel Agent for a copy of the Air France Holidays Brochure.
Then hop across to France.

AIR FRANCE HOLIDAYS

To: Air France, Department P.U., 69 Boston Manor Road, Brentford, Middlesex TW8 9JQ
Please send me a copy of the Air France Holidays Brochure.
Name
Address
Air France Holidays, a member of ABTA DT 22 2

fallen below 100,000 in 1928 when Lord Burnham (Lawson's grandson) and his family sold *The Telegraph* to the Berry brothers.

One of the new proprietors, Sir William Berry (later Lord Camrose) took editorial charge of *The Telegraph* and returned it to the principles which had made it so successful in its pioneering days—the careful balance of quality news and human interest and of presenting the plain truth, the unadorned facts completely and trustworthily. During the thirties, the Berry brothers also bought the *Morning Post* and combined it with *The Telegraph*. And they once again demonstrated that there was a large reading public for a paper that could combine serious journalism with human interest in the more sensational aspects of the news.[6]

By 1939, *The Daily Telegraph*'s daily circulation had climbed to 750,000. During the events leading up to World War II, the paper took a very responsible, though unpopular position. In the thirties, the British wanted to believe Hitler's repeated assurances he would never attack France or England. Some British papers ignored the problem, offering mainly entertainment and very little information about developments on the European continent. Other papers even opposed Britain's preparation for war and conscription. But right up to the nation's declaration of war on Germany in September, 1939, *The Telegraph,* despite the unpopularity of its warnings, was the strongest and most insistent voice against appeasement.

During the war, *The Telegraph*'s Fleet Street plant was set on fire by German bombings. When supplies of newsprint ran low, it, along with *The Times,* cut back part of its circulation in order to have six pages for more complete coverage of the war.[7]

After the war, *The Daily Telegraph* became the first quality newspaper to sell over a million copies daily. With the coming of television, curiously, *The Telegraph,* along with the other leading London quality dailies—*The Times* and *The Guardian*—picked up readers while the sensational popular dailies lost nearly 20 percent of their readers to the tube. At the end of 1977, *The Telegraph*'s circulation was approximately 1,326,000, with the *Sunday Telegraph,* a counterpart of similar nature published by *The Telegraph* but with a totally separate staff, selling 821,000 copies. Some 70 percent of *The Telegraph*'s copies are distributed through wholesalers and retailers directly to homes, with the remainder attributed to casual sales at distribution points.[8]

Ever since the earliest days of *The Telegraph* when Edward Lawson put correspondents in Paris, St. Petersburg and New York, with a fourth patrolling between Berlin and Vienna, the paper has always rightly prided itself on complete and accurate coverage of international affairs. Through the years, the paper has covered the world, with special attention to Commonwealth countries. Foreign correspondent E. J. Dillon lived and hid among the Armenians to report the atrocities being committed against them by the Turks. *Telegraph* correspondents carried the exclusive first news of the German capture of Paris. One

[6] Green, *op. cit.,* p. 6.
[7] Olson, *op. cit.,* pp. 22–24.
[8] K. C. Shard, Marketing Director, *The Daily Telegraph,* in letter to H. Fisher, dated February 9, 1978.

of the paper's most colorful nineteenth century writers, George A. Sala, described a typical foreign news for *The Telegraph* in these words:

> Wars and rumors of wars, the price of gold at San Francisco, depreciation of the rupee at Calcutta, corners in pork and grain at Chicago and in Erie Railroad shares in New York, coal miners and trainworkers strike, a famine in Russia, a beer riot in Munich, a balloon accident in Rangoon, a kidnapping by brigands in Sicily, an anti-clerical demonstration in Rome, an attack on missionaries at Shanghai, a diplomatic ball at Peking with a full explanation of the political motives which prompted the Russian Minister to have an attack of measles on the very evening previous to the British plenipotentiary's dance." [9]

In recent decades, *The Telegraph* has continued to match that consuming interest in foreign news coverage. It has provided thorough coverage in recent years of Africa's tribal strife, the Vietnam war, India's political problems, the Middle East conflict and the Western Hemisphere as well as the European scene. In fact, its comprehensive coverage of world news makes up a third of the total reading content of each day's paper. On a typical day, international stories share the front page and occupy three additional full pages. To provide such extensive coverage, *The Telegraph* keeps a staff of 15 full-time foreign correspondents in key capital cities of the globe, plus over 100 part-timers located throughout the world.[10] Three international wire agencies—Reuters, Associated Press and United Press International—supplement the work of *The Telegraph*'s overseas staff. Among its distinguished foreign correspondents, the paper lists Christopher Buckley, John Ridley, Anthony Mann and John Wallis.

Nor does *The Telegraph* neglect coverage of its own government. A staff of eight reporters keeps a watchful eye on Parliament and each day, in addition to national political and party news, there is a full review of the previous day's activity of the nation's lawmakers called "Yesterday in Parliament." One team of three reporters works in the lobbies and corridors of Parliament to give a full account of all the Members and Ministers' on- and off-duty activities. Another team supplies a full daily report of the debates of both Lords and Commons.

While *The Telegraph* could not be considered an outstanding "crusading newspaper," it does engage in thorough investigative reporting when the situation calls for it. Recent activities by Labour governments and trade unions have made necessary investigation of their compromises of workers' freedoms. One team analyzes strikes and union maneuverings. Another team of three digs into questionable business practices. Recently, the paper has been watchdogging the numerous quasi-autonomous National Government organizations attached to official departments which have been costing taxpayers heavily in the form of hidden expenses. As a result of other digging, the paper's reporters have helped to convict swindlers, especially in motor insurance. Crime, sex and other sensation does get into *The Telegraph*'s news columns, but as a part of the day's events to be reported and sans the screaming headlines and keyhole peeping of the popular dailies.

[9] Green, *op. cit.*, p. 3.
[10] There are three full-time overseas correspondents in Washington, D.C., two in New York, and one each in Moscow, Peking, Bonn, Paris, Stockholm, Madrid, Salisbury, Nairobi, Cairo and Tel Aviv.

Since, "in the very first days of *The Telegraph* it was decreed that all sections of interest should be catered for,"[11] the paper covers numerous fields. Specialist reporters cover areas such as science, medicine, law, finance, property, fashion, tourism, motoring and agriculture, among others. Pages are regularly given to concerts, operas, books, the theater, radio, television, painting and art. Yet another page carries guides to current radio, television, theater, cinema and art entertainment. Sports are given full treatment, usually in the final three pages just preceding the paper's back page. Generally, one page is devoted to a special feature and shorter feature or background articles may appear throughout the paper. There is also a page for the paper's forthright editorial opinions and for "Letters to the Editor." The daily column by a guest writer treats a wide variety of subjects. However, "no local news are printed unless it is of national interest."[12]

The front page of *The Daily Telegraph* presents a serious, dignified "gray" appearance. Makeup is vertical, with news items extending lengthwise down the page in eight columns. A single picture, usually fairly large, graces the upper center of the page. Layout is orderly, with contents evenly divided between top national and international stories. The "Late News" box, "Today's Weather" and the "Index to Other Pages" contribute to the paper's careful organization and neat appearance. A typical daily runs from 32 to 36 pages in length, and its serious, dignified appearance holds consistently throughout. Inside pages may carry up to three pictures, but many pages appear without photographs. Cartoons are used well.

The Daily Telegraph has always had the benefit of family ownership. Even today, there is family group ownership under the chairmanship of Lord Hartwell. The paper's financial solvency and stability rises in part from the personal care and management of its well-heeled family owners, in part from its lucrative advertising revenues and in part from its strong circulation figures and the income they represent. But the paper is not entirely free from worry. There is always the danger that changes will affect England's delicate circulation balance. In recent years, there has been growing concern among *Telegraph*'s leaders about the mechanical unions' increasing resistance to reduction of current overstaffing and new labor-saving techniques the paper wishes to introduce.[13] And there is concern at *The Telegraph,* as elsewhere, that the heavy influence of unions and shop stewards on employment practices may actually be interfering with the press freedom to report all the news. To date, *The Telegraph* has been one of few British dailies free and bold enough to report fully the problems of overmanning and other union excesses. At the moment, however, *The Telegraph* continues to enjoy rather steady circulation and financial security.

The Daily Telegraph's ranking among London's three top quality dailies and with the world's best elite newspapers is well justified. Its primary aim is comprehensive news coverage—"the clear, simple, accurate presentation of news—

[11] Green, *op. cit.,* p. 7.
[12] Heren, *op. cit.*
[13] "Press Freedom Report," *IPI Report,* 24:12, December, 1975, p. 2.

news that has been looked for, worked at and thought about."[14] Its historian notes: "The emphasis here has been laid all on news, news, news, because that is where the success of *The Telegraph* began and how it was recreated."[15] To achieve this aim, the paper seeks to present national and international news as comprehensively and as objectively as possible. It is also a paper of forthright opinion, presenting its views from a distinctly conservative viewpoint, but yet independent of all party or group affiliations.

The Telegraph stands solidly on noble principles—free enterprise, the importance of the individual and diversity and against social injustices and all extremes of social organization—socialism, Marxism and the corporate state. At the same time, it never forgets the interests of its middle class readers and offers them a smorgasbord of human interest materials that range from the dead serious to those that border on being sensational without being sensationalized. It is for these reasons that nearly a million and a half readers reach for *The Daily Telegraph* each day. At their fingertips is an elite newspaper that satisfies their thirst for all the news and their hunger for human interest materials.

O Estado de S. Paulo

(BRAZIL)

O ESTADO DE S. PAULO, Brazil's foremost paper, has often been called "The New York *Times* of Latin America." In recent years, to maintain that status, *O Estado* has had to exercise courage never demanded of *The New York Times*. Since 1972 in particular, it has faced heavy challenges to its freedom to publish what it feels Brazilians should know. Terminology used to describe the paper's responses to these challenges reveals the nature of its stance: "courageous," "durable rebel," and "defiant." Because of such courage, *O Estado,* in the words of *Time* magazine's editors "stands out as a durable, responsible independent"[1] newspaper.

São Paulo, the largest city of Latin America's largest country, serves as the home base for *O Estado de S. Paulo* (The State of São Paulo). With a growing staff of writers, editors and full-time correspondents that now numbers over 450, the paper sets a journalistic pace difficult to match, at least in Latin America. Its comprehensive news coverage has made it required reading for Brazil's better-educated professionals and business leaders. Its power as a social

[14] Smith, *op. cit.,* p. 46
[15] Green, *op. cit.,* p. 7
[1] "Brazil's Durable Rebel," *Time* (January 27, 1975), p. 88.

and political force is considerable. Its growing circulation, up from 180,000 a decade ago to around 200,000 today, combined with its lucrative income from advertising and its private family ownership have given it financial stability to ride out oppression, censorship and other challenges to its freedom.

From its earliest beginnings, this impressive Brazilian daily has been a staunch supporter of liberal democracy. When it was founded in 1875 by a group of 17 men, its slogan became "Representation and Justice." During the remainder of the decade of the 1870's, the fledgling newspaper worked success-fully to get slavery abolished in Brazil. For a time named A *Provincia de São Paulo* until its province became a state, it was a good, but undistinguished newspaper in those early years.

Then the paper was bought by Julio de Mesquita, the grandfather of the present director, Julio de Mesquita Neto. In the hands of the Mesquita family, *O Estado de S. Paulo* has constantly improved its coverage and its quality, has always played an important role in the political climate of the country and has consistently championed independence and freedom. Under the Mesquita fam-ily, *O Estado*'s prestige and credibility have grown steadily.

After the monarchy was overthrown, Mesquita began working for the es-tablishment of a republic in Brazil. As a result, numerous regimes have tried to suppress *O Estado*, but they have always failed, partly because of the paper's power base among the nation's wealthy, moderate conservatives. In 1924, for example, Julio de Mesquita was imprisoned for his advocacy of a more demo-cratic structure, but the paper could remain firm because of its well-to-do sup-porters.

When Julio de Mesquita died in 1927, his son, Julio de Mesquita Filho took control of *O Estado*. In the 1930's and 1940's, he continued the battle against oppressive government begun by his father. Aided by his brother and six of their children, Swiss-born Mesquita Filho gave his paper the stamp of excellence it still bears today. Twice he was forced to flee into exile. For five years (1940–1945) Dictator Getulio Vargas seized complete control of the paper. But in 1964, after his comeback from his second exile, Filho immediately began to mold political influence once more through his paper. When it seemed that left-ist Joao Goulart was headed towards a total dictatorship, Mesquita Filho joined with the military in overthrowing Goulart. Then, when the military assumed control and turned authoritarian, *O Estado* found itself opposing the military dictatorship. The esteem held by his fellow newspapermen for Filho's courage in fighting for greater freedom and democracy is reflected in their 1966 election of him as President of the Inter-American Press Association.

In 1969, today's editor-director of *O Estado* and the son of Filho, Julio de Mesquita Neto, took over when his father died. He is now almost solely respon-sible for the paper's total operation. He has courageously continued to guide *O Estado* in its high quality, independent path. His editor-in-chief has been the highly professional and courageous Marcelino Ritter, undoubtedly one of the most intelligent and versatile journalists in all Latin America. In recent years, Julio de Mesquita Neto has consistently defied governmental moves against his

TEMPO EM SÃO PAULO

Nublado, nevoa úmida, chuvas esparsas no decorrer do período. Temperatura estável. Página 26

O ESTADO DE S. PAULO

JULIO DE MESQUITA NETO
DIRETOR RESPONSÁVEL

JULIO MESQUITA (1891 - 1927) — JULIO DE MESQUITA FILHO (1927 - 1969) — FRANCISCO MESQUITA (1927 - 1969)

Capital e Interior de São Paulo Crs 4,00 | ANO 99 | QUARTA-FEIRA, 22 DE FEVEREIRO DE 1978 | Nº 31.575 | Domingo: Crs 8,00. Assinatura Crs 960,00

Os heróis do Cairo

Os sobreviventes do comando egípcio enviado a Chipre para resgatar os refens tomados pelos palestinos em Nicósia, após o assassínio do diretor do diário Al Ahram, foram recebidos na volta ao Cairo como heróis. Os 15 soldados mortos pelas forças da Guarda Nacional cipriota serão enterrados hoje, depois de condecorados postumamente com a "Estrela de Sinai" pelo presidente Anuar Sadat. **Página 7**

Lista que Egydio levará a Brasília não inclui Natel

De serviço local
e de sucursal

O governador Paulo Egydio afirmou categoricamente ontem que, após a convenção nacional da Arena, levará a Brasília como candidatos ao governo do Estado apenas os quatro nomes do grupo que segue sua orientação política — Delfim Netto, Raphael Baldacci, Olavo Setúbal e Murilo Macedo. Admitiu também que, além de se preocupar com a sucessão estadual, "o grupo pretende continuar explorando a possibilidade de formação de um partido político, quando chegar o momento oportuno".

Egydio fez essas declarações em sua residência, após reunir-se com Delfim Netto e com o deputado Nabi Abi Chedid. Foi categórico também ao negar a presença, em São Paulo, de qualquer emissário de Brasília: "Não é verdade. Eu funciono aqui com total independência. Eu não procuro saber se veio um emissário, se disse isso, se pediu aquilo. O que eu estou fazendo é de minha responsabilidade pura e exclusiva. Agora temos dois grupos dentro de uma mesma legenda partidária e pode ser — eu não

elimino essa possibilidade — que, amanhã, em função do interesse político do Estado, se estabeleça um acordo entre esses dois grupos".

Em Brasília, o coronel Toledo Camargo reafirmou ontem que o Palácio do Planalto só se manifestará sobre o problema das sucessões estaduais depois da convenção nacional da Arena, que devem homologar o nome do general João Baptista Figueiredo e o de Aureliano Chaves como candidatos à Presidência e à Vice-Presidência da República. Com essa afirmação, Camargo recusou-se a comentar a declaração do secretário Adhemar de Barros Filho, segundo a qual o Palácio do Planalto poderia intervir na sucessão paulista "se os políticos não promoverem o entendimento".

O próprio tenente-brigadeiro Délio Jardim de Mattos, ministro do Superior Tribunal Militar, desmentiu ontem que tenha estado em São Paulo na semana passada, como emissário do general João Baptista Figueiredo, para ouvir as forças arenistas do Estado que disputam a sucessão do governador Paulo Egydio Martins. **Página 4**

A Etiópia garante que não atacará a Somália

WASHINGTON — A Casa Branca informou ontem que o presidente Jimmy Carter recebeu garantias pessoais do tenente-coronel Mengistu Hailé Mariam, chefe do governo da Etiópia, de que as tropas etíopes não tentarão cruzar a fronteira somali e interromperão a atual ofensiva quando recuperarem o território ocupado pelas forças do país vizinho.

As garantias do dirigente etíope — e também a promessa de receber em breve um novo embaixador norte-americano, para normalização das relações com os Estados Unidos — foram transmitidas a Carter pelo vice-diretor do Conselho Nacional de Segurança, David Aaron, a Adis Abeba na semana passada para conferenciar com o governo do país africano sobre o perigo de evolução e internacionalização do conflito.

O presidente da Somália, Siad Barre, por sua vez, disse a um jornal do sultanato de Omã que o Ocidente comete um "grande erro" ao manter uma atitude negativa em relação ao seu país, porque isso fará com que a União Soviética se sinta estimulada a ampliar suas ações na região do "Chifre da África".

Barre tentou justificar a presença de suas tropas em território etíope dizendo que a Somália foi obrigada a entrar na luta quando viu que as forças da Frente de Libertação da Somália Ocidental (FLSO) eram combatidas diretamente por unidades do Pacto de Varsóvia.

No Kuwait, o diário As Siyassah informou que, nas últimas semanas, cerca de 30 navios descarregaram armamentos norte-americanos, ingleses e alemães, em um porto a 130 quilômetros de Mogadiscio, e que o Irã se transformou no principal fornecedor de armas para as tropas somalis. **Página 6**

Os russos apóiam a Síria contra o Egito

MOSCOU — O presidente soviético Leonid Brejnev apoiou ontem integralmente a "Frente de Rejeição", formada pelos países árabes contrários às iniciativas egípcias, e informou que a União Soviética é partidária da reconvocação da Conferência de Genebra sobre o Oriente Médio.

Em discurso pronunciado durante banquete oferecido ao presidente sírio Hafez Assad, Brejnev também elogiou a participação da Síria nas decisões adotadas pela "Frente de Rejeição", integrada ainda pela Líbia, Argélia, lêmen do Sul e pela Organização de Libertação da Palestina, reafirmando sua intenção de reduzir a qualquer das formas "de capitulação" diante da "agressão israelense".

Assad chegou segunda-feira a Moscou para uma visita oficial de três dias, tendo mesmo rumores de que Damasco já teria recebido armas russas no valor de 1 bilhão de dólares, financiadas pela Líbia.

A agência TASS noticiou os encontros dos líderes sírios e soviéticos, afirmando que a cooperação entre os dois países "se estende ao campo da defesa, importante para Damasco e notória". A TASS informou que as reuniões se deram "em um clima de amizade", tendo Brejnev e Assad concordado em condenar as iniciativas de paz do presidente egípcio Anuar Sadat, por "prejudicarem os interesses árabes".

"No banquete oferecido em sua honra, após agradecer o apoio soviético, o presidente sírio insistiu na retirada israelense dos territórios árabes ocupados na guerra de 1967 e reiterou sua posição favorável à criação de um pátria palestina independente. Assad concluiu seu pronunciamento, dirigido simultaneamente contra Damasco, dizendo que a paz no Oriente Médio só poderá ser concretizada na base das resoluções das Nações Unidas e com a participação soviética. **Página 7**

CVM apura operação com ações da Acesita

De sucursal do
RIO

A Comissão de Valores Mobiliários está investigando operações feitas no dia 15 na Bolsa de Valores do Rio de Janeiro, de valor superior a 11 milhões de cruzeiros, envolvendo ações da Acesita e que foram negociadas com a utilização de informações de caráter sigiloso. A denúncia encaminhada à Comissão indica que as operações a termo, com preços de 30 e 60 dias, teriam sido feitas por ordem de João Jabour,

um dos maiores acionistas privados do Banco do Brasil e que, como integrante do Conselho Fiscal do BB, teria tomado conhecimento da transferência do controle acionário da Acesita, do Banco do Brasil para a Siderbrás. Se confirmada a denúncia, João Jabour pode ser enquadrado como beneficiário de uma "insider information", pela qual um fato conhecido por administradores e utilizado em prejuízo dos demais acionistas, irregularidade prevista na Lei das Sociedades Anônimas. **Página 26**

Vance pede mais verba para ajuda externa dos EUA

WASHINGTON — O secretário de Estado Cyrus Vance pediu ontem a aprovação do Congresso para um programa de ajuda ao exterior no valor de 9,5 bilhões de dólares, argumentando que o governo do presidente Jimmy Carter pretende ampliar seus planos neste setor, nos próximos quatro anos. Na semana passada, a Casa Branca havia anunciado que o programa de ajuda externa em 1979 seria de 7,6 bilhões de dólares — 518 milhões de dólares menos que o aprovado para o exercício de 1978.

Da verba pedida ontem, 4,5 bilhões de dólares serão reservados à ajuda militar e econômica bilateral, destinando-se quase dois terços a Israel e ao Egito. Vance salientou a importância da ajuda econômica e militar aos países do Oriente Médio e da África e disse que a ajuda ao exterior é um dos instrumentos mais eficientes de que os Estados Unidos dispõem para promover o desenvolvimento econômico nos países do Terceiro Mundo.

URSS ameaça país que usar bomba N

MOSCOU — A União Soviética advertiu os países do Ocidente de que devem desistir de incorporar a bomba de nêutrons ao arsenal da Organização do Tratado do Atlântico Norte — NATO — ede sua eventual utilização contra forças do Pacto de Varsóvia, se não quiserem sofrer as consequências de um "contragolpe contundente e devastador".

Na advertência, divulgada ontem pelas agências soviéticas Novosti e TASS, o Cremlin afirma que o contragolpe, com as armas escolhidas por Moscou, causará dezenas de vezes maiores do que o da bomba de nêutrons, podendo levar o mundo a uma catástrofe nuclear. **Página 7**

Quando São Paulo pára

As enchentes voltaram a tumultuar a vida da cidade na tarde de ontem, após temporal de uma hora, que inundou principalmente a Baixada do Glicério, avenida do Estado, 23 de Maio, Brooklin, Ipiranga, Água Rasa e parte do ABC. **Última página**

A renda do brasileiro: US$ 1.440

De sucursal de
BRASÍLIA

Estimativas feitas pelo IBGE e pela Fundação Getúlio Vargas indicam que o Produto Nacional Bruto subiu de Crs 1.533,2 bilhões em 1976 para Crs 2.386 bilhões em 1977, equivalentes a US$ 163 bilhões, o que eleva a renda per capita do País para 1.440 dólares, considerando-se a população atual de 113 milhões de habitantes. Segundo os cálculos, o setor agrícola participou no ano passado com 13,2% na composição do PNB; o setor secundário, com 37%, e o terciário, com 50,8%.

Por outro lado, o ministro Reis Velloso, do Planejamento, informou ontem que, segundo pesquisa da Fundação Getúlio Vargas, os empresários esperam um desempenho econômico bastante favorável no próximo trimestre deste ano: apenas 25% prevêem queda na demanda, enquanto 75% acreditam em aumento ou manutenção do nível de atividades em relação ao último trimestre de 77. Da mesma forma, 82% dos empresários esperam aumento ou manutenção da capacidade instalada das indústrias e apenas 18% prevêem ociosidade. Também há otimismo quanto ao nível de emprego, que no quarto trimestre do ano passado diminuiu em 26% das empresas e aumentou ou se manteve estável em 84%; para este trimestre, apenas 9% dos empresários aguardam redução.

Em São Paulo, a Associação Comercial informou ontem que em janeiro deste ano as vendas do comércio varejista cresceram 3,2% em relação a janeiro de 1977. O Serviço de Proteção ao Crédito, por sua vez, registrou um total de 366 mil consultas, contra 302 mil em janeiro do ano passado. **Página 25**

IR espera arrecadar 63 bilhões

De sucursal de
BRASÍLIA

A Secretaria da Receita Federal espera que a arrecadação do imposto de renda de pessoas físicas (ano-base de 77) chegue a 63 bilhões de cruzeiros, 50 bilhões dos quais obtidos com a retenção na fonte e o restante em declarações. Adilson Gomes de Oliveira, secretário da Receita Federal, lembrou ontem que as declarações das pessoas físicas cao imposto a pagar ou a receber deverão ser entregues até o dia 7 de abril e que não haverá novidade quanto à dedução para o Fundo 157.

O serviço noticioso internacional de "O Estado" é elaborado com telegramas das agências AFP, AP, DPA, Latin, Reuters, UPI e Ansa.

paper. Although *O Estado,* because of its family ownership and high circulation, is proving to be a highly profitable venture that could provide a luxurious life of ease, Julio and his brother Ruy devotedly spend most of their time managing and improving the paper.

One key reason for *O Estado'*s high quality, extensive coverage and intelligent, dependable insights lies in its highly paid and well-educated staff. All reporters have university degrees and a number have doctorates. At least 95 percent of the entire staff have graduated from a university. They provide their readers, mostly from the educated and well-to-do professional classes, with a journalistic package unexcelled in South America and perhaps in the world. In addition to excellent and comprehensive coverage, the paper's pages are packed with serious information, including full texts of all major speeches and press conferences, translated articles from foreign papers, stories from five wire services, national news of all types and local items in profusion.

To supplement its regular heavy fare of news, features, editorials and interpretive pieces, *O Estado* frequently runs special articles on a wide range of domestic and foreign subjects. These articles often continue in serial form for a dozen or more issues. They are well written, well researched and more thorough than many articles found in the country's magazines. In its desire to reach the country's intelligent, well-educated classes, *O Estado* also prints numerous well-written scholarly essays by intellectuals—notably leading literary figures and professors from the University of São Paulo. Speaking of *O Estado'*s total contents, one rival Brazilian journalist from São Paulo remarked,

> There is no doubt about it. *O Estado* is thorough and encyclopedic—actually filled with more reading material than a person can find time to read; it is the nearest thing in Latin America to the New York *Times.*[2]

When it comes to foreign news presentation, a survey of newspapers will almost certainly find *O Estado* at or near the top. In the past, several studies have led to precisely that conclusion. A UNESCO study in 1953 showed that during a selected week in 1951, *O Estado* provided more foreign news than any of 16 other leading newspapers in the world. In another 1960 study, the paper was found to be second only to *The New York Times* in space given to foreign news over a 30-day period; *O Estado* had 200 column inches per day and the *Times* just 19 column inches more, with 219. None of the 11 North and South American dailies in this latter study came close to providing the foreign coverage of these two papers. In addition to the input from its five wire services, *O Estado* has had 12 full-time foreign correspondents stationed in the leading newsmaking capitols of the world. Today, approximately 15 percent of the paper's total space is devoted to foreign news, to say nothing of its numerous interpretive and background articles on overseas situations. For the excellence of its international coverage, *O Estado* has been singled out for special recognition by the United Nations, by the International Press Institute and by several European and American universities.

[2] Antonio L. O. Figueiredo, columnist for *Diarios Associados,* in interview with Dr. John Merrill, November 10, 1966.

A typical weekday edition of *O Estado* may vary from 28 to 48 pages in length, and the huge Sunday edition may run to 150 or more pages. Its general appearance is so serious it has sometimes been called the "gray giant of Brazilian journalism." Another factor contributing to its sober visage is the full, efficient use of space without crowding. Other than the two large pictures which normally occupy the front page, the lead page appears business-like with its mix of national and international lead stories. The nameplate at the top is set off by the latest weather report on one side and the name and title of the paper's director on the other. Headlines are set in large lower-case type, sometimes with subtitles. There is a page directory to story and feature placement inside the paper.

Inside *O Estado,* pages two and three carry editorials and letters to the editor. Only an occasional small cartoon and no pictures enliven the serious gray appearance of the pages. The editorials are conservative, assume a strong anti-Communistic stance and are generally supportive of private enterprise. Pages of Brazilian news usually precede the paper's several pages of international news and features. Generally speaking, on an average day, the reader will find two to four pages of cultural news and information, several business pages, a page on education, two or three pages of sports and news of São Paulo and the interior. To round out the paper's offerings, there are several pages of well written, interesting and highly informative feature articles. Important stories and materials are frequently set in heavy black type. *O Estado* is divided into two parts, which are not clearly delineated as two separate sections. On Sundays and other special days, there is an additional color section which centers on a single topic. It carries a large number of advertisements which generate much of the paper's financial support and profit.

Although *O Estado* considers itself "liberal," many outsiders would label it "conservative." Perhaps the latter designation stems from the fact that in recent years the paper has fought persistently against leftist tendencies in the country and against Communist attempts to infiltrate the government. Also, alone among the Brazilian newspapers, *O Estado* has been a firm supporter of United States' policies. Its honesty, good manners and refinement add further to the conservative image. But the paper also fights for worthwhile social reforms and progressive causes. And, of course, it has struggled most valiantly in the interests of press freedom and journalistic independence from governmental surveillance.

While *O Estado* has always championed freedom, its strongest challenges to its defense of editorial independence have occurred since 1972. In September of that year, the Brazilian government issued a decree which read in part:

> By order of the Minister of Justice, it is prohibited to publish news or comment of any kind on the subject of free politics, development of democracy or matters pertaining to these subjects; on amnesty for those people who have had their civil rights suspended on demands for reduction of sentence; and on critical comment on official financial and economic matters. . . .[3]

[3] "Latin America: Brazil," *IPI Report,* 22:1 (January, 1973), p. 6.

The decree and subsequent actions resulted in three types of restrictive regulation and censorship of the press. Some newspapers and magazines exercised self-censorship so thoroughly they were even praised by the authorities. Others, more suspect to the Government, got their instructions by telephone directly from the censors on what to include or exclude. O Estado found itself in the third, most restricted category, under which journals were submitted to prior censorship.[4]

As government strictures increased and press freedom for all papers disappeared, O Estado was subjected to increased restriction. At first, there were telephoned warnings from the police and unannounced night visits by censors to the paper's editorial offices.[5] Shortly thereafter, early in 1973, O Estado's editor was forbidden to publish a report which denied the existence of a real free press in Brazil.[6] Later that same year, Brazilian censors moved right into the newsroom at O Estado when the newspaper refused to go along with self-censorship. At this time, the paper set in type what it wished to publish and then stood by while censors blue-pencilled forbidden items and comments. In place of the censored stories, O Estado would then run recipes, innocuous letters to the editor or excerpts from Poet Luis Vaz de Cameo's epic work Os Lusiadas on Portuguese adventures in the Far East.[7] One well-informed observer has recently noted that in Brazil, "Printing of poetry in the middle of an article was not only a courageous act, which is still typical of O Estado de S. Paulo today, but in public eyes a constant warning about attacks on freedom of information."[8]

The Inter-American Press Association pointed out at the time that the censor's interventions were completely arbitrary and whimsical, so that news permitted one day might be forbidden the next, resulting in a permanent state of insecurity.[9] O Estado was forbidden to publish the IAPA observation. For his defiance of Government orders that O Estado should censor itself, the paper's director and publisher, Julio Neto received the International Federation of Newspaper Publishers' 1974 Golden Pen of Freedom award.

In January, 1975, when O Estado celebrated its 100th anniversary, publisher Neto said he really could only admit to 95 years of independence, since the paper had been in the hands of government for five years. About the same time, the government, to curry public favor, began to relax its restrictions on the paper somewhat. But its unrelenting campaign to outlaw the Communist Party continued to entrap some journalists. President Geisel removed the censors from the offices of O Estado but told them to keep checking on the paper and to stop stories involving "national security."

Some censorship has continued, most of it stemming from military intervention. At its October, 1977 conference, the IAPA was still considering press

[4] "Press Freedom Report: Brazil," IPI Report, 23:1 (January, 1974), p. 13.
[5] "Latin America: Brazil," op. cit.
[6] "A Quick Look Around," IPI report, 22:4 (April, 1973), p. 7.
[7] "News of the World's Press," IPI Report, 22:11–12 (November–December, 1973), p. 2. See also "Brazil's Durable Rebel," op. cit.
[8] Gerald Sievers, "Brazil: Making Out in the Grip of the Censor's Army," IPI Report, 27:3 (March, 1978), p. 9.
[9] "Press Freedom Report: Brazil," IPI Report, 23:1 (January, 1974), p. 13.

freedom in Brazil "like a government concession." Julio de Mesquita Neto, *O Estado*'s director told that meeting:

> Freedom of information still remains as a "compromise" by the government, a kind of "gift" and proof of its tolerance. We haven't been able to witness any initiative which would consider this freedom an actual right which the government has to respect.
>
> The roots of this paradoxical situation have been explained more than once: the coexistence in Brazil of two judicial orders, one constitutional and the other inconstitutional. Therefore on one hand we have the constitution which recognizes the freedom of expression and opposes censorship and on the other hand we have a number of laws which can annul in practice all constitutional rights by a simple action of the political power. . . .
>
> . . . While this picture persists we cannot afford to be optimistic as regards freedom of expression and in our hearts we ask if soon heavy prior censorship won't be in operation again.[10]

In mid-1978, eleven Brazilian editors reported a four-week period of harassment in which papers were seized, two journalists beaten up and others arrested.[11] Among those arrested under the outdated Law of National Security was Carlos Chagas, *O Estado*'s well-known political correspondent. Nonetheless, at this writing, the general freedom of the press situation seems to be improving considerably. Prior censorship has been lifted, even for radio and television, and newspapers and magazines are again publishing what they please, including criticism of the government. Papers now report fully on political opposition, moves to provide amnesty for political prisoners, torture, demonstrations, the economy, the Catholic Church and other matters previously made taboo by the censors. But Julio de Mesquita Neto continues to observe that removal of censorship must be considered a "gift" which the Government can take away as easily as it was given.[12]

Despite—or perhaps because of—*O Estado*'s oppression, Brazilians continue to find in it well-informed, serious and responsible journalism and readiness to publish, irregardless of the consequences, what its editors see to be the truth. Amid Brazil's shifting political tides, *O Estado*'s editors maintain a firm determination to remain independent. Publisher and editor Julio de Mesquita Neto recently voiced that stand in these words:

> *Estado* will not change its opinions. Under a totalitarian regime, we will be oppressed and continue to fight for freedom. Under a free regime, we will worry about the dangers and excesses of democracy. It's really easier for Brazil to change than it is for *Estado* to change.[13]

The rest of the world interested in a free, responsible elite press can be gratified for *O Estado de S. Paulo*'s example of enduring courage.

---

[10] Sievers, *op. cit.*, p. 16.
[11] "Brazilian Editors Cite Arrests, Torture, Bans and Sackings," *IPI Report,* 27:5 (June, 1978), p. 16.
[12] "Situation in Brazil Much Improved, Says AP," *IPI Report,* 27:5 (June, 1978), p. 15.
[13] "Brazil's Durable Rebel," *op. cit.*

Le Figaro

(FRANCE)

LE FIGARO, long one of the great names in French newspaper journalism, has been experiencing disturbing upheavals during the past decade. Recently, Paris' oldest daily, which has contained some of the nation's best journalistic writing, has found its pages to be a political battleground. Its present owner, a right-wing politician hungry for press power, has been using the paper for his political purposes and has been firing staff members who dare oppose him. As a result, while it remains France's second best daily, Le Figaro's objectivity, political independence, quality of writing and even circulation have begun to slip noticeably.[1]

The current conservative leanings of Le Figaro are a far cry from its origins and traditional editorial stance. It began in January, 1826, as a tiny satirical sheet edited by Maurice Allhoy. The original Figaro, as its name might imply,[2] filled its columns with the artistic life of Paris—feminine fashions, theatrical activities, and gossip. Although the paper has retained some of these features, it has added through the years many serious dimensions never imagined in early nineteenth-century Paris.

Le Figaro in its infancy admirably filled a journalistic gap left by the influential papers of Paris, presenting witty commentary on literature, politics, manners and morals. However, in those early days, it apparently went along with the common French practice of staff members taking sizeable bribes for favorable reviews.[3] It was Henri de Villemesant who brought popularity to the paper when, in the 1850's, he started hiring talented writers as Léo Lespès, Rochefort, Alexandre Dumas, and Baudelaire.[4] In 1856, the paper became a bi-weekly and began a letters column which precipitated some of the most vigorous political dialogue in France. Villemessant would usually reply to letters with one-line retorts which exemplified his talent for biting satire.[5] Le Figaro became a daily in 1866. Villemessant was one of the first editors to departmentalize the news, and compared a newspaper to a department store in which the buyer must know where to locate the various merchandise.[6] He also introduced local reporting and personality interviews and published fresh, recent news.

---

[1] For a further discussion of Le Figaro's present problem, see "Citoyen Hersant," Time (March 13, 1978), p. 100, and "Figaro Shorn," The Economist, 263:6980 (June 11, 1977), p. 61.

[2] Figaro was the Barber of Seville, put on the stage by Beaumarchais and to music by Mozart.

[3] "Fools and Opposition," Time (June 5, 1950), pp. 70–74.

[4] Eugène Tavernier, Du Journalisme (Paris, H. Oudin, 1902), p. 199.

[5] Ibid., p. 237.

[6] Ibid., p. 302. Compare René Pucheu, "Dans la Lumiere du Figaro," Presse-Actualité, Paris (February, 1967), pp. 6–17.

XX

MERCREDI 22 FÉVRIER 1978
ÉDITION DE 5 HEURES — 1,40 F

ADMINISTRATION, ABONNEMENTS PUBLICITÉ : 25, AVENUE MATIGNON 75380 PARIS CEDEX 08. TÉL. 256-80-00
DIRECTION, RÉDACTION, SERV. VENTE IMPRESSION : 37, RUE DU LOUVRE 75081 PARIS CEDEX 02. TÉL 233-44-00

COMMISSION PARITAIRE N° 57.984
Algérie, 1,30 din. ; Maroc, 1,60 dh ; Tunisie, 130 mil ; Espagne, 35 p. ; Italie, 350 lires ; Autriche, 12 sch. ; Belgique, 12 FB ; Luxembourg, 12 FL ; Portugal, 17 esc. ; Suisse, 0,90 FS ; Allemagne, 1 DM ; Grande-Bretagne, 20 p. ; Hollande, 1,25 FL ; Canada, $ 0,75.

LE FIGARO

« SANS LA LIBERTÉ DE BLAMER, IL N'EST PAS D'ÉLOGE FLATTEUR » BEAUMARCHAIS.

sommaire

Sondage Figaro-Sofres à 18 jours des élections

Stagnation de l'électorat

Majorité 45 %, opposition 50 %

En dépit des efforts considérables des candidats de la majorité dans les circonscriptions, on constate, dix-huit jours avant le premier tour des élections législatives, une grande stagnation de l'électorat. C'est ce qui ressort du sondage SOFRES effectué pour le compte du « Figaro » entre le 14 et le 17 février. Comme au début de ce mois, les intentions de vote au premier tour donnent 45 % des suffrages à la majorité et 50 % à la gauche, les écologistes et divers centre gauche recueillent toujours 5 %.

Les variations à l'intérieur de chaque camp ne dépassent pas un point. Une si faible marge ne permet pas de conclure à une modification significative de la tendance. Ainsi, à la date du 21 février, le P.C. obtiendrait 21 % des voix contre 20 % le 7 février et, au sein de la majorité, le R.P.R. gagne également un point (22 contre 21).

Ces résultats ne portent donc pas à l'optimisme. Sans doute d'ici au 12 mars une fraction de l'électorat encore hésitante peut, étant donné l'importance de l'enjeu, rétablir l'équilibre en faveur de la majorité. Mais les possibilités se restreignent de jour en jour. Plus on approche du scrutin, plus les électeurs déclarent avoir fait pratiquement un choix définitif. Cette détermination est particulièrement élevée dans l'électorat communiste (92 %). Cependant, on compte encore 20 % d'électeurs socialistes potentiels qui sont susceptibles de changer d'avis. C'est dans leur direction que doivent porter les efforts.

Autre constatation : le sentiment des personnes interrogées rejoint progressivement les intentions de vote. Alors qu'au début de ce mois 45 % souhaitaient, au fond d'eux-mêmes, la victoire de la majorité et 43 % la victoire de la gauche, aujourd'hui la majorité et l'opposition sont à égalité (45 % pour chacune). De même, en ce qui concerne les pronostics, les deux camps sont à égalité (39 % pour chacun).

A ce jour, l'électorat reste donc figé sur les positions qui sont les siennes depuis cinq mois. La rupture de la gauche n'a pas permis à la majorité de combler son handicap. Elle semble, au contraire, l'avoir aggravé en permettant à François Mitterrand de prendre ses distances à l'égard des communistes.

Tout dépendra maintenant de la façon dont se fera le report des voix au second tour. Notre sondage montre que de mois en mois la discipline de vote est mieux observée, tant de la part des formations de la majorité que de celles de la gauche, avec toujours des réserves de la part des socialistes.

Deux hypothèses se présentent :

Dans la première, le transfert des voix s'effectue normalement et la majorité, eu égard à son lourd handicap, risque fort d'être battue.

Dans la seconde hypothèse, le transfert des voix se fait mal, par exemple si le P.C. refuse de se désister en faveur du P.S., ou si, au moment décisif, une partie de l'électorat de gauche n'observait pas les consignes. La majorité pourrait alors disposer de plus de sièges que la gauche. A cet égard, les dernières élections partielles d'Issy-les-Moulineaux et de Chennevières permettent quelques espoirs.

On entre ici dans le domaine de l'insondable. Tout pronostic est d'une grande fragilité. C'est la raison pour laquelle nous ne publions pas de simulations pour la répartition des sièges. Comme l'observe la SOFRES, les modèles de simulations qui permettent de passer des voix aux sièges sont des modèles probabilistes qui prennent en compte un certain nombre de mouvements contradictoires, mais posent comme hypothèse que ces mouvements se compenseront. Or ces conditions sont rarement remplies dans la réalité. « A fortiori », il n'est pas admissible de prétendre obtenir, à partir de tels modèles, des résultats au niveau de chaque circonscription.

Charles REBOIS.

Page 4 : nos tableaux et notre analyse

Les Français à l'heure du choix

17 Les jeunes : le rêve d'abord

Page 2 : l'enquête de Bernard BONILAURI

Raymond Barre à « L'Événement » :

La gauche paierait le S.M.I.C. à 2.400 F en monnaie de singe

Raymond Barre — qui n'aime pas le mot optimisme — « a le sentiment que la majorité peut l'emporter et l'emportera ». Et ce sentiment il a tenu à le faire partager, hier, soir, à l'opinion publique en participant, sur TF 1, à l'émission « L'Événement ».

S'élevant au-dessus des querelles de partis tout en prenant toutes ses responsabilités dans le combat électoral, le premier ministre s'est attaché à préciser les grandes lignes de « la politique de progrès, d'équilibre et de raison » qui sera suivie après le succès de la majorité, c'est-à-dire de tous ceux qui ne veulent pas l'application du programme commun.

Mais Raymond Barre a aussi longuement parlé en ministre des Finances rappelant que le programme de Blois prévoit une pause des charges sociales et fiscales. Le S.M.I.C. à 2 400 F ? Oui mais à condition qu'il ne soit pas versé en monnaie de singe. Réduire les inégalités ? Oui mais « je suggère qu'on ne se lance pas dans une improvisation fiscale avec un impôt sur les grandes fortunes ».

Interrogé enfin sur son rôle par rapport aux formations de la majorité, Raymond Barre a dit clairement : « Je ne vois pas pourquoi je prendrais la tête d'une tendance. Un bon nombre de Français ne le souhaite pas. Cela dit, l'organisation des deux grands courants de la majorité était nécessaire, utile et souhaitable. Et pourquoi n'aurai-je pas de sympathie pour l'U.D.F. qui marque son soutien au président de la République et au gouvernement ? Ce que je souhaite, a encore dit Raymond Barre, c'est l'entente et l'ouverture de la majorité. »

« C'est essentiellement sur le bon sens des Français que je compte lorsque je dis que l'issue des législatives sera favorable à la majorité. »

D'entrée de jeu, Raymond Barre a réaffirmé sa confiance quant à l'issue du scrutin des 12 mars et 19 mars. Il est convaincu que *« l'effort de réflexion des Français les conduit à modifier les positions qu'ils avaient pu arrêter par idéologie ou mauvaise humeur »*.

Le premier ministre conçoit qu'il y ait du mécontentement chez ses compatriotes, mais si dans un premier temps, ils tendent à imputer les difficultés au gouvernement, *« quand ils réfléchissent, ils comprennent que ce sont des problèmes d'ordre international qui sont à l'origine de nos difficultés »*.

Interrogé sur le franc, Raymond Barre reprend les arguments qu'il avait eu l'occasion de développer à la sortie de l'Elysée : « Le franc se tient [illegible] », réaffirme-t-il *(voir page 3)*.

Quant aux innombrables comptes en Suisse dont se gargarise Georges Marchais, cela n'émeut pas le premier ministre qui croit plus au secret bancaire suisse qu'à tout ce qui peut être avancé sans preuves.

« M. Marchais ressemble de plus en plus à Ali Baba, il a de l'argent partout », dira-t-il, avant de redevenir plus grave pour affirmer qu'une des responsabilités des hommes politiques est de *« conduire le changement »*.

« La majorité ne doit pas se borner à critiquer le Programme commun, mais tenir compte de ce qu'il avait de désir d'espérances. Nous ne devons pas nous contenter de gérer la crise, mais adapter la France aux temps nouveaux. »

Evolution qui, selon le chef du gouvernement, doit être conduite *« raisonnablement »*.

Le premier ministre affiche ensuite sa confiance de voir le franc se stabiliser et avoir une bonne tenue sur le marché des changes. Citant les propos du chef de l'Etat, Raymond Barre dit : *« Le franc n'est pas malade de l'économie mais de la politique. »*

Raymond Barre pense qu'au lendemain des élections, beaucoup d'entreprises qui depuis plusieurs mois hésitaient, se décideront à investir. Le premier ministre se prononce pour la relance par l'investissement productif des entreprises et contre la relance par la consommation.

En septembre 1975 il y a eu une relance mais six mois après, le franc est sorti du serpent monétaire européen, les rémunérations se sont emballées.

« Il ne faut pas poser le problème en termes de relance, il faut doser les stimulants. » En septembre 1976 on a dit, « ce sera la récession » or, en 1977, nous avons soutenu la consommation des ménages.

(Suite page 3, col. 1 à 3.)

Page 3 : l'article d'Antoine-Pierre MARIANO

Page 31 : l'article d'André FROSSARD

Création d'un commissariat à l'énergie solaire

Le soleil, énergie de l'an 2000

Le Conseil des ministres doit décider ce matin de créer un Commissariat à l'énergie solaire (C.E.S.). Cet organisme, dont le schéma devrait être calqué sur celui du Commissariat à l'énergie atomique, sera appelé à jouer un rôle capital dans les années à venir. En outre, le C.E.S. reprendra les attributions de la Délégation aux énergies nouvelles.

On ne doit plus rire de l'énergie solaire. Il y a trente-trois ans, quand le gouvernement français a créé le Commissariat à l'énergie atomique, personne n'imaginait qu'un jour les centrales nucléaires civiles deviendraient l'un des atouts majeurs pour le développement économique des vingt dernières années du siècle.

Avec le Commissariat à l'énergie solaire, les pouvoirs publics font un pari d'une ampleur au moins similaire. Car, le soleil ne restera plus longtemps une curiosité, propriété de l'Internationale des professeurs Nimbus.

Certes, dans l'immédiat, il y a peu à attendre du soleil. Mais, si l'on dispose un jour d'une énergie inépuisable et très bon marché, on le devra à l'énergie solaire. Les experts sont, en effet, persuadés que, dans quelques dizaines d'années, nous saurons reproduire et contrôler des réactions thermonucléaires analogues à celles qui se déroulent sans fin dans l'astre solaire.

Ainsi, au bout du compte, l'antagonisme que montent en épingle les écologistes entre l'énergie solaire et l'énergie nucléaire disparaîtra. Et vers l'an 2000, le Commissariat à l'énergie solaire pourra absorber le C.E.A...

L'humanité s'engage ainsi dans une curieuse aventure. Au moins pendant encore cinquante ans, le monde va cruellement manquer d'énergie. Mais après, ce sera l'Eldorado. Et les premiers pas de l'énergie solaire vont nous familiariser avec une nouvelle source de chaleur et d'électricité qui deviendra progressivement prépondérante.

Cela dit, il y a énergie solaire et énergie solaire. Il ne faut pas confondre capteurs, plans et cellules photovoltaïques, ni les centrales solaires avec les moteurs solaires.

Christian GUÉRY.

(Suite page 10, col. 6 à 8.)

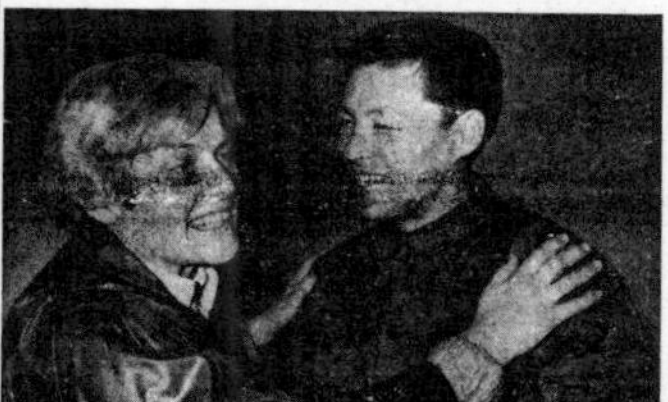

Le 7 novembre dernier, on le sait, une étudiante française, Odile Pierquin, épousait à Pékin M. Tian Li. Les amoureux de Pékin sont arrivés, hier, à Roissy. Ci-dessus : Mme Pierquin embrasse son gendre pour la première fois. La France est aussi le pays du sourire.

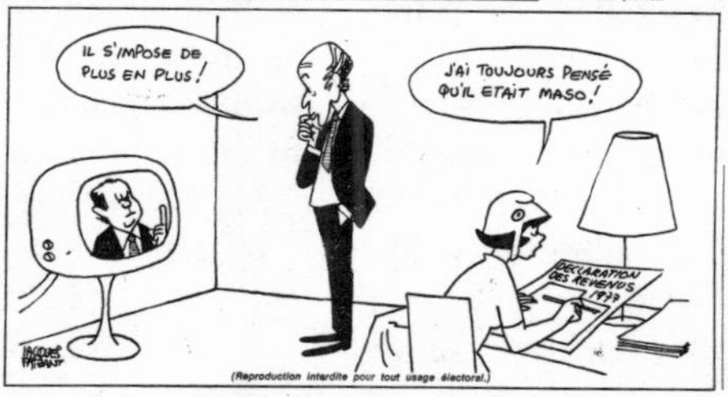

(Reproduction interdite pour tout usage électoral.)

CAVALIER SEUL

Utiles

LES nouveaux philosophes, invités au Mexique, et qui semblent déçus, craignent que leurs discours « ne soient utilisés d'un côté ou de l'autre ».

N'est-ce pas le sort de tout discours utile d'être utilisé un jour ou l'autre ? On espère que nos jeunes et brillants intellectuels ne décideront pas pour autant de tenir désormais des discours inutilisables, comme la philosophie n'a que trop tendance à en produire.

Mais on peut apaiser leurs craintes : ils ont fait entendre une voix, plus nouvelle que leur philosophie, qui du reste n'existe pas encore, et c'est une voix juste, qui dit vrai.

Qu'ils persistent avec le même courage à se montrer ainsi véridiques, et ils auront la surprise de s'apercevoir bientôt que leurs discours, de plus en plus utiles, seront de moins en moins utilisés.

André FROSSARD.

Dossier (page 15)

Le coup de Prague : les staliniens frappent et gagnent

PAR FRANÇOIS FEJTO

Liban : la force syrienne

Les violents accrochages de Fayadie ont irréversiblement remis en question la présence militaire syrienne au Liban. Les chrétiens supportent de plus en plus mal cette « occupation » et appellent maintenant cette armée de près de trente mille hommes une « force de frappe arabe ».

(Page 16 : la dépêche de Thierry DESJARDINS)

F.N.S.E.A. : 32e congrès

La Fédération nationale des syndicats d'exploitants agricoles tient aujourd'hui et demain, à Versailles, son 32e congrès. La principale organisation paysanne qui se dit forte de 650 000 adhérents paysans, va, pendant quarante-huit heures, réfléchir sur la « démocratie économique ».

(Page 9)

Légumes : bientôt la baisse

Après la flambée des prix enregistrée depuis une semaine en raison des températures, les professionnels prévoient, sans doute pour la fin de cette semaine, un retour des cours à la normale. Les légumes restent abondants, la température s'adoucit, toutes raisons pour voir baisser les prix sur les étiquettes.

(Page 9)

Demain, notre supplément "L'immobilier-bureau"

La politique étrangère et les élections

Deux camps coupés en deux...

PAR PAUL-MARIE DE LA GORCE

VICTOIRE posthume du général de Gaulle, le mot « indépendance » s'est imposé semble-t-il au vocabulaire de tous les partis. Il est loin le temps où il attirait au contraire le mépris des esprits forts, l'aversion des fanatiques de la supranationalité, les mines offusquées des orthodoxes de l'atlantisme ou la fureur des adversaires éternels de la politique nucléaire française. L'acquit de la politique étrangère menée jusqu'en 1974 est tel qu'il était presque impossible que cette politique fût alors abandonnée et qu'il serait presque inimaginable qu'elle le fût demain. C'est sans doute la raison de la faible place de la politique étrangère dans les controverses électorales.

Il est vrai que, des communistes aux giscardiens, en passant par les socialistes et le R.P.R. on récuse la politique des blocs, l'alignement sur les hégémonies, l'esprit de guerre froide. Dans ses derniers entretiens télévisés, le président de la République a tenu sur ce point des propos incontestables.

Personne n'ose envisager un retour de la France au sein de l'O.T.A.N. : les communistes accusent volontiers le gouvernement de s'y préparer discrètement; mais ils sont mal informés ou cèdent à la tentation de la polémique, et si l'un d'eux devenait ministre des Armées ou de l'armement, il constaterait qu'en dépit des propos officiels, mais contradictoires et ambigus, tenus en 1976, les directions ont été maintenues rigoureusement y compris pour la doctrine d'emploi, les plans et le déploiement des forces françaises.

De même ne pourrait-on remettre en cause ni les références aux motions des Nations unies sur le Proche-Orient, ni le principe du droit à l'existence de tous les Etats de la région, ni l'appui donné à l'idée de patrie palestinienne. Quant aux progrès de l'Europe, ils ne sont conçus, en principe, que sans restriction pour l'indépendance nationale. L'Afrique fut, certes, le principal terrain des désaccords. Mais ceux-ci ne sont-ils pas en train de s'atténuer ? Les erreurs des responsables français après la visite de M. Giscard d'Estaing à Alger ont été critiquées, et leurs conséquences inévitables sur les exportations françaises ont été dénoncées, mais nul ne peut nier les efforts faits aujourd'hui par Paris pour rétablir de bonnes relations avec l'Algérie et chacun en souhaite le succès. On a pu regretter — ou stigmatiser — l'appui donné à la Mauritanie et au Maroc dans l'affaire du Sahara occidental, par des ventes d'armes, ou par une assistance technique.

Mais le gouvernement actuel veut manifestement en revenir à plus de neutralité et une autre équipe ne pourrait, du jour au lendemain, sacrifier la coopération de la France avec Rabat et Nouakchott. De même, tous les gouvernements français, tout en proclamant leur volonté passionnée d'indépendance ne pourraient qu'essayer de maintenir des relations cordiales avec les Etats-Unis et aucun ne voudra compromettre le dialogue direct et privilégié entre Paris et Moscou qui demeure aujourd'hui l'une des principales cartes de la politique étrangère française.

Mais ces convergences ne doivent pas dissimuler les nuances ou les désaccords. Et c'est au sein de chacun des camps opposés que l'on peut le mieux les discerner. Laissons de côté les homélies habituelles aux socialistes et aux communistes sur la politique de désarmement : ce n'est pas parce que l'on enverra des diplomates français séjourner dans les hôtels de Genève et de Vienne pour prendre part aux interminables conférences qui s'y traînent, que cela sera de la moindre efficacité.

(Suite page 4, col. 1 à 3.)

After Villemessant, *Le Figaro* passed through a number of editorships: Francis Magnard, Fernand de Rodays, Antonin Périvier, Gaston Calmette, Alfred Capus, and Robert de Flers. In 1922 the paper fell victim to François Coty's venture into journalism. A millionaire cosmetics manufacturer, Coty bought the paper and used it to support him in his political adventures. Until after his death in 1934 the paper declined; however, his ex-wife (Mme. Yvonne Cotnareanu) took over and gave the editorship to Pierre Brisson, Lucien Romier, and Pierre Lafitte who were capable journalists and who built the paper into one of the best in pre-World War II France. A critique of the European press by an American scholar in 1937 referred to *Le Figaro* as "particularly well written, giving much attention to literary and theatrical affairs."[7]

Shortly before Hitler's armies swept through France in 1939, *Le Figaro* was established as the leading morning paper of the country and while its circulation was not a record one, it had prestige and an impressive array of by-lines. In 1940, when Paris fell to the Germans, Pierre Brisson, who was then the top editor, moved the paper to Lyons in the unoccupied zone and continued publication under the Petain regime. He had decided to stop circulation of *Le Figaro* as early as November, 1942, rather than be forced by the Vichy Government and the German censorship to express opinions that he knew would be hostile to the majority of his readers. Even while the German garrison and the Gestapo were still active in Paris in August, 1944, *Le Figaro* resumed publication.[8]

The period 1945 through 1950 was one of the high-water marks in the paper's history; its circulation reached almost 450,000. It was also during this period that *Le Figaro* began a campaign against the rapid growth of Communism in France. François Mauriac, *Le Figaro* columnist and outstanding novelist, launched a daily attack on *L'Humanité,* Communist organ and a leading Paris paper at the time.[9] *Figaro* also was backing a movement to bring General de Gaulle back into power. In 1946, it was called the "favorite paper of the Frenchman who believes himself to be an enlightened liberal." By 1947, however, it was being called "conservative."[10] Since then, *Le Figaro* has generally been considered conservative and the chief representative of the French *bourgeoisie*. It has been pro-United States, except at certain times when de Gaulle veered antagonistically away from American politics.

From the conclusion of World War II, *Le Figaro*'s prestige and circulation rose steadily until it began to run into strikes and ownership problems in the late 1960's. By 1968, it was considered one of the best dailies in Europe and it was circulating close to a half-million copies to leading Frenchmen in every part of the nation and in many parts of the world. Writing in 1950, Theodore H. White said that *Le Figaro* "combines the widest coverage of world news with elegantly written prose and distinguished by-lines."[11] In 1958, it was called the

[7] Robert Desmond, *The Press and World Affairs* (New York: Appleton-Century-Crofts, 1937), p. 217.
[8] Brisson controlled the paper and ignored Mme. Cotnareanu's attempts to oust him. In 1950, she sold half her stock to a pro-Brisson group headed by Jean Prouvost.
[9] J. Alvarez del Vayo, "Who's Who in the French Press," *The Nation* (June 22, 1946), pp. 745–747.
[10] E. Putman, "Press in Europe," *New Republic* (November 3, 1947), p. 35.
[11] Theodore White, *The Reporter* (November 7, 1950), p. 28.

"bible of France's upper-middle class" and was praised for its foreign news, music, literary and theater coverage.[12] In 1964, John Hohenberg of Columbia University praised its foreign coverage, calling it "thoughtful and well-ordered,"[13] and in 1966 Kenneth Olson alluded to its "excellent foreign coverage and backgrounding" and called it the "most influential" of the French dailies, particularly with the upper-middle class.[14] *Le Figaro* was France's only daily to cover the Jack Ruby trial in Texas and the only one to send a reporter on President Johnson's trip to Southeast Asia in 1966.

In the 1960's, *Le Figaro*'s contributors included some of France's most famous literary figures, among them François Mauriac, Paul Claudel, and Georges Duhamel. Its special weekly literary edition, *Le Figaro Littéraire*, was generally considered the finest such paper in Europe. It also claimed outstanding writers from specialized fields, such as economist André Siegfried and political writer Raymond Aron. The latter, who was with *Le Figaro* for about 30 years, was France's most respected political columnist.

Then, late in 1968, the paper's staff-management problems struck the first time. Jean Prouvost, France's largest manufacturer of woolen goods and owner of *Paris-Match* and *Paris-Soir,* bought financial control of *Figaro* in 1949. Since Prouvost had collaborated with the Vichy regime during World War II, Gaullists and leftists had banded together when he purchased the paper to keep him out of its editorial affairs. The agreement had given editor Pierre Brisson and *Le Figaro*'s editorial and reportorial staff of 250 full control of the paper's contents. Then, when Brisson died in 1964, Prouvost began to assert his rights as owner to run his own paper. The editorial staff resisted, and the mounting tension broke into a one-day strike in 1968, a strike that marked the first time the paper had missed an edition in its 102-year history. To get the paper back in production, Prouvost offered the editorial workers a weak voice in management—an arrangement that left the strikers disgruntled at best, but kept the paper operating until 1969.[15]

The argument over editorial control of *Le Figaro* broke into the open again in May, 1969, when Prouvost refused to allow the editorial "leasing company" enough votes to give them veto power on the paper's board of directors. This time, there was a long and spectacular strike, followed by litigation by both the leasing company and the French Journalists' Association, until the court recognized the rights of the editors and named a receiver for *Le Figaro*. Finally, in 1971, Prouvost and the Association of Journalists of *Le Figaro* agreed to operation of the paper by two companies, one to tend to ownership matters and the other to editorial affairs. This arrangement worked until 1975, when another change—and more trouble—struck *Le Figaro*.[16]

When, in 1975, conservative, aging owner Jean Prouvost (he died in Octo-

---

[12] Jean Gênet, "Letter from Paris," *New Yorker* (October 4, 1958), p. 108.
[13] John Hohenberg, *Foreign Correspondence* (New York: Columbia University Press, 1964), p. 445.
[14] Kenneth Olson, *The History Makers* (Baton Rouge: Louisiana State U. Press, 1966), p. 193.
[15] "Figaro's Prerogatives," *Time* (October 25, 1968), pp. 70–72.
[16] Jean Schwoebel, *Newsroom Democracy: The Case for Independence of the Press,* Monograph, (Iowa City: Iowa Center for Communication Study, 1976), pp. 45–47.

ber, 1978), in need of cash, sold *Le Figaro* to Robert Hersant, the news personnel at the paper went on a one-day protest strike. They opposed Hersant's takeover on several grounds. He had been convicted of collaborating with the
Germans during the Occupation. For ten years, after the war, he had been the
leader of an anti-Semitic youth group. He had used questionable means to build
his publishing empire of 12 dailies, 9 provincial papers, 11 magazines, a news
agency and 6 modern printing plants. More frightening, when he had acquired
the regional newspaper *Paris-Normandie* with the aid of government (as was
the case with his purchase of *Le Figaro*) after bribing its stockholders, he had
destroyed the paper's journalists' association.[17] Finally, they feared he would
use the paper for political ends and as a pro-government tool.

About the same time, other issues were plaguing the French press, and *Le
Figaro* in particular. With equipment aging, readership and advertising revenues falling off dramatically and the price of newsprint up, unions resisted any
changes that would result in dismissal of employees. Under these conditions,
newspaper chains were quickly formed, including Hersant's, and the *Le Figaro*
staff made this an issue in their fight, warning that such concentration meant
less diversity of information and, ultimately, less freedom of the press.

Developments since Hersant purchased *Le Figaro* in 1975 have vindicated
the paper's editorial staff's worst fears. He at once took control of the entire
paper, justifying his moves on falling readership, overstaffing, a printer's union
monopoly and a pressing need to modernize *Le Figaro* equipment. The battle
was drawn when Hersant, in the interests of cutting costs, brutally began making scores of *Le Figaro* journalists redundant and declared it was he who was
upholding press freedom by keeping *Figaro* afloat rather than those concerned
with editorial independence in the newsroom. Hersant's dual roles of publisher
and politician became more and more intertwined. In 1976, he strengthened his
hand still further by acquiring *France Soir* (circulation: 443,000), Paris's largest
afternoon daily.

The fight turned into open warfare in June, 1977, when the paper's long-
time managing editor, Jean d'Ormesson engaged the owner in a curious newspaper headline battle. One day d'Ormesson announced in *Le Figaro* he was
quitting because his authority had been usurped by Hersant. The next day, Hersant hit back with a front page attack "on self-serving prima donnas whom he
blamed for getting *Figaro* into the financial mess from which he had extricated
it over the past year."[18] The paper's top political commentator, Raymond Aron
quit with d'Ormesson, saying Hersant was taking on too much by becoming, at
the same time, *Figaro*'s owner, administrator, political director and editor while
also serving as a member of Parliament and campaigning in the 1978 elections.
By this time, Hersant had dismissed half of the paper's 400 journalists, many of
the paper's best, and was using *Figaro* as a political vehicle to help the ruling
center-right coalition win the 1978 elections and to keep himself in the National
Assembly. He took personal charge of *Figaro*'s pre-election coverage, featuring

[17] Lance Tapley, "Press Crisis in France," *The Nation* (August 2, 1975), pp. 82–3.
[18] "Figaro Shorn," *The Economist*, 263:6980 (June 11, 1977), p. 61.

himself and omitting any mention of his opponent in the paper and using the paper to defend the actions of the majority coalition.[19] At one point just before the elections, Hersant even issued a special edition of *Le Figaro* to be distributed as personal propaganda in his district.[20] At this point in time, there appears to be little doubt Hersant intends to turn his formerly moderate, independent paper into a propaganda organ of the Giscard regime.

Throughout the long war raging over its control and contents, the physical appearance of *Le Figaro* has not substantially changed. As has been the case for years, a typical issue consists of 32 standard-sized pages with the normal 8-column format. The front page contains several large headlines, followed by brief beginnings of stories which are then continued on the inside pages. Columns are frequently grouped two or three together, each containing several short articles which are continued inside. Most page one stories—there are typically eight or nine—are of national or international origin. Frequently stories carry a correspondent's by-line. One or two pictures, often a cartoon and a single advertisement also typically appear on the front page. The paper's name banner at the top of the front page is flanked by the paper's address on the left and by an index to its inner contents on the right. In general, the front page appears serious, gray, reserved, even a trifle dull.

Page two contains features or stories on France, plus advertising. Throughout the paper, pages are given heading titles according to key subjects treated. Near the beginning, there are usually several pages on French and European politics and on economic affairs in the region. Single pages featuring Paris news, religion, medicine, sports, women, commentary and reader feedback entitled "Le Figaro Dialogue" occupy the paper's early and middle portions. Foreign articles appear after the national and economic news, now buried somewhat deeper in the paper than formerly. There is a page for deaths, births and other announcements, another on society news and still other pages with articles on high culture and education. Several pages are given to entertainment. Usually there is a page of news and features on the cinema, music and the theatre, another on art and literature and a third on television. Schedules for radio, television and individual cinemas are found among these pages.

An analysis of a randomly-selected week of *Le Figaro*'s contents indicates that, although it is known in France as an "information" paper, it gives considerable emphasis to political affairs. Foreign and economic news and the "high arts" (serious music, literature, art) also receive generous attention. Its many features are of a hybrid nature—a cross between editorials, commentaries, essays, and literary criticism and factual news accounts. In tone, the paper is very serious, although its rather haphazard use of headlines detracts somewhat from its generally dignified appearance. Pictures are employed sparsely throughout, some pages carrying none at all.

Since Hersant took ownership, the bulk of *Le Figaro*'s former staff has been replaced. Many of its writers and editors today are comparative unknowns, al-

[19] "Citoyen Hersant," *Time* (March 13, 1978), p. 100.
[20] Claude-Jean Bertrand, Université de Drioit d'Economie de Sciences Sociales de Paris, Paris, France, in letter to J. Merrill, dated March 1, 1978.

though its editor-in-chief is Max Clos, a former A.P. correspondent who covered the French-Indochina War and who has reported from most of the world's hot spots during the past quarter century. *Le Figaro*'s circulation has dropped steadily since Hersant's takeover in 1975. At that time, circulation figures were about 400,000. Two years later, circulation stood at about 350,000, and in 1978, one source indicates the count has fallen to about 223,000.[21] However, the paper's advertising revenues have been rising and today it is "more than ever the newspaper which carries the biggest share of real estate advertising."[22] An opinion poll in the French news magazine *Le Point* late in February, 1978, "showed that *Le Figaro* has just about the most homogeneous readership any Paris paper has: well-to-do and pro-"majorité" (Giscardians, Gaullists and centrists).[23]

Today, *Le Figaro,* once Paris' finest morning paper and one of Europe's best, finds itself barely holding its own among the world's quality newspapers. Its future standing as a quality paper lies in the outcome of its present internal struggle between a powerful press lord with political ambitions and those who desire *Le Figaro*'s editorial integrity and independence.

Frankfurter Allgemeine

(WEST GERMANY)

WITHIN A REMARKABLY SHORT TIME, the *Frankfurter Allgemeine Zeitung* ("Frankfurt General Newspaper") has become "West Germany's most prestigious daily, with an international reputation for seriousness and thoroughness."[1] Its 30-year history has in many respects paralleled and reflected the recovery and development of the nation. Commonly designated the *F.A.Z.,* the paper presents some of the most responsible reporting, weighty content, neat and orderly makeup and serious and dignified journalism found anywhere in the world. When compared with Germany's other national dailies—*Die Welt, Süddeutsche Zeitung* and *Frankfurter Rundschau*—it can claim both the best national and international distribution. What is more, *F.A.Z.* may be the country's most influential paper, for it is estimated some 90 percent of its readers are the most important decision-makers in Germany's thriving and expanding economy.[2]

[21] "Citoyen Hersant," *op. cit.,* p. 100.
[22] Christopher Henze, Paris, in letter to H. Fisher, dated March 15, 1978.
[23] Bertrand letter, *loc. cit.*
[1] John Sandford, *The Mass Media of the German-Speaking Countries* (London: Oxwald Wolf Publishers, Ltd., 1976), p. 211.
[2] *Ibid.*

Frankfurter Allgemeine

ZEITUNG FÜR DEUTSCHLAND

D 2954 A

Mittwoch, 22. Februar 1978, Nr. 43 D-Ausgabe   Herausgegeben von Bruno Dechamps, Jürgen Eick, Fritz Ullrich Fack, Joachim Fest, Johann Georg Reißmüller, Erich Welter   1 DM

Nato-Staaten legen in Belgrad eigenen Entwurf vor

V. M. BELGRAD, 21. Februar. Die Belgrade Folgekonferenz von Helsinki ist in ihre endgültige Schlußphase getreten. Den Anstoß dazu gab am Montag die zum Schluß genommen war, daß die „Stunde der Wahrheit" angebrochen sei und entsprechend „markiert" werden müsse. Der Schweizer Delegierte Brunner erklärte zur allgemeinen Überraschung in der Plenarsitzung, ein Konferenz habe drei Möglichkeiten eines Schlußdokumentes. Die eine sei das „substantielle" Dokument gewesen, das sowohl die westlichen wie die neutralen Delegationen gewünscht hätten, aber das wegen der sowjetischen Weigerung offensichtlich nicht realisierbar sei. Die zweite Möglichkeit sei den Mißerfolg mit einigen nichtssagenden Floskeln und hohlen Formulierungen zuzudecken. Die dritte sollte sonst als dritte Möglichkeit nur, ein kurzes Dokument festzustellen, das im „nackter" Form nichts anderes als die Tatsache der stattfindenden Konferenz festhalte. Diese sei kein „Vorschlag", sondern nüchterne Eingeständnis der entstandenen Situation.

Ehrenberg sucht für die Rentenversicherung neue Beitragszahler

Die freiwillig Versicherten sollen regelmäßig einzahlen / Forderungen des DGB

Kg. BONN, 21. Februar. Bundesarbeitsminister Ehrenberg will mit dem geplanten Rentenanpassungsgesetz auch weitreichend in die freiwillige Versicherung eingreifen. Dies geht aus dem Referentenentwurf hervor, der den interessierten Verbänden und Organisationen zur Stellungnahme zugeleitet worden ist. Versicherte, die von den Möglichkeiten der freiwilligen Versicherung, so wie sie 1972 eingeführt worden, Gebrauch machen, sollen künftig mit ihren Beiträgen nur dann dynamische Rentenansprüche erwerben, wie sie regelmäßige Beiträge entrichten. Beitragsansprüche, die nicht auf einer regelmäßigen Beitragszahlung beruhen, sollen nicht mehr an den regelmäßigen Rentenanpassungen teilnehmen. Damit hat Ehrenberg Forderungen entsprochen, die seit langem im Deutschen Gewerkschaftsbund, in jüngster Zeit auch im sozialdemokratischen Lager erhoben werden. Dabei ist das heutige Recht der freiwilligen Versicherung maßgeblich 1972 von der SPD/FDP-Koalition geschaffen worden. Im einzelnen ist folgende vorgesehen: Für die bisher geleisteten freiwilligen Beiträge wird ein

[... Fortsetzung Seite 2]

Andreottis Regierungsverhandlungen kommen nur mühsam voran

Gegensätze in der Steuer- und Lohnpolitik / Kommunisten fordern Polizeigewerkschaft

Vo. ROM, 21. Februar. Die Verhandlungen des mit der Regierungsbildung beauftragten bisherigen christlichdemokratischen Ministerpräsidenten Andreotti über das Regierungsprogramm, die mit den stützenwerdenden Sekretären und Fachleuten der ersten Partien am Montag begannen, kommen nur mühsam voran. Es besteht aber der Eindruck, daß die Entscheidung erst in der nächsten Woche fallen wird und auch die Einberufung des christlichdemokratischen Parlamentsfraktionen und des christlichdemokratischen Parteivorstandes bis dahin verschieben wird.

Sadat ordnet Schließung der ägyptischen Botschaft in Nikosia an

Kein Abbruch der Beziehungen / Gegenseitige Vorwürfe wegen der Geiselbefreiung

HJK. ATHEN, 21. Februar. Nach den Kämpfen zwischen aus Ägypten eingeflogenen Kommandotruppen und Nationalgardisten Zyperns am Sonntag auf dem Flugplatz in Larnaka hat Präsident Sadat die Schließung der ägyptischen Botschaft in Nikosia angeordnet.

Ein Rundfunksender prozessiert gegen sich selbst   Seite 2

Für mehr Bundeskompetenzen im Bildungswesen

MÜNCHEN, 21. Februar (dpa). Der FDP-Bundesvorsitzende und Bundeswirtschaftsminister Graf Lambsdorff hat für eine Bundeskompetenzen im Bildungswesen kämpfen.

Groß: Niedersachsens FDP kein Mehrheitsbeschaffer für Schmidt

HANNOVER, 21. Februar (Reuter). Die niedersächsische FDP sieht es nach vor Worten ihres Landesvorsitzenden Groß nicht als erste Aufgabe an, die SPD/FDP-Regierung in Bonn zu stützen.

Prag soll politische Häftlinge freilassen

PARIS, 21. Februar (dpa). Zum Jahrestag der kommunistischen Machtübernahme in der Tschechoslowakei haben 33 Schriftsteller, Künstler und Gelehrte für die Freilassung der Tschechoslowaken Vaclav Havel und das Journalisten Jiri Lederer sowie eine Amnestie für politische Häftlinge in der Tschechoslowakei plädiert.

Mitglied einer internationalen Helsinki-Gruppe verhaftet

MOSKAU, 21. Februar (dpa). In der ukrainischen Hauptstadt Kiew ist am 15. Februar der 52 Jahre alte Physiker Pjotr Wins, ein Mitglied der Moskauer Bürgerrechtler-Friedensgruppe, verhaftet worden.

Warschauer „Nebenuniversität" eröffnet zweites Semester

hs. WARSCHAU, 21. Februar. In Warschau ist jetzt das zweite Semester der Vorlesungen der „Gesellschaft für wissenschaftliche Kurse" — jener Bürgerinitiative, die es sich zum Ziel gesetzt hat, die Lücken des offiziellen akademischen Lehrbetriebs zu füllen.

Assad bei Breschnew

MOSKAU, 21. Februar (AP). Der sowjetische Staats- und Parteichef Breschnew hat am Dienstag Regierungschef Assad von Syrien zu Gesprächen empfangen.

Nichts dazugelernt

Kg. Die Rentenanwärter haben nichts dazugelernt. Anstatt sich darauf zu bedenken, den Rentenausgaben den verfügbaren Einnahmen anzugleichen, wird versucht, immer mehr Bürger der Beitragspflicht zur Rentenversicherung zu unterwerfen.

Apels neues Geschirr

Von Karl Feldmeyer

Für die Bundeswehr hat ein neuer Abschnitt begonnen. Der neue Verteidigungsminister Apel ist der erste in diesem Amt, der den Zweiten Weltkrieg nicht als Soldat erlebt hat.

Like hundreds of other German journals, the *F.A.Z.* came into being in the early post-World War II period when the new German Federal Republic was being shaped. Unlike many other German newspapers, the *F.A.Z.*, put together by many of the staff of the great pre-war *Frankfurter Zeitung,* had some continuity with the past. Unlike several German papers, too (such as *Die Welt*), it did not take on the journalistic styles of occupation armies, but remained—and still remains—distinctively German in its makeup.

The *Frankfurter Allgemeine* appeared for the first time on November 1, 1949, very shortly after the Occupation Forces lifted licensing of German newspapers. During the licensing period, numerous small regional or local papers (Heimatpresse) had sprung up, but there was no daily of national scope in central Germany until *F.A.Z.* came along to fill the gap. The new paper was launched by a consortium of dedicated journalists who had labored to make the pre-war revered old *Frankfurter Zeitung* the respected daily it was. The *Frankfurter Zeitung* had been closed down by Hitler in 1943 and many of its staff members had gathered in Mainz during the early occupation years to establish the *Allgemeine Zeitung* there. But, with the founding of *F.A.Z.*, they eagerly returned to Frankfurt-am-Main to work for the new paper. From the beginning, they sought to make *F.A.Z.* an independent newspaper designed "to work and speak—both inside and outside the country—for the whole of Germany."[3] Today, the paper's subtitle, "Newspaper for Germany," still reflects that aspiration.

The first edition of *F.A.Z.* defined the new paper's mission: "The truth of the facts must be sacred . . . strict objectivity in its coverage . . . fair treatment of opposing viewpoints . . . the preservation of the ideals of freedom and justice, which our profession shall serve."[4] An editorial in a later edition declared the paper's intentions even more succinctly:

> The object of the enterprise is to preserve the light of freedom from the many outside forces. We despise chauvinism; we don't place the nation above humanity! But we love equally as little the dishonorable role of national imprisonment. Mainly because we (the German people) do not recognize ourselves as Europeans, we need not be an inferior member in the European community. Germany cannot be excluded from the great ideals of freedom and justice.[5]

Although officially there has never been a connection between the famous pre-war *Frankfurter Zeitung* and *F.A.Z.*, the founders saw themselves as part of the fine traditions of the older paper. Even today, the staff remains proud of the connection, however tenuous, and in its promotional materials *F.A.Z.* continues to use the slogan "The young international newspaper with an old tradition." The relationship has always been reflected, too, in the appearance of *F.A.Z.* In 1949, the highly respected Swiss daily *Die Tat* noted the strong resemblance between the pre-war paper and *F.A.Z.*: ". . . its quiet, sophisticated and reserved

---

[3] *F.A.Z.: The Face of a German Newpaper (Frankfurter Allgemeine Zeitung,* n.d.), p. 6.
[4] Georg Bitter, *Zur Typologie des Deutschen Zeitungswesens in der Bundesrepublik Deutschland* (Munich; Eduard Pohl & Co., 1951), p. 68.
[5] *Ibid.,* p. 69.

layout . . . the inside pages with outstanding predominance of the intelligent, polished and learned commentaries of daily news and a quiet intellectual distance to other worldly matters—all this would remind one of the *Frankfurter Zeitung.*"[6] Today's gray front page, bare of any pictures or color, with its neat columns of dignified type continues to bear the resemblance, as do the serious in-depth approach to the news, the heavy content and the thoroughness of the inside pages. The reminder still persists, too, in some of today's headlines, which continue to use the old German gothic text type common in pre-Hitler Germany.[7]

Without a doubt, *F.A.Z.* is the heaviest and most serious in makeup and writing of any newspaper in Germany today. With the possible exception of Switzerland's *Neue Zürcher Zeitung* and France's *Le Monde,* there are no dailies in the world more staid in appearance or academic in content. Although the *Frankfurther Allgemeine* does use some pictures on its inside pages, they are small. Stories rather than photographs and large headlines dominate the *F.A.Z.* Pages and pages of closely set type under conservative headlines face the reader. Stories laden with excellent content are presented in horizontal rectangles for easy reading. Thus, the dress and contents of *F.A.Z.* both reflect the paper's total character of seriousness and thoroughness.

Probably no other daily in the world is as well organized as F.A.Z. The editors have devised a master plan for the makeup and content of every page, even down to small details. Furthermore, the paper follows the plan consistently, though not inflexibly. Because of this pre-planning, the readers of *F.A.Z.* can predict with a high degree of accuracy just where in the paper they can find certain types of articles. Almost invariably, the main part of the paper is divided into three main sections or "books" every day: politics, economics and *feuilleton.* These three divisions of *F.A.Z.* total between 20 and 32 pages on work weekdays, with the political and economics sections usually running less than 12 pages each. A breakdown by percentages of the contents of the F.A.Z. gives further insight into the emphasis given each section. National and international news accounts for 13 percent of the paper's total volume and editorials and analysis another 7 percent; business news occupies 12 percent and sports another 3 percent; and the *feuilleton* section 8 percent. About 50 percent of all space is filled by advertising and the remaining 7 percent by features and entertainment materials.[8] Supplements, special sections or advertising flyers are added to this initial three-book paper, especially on weekends, but never inserted between the books. Thus, the paper's predictable order remains intact.

F.A.Z. gives high priority to its first section, which carries political news from Germany and the world-at-large, but it is careful to separate facts from opinion. On the front page, the first four left-hand columns of the six-column page contain the leading news items of the day, with the biggest story placed in the extreme left-hand column. The political editorials for the day occupy the two

[6] *Ibid.*
[7] Reinhard Mundhenke, managing director, *Frankfurter Allgemeine Zeitung* in questionnaire and other typed information sent January 26, 1978.
[8] Mundhenke questionnaire.

right-hand columns and usually run the length of the page. The editorials are headlined in ornate old German gothic type. All headlines are small and accurately descriptive of stories' contents. About ten or a dozen stories appear on this front page, some of them continued later in the section. Editorials are by-lined with the writer's full name; stories are either initialled or left unsigned.

The second page of this "Politik" section presents an index to the paper's contents for the day, carryovers from the first page and additional stories from home and foreign correspondents. Most of "Politik's" pages are devoted to the day's significant national and international news. The first advertisement always runs across the bottom of page three. Every day, there is a page of "faits divers" under the page headline "Deutschland und die Welt," as well as "Briefe an die Herausbeber" (Letters to the Editor). From time to time, there is a documentary page entitled "Die Gegenwart" (The Present). The back page of this section (this page is always important in German papers) continues editorial opinion articles begun on the first page and presents a background article on a topic of political importance.

The paper's second major part, "Wirtschaft" or the economic section is made up typographically in a manner similar to "Politik." On the first page, an economic editorial appears every day next to the articles covering news and developments in the business and financial world, but the arrangement becomes a mirror image of the front page of "Politik." This time the editorials range down the left side of the page, key economic stories cover the middle columns and short economic news items the right-hand column. Several pages follow which thoroughly cover national and international economic problems and developments. The list of stock exchange quotations in this section is so comprehensive that it has become "must" reading for anyone wishing to be fully informed about the market. After several pages of advertising—this is where the bulk of the paper's advertisements are placed—the last two pages are given to sporting event news and background information.

The final main major part is the "Feuilleton" or arts pages section. In F.A.Z., it is dedicated to major reports on cultural subjects. usually this third section covers four to eight pages, and there are only a few articles—usually two to four—per page. A major cultural feature article occupies the first page of the section. Reviews of TV programs, movies, operas, and concerts and books and reports on art galleries and museums generally fill the inside pages of this section. These pages also feature a short chapter from a continued serial story. The last page of "Feuilleton" contains the daily television schedules, the weather forecast, and weather and celestial charts.

The weekend (Saturday) edition may expand to as many as 180 pages, with the same heavy emphasis on political, economic and cultural news and an added section, called "Bilder und Zeiten" (Pictures and Time). This section, printed on slick, high-grade paper, is one of the finest such sections found in a newspaper anywhere. It represents the lone F.A.Z. departure from its sombre, almost picture-less visage. It contains literary articles, book reviews, personality sketches, international reports, many fine photographs and other cultural materials. The only four-color advertisements carried by *F.A.Z.* appear in this section each week. Color in the *F.A.Z.* is confined to an occasional advertisement.

Other special supplementary sections are carried on certain days of the week. On Wednesdays, the *F.A.Z.* editorial staff regularly presents "Natur und Wissenschaft" (Nature and Science). Each Thursday, there is a travel supplement. Several times each year, a voluminous special literary supplement appears. A supplement entitled "Schallplatten und Phono" (Records and Phono) likewise puts in an appearance frequently. Special supplements on various countries are publishers in *F.A.Z.* at irregular intervals.

To prepare its excellent package of thorough and objectively reported and carefully written news, features, editorials, *feuilletons* and special sections, *Frankfurter Allgemeine* keeps a staff of 161 full-time editorial personnel. Most —105 of them—work in the paper's Frankfurt offices assigned to one of the paper's sections. Besides the editorial staff, *F.A.Z.* has 689 other employees working in administrative or managerial capacities. Since the paper contracts for its printing, it has no technical staff.

The *F.A.Z.* editorial staff is directed by an editorial management board composed of editors Erich Welter, Bruno Dechamps, Jürgen Eick, Fritz Ullrich Fack, Joachim Fest and Johann Georg Reissmüller and managing directors Reinhard Mundhenke and Hans Wolfgang Pfiefer.[9] This board makes cooperative decisions about the paper's editorial policies and daily content. In general this administrative arrangement has worked successfully, although there have been times of stress, even at the respectable *F.A.Z.* In 1970, for example, Jürgen Tern, then one of the paper's six-man publishing board, was dismissed when his editorials sympathized too strongly with Willy Brandt's "Ost-Politik" policies to suit the conservative tastes of editor Erich Welter.[10]

In the *F.A.Z.* organization, the person who holds the title of chief editor actually serves as a coordinator between the newsroom and technicians who make up the paper; thus, he does not have the functions usually held by a chief editor. The task with *F.A.Z.* includes editing, fitting and arranging stories and written materials in consultation with the newsroom and the technicians. A "chief correspondent" on the staff assigns stories to be covered and editorials to be written in a fashion akin to the functions of an assignment editor in an American television station newsroom.

Members of the paper's editorial management board prefer staff members who have a combination of academic training and practical experience. The overwhelming majority of *F.A.Z.* editors and correspondents hold university degrees. The *F.A.Z.* expects of its editorial and writing staff, besides good writing abilities, integrity, sincerity and good judgment.

The *F.A.Z.* excels in its foreign news coverage and interpretation, and its network of foreign reporters is unrivalled in Germany. It keeps a staff of 31 full-time foreign correspondents in 22 of the world's strategic urban centers outside

---

[9] Mundhenke questionnaire.
[10] "Ferment in Frankfurt," *Newsweek* (June 29, 1970), p. 56.

the Federal Republic and part-time stringers in 25 other important cities outside the country.[11] Between 50 and 60 percent of *F.A.Z.* foreign news stories are credited to its own correspondents—identified by the reporter's initials at the beginning of the story. The reportage of the *F.A.Z.* foreign staff is supplemented by the paper's receipt of news wire services from AP, DPA, Reuters and AFP. Many outstanding foreign correspondents have served *F.A.Z.*, among them Jan Reifenberg, Washington; Sabina Lietzmann and Hans Jürgensen, New York; Ulrich Grudinski, Hans-Joachim Rudolph and Karl Heinz Bohrer, London; Karl Jetter, Thankmar Frhr. v. Munchhausen and Andreas Graf Razumovsky, Paris; Leo Wieland, Moscow; Walter Haubrich, Madrid; and Josef Schmitz van Vorst, Rome.

F.A.Z. can also claim Germany's best corps of home correspondents. It maintains 25 full-time reporters in editorial bureaus in all the Federal Republic's land-capitals, including the national capital in Bonn. It does not cover the national capital with the saturation achieved by *Die Welt,* but its national news must be regarded as excellent.

Besides the paper's full-time staff, more than 450 journalists in various places in Germany and abroad are regular contributors. In addition, more than 500 specialists, reviewers, and critics are at the newspaper's disposal with contributions in their own fields.[12]

The *F.A.Z.* is organized as a non-profit, limited liability company (FAZIT-Stiftung) under the name Frankfurter Allgemeine Zeitung GmBH. The majority of the stocks of this publishing company are controlled by Professor Helmut Diederich, Jürgen Eick, Professor Walter Hamm and Professor Erich Welter. The board of publishers, composed of Bruno Dechamps, Jürgen Eick, Fritz Ullrich Fack, Joachim Fest, Johann George Reissmuller and Erich Welter, holds the *F.A.Z.* in trust. The remaining interest is held by two groups: the Frankfurter Allgemeine Zeitung GmBH itself and the Frankfurter Societäts-Druckerei GmBH. Throughout the financial crisis years of the mid-1970s, when much of the German press operated at a loss, the *F.A.Z.* managed to break even or make a profit, thus giving it financial independence.[13]

The *F.A.Z.*, which has a circulation of about 300,000 today (75 percent by subscription; the balance in street sales), can claim for itself "the nearest thing to a national distribution among the 'quality' dailies" of Germany. Although circulation is naturally heaviest in Frankfurt and its environs, distribution is fairly equal in the areas north and south of the Main River. About 10 percent of the circulation goes abroad. The editor of *F.A.Z.*, Dr. Erich Welter says that his paper is designed for the intelligensia, businessmen, politicians, academicians and educated people of all classes. It has a predominantly male readership. A 1976 readership analysis indicated the *F.A.Z.* has the best reach of all German-language daily and economic newspapers among the nation's opinion leaders

---

[11] Full-time *F.A.Z.* foreign correspondents are located in Athens, Brussels, Jerusalem, Johannesburg, Lisbon, London, Madrid, Moscow, Nairobi, New Delhi, New York, Paris, Peking, Rio de Janeiro, Rome, Stockholm, Sidney, Tokyo, Warsaw, Washington, Vienna and Zurich.

[12] *F.A.Z.: The Face of a German Newspaper, op. cit.,* p. 8.

[13] "German Papers on the Critical List," *Economist,* Vol. 254 (February 15, 1975), p. 43.

and decision-makers. A high proportion of the copies—some six percent—goes
to university students.[14]

Another mark of *Frankfurter Allgemeine*'s quality may be found in its international audience. One-tenth of each edition—some 30,000 copies—goes to
opinion-leaders and intelligensia in 130 countries of the world. A 1965 survey
showed that 31 percent of Swiss businessmen read the economic section regularly and another 31 percent occasionally. A 1963 *Time-Life* study of Common
Market countries found that 29 percent of the businessmen polled read *F.A.Z.*
regularly. Foreign readers have indicated the economic section is particularly
valuable to them. *F.A.Z.* has also been one of West Germany's most prominent
and most widely quoted papers in the foreign press.

Like most of the newspapers in modern West Germany, the *F.A.Z.* is unattached to any political party and takes pride in the fact that it speaks as an independent, often critical voice. It does lend its backing to politicians whose
policies it feels are worthy of support; for example, it was a strong supporter of
Konrad Adenauer.[15] Generally speaking, it might be termed "a paper of the
middle." Its staff considers its political point-of-view to be "center—with a liberal
touch (in the European sense)."[16] But another informed source terms it conservative and "right-wing—in particular, a determined advocate of private enterprise."[17] Whatever political position *F.A.Z.* may actually represent, its readers
can be certain the paper's primary interest is in providing what its editors call
"nonpartisan information." Perhaps Fritz Ullrich Fack, one of the paper's editors, stated the guiding editorial principle of *F.A.Z.* vis-a-vis politics and all
touchy issues most clearly: "Critical distance in all spheres."

In nearly every respect, the *Frankfurter Allgemeine* represents excellence
in quality journalism. Within Germany, its thorough economic coverage makes
it, in the eyes of many, the voice of German industry and business. Germans
also respect its thorough, astute political reportage and its enlightening *feuilletons*. Many Germans consider it "the most respected paper of really national influence."[18] And its reputation for being serious, thorough, reliable, respectable,
well written and reported, orderly—and a long list of other complimentary de-
scriptions that could be added—is international. One press critic rated *F.A.Z.*
". . . among the best in the world, offering a rich blend of news, interpretive
writing and cultural features seldom found in American papers."[19] Perhaps the
editors of *Newsweek* magazine came closest to summing up *Frankfurther Allgemeine*'s place and prestige as an elite newspaper when they wrote: "(It) has not
only earned a reputation as the most respected paper in its own country, but it is
often ranked as one of the ten best in the world."[20]

[14] Mundhenke questionnaire.
[15] Kenneth E. Olson, *The History Makers: The Press of Europe from its Beginnings through 1965*
   (Baton Rouge: Louisiana State University Press, 1966), p. 132.
[16] Mundhenke questionnaire.
[17] Sandford, *op. cit.*, p. 212.
[18] Olson, *op. cit.*, p. 129.
[19] M. L. Stein, "West Germany's Adversary Press," *Saturday Review* (May 8, 1971), p. 48.
[20] "Ferment in Frankfurt," *op. cit.*, p. 56.

The Globe and Mail

(CANADA)

BESIDES HAVING THE USUAL journalistic qualities characteristic of an elite newspaper, Toronto's *Globe and Mail* receives renown and respect unapproached by
any other Canadian paper. It comes closest to being a national newspaper of all
Canadian dailies. It is the nation's best-known daily. With over 263,000 copies
sold each day, it claims the country's largest morning circulation. Its editorials
and news stories are highly respected, widely quoted and frequently reprinted in
the remainder of the Canadian press and elsewhere outside the country. It is
Canada's most influential paper among leaders in civic and professional circles.
Because of these reasons, *The Times* of London has called *The Globe and Mail*
the only newspaper which is capable of "setting the tone of newspaper play" on
a national basis in Canada.[1]

Although its circulation is concentrated mainly in the central south and
southeast, *The Globe and Mail* is designed to appeal to readers in all parts of
Canada's vast expanse. Jet air service makes it obtainable on newsstands across
the nation on the day of publication. This rapid delivery allows it to be an important source for smaller papers about the country. The *Canadian Press,* a national news-gathering agency, frequently picks up its front page stories and
distributes them to other Canadian newspapers with credit given to *The Globe
and Mail.* The paper today maintains more out-of-province and out-of-country
bureaus and subscribes to more news services than any other Canadian paper.
It publishes its own weekly magazine and an international airmail edition. The
latter, which replaces the former "Overseas Edition," covers an additional
32,000 subscribers from coast to coast. Recently, the paper has begun limited
dealer sales of regular airmailed copies in the USSR.[2]

Credit for the founding of *The Globe and Mail,* which has evolved from the
merger of three newspapers, usually goes to Scots-born George Brown. He
started *The Globe* in 1844 and, through it, exerted great influence on the early
development of Canada and helped bring about the Confederation. As architect
of the Reform Party (later to become the Liberal Party), Brown used *The Globe*
to speak out for responsible government, individual freedom, and the desirability
of preserving strong ties with Britain. *The Globe* was owned by Brown until his
death in 1880, when it was bought by the Jaffray family.

[1] "Profile of the World's Press: The Globe and Mail," *The Times,* London, September 23, 1975.

[2] Richard S. Malone, Publisher and editor-in-chief, *The Globe and Mail,* Toronto, in letter to H. Fisher,
dated January 11, 1978.

The Globe and Mail

134th YEAR, No. 40,003 • METRO EDITION — TORONTO, WEDNESDAY, FEBRUARY 22, 1978 — 62 PAGES • 15 CENTS • 20 CENTS OR HIGHER OUTSIDE TORONTO AREA (RTZ)

Cloudy periods
High near −3
Weather details on Page 2

Ottawa to borrow abroad in bid to bolster the sagging dollar

By JOHN KING
Globe and Mail Reporter

OTTAWA — The federal Government plans to borrow funds outside Canada for the first time since 1968 in a move aimed at temporarily supporting the dollar, Finance Minister Jean Chretien announced last night.

The Canadian dollar has been trading for less than 90 cents (U.S.) for a week, at one point hitting the lowest level in 45 years.

The borrowing plan is being arranged now and details will be announced later, Mr. Chretien said in a statement.

As an interim step, the Government will shortly be withdrawing some money from the $1.5-billion revolving standby credit that it arranged last October with the Canadian chartered banks.

The purpose of the borrowing, Mr. Chretien said, is to assist in financing the current account deficit of the balance of payments and

Bank of Canada intervenes
Page B1

to supplement the flow of capital into Canada that occurs through other channels.

The Government last borrowed abroad in May and June of 1968, when it borrowed 250 million Deutschmarks (worth $77.7-million) in West Germany and $100-million (U.S.) in the United States.

The initial withdrawal from the revolving standby credit will be made while the foreign borrowing is being arranged, a Finance Department spokesman said last night. Precise amounts and markets had not been decided.

If the Government thought the dollar was sufficiently strong, it might repay the loan from the standby credit with the foreign borrowing, so the $1.5-billion

SUPPORT—Page 2

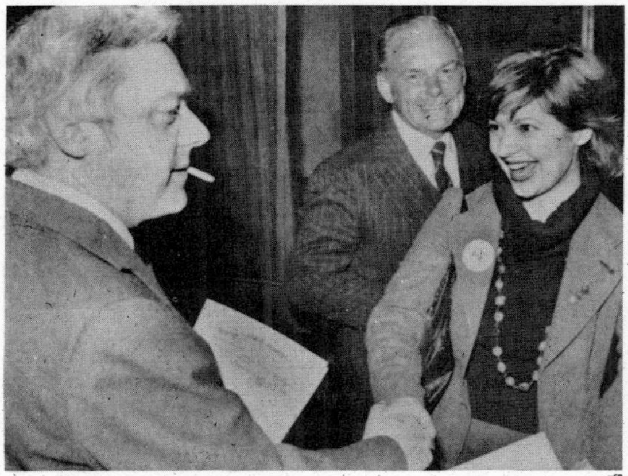

—CP

Pierre Lamontagne, a lawyer for the RCMP, is congratulated by assistant Victoria Percival on hearing of decision to close the Keable inquiry. Maurice Nadon, middle, former RCMP commissioner, was testifying when the inquiry came to an abrupt end.

1980 earliest date

Compulsory car insurance on the way, Ontario says

By PETER MOSHER

The Ontario Government says it plans to make it compulsory for car owners to buy insurance some time after 1979.

The announcement was one of the few surprises in a Speech from the Throne read at the opening of a new Legislature session yesterday. Premier William Davis said the speech outlining the legislative plans of his minority administration had "no gimmicks, nothing fancy" because the times call for less Government intervention.

Besides the promise to move to compulsory auto insurance, the speech read by Lieutenant-Governor Pauline McGibbon promised action to try to improve economic conditions in Northern and Eastern Ontario, restrictions on liquor advertising and raising of the legal drinking age to 19 from the present 18.

There also will be legislation designating areas of the province where the French-speaking population is large enough to guarantee accused people a trial in French, the Government said. More money will go to youth employment programs, apprenticeship training in trades and special education for children with learning disabilities.

The absence from the speech of large-scale and long-term projects to stimulate the economy brought criticism from the leaders of the two opposition parties, although Liberal Leader Stuart Smith and New Democratic Leader Michael Cassidy both said they liked some of the specific proposals as far as they went.

A dominant theme in the Throne Speech was more individual responsibility and a "reordering of priorities to do better with relatively less."

The speech "represents the realities that the Government and the people of the province face," Mr. Davis told reporters at a press conference. "There's a general feeling there's a lot of legislation already on the books."

He said the move to compulsory automobile insurance, approved in principle by Cabinet but not to be brought in before December, 1979, at the earliest, is not a contradiction of the basic conservative philosophy of the speech because it has been discussed for years. The size of claims is increasing, and the Government is afraid a fund paid into by uninsured drivers is not enough to cover huge settlements.

The promise of compulsory auto insurance is a change in Government policy. Sidney Handleman, when he was Minister of Consumer and Commercial Relations, said such a move would make little difference unless there were ways of apprehending those who would continue to drive illegally without insurance.

Now out of the Cabinet, Mr. Handleman said yesterday that about 95 per cent of drivers in Ontario are insured and most of the others would find ways to beat the proposed law.

Larry Grossman, who succeeded Mr. Handleman in the portfolio responsible for regulating insurance, said about 30,000 of the 140,000 drivers now uninsured would buy insurance if it became compulsory. He agreed it might be difficult to find those who bought policies and then cancelled them as soon as they obtained their automobile registration.

Among the promises in the 25-page Throne Speech:

—For Eastern Ontario, where both opposition parties have cut into traditional Tory strongholds, there will be a drainage and land reclamation project to prevent flooding in the South Nation River watershed southeast of Ottawa to Brockville. This will lead to better farming and forestry in 900,000 acres of land — some of it on Edwardsburgh Township land that the Government assembled but does not yet know what to do with.

—There also will be a study of a commuter air service in Eastern Ontario, possibly financed privately. The Government's NorOntair service in Northern Ontario is highly regarded in the area, and the Government may be hoping to duplicate its success in the East.

—For the North, which always has been loud in its cries for better services and always comes in for special mention in any Throne

ONTARIO — Page 2

☐ Tories' failure to lead criticized — Page 5
☐ Much ado about little — Page 6
☐ Quebec to help cultural industries — Page 9

Quebec will appeal court order halting provincial probe into RCMP operations

MONTREAL (CP-Special) — The federal Government won an order from the Quebec Court of Appeal yesterday stopping all proceedings of the province's Keable inquiry into police illegalities. Quebec quickly announced that a final round will be fought in the Supreme Court of Canada.

The order halted the inquiry abruptly with former RCMP commissioner Maurice Nadon on the stand, and forced cancellation of the long-awaited appearance today of former solicitor-general Jean-Pierre Goyer.

The court ruled that the inquiry, under Montreal lawyer Jean Keable, had overstepped its consititutional powers as a provincial commission in seeking to force a federal minister — former solicitor-general Francis Fox — to turn over secret files of the RCMP.

But the ruling, made on Ottawa's appeal of the case it lost before Quebec Superior Court in December, did not go as far as the federal Government had wanted. Ottawa had argued that the entire mandate to investigate a federal entity, the RCMP, was illegal. The current Solicitor-General, Jean-Jacques Blais, said in Ottawa yesterday that this means the whole inquiry could be restarted through a new Quebec order-in-council.

However, he pronounced himself elated at the decision, saying Ottawa had got "exactly what we wanted." The commission "all shuts down . . . the whole works stops."

The ruling ended a series of federal defeats in lower Quebec Courts on the issue. Ottawa began the action after the Keable inquiry sought from the RCMP operating manuals, Telex systems, files on the Parti Quebecois and other documents.

In Quebec, Justice Minister Marc-Andre Bedard, in announcing the appeal, reserved his criticism for the judgment of the former Solicitor-General rather than for the court's decision.

He said the federal Government's position that it can withhold information from the provincial inquiry had paralyzed the investigation of police activities "that put in jeopardy and still threaten, perhaps, individual rights and liberties of the citizens of Quebec."

Mr. Blais said the ruling will not effect Ottawa's own McDonald royal commission on RCMP activities. It has often followed in the tracks of the Keable inquiry.

The decision granted the federal Government a writ of evocation ordering that the Keable inquiry suspend all work and give all documents to the Court of Appeal within 15 days. The order remains in effect until a final ruling on the commission's constitutionality.

The majority opinion, written by Judge Rodolphe Pare, was concurred in by Judge Amedee Monet, while Judge Fred Kaufman registered a partial dissent, saying it was not necessary to stop "all further proceedings" of the inquiry.

Bus surcharge

35¢ to go past subway on GO

GO Transit will charge some bus riders 35 cents extra to go downtown to persuade them to take the subway.

But the subway cash fare is 55 cents and it will still be cheaper to stay on the bus.

Bill Howard, executive director of the Toronto Transportation Terminal, said that GO was not trying to compete with the TTC and there was no reason to make the surcharge match the TTC fare.

"Getting through heavy city traffic ties up buses unnecessarily so we want to discourage people from using our bus service to take them all the way downtown," said Tom Henry, a spokesman for Toronto Area Transit Operating Authority. "We want them to take the subway whenever possible."

He said the surcharge will start April 1, and will be in addition to a general increase at that time.

He said those who ride past subway stations that are regular GO bus stops will pay the surcharge.

For instance, passengers on the Newmarket run who don't leave at the Finch subway station will pay the charge.

Details of the general increase have not been released.

Double-decker coaches
Page 5

Clark supports Davis on French-rights stand

OTTAWA (CP) — Opposition Leader Joseph Clark says he "sympathizes entirely" with Ontario's refusal to make French an official language in the province, arguing that it is more important to make practical language reforms than to pass symbolic declarations.

On the second anniversary of his election as Progressive Conservative Leader, Mr. Clark outlined in an interview steps he would take to keep French Canada in the political mainstream should he win the next election with little support in Quebec.

They include plans to appoint senators from Quebec who could sit in Cabinet, efforts to entice support from Premier Rene Levesque for constitutional and economic reforms, pledges to remove irritants from the Official Languages Act without undermining French and English language rights and promises to honor Liberal Government commitments to minority-language education in the country.

At the same time, Mr. Clark said Premier William Davis of Ontario is right when he argues that simply declaring a language official creates "expectations and legitimate demands that the system can't fill.

"I can sympathize entirely with the Davis position," Mr. Clark said. "He is saying that he is going to make the practical reforms that will put us in the position to fill those demands. He's acting practically rather than by the declaration of some kind of principle."

Mr. Davis has been attacked by Prime Minister Pierre Trudeau's top spokesman on federal-provincial relations, Marc Lalonde, for refusing to declare French an official language in Ontario. Symbols, Mr. Lalonde has said, are important in the battle to keep Quebec in Confederation.

Mr. Clark said he would attempt to see that francophones continue to be attracted to the federal civil service and that Canadians can deal with the Government in both official languages.

But any government he leads is "not going to force people to become bilingual, to try to learn languages they can't."

Mr. Clark's Conservatives currently hold only three federal seats in Quebec, and he feels he's likely to capture only between five and 25 of the 75 ridings during the next general election.

In the past, the party has attempted to win Quebec seats by holding certain ridings open to prominent candidates — Claude Wagner, former provincial Liberal Cabinet minister and judge, was one.

Now the strategy has changed. Candidates with strong local ties to ridings are being nominated and are working year-round to win. It's a system that has worked for the Social Credit Party in the province, and one Mr. Clark feels will work for him.

"The star system obvious-

DAVIS — Page 2

Davis gets no advice about uranium pacts from split committee

By THOMAS CLARIDGE

Premier William Davis's hopes for guidance from a legislative committee as to what his Government should do about $7-billion in uranium contracts were dashed effectively yesterday when the committee split three ways along party lines.

The Premier had asked the Select Committee on Hydro Affairs for a decision on whether the proposed contracts with Denison Mines Ltd. and Preston Mines Ltd. would be in the public interest.

After holding 29 meetings and hearing 40 witnesses and its own staff, the committee voted down a Government backbencher's motion supporting the contracts, but then rejected separate Liberal and New Democratic Party motions that criticized the proposed 40-year supply agreements. Committee chairman Donald MacDonald said he would write the Premier advising him that seven opposition members on the committee felt the contracts were not in the public interest and six Government members favored the pacts.

The committee's actions won't bind the Government, but when asked for comment later yesterday Mr. Davis made no attempt to conceal his unhappiness at the outcome.

"They didn't say what we should do, as I understand it," he said. "Doesn't that surprise you?"

Mr. MacDonald opened the meeting with advice that the only question to be determined was whether the contracts with Denison and Preston for provision of 200 million pounds of uranium were "in the public interest of Ontario."

The stands taken by the

URANIUM — Page 2

Your morning smile

A father down the block said his teen-age son took an aptitude test and was found to be well-suited for retirement.

Brewery revives Grand Prix idea, wants racing at CNE

By ROSEMARIE BOYLE

There may be Grand Prix racing at Exhibition Place next Thanksgiving after all.

Carling O'Keefe Breweries of Canada Ltd. will go before the executive committee of the Canadian National Exhibition this afternoon for approval to stage the race within the grounds.

Graham Leggat, spokesman for Carling O'Keefe, said yesterday that his company will propose holding the race during the Thanksgiving weekend, Oct. 6-9, but will not allow racing on Sunday.

The whole race would take place within the CNE grounds. A previous proposal by Labatt's Ontario Breweries and Mosport Park Ltd. suggested that part of Lake Shore Boulevard might be closed and used as part of the racetrack.

The Canadian Grand Prix has been held at Mosport, about 60 miles north-east of Toronto, for the past decade. Labatt's and Mosport Park wanted to bring the international racing competition, which leads to points for the world racing championship, to Toronto to attract larger crowds.

Last Dec. 6, Toronto City Council voted 18-4 against giving Labatt's exemption from the city's anti-noise bylaw and permission to hold auto racing on a Sunday.

Opponents of Grand Prix racing at the CNE have vowed to fight the latest proposal from Carling O'Keefe on the same grounds as before, according to architect Howard Walker of the Anti-Grand Prix Coalition.

They object to the probable noise and pollution, traffic congestion, policing problems and the over-all intrusion into the neighboring community of Parkdale.

Mr. Leggat said Carling O'Keefe was approached by Canadian racing driver Peter Ferguson of the Grand Prix Festival Committee to sponsor Formula One auto racing at the CNE.

Mr. Ferguson refused to comment yesterday on the proposal until it is presented to the CNE. Mr. Leggat added that Carling O'Keefe is in the midst of making all necessary applications and arrangements to sponsor and hold the race. He refused to say whether the company has approval from the international racing federation.

Raymond Bremner, Toronto works commissioner, said the city would have little control over the race if the CNE approves it. The CNE directors, as a board, are "masters of their own premises . . . but they would still have the anti-noise bylaw to contend with."

Mr. Bremner said the race sponsor would have to submit a noise-impact study to the city for clearance.

Metro Chairman Paul Godfrey said he wants to see all the facts and figures before he makes up his mind about the proposal. "I'm open-minded." He met Mr. Ferguson yesterday to discuss the proposal.

Toronto Mayor David Crombie is to write a letter to the CNE executive committee today asking that all information about the latest scheme be shared with the city. Several Council members, including Aldermen John Sewell and Patrick Sheppard, plan to attend the CNE meeting to protest against the race.

Toronto Alderman Arthur Eggleton, who has voted for Grand Prix racing at the CNE all along, is the city's only representative on the CNE executive committee. Nora Pownall, an Etobicoke controller, represents Metro.

FANFARE

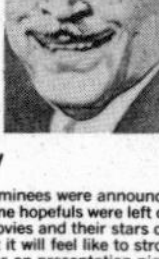

The latest from Fats Waller
Dreamy Limehouse, a song written by Fats Waller, was discovered by his son Maurice in a cardboard box. Never before published, it is presented for the first time in Fanfare. Fanfare Page 10.

The great Academy race is on
The Academy Award nominees were announced yesterday, and while some hopefuls were left out in the cold, other top movies and their stars can begin to anticipate what it will feel like to stroke Oscar's slim silver curves on presentation night. Fanfare Page 5.

Canada

Settlement with Algoma costs Steelworkers $10,000
The Steelworkers union got off with $1 on some claims from the Oct. 14, 1976, protest day, and it has settled with Algoma Steel for $10,000, but two big claims pending may cost it in the hundreds of thousands. Page 3.

Chance of travelling in space slim if the candidate is fat
You don't have to be fit but you can't be fat if you want to go up in the space shuttle. Page 4.

Canada in need of economic miracle
Unless the Government conjures up a miracle Canada's economy will remain sick, says Globe and Mail publisher Richard S. Malone. It could learn a lot by studying the modern German miracle worked by former Chancellor Ludwig Erhard. Page 7.

The World

China's Gang of Four will be allowed to live
The radical Gang of Four, "unrepentant" though they are, will be permitted to live, China's Hsinhua news agency reports. It was the first official word that the four, arrested in October, 1976, would not be executed. Page 12.

Brazil says drought should boost coffee prices
So you thought coffee was going to come down in price, eh? Well the word from Brazil is that it is hoping to use the loss of 10 per cent of the crop in a drought to justify price increases. Page 12.

Bridge	Fanfare 16	Osgoode Hall	B2
Crossword	Fanfare 16	Recreation	35, 36, 42

Then, in 1872, Sir John A. Macdonald, with financial backing from the Conservative Party, began *The Mail* in Toronto. A second Conservative paper, *The Empire*, was founded in 1887, but was taken over by *The Mail* in 1895 to continue as the *Mail and Empire*. For almost forty years *The Globe* and the *Mail and Empire* competed in Toronto, the former reflecting Liberal thought and the latter, Conservative. Then, in 1936, George McCullagh, a former financial writer for the paper, bought *The Globe*, which had a circulation of some 78,000 at the time, from the Jaffray family. In less than a month, McCullagh had also bought the *Mail and Empire* (circulation 118,000) and the two papers were consolidated under the new name, *The Globe and Mail*.[3]

McCullagh breathed new life into the paper and its pages showed a spirit reminiscent of the days when George Brown had edited the old *Globe*. The new owner announced his paper's independence at once, but through World War II *The Globe and Mail* generally supported the Progressive Conservative Party.

Harry G. Kimber, who had been general manager, became publisher when McCullagh died in 1952. Three years later the paper was bought by R. Howard Webster, a Montreal financier. In 1957, Oakley Dagliesh, who had been editor for ten years became editor and publisher. After Dagliesh's death in 1963, Webster assumed the title of publisher and named James L. Cooper as his editor-in-chief.

Early in 1966, *The Globe and Mail* became a part of F. P. Publications, Limited, a newspaper group including six other newspapers. In 1973, the Montreal *Star* was added to the F. P. group, increasing the size of its holdings to eight dailies. In April, 1974, Richard S. Malone, formerly the publisher of the *Winnipeg Free Press* and President of the F. P. newspaper group, was appointed publisher and editor-in-chief of *The Globe and Mail*. He also continued in his appointment as president of F. P. Publications, Limited.

During the past 25 years or so, *The Globe and Mail* has asserted complete independence. Politically, this means its views, while tending to be somewhat conservative, are dictated to by no political party. Its editors feel free to criticize any government irrespective of party domination. In the 1974 federal election, it supported the Conservatives, while in the 1972 campaign it had endorsed the Liberal Party's views. A few years ago, the paper told a special Senate committee on the mass media, *"The Globe and Mail* is independent, but by no means neutral. Its independence of any political party or fraction gives its editors freedom to criticize or support parties or policies as they see fit." In social and economic affairs, the paper still leans towards Conservative bias.

Today, *The Globe and Mail* is probably the best example in the general Canadian press of a journal which, as one observer has noted, has "a calm and level-headed tone" thus causing it to "accurately mirror a calm and balanced nation."[4] The paper takes pride in being Canada's "paper of record," devoting considerable space to materials such as texts of parliamentary debates and political manifestos. The same writer called *The Globe and Mail* "Canada's superior

---

[3] "Industrialist's Bid Wins Toronto *Globe*," *Editor and Publisher*, (February 19, 1955), p. 8.

[4] Stuart Keate, "How Good are the Newspapers of Canada?" *Nieman Reports*, 20:3 (September, 1966), pp. 28–32.

paper," and placed the Montreal *Star* close behind it. However, others, among them *The Globe and Mail*'s own editor, feel the *Winnipeg Free Press* (see profile) is the second best quality daily in Canada today.

Perhaps one of *The Globe and Mail*'s greatest strengths is the excellence and thoroughness of its foreign coverage. It maintains bureaus in three key cities—London, Washington and Peking. It also has 22 part-time correspondents on every continent.[5] To supplement the efforts of its own staff, it takes wire agency input from Dow Jones, Canadian Press, AP, Reuters and UPI. It also gets foreign news information from the syndicated services of the New York *Times*, *U.S. News and World Report*, *Le Monde* and from London's *Times, Economist* and *Financial Times*. These combined inputs typically result in several front page foreign news items and two full inside pages of further overseas stories, plus a page of feature articles and background information entitled "The World."

The Globe and Mail's coverage and insights on China have been especially noteworthy. Its Peking bureau has been particularly effective. A recent series on China by Peking correspondent Ross Munro was given wide recognition both in American newspapers and in leading English quality dailies such as *The Times* and *The Observer*. As a result of that series, Munro was asked by the Chinese government to leave China, but the bureau has been allowed to continue operation with a new staff member.[6] The Peking bureau has been served by at least three distinguished overseas correspondents—Colin McCullough, Norman Webster and Ross Munro. *The Globe and Mail*'s own news service on Communist China, established in 1958, has been the major, and very often the only, source of news from that country for many newspapers of the Western world. *The New York Times*, for instance, has regularly used this service.

The paper likewise displays intense interest in thorough coverage of national, Ontario and Toronto news. Six reporters are stationed at Ottawa to provide thorough coverage of Parliament and other governmental activity. The amount of Canadian national news coverage roughly equates space given to international news—typically some five percent each of the total space in the paper. Another six percent of space is given to state and local news coverage. One page is entitled "The Provinces," another "Metro News." Sports news coverage is likewise complete and thorough, taking some seven percent of all space. A daily issue will normally carry four to eight pages of sports news and contains numerous action pictures. Sports and classified advertisements form the paper's third section. Advertisements total 48 percent of all the paper's space.

Another of *The Globe and Mail*'s strengths is its emphasis on business and finance, which comprises about 15 percent of its space. Its editors consider its broad coverage of Canadian business affairs one of the paper's finest qualities. The financial supplement "Report on Business", added in 1962 and usually 16

[5] As of early 1978, stringers were located in London, Paris, Washington, Bahamas, Belgium, Guatemala, West Germany, Italy, Ireland, Israel, Jamaica, Japan, Kenya, Lebanon, Rhodesia, South Africa, Spain, Sweden, India, Australia, Zambia and Thailand. (R. S. Malone, in response to questionnaire, dated January 10, 1978).
[6] Malone letter, *loc. cit.*

pages in length, forms the second section of the paper. This section now appears five days a week, and is likewise published as a separate airmail edition. For the convenience of busy businessmen, the front page of this section carries a column of encapsulated versions of the day's news stories. As in the remainder of the paper, pictures are well chosen and form an important part of the paper's information.

The Globe and Mail's editorial and op-ed pages provide one of the most dignified and attractive two-page opinion sections found among the world's elite newspapers. "Its editorials, hard hitting and pungent, are sometimes imbued with a self-righteous, omniscient flavor that public figures find objectionable."[7] Editorial opinions are given with intelligence and clarity. The writer keeps himself out of the news columns, which are backed by interpretive pieces written by specialists. Feedback from readers is given full play; frequently a full page is devoted to letters to the editor, sometimes with appropriate accompanying photographs. The editorial page typically carries an incisive cartoon.

The Globe and Mail emphasizes national and international general news and business and finance information designed to appeal to its substantial following among judges, lawyers, doctors, diplomats, businessmen, clergymen, bankers, teachers and other influential readers. But it has not deserted the wider interests of its readers. There is a regular "Feature Page," plus numerous background articles and interpretive pieces. When a special fourth section is published, its entire space is usually devoted to a single topic. In recent years, one special section added has been a weekly youth section, "Fanfare," and also a weekly television supplement, "Broadcast Week." The front pages of both are done in attractive color. Weather information is complete, up-to-date and national in scope. For the readers' lighter moments, there are entertainment guides, a crossword puzzle and even a "Your Morning Smile" to lighten the otherwise businesslike front page.

The paper's front page is generally serious and orderly, containing a mix of the top Canadian and international stories of the day and from one to three pictures. Makeup is neat, with many stories laid out in horizontal fashion. The left-hand column gives news briefs and provides information about the paper's remaining contents. Correspondents frequently receive by-lines for their stories. Spot color enlivens the front page index box each day, and there is three-color art or a color photograph at least once a week. Vivid, pleasant, carefully registered color is also employed for magazine inserts, editorial features, maps and advertising—making *The Globe and Mail* one of the biggest users of color among quality papers anywhere.

The *Weekly Globe and Mail* was started in 1957, with a magazine supplement and other special features. It has been replaced by the *Saturday Globe and Mail,* which gives greater emphasis to features, news summaries and political roundups for weekend reading.[8] It is not unusual for this edition to run more than 100 pages in length, and its contents roughly equate the Sunday editions of other quality papers which print one.

To produce its attractive product, *The Globe and Mail* employs modern

---

[7] "Profile of the World's Press: The Globe and Mail," *loc. cit.*
[8] Malone letter.

equipment. Video display terminals are used extensively; total story input and editing is carried out by VDTs. Composition is letter press, cold type via computer and direct VDT input, and printing is direct, utilizing plastic press plates.

With this equipment, the paper publishes five daily editions, with 42 pages being the average weekday size. The daily and its supplements represent the efforts of a total staff of 1,021, of which 222 are involved in technical activity, 41 in administrative and managerial roles, and 263 in writing and editorial tasks. The paper tries to recruit experienced writers for its editorial positions; where they are not available, staff members are trained on the job.[9]

The watermark of *The Globe and Mail*'s excellence as a high-quality newspaper is its impressive list of awards and citations. Over the past ten years, it has received seven National Newspaper Awards for foreign correspondence, editorial writing, spot news and drama criticism, and eight Maclaren Awards for typographical excellence. In 1973, it won the Rowland Michener Award for Investigative Reporting. Its 1976 efforts brought the paper two National Business Writing Awards and the Joseph P. Kennedy Award for stories on the retarded. Prior to 1968 the paper received, among others, 13 National Newspaper Awards in various categories, two Bowater Awards for Economic Writing and the U.S. Soil Conservative Society 1964 America Award.[10]

In addition to cherishing its political independence, *The Globe and Mail* supports the high principles of freedom of speech, religion, trade and the free enterprise system. While it takes stands on issues, its approach is always open and provocative, and it continually attempts to inform its readers with a well-rounded and reasoned picture of any given situation. Its approach and its scope are national rather than local, and by its broad, well-balanced, high-quality coverage of the international scene and of Canadian business and governmental affairs, it both keeps its readers well informed and sets the pace for all of Canadian journalism. Thus, *The Globe and Mail*—this serious paper so excellently produced in all respects—deserves its place among the world's great newspapers.

The Guardian

(ENGLAND)

THE GUARDIAN holds the distinction of being Britain's only newspaper which has risen from the rank of a small provincial Manchester weekly to become one of the country's top quality national dailies. Its gradual but steady rise to such

[9] Malone questionnaire.
[10] *Ibid.*

heady prominence stems from several strong journalistic roots, among them appeal to young intellectuals, insistence on balanced and fair reporting, good international coverage and relative financial security.

But perhaps the paper's chief strengths lie in its consistent emphasis on social reform and progressive liberal thought. T. S. Matthews once remarked appropriately that *The Guardian* keeps reminding its readers civilization both exists and is worth saving. And the deputy editor of the rival *Times* of London, Louis Heren, summing up these two *Guardian* strong points recently wrote: "*The Guardian* is on the moralistic left and appeals to non-conformist school teachers, while defending the rights of unmarried mothers."[1]

In the past, *The Guardian* has been called "Britain's non-conformist conscience," a role in which it still sees itself. Its priority is "the people who govern the country and the way the country is governed."[2] But, as its coverage demonstrates, its interests are numerous—economics, finance, industry, business, sports, science, current history, contemporary literature and art. At times its features take it as far afield as archeology, engineering, philosophy and man's early beginnings.

Today, *The Guardian* continues to underwrite its 1966 self-description—an analytical ("analyzes news like no other paper"), careful ("looks carefully at everything of importance"), serious ("never sensational and tries not to be superficial"), honest ("doesn't mold facts to suit its line") and truthful ("strong opinions . . . are not allowed to get in the way of truth") newspaper. It takes pride in its social awareness ("has great humanity, cares about social problems") and high writing standards ("grammatical standards are set extremely high"). Its primary concern is with intellectual content but it does not lose sight of entertainment values.

One revealing measure of a daily's content and appeal is the readership it attracts. Officials of *The Guardian* say they are trying to reach those "with an intelligent, free-thinking, international outlook."[3] Surveys indicate their quest is successful. Daily circulation is about 280,000, of which 75 percent are subscriptions. (There is no Sunday edition.) Since readership statistics in England indicate each copy of a newspaper attracts three to four readers, well over a million people will read *The Guardian* on an average day. More significantly, the studies indicate these *Guardian* readers are "a lot younger, better off and better educated than the general run of the population."[4] In a country where the median age of the adult population is 43 years of age, that for *Guardian* readers is a tender 33, whereas that for *The Times* is 38, for *The Daily Telegraph,* 42, and for the *Daily Express* and the *Daily Mail* about 47. Three-fourths of *The Guardian*'s readers are "white collar" with incomes generally running over £5,000. per annum. Over 30 percent have gone to college.

The statistics do not adequately reveal *Guardian* readers' life styles. Further study of reader profiles indicates many are the thoughtful, discriminating, elite

[1] Louis Heren, "Fleet Street and the Free Press," *Saturday Review,* June 11, 1977, p. 24.
[2] "*The Guardian* in London and Manchester," a Brochure (London, *The Guardian,* 1977), p. 3.
[3] Kit Harding, Public Relations Officer, *The Guardian,* in response to questionnaire, February 6, 1978.
[4] "*The Guardian* in London and Manchester," *op. cit.,* p. 9.

SQUIRE
The Padlocks with the 5-year guarantee

THE GUARDIAN

Printed in London and Manchester Wednesday February 22 1978 15p

rhp BRITISH PRECISION BEARINGS

NEWS IN BRIEF

Schmidt warned on US quarrel

CHANCELLOR SCHMIDT has been privately warned by members of his Cabinet that his quarrel with the Carter Administration over economic policy is straining US-German relations. Among those opposed to Mr Schmidt is the Defence Minister, Hans Apel, regarded as the man most likely to succeed as leader of the Social Democrats. **Page 6; Leader comment, page 14.**

Abortion Bill progresses

ABORTION returned to the parliamentary arena yesterday when Conservative Sir Bernard Braine's private member's Bill to amend the 1967 Abortion Act was given a second reading by a majority of six. **Back page. Parliament, page 4.**

Budget travel

IF YOU cannot avoid the ruinous expense of owning a car, how can you best get someone else to meet the costs? Would you do better taking to a moped? Where can you get holidays for £17 a week? How should you play the season ticket game on British Rail? These and other answers can be found in Living Better on a Budget, which looks at ways of travelling more cheaply. **Pages 17 to 19.**

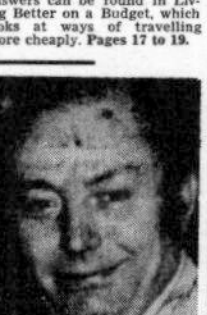

A FORMER boy soldier, William "Billy" Rice—above—was sent to prison for ten years at Preston yesterday for ferrying explosives through England to a Protestant extremist organisation, believed to be the Ulster Volunteer Force. **Back page.**

THE European Human Rights Commission has rejected a complaint by an Irishman, Patrick Gallagher, against his extradition from Holland last November. Mr Gallagher, aged 38, was extradited to Dublin to stand trial for robbing a post office and in December gaoled for six years.

THE Guardian regrets that production difficulties on Monday night meant that many readers in the London area did not receive their normal delivery. We apologise for the inconvenience caused.

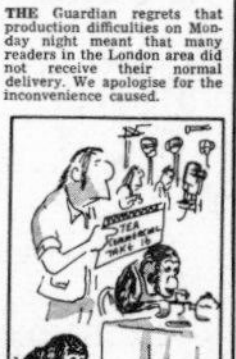

INSIDE

The weather

RAIN, heavy in places. Cold in the north. **Details, back page.**

Italian behind move for peace in the Horn

From James MacManus in Mogadishu

A senior member of the Italian Communist Party has arrived in Somalia on a secret mission from Moscow to explore prospects for a negotiated end to the war in the Horn of Africa, according to sources here.

Mr D. Giadresco, head of the Communist Cooperative Commission in Italy, arrived from Rome on Monday and was discreetly welcomed by senior aides of President Siad Barre, said the sources.

Although his visit has not been publicised, enquirers are told that Mr Giadresco is to inspect a cooperative road building scheme set up in the northern town of Berbera by party members from his home town of Ravenna in central Italy. It is understood, however, that the real reason is a move by Russian and pro-Soviet officials in Mogadishu to seek common ground for a ceasefire and staged withdrawal of Somali forces from the Ethiopian Ogaden region.

Mr Giadresco is said to know President Barre well and to have visited Somalia several times since 1971. He is

Ethiopia's weak spot, page 5; Russia raises the stakes, page 15

regarded as a firmly pro-Soviet figure in a party whose relations with Russia have recently been strained by endorsement of the politics of Euro-Communism.

In early November, before the expulsion from Somalia of some 3,000 Russian military advisers and their families, Mr Giadresco travelled to Mogadishu and tried to negotiate, on behalf of the Italian Communist Party, a military withdrawal from Ethiopia by Somali regular and guerrilla units. That public visit ended with a joint statement saying that the Italian Communist party and the Somali government agreed to disagree on the issue.

It now appears that President Barre, whose accession to power in 1969 introduced an era of "scientific socialism" and massive Russian military aid in Somalia, has decided to keep the diplomatic lines to Moscow open. Although no formal break in relations followed the expulsion of Russian advisers, feelings between the Russian mission in Mogadishu and the Government have been embittered to the point of precluding meaningful discussions.

Yesterday the whitewashed walls in the capital were covered in political graffiti denouncing Russian and Cuban support for the "imperialist" regime in Ethiopia and calling for an end to all Russian "interference" in Africa.

Yet several members of the Central Committee of the ruling Somali Socialist Revolutionary Party appear to regret Somalia's slide towards the West, particularly in the search for arms.

The key ideologue in the party, Mohammed Aden Sheik, is said to have endorsed Mr Giadresco's visit and to have worked hard on President Barre to find some rapprochement with the Soviet Union. It appears therefore that the President, in spite of his undoubtedy bitter feelings towards what is regarded widely here as Russian treachery in supporting Ethiopia, has not entirely ruled out the possibility of a negotiated compromise to end the war. If true, this would be the first sign in months that Somalia's military leaders might welcome a diplomatic escape route from the painful predicament which confronts them in the Ogaden.

Nonetheless, the prospects of a peaceful settlement remain dim. In the Somali media the war is now more than ever portrayed as a national crusade. Since the Ethiopian government regards the conquest of the Ogaden in the same light, there seems only a slim chance of successful private negotiations at this stage.

40,000 unemployment drop fails to lift gloom

Ministers and unions clash over job trends

By Rosemary Collins, Labour Staff

The number of people out of work fell this month, but not enough to convince Whitehall officials that the worst levels of unemployment have necessarily yet been reached.

The mid-February unemployment total stood at 1,508,674, 39,870 fewer than the previous month, which represents 6.3 per cent of the working population.

Unemployment is now still 77,600 higher than it was in mid-February 1977 and the prospects led to a sharp rift between senior Ministers and leading trade unionists at yesterday's monthly meeting of the TUC and Labour Party liaison committee.

The final paragraphs of a document presented to the meeting by Mr Albert Booth, the Secretary for Employment, caused the trouble and will be deleted from a version to be published later.

According to the Department of Employment document "the social trend towards shorter hours and earlier retirement is likely to continue in the period ahead," but the Government "does not regard these as desirable ways of dealing with the current problem of high unemployment."

The document points out that reducing the retirement age would be costly and would also reduce the resources available to ensure that pensions are high enough to provide an adequate standard of living for those already retired. Work-sharing, according to Mr Booth's Paper, would have an "uncertain" effect on unemployment levels, as would reducing working hours or extending holidays, and "such approaches carry high risks of upsetting the major economic objectives of controlling inflation and maximising the rate of recovery because of their effects on industrial costs and competitive position."

The tenor of this paragraph was felt, particularly by Mr Jack Jones, the Transport and General Workers' Union leader, to be unhelpful and to run counter to much of the medicine prescribed by union leaders as a current remedy for unemployment. Mr Jones is a keen advocate of earlier retirement, and the TUC as a whole puts forward in this year's Budget strategy document a proposal, that the basic working

City Notebook, page 20

week in industry should be shortened to 35 hours.

The Government line, as put forward yesterday by Mr Booth, is to create extra jobs to absorb the increase in the labour supply rather than to try to cut the labour supply by the methods now being advocated by the unions. Mr Booth spelt out to his trade union and Labour Party colleagues the extension of various job schemes announced in the House of Commons earlier this week and calculated by the Department of Employment to be keeping 320,000 in jobs they might not otherwise have. The actual effect on the unemployment register is thought to be slightly less than this.

The Government has apparently accepted estimates that the number of people entering the job market is likely to increase by around 170,000 a year over the next four years, a calculation which has helped to spread pessimism in Whitehall over medium and longer-term employment prospects.

The new figures were being treated with a good deal of caution in official circles, where there is concern that last year's pattern of a winter levelling-off of unemployment followed by an unexpected and unseasonal rise may be repeated.

This month's total includes 49,701 school-leavers, a drop of 11,414 on last month, which means that 90 per cent of the 663,000 boys and girls who left school in the last academic year have now either found jobs or entered into training or further education.

The seasonally adjusted total of adult vacancies, at 187,000, is the highest since March, 1975, and the vacancy figures in general are regarded as encouraging. The total number of unfilled vacancies was 172,065, which is 13,144 more than in January.

Simon Hoggart writes: The Prime Minister gave the liaison committee meeting a grim warning of the possibility of a world trade war through a growth of protectionism throughout the world if growth rates failed to improve.

"It is because I am deeply concerned about this situation that I am in consultation with President Carter," Mr Callaghan said. He thought a tendency towards protectionism could only be harmful, and he feared that the French would be "at the head of the queue" in starting such a movement. He confessed to taking a more gloomy view of the world economic outlook than Mr Denis Healey, the Chancellor, but Mr Healey did threaten that action might have to be taken against the Japanese, who, he said, [illegible] exporting to [illegible] importing from nobody.

Flood alert after blizzards

By Staff Reporters

After the weekend blizzards, high tides and melting snow brought flooding to parts of south Devon yesterday. The worst hit area was the South Hams district where the town of Kingsbridge was under four feet of water in places.

Along the south Devon coast county council workmen issued villagers with sandbags in anticipation of more flooding caused by gale force winds and high tides. The forecast for the South-west is heavy rain in places, with the temperature rising to a maximum of 10C and rapid thawing of snow.

The Minister in charge of the snow emergency, Mr Denis Howell, spent yesterday consulting officials in Devon and Somerset and setting up information centres. He said the first objective was to get things cleared up and after that the cost of the operation could be discussed. He drew a parallel with the flood-hit local authorities on the east coast of England, who have to meet costs only up to the equivalent of a penny rate with the Government meeting the rest.

Meanwhile up to 1½ million gallons of milk a day are being poured away, stored in emergency containers or fed to livestock because bulk tankers cannot reach 14,000 dairy producers in the South-west.

Mr Howell said the army would be drafted into Somerset to help with road clearing. Dorset police have banned private cars from badly-hit areas because they were hampering rescue and clearance operations.

Welsh farmers hit, page 2; Living in a cold climate, page 15; Snowdrift baby, back page

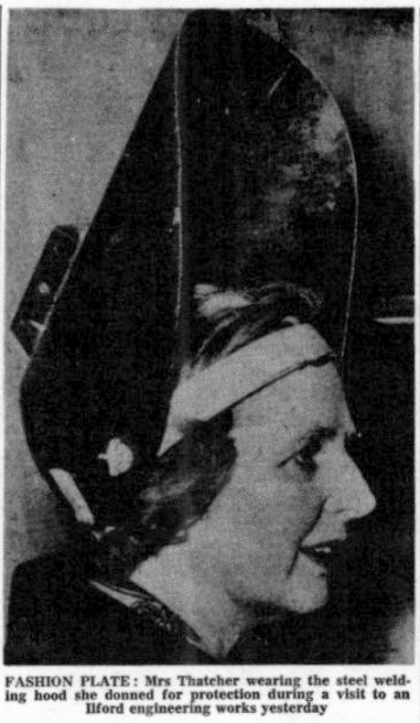

FASHION PLATE: Mrs Thatcher wearing the steel welding hood she donned for protection during a visit to an Ilford engineering works yesterday

Thatcher stands firm on race

By Melanie Phillips

Mrs Thatcher yesterday denied that she had adopted the policies of the National Front and was making racial hatred respectable. In a speech in Ilford North she said that she "condemned and hated" the National Front, and that repatriation was not part of the Conservatives' "scheme of things."

She was defending herself against allegations by the Home Secretary, Mr Rees, who claimed that she was "making respectable racial hatred and inciting the threats to public order that we have seen in some of our towns and cities." Mrs Thatcher called Mr Rees's remarks "absolute nonsense," but she refused to join those calling for Saturday's National Front march through Ilford to be banned.

The Conservative candidate for Ilford North, Mr Vivian Bendall, has said that he will ask the Police Commissioner to ban the march if the National Front does not call it off. When asked at a press conference whether she supported Mr Bendall in this, Mrs Thatcher replied: "He knows the area very much better than I do. The march must be left in the hands of the police."

Mr David Lane, chairman of the Commission for Racial Equality has also called for Saturday's march to be banned and yesterday the Prime Minister attacked "some" Conservative leaders for "preaching a doctrine that will result in conflict and confrontation. I ask the people of Ilford to show that they do not want this," he said. "We are working to preserve our tolerant society which is just and fair towards all people regardless of creed or colour. But we shall not allow that tolerance to be taken advantage of by vandals and thugs. Hooliganism in the streets or elsewhere will be firmly dealt with by the courts in the interests of us all."

Mrs Thatcher, who was speaking after a morning of canvassing in Ilford, said that she stood by everything she had said on immigration and would not be "bullied or intimidated." Answering the Home Secretary's comments, she said: "Mr Rees is having great difficulty in making up his mind whether his policies hold out a clear prospect of an end to immigration, or whether he should attack us for saying it."

She claimed that she herself had not raised immigration as an issue; all she had done was

Turn to back page, col. 1

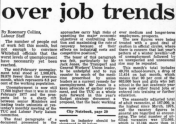

Interim 10p in pound for Poulson creditors

By Michael Parkin

Creditors of the bankrupt former architect, John Poulson, are to be paid an interim dividend of 10p in the pound—far more than they could have ever hoped for when the Mersey Regional Health Authority first put in a claim for £2.5 millions over defects in a hospital designed by Mr Poulson's firm.

After negotiating with the trustee in the Poulson bankruptcy the health authority withdrew its claim "because of Mr Poulson's insolvency." An authority spokesman said that the claim had been pitched at £2.5 millions because the first indications were that defects at the Leighton District Hospital, Crewe, would cost that much to remedy.

A consultant has now looked at the hospital and his first report suggests that the remedial work will cost about £1.3 millions. The main defects are in the floors of corridors and operating theatres, and in window casements and drains.

Mr Poulson included some experimental design ideas, approved by the Department of Health, when the 720-bed hospital was built in 1972. It cost £6 millions and was one of the cheapest hospitals of its size built in Britain. The health authority calculates that even with the additional expense of remedial work, the final cost will be about average for hospitals of this type.

The £2.5 millions claim and some smaller claims delayed the fixing of the interim dividend of 10p which was approved by the bankruptcy court yesterday. Within the next few months the trustee hopes to settle other claims and pay the final dividend.

The biggest of these outstanding claims is one for not more than £130,000 by Leeds City Council over defects in another Poulson building, the Leeds international swimming pool. This sum includes £50,000 claimed by a contractor for disruption to his building programme for the pool.

Leeds people call the international pool "Fu Manchu's Palace," from its likeness to a Chinese pagoda. It has proved a millstone for the city council. The roof was found to be defective and it began to rot from condensation. The pool loses far more money than it takes, and councillors have been calling for its demolition—after a life of just over 10 years—and the sale of the site.

So far the trustees in bankruptcy have collected assets of £323,759, much of it bribes and gifts given by Mr Poulson as sweeteners to councillors, civil servants and others. It was hard work. Mr Poulson was adjudged

Turn to back page, col. 7

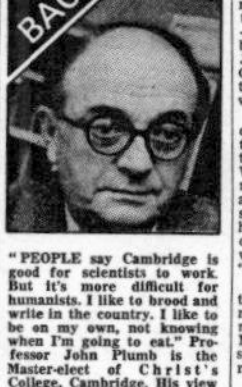

"PEOPLE say Cambridge is good for scientists to work. But it's more difficult for humanists. I like to brood and write in the country. I like to be on my own, not knowing when I'm going to eat." Professor John Plumb is the Master-elect of Christ's College, Cambridge. His view of the bachelor life appears in Guardian Women on page 11.

Cocktail stains Carter's image

From our own Correspondent in Washington

A storm in a teacup — or more precisely a drink down the front of a woman's blouse — has surfaced here over the behaviour of Mr Hamilton Jordan, one of President Carter's assistants and one of the architects of his electoral victory.

The story of how Mr Jordan came to spit his cocktail, for that is what is alleged, was told in Sunday's issue of the Washington Post — the same newspaper which recounted an earlier Hamilton Jordan scrape in which he was said to have plucked at the neckline of the Egyptian ambassador's wife and expressed a desire to "see the pyramids."

In response to the latest story the White House publicity machine has closed ranks and made itself a laughing stock. Mr Jordan has issued a massive affidavit denying the report.

Twenty-four pages of the White House document are devoted to the evidence of the bartender, who admits that he was not around when matters came to a head. The Washington Post said yesterday that it stands by its version of the incident. So does the woman.

The bartender, Mr Marshall, said: "I saw no spitting, no touching. I saw a cocktail stand-up situation in a very crowded bar."

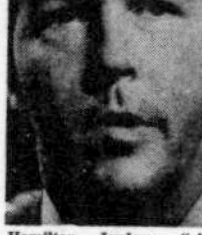

Hamilton Jordan: "An unpleasant encounter"

According to Mr Marshall, "There were a few heated words spoken, but no spitting," after Mr Jordan was surrounded by young women at the bar.

Through President Carter's press secretary, Mr Jody Powell, Mr Jordan said: "I did not say or do anything that night to any woman that was improper, and I categorically deny that I spat my drink on anyone. I did have an unpleasant encounter with a woman at the bar, but it was not precipitated by me or anything that I had done."

But the woman, who was not named, was reported to have said she turned around "and he spat again, over a girl's head and down my blouse.

Mr Jordan is an indispensable man around the White House, but he has now become an embarrassment to a President who is already under criticism for failing to live up to his righteous image.

White House press briefings yesterday were as much absorbed with the troubles of Mr Jordan as with affairs of state.

Bailiffs' reprieve for council house cows

By John Ezard

At least one comfort emerged last night for council tenants in severe rent arrears in Hereford and Worcester. Bailiffs are under a legal obligation to milk their cows before seizing the animals in distraint.

This is a requirement in a tangle of medieval common law which Wychavon Council has been using over the past few months against debtor tenants. Under the laws from the Statute of Marlborough (1267) onwards, bailiffs are also entitled to seize domestic pets. But they must not lay hands on any wild animals that may happen to be about the house.

The improbable method is working beautifully for the council. Already it has reduced previously mounting arrears by £20,000, an unprecendented 30 per cent of the total." I cannot see that—on the evidence so far—the elected council will wish to withdraw this particular method," Wychavon's chief executive, Mr P. G. Rust, said last night.

However, the housing charity Shelter, can see so many disadvantages that today Mr Graham Godden, a Midlands official, plans to tour the Boycott Estate, Droitwich, advising debtor tenants to go into a state of "siege" by locking their doors and windows.

The point about windows is that the Distress Act (1689) and other legislation up to the Law of Distress Amendment Act (1908) appears to give bailiffs a right of entry through open windows.

But locks may not be enough. It is arguable that, if a bailiff can get into the garden he can trigger the legal process of distraint by "seizing" a possession like a wheelbarrow, then look through the window and mentally "seizing" the colour television set. Technically, the set might then count as impounded and it would be improper for the tenant to use it.

This legal weapon has also been adopted by other councils, including Wyre Forest, Bromsgrove, North Tyneside, Newcastle and Kensington-Chelsea. Wychavon has recently authorised bailiffs to visit 71 of its 9,600 tenants. Three families have been physically distrained. The council is reviewing a further 20-30 cases.

"This method of rent collecting is immoral and self-defeating," Mr Bob Widdowson, Shelter housing aid trust director, said yesterday. "Many of the tenants are unemployed and rents are high. No attempt is made to assess a tenant's circumstances—the reasons for the arrears—and no consultations with social services are held."

It also contravened a 1966 Law Commission report urging that a court's leave should be granted in every case where goods are seized. "It's rather like walking in with a shotgun and saying we're going to blast your heads off if you don't pay. Of course it works but you have to consider the social cost of it."

But Mr Rust accused Shelter of overstating the case. In the cases so far, "officers of the council were satisfied there was an ability to pay which was not being reflected in rent arrears." Some tenants had been getting rent money from social security but not paying it. The method was a last resort alternative to evicting people. But, "since the reaction of Shelter," tenants were now being sent an advance warning that bailiffs might be visiting.

THE NEW FACES

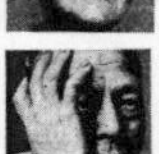

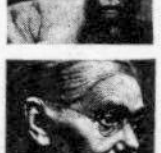

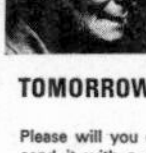

TODAY THEY NEED YOUR HELP

RUKBA is the Charity which looks after the new poor of the middle and professional classes who are aged, and struggling to live on insufficient means.

Always worried, mostly lonely and infirm, many of them disabled. Your donations *NOW* will enable RUKBA to give them the security of immediate lifelong annuities and, when necessary, the care of a Home or sheltered Flat. We are already helping over 4,500, but many more deserving people, who once thought their futures well secured, are now in really desperate need. Please help us to bring back some dignity and independence into their lives. They are not the sort who will ask for themselves but we take pride in asking for them.

TOMORROW YOU MAY NEED HELP!

Please will you complete the coupon below and send it with a generous donation in support of THE ROYAL UNITED KINGDOM BENEFICENT ASSOCIATION (Founded 1863).

RUKBA

To: The General Secretary
RUKBA
6 AVONMORE ROAD
LONDON W14 8RL

I'd like to help – here's my contribution.

Name (BLOCK CAPITALS) ____________

Address ____________

GN278

of the society who attach importance to social and cultural enrichment activities, such as books, records, sports, music, the theater and good restaurants. And they are financially prudent, investing in insurance, bank accounts and homes in preference to clothes and cars.

Most intriguing of all is the psychological profile of *Guardian* readers. A 1973 British Market Research Bureau survey showed them to rate high in tender-mindedness ("kindly, imaginative and sensitive"), imagination ("intensive subjectivity and inner mental life") and radicalism ("experimenting, analytical, free-thinking").[5] The study also found numerous opinion leaders among *Guardian* readers, people described as "adventurous, thick-skinned and socially bold."

Other surveys indicate that readers value *The Guardian* most for its lack of bias. Without a doubt, the paper, along with its more conservative counterpart, *The Times,* is a national institution in Britain, reporting all sides of life widely. But editorially it is highly opinionated. Its human interest appeals attract a wide spectrum of readers. With such an all-inclusive approach, *The Guardian* has made a significant impact on the British society.

The Guardian's small-format *Guardian Weekly* is also read widely in intellectual circles, even in other countries. In the United States, this version is the most widely read foreign paper imported into the country. Since *The Guardian* has no Sunday edition, the *Guardian Weekly,* an anthology of its best stories, fills this weekend need, with most of its 40,000 copies going abroad.

The Guardian's roots extend back to 1821, when John Edward Taylor, an ardent Liberal active in parliamentary reform, founded the *Manchester Guardian.* Taylor, son of a Manchester Unitarian minister, and a dozen of his friends hoped the paper would aid the Liberal cause. Their more immediate goal was to gain representation at Westminster (Manchester's 150,000 inhabitants had no MP at the time) so they could press for social reforms. They were still smarting as a result of the Peterloo Massacre two years earlier, when eleven people died as troops broke up a reform meeting. A prospectus published prior to the paper's first issue stated in part:

> It will zealously enforce the principles of civil and religious Liberty, in the most comprehensive sense of those terms; it will warmly advocate the cause of Reform; it will endeavour to assist in the diffusion of just principles of Political Economy. . . . The Foreign Intelligence of the week will be regularly and succinctly detailed, whilst particular attention will be paid to Parliamentary Debates. . . .[6]

The *Manchester Guardian* demonstrated its dedication to these principles by taking a leadership role in the events that led to the Reform Act of 1832 and a fairer distribution of voter representation and privileges. Ever since, the paper has championed reform.

Getting out the starting gate, *The Manchester Guardian* faced heavy local competition; six other weeklies were already publishing in Manchester. None-

[5] B. Mabey and M. Bird, "Personality and Media Selection," pamphlet, British Market Research Bureau, London, 1973.
[6] *The Story of the Guardian* (London: The Guardian, 1964), p. 5.

theless, in two years *The Guardian* was selling 1,750 copies each week. The following year sales again doubled. By 1833, it claimed Manchester's largest circulation—nearly 4,000.[7]

In 1855, when the stamp duty on newspapers was abolished, the *Manchester Guardian* became a daily, one of the first of numerous morning dailies to spring up in the provinces. It dropped its price from twopence to a penny. Thereafter, the paper grew rapidly in circulation, coverage, and prestige. Until 1861, it went through a series of editors and that year J. E. Taylor II became editor. At this time *The Guardian,* with a circulation of more than 20,000, was becoming well known as a sound and thoughtful provincial daily. In 1870 it had its own war correspondents in the Franco-Prussian War—three with the French and one with the Germans.[8]

During the 57-year editorship of Charles Prestwick Scott, who joined *The Guardian* in 1871, the paper became world famous. Scott was brought to the paper by his cousin, J. E. Taylor II. An Oxford graduate, Scott had worked briefly as an apprentice journalist at *The Scotsman* in Edinburgh. After a year with *The Guardian* and while he was but twenty-five years old, Scott was appointed editor.[9] He was determined to improve the quality of the paper. He insisted on good writing and pounced on sloppiness. At one point he wrote: "People talk as though a journalist were of necessity a pretentious and sloppy writer; he may be, on the contrary, and very often is, one of the best writers in the world. At least, he should not be content to be much less."[10] Among the outstanding journalists Scott gathered around him were John Masefield, William Archer, Laurence Housman, J. M. Keynes, Arthur Ransome, Arnold Toynbee, J. M. Synge and W. T. Stead.

Scott took such interest and pride in the editorial page that he both considered himself the keeper of the paper's conscience and tried to make the paper the nation's conscience. He instilled in his staff the conviction that *The Guardian* was a special paper, unlike other papers, in a class by itself. He enforced his high ideals firmly. Besides demanding good writing and deploring articles which displayed lack of deep thought, he insisted the paper must have "courage and fairness, and a sense of duty to the reader and community."[11] Scott's desire for fairness is evidenced in his famous words: "Comment is free, but facts are sacred. Propaganda . . . is hateful. The voice of opponents . . . has a right to be heard. . . . It is well to be frank; it is even better to be fair."[12]

During his editorship, Scott's sense of fairness led to stands on issues that sometimes made his paper unpopular. In 1886, he supported the "Irish question" (the Home Rule issue) in the face of much opposition. On numerous other

[7] *Ibid.,* p. 2.

[8] T. S. Matthews, *The Sugar Pill: An Essay on Newspapers* (London: Victor Gollancz, Ltd., 1958), p. 92.

[9] William H. Mills, *The Manchester Guardian: A Century of History* (London: Chatto and Windus, 1921), pp. 105–107.

[10] Matthews, *op. cit.,* p. 93.

[11] J. L. Hammond, *C. P. Scott of the Manchester Guardian* (New York: Harcourt, Brace and World, 1934), p. 33.

[12] D. Hudson, *British Journalists and Newspapers* (London: Collins, 1945), p. 45.

occasions he took stands which did not enhance *The Guardian*'s popularity. For example, during World War I, a highly nationalistic period, Scott's paper presented the minority views on pacificism and internationalism.

In 1907, after the death of J. E. Taylor II, Scott bought *The Guardian*. Scott's wife had just died, and he made the paper his whole life for the next 24 years. In 1921, when *The Guardian* was a hundred years old and Scott had been editor-in-chief for a half-century, all of Britain, regardless of ideology or party, congratulated him. The *Observer* called him "the greatest and in every way the best of all recorded editors." Lloyd George termed him "the noblest figure in modern journalism." Eleven years after these accolades, Scott died, ending a period of exceptional color and quality for *The Guardian*.

During C. P. Scott's editorship, his oldest son John Russell Scott served as business manager of the paper. He built up the paper's financial reserves and bought the *Manchester Evening News* in 1924. When the elder Scott retired in 1929, he was succeeded as editor by his younger son, Edward. Shortly after his father's death in 1932, Edward died in a boating accident. *The Guardian*'s chief editorial writer, W. P. Crozier was then appointed editor, a capacity he filled for the next 12 years until his death in 1956. Wadsworth had been a journalist for 40 years when he became editor. He was friendly and open, well liked. He encouraged the light touch and made the paper's style much more contemporary and colloquial than it had ever been. T. S. Matthews, who once observed that Scott made righteousness readable but Wadsworth also made it witty, summarized well how the paper developed under its editors over the 85-year period between 1871 and 1956: "Scott had made *The Guardian* a great paper: Crozier had kept it going. Wadsworth developed it and made it better than ever."[13]

Following Wadsworth's death, foreign editor Alastair Hetherington became chief editor, just a week before the Suez crisis. His stand against Britain's attempts to take over the canal cost *The Guardian* thousands of readers for a time. But under Hetherington, a conservative Liberal and an intellectual, *The Guardian*'s readership eventually rose well above 300,000 and the paper began to challenge the circulation superiority of *The Times*.

Although Hetherington was accused by his critics of being too easy with staff discipline, he was responsible for selection of staff members who brightened the paper's appearance, improved its news coverage and increased the frequency with which it came up with socially significant stories. Hetherington insisted on balanced and fair reporting and comment; during the 1970 elections *The Guardian*'s objectivity stood out partly because he had memoed staff emphasizing the need for scrupulous fairness.[14]

In 1975, Hetherington was succeeded by the present editor, Peter Preston, who, at 36, had had a varied career for the paper—as diarist, features editor and night editor. Preston continues to uphold the paper's high qualities he inherited; under him, the paper has already won several distinctions.

After C.P. Scott's death in 1932, his family gave *The Guardian* to a trust.

[13] Matthews, *op. cit.*, p. 107.
[14] Tom Baistow, "A Fair Cop for *The Guardians*," *New Statesman*, July 24, 1970, p. 79.

Called the Scott Trust, it has control of all voting shares and acts as proprietor of the publishing company it holds—The Manchester Guardian and Evening News, Ltd. Members of the Trust are three grandsons of C. P. Scott and three senior employees of the paper. Peter Gibbings serves as the present Trust Chairman. A few non-voting, fixed-dividend shares remain in public hands but they represent only a small part of the paper's capital and the fact is that the newspaper is run in a nonprofit-distributing manner.

The Trust ensures the paper's financial independence and has led to sound commercial planning. For example, when the paper's growing circulation put a strain on the Manchester-based distribution system in 1961, printing was also started in London (already in 1959 the word "Manchester" was dropped from the paper's title). Today, the paper is published simultaneously in both centers, but the main offices are in London. *The Guardian*'s Manchester offices were moved to London in 1970 and in 1976 the London offices were moved into a handsome new building on Farrington Road. These moves have paid off in terms of increased sales and more balanced national coverage.

Up-to-date equipment is employed in composing *The Guardian*. Raw copy is converted into punched tape, which is corrected on video display units and justified by computer. High speed casters controlled by computer convert the final tape into slugs of hot metal at the rate of 14 lines per minute, which then are put into page-size metal frames. High quality proofs of these frames are then picked up by a photo-electric scanner and transmitted electronically to *The Guardian*'s office in Manchester, where plastic printing plates are made from the facsimile pages received from London. In London, a flong is prepared, put into a casting box and molten lead pumped in to form the curved print cylinders, from which the pages are printed.

Several features contribute to *The Guardian*'s bright, attractive, smart appearance. A small cartoon, small pictures of personalities and a small ad or two usually grace the front page—a contrast to pre-1952 days when personal advertisements comprised the front page. One outstanding characteristic is the clear organization of the paper into sections, such as "Overseas News," "Home News," "Arts Guardian," "Financial Guardian," "Small Business Guardian," "Guardian Women," and "Sports Guardian." Virtually every issue contains feature or special report pages. Two full pages are given to editorial comment and feedback.

Early in 1978, a staff of 1,003 was serving *The Guardian*, 428 of them technical, 252 administrative and 273 editorial personnel. A staff of 100 supplies advertisement copy, including at least two full-page color ads every week. Together, they turn out four editions each day. Forty-one reporters cover government, one indicator reflecting the paper's vision of "admonishing and instructing the national conscience" and its claim to be national in charcter.

No local news is printed unless it is of national interest; local news is left to the provincial dailies. But, domestically, the paper does keep offices or bureaus in Bristol, Leeds, Edinburgh and Glasgow. In addition, local correspondents or stringers are located in every major town and city of Britain.

Ever since its founder, John Taylor, promised "foreign intelligence will be regularly and succinctly detailed," *The Guardian* has always excelled in its international coverage. At present, eight full-time correspondents located in key geographical locations and 33 stringers dispersed world-wide, supplemented by input from six wire services, assure that *The Guardian* devotes strong attention to international news.[15] The paper also keeps a team of trained reporters ready at all times to fly to any trouble spot in the world at a moment's notice. A recent Royal Commission on the British Press indicates 27 percent of the daily's news space is devoted to foreign news—clear evidence of the paper's cosmopolitan outlook. The paper has a long list of distinguished foreign correspondents, among them Alistair Cooke and James Cameron. In the years 1973 to 1977, six correspondents received awards for outstanding reportage of international stories.

The Guardian's and its staff's long list of awards for quality work adds to its prestige. In the past 15 years, in addition to recognition given its overseas correspondents, special awards have gone to staff members, often more than once for "Journalist of the Year," "Columnist of the Year," "Reporter of the Year," "Woman Journalist of the Year," "Scoop of the Year," "Critic of the Year," "Men's Fashion Writer of the Year," best English science writer, best political writer, and for sports and photography excellence. In 1973, Alistair Cooke, *Guardian*'s U.S. correspondent for 12 years, received an honorary knighthood, partly for his work with the paper. In 1971, its 150th Anniversary year, the paper won the annual Newspaper Design Award. A year later, the Granada television program, "What the Papers Say" named *The Guardian* as "Newspaper of the Year," citing its excellent writing, reporting, integrity and individuality.

Editorially, *The Guardian* calls its political stance "very liberal" as it seeks to appeal to a reading public that is "intelligent, free-thinking and with an international outlook."[16] The paper also considers itself "radical," which means "holding the most advanced views on political reform by democratic methods." It is the underlying radicalism applied to all of life which *The Guardian* believes makes it possible for the paper to support no party officially and yet avoid the danger of being uncommitted or indifferent. Ideologically, the paper thinks of itself as "center-left," a position, though unpopular in some quarters, which shows *The Guardian* has not broken with the basic liberal-radical views of the earliest days of its history.

Throughout its 150-years-plus history, *The Guardian*'s journalistic quality has been as consistent as its liberal views and its appeal to the informed and the intelligent. This time-tested combination unmistakably has made *The Guardian* one of the world's truly great newspapers, not just for a brief moment, but across the decades.

[15] As of early February, 1978, *The Guardian* had full-time correspondents in India, Africa, eastern Europe, Belgium, Cyprus, France, Israel and the U.S.A. It was taking the following wire services: AP, UPI, Reuter, Extel, AP-Dow Jones, and PA.
[16] Harding questionnaire.

Ha'aretz

(ISRAEL)

SEVERAL OUTSTANDING characteristics combine to make Israel's morning daily
Ha'aretz (The Land) of Tel Aviv the country's leading quality newspaper.

First, *Ha'aretz* justly takes pride in its independent, "no-strings-attached"
status. Whereas most Israeli newspapers are voices of trade unions, political parties, or other organizations or groups, *Ha'aretz* remains nonpartisan.[1] That
stance has led to another plus—the paper, while maintaining strong loyalty to
the nation, has become increasingly fearless in its battle against governmental
and societal failings and injustices. It places strong emphasis on foreign news
and takes special interest in appealing to business and political leadership. Its
editorial and reportorial standards are high and its appearance is sober and
serious, sophisticated without being snobbish.

The oldest paper in the country, *Ha'aretz* was started in 1919 by "a group
of prominent Russian Jewish Zionists who immigrated into Israel after World
War I,"[2] when Tel Aviv was yet a small town and the Hebrew-speaking population of Palestine numbered only about 50,000. For the first ten years until the
British news agency Reuters opened services in Tel Aviv, the paper got the bulk
of its news from Cairo by train, a day or so late. "Its early years were marked by
struggles with competitors and against economic difficulties."[3] *Ha'aretz* did not
really prosper until it was purchased in the mid-thirties by a wealthy German
businessman and department store owner, Zalman Schrocken, who regarded
publishing as a sideline. The paper's main expansion came during the years just
prior to and immediately after World War II, when there was a mass influx of
European Jews into Palestine.

In 1939, Zalman Schrocken's son Gershom became the editor-in-chief.
During the past 40 years, he has served as editor, publisher and owner. In that
period, he has made *Ha'aretz* a true "information" paper and has upgraded it in
numerous ways. Today, Gershom's son Amos acts as general manager, making
Ha'aretz a three-generation family newspaper.

Ha'aretz's weekday editions, usually from 12 to 20 pages in length, circulate
to about 55,000 readers, about 85 percent of which are regular subscribers. The
thicker weekend (Friday) edition, usually some 60 to 70 pages long, circulates

---

[1] Aviv Akrony, Cultural Attaché of Israeli Consulate (Chicago) in interview with John Merrill, April 22,
1966. See also entire issue of *Gazette*, Leiden, 7:1 (1961) given over to Israeli press.

[2] Gershom Schrocken in reply to questionnaire mailed to Harold Fisher, January 10, 1978. (Hereafter
called Schrocken questionnaire.)

[3] "World Press—II," London *Times*, 1975.

about 75,000 copies. There is a daily airmail edition of 4,000 copies, most of which reach readers in the United States.[4] The paper's chief competitor is another quality daily, *Ma'ariv*, an afternoon paper also published in Tel Aviv and circulating about 100,000 copies. *Ha'aretz*'s seriousness is reflected in the intellectual appeal of its writing, the use of only a few pictures (one, two, sometimes three on the front page and a few scattered throughout the issue) and the presence of but a single advertisement on the front page.

Schrocken continually seeks to upgrade the quality of *Ha'aretz*. In 1939, he organized a morgue, which he has since built into Israel's most complete newspaper archive.[5] He has brought to his staff "one of the world's finest political cartoonists," whose full-page cartoons caricature the Israeli view of the world's leaders.[6] He gives full rein to the talented staff he has gathered about himself. Interestingly, journalistic experience and academic training in the field have traditionally not been important to Schrocken when he hired staff members. He has looked first for people "with university degrees, general education and command of English, at least, preferably more languages."[7] Although he now employs an increasing number of writers and reporters with journalism training and/or newspaper experience, Schrocken still regards native intelligence, quick adaptability, versatility and general erudition as the most desirable characteristics to seek in a potential staff member.

The sensitivity of Israel to international affairs is reflected in the paper's emphasis on foreign news, which usually appear on the front and third pages. *Ha'aretz* has had as many as nine full-time correspondents in the world's leading capital cities.[8] In addition, it receives the services of the United States, British, French and Jewish news agencies.

There can never be doubt about the newspaper's loyalty to Zionist fundamentals and the better interests of Israeli nationhood. But, at the same time, *Ha'aretz* has distinguished itself in recent years with incisive investigative reporting and bold exposés of governmental and military encroachments on public and press freedoms. In 1973, it severely criticized Moshe Dayan, after supporting him for years, for "urging accelerated Jewish settlement and land purchase in the occupied West Bank."[9] In 1974, it was fined for daring to criticize the military leadership for censoring releases to the press.[10] Early in 1977, *Ha'aretz* exposed the violation of Israeli exchange controls by former Prime Minister Yizchaq Rabin and his wife—information that led to Rabin's resignation and the defeat of the Labour Party in the May elections. The paper followed with a series of articles which laid bare the damaging effects of foreign exchange control to the development of the economy—information which finally led to the lifting of

[4] Schrocken questionnaire.

[5] Gershom Schocken in letter to Harold Fisher, January 10, 1978.

[6] "World Press—II," *loc. cit.*

[7] Schrocken questionnaire, *loc. cit.* All staff must, at minimum, be bilingual, since the paper is published in Hebrew.

[8] Correspondents are presently located in Washington, New York, London, Paris, Bonn, Brussels and Bale; in the past, there have been reporters in Copenhagen and Firenze as well.

[9] "World Press—II," *loc. cit.*

[10] "Press Freedom Report, 1974," *I.P.I. Report,* Vol. 24, No. 1 (January, 1975), p. 17.

הארץ

V. 60 / 17917/FEBRUARY 22 '75

בפעם הראשונה, בגלוי:

קהיר: לאש"ף אין זכות לייצג את הפלשתינאים

"הארגון ביצע שורשים של מעשים מתועבים" * מסקר יחידת הקומנדו המצרי * "בגדודה הקטפונים, שדור בגבם של המצרים" * סאדאת מקבלת פנים לחיילים שחזרו, אך שלח את שרי משרד בריאות

נשיא קפריסין "מוכן להיפגש עם סאדאת לשיפור היחסים"

ראש הממשלה... משוחח ...

צעדי חירום במדיניות ה,שוק" לבלום האטה הכלכלית

נשיא הבנק...

הצטרף לקופה שהוכיחה את עצמה!...

"עתיד"

קופת תגמולים מרכזית ליד בנק המזרחי המאוחד בע"מ

מחקר של אוניברסיטת תל-אביב קובע כי הרווחים המצטברים של קופת "עתיד" במשך 6 השנים האחרונות, הן הגבוהים ביותר מבין המומל של הבנקים הגדולים שנבדקו במחקר ...הצטרף גם אתה לקופה טובה באמת.

בגין הציע לאתרטון כינוס תת-ועדה ישראלית-מצרית

הערב בחירת דולצין ליו"ר ההנהלה הציונית

ראונ מאירן בקונגרס לאשר מכירת הנשק כ,,חבילה אחת"

מאת יואב קרני, וושינגטון

אפסקת הנשק בדיון מברכז בדיון אסד במוסקבה

היום יחודש המסחר באג"ח בלי הגבלה בתנודות שערים

דוכאה עוד התפרעות בכלא הצבאי במגידו

אש אוסטרלית בדרום לבנון

25 שנות מאסר לאנס חליוואה

ביומיים: לנוכח שרשרת מעשים נוראים ומדהימים בחומרתם מתנצלת המשטרה מעל גל של שיקול אחר

חקלאות
ראה עמודים 14—15

the controls in November.[11] As early as 1971, the paper carried a series of articles which called attention to the development of organized crime in Israel. Last year, at great personal risk to himself, the paper's police reporter revealed the alarming growth of organized crime (police had said it did not exist). His series spurred the appointment of a commission of investigation whose report in early 1978 vindicated *Ha'aretz* and brought official government action against the drug and diamond smuggling rings.[12]

Nor is the paper afraid to speak out against those who manipulate business for personal gain. In 1975, for example, it produced a series of investigative articles which played a role in revealing financial fraud involving heads of corporations in Israel and certain European banks.[13]

Ha'aretz's "Independent Liberal" views are further illustrated in its stands for civil rights, economic progress and defense of a healthy environment. Its economic and parliamentary reports (there are ten reporters covering governmental affairs) and its interpretive pieces are influential. It has fought consistently for better treatment of the Arab minority. It has crusaded for conservation of natural resources and for national beautification projects. It is the leading press proponent of separation of religion and state.[14]

Ha'aretz is produced by Ha'aretz Publishing, Ltd., a family owned operation managed by Amos Schrocken, a son of the paper's editor and publisher, a graduate of Harvard's Business School and a former employee of Fairchild Publications in New York. The company employs a staff of approximately 400, of whom about 100 are engaged in technical production aspects of the paper. The editorial staff of *Ha'aretz* totals about 100, including governmental reporters and the overseas staff. Together, the staff produces an 18–24 page, two-section *Ha'aretz* daily.

In general, *Ha'aretz* presents a serious, gray, somewhat dull appearance. The paper's nine narrow columns give a vertical look to the paper and there is little deviance from this pattern. Like papers in all Semitic languages, *Ha'aretz* folds on the right hand side and opens on the left, and copy reads from right to left across the page. The nameplate is placed in the upper right-hand corner of the front page and is flanked on its left by a small advertisement. Normally, the front page carries only one other advertisement, a large one placed in the lower left-hand corner. Headlines are set in bold, heavy script. Most headlines have sub-titles and important sub-sections or paragraphs of an article are introduced by a small heading in small, bold type. Some of the headlines are framed to attract attention to them. Wide top and bottom borders and adroit employment of white space do much to avert a crowded look and give the appearance of spaciousness. However, this serious paper is loaded with information; the front page normally is filled with a dozen or more articles. Most of the stories are concluded on the first page, although some are continued, usually to page two.

The remainder of the first section carries local, state and international

[11] Gershom Schrocken in letter to Harold Fisher dated March 1, 1978.
[12] *Ibid.*
[13] "World Press—II," *loc. cit.*
[14] "Newspapers of the World—XVIII," London *Times* (April 7, 1965), p. 11.

news, investigative pieces and other feature materials. There is a business page which places heavy emphasis on stock quotations and finance. Sports are usually confined to a single page or two. Throughout this first section, as for all the paper, there is an average of one to two photographs per page; in general, the paper's photographs lack attractiveness and are frequently rather poorly reproduced, with insufficient clarity and contrast. *Ha'aretz*'s infrequent cartoons invariably display a cynically humorous twist and their pro-Israeli bias is obvious.

Advertising covers about 45 percent of the total space in *Ha'aretz,* considerably less than most Western newspapers. In general, advertisements are somewhat crowded and not visually attractive; however, some rather striking techniques are employed, such as large black-inked areas broken only by a single word, phrase or symbol.

The second section of *Ha'aretz* is devoted to a wide range of human interest materials—features, commentary, the arts and entertainment. There is often a page of religious news and features. Cinema, theater, and television schedules are regularly printed in this section. Occasionally, the bulk of this part is given to emphasis on a single topic, such as style or art. In such cases, numerous photographs may be included. Personal classifieds and retail advertisements usually conclude this section.

Throughout the week, *Ha'aretz* is aimed at the intellectuals, professionals and businessmen of better-than-average education and sophistication. However, its Friday edition seeks to appeal to a much larger and more entertainment-minded audience. In 1963, it initiated a 48-page, heavily illustrated magazine supplement in color, which is inserted in the Friday edition and contains human interest materials of all types, such as sports, fashion, entertainment and adventure pieces. Noteworthy Hebrew writers contribute poetry and fiction to the special literary pages of the Friday edition and special editions published on the eves of holidays.

With its emphasis on serious, sophisticated and well-informed writing, *Ha'aretz* typifies the best in Israeli quality journalism. Through its nonpartisan independence and high quality investigative reporting, it serves as an effective "watchdog" against excesses and in the interests of the Israeli public. And by its broad international reportage, it reflects and extends Israel's cosmopolitan interests or, what one author has called "the outward-mindedness of a small country."[15]

[15] Harry Golden, "The Israeli Press," *Publisher's Auxilliary* (June 20, 1964), p. 4.

Helsingin Sanomat

(FINLAND)

IN FINLAND, every fourth person over twelve years of age regularly reads the *Helsingin Sanomat,* the country's biggest and finest quality newspaper. Like other Scandinavians, Finland's nearly five million people are avid readers. In addition to taking a local paper and several periodicals, almost every Finnish home subscribes to one of the country's approximately 60 dailies, and the *Helsingin Sanomat* is their favorite. It is, in fact, the only newspaper in the country with a circulation of over 100,000 copies.[1] As of mid-1978, its daily circulation stood at 366,000, with sales of Sunday papers running 418,000.[2] About 97 percent of the paper's readers are subscribers. Only about one-third of its circulation is in Helsinki; the remainder spreads out over the entire nation even into the Arctic Circle as a truly national newspaper.

Helsingin Sanomat is an independent paper, both politically and economically. In Finland, about 54 percent of the newspapers are independent and the other 46 percent have party affiliations. *Helsingin Sanomat* declared itself free of party affiliations in 1932, and has remained that way since. The paper prizes its independence; it strongly advocates democracy, social justice and freedom of thought and has fought hard for liberal and constitutional ideas. It strives to achieve these goals through unbiased, dependable and fast news coverage. Because of its independence, its columnists represent various sectors of public opinion in the country and almost everyone can find his views in the paper— another reason for its popularity.

One family has owned and operated *Helsingin Sanomat* from its inception. Eero Erkko founded the paper in 1889 and today his grandson, Aatos Erkko is its publisher and chairman of the Sanoma Publishing Company, which also publishes an afternoon paper, periodicals, magazines, catalogues and books and holds the ownership of two print plants near Helsinki. It also owns stock in Suomen Tietotomisto—Finska Notisbryan (STT—the Finnish News Agency), Rautakirja (a newspaper distributing outfit), Levikintarkastus (a newspaper circulation control company), and is a member of Sanomalehtien Liitto (Association of Finnish Dailies). By its wise management, the Erkko family has kept the paper solvent, vigorous and growing until today their Company is Finland's largest publishing empire. More important, considering the competition and the po-

---

[1] Kenneth E. Olson, *The History Makers: The Press of Europe from its Beginnings through 1965* (Baton Rouge: Louisiana State University Press, 1966), p. 91.

[2] Aatos Erkko, publisher, *Helsingin Sanomat* in response to questionnaire dated April 29, 1978.

VIEHÄTTÄVÄT VOITTAJAT

Viestin viehättävät voittajat Taina Impiö (vas.), Marja-Liisa Hämäläinen, Hilkka Riihivuori ja Helena Takalo.

Hilkan hirmuinen hiihto ratkaisi

Hilkka Riihivuori pohjusti hirmuisella hiihdollaan naisten viestin maailmanmestaruuden Lahdessa. Hilkka kiskoi Neuvostoliiton ja DDR:n mahdottomalta tuntuneen etumatkan kiinni.

Hiihdon MM
Lahti 17.—26. 2

Lahti (HS) Hilkka Riihivuoren, 25, hirmuinen hiihto kolmannella osuudella ratkaisi Suomen naisille maailmanmestaruuden 4 x 5 kilometrin viestissä, Viestivoittoa pohjusti hienosti avausosuuden hiihtänyt Taina Impiö, 21, joka tuli ensimmäisen vaihtoon ensimmäisenä. Marja-Liisa Hämäläinen joutui kakkososuudella päästämään sekä Neuvos-

toliiton että DDR:n ohitseen. Hilkka Riihivuori pääsi lähtemään omalle taipaleelleen puoli minuuttia kärkikaksikon perässä.

Yleisön huutaessa Hilkka veti sekunti sekunnilta eroa kiinni. Hän tuli viimeiseen vaihtoon ensimmäisenä uskomattoman hiihtonsa jälkeen.

Helena Takalolla, 30, viiden kilometrin maailmanmestarilla oli varaa odotel-

la maalilinjalla Neuvostoliiton Galina Kulakovan matkaan lähtöä.

Etukäteistaktiikan mukaan Helenan piti vain rotkua Kulakovan kannassa ja mennä sopivaksi katsomassaan paikassa ohi. Eikä Helenaa pidätellyt mikään. Kolmen kilometrin kohdalla hän painaloi Kulakovan ja DDR:n Christel Meinelin ohi. Sen jälkeen ei Suomen voitosta enää

ollut epäilystä. DDR tuli yllätäen kilpailussa toiseksi ja Neuvostoliitto kolmanneksi.

. Suomen naisten mitalitili oli mahtava: kaksi kultaa, yksi hopea ja yksi pronssi. Suotta ei kukkia lehdistötilaisuudessa jakanut kuniatoimikunnan puheenjohtaja Keijo Liinamaa puhunut "viehättävistä voittamattomista."

MM-sivut 23—27

Uusi hallitus saa vastaansa Suomen Pankin

Suomen Pankin ja uuden hallituksen yhteentörmäys näytti olevan edessä, kun pääministeri Kalevi Sorsan (sd) kolmannen hallituksen ohjelmaneuvottelut käynnistettiin keskiviikkona. Suomen Pankki ei ole halukas sellaiseen ulkomaisen lainan määräkin, jota hallituksenmuodostajat katsovat tarvittevansa valtion talouden katteeksi.

Uuden hallituksen ohjelmaa valmistelemaan asetettiin keskiviikkona työryhmä. Ohjelmaluonnos aiotaan saada valmiiksi ensi viikon alussa. Tavoitteena on saada uusi hallitus kokoon jo ensi keskiviikoksi tai torstaiksi.

Hallitusneuvotteluista jättäytyivät pois jo ennen ensimmäistä ohjelmaneuvottelua Skp:n taistolaiset, kun heidän esityksensä hävisivät Skp:n politbyroon äänestyksessä 7—5.

Keskiviikkona ounasteltiin myös Sorsan toisen hallituksen valtiovarainministerin Paul Paavelan (sd) jättäytyvän syrjään uudesta hallituksesta. Paavela ei ollut mukana keskiviikon hallitusneuvotteluissa valtiovarainministeriön edustajana eikä hän osallistunut myöskään Sdp:n puolueetoimikunnan kokoukseen illalla.

— Sivu 7.

Uutta enemmistöhallitusta rakentelevan viiden puolueen edustajat kokoontuivat pääministeri Kalevi Sorsan (selin) johdolla keskiviikkona Valtioneuvoston juhlahuoneistossa.

Jarmo Hietaranta

— Sivu 19.
— Sivu 21.
— Sivu 7.
— Sivu 16.

Egypti katkaisi suhteensa Kyprokseen

Kairo (Reuter) Varaulkoministeri Butros Butros-Ghali ilmoitti keskiviikkona, että Egypti on katkaissut diplomaattiset suhteensa Kyprokseen.

Butros-Ghali sanoi, että suhteiden katkeaminen on tulos presidentti Anwar Sadatin samana päivänä julkistamasta päätöksestä kieltäytyä tunnustamasta enää Spyros Kyprianouta Kyproksen presidentiksi.

Larnakassa viime sunnuntaina sattuneen egyptiläisten ja kyprolaisten sotilaiden verisen yhteenoton vuoksi.

Lähi-idän uutistoimisto Mena kertoi, että Egyptin Kyprokseen toimiva suurlähettiläs palaa kotimaahan perjantaina. Kyproksen Kairon-suurlähettiläs ilmoitti keskiviikkona myös lähtevänsä asemapaikastaan.

— Sivu 19.

OECD kehottaa Suomea

Kulutusta on varaa lisätä

Yksityistä kulutusta pitäisi lisätä Suomessa, kehottaa taloudellisen yhteistyön ja kehityksen järjestö (OECD). Tähän on hyvät edellytykset, koska vaihtotase saattaa muuttua tänä vuonna ylijäämäiseksi.

Vaikka kulutusta lisättäisiin, siitä ei ole OECD:n mukaan inflaation vauhdittumisen vaaraa. Järjestö uskoo Suomen pystyvän pitämään inflaation kurissa eli noin kuudessa prosentissa.

OECD kehottaa Suomea nopeuttamaan myös valtion ja kuntien suunnittelemien investointien toteuttamista.

— Sivu 21.

Työttömien määrä väheni tuhannella

Työttömyyskortistoihin ilmoittautuneiden työttömien määrä on vähentynyt tammikuusta runsaalla tuhannella. Helmikuun puolivälin ennakkotietojen mukaan työttömiä on nyt 195 300. Vastaava luku oli tammikuun puolivälissä 196 400.

Työttömistä 195 300 suomalaisesta oli helmikuussa pakkolomalla 25 000 kuten tammikuussakin. Lyhennetylle työviikolle on joutunut sen sijaan lähes 7 000 työntekijää tammikuun määrää enemmän. Lyhennettyä työviikkoa teki nyt 45 700, tammikuussa 38 800.

Keskiviikkona maan halituseuvotteijoille kerrotaan tutkijoiden uusien työttömyystietojen mukaan työllisyys on parantunut nyt selvästi lisesti eniten kehittyväisellä.

Työttömyys lisääntyi joulukuusta tammikuuhun yli 30 000 työttömällä. Työttömyyden kasvun pyrähtäminen syitä ei keskiviikkona ennakkotietojen pohjalta vielä osattu arvioida. Yhtenä arveluna esitettiin, että helmikuussa armeijaan menneet, joita oli tavanomaista enemmän, saatiaisivat näkyä uusissa, odotettua suotuisammissa työttömyysluvuissa.

Ahvenanmaalle kaksi jäätietä

Viime aikojen pakkaset ovat jälleen monen vuoden tauon jälkeen vahvistaneet jäitä niin, että epävirallisia jääteitä mantereelta Ahvenanmaalle ovat jälleen avoinna.

Piirrettiin tänään matkan ajaa 150—250 henkilöautoa, jotka nuorin osa ahvenanmaalaisia.

Epävirallisesti on avoinna kaksi reittiä, joista toinen lähtee Ahvenanmaalta Sandbroudista Ahvenanmaan koillispuolelta ja jatkuu sieltä Enklingeen, Asterholmaan, Näotbyhyn, Kaisvoliin ja Rysättyylään asti sieltä Turkuun.

Toinen reitti taas on Sandbund — Enklinge — Asterholma — Appö — Lauppamen (Kustavi) — Turku.

Molemmilla reiteillä on railovaaroja. Reitin varrella ei liikenteessä Enklingen — Kumlingen, Lappon — Asterholman asti Inö — Lauppasen välillä sekä Kaisaaren luona.

HS tukee nuoria tanssijoita

Nuorille tanssijoille järjestettiin kilpailu ensi kerran Kuopio heveäll ja on »viikolla. Helsingin Sanomat lahjoittaa kilpailun palkinnoksi kaikkiaan 16 000 mk. Sekä 15—22-vuotiaiden tyttöjen että poikien sarjassa on 1 palkinnon määrä 6 000 mk, II 2 000 mk ja III 1 000 mk.

Kilpailin on lajissaan maamme ensimmäinen. Aikaisemmin ei ole lainkaan järjestetty ammatti-

tason tanssikilpailuja, joiden palkinnoilla olisi ollut epävirallinen jättävät mainittavia Ahvenanmaan asemapaikastaan.

Tanssikilpailu, joka edustaan tanssia maamme tähdillä, mukana nuorin esittävän viikonloppu ja on vilkastuttaa eri virittäädön tulonta Kuopion tanssiviikkoa. Ajatus kilpailun järjenäemisestä on herkästy Suomen Tanssitaiteilijain Liitossa.

— Sivu 16.

litical pressures to which the *Helsingin Sanomat* has been subjected through the years, its consistent struggles for independence and freedom and its rise to the nation's circulation leadership are further remarkable attributions to the foresight, courage and effective management of Eero Erkko and his descendants.

Eero Erkko, son of a southern Finnish farmer, founded *Helsingin Sanomat's* forerunner, *Paivalehti* in 1889 amidst heavy competition from other papers and strong suppression of press freedoms. At the time, some 51 Finnish and 44 Swedish papers, the latter appealing mostly to the middle and upper classes, could be found in the principality of Finland, which was then ruled by Nicholas II. The Tsar imposed censorship on the press and suppressed scores of newspapers that dared oppose him.[3] Among those who fought the Tsar's policies, often by founding underground newspapers, was a cultural, liberal and realistic literary group called the Young Finns. Erkko, one of the leaders of this group, set out boldly with his closest journalist and writer friends to pursue the dream of Finnish independence by starting the *Päivälehti*. It quickly became "the first important Finnish-language newspaper which by means of radical Finnishness managed to combine a liberal and democratic policy in public affairs."[4] Because of its daring liberal views, the *Päivälehti* was suspended eleven times. In 1903, Erkko, as its chairman and editor-in-chief was banished on twenty-four hours' notice. He fled to the United States, where he started and edited a Finnish newspaper in Brooklyn.

Meantime, the *Päivälehti*, under the direction of Santeri Ivalo, a well-known historical novelist and one of the paper's editors, continued the liberal views and strong defense of the constitutional rights of the Finnish people which Erkko had championed. Because of the political climate, *Päivälehti* was forced to suspend publication and close down on July 3, 1904.

A few months later, to fill the gap, the Sanoma Publishing Company was formed and on September 24, 1904, the *Helsingin Sanomat* (Helsinki Mail) appeared six times a week to take up the banner of its predecessor. Nothing but the name had really changed. The new paper supported the Young Finns Constitutional Party, which had come into being shortly before. It placed strong emphasis on news. Almost at once, it moved into circulation leadership. "In 1914, publication began on Mondays as well, making the *Helsingin Sanomat* a seven days a week paper for the first time."[5] When he returned from exile in 1905, Eero Erkko was arrested and held in prison until his release in 1918. But, until his death in 1927, he was always the central figure in the expansion of Sanoma Publishing Company and *Helsingin Sanomat*.

Eljas Erkko, Eero's son, took over the direction of the paper in 1927 when his father's health failed. His dynamic personality dominated the *Helsingin Sanomat* until he died in 1965. He was one of the world's best-known publishers and was often referred to by his countrymen as "Finland's press king," and his paper simply as "the Erkkos paper." He freed his paper from all political

---

[3] Olson, *op. cit.*, p. 83.
[4] Torsten Steinby, *Finland's Press: In Quest of Freedom*, Helsinki, 1971, p. 41.
[5] Brochure, "Sanoma Publishing Company," Sanomaprint, Helsinki, 1976.

party affiliations in 1932 by dropping associations with the Progressive party. He greatly expanded the paper's coverage, began sending out special foreign correspondents and signed news agreements with world agencies and important newspapers. In addition to making his paper the largest and best in his country, Eljas Erkko also achieved personal fame. He distinguished himself as a commander in the 1918 war of liberation and later became Foreign Minister of his country.[6]

In 1965, Eljas' son and the third generation of *Helsingin Sanomat*'s great family of publishers, Aatos Erkko took charge. He is both publisher of *Helsingin Sanomat* today as well as chief executive and chairman of the Sanoma Publishing Company. Under him, the Company has expanded and diversified its interests until today its varied activities provide a livelihood for almost 5,000 people, including 1,600 newspaper distributors and some 400 retirees. Of that number, a total staff of 1,262 serve *Helsingin Sanomat,* including a writing and editorial staff of 230 journalists. The paper is guided by its former editor and chief publisher, Aatos Erkko and its collective team of senior editors-in-chief—Heikki Tikkanen, Teo Mertanen, Keijo Kalavaara and Simopekka Nortamo. As part of its diversification, the Company publishes an afternoon broadsheet counterpart of the *Helsingin Sanomat,* called the *Ilta-Sanomat,* which had a circulation of about 120,000 in 1976. It produces several family, women's, children's and other specialized magazines and books. The Company has a printing division called Sanomaprint; half of the work of its two plants is production of materials published by Sanoma and the other half comes from outside contracts.

Since its founding, the *Helsingin Sanomat* has always been located on Ludviginatu (Ludvig Street), Helsinki's equivalent of London's Fleet Street. Under Aatos Erkko, a large, new and modern newspaper production plant has been planned and constructed on a site 16 kilometers north of the old location. Plans are under way for a new main office building.

Besides its political independence and benevolent ruling family, many other factors contribute to *Helsingin Sanomat*'s being Finland's leading newspaper.

First, there is the paper's openness which reflects a neutral or multivalued picture of controversial political questions. It seeks to be politically independent, not aligned with any party, taking a liberal, middle-of-the-line position. In a 1977 content analysis study of the Finnish media, the Honorable Osmo Wiio, member of the Finnish Parliament and professor of the Finnish Institute for Human Communications, found that "The most open medium in the message system would be *Helsingin Sanomat,* the largest newspaper in the country. Most Finns agree."[7] According to Professor Wiio, "This means that the contents of the paper are 'unpredictable'. . . . it is open to all kinds of views and opinions."[8] and he further cites a case study by one of his doctoral students which showed the *Helsingin Sanomat*'s reportage of a long strike to be "quite bal-

[6] Olson, *op. cit.,* p. 93.

[7] Osmo A. Wiio, "Open and Closed Mass Media Systems and Problems of International Communications Policy," *Studies of Broadcasting,* No. 13, 1977, p. 80.

[8] Osmo A. Wiio in personal letter to H. Fisher, dated April 9, 1978. Professor Wiio is generally considered one of Finland's best authorities in the field of mass communications.

anced" treatment of the union's and the employer's sides of the story. Wiio also observes that this pluralism of the paper has not always been unanimously applauded, some people feeling too much space is given to leftist ideas and that the culture department particularly tends to be left-leaning. In spite of such criticism, Professor Wiio considers the paper to be "mostly unbiased in its reporting." On the whole, this practice of openness, of pluralism nets the paper many readers across party lines, a reputation for thorough coverage of events from all points of view and the satisfaction of stimulating lively discussion and debate among its numerous readers.

Another noteworthy quality which sets the *Helsingin Sanomat* apart as Finland's best is its serious concern with full coverage of the news. Its foreign coverage is among the best in the world; Professor Wiio says the foreign section is "excellent and competes with the best papers anywhere."[9] There are six foreign correspondents stationed in Geneva, London, Washington, Moscow, Peking (shared jointly with *Dagens Nyheter*) and Stockholm (for the Nordic countries), plus three part-time international staff in Denmark, Norway and Brazil. In addition, its newsmen travel extensively around the globe. The work of these correspondents is supplemented by wire service input from AP, UPI and Reuters, plus all European agencies via STT, the Finnish National News Agency. Newspaper syndicated services from Washington *Post*-Los Angeles *Times,* New York *Times, Newsweek* and *The Financial Times* also enrich the international content of *Helsingin Sanomat.*

The fact that *Helsingin Sanomat* has the largest domestic news coverage from all parts of Finland of any newspaper further establishes it as a great national newspaper. An editorial staff of 180 reporters and photographers work in Helsinki, providing comprehensive coverage of national government and all events of significance in the capital. In addition, regional reporters and photographers are located all over the nation. The paper is noted for its regular and thorough, but non-sensational investigative reporting.

But the *Helsingin Sanomat* is considered the best in Finland for other reasons as well. It is famous in Finland for its business news, sport pages and arts and literature section. It continuously publishes long and short feature and background articles and debates representing the full variety of opinions from all parts of the political and ideological fields. The Sunday edition often contains from ten to twelve full pages of special features. Its pictures are numerous and informative. There is high quality entertainment material for the entire family. There is much for everyone, and especially those with broad interests and liberal views, in *Helsingin Sanomat.*

The newspaper also evidences an invigorating independence and progressive spirit in its editorial expression. It puts no restrictions on its editorial policy of what or what not to publish other than that the paper should exercise "responsibility with aim towards common sense and professional ethics."[10] Editorial policies are thrashed out at conferences of the top executives. Although it is

[9] *Ibid.*
[10] Erkko questionnaire.

never reluctant to present its own opinions in clear and unequivocal language, it is also always ready to make other opinions available to its readers. Most of the paper's views represent the liberal middle way, although it has never allowed itself to become the mouthpiece of the political parties of the center. Its columnists represent various sectors of public opinion in Finland, and the columns are popular and often the cause of heated debates and heavy reader reaction. The paper's Letters to the Editor section is popular and an important source of reader-newspaper interaction.

For decades, *Helsingin Sanomat* has been the leading advertisement medium in Finland, carrying more ads than any other newspaper. Its advertiser dominance comes partly from its excellent and complete news coverage and partly from the excellent services it provides advertisers. An increasing number of its advertisements appear in color. Its classified advertisements, with sectors, among others, for jobs and vacancies and the real estate market are read nationwide. The amount of display advertising provided by national producers and especially the retailers of the metropolitan Helsinki area is impressive in comparison with that of any other Finnish paper. *Helsingin Sanomat* is one of the few remaining great newspapers to give over its entire front page to advertising. With the front page unavailable for news, the editors have made the first inside right page (page 3) opposite the editorial page (page 2) the main news page.

The *Helsingin Sanomat* daily averages 38 pages per day on weekdays and 54 pages on Sundays, with the largest number of pages for a single issue to date being 92 pages. It is published daily in three editions, two for the provinces with a deadline of 11:00 P.M. and the last for the Helsinki area. To obtain and prepare the wide range of diverse news material these thick editions require, the news department is divided into sections and editorial technical matters are handled by a central editorial section. They have available to them an excellent press archives library manned by a staff of 90 persons which contains over four million newspaper clippings. To turn out their large production efficiently, the production departments employ about 600 people. Four letterpress presses have been used to publish the paper. The text has recently been composed with the aid of computers, part of it on hot metal, but, as of the end of 1978, makeup was being computerized and all text was transferred to photocomposition and offset printing.

In order to keep its quality high, the Sanoma Publishing Company engages in teaching future journalists. Annually, it takes about 20 new students into its two-year study-work experience, professional Sanoma School of Journalism. Students are picked on the basis of their talent and promise. About half of those who complete the course find employment with the paper. The Company also has a school for teaching the printing trades and another for training marketing and sales personnel.

Helsingin Sanomat today finds itself, like other Finnish newspapers, in a position relative to the East and to the West which calls for considerable journalistic skill and diplomacy. Steering a path through the midst of the ideological storms raging around it is no easy task for a nation or a newspaper which desires to function freely and intelligently. Finland, a Scandinavian country oriented towards western Europe but geographically in the middle, is managing to cope with these storms and to live with both ideological "camps." Its best and most popular newspaper, *Helsingin Sanomat* speaks out daily with courage. Because it stands firmly on the principles of freedom, democracy and social justice and carefully maintains its full independence from establishment pressure groups within and without,[11] it can keep the nation informed of all sides of issues and entertain a wide range of opinions. In this way, it helps to preserve Finland's national independence and equilibrium and to perpetuate its own tradition as a dignified and reliable quality national newspaper, the country's largest and best. And these same qualities also help to rate *Helsingin Sanomat* as one of the world's greatest dailies.

The Hindu

(INDIA)

OF INDIA'S APPROXIMATELY 60 English-language dailies, five rank as the nation's representatives of the quality press—*The Times of India* (Bombay), *The Statesman* (Calcutta), *The Hindustan Times* (New Delhi), *The Indian Express* (Bombay), and *The Hindu* (Madras). Every one of this "Big Five," each outstanding in its own way, could be called a "national" newspaper because of its circulation and interests. During India's recent State of Emergency, the first four showed even greater open defiance of the government's restrictive moves against the press than *The Hindu*. But among the "Big Five," *The Hindu* enjoys the highest reputation for reliability and concern for truthful and comprehensive coverage. Among them, too, it commands the widest international respect as an authoritative expression of liberal and cosmopolitan attitudes. It is usually considered India's most serious English-language daily.

As *The Hindu* celebrated the 100th anniversary of its founding on September 4, 1978, its editor, Mr. G. Kasturi outlined for a distinguished crowd gathered for the occasion the paper's record and future intent. He said, in part:

> . . . In the ranks of its editorial staff, *The Hindu* has always been fortunate to have men of intellectual substance and integrity—qualities so essential to sustain the understanding and support of the public day after day. . . .
>
> We—those who own and manage *The Hindu* today—would like to state that we continue to nurture the same feeling of a national trust about this newspaper, as those venerable predecessors of ours did in the past. In the pursuit of our ob-

---

[11] Erkko questionnaire.

THE HINDU
India's National Newspaper
CENTENARY YEAR 1977-78
Vol. 101. No. 43.
16 Pages.
Printed at Madras, Coimbatore, Bangalore & Hyderabad.
45 p
MADRAS
WEDNESDAY
FEBRUARY 22, 1978.
Air Surcharge 15 p

Concessions for Second Class Passengers

Sleeper and Reservation Charges Reduced

Big Surplus in Ry. Budget

From Our Special Correspondent

NEW DELHI, Feb. 21.

There will be no increase in either the railway passenger fares or freight during 1978-79. The charge for sleeper accommodation for second class passengers will also be reduced to Rs. 5 for the entire journey as against the present Rs. 5 for the first night and Rs. 3 for subsequent nights for three-tier accommodation and Rs. 5 for the subsequent nights for two-tier berths.

Reservation charges for second class sitting and sleeper accommodation will be reduced from 50 Paise to 25 Paise while surcharge on super-fast express trains will be reduced from Re. 1.50 to Re. 1 for second class passengers. In the case of super-fast trains which have ceased to be such, the surcharge will be abolished altogether.

These are among the major concessions announced to-day by Mr. Madhu Dandavate, Railway Minister, when he presented a Rs. 65.43-crore surplus budge for 1978-79.

The Railway Minister also announced that as against the estimated surplus of not more than Rs. 32.5 crores for 1977-78, the actual surplus for the year is expected to be Rs. 89.32 crores, i.e., Rs. 57 crores higher.

"This is", he said, "after providing for Rs. 140 crores towards Depreciation Reserve Fund, Rs. 40 crores for Pension Fund and after making full payment of dividend to the General Revenues to the extent of Rs. 227 crores. In this context, it is significant to note that whereas the actual surplus generated in 1976-77 was Rs. 87.24 crores, the surplus expected in 1977-78 is Rs. 89.32 crores without any further increase in fares and freight rates and despite escalated costs". He held out the hope that during 1978-79 also, "if the amount earmarked for additional expenditure on staff and increased provision for Depreciation and Pension Funds is taken into consideration, the comparable surplus would be higher than that for the current year".

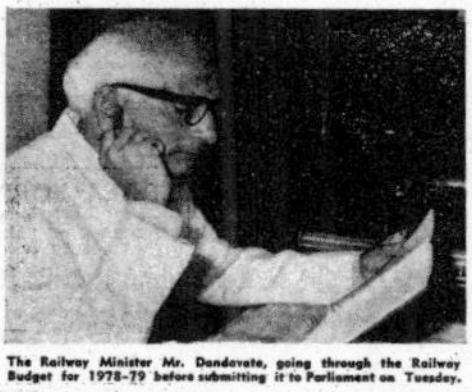

The Railway Minister Mr. Dandavate, going through the Railway Budget for 1978-79 before submitting it to Parliament on Tuesday.

Women Staff for Booking Counters

Mr. Dandavate announced that as part of the drive to root out malpractices in booking and reservation offices, "I have decided that as a matter of general policy, only women should be employed as reservation or booking clerks and supervisors in the major booking offices, starting with the metropolitan cities. We may be accused of being partial to the fair sex but our experience has shown that malpractices in reservations are comparatively less where women are employed at the counters". He was also considering the computerisation of passenger reservations in the four metropolitan cities. To start with, the feasibility of introducing this system in Delhi area is being explored in collaboration with the Electronics Corporation of India Limited, Hyderabad. "I only hope", he said, "that human deficiencies would not be replaced by mechanical errors of the machine".

The other concessions to passengers are: Hill concessions for specified stations which were available prior to 1975 will be restored and they will be available all the year round. The facility of rail travel concession to teachers of recognised educational institutions while undertaking educational tours in parties of not less than four will be extended to individual teachers also subject to the condition of their producing the requisite certificate from the District Education Officer concerned. Some of the facilities of rail travel concessions have also been extended to post-graduate students subject to the group size being five provided the head of the institution certifies that the size of the post-graduate group is less than ten. Similar other concessions were also announced in respect of "Indrail passes" which would be extended to non-resident Indians and issue of rail travel coupons to journalists.

All the long-distance mail and express trains will be having in the next two to three years second-class three-tier coaches with padded cushions and improved amenities. This, the Minister said, "will greatly wean away most of the passengers from the first-class to the second-class, thereby achieving our ultimate objective of having predominantly one type of accommodation in the long-distance trains. This will mean gradual doing away with the different classes on the Railways". In furtherance of this concept of Janata trains, "I have decided that the first-class air-conditioned accommodation will not be increased hereafter and will be progressively phased out. No new first-class air-conditioned coaches on additional account will be built in the future", he added.

The Planning Commission had provided to the Railways Rs. 2,202 crores (excluding Rs. 80 crores for the metropolitan transport schemes) for the Fifth Plan, which will be terminated a year in advance. Plan expenditure on the Railways up to March 31, 1978 will be approximately Rs. 1,901 crores excluding Rs. 53 crores on the metropolitan transport schemes. Passenger traffic handled by the Railways up to the end of the present financial year is expected to be 25 per cent higher and goods traffic in terms of originating freight 30 per cent higher than at the commencement of the Fifth Plan. The originating freight traffic at the end of March 1978 will be of the order of 240 million tonnes and at the end of 1978-79, about 248 million tonnes. This, the Minister said, "compares favourably with the anticipations of the Fifth Plan as originally drawn up, according to which freight traffic should attain the level of 250 million tonnes at the end of 1978-79".

Study into Capital Structure

The anticipated surplus in 1978-79 will help the Railways reduce their indebtedness to the General Revenues from Rs. 366.68 crores at the end of March 1978 to Rs. 345.3. crores at the end of March 1979. The Railways had still a long way to go in the matter of being able to function as an economically viable unit in spite of the surpluses achieved in 1976-77 and 1977-78 and the expected surpluses in 1978-79. "I am exploring avenues", he said, "for overcoming the adverse effects of this indebtedness in consultation with the Ministry of Finance". He was also thinking of having an in-depth study made into the capital structure of the Railways by a committee as recommended by the Railway Convention Committee in 1971.

Giving the budget estimates for 1978-79, Mr. Dandavate said the gross traffic receipts for the year were estimated at Rs. 2,220 crores or Rs. 88 crores more than the revised estimates for the current financial year. The revenue-earning goods traffic was expected to be 222 million tonnes or eight million tonnes more than the revised target of 214 million tonnes for the current wear. Passenger traffic as well as earnings were expected to increase by five per cent. As regards working expenses, the estimates are placed at Rs. 1,701 crores which is Rs. 90 crores higher than the revised estimates for the current year. This increase in working expenses, the Railway Minister said, "is mainly due to the grant of dearness allowance to the employees, revision of rates of night-duty allowance for various categories of staff, implementation of assurance relating to ten-hour rule for loco running staff and acceptance of labour tribunal awards relating to hours of employment regulations. Increased provision has also been made for better maintenance of track and rolling stock and fuel requirements for the anticipated increase in traffic". The appropriation to the Pension Fund was also being increased from Rs. 40 crores in the current year to Rs. 50 crores in 1978-79.

In order to assist the civil and police authorities in protecting railway track, 11,000 Railway Protection Force men and 14,000 gangmen have been deployed for patrolling the track in vulnerable areas in co-ordination with the local administration. The Railways are spending about Rs. one lakh a day on these patrolling arrangements. After introduction of these measures, several cases of suspected sabotage were detected in time and accidents averted. To eliminate fish-plates which are potential targets of mischief, the Minister said the Railways were going in for introduction of long and short welded rails on trunk routes. At present, 32,000 km. of track have already been provided with welded rails.

Mr. Dandavate was also anxious that arrears of track renewal works should be overtaken as quickly as possible. Taking into account the backlog and also the accruals during the next five years, the total renewals of tracks to be carried out would be 14,650 km. requiring an investment of about Rs. 500 crores. The Railways have approached the Planning Commission for an increased allotment for 1978-79 for this purpose. In view of a number of accidents at the level-crossings and the need for greater safety, "I have decided that such of the unmanned level-crossings as are potential hazards to safety of passengers shall in future be upgraded to manned level-crossings in a phased manner, entirely at the cost of the Railways", he said.

The Minister gave details of the development programmes for new lines, gauge conversions and surveys and said, 28 new railway lines and restoration schemes which still require about Rs. 180 crores for their completion were on hand during the current year. The process of restructuring the Railway Board has been completed according to schedule by December 31, 1977. The Board has now only five members, assisted by three Advisers who do not form part of the Board, against the original five regular members and eight additional members. More powers have now been delegated to the General Managers so that the decision-making process may be expedited. In order to strengthen the divisional organisation, he is also considering the transfer of some higher grade posts from the zonal headquarters to the divisions so that the divisional administration could be manned at a higher level than at present and the increased powers to be delegated to the divisional organisations could be utilised effectively.

See also Page 10

221 Poll Observers to be Appointed

FROM OUR SPECIAL CORRESPONDENT

NEW DELHI, Feb. 21.

As an additional precaution for a free and fair poll, the Election Commission has decided to appoint 221 observers in the five States and a Union territory which are to elect new members to the Assemblies this week.

This innovation, the Chief Election Commissioner, Mr. S. L. Shakder told a press conference to-day, had been planned to ensure that election rules and practices were observed. It would be open to him, he said to order a re-poll if considered necessary in the light of the report of an observer. Primarily, however, the reports of the observers would be useful as a contemporary record.

The observers would be the representatives of the Election Commission and would not receive instructions from the Government, he said.

Mr. Shakder, who had toured the States concerned was confident that the polling would be peaceful. The heat generated by some incidents of stone-throwing in Maharashtra according to his information, had subsided. This trouble was essentially caused by the skirmishes between the supporters of the two Congress parties. Even the incident where the car of the Janata Party President, Mr. Chandra Shekhar, was hit, had resulted from the Congress rivalry. At the instance of Mr. Shakder constituency committees, comprising representatives of political parties and candidates, had been set up throughout Maharashtra which would help in enforcing the code of conduct.

Considering the past record of the States, which would go to poll now, Mr. Shakder did not apprehend capturing of booths and, therefore, had not taken any precaution in this regard. The election staff, however, had been asked to be vigilant, while the State police would be supplemented by Home Guards, Forest Guards and similar other forces. Because of the decision to complete the polling in all areas in one day, there would be strain on the administrative machinery, he said, but steps had been planned to cope with the pressure.

In all there would be more than 1.11 lakh booths—each one catering to 750 to 1,000 voters as against the previous range of 900 to 1,200. To ensure against intimidation of the voters belonging to the weaker sections there would be a larger number of booths in the areas inhabited by them. In no case would a voter be required to walk more than 1.5 km.

The electorate total 8.6 crores and seats involved are 1 022 (excluding two which had chosen their representatives without a contest). Independents outnumber the candidates sponsored by political parties. The State-wise breakup of the contestants is: Andhra Pradesh 1,538, Karnataka 1,165, Maharashtra 1,819 Assam 938, Meghalaya 262 and Arunachal Pradesh 84.

Mr. Shakder was satisfied with the preparation of the electoral rolls about which there had been no complaints from the political parties. The rolls included the names of those who were 21 or above on January 1, 1977. He conceded that because of the present lacuna in the election law those who crossed the qualifying age last year would be left out. He said he had suggested removal of such shortcomings in the comprehensive list of poll reforms submitted to the Government.

The counting of votes for the Karnataka Assembly elections will begin on February 26 and will be completed the following day. The counting in the case of other States will begin on February 27.

The schedule for Karnataka has been advanced to enable the State to have a popular Government by February 28—within two months' of the promulgation of the Central rule—otherwise the Presidential proclamation would be required to be approved by Parliament.

52 Injured as Two PTC Buses Collide

MADRAS, Feb. 21.

Fiftytwo persons, including 18 women and two children, were injured in a head-on collision between two PTC buses on the College Road in Nungambakkam near the Directorate of School Education this morning. While four of the injured were hospitalised, the rest were treated as out-patients.

The drivers of the two buses were among the injured. The front portions of both the vehicles — plying on routes 17-D (K.K. Nagar-Parry's) and 23-A (Egmore-Tiruvanmiyur) — were badly damaged.

The Deputy Commissioner of Police (Traffic), Mr. G. Veeraraghavan, and PTC officials visited the spot.

The police arrested the driver of route No. 17-D bus, Radhakrishnan (30), on a charge of rash and negligent driving.

A traffic Police official said more passengers would have been injured had it not been a Government holiday to-day.

CPP Concern over Centre's Hindi Policy

FROM OUR SPECIAL CORRESPONDENT

NEW DELHI, Feb. 21.

The Congress Parliamentary Party Executive to-day expressed concern over the tendency of the Centre to impose Hindi on the non-Hindi States. It took exception to the practice followed of late, by the Union Government of sending letters in Hindi without an English translation, to the Southern States.

The matter was raised by Mr. K. Gopal, Party Secretary, who demanded that the assurances given by Mr. Nehru that English would continue to be used as long as it was wanted by the non-Hindi States, be respected. The despatch of Hindi letters to the Southern State Governments ran counter even to the guidelines supposed to be observed by the present Government. His concern was all the greater because of the belligerent attitude of a section of the ruling party. The Executive endorsed the sentiments expressed by him.

The Kerala Government, it was stated at the meeting, had decided to reply to the Hindi letters in Malayalam. This point was made to show that the Centre's attitude would merely lead to confusion and create problems in communication between New Delhi and some State capitals.

PANEL ON CENTRE-STATE TIES

The Centre-State relationship, in the context of the recent controversy, also figured in the Executive's discussions, and members seemed to favour re-assessment of the fiscal relationship, though not the type of review demanded by the West Bengal Chief Minister, Mr. Jyoti Basu. The Executive set up a panel to prepare a paper on the subject for fuller discussion by the general body.

Madras Weather

NUNGAMBAKKAM on Feb. 21: Max.: 31.1°C (88.0°F); Min.: 25.1°C (77.1°F); Humidity at 5-30 p.m.: 78 per cent.

MEENAMBAKKAM on Feb. 21: Max.: 31.7°C (89.1°F); Min.: 24.5°C (76.1°F); Humidity at 8-30 p.m.: 78 per cent.

Forecast (valid until Thursday morning): Sunny day with partly cloudy skies. No significant change in night temperature.

PM Pulls up Party MPs for Raising Language Issue

NEW DELHI, Feb. 21.

The Prime Minister, Mr. Morarji Desai, to-day pulled up a section of Janata members in the Lok Sabha when they interrupted Mr. Dandavate to demand that he should present the Railway budget in Hindi.

The demand was voiced first by Mr. Maniram Bagri and a few others. But the Speaker, Mr. K. S. Hegde, said both English and Hindi were permitted in the House and he asked Mr. Dandavate to continue with the speech.

When Mr. Bagri soght to join issue with the Speaker, Mr. A. Bala Pazhanoor (AIADMK), Mr. Vayalar Ravi and a few others angrily protested against the demand for switching over to Hindi.

At this stage, Mr. Desai, intervened and requested Mr. Pazhanoor and others not to get excited. Turning to his own party members, the Prime Minister firmly admonished them for the manner in which they sought to raise the language issue.—Samachar.

Bonus Restored to LIC Staff

FROM OUR LEGAL CORRESPONDENT

NEW DELHI, Feb. 21.

A seven-judge Constitution Bench of the Supreme Court has unanimously struck down as unconstitutional the Life Insurance Corporation (modification of settlement) Act, 1976—enacted during the Emergency—nullifying (without providing for any compensation) the bonus payable under the "settlement" dated January 24, 1974, entered into between the LIC class III and IV employees' representatives and the LIC management.

Mr. Justice P. N. Bhagwati, who delivered the main judgment of the Bench speaking for himself, Mr. Justice V. R. Krishna Iyer and Mr. Justice D. A. Desai, also ruled that the bonus payable under the "settlement" to the LIC employees was a right to property and therefore, the impugned Act of 1976 depriving the workmen of this property without providing for any compensation was violative of sub-article two of Article 31 of the Constitution.

(According to this Constitutional provision, no property of a person could be acquired by the State without a law providing an "amount" for such acquisition or prescribing relevant principles for the amount etc.).

The out-going Chief Justice, Mr. Justice M. H. Beg, in a separate judgment, while concurring with the conclusion of Mr. Justice Bhagwati, held that the impugned Act infringed Clause (1) (f) of Article 19 (of the petitioners LIC employees concerned)—dealing with the fundamental right to hold property etc. His Lordship also held that this Act was discriminatory and so also violative of Article 14 of the Constitution (equality before law).

Mr. Justice Y. V. Chandrachud, speaking for himself, Mr. Justice S. Murtuza Fazl Ali and Mr. Justice P. N. Shinghal, concurred with the conclusion of the main judgment of Mr. Justice Bhagwati that this Act hit Sub-Article 2 of Article 31. His Lordship, Mr. Justice Chandrachud, said that his reasons would be given later.

The main judgment, while allowing the writ petitions of the employees concerned questioning the validity of the impugned Act, directed the Union of India and the LIC management (respondents) by a writ of mandamus, "to forbear from implementing or enforcing the provisions of the Act and to pay annual cash bonus for the years April 1, 1975 to March 31, 1976, and April 1, 1976 to March 31, 1977 to class III and class IV employees under the terms of settlement dated January 24, 1974."

As a result of to-day's judgment, the LIC employees concerned would be entitled to get bonus for the period of two years ending March 31, 1977, at the rate of 15 per cent of their wages under the "settlement".

See also Page 9

Praise for Ry. Minister from All Sides

NEW DELHI, Feb. 21.

The Railway Minister, Mr. Madhu Dandavate's Janata-oriented surplus budget for 1978-79 presented in the Lok Sabha to-day earned him encomiums from several members belonging to all parties.

"Many, many thanks" members were heard saying as they went up to Mr. Dandavate and warmly shook hands when he concluded his budget speech which occupied exactly 55 minutes.

Mr. Biju Patnaik, Minister of Steel and Mines, was the first to give a pat to Mr. Dandavate.

Members vied with one another in applauding Mr. Dandavate when he annonced that women would be employed as reservation and booking clerks at the reservation counters in all major railway stations starting with metropolitan cities.

Reason: Experience has shown that malpractices in reservations were comparatively small where women were employed at the counters.

Mr. Dandavate said amid thumping of desks by members that he would not mind even being accused of showing partiality to the fair sex if management of reservation counters by women did good to both Railways and the rail-users.—Samachar.

'Janata Khana'

NEW DELHI, Feb. 21.

The Railways has decided to supply "Janata Khana" on all major long distance trains at one rupee per food packet.

Announcing this in his Budget speech, Mr. Madhu Dandavate said this was being done in response to the demand of the travelling public for supply of food at cheaper rates.

"Three varieties of food packets will be sold on trains to suit the tastes of people from different parts of the country. This will be in addition to the normal catering arrangements already existing on trains and at stations", he said.

China Inviting Desai

From K. V. Narain

TOKYO, Feb. 21.

The Chinese Government is expected to invite the Prime Minister, Mr. Morarji Desai, to pay a visit to China, according to a Peking report received here to-day quoting diplomatic sources in the Chinese capital.

The sources said that Mr. Wang Ping-nan, President of the Chinese People's Association for Friendship with Foreign Countries, who left Peking yesterday, leading a delegation on a visit to India, Pakistan and Bangladesh is taking the Chinese Government's invitation with him to be presented to Mr. Desai on whom he will be calling.

Mr. Desai has been saying that India does not desire to have disputes with China, Nepal or other neighbours and is hoping for the solution of all disputes with them without resort to force. He has reiterated India's desire to improve relations with China provided the latter also so desired.

The invitation which Mr. Wang is taking with him would indicate that China is also willing now to respond positively to the desire of Mr. Desai. Such a gesture from China can be expected to mark a significant breakthrough in the long-strained Sino-Indian relations and place them in a new perspective.

AP reports from Tokyo:

Mr. Wang is reported to have said at the airport before his departure that the Chinese people have a long-standing traditional friendship with the peoples of Pakistan, Bangladesh and India.

"Our aim is to promote this friendship and learn from the peoples of these three countries. We hope that the visits will make due contributions in deepening mutual understanding and friendship between the peoples of China and the three countries".

Koirala Acquitted in One Case

KATHMANDU, Feb. 21.

The Special Tribunal to-day acquitted the former Prime Minister of Nepal, Mr. B. P. Koirala, of the charge of treason in what is known as the Dharan Bomb Case, hearing in which began here yesterday.

The judgment came shortly before the tribunal rose for the day after defence lawyers had completed their arguments.

The former Prime Minister is facing charges of treason in five more cases and sedition charge in another, all of which will be heard by the Special Tribunal which will be in session till Monday.

Cases against Mr. Ganesh Mansingh will also be heard by the Tribunal.

It will hear two cases of treason against Mr. Koirala to-morrow

jectives, we are governed by an ardent desire to help protect the independence and integrity of the nation. If only to remind ourselves of our objective and concerns, rather than to make it a slogan of publicity, we print every day the inscription, "India's National Newspaper," under the masthead on the front page. We shall continue to set ourselves high aspirations. . . . We do not stand for any sectional interest or group; our approach is wholly national.

. . . the very essence of a newspaper is to take a critical look at what goes on around it. This *The Hindu* has often revealed and, in the process, it has incurred the displeasure or the wrath of Authority, and sometimes of the public as well. *The Hindu* has also supported Authority when such support seemed warranted in the national interest. It has tried to give the lead on matters of vital public importance. . . . Let me assure the public, *The Hindu's* readers, its friends and foes, and, in fact, all citizens, that the motivation has always been—and will continue to be—to serve the larger and long-term considerations of the country by maintaining an independent stance.[1]

During the first 70 of its 100-year existence, *The Hindu* played an active role in the struggle for Indian independence. Since India gained its own freedom, the paper has done its share to further the nation's development and growth. Through the years, it has demonstrated great concern for accuracy, reliability, honesty and authoritativeness. The wide assortment of Indian national leaders and intellectuals, as well as English-speaking foreigners, who regularly and carefully read *The Hindu* value it for its intelligent tone, its literate style, its progressive spirit, its cosmopolitan emphasis and its forceful expression of opinion. Undoubtedly, this paper has played a notable part in the development of Indian intellectualism and the growth of the free-press philosophy, as well as championing the struggle for national and individual freedoms.

Six enthusiastic, adventurous young intellectuals founded *The Hindu* in 1878 as a weekly. Of the six, two were school headmasters and four were law students. All were imbued with a keen sense of Indian nationalism and a desire to provide a voice for Indian opinion. Their lack of finances forced them to borrow the one and three-fourths rupee cost of running off the 80-copy first edition on a treadle-operated press. They appointed one of their number, G. Subramania Aiyer, an eminent intellectual and freedom fighter, as editor, a position he held for the paper's first two decades of existence. Another of the original six, M. Veeraraghavachariar became managing editor. This initial issue of *The Hindu* signalled its long struggle for independence by opposing the Anglo-Saxon press support for a Madras High Court appointment.[2]

Although copies of *The Hindu's* first three years as a weekly have not been preserved, the editorials and all other extant evidence indicate it was a paper deeply concerned with social issues and justice. The first editorial, in fact, pledged the paper to the principles of fairness and justice. From the beginning, it carried the people's grievances to the colonial government. It distinguished itself from the remainder of the press by fighting the public injustices. Its most

[1] From text of address given by Mr. G. Kasturi, editor, *The Hindu,* in Madras on the occasion of the paper's 100th Anniversary, September 4, 1978.

[2] "*The Hindu* 100 Years Old," in special centenary edition of *The Hindu* September 4, 1978, and booklet, *The Hindu Centenary* (Madras: B.N.K. Press Private Ltd., 1978).

important exposure was what was called the Salem Riots scandal, in which a number of respected public leaders had been prosecuted on trumped-up charges.

In 1883, *The Hindu* became a tri-weekly and moved to a new location. By 1885, it boasted the second largest readership in south India and was threatening the virtual monopoly of British-owned newspapers. In April, 1889, it became an evening daily, and since then has been the "main daily purveyor of news to thousands of news-hungry people."[3] During those early days, it had two classes of subscribers based on ability to pay. Reading rooms and people with incomes of over 200 rupees per month were charged one rate, and all other a lower one.

In 1898, after two decades of distinguished service in the interests of nationalism and independence, Aiyer left *The Hindu*. His editorial role was taken by Karunakara Menon. About this time, because of falling circulation and general hard times, the paper passed through a financial crisis. When, in 1905, S. Kasturiranga Iyengar, an experienced lawyer and avowed nationalist, took over as editor-owner, the paper had only 800 subscribers. Although he had had no journalistic training or experience, Iyengar immediately reorganized the paper, improved its contents, introduced more features to attract more readers and subscribed to a regular foreign news service. By the end of his first year with the paper, it was operating at a profit.

The years before World War I marked a period of consolidation and progress for *The Hindu* despite obstacles introduced by the colonial government. Iyengar insisted on vigorous writing, good reporting and thorough explanation, especially of the nationalist-versus-colonial government struggle. By 1912, *The Hindu* regularly published 18 pages daily, sometimes more. It carried telegrams from its own correspondents in Delhi and other state capitals. It subscribed to the Associated Press of India news service, then operated by Reuters. It regularly featured coverage of the courts and legislative bodies, as well as science, farming and sports news and a weekly book review.

World War I created serious technical and economic difficulties and circulation dropped to 3,000 from a high of 11,000 in 1912. With the end of the war, prosperity returned. In 1921, the paper installed Madras' first rotary presses, Linotype machines and stereotyping facilities. The circulation subsequently rose to over 17,000. However, in the meantime, the paper's strong nationalistic stance, its exposure of the Punjab atrocities and the Jallianwalabagh massacre and its insistence that colonial rule should be based on justice and humaneness rather than force led to the levying of a heavy security deposit by the government. Letters from readers supporting and praising *The Hindu* poured in from the public and the paper responded by remaining firm in its criticism despite the fine. During those early years under Iyengar when it was often in trouble with the British authorities, the paper never became emotional or bitterly hostile, but kept up an intelligent approach, speaking to the British conscience in calm, logical and sensitive tones.

Although *The Hindu* had been independent at its founding, under Iyengar

---

[3] Nadig Krishna Murthy, *Indian Journalism* (Mysore: Prasarange of University of Mysore, 1966), p. 175.

it became increasingly identified with India's Congress Party. However, Iyengar always encouraged fair play on the part of all parties. Iyengar, a quiet and reserved person, desired to pattern the appearance of *The Hindu* after *The Times* of London, including even the full front page of advertising (a practice *The Hindu* did not drop until 1958—the last Indian daily to do so). It was mainly Iyengar who imbued the paper with its concern for accuracy. Although it presented a liberal political philosophy, it was considered a conservative paper because of the serious way it wrote and displayed its news and views. When Iyengar left his paper in 1923, it was a modern newspaper with steadily growing influence.

For three years, until his death in 1926, S. Rangaswami served as *The Hindu*'s editor. His principal achievement was to initiate a sports page. Then Kasturi Srinivasan, Kasturiranga Iyengar's son, became editor and in the next four decades contributed significantly to the paper's becoming a national institution and one of the great newspapers of India. He was an admirer of Mahatma Gandhi's methods, although he never failed to editorialize against them when he felt they were too extreme. He was one of the outstanding fighters for press freedom in India's journalistic history.

Under Srinivasan, the decade of 1928–1938 proved to be a period of significant expansion of *The Hindu*'s staff and its news coverage and services. During this period, it became the first newspaper in the country to get a teleprinter connection direct to the national central telegraph office. In 1935, it changed its crest to include significant Indian symbols—the sun as the source of knowledge and vitality, the conch as the voice of the people, the lotus for purity and independence, the elephant for strength and power, and the "Kamadhenu" (winged figurine) to suggest auspiciousness. In 1939, it moved to its present location on Mount Road. Then, in 1940, after a reader survey, it decided to publish mornings instead of evenings.

World War II presented multiple problems, among them intensified government hostility, censorship, scarcity of newsprint and rising prices. Consequently, *The Hindu* was forced to raise its prices while reducing the number of pages, resulting in a sharp drop in circulation. But the dip was only temporary, for circulation picked up to a record high of 46,000 in 1946. During the war years, the paper gave extensive first-hand coverage of the fighting, stood firmly against fascism and staunchly supported the Indian freedom movement. It reported the country's struggle for independence sensitively and responsibly.

After India won its independence in 1947, Kasturi Srinivasan was instrumental in forming an independent national news agency called the *Press Trust of India*. In 1949, he became the organization's first president. Actually, the Trust was a junior partner of *Reuters* until it achieved the status of a full-blown independent national news agency in 1952. During Srinivasan's editorship, the paper established a network of foreign correspondents and extended its coverage into the remote regions of India. The paper's editorials, mostly written by K. P. Viswanatha Iyer, began to draw attention at home and abroad. During this period, many outstanding journalists worked for *The Hindu,* among them B. Shiva Rao, K. Balaraman, K. S. Shelvankar, S. K. Gurunathan and H.

Venkatasubhiah. Although the paper was plagued by a work stoppage in 1958, by the time of Srinivasan's death in 1959, its circulation had passed the 100,000 mark.

At Srinivasan's death, *The Hindu*'s senior assistant editor, S. Parthasarthy took over as the paper's editor. Srinivasan's son, Srinivasan Parthasarathy took over as publisher and quickly became popular until an untimely death cut short his career in 1965. During this period, *The Hindu* strengthened its reputation for excellence in foreign coverage. It also scored a scoop when it became the first Indian paper to carry the news of the assassination of President J. F. Kennedy of the United States in 1963. Although some of the early morning editions were already airborne to readers, they were recalled and a new front page with the shocking news inserted.

When today's editor, G. Kasturi assumed the paper's editorship in 1965 upon the retirement of S. Parthasarathy, he launched a policy of appointing trained full-time correspondents in all the state capitals and district headquarters towns in the nation. He inspired a new spirit of enquiry and a fearlessness which would not yield to official desires or displeasures. Reporters were re-trained and given greater freedom in their reporting and writing. Aided by a fleet of four airplanes procured by the paper in 1963, he was able to assure same-day delivery all over India. Under him, too, *The Hindu* has achieved several international distinctions. He has guided the paper through several crises— the 1972 drought, high prices, inflation, shortage of newsprint, deaths of key members of the paper's staff and the Emergency and subsequent censorship of the Indian press. Amid the difficulties, *The Hindu* has improved its pages and gained in reader popularity.

In recent years, Kasturi has instituted several editorial improvements that have served to enhance further *The Hindu*'s quality and popularity. He began by making the Letters to the Editor section more lively through encouraging reader debate on controversial subjects. In 1975, after the newsprint crisis had abated, he introduced a Saturday sports section and an education page. Later in the same year, he developed a weekly international edition which quickly gained readers in the United States, Canada, Britain, Western Europe, Japan, Malaysia and Singapore. In 1976, he introduced a pictorial section in the Sunday magazine and a year later added color features and advertisements in the same magazine. Toward the end of 1977, he introduced three further innovations, making *The Hindu* the first Indian newspaper to offer a special section to its readers six days a week. The first addition, called "Outlook" presents verbatim reports on lengthy discussions by a panel of experts on important topics chosen by Kasturi. The second, a one-page feature called "Special Report," contains short articles from special correspondents. The third, "Open Page," is a readers' page allowing them to discuss and suggest solutions to burning problems. Finally, in mid-1978, Kasturi added a sports weekly section called "The Sportstar," which covers sports activities in India and often carries color photographs.

In the 1970's, *The Hindu* lost two key leaders who had long been associated with its policies and who had provided it with continuity of quality journalism. In 1974, Kasturi Gopalan, the paper's publisher, passed away after six decades of service. Among his many contributions to the paper was the sports page, of which he is usually considered the "father." Then, in 1977, managing editor G. Narasimhan died after nearly 40 years of distinguished service. He is especially remembered for the confidence and loyalty he generated in the paper's staff members.

In the mid-1970's, the entire Indian press passed through a crisis which threatened its freedom and very existence. Pressures began in 1974 when the government forced dismissal of the *Hindustan Times'* editor George Verghese, apparently as a move against the power of the press to criticize government. Then, in June, 1975, Prime Minister Indira Gandhi declared a State of Emergency and imposed press censorship. Three months later, after *The Times of India,* the *Indian Express,* the *Hindustan Times* and *The Statesman* had criticized Mrs. Gandhi's policies such as the nationalization of 14 major banks, the government began to impose its plan to restructure the press. A year later, the government had placed representatives on the boards of directors of the first three and was putting heavy precensorship restrictions on *The Statesman* to get it to capitulate. Although *The Hindu* escaped some of the restrictions, probably because of its record as a family-owned newspaper, it also felt the heavy hand of government on its freedom. At one point, it was forced to scrap an editorial on the State of Emergency. It was especially angered by the government's repression of information about excesses of the family planning drive in the north and it joined in the drive to oust Mrs. Gandhi's "authoritarian and repressive regime." Shortly after the Janata Party came to power in 1977, *The Hindu* again demonstrated its political independence by strongly criticizing the ruling party's attempts to create one-party rule in the country.

Although *The Hindu* is a corporation with the public holding part of the preference shares of stock and having some voice in management, it is basically owned by Kasturi and Sons, Ltd. It holds the unique distinction in India of having been a family-owned newspaper through its century of existence, a factor which has proven to be a source of strength in crises. As R. V. Murthy has noted in *Journalism in Modern India,* "The Hindu has had the rare good fortune of having a series of editor-proprietors, all hailing from the same family, who have sedulously reared the paper to its present size and proportions."[4]

From its earliest beginnings, *The Hindu* has always provided good national and international coverage. Today, it keeps correspondents in London, Tokyo, Singapore and Washington, D.C., and depends heavily on their live reports. Their stories are supplemented by input from two major wire services: Press Trust of India (and through it, Reuters) and United News of India (and through it, AP and AFP). Further information on the international scene comes from subscriptions to *The New York Times, Christian Science Monitor* and Gemeni news services and reprint arrangements with England's *Guardian.* Distinguished correspondents who have served *The Hindu* overseas include Dr. R. Shelvankar and K. Balaraman. To cover national developments, the paper keeps

---

[4] R. V. Murthy, "The Business Side," in Roland Woleseley (ed.), *Journalism in Modern India* (New York: Asia Publishing House, 1964), p. 177.

a staff of six reporters in New Delhi in addition to those stationed in state capitals and district headquarters.[5]

Altogether, in January, 1978, *The Hindu* had a staff of 1,009, with 164 of them directly engaged in editorial tasks, 367 in administrative roles and 478 in technical duties. To achieve its high quality standards and to appeal to its better-educated readership, the paper demands excellent staff qualifications. Editorial and administrative personnel must have at least a college degree, with a post-graduate degree and experience in journalism or newspaper work preferred. All technical staff have had specialized training for their work.[6]

The Hindu presents such a serious appearance that a London *Times* correspondent once noted that "its heavy single columns march across the pages like Prussian guardsmen, gray and disciplined."[7] Although the paper varies its makeup, its look is somber, lightened only by a single front page picture and very few inside. Except for three small advertisements, the front page is all "business," with an eight-column mixture of key international, national and local news of the day. Stories usually conclude on the same page—one of Kasturi's innovations. Only a few reporters receive by-lines. The personal advertisements and public announcements which formed page one until 1958 now appear on page two. Inside, there are one or two pages of international news and several of national and local origin. The paper also features regular coverage of sports, finance, commerce and business news and of the cultural and entertainment worlds. Editorials and letters to the editor are usually situated on page eight. One-page and shorter features on numerous subjects are scattered throughout *The Hindu*'s normal 16 pages (up to double that on Sundays). About 55 percent of the total space is devoted to advertising, and the remaining "news hole" is composed of international (some 5 percent), national (20 percent), state and local (about 19 percent), sports (nearly 14 percent) and business news (over 5 percent), of editorial page materials (nearly 7 percent), of features and entertainment (27.5 percent) and of book reviews (nearly 3 percent).[8]

Except for a few isolated interims occasioned by strikes or newsprint shortages, the circulation of *The Hindu* has grown steadily since its 80-copy initial issue. The increase of readers has been particularly noteworthy in the past two decades; in 1958, circulation reached over 84,000 copies, by 1968, nearly 140,000 copies and in 1978, by the time of its centenary, regular circulation stood at 281,146 copies. The paper touched an all-time high of over 300,000 copies in 1977 for the daily and of nearly 305,000 Sunday papers in March, 1978. A recent readership study conducted by a Bombay-based research group showed that ten percent of all adults in Madras read *The Hindu*, with just three percent and one percent for the city's other two English dailies. The survey also indicated that 85 percent of *The Hindu*'s readers are young (between the ages of 15 and 24), that 80 percent have a college education and that nearly half are professionals or traders. Most readers are devoted to *The Hindu* and few say

[5] N. Ravi, Assistant Editor, *The Hindu*, in response to questionnaire, dated September 23, 1978.
[6] *Ibid.*
[7] "Newspapers of the World—VI," London *Times* (March 3, 1965).
[8] Ravi questionnaire.

they would switch to a competitor. In its makeup, content and writing, the paper's editorial staff has long made conscious efforts to appeal to these educated, above average readers. Because a paper in India is usually read by several people, it has been estimated that *The Hindu* has well over a million readers daily.

Because India's transportation system is slow, *The Hindu* has resorted to modern techniques to speed delivery. In 1963, it acquired a fleet of airplanes to deliver papers within hours of publication. In the 1970's, it has gone to a system of electronic facsimile transmission of publishable copy to satellite printing plants at Coimbatore, Bangalore, Hyderabad and Madurai, thus eliminating the need for its air fleet.

The Hindu has gained recognition among the world's quality dailies. In 1965, *The Times* of London named it one of the world's ten best newspapers, calling it "a distant and authoritative voice on national affairs . . . an expression of the most liberal southern (Indian) attitudes. . . . (thus) a national voice with a southern accent." Three years later, it received the 1968 World Press Achievement Award of the American Newspaper Publishers Association, which cited it for providing its country with a model of journalistic excellence. Today, its long and continuing traditions of service to India's national interests, of struggle for press freedom, of political independence, of practicing serious journalism with reliability and authenticity, of providing comprehensive national and good international coverage, and of keeping its "opinion leader" clientele informed leave little doubt that *The Hindu* is both one of India's most highly respected and influential dailies and one of the world's finer quality papers.

IZVESTIA

(U.S.S.R.)

SEVERAL FACTORS OPERATE in the Soviet Union to make circulation of a true national daily difficult. Physical distances are formidable, since the U.S.S.R. covers a sixth of the earth's land mass, or an area three times the size of the United States. The vast distances between east and west span nine time zones, making same-day publication and distribution a virtual impossibility. Soviet transportation facilities, while dependable, simply do not reach remote areas rapidly. Population is unevenly distributed, with 70 percent of the people living west of the Ural Mountains, a factor which makes per unit cost of newspaper distribution in the rest of the nation exorbitant. At the same time, the Soviet Union is

Пролетарии всех стран, соединяйтесь!

ИЗВЕСТИЯ
Советов народных депутатов СССР

Газета выходит с марта 1917 года

№ 45 [18805] ● Среда, 22 февраля 1978 года ● Цена 2 коп.

ВСЕ — НА ПРАЗДНИК ТРУДА!

(ТАСС).

Это воины — представители славных Советских Вооруженных Сил, стоящих на страже нашей Родины. Лейтенант Сергей Федоров, матрос Владимир Князев и рядовой Николай Мальцев достойно встречают 60-летие Советских Вооруженных Сил. Все они отличники боевой и политической подготовки.
Фото Г. Дубинского.

НАДЕЖНЫЙ СТРАЖ МИРА И СОЦИАЛИЗМА

ШЕСТЬДЕСЯТ лет назад, в суровые годы гражданской войны, молодая Советская Республика создала свои Вооруженные Силы...

(Окончание на 2-й стр.)

ВЫСОКАЯ НАГРАДА РОДИНЫ

Указ Президиума Верховного Совета СССР

О награждении Героя Советского Союза Маршала Советского Союза Москаленко К. С. орденом Ленина и второй медалью «Золотая Звезда»

За умелое руководство войсками, мужество и героизм, проявленные в борьбе с немецко-фашистскими захватчиками в годы Великой Отечественной войны...

Председатель Президиума Верховного Совета СССР
Л. БРЕЖНЕВ.
Секретарь Президиума Верховного Совета СССР
М. ГЕОРГАДЗЕ.

Москва, Кремль, 21 февраля 1978 г.

Указ Президиума Верховного Совета СССР

О присвоении звания Героя Советского Союза маршантам и генералам Советской Армии и Военно-Морского Флота

Председатель Президиума Верховного Совета СССР
Л. БРЕЖНЕВ.
Секретарь Президиума Верховного Совета СССР
М. ГЕОРГАДЗЕ.

Москва, Кремль, 21 февраля 1978 г.

Указ Президиума Верховного Совета СССР

О присвоении звания Героя Советского Союза генерал-лейтенанту авиации Бабаеву А. И. и генерал-лейтенанту авиации Дольникову Г. У.

Председатель Президиума Верховного Совета СССР
Л. БРЕЖНЕВ.
Секретарь Президиума Верховного Совета СССР
М. ГЕОРГАДЗЕ.

Москва, Кремль, 21 февраля 1978 г.

Указ Президиума Верховного Совета СССР

О присвоении звания Героя Советского Союза генерал-лейтенанту в отставке Руссиянову И. Н.

Председатель Президиума Верховного Совета СССР
Л. БРЕЖНЕВ.
Секретарь Президиума Верховного Совета СССР
М. ГЕОРГАДЗЕ.

Москва, Кремль, 21 февраля 1978 г.

Указ Президиума Верховного Совета СССР

О присвоении звания Героя Социалистического Труда полковнику медицинской службы Сиефанову Е. М.

Председатель Президиума Верховного Совета СССР
Л. БРЕЖНЕВ.
Секретарь Президиума Верховного Совета СССР
М. ГЕОРГАДЗЕ.

Москва, Кремль, 21 февраля 1978 г.

Указ Президиума Верховного Совета СССР

О присвоении звания Героя Социалистического Труда

Председатель Президиума Верховного Совета СССР
Л. БРЕЖНЕВ.
Секретарь Президиума Верховного Совета СССР
М. ГЕОРГАДЗЕ.

Москва, Кремль, 20 февраля 1978 г.

Указ Президиума Верховного Совета СССР

О присвоении звания Героя Социалистического Труда

Председатель Президиума Верховного Совета СССР
Л. БРЕЖНЕВ.
Секретарь Президиума Верховного Совета СССР
М. ГЕОРГАДЗЕ.

Москва, Кремль, 20 февраля 1978 г.

В ОБСТАНОВКЕ ДРУЖБЫ И ВЗАИМОПОНИМАНИЯ

Во время переговоров.
Фото С. Косырева.

По приглашению ЦК КПСС, Президиума Верховного Совета СССР и Совета Министров СССР 20 февраля с официальным дружественным визитом прибыл Генеральный секретарь Партии арабского социалистического возрождения, Президент Сирийской Арабской Республики Хафез Асад во главе партийно-государственной делегации САР...

21 февраля в Кремле начались советско-сирийские переговоры.

Темп прежний — ударный

А. ЕЖЕЛЕВ, соб. корр. «Известий».
ЛЕНИНГРАД.

ОБМЕН ТЕЛЕГРАММАМИ

(ТАСС).

От Президиума Верховного Совета СССР

divided into 15 national republics, many of them representing strong ethnic loyalties who would prefer their newspaper in their own languages.

Despite such obstacles, the Soviet Union does, indeed, have a strong national press. Although the nation does have a highly local and regional press— "some 8,000 newspapers with a total circulation of 150 million copies and some 6,500 journals and magazines with a total number of more than 166 million copies per issue are published in the U.S.S.R."[1]—it also has a strong centralized national press, which influences the entire country. Three Russian-language newspapers are generally considered to comprise the heart of the national press—*Pravda, Komsomolskaya Pravda* and *Izvestia*. Of the three, *Komsomolskaya Pravda,* as "a nation-wide youth daily newspaper, has the largest newspaper circulation in the country in 1978—about eleven million."[2] Russia's second largest—and most authoritative—newspaper, *Pravda* (Truth) has today's second largest nation-wide circulation, with some 10.6 million copies daily. The Soviet Union's third largest daily, *Izvestia,* with a daily circulation in excess of 8 million, is in reality the nation's second most prestigious paper, after *Pravda.*[3]

Maintenance of a central press with nation-wide distribution is vital to the Soviet system. Since before the Bolshevik Revolution, newspapers and all the mass media have served as instruments by which the Communist Party makes its wishes known to the people. Under Joseph Stalin, the newspaper "was the means to maintain contacts with the working masses of our country and rally them around the party and the Soviet state."[4] A few years later, Nikita Khrushchev made virtually the same point at a conference of journalists in Moscow: "As soon as some (Communist Party) decision must be explained or implemented, we turn to you, and you, as the most trusted transmission belt, take the decision and carry it to the very midst of the people."[5] To this day, the national newspapers continue to serve the same function.

But a central press exists in the Soviet Union for a second, almost-as-vital reason: it serves as a sounding board for internal criticism and correction of the Soviet system. This criticism, as one authority explains, comes from the top down, from the party or government organs in the form of articles and editorials to bring pressure on industrial, political and social groups to improve their productivity and allegiance to the Soviet nation. It also comes from below, via letters to the editors and conferences from individuals, collectives and, frequently, trade union organizations "with complaints of official shortcomings, mistakes or excessive bureaucracy in public life."[6] Both the party instrument and critical

[1] Sepp Horlamus (ed.), *Mass Media in C.M.E.A. Countries* (Prague: International Organization of Journalists, 1976), p. 209.

[2] Alexei N. Burmistenko, foreign editor, *Journalist* Magazine (Moscow), in letter to H. Fisher, dated April 28, 1978.

[3] *Ibid.*

[4] T. M. Reshetnikov, *Partiya o pechati* (Sverdlovsk, 1934), pp. 16–17. Quoted by Mark Hopkins, "Media, Party and Society in Russia," in Alan Wells (ed.) *Mass Communication: A World View* (Palo Alto: National Press Books, 1974), p. 43.

[5] Quoted by Mark Hopkins, "Media, Party and Society in Russia," in Alan Wells (ed.), *Mass Communication: A World View* (Palo Alto: National Press Books, 1974), p. 43.

[6] Antony Buzek, *How the Communist Press Works* (New York: Frederick A. Praeger, 1964), pp. 52–3.

functions contribute to the emphasis of Soviet newspapers on the Party and the socialist system in their pages and a resultant de-emphasis of news events.

Izvestia or *Izvestiya Sovetov Deputatov Trudyashtchikhsya* (News of the Councils of Working People's Deputies) as it is known by its full title, is "the press organ of the Presidium of the Supreme Soviet of the U.S.S.R." (Soviet Parliament).[7] Because of its high position in government, *Izvestia* holds a position of prestige second only to *Pravda,* the Communist Party paper. It has a general political orientation, specializing in publishing state political news. As one source notes, special attention is paid to the activities of the Soviets.[8] In addition to publishing information about the government's activity in accord with Party ideology, it regularly prints sketches about the work of the deputies in columns entitled "A Deputy and Life," "Sketches about Deputies" and "Local Soviets."[9] The pages of *Izvestia,* as the voice of the Kremlin, stress the practical problems of government, the business of the Soviet Parliament and the work of national planning more than the ideals of theoretical communism. From one point of view, it is a "newspaper of record," explaining the work and actions of government.

Izvestia also out-distances *Pravda* in the amount of foreign news and commentary it publishes. It has a network of foreign correspondents in 22 of the world's key cities, with just four in communist countries. In addition, it has roving reporters and foreign news analysts whose columns often are similar to those in Western papers. It also gets much of its input from the U.S.S.R.'s two major wire services, TASS and Novosti. *Izvestia* carries many of the same stories found in *Pravda,* but it gives more attention to the relations of the U.S.S.R. with other governments. Although *Pravda* is more widely known and read in the West, it is *Izvestia* that speaks officially on government foreign policies.

Izvestia came into being during the stormy revolution which toppled Imperial Russia and forced the tsar to abdicate on March 15, 1917. During the last years of the tsar's regime, the press in Russia was at low ebb; in 1913, there were only 859 newspapers circulating some 2.7 million copies, or less than one for every 40 Soviet Union inhabitants.[10] On March 13, 1917, two days before the tsar was deposed, the new voice of the Bolsheviks and Social Revolutionaries had first appeared under the title *Izvestia Petrogradskogo Soveta rabotchikh i soldatskikh deputatov.* On March 28, the Soviet (Council of Workers and Soldiers) published in *Izvestia* that they were assuming control of the armed forces, and thus the new paper was, from the start, the press organ of Soviet government. At the time of the Second All-Russian Congress of the Soviets on November 9, 1917, that role was made official.[11] During the month of October, 1917, the peasants, directed by the Marxists, took over Petrograd and all non-Bolshevik publications were made subject to pre-censorship. *Izvestia* was re-

[7] Horlamus, *op. cit.,* p. 211.
[8] *Ibid.*
[9] Horlamus, *op. cit.,* p. 211.
[10] Buzek, *op. cit.,* p. 65.
[11] Horlamus, *op. cit.,* p. 211.

sponsible for publishing the documents the October Revolution had spawned—the Decree on Peace and the Decree on Land.[12] A year later, the 1918 Constitution stipulated that the power of the press was transferred into the hands of the laborers and peasants; but that power, in fact, stayed in the hands of Communist Party leaders.

During the years that followed, *Izvestia*'s activity was linked with the name M. I. Kalinin, and famous people such as Bernard Shaw, M. Gorky, Henri Barbusse and V. Mayakovsky were among its contributors.[13] World War II proved to be a difficult period for the paper, as for many Soviet journals, because of newsprint and personnel shortages and physical damage to equipment by the invading Germans.

Although *Izvestia* was publishing over two million copies before World War II, the combination of wartime restrictions and the rigidity imposed on the press by Stalin led to a post-war drop in circulation. During this period, the press—including *Izvestia*—was generally dull and uninteresting. Then, at a 1953 conference convened by the Central Committee, Party Secretary Nikita Khrushchev urged editors to use new methods of presentation to make the press more efficient and more attractive to readers. Soviet journals were slow to adopt the suggested new practices. It was Khrushchev's own son-in-law, Alexei Adzhubei who, as its editor-in-chief, first put a fresh spirit in *Pravda* in 1956. Then, in 1958, he was transferred to *Izvestia* and became its editor. With the aid of a Party decree directing reorganization of *Izvestia*, Adzhubei began transforming the paper. He made the paper's presentations more vivid by introducing shorter articles, more human interest stories, more pictures, better makeup and headlines and even added some women's features and on-the-spot reporting.[14]

As a result, *Izvestia*'s circulation soared. Whereas its circulation had been only about one million, as an evening paper under Adzhubei it became much more popular. By 1961, its circulation had trebled to 4.1 million copies daily. By 1964, circulation had jumped to 6 million and it was being read all over the Soviet Union. The next year, circulation was reported at 8 million, but in 1966, it suddenly dropped by nearly a half million because government officials began insisting that press runs should more closely match the actual sales.[15] But actual sales kept growing and today *Izvestia*, the paper which started with a mere 35,000 copies in 1917, publishes well in excess of 8 million copies daily, making it one of the world's highest circulation newspapers.[16] Most of its readers get their six-day-a-week *Izvestia* (it does not publish on Sundays) by subscription. It is published as an evening paper in Moscow, but it comes out as a morning paper in the rest of the country.[17]

After Khrushchev lost power in 1964, the new regime dismissed Adzhubei

[12] *Ibid.*
[13] *Ibid.*
[14] Kenneth E. Olson, *The History Makers: The Press of Europe from its Beginnings through 1965* (Baton Rouge: Louisiana State University Press, 1966), p. 322. Compare Buzek, *op. cit.*, p. 84.
[15] "Soviet Circulation Battle," *Time* (February 17, 1967), p. 78.
[16] Horlamus, *op. cit.*, p. 212.
[17] Burmistenko letter.

as editor of *Izvestia*. His place was taken by Vladimir Stepakov, who, in turn was succeeded in late 1965 by Lev N. Tolkunov. Under these two editors, the paper remained lively and even today it reflects the changes brought about by Adzhubei. Tolkunov has continued to improve the paper's appearance by innovations such as boxing headlines in color, increasing the number of pictures, improving the newsprint and typography. Tolkunov has also cut down on full quotations of party and governmental pronouncements. It does not carry advertisements, but it is the only large central newspaper which features sports in Russia. In 1970, Tolkunov led an eleven-member party of the Soviet Union of Journalists on a three-week tour of United States' newspapers.

In keeping with its role in criticism, large numbers of letters pour in to *Izvestia*'s main office in Moscow's Pushkin Square. As far back as 1956, the paper received nearly 66,000 letters during the year. Now, "about half a million letters are received by the Editorial Board annually."[18] All of the letters are not published, of course, but they are read and those which are not printed are answered. A staff of about fifty, mostly women, handle the increasing flow of letters. All complaints (there are many) are investigated. Through letters to *Izvestia* and to other Soviet newspapers, the people can feel a part of the country's journalism. Editorial conferences (*letuchkas*) at *Izvestia* consider readers' letters several times a week to determine which ones will be used, and which ones should precipitate sending out a special reporter to look further into the situation. Letters are encouraged and *Izvestia* selects as many as possible which bring light to abuses, deal with moral matters, suggest improvements, and contribute in some way to national progress. In addition to writing letters, readers of *Izvestia* often visit the paper's "reception" department (adjacent to its "letters" department) to complain and to discuss problems personally.[19]

Never a thick paper, *Izvestia* usually runs four pages on weekdays and six on Saturdays. Its makeup attracts readers. Typeface size and styles are diversified. The occasional color printing, the numerous photographs inside the paper, the use of rectangular boxes and lines to divide materials, the clean and neat columns, and the occasional use of color for borders all give the paper an aura of careful planning and dignified appearance. Articles vary widely in length from a few lines to as long as 3,000 words. Although *Izvestia* means "News," the paper contains few hard, last-minute news items. What news it does publish is often related to world affairs and they invariably appear on the inside of the first page and on page three. Most of the paper's articles educate or agitate, which are considered the primary functions of a newspaper in the U..S.S.R. No permanent features are carried in *Izvestia* and editorials appear only occasionally. Instead, the paper concentrates on discussions (in which readers can participate by writing letters or speaking to the paper's officials), features (largely related to world affairs and Soviet national progress), and special essays

---

[18] Horlamus, *op. cit.,* p. 212.

[19] "Newspapers of the World—II," London *Times* (February 24, 1965). Compare Buzek, *op. cit.,* pp. 223–224, and "The Soviet Press . . . A Fresh View by Three U.S. Newspapermen," *The Quill* (October, 1966), p. 18.

by intellectuals and high government officials. And there is the most essential part of the contents—the letters from readers.

Izvestia also publishes a 16-page weekend supplement called *Nedelia* ("The Week"), a tabloid pictorial magazine complete with comics, cartoons, and short articles satirizing Western life. Today, *Nedelia* either sells separately or as a part of the Saturday issue of *Izvestia*. It enjoys great popularity, probably because it seems to have excellent contacts with readers.

The contents of *Izvestia* are carefully controlled to serve the interests of the Russian government. This leads to omissions of some stories, unusual angles on others, and, sometimes, deliberate distortion of the facts. For example, when Dag Hammarskjold, the U.N. Secretary-General who had defied Khrushchev, died in 1961, the paper editorialized on U.N. proceedings that day without mentioning the general's death, except for a brief news item on the last page.[20] During the Kennedy quarantine of Cuba, all naval vessels were reported by the paper to have been refused passage to the island (but peaceful cargoes were never detained). In the mid-seventies, it twisted facts about U.S. Defense Secretary James Schlesinger when he warned the United States against being lulled to sleep on military preparation because of detente.[21] However, in recent years, as the Cold War has faded, there appears to be some less distortion of the facts.

Like the other large Soviet national dailies, *Izvestia* has always raised—and continues to lift—the cultural level of the Soviet people. In its earlier days, it played a role in teaching illiterates to read. It has consistently refused to publish what is considered harmful, degrading or purely entertainment. Such subjects as sex, murder and other crime, romance and frothy social items do not find a place in the pages of *Izvestia*. Even human interest material appears only rarely.

Instead, the paper publishes a steady diet of cultural and political items, readers' letters, serious essays and governmental announcements, all designed to keep the readers' minds on serious matters. From the Soviet perspective, this makes *Izvestia* the best of Communist elite papers, without a doubt as prestigious and influential as any other daily in the world. If the purpose of *Izvestia* as an organ of the Soviet government and the resultant limitations of that relationship are borne in mind, critics everywhere must agree it is indeed one of the world's most important serious "prestige" dailies.

[20] Olson, *op. cit.,* p. 327.
[21] Elizabeth Pond, "Soviet Press Raps Schlesinger," *Christian Science Monitor* (July 25, 1975).

Jornal do Brasil

(BRAZIL)

IN BRAZIL, where press freedom has been erratic at best, repressed at times and often contradictory in recent years, one newspaper has steadily been improving its status and image as a quality daily. That paper is Rio de Janeiro's *Jornal do Brasil,* now considered by many Brazilians to be, along with *O Estado de S. Paulo,* one of their rapidly modernizing nation's two best dailies. Like *O Estado,* the *Jornal do Brasil* has been distinguishing itself in its fight for press freedom and in its serious approach to journalism.

Compared with many of the world's leading newspapers, *Jornal do Brasil's* circulation is not large, but its 155,000 daily copies and 265,000 copies on Sundays go to the nation's educated and elite opinion leaders in Rio de Janeiro, Brasilia and elsewhere across Brazil's vast expanses. Its daily circulation still cannot match the 200,000 level of the nation's foremost paper, *O Estado.* However, the *Jornal's* circulation has been climbing steadily in recent years. Most of the issues are bought in street sales (78 percent), with only 22 percent of the circulation accounted for by subscriptions.[1]

Jornal do Brasil was founded on April 9, 1891, by Rodolfo Dantas, Joaquim Nabuco, Constancio Alves and Aristides Espinola. Formerly, it was located on Avenue Rio Branco in Rio de Janeiro, but recently it has moved to its present modern quarters at 500 Avenida Brasil in the same city. There, the paper is printed on linotype presses with computer control for the advertisements. Supplements are printed with offset machinery. Color is used in the Sunday edition for the Sunday magazine and in the children's supplement.

The *Jornal* enjoys private ownership under Dr. Manoel F. do Nascimento Brito, who also publishes the paper. Its oversight is managed by a board of directors which includes Brito, Condessa Pereira Carneiro, Lywal Salles and Bernard Campos. Its editor-in-chief is Walter Fontoura.[2]

Several distinguishing marks make *Jornal do Brasil* one of Brazil's top quality newspapers. It provides thorough and serious coverage of national and international news. Its stress on finance and economics keeps the dynamic business community in one of the world's fastest growing areas abreast of national and world products, markets and trends. It carries excellent feature materials and commentary and its investigative pieces are thorough exposés without peer in the country. It champions human rights and betterment and represents the best

[1] Walter Fontoura, editor-in-chief, *Journal do Brasil,* in response to questionnaire, May 31, 1978.
[2] Fontoura questionnaire.

liberal political thought in the nation. By its reportage of the development of the entire country, it brings Brazilians everywhere a sense of unity and of pride. The serious and thorough traits which characterize its news carry through to its treatment of entertainment; the paper's space and commentary given to the cinema, the theater, music, art, literature and the electronic media attest to its interest in enriching cultural and entertainment activities.

Like the remainder of the Brazilian press today, the *Jornal do Brasil* finds itself in erratic and contradictory circumstances vis-a-vis the government. The *Jornal* does not support the authoritarian Brazilian regime; rather it seeks to remain non-partisan and "takes a basic stand of support of civil liberties and human rights" and in its philosophy champions "free enterprise, western-type democracy and Christian principles."[3] Yet it must also, in the interests of loyalty to the development of the nation, support a government that professes a consuming interest in modernization, even if it comes by dictatorial means.

Although it has not experienced as much direct governmental harassment and interference as that suffered by some of its sister Brazilian papers, *Jornal do Brasil*, like them, finds itself caught up in the growing pattern of recent official intervention. In 1972, for example, the Ministry of Justice published a decree banning critical reports of the nation's economic situation, a direct affront to the *Jornal*'s thorough financial coverage.[4] The same year, the government was issuing other decrees, including one suppressing editorial independence, and the press then, as now, found difficulty in getting specifics about the new ruling.[5] Pre-publication censorship was introduced in 1973 as the most direct form of control; *Jornal do Brasil* was among the papers which underwent a slightly lighter form of intervention—instructions from the censor over the telephone. It had been more cautious than its rival *O Estado de S. Paulo*, which had to submit its materials to the censor before publication.

By May, 1975, however, *Jornal do Brasil* found itself among the directly oppressed as the government initiated proceedings against it for libelling the security authorities by reporting that a former member of parliament had been tortured.[6] The press situation relative to its freedom remained confusing: on the surface, there were moves to relax censorship, but at the same time oppression, particularly against anyone or any publication favoring socialism and the outlawed Communist Party, mounted.

The noose tightened again in 1977, and *Jornal do Brasil* felt the heavy hand of the censor once more. Like the other quality journals, the paper had reported governmental, especially military, torture of citizens. For its reports, the authorities punished the *Jornal* in two ways. First, virtually all government advertising was withdrawn from its pages. Then, when the paper wrote in an editorial, "It is much worse than trying to cover the sun with a sieve for a state to try to confront the enemy outside without representing the people's will internally," the editors were forced to replace the entire column with commercial ad-

[3] Fontoura questionnaire.
[4] "A Quick Look Around: Brazil," *IPI Report*, 21:12 (December, 1972), p. 6.
[5] "Latin America: Brazil," *IPI Report*, 22:1 (January, 1973), p. 6.
[6] "The Press Under Pressure: Brazil," *IPI Report*, 24:4/5 (April/May, 1975), p. 12.

JORNAL DO BRASIL

Rio de Janeiro — Quarta-feira, 22 de fevereiro de 1978   Ano LXXXVII — N.º 316

Egydio tira Natel da lista de sucessores

O Governador Paulo Egydio Martins excluiu o Sr Laudo Natel da sua lista de candidatos à sucessão paulista. Ele declarou, em entrevista coletiva ontem à noite, que só levará ao Governo federal os nomes dos quatro políticos que assinaram, na semana passada, o pacto de coalizão que lhe delegou a arbitragem do processo.

Assinaram esse pacto o professor Delfim Netto, o Prefeito Olavo Setúbal e os secretários Murilo Macedo e Rafael Baldacci. O Sr Delfim Netto estava ao lado do Governador na entrevista e, à tarde, ambos estiveram reunidos no Palácio. A candidatura do Prefeito Olavo Setúbal foi apoiada por manifesto dos alunos de Direito da Universidade Mackenzie.

Dez dos 17 deputados que integram a bancada federal de São Paulo prepararam um documento reconhecendo, como os quatro candidatos e a maioria dos secretários de Governo, que a sucessão no Estado será coordenada pelo Sr Paulo Egydio. Ele não foi divulgado porque houve divergências, entre seus signatários, sobre a redação final.

O Brigadeiro Délio Jardim de Mattos desmentiu que tivesse recomendado, em nome do Governo federal, o "desaquecimento da sucessão paulista", missão atribuída pelo Sr Delfim Netto ao "agente X-9". O Presidente Geisel estará em São Paulo no dia 24, para visitar a nova Praça da Sé e as obras do metrô. (Página 3)

Com o General Figueiredo à sua direita, Geisel toma um café depois da solenidade

África do Sul não teme o embargo da ONU

O Ministro da Defesa sul-africano, Pieter Botha, afirmou que o país "não se deixará, nem vai ficar de joelhos", em consequência do embargo de armas recentemente imposto pela ONU. Explicou que a África do Sul era advertida há algum tempo para a eventualidade da medida e preparou-se para enfrentá-la.

Sobre a invasão de Angola por guerrilhas sul-africanas, há dois anos, disse ter sido "uma experiência bastante positiva, um momento heróico de nossa História, levando-se em conta o número limitado de efetivos empregados". Admitiu que a ANITA, "muito bem-vista em várias capitais da África", continua recebendo ajuda, mas não da África do Sul. (Página 12)

Israel denuncia que Brasil abriga nazistas

O Instituto Yad Vashem, de Israel, revelou ao JORNAL DO BRASIL que inúmeros criminosos de guerra nazistas moram no Brasil, entre eles Wilhelm Balcys, que chefiou as SS no campo de concentração de Treblinka, e Zenonas Ignatavicius, capelão durante a Guerra e desde 1970 vigário-geral dos lituanos no Brasil.

Balcys, que tem também o nome de Stasis Dobekvicius, não foi encontrado ontem à noite em São Paulo, no endereço fornecido pelo Instituto israelense. Ele estaria morando no bairro da Mooca, numa cidade pertencem há 15 anos ao Sr Angelo da Silva, que afirma ter o antigo proprietário — "um húngarês" — morrido "há muito tempo". (Página 11)

EUA dão ao Golfo mesmo valor da OTAN

A segurança do Oriente Médio e dos lençóis petrolíferos do Golfo Pérsico "é tão vital para os Estados Unidos quanto a segurança da OTAN e dos aliados asiáticos", afirmou o Secretário de Defesa, Harold Brown. Acrescentou que Washington pretende com sua força estratégica na Ásia e ampliar a frota no Pacífico.

"Somos a continuaremos sendo uma importante força no Pacífico, na Europa — através da Europa e fraco na Ásia", declarou ainda o Secretário de Defesa, para quem o poderio militar da União Soviética na Ásia e as "incertezas do Pacífico" tornam necessária a presença militar norte-americana. (Página 14)

Discurso de Pinochet irrita os argentinos

O Governo e os meios militares argentinos manifestaram desagrado, e em alguns casos até revolta, com o discurso do Presidente do Chile, General Augusto Pinochet, depois da assinatura do acordo para solução diplomática de divergência na zona austral, dizendo o que o canal de Beagle não entra nas negociações.

Ao voltar a Buenos Aires, o General Jorge Rafael Videla reuniu-se imediatamente com os demais componentes da junta militar, para tratar do acontecimento depois de firmado o acordo em Puerto Montt, no Chile, mas o Governo resolveu não emitir nota por enquanto, para não perturbar o trabalho das comissões de negociação, que foi iniciado ontem. (Página 13)

PNB alcançou os 163 bilhões de dólares em 1977

O PNB (Produto Nacional Bruto) brasileiro alcançou 163 bilhões de dólares em 1977 — o que corresponde a uma renda per capita de 1 mil 440 dólares (Cr$ 23 mil 750 ao câmbio atual) — revelou ontem o Ministério do Planejamento, Reis Velloso, com base em dados preliminares da Fundação Getúlio Vargas sobre as contas nacionais do ano passado.

O Ministro adiantou também que, de acordo com sondagem conjuntural da FGV, as empresas estão encarando com otimismo a atividade industrial no primeiro trimestre deste ano. Apenas 9% deles esperam queda no nível de emprego no período. (Página 19)

Cordeiro passa mal na solenidade de Monte Castelo

O Marechal Cordeiro de Farias, o mais velho dos oficiais da FEB ainda vivo, passou mal "devido ao calor e à emoção" na solenidade de comemoração do 33º aniversário da Tomada de Monte Castelo. O Presidente Geisel presidiu a solenidade no Monumento aos Mortos da II Guerra Mundial. O General Figueiredo também compareceu.

Às 17h, mesma hora em que se consolidava a Tomada de Monte Castelo, ex-pracinhas e oficiais entravam no quartel do ex-Regimento Sampaio (atual 1º Batalhão de Infantaria Motorizada), tropa que ganhou a batalha, ao som da Canção do Expedicionário. O Marechal Cordeiro de Farias esteve também na Vila Militar. (Página 7)

Portella está negociando a eleição de ex-cassados

O Presidente da Câmara dos Deputados, Marco Antônio Maciel, tornou-se ontem o primeiro integrante da cúpula do Governo a reconhecer que a reforma política que está sendo negociada pelo Senador Petrônio Portella inclui-se a supressão do Artigo 185 da Constituição, que torna inelegíveis aqueles que tiveram seus direitos políticos suspensos por força de Atos Institucionais.

Essa supressão foi também admitida, indiretamente, pelo Senador Petrônio Portella, ao afirmar que "o problema do 185 será ser colocado entre anistia ou revisão, como um dilema, pois estamos em condições de estudar uma forma capaz de reintegrar aqueles contra os quais não existam razões para continuar fora da atividade política".

Enquanto o porta-voz do Governo, Coronel Toledo Camargo, afirmava que "não há no Governo nenhum estudo sobre anistia a presos políticos", o Senador José Sarney advertia que essa discussão "não pode ser tema de radicalização".

O presidente da Comissão Internacional Pontifícia de Justiça e Paz, Cardeal Bernardin Gantin, já em Brasília, a convite da CNBB, disse que não tem tempo, nem intenção, de manter contato com o Governo para discutir a questão dos direitos humanos. (Página 4)

Juiz decreta a prisão de Sérgio Fleury

O delegado Sérgio Paranhos Fleury teve ontem prisão decretada pelo juiz da 1.ª Vara Criminal de Guarulhos. O delegado foi pronunciado por ter acompanhado as investigadores Capão, Traili, Bruno e Pininho — cujos mandados de prisão também foram expedidos — nas execuções sumárias de três traficantes de entorpecentes.

Atualmente na direção do DEIC (Departamento Estadual de Investigação Criminais), um dos principais órgãos da polícia paulista, o delegado Fleury pode ser preso a qualquer momento. A próxima etapa do processo é o julgamento pelo Tribunal do Júri de Guarulhos. Seu advogado poderá impetrar habeas-corpus para que seja julgado em liberdade. (Pág. 16)

D Ivo critica conformismo da população pobre

Qual a causa de sua pobreza? Falta de estudos, desemprego, destino e vontade de Deus. O que faz para melhorar sua situação? Reza, procura trabalhar mais, procurar mais conhecimentos. E quando isso vai acontecer? Com a sorte grande, quando Deus quiser. O que o tornar se tente? Esperançoso, conformado.

Estas foram as respostas predominantes numa pesquisa realizada entre os pobres de oito municípios gaúchos da diocese de Santa Maria, o que levou o Bispo, D Ivo Lorscheiter a criticar ontem tal grau de conformismo. Afirmou ainda ser "exigência de fraternidade e justiça converter todos os homens em responsáveis, conscientes e corajosos do seu próprio destino e da sua efetiva ascensão social". (Pág. 7)

Acordo nuclear já firmado não é mais tema de Geisel

O Embaixador da Alemanha no Brasil, Jorg Kastl, afirmou ontem em Brasília que durante a visita do Presidente Geisel a Bonn, a partir de 6 de março, os dois Governos irão formalizar um acordo já formalizado e que funciona muito bem". Acrescentou que os dois países já reiteraram sua disposição de cumprir o Acordo Nuclear como foi assinado em junho de 1975.

Disse que a visita do Presidente Geisel ao seu país trará novos impulsos para a concretização de cooperação bilateral: "Já temos vários projetos em vista mas os conteúdos ainda não foram definidos". Atualmente, Brasil e RFA elaboram acordos para extração de álcool e gaseificação e liquificação do carvão.

Explicou o Embaixador que, no momento, o Brasil está empenhado em atrair pequenas e médias empresas da RFA, mas que existem algumas dúvidas dos empresários alemães com relação à legislação brasileira, as "dificuldades normais para encontrarem parceiros brasileiros que sejam estáveis e oportunos".

No Rio, o presidente da Furnas — Centrais Elétricas, Licínio Seabra, disse que o atraso de um ano na construção das usinas Angra-2 e Angra-3 não poderá ser recuperado. As duas usinas deverão entrar em operação em 1983 e 1984, mas só o farão em 1984 e 1985. (Pág. 4)

vertisements.[7] Before 1977 had run its course, various other sectors of the Brazilian press had suffered closure, censorship, kidnapping, reporter detentions and charges of subversion.

During 1978, conflicting reports on the freedom of the press to report and comment openly on government and authorities have continued to emerge from Brazil. In March, the situation was depicted as one of growing government oppression of the press.[8] By mid-year, the Associated Press reported newspapers and magazines were publishing what they pleased, including direct criticism of the government, political opposition, reports of torture, demonstrations, the economy and even unfavorable articles about the Church.[9] But at almost exactly the same time, eleven Brazilian journalists, among them *Jornal do Brasil* correspondent Luis Alberto Manfredini, protested their arrest, detention and harassment as suspected "subversives" by the officials of the town of Curitiba.[10] Perhaps the confusion can be partially comprehended when one considers Brazil's diversity, uneven development (ultra-modern cities and retarded rural areas), the desire of an authoritarian government to keep out all subversives and official insistence that newspapers should give priority to supporting official efforts to modernize the nation.

Amid the confusion of trying to follow the government's changing moods, the *Jornal do Brasil* itself has been understandably ambivalent at times. In 1967, for example, it pointed out boldly that during the three-year rule of Castelo Branco (1964–1967), the national executive had promulgated 19,259 decrees and 312 decree-laws, plus other dictatorial acts.[11] However, in 1971 the paper ignored the impact of the trans-Amazon highway upon the Indian tribes of the Amazon and upon the ecology of the country as it praised the project as "a fundamental part of the Plan of National Integration" and "the opening of the nation's new frontier."[12] It is possible that *Jornal's* editors, in their enthusiasm to support national development, failed to consider the negative effects of progress.

Publisher Manoel F. do Nascimento Brito has procured a large staff for the publication of his morning daily, *Jornal do Brasil,* its Sunday counterpart and its sister weeklies. In all, there are 2,161 employees, with 1,223 of them working in administrative and managerial tasks, 482 in technical aspects of publication and 456 on the editorial side. The paper does not take on a journalist unless he or she has a university degree in journalism; unfortunately, the quality of Brazil's university training in journalism is questioned by some. The *Journal* keeps a large staff of 45 reporters and photographers at Brasilia and their work is reflected in the several pages of news and numerous features and commentary

[7] "New 'Dark Continent'," *IPI Report,* 26:7 (August, 1977), p. 4.
[8] Gerald Sievers, "Brazil: Making Out in the Grip of the Censor's Army," *IPI Report,* 27:3 (March, 1978), pp. 8–9 and 16.
[9] "Situation in Brazil Much Improved, Says AP," *IPI Report,* 27:5 (June, 1978), p. 14.
[10] "Brazilian Editors Cite Arrests, Torture, Bans and Sackings," *IPI Report,* 27:5 (June, 1978), p. 3.
[11] Luis Barbosa, "Vinte mil atos, leis decrêtos em três anos," *Jornal do Brasil* Caderno Especial (March 13, 1970).
[12] Quoted in Riordan Roett, *Brazil: Politics in a Patrimonial Society* (New York: Praeger Publishers, 1978), pp. 152–3.

items on national government the paper publishes daily.[13] *Jornal do Brasil* could not be considered a true "newspaper of record." It does not, for example, give President Ernesto Geisel's speeches verbatim; however, it does report fully on all activities of government.

Jornal do Brasil's thorough written and photographic coverage of international news deserves note. Besides featuring the key world events on its front page, the *Jornal* normally carries about 3–4 full pages of international news. In addition, it gives space to features of international interest and reflects on the world scene in its editorials. For a paper of its size, it maintains a large staff of 14 foreign correspondents located in Buenos Aires, Madrid, Paris, Rome, London, Moscow, Bonn, Tokyo, Jerusalem, Washington, New York and Los Angeles. The paper's correspondents receive by-lines for their stories, so it is not unusual to see the well-known names of distinguished *Jornal* correspondents, such as that of N. A. Spinola on Washington stories, Arlette Chabrol on those from France and Mario Chumanovich on pieces from Jerusalem. Other indicators of its interest in world affairs are the numerous press wire and syndicated services it receives. Presently, the paper takes news from seven wire agencies: UPI, AP, Reuters, AFP, ANSA, DPA and EFE. It also gets syndicated materials from *Le Monde,* The New York *Times, L'Express,* The *Economist* and the London *Times,* plus wirephotos from AP and UPI.[14]

In keeping with its aim to reach primarily the urban middle and upper classes, *Jornal do Brasil* appears serious, written for the intelligent, and somber and gray. Within its usual 48 pages each morning, the reader can find a wide array of material to satiate his entire range of interests. The front page offers a mixture of national and international news items across the right hand two-thirds of the page, with a narrow column containing weather, the latest monetary exchange rates and similar information vertically down the left-hand side. The *Jornal* is one of the world's few remaining papers to place classifieds on the front page; they run across the bottom portion of that page. Although the paper's normal makeup format is 8–10 columns 4.5 centimeters wide and 54 centimeters deep, a variety of arrangements are employed. Two—sometimes more—columns are often combined into one wider one and stories are frequently arranged in horizontal blocks. Normally, the paper carries a single front-page picture in the upper right quadrant. Variations in blackness of ink, type style and adroit use of white space bring variety and interest to the reader.

Usually, the paper is broken into several sections, the main one offering news and editorial commentary, another culture and entertainment and a third classifieds. Page two of the main section presents entertainment feature material. Several pages of national and local news and features, mostly from Brasilia or the paper's home city, Rio de Janeiro, follow. An editorial page, with commentary by the paper's editors, a cartoon and letters to the editor and an opposite page with bylined guest commentaries come next. They are usually followed by the 3–4 page section of foreign news, which in turn is followed by the paper's

[13] Fontoura questionnaire.
[14] *Ibid.*

excellent 5–6 page presentation of economic and financial news and features. After a page of obituary notices and religious announcements and a society page, the first section ends with three well-illustrated pages of sports news, interviews and commentary.

The second ten-page section contains cultural and entertainment materials. A couple of pages are given to interviews and commentary on the cinema and to a review of a major film. The section also features pages on classical and popular music, books and literature, radio and television schedules, travel and one containing comics, a crossword puzzle and the horoscope. The third major section, often running to a dozen or more pages, is composed of classified advertisements.

Editor Fontoura indicates the ratio of the total contents of the *Jornal* might be characterized as follows: international news, 10 percent; national, 15; local, 5; analysis of news, 2.5; editorials, 2.5; features/entertainment, 2; sports, 5; travel/leisure and home, 1; business, 15; and advertising, 40 percent. Decisions as to the main topics of editorial content are arrived at by daily editorial conferences between the publisher, editor-in-chief and senior editors.[15] Where issues or events are debatable, especially those involving Brazilian foreign policy and national politics, the paper's staff tries to present all sides. The paper also has an editorial policy of providing reporters with adequate time for thorough investigation of stories they are assigned to cover.

As evidence of its high quality work, *Jornal do Brasil* and its staff claim an impressive list of citations and awards—in fact, 45 of them between 1958 and 1977. The awards have been given to the paper for its excellence in photography, reporting, coverage of national, economic, literary and sports subjects, editorials, makeup and journalism in general. At least three of the citations have been international in scope and several of the staff members, including owner-publisher Dr. M. F. Nascimento Brito, have received individual awards.

Besides its serious approach to journalism and its defiance of government, *Jornal do Brasil* has other earmarks of the quality elite newspaper. Some of its more remarkable qualifications are its reliability, its editorial independence and its unusual layout. In its independence, it serves as a "watchdog" in the interests of a free press in Brazil. It also plays a vital national role in its thorough presentation of materials affecting foreign policy and the interests of the nation's dynamic internationally-minded business community. In authoritativeness, it is catching up with the nation's leader, *O Estado de S. Paulo*. For an increasing number of influential Brazilians and among those informed about the quality press around the world, the name *Jornal do Brasil* has become synonymous with excellence in elite journalism.

---

[15] Fontoura questionnaire.

Los Angeles Times

(UNITED STATES)

FOR ITS FIRST EIGHTY YEARS or so, the *Los Angeles Times* built up and perpetu-
ated an image of stodgy conservatism. Through those years, it was generally not
considered either progressive or even very fair in its editorial positions. Otis
Chandler, today's publisher, recalls: "We tended to be very conservative, and we
used to bias the news—we didn't print both sides of labor-management disputes, we wouldn't print much Democratic news, we were narrow in our religious
coverage. . . ."[1]

Today, that "behind-the-times" image has long been forgotten, and the *Los
Angeles Times* is thought of as respectable, independent, thorough and up-to-
date—in short, as *Time* magazine recently observed, "one of the nation's most
serious, best-reported dailies."[2]

The person chiefly responsible for this notable metamorphosis is *Times*
publisher Otis Chandler. Shortly after he took the paper's reins in 1960 at the
age of thirty-three, he began to initiate changes—and he hasn't stopped yet.
Rapid changes were taking place in the American society in the early 1960's
and Chandler had the insight and courage to change his paper enough that it
moved into the vanguard of alert, progressive, sprightly quality newspapers. By
1964, his West Coast newspaper, until then considered a prime example of
provincial journalism, had won a citation from journalism educators for "en-
hancing public understanding of great national and international issues by providing thoughtful, searching background articles by respected, competent
Washington and foreign correspondents."[3]

Chandler and his chief editor, Nick Williams, began the *Times* turnaround
in the early 1960's by placing the emphasis squarely on writing and editing. To
achieve editorial excellence in these two areas, Chandler and Williams used a
three-point guideline devised by the latter: (1) upgrading staff whenever possible as staffers left to retire or to take other jobs; (2) seeking better editorial personnel, even though they cost substantially more money; and (3) adding new
and better talent for jobs which were not previously open.[4] The resulting overall
improvement in all editorial departments probably cannot be matched in American journalism history. Already in 1965, London's *Economist* was calling it "by

---

[1] Frank Riley, "The Changing Direction of the *Times*," *Los Angeles Magazine* (June, 1966), p. 29.

[2] "Invasion from the North," *Time* (April 17, 1978), p. 103.

[3] Otis Chandler, "The Role of the Metropolitan Daily in Today's Changing Environment," *Journalism
Educator* (Fall, 1964), p. 94.

[4] *Editor and Publisher* (October 8, 1966), p. 28.

all odds the best California newspaper—most complete, and soundest in news judgment and honest in preparation," a condition surprising because "a few years back it was a shoddy sheet of extreme right-wing viewpoint and with a Hollywood divorce focus for its news measurement."[5]

In 1966, the *Times* instituted several significant changes that continue as an integral part of its success today. It converted its rather stodgy eight-column pages to a modern, six-column format, with column rules eliminated. On page two, the paper began a full-page news summary, providing readers with a concise and comprehensive roundup of the major news developments in all the principal news areas. About the same time, it also began carrying special background or interpretive articles which have ranked among journalism's best, such as a series by John Randolph on Korea, another on the press and the courts by Gene Blake, a third by Jack Jones on the civil rights issues and yet another on Southern California's future by Sterling Slappey.

Through the years that he has been at the *Times* helm, Chandler has taken a number of other steps to increase both the quality and the quantity of his paper's domestic and international coverage. In 1965, the *Times* reported the Watts riots thoroughly, after which the liberal *Frontier* magazine noted the paper's "sharply improved quality of reporting" and the fact that "news coverage, local, national and international, has been vastly increased under an editorial budget that has doubled to $8 million in the past six years."[6] Chandler has also encouraged today's editor, William Thomas, to complete demolition of the old conservative image. Thomas has responded by supplying, in addition to continued excellence in writing and editing, efforts to furnish readers with a stylish, fair and complete informational package which addresses the issues of the day and a new "lifestyle" designed to appeal to readers' special interests.

The shift Chandler engineered can be seen in the *Times'* expansion during the past 15 years. The paper's Washington bureau jumped from three men in 1963 to 24 today. In 1962, the *Times* had but a single overseas correspondent, as contrasted to 18 bureaus today. Its spotty domestic coverage of 15 years ago has been upgraded. The development of the joint *Los Angeles Times*-Washington *Post* syndicated services in 1962 "to exchange Washington, foreign and regional interpretive news" has further improved the serious, comprehensive coverage of the *Times*.

Chandler's "new look" spurred another effect: increased circulation. When he took over the *Times* in 1960, circulation was sputtering along at about 525,000 daily and 900,000 on Sundays. By 1967, the figures had risen to 850,000 on weekdays and around 1,200,000 Sundays. Despite inflation, general decline in newspaper readership and other problems, the trend continues. Early in 1978, the circulation count stood at 1,020,987 copies on weekdays and 1,309,677 for Sundays. With the upward swing, the *Times* circulation ranks among the nation's largest dailies, improved from fourteenth in 1956 to third behind the New York *Times* and the Chicago *Tribune* in 1967 to second today

[5] *The Economist* London (May 22, 1965), p. 12.
[6] "Making News Two Ways," *Frontier* (June, 1966), p. 23.

Los Angeles Times

LARGEST CIRCULATION IN THE WEST, 1,020,987 DAILY, 1,309,677 SUNDAY

VOL. XCVII EIGHT PARTS—PART ONE 118 PAGES WEDNESDAY MORNING, FEBRUARY 22, 1978 CC † DAILY 15c

CITIES, STATES

New Fiscal Problem: Too Much Money

BY ROGER SMITH
Times Staff Writer

Three years ago many of the nation's cities and states were facing financial chaos. Inflation was pushing up costs and the recession hurt revenues generated by income and sales taxes. Higher taxes or massive cuts in services seemed the only alternatives.

Now the signs are everywhere that the crisis has abated, if not ended. The predominant problem today is not how to deal with impending deficits but what to do with billions of dollars in budget surpluses.

By the end of this fiscal year California expects a $3.2 billion surplus. Texas anticipates $3 billion and New York $360 million.

Cities do not have big surpluses but fears of financial collapses have vanished. Municipal bond ratings are up and sales are better than ever.

A nationwide survey by Times reporters shows that widespread cost cutting over the last three years, combined with inflation-linked increases in tax revenues, has steadily renewed state and local coffers.

But the reaction to the new-found wealth is mixed. Some officials, including California Gov. Brown and New York Gov. Hugh L. Carey, want to cut taxes immediately. Others, including big city mayors and federal officials, want to divert the surpluses to problems that still plague many urban areas: unemployment, declining tax bases and soaring welfare costs.

The debate could determine what responsibility states must shoulder in meeting urban problems and how much tax relief taxpayers can expect in coming months.

Elected officials are plainly worried about the growing state and local tax bite. In fiscal 1977 state and local tax collections totaled $174 billion. Over the last 30 years federal taxes have remained relatively constant at about 23% of national income but state and local collections have increased from an 8% share to 14% in the same period.

The rate of increase would have been much larger had it not been for reforms instituted by many cities and states during the 1974-76 recession. Faced with declining tax collections as sales and incomes fell off—and stiff resistance to higher taxes—city and state officials began major cost-cutting efforts to keep their budgets in balance.

Georgia Gov. George D. Busbee cut the state budget 9% and eliminated 1,600 state jobs in 1974. The Chicago school board cut 1,000 teachers from the payroll last year and imposed a hiring freeze. New York City, which faced default on its bond obligations, laid off 61,000 workers, imposed tuition at the city university and raised the subway fare 40%.

In San Francisco the new austerity took the form of a confrontation with

Please Turn to Page 14, Col. 1

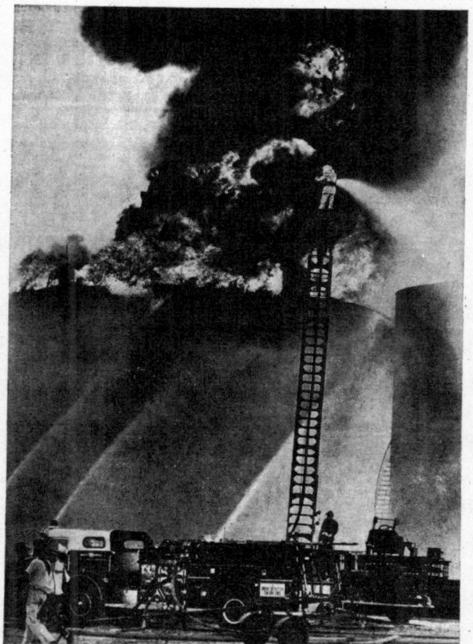

FACING AN INFERNO—Fireman on ladder aims hose to cool tank next to one aflame in Rialto.
Times photo by Bruce Cox

U.S. Bares Indictment of Torrijos' Brother

'72 Charges Accuse Him of Smuggling 155 Pounds of Heroin Into New York

BY JOHN H. AVERILL
Times Staff Writer

WASHINGTON—A secret six-year-old indictment accusing the brother of Panamanian leader Gen. Omar Torrijos of smuggling a huge shipment of heroin into the United States in 1971 was unsealed by the Justice Department Tuesday night.

The indictment charged that Moises Torrijos, now Panama's ambassador to Spain, and four other persons smuggled 155 pounds of heroin aboard a Braniff Airlines flight from Panama to New York City on July 8, 1971.

The Justice Department unsealed the indictment, handed down on May 16, 1972, as the Senate spent a day in unusual closed session looking into allegations that Omar Torrijos and his family were involved in narcotics trafficking.

The Senate Intelligence Committee reported that it had found no hard evidence directly linking Gen. Torrijos to drug dealing.

But among other things, the Senate—which is debating two treaties to end U.S. control of the Panama Canal—was told that reliable intelligence reports pictured Torrijos as aware of drug trafficking by his brother and other Panamanian officials and "did not take sufficient action" to stop it.

Sen. Birch Bayh (D-Ind.), chairman of the Senate Intelligence Committee, also disclosed that a State Department official, apparently under instructions from the Nixon White House, tipped off Gen. Torrijos in 1972 that his brother faced arrest in the Canal Zone by U.S. agents.

"Moises was on a ship bound for Cristobal, where customs agents were preparing to arrest him," Bayh said. "Gen. Torrijos, acting on the information provided by the American official, contacted Moises, who then left the ship at an earlier stop."

Bayh also said that a month later, "at the direction of the White House," Moises Torrijos was briefed on his indictment by officials of the U.S. Bureau of Narcotics and Dangerous Drugs, now known as the Drug Enforcement Administration.

Bayh's disclosure about the Torrijos brothers came only two days after the Panamanian leader was quoted as saying that he would arrest his brother himself or turn him over to U.S. officials if the United States provided evidence to support the drug charges.

But according to Bayh's report to the Senate, Torrijos has known of the charges against his brother for more than five years.

Bayh, according to Senate sources, spent much of the closed session reading the findings of his committee to the Senate. A 20-page censored version of Bayh's voluminous report was distributed to reporters.

The existence of the indictment against Moises Torrijos was confirmed by Bayh before the Justice Department unsealed it. A department spokesman said that Atty. Gen. Griffin B. Bell decided to make the indictment public because its existence was widely known.

A government official described the 155 pounds of heroin mentioned in the indictment as "an unusually heavy amount," but said it was not a record seizure. (Los Angeles police said that 155 pounds of heroin would have a street value of $67.5 million.)

In outlining the intelligence reports involving Torrijos, Bayh stressed that they "were largely secondhand and of varying reliability."

The Senate's closed session had been requested by Robert Dole (R-

Please Turn to Page 9, Col. 1

Coal Bargainers Agree to Resume Talks on Contract

BY BRYCE NELSON
Times Staff Writer

WASHINGTON—Leaders of the United Mine Workers union and the soft coal operators association agreed Tuesday to resume face-to-face negotiations as the Carter Administration struggled to end the record 78-day-old coal strike.

The agreement was the most hopeful sign since negotiations broke down between the two sides early Saturday morning when the UMW's bargaining council unanimously rejected the "final" offer of the Bituminous Coal Operators Assn.

The talks could resume as early as today.

Labor Secretary Ray Marshall met with both industry and union leaders Tuesday, according to White House Press Secretary Jody Powell.

Powell spoke of Tuesday's developments with guarded optimism, saying that "we are somewhat encouraged that these discussions are taking place."

At the same time, an Administration official said the settlement the UMW made with the Pittsburg & Midway Coal Mining Co. Monday "does figure in a major way into these discussions."

Meanwhile, the effects of the strike continued to be felt throughout the economy. Mandatory curtailment of electric power to industries caused layoffs to mount to nearly 3,000 workers in the Indiana cities of Terre Haute, Kokomo, Peru and Anderson.

Elsewhere, utilities were staving off widespread power cutbacks that had been forecast this week.

Spokesmen for the auto makers said they had been temporarily spared the most severe effects of the strike, and a General Motors spokesman said the "main crunch" had been delayed for a week.

The strike was also felt in the Kansas City area where leaders of 152 industries were told to devise plans by next week to close down two days a week to conserve electricity. Included would be a Trans World Airlines overhaul base employing 6,000.

The tentative agreement to resume negotiations was first announced by BCOA Chairman E. B. Leisenring Jr. in a letter to West Virginia Gov. John D. Rockefeller IV. Rockefeller and the governors of Pennsylvania, Ohio and Kentucky had urged the operators to resume negotiations, taking into account the settlement made with the P&M Coal Mining Co.

"On behalf of myself and my colleagues, I assure you that we are willing to return to face-to-face bargaining," Leisenring wrote. He indicated, however, that he did not regard the P&M settlement as a necessary model for the BCOA, a group of 130 companies that produce 80% of the coal mined by the UMW.

Please Turn to Page 14, Col. 3

Brown Tells Reelection Bid in Routine-Looking 'Memo'

BY GEORGE SKELTON
Times Sacramento Bureau Chief

SACRAMENTO—Gov. Brown, in his own calculatedly casual way, let it be known officially Tuesday that he is running for reelection to a second term.

It caught no one by surprise. There never had been the slightest hint he would not run.

The 39-year-old Democrat's recent public travels, in fact, have more befit a campaigning politician than a sitting chief executive.

The only mystery had been just how Brown would formally announce his candidacy. And that came Tuesday in a routine-appearing, three-paragraph "memo" distributed by his press office to Capitol reporters. It began:

"Gov. Edmund G. Brown Jr. announced today that his chief of staff and Executive Secretary Gray Davis will take a leave of absence to manage his reelection campaign."

It was the first time Brown had publicly acknowledged he is running for reelection.

The memo went on to announce, as reported in The Times Feb. 2, that Davis would temporarily be replaced as the governor's top aide by Business and Transportation Secretary Richard T. Silberman, a wealthy San Diego businessman.

After the November election, the memo continued, Davis and Silberman will return to their present jobs.

The memo concluded that Brown would answer questions about campaign details at a Capitol press conference this morning.

"All the details will emerge in good time," Davis told The Times, borrowing the "will emerge" answer Brown has given to countless queries during his Administration.

So low-key was Brown's announcement that he did not even schedule the almost obligatory-by-tradition statewide tour of candidacy declaration news conferences normally held at airports and press clubs.

"We didn't see any great need for fanfare," Davis said. "We're confident the message will go forth from Sacramento."

It was a 180-degree contrast from the way Brown, then the secretary of state, announced his long-anticipated gubernatorial candidacy four years ago.

He flew to four cities that day, declaring that Californians could have "blue skies, a prosperous economy and a educational system second to none" if the voters would elect him

Please Turn to Page 17, Col. 1

Million-Gallon Gasoline Tank Explodes in Rialto

BY TOM PAEGEL and JERRY BELCHER
Times Staff Writers

A tank containing more than a million gallons of high-octane gasoline exploded in a massive fireball in Rialto Tuesday, critically burning a motorist on a nearby street and sending a black pillar of smoke into the sky that was visible for miles.

The blaze that resulted from the 8:38 a.m. explosion was finally extinguished at 5:30 p.m. after a daring effort by fire fighters clad in reflective, fire resistant suits.

The fireball from the explosion of the Texaco-leased tank boiled 200 feet into the air and fanned out an estimated 200 yards on the ground—enveloping a pickup truck driven by Terry Lee, 24, of Rialto, a city centered just west of downtown San Bernardino.

Lee was driving along Riverside Drive, adjacent to the tank farm that

Please Turn to Page 3, Col. 5

FILM ACADEMY LISTS OSCAR NOMINATIONS

Nominations for the 50th annual Academy Awards were announced Tuesday. For Gregg Kilday's account of the nominations, see Part 2, Page 1. Times Arts Editor Charles Champlin's commentary on the nominations appears in Part 4, Page 1, and a complete list of the nominations in Part 4, Page 12.

Supreme Court Opens Way for Oil Drilling in Atlantic

BY PHILIP HAGER
Times Staff Writer

WASHINGTON—The Supreme Court Tuesday refused to block plans for extensive exploratory oil and natural gas drilling on the outer continental shelf off the coasts of New York, New Jersey and Delaware.

The justices, in a brief order, let stand a federal appeals court decision approving the sale of $1.1 billion in offshore leases to oil companies by the government in 1976.

Both President Gerald R. Ford and President Carter had urged offshore development, provided there were adequate environmental safeguards. Last August, Carter expressed support for a rapid increase in offshore oil and gas development along the eastern seaboard, saying it could reduce the nation's dependence on foreign fuel.

The court's action Tuesday was a blow to environmentalists, New York officials and citizens' groups in New York that had claimed environmental impact statements on the potential effects of transporting oil ashore were inadequate. The use of tankers, they said, could result in damaging oil spills.

The Department of the Interior, supported by the major oil companies, urged the justices to reject the claims by opponents.

The leases involve 93 tracts of submerged lands—covering nearly 900,000 acres—in the Baltimore Canyon area off the Middle Atlantic states. The $1.2 billion from the lease sale was paid to the U.S. Treasury by a group of 20 oil companies. Although six of the companies have obtained permits to begin exploratory drilling,

Please Turn to Page 12, Col. 1

FEATURE INDEX

TERRORISTS DISORGANIZED

Hostage on Cyprus: No Time for Fear

BY JOE ALEX MORRIS JR.
Times Staff Writer

NICOSIA, Cyprus—"It was such a comedy I did not have time to be afraid."

That was how an Arab hostage described the dramatic events in the Cyprus Hilton Hotel when two Arab gunmen broke up a meeting of the Afro-Asian People's Solidarity Conference on Saturday.

The man, who works for an international organization here and asked not to be identified, was in the lobby when the gunmen rounded up frightened delegates shortly after killing the conference's secretary general, Youssef Sebai of Egypt. The Arab later was released before the gunmen took their final group of 11 hostages to a plane at Larnaca airport.

"We were all herded into the cafeteria, maybe 80 people altogether. Their first question was 'Who is from Vietnam?'"

After separating the Arabs from the Asian and African delegates, they asked two policemen present to put their weapons on a table. Then they asked if anyone else had weapons, and three plainclothes policemen stepped forward docilely and deposited their guns.

"The five guns were lying there, right next to the hostages. Anyone could have picked one up and started shooting," the man said.

The two gunmen were identified as Samir Mohammed Hadar, 28, a Palestinian with an Iraqi passport (identified initially as a Jordanian), and Zayed Hussein Ahmed Ala, 26, apparently from Kuwait. The witness said he was sure the second man, who spoke with a Kuwaiti accent, was the one who had killed Sebai.

At one point, he recounted, the Palestinian shouted to the Kuwaiti, "How many bullets did you put in him, two or three?" The Kuwaiti told him to shut up, he reported.

The drama did not end until late Sunday evening at Larnaca airport, to which the terrorists and their hostages had returned after their commandeered Cyprus Airways jetliner had flown to Djibouti. But 15 Egyptian commandos were dead, killed by Cypriot national guardsmen during an attempt to storm the plane, before the gunmen meekly surrendered.

Please Turn to Page 7, Col. 1

THE WEATHER

National Weather Service forecast: Fair and warm today and Thursday with highs both days about 80. High Tuesday 80; low, 50.

Complete weather information and smog forecast in Part 3, Page 14.

only to the New York *News* during the week and third behind New York's *News* and *Times* on Sundays. About 75 percent of the *Times'* sales are by subscription and it leads all newspapers in the nation in home-delivered circulation.[7]

How did the *Times* evolve to its present position of prestige and respect? Actually, the paper has been an important institution in Southern California ever since it was founded by Thomas Gardiner and Nathan Cole in 1881. For financial reasons, they were forced to sell the controlling interest in their paper in August, 1882, to Harrison Gray Otis, a Civil War colonel from Ohio. By 1886, he had become the sole proprietor of the *Times*. As he took over as editor-publisher, he also waged "a tireless campaign to further the growth and prosperity of the area" of Southern California.[8] In 1884, he incorporated the *Times* under a public corporation, The Times Mirror Company, now one of the nation's largest publicly-held publishing firms.

In his paper, Otis fought and won a long battle for free harbor facilities at San Pedro against the private interests that wanted to control the area's docking and shipping. The *Times* also campaigned tirelessly for an adequate water supply for southern California's burgeoning population and for the Owens River aqueduct system to transport it.

Otis, who became a general during the Spanish-American War, claimed two other distinctions as editor-publisher. When the *Times* plant was bombed in 1920 and 20 men were killed, Otis teamed up with his son-in-law Harry Chandler and editor Harry Andrews to continue publication without missing an edition. Then, in 1911, he directed the construction of a new plant, then the most modern newspaper facility on the West Coast.

Upon Otis's death in 1917, Harry Chandler took over as publisher to shape and develop what his father-in-law had begun. He sparked *Times* campaigns for "agricultural diversification, for industrial growth, and for a highway system that would serve both agriculture and industry."[9] In 1922, the *Times* opened the first newspaper-owned radio station, and six years later became the first newspaper to make use of airplanes for newspaper delivery.

The decade of the 1930's and the early 1940's were fruitful years for publisher Chandler. In 1935, he constructed a new, modern six-story building which still serves today as the mainstay of the *Times* three-building complex in Times Mirror Square in the Los Angeles civic center. Under him, the *Times* won its first Pulitzer Prize Gold Medal in 1941 for "disinterested and meritorious public service." Under him, also, the paper became the first Western newspaper to win the Ayer Award for news makeup and typography. Through a Supreme Court reversal of an earlier decision, he won the right for the *Times*—and all newspapers—to comment editorially on the conduct of the courts and court trials.

Norman Chandler, who had gradually been assuming the responsibilities of the *Times*, became its publisher when his father Harry died in 1944. Under

---

[7] Brochure, "Facts About the *Los Angeles Times*," The Times Mirror Company, Los Angeles, 1977, p. 5.

[8] *Ibid.*, p. 24.

[9] "*Facts About the Los Angeles Times*," *op. cit.*

Norman's leadership, the paper responded to post-war change and the rapid
growth of California in several ways. It expanded its editorial content until it became the world leader in volume of news and features. It increased its daily
readership and advertising space. It worked to improve the area's cultural development. In 1959, Norman Chandler launched a program of planned diversification in the fields of publishing, printing, education and the graphic arts. A year
later, he turned over the work of publishing to his son Otis in order to devote full
time to the Times Mirror Company as its president and board chairman. Under
Otis Chandler, since 1960, the *Times* has witnessed the greatest changes of its
entire history.

Ever since its incorporation in 1884, the Times Mirror Company, of which
the *Los Angeles Times* is a division, has grown in size and worth. It has, in fact,
expanded into a major diversified international holding company, interested
primarily in the media. At present, the Company has over 35 branches. In addition to the *Times,* it publishes three newspapers: *Newsday* in New York, the nation's largest suburban paper (daily circulation: 468,000); *The Dallas Times
Herald* (235,000); and the Orange Coast *Daily Pilot* (46,000). In addition, the
Company holds the Publishers' Paper Company in Oregon, seven book publishing firms and six information services. Its empire extends to the publication of
seven magazines, ownership of two television stations, operation of 19 cable systems and publication of most of the nation's large telephone directories.

The *Times* seeks to be relevant to the issues of the day. Each day, current
issues and their place in the paper are discussed and decided upon by an editorial board comprised of publisher Otis Chandler, editor William Thomas, associate editor Jean Taylor, managing editor Frank Haven, the editorial writing staff
and representatives from the paper's political, financial, foreign and national
staffs. This forum serves as a sounding board from which emerges many of the
Times editorials.

Times editorials are hard-hitting, but fair. Editor William Thomas says: "We
try to air all sides on our Op-Ed page and in our Opinion section."[10] The Opinion section, which appears in the Sunday edition, is considered one of the best
such departments in world journalism. Usually an eight-page section, it gives
the serious reader a wealth of interpretation, background and opinion on local,
national and world issues. These "depth" pieces have covered such topics of
concern to readers as mobs, education, culture, the people's revolution in China,
the Middle East peace talks, Ethiopia's revolution and the United States' role in
Africa.

In its daily editorials, the *Times'* own editors, under the direction of Anthony Day, treat a wide range of subjects, steer a moderate course and take a
responsible, thoughtful position on the big issues of the day. This two-page pot-
pourri of editorials and syndicated columns supplies readers with a wide range
of informed opinion. Publisher Otis Chandler tries to maintain a political balance in these pages by dividing his contributors into three main classes: liberal,
moderate and conservative. Liberal contributors include columnists such as

10 William F. Thomas, editor, *Los Angeles Times,* in response to questionnaire, dated January 23, 1978.

Walter Lippmann, Robert Hutchins and Drew Pearson. A long list of contributors represent the moderate and conservative views. Among them are Roscoe Drummond, Stewart Alsop, Max Freedman, George Will, J. F. ter Horst, William Raspberry, Max Lerner, Jimmy Breslin, David Broder, Ellen Goodman, Ernest Furgurson, James Kilpatrick, Joseph Kraft and William F. Buckley, Jr.

Otis Chandler tries to maintain a politically independent and balanced stance throughout the paper. Through the years, his paper has moved from staunch Republican to Republican-moderate, to political independence. Before 1960, it was dogmatic in its Republican conservatism. Then, it supported liberal Republican Nelson Rockefeller in the 1964 primaries, although it wound up backing Barry Goldwater in the Presidential election. But it was careful to oppose many of Goldwater's reactionary policies. Today, it no longer routinely endorses candidates for the California governorship, the U.S. Senate and the Presidency.

Within two years after Otis Chandler took over the publisher's chair from his father, the *Times* was already well on its way to becoming one of the very few internationally significant dailies in the United States. In 1962, Chandler strengthened his paper's existing Paris bureau, created a Far Eastern bureau in Tokyo, a Latin American one in Rio de Janeiro, and others in Mexico, Hong Kong and the United Nations headquarters in New York. During the next two years, he added bureaus in London, Bonn, Rome, Moscow, Vienna, and Saigon (the last two now closed). In 1966, bureaus were opened in Bangkok, Buenos Aires and New Delhi. Today, the paper can boast 18 foreign bureaus, those listed above plus others in Athens, Brussels, Cairo, Jerusalem, Johannesburg, Madrid and Nairobi. It counts among its distinguished foreign correspondents William Tuohy, Joe Morris, Jack Foisie and Robert Elegant. The *Times* also supplements its foreign coverage with input from nine news wire agencies (all the major wire services except TASS) and numerous syndicated services. But bland, stereotyped stories lifted directly from the wires have virtually disappeared from the *Times,* replaced by exclusive stories from the paper's network of correspondents and in-depth reporters.

The foreign correspondent for the *Times* enjoys greater freedom than many of his American counterparts. Like the overseas reporters for the best European quality dailies, he is not bound by deadlines, nor is he under pressure to file every day. Reminiscent of correspondents for the *Neue Zürcher Zeitung,* he digs in depth and takes his time providing interpretation of events. His is interested in the "why" as much as the "what" of the story.

Perhaps more than any other United States paper, the *Times* seeks experts for its foreign bureaus and men who will be permitted to stay in one area long enough to understand the situation behind events fully. First, the *Times'* requisites for staff are very high, and even higher for foreign correspondents. To even gain consideration for a *Times* post, an applicant must have a proven record of at least five years of experience with other newspapers, magazines or other media. At the same time, as one observer has commented, being a correspondent for the *Times* "is the closest one can come to a career service" in overseas journalism since the days when London *Times* correspondents enjoyed such status. Highlighting the fantastic job the *Times* has done in improving its foreign coverage, this observer adds: "When one considers that it costs the *Times* an estimated $50,000 to establish a bureau, it indicates that the *Los Angeles Times* has lost its parochial outlook and is dedicated to the enormous task of providing its readers a truly world-wide view."[11]

The quality and extent of the *Times* foreign coverage has been greatly enhanced by two syndication services of its own. The first, the *Los Angeles Times*–Washington *Post* News Service, established in 1962, now provides exclusive staff-produced news and features to over 430 newspapers around the world. For its average daily transmission of 40,000 words, the service draws from the far-flung staffs of the two papers plus the staffs of their related dailies and from the *Guardian* of Manchester and the AFP wire agency. This syndication service has come to be considered one of the profession's best, especially in its covering and interpretation of developments outside the United States. A second service operated by the *Times* is its own *Los Angeles Times* Syndicate, a feature service taken by and published in over 2,000 papers around the world. Its features on world affairs include articles by Georgie Anne Geyer and other staff members with international expertise.

Since Otis Chandler's take-over, his paper's national coverage has also improved markedly. In 1960, it kept only a three-man staff in Washington, D.C. The *Times* now has 24 correspondents at the national capital and its coverage of national affairs is extensive and thorough. Nor has it neglected the remainder of the country; today it operates domestic bureaus in Atlanta, Chicago, Houston, New York, San Francisco and Denver in addition to the Washington corps.

The *Times* has handled well its challenge to provide effective state, area and city news and feature coverage of Los Angeles and southern California's burgeoning population. It covers regional news daily in three sections—the main news, Metro and View. In the 1960's, it won recognition for its work on the Watts riots; lately, it has provided thorough information on Proposition 13 tax reform legislation. But its main service has been through the development of several local sections and one edition. In 1968, it opened a new $8 million plant to produce the Orange County edition. Published daily, this edition reaches some 160,000 readers in the county. Then there are six suburban sections, five publishing twice weekly and one once. All seven have full-time staffs of reporters and photographers to cover local civic, social and cultural events. All seven provide concentrated coverage of news and advertising opportunities within their select area in addition to the other materials in the main edition. In recent months, the *Times* has opened news bureaus in Long Beach, San Bernardino and Santa Barbara. Most recently, the *Times* opened a 26-member editorial office in San Diego, 110 miles to the south of Los Angeles because of the rapid growth of population—and a newspaper market—there.[12]

Several leading newspapers across the United States have taken on a new look which is epitomized in the special sections they have added. The *Los*

[11] Ted Weegar, assistant managing editor, *Los Angeles Times* to J. Merrill, dated July 19, 1966.
[12] "Invasion from the North," *loc. cit.*

Angeles Times has been a leader in adopting this new lifestyle. Recently, it added a "Fashion 78" section to its Friday edition. Vance Stickell of the *Times* says the section was started because

> . . . we had a void to fill. We weren't giving fashion advertisers the reproduction they wanted. We also were trying to retain readers and attract new ones. The section gives the working women a reason to read the newspaper, while at the same time it features articles for the affluent west-sider who doesn't work.[13]

The *Times* carries two other weekly sections: "Food" on Thursdays and "You," a tabloid magazine covering entertainment and consumer information, on Tuesdays.

The *Times* is a big paper, often running more than 200 pages in its weekday editions. During 1976, for example, it published an average of 105 pages daily and 416 pages on Sunday. It consumes more newsprint than any other American daily and accounts for over 20 percent of all newsprint used in the western states. In 1976, it used 330,000 tons of newsprint, or more than 400,000 rolls—enough newsprint to reach to the moon nearly eleven times!

The typical *Times* daily contains at least five parts, sometimes more. Part I, the main news section, includes a page two "News in Brief" summary of all news. The major international, national, state and local news of the day are spread across the remainder of this 32-page section. Part II contains metropolitan and regional news, the editorial and op-ed pages and analyses by columnists. Part III gives sports, business and financial news; Part IV, the "View" section, covers community, social and cultural events; and Part V is, on the average, the world's largest classified advertising section. In addition, there may be special feature sections from time to time. The *Sunday Times* regularly carries sections and features called "Home Magazine," "Calendar," (focusing on art and literature), "The Book Review," "Outlook," "Opinion," "TV Times," "Real Estate," and "Travel." To prepare their stories and features, reporters have access to the paper's editorial library, which contains over 8 million clippings and a million photographs from past issues, all easily available via a computerized access system. Although the paper is really quite well organized, some are critical of its makeup, saying "You can't find anything in it," and that, because of the paper's numerous advertisements, stories "jump from page to page."[14]

The *Times* editorial offices and production facilities would satisfy most journalists' dreams of a utopian work setting. The reporter's edited copy is retyped on an electric typewriter. An optical scanner then "reads" the copy and transmits it to a master computer, from which it is displayed on a video terminal. That print-out is photographed and pasted onto pages, from which a photocomposition system sets it into type. The paper's 52 presses at Times Mirror Square and in Orange County are capable of producing nearly a million 64-page newspapers per hour. The *Times* also uses an electronic layout system, a microwave

13 "Newspapers 'New Lifestyle'," *Media Decisions* (April, 1978), p. 72.
14 "Invasion from the North," *loc. cit.*

link to send the entire newspaper to the *Times* Orange County facility, an advanced platemaking system using lasers, and plastic letterpress printing plates instead of conventional lead ones.

A paper's interest in serving the public is indicated in part by the number of community events and philanthropic causes in which it engages. In these respects, the *Times* has an enviable record. In 1944, it established the Los Angeles Times Fund, which has provided over $10 million worth of benefit to California's youth to date. A *Times* Summer Camp Fund has sent over 150,000 underprivileged children to camp. Annually, it sponsors an Indoor Games meet, a charity professional football game and a national stock car race to supply monies for its philanthropic funds.

Perhaps one of the clearest indicators of a paper's quality and service is the number of awards it receives. To date, the *Times* and its staff members have taken a total of nine of journalism's most valued award, the Pulitzer Prize, three of them Gold Medals for Public Service. It has garnered 12 coveted Society of Professional Journalists/Sigma Delta Chi awards, nine from the Overseas Press Club and one member (Jim Murry) has won "America's Best Sportswriter" award eleven times in the past 12 years. In addition, it takes numerous less significant awards each year.

Much of the greatness of the *Los Angeles Times* must be attributed to the wise editorial policies and guidance it has received. The paper bases its overall editorial policies on two major premises:

> 1. The maintenance of the concept of individual liberty through watchful vigilance at home and abroad.
>
> 2. The preservation, as an essential to the concept of individual liberty, of the free enterprise system in the United States and wherever else, and to the extent that the wishes of other peoples permit it.[15]

As the *Times* has become more liberal and diversified, it has adhered firmly to these two premises. Management has always considered the *Times* to be in the public domain and that the public's best interests are to be served. It has seen itself blessed with constitutional guarantees of freedom which in turn carry heavy responsibilities to make a quality publication out of the *Times*. Today's editor, William Thomas, believes such high purposes are served, at least in part, by "the diversified nature of the stories and features we provide, along with the scope and the thoroughness of our news and feature efforts."[16]

Today, without question, the *Los Angeles Times*' high journalistic standards and quality and its political independence in themselves place it among the great dailies of the world. But it bears another mark of greatness; it is not satisfied to stand still; rather it continues to improve in numerous ways. Its steady and continuing editorial and production upgrading, its willingness to build a new image and its efforts to serve the needs of California's exploding population mark it as a paper "on the move" to an ever-higher rank among the world's elite.

[15]. "The Los Angeles Times," Brochure, Times Mirror Company, 1966, p. 26.
[16] Thomas questionnaire.

The (Louisville) Courier-Journal

(UNITED STATES)

ON NOVEMBER 8, 1868, the approximately 100,000 citizens of Louisville, Kentucky, had a new daily newspaper available to them: *The Louisville Courier-Journal*.[1] The two rival Democratic newspapers of the city—the *Louisville Courier* and the *Louisville Journal* had merged, and the new hyphenated paper was starting a history destined to place it in the front ranks of American daily newspapers.

W. N. Haldeman was in charge of the new paper's business operations and Henry Watterson was the editorial manager. Very early the paper established itself as a prestigious newspaper, and today, some 110 years later, it is more highly respected than ever. It has been fortunate to have been guided by strong, liberal-minded men dedicated to quality journalism and considering the paper as a kind of public conscience. Throughout its history *The Courier-Journal* has been a champion of forward-looking, courageous, vigorous journalism, never satisfied to rest on its laurels. It has consistently taken editorial positions which have jarred the complacent thinking and action of those desiring to perpetuate the status quo.

The newspaper's courage has often resulted in economic and political pressures being used to get it to moderate its editorial positions. Advertisers have threatened to withdraw their advertising—and some have actually done it—and politicians and pressure groups have applied their pressures. But *The Courier-Journal* has stood fast, withstanding attempts by outside forces to dictate or influence its news reporting or editorial policy.

This courageous stance was largely set by its famous editor, Henry Watterson,[2] who at one time rose to fury in righteous indignation when a Post Office official in Washington wrote him suggesting that an anti-Prohibition editorial was nothing but disguised advertising. "Sir," replied Watterson, "I return you these enclosures with the scorn and contempt they fully merit. An official who could transmit to *The Courier-Journal* an anonymous accusation that it printed a paid advertisement as an editorial is unfit for public service, and the individual, be he the third assistant postmaster, or another, who gives expression to such a charge, is a scoundrel and a liar."[3]

[1] In the beginning the nameplate (newspaper's title across the top of the front page) included the name of the city, but not today.

[2] Watterson, a fiery and progressive journalist, was in editorial command of the paper for its first 50 years. He is one of the truly outstanding journalistic figures in American history, and the imprint of his character and personality is still on the newspaper.

[3] Joe Creason, *Mirror of a Century* (a special publication published by the newspaper on its centennial), Nov. 10, 1968, p. 4.

The Courier-Journal

60 Pages ******* Louisville, Wednesday, February 22, 1978 Home delivery: Metro 75¢ week, other 80¢ week Newsstand 15¢

Sheriff tax funds held in banks cost governments

By MIKE BROWN
Courier-Journal Staff Writer

Local and state governmental units — including the financially strapped Jefferson County schools — may be losing thousands of dollars each year because tax money collected by the sheriff sits for several weeks in bank accounts that pay no interest.

The Courier-Journal also has found that former Sheriff James K. Larkin Sr. kept tax collections in local banks for longer than the normal time set by law before sending the money on to the various taxing agencies.

Larkin, who left office last month, said he never got interest on tax money because he had found that this was prohibited by state law.

The extra time his office held the tax money was necessary for processing the county's thousands of payments, he said, and fully legal under an extension provision of the law.

However, a number of officials, including representatives of the state attorney general and the Revenue Department, say they know of no specific prohibition on tax investments by the sheriff, although they say it's a question that needs study.

Joe Greene, the new sheriff and an employee under Larkin, said yesterday that he had assumed there was a law forbidding investment of the tax money. Because of the points raised by The Courier-Journal's inquiry, he said, he plans to look into the matter.

Greene said he thought any interest would go to defray the cost of his office operation. However, lawyers at the Revenue Department and attorney general's office said any interest would go to the taxing districts themselves.

Several years ago Larkin started a new computerized processing system at the Citizens Fidelity Bank & Trust Co. to speed up the handling of tax payments.

An official of the bank said tax payments now are deposited in a non-interest-bearing "demand" account and are ready for withdrawal within two days of receipt.

Larkin withdrew some of the funds — he estimates about one-fifth — for transfer to similar accounts in other local banks. That was done "to keep peace" with all the banks, he said.

Non-interest-bearing accounts were also used by Larkin's predecessor, Allen Hamilton, who said he also thought investments were illegal.

However, other governmental agencies routinely make short-term investments in federal government and bank securities, and the sheriff's dependence on non-interest-bearing accounts is privately questioned by some officials.

"Between you and me, it's sure a waste," said one local official, referring to the lost interest. "It's a shame," said another. "I can't understand it," added a third. "If there are laws, they should be changed."

As an example, Jefferson County Fiscal Court on Dec. 28 invested $3 million until just Jan. 5, making $4,166 in interest at a rate of 6.25 percent.

The Louisville Sinking Fund, which handles local occupational taxes, on Jan. 13 invested $60,000 until Jan. 18 at 6 percent. On Jan. 19, it invested $2 million for just one day.

Mrs. Ernestine Roach, the receiver of Jefferson Circuit Court, said she recently invested $500,000 in federal securities on a day-to-day basis.

The sheriff collects more than $100

See GOVERNMENTS
Back page, col. 1, this section

River Region workers not getting paid while head is

By ROBERT L. PEIRCE
Courier-Journal Staff Writer
© 1978, The Courier-Journal

The executive director of the River Region Mental Health-Mental Retardation Board has been guaranteed a monthly paycheck of $3,750 at least through March while more than 400 other board employees continue to work without pay.

Dr. James A. Halikas can collect his paycheck at least through March because River Region paid a large part of his paycheck three months in advance to the University of Louisville. The salary payment and a payment of fringe benefits were made Jan. 13 before the Louisville-based mental-health agency ran out of money to pay other employees and was forced into bankruptcy court.

The university passes the money along to Halikas.

Halikas apparently won't get, at least for the moment, another $1,533 a month that he receives directly from River Region. The last such payment was made to him Jan. 31, according to River Region officials.

Halikas said he had no comment on whether it was fair that he receive salary while other employees do not.

Last Wednesday when employees did not receive paychecks, he told a reporter that he was not being paid either. However, he said yesterday that he was

See DIRECTOR
Back page, col. 2, this section

High beams

National Weather Service

LOUISVILLE area — Sunny and continued cold; increasing cloudiness tonight with 30 percent chance of light snow. High today, near 35; tomorrow, upper 30s. Low tonight, near 25.

KENTUCKY — Sunny and cold; increasing cloudiness tonight with chance of light snow. Highs today and tomorrow, 30s. Lows tonight, upper teens to mid-20s.

High yesterday, 30; low, 20.
Year ago yesterday: High, 38; low, 29.
Sun: Rises, 7:25; sets, 6:29.
Moon: Rises, 6:25 p.m.; sets, 6:57 a.m.

Weather map and details, Page B 4.

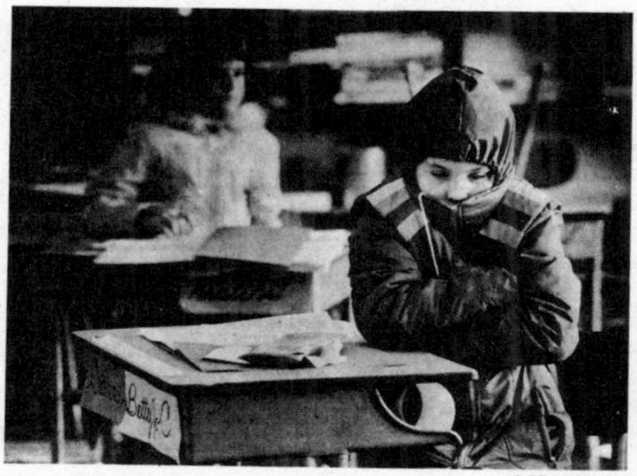

Staff Photo by Bill Luster

As to the impact of the coal strike, ask Deanna Lindsey, 9, a third-grader at the Middle Road Elementary School in Jeffersonville, Ind. Schools there have turned back the thermostats to conserve dwindling coal stockpiles. Deanna said she was freezing.

UMW, industry negotiators meet separately with Marshall

From New York Times and AP Dispatches

WASHINGTON — Coal industry and union bargainers resumed negotiations yesterday in an attempt to end the United Mine Workers strike before the government imposes a settlement.

Top industry officials and union bargainers shuttled in and out of the Labor Department for separate meetings with Labor Secretary Ray Marshall. Marshall sent the bargainers home by early evening, saying he would stay in contact with both sides by telephone.

The White House said it was "somewhat encouraged" by the bargaining resumption but not sure the talks would be productive.

The new round of talks came as the White House consulted with congressional leaders about direct governmental intervention to end the walkout — but once again stopped short of acting in hopes that a voluntary agreement could be worked out.

An administration official said a proposed settlement reached by the UMW and an independent coal operator — the P&M Coal Co. — on Monday "does figure in a major way" in the new talks.

As government pressure mounted for an end to the lengthy strike, officials of the Bituminous Coal Operators Association, the 130-member employers group, announced they were agreeable to new talks. However, they criticized aspects of the independent settlement.

BCOA Chairman E.B. "Ted" Leisenring said the union's settlement with P&M did not adequately deal with several major issues in the dispute.

But a BCOA statement made clear that negotiators for "the majors" — the 130 coal companies that produce about half the annual tonnage — would con-

See UMW
Page 2, col. 1, this section

More stories about the strike

- The health-care program for coal miners, already weakened by years of financial trouble, suffers another setback, Page B 3.
- Residents of the White House need not worry about an energy shortage because the utility serving them uses imported oil and non-union coal, Page B 3.
- Kentucky employes of P&M Coal Co. wait anxiously for a look at the tentative agreement reached between their company and the UMW, Page B 3.
- Layoffs forced by the nationwide coal strike jump to 3,000 in Indiana, Page B 3.

Coal shortages filling some truckers' pockets

By MIKE WINERIP
Courier-Journal Staff Writer

CAMPTON, Ky. — Phillip Bryant rarely eats or sleeps these days. He's too busy making money hauling coal out of the Kentucky River fields.

He made two nine-hour, 450-mile roundtrips to the Hamilton, Ohio, municipal electric plant yesterday. On Monday he made three hauls to a Winchester, Ky., utility plant and one to Hamilton. He even made a haul on Sunday, something that never happens in normal times.

And making trips makes money for Bryant — more than $100 a day, even though he doesn't own his truck. A friend who owns his coal rig cleared nearly $2,000 last week, Bryant said.

"I'm running back and forth as hard as I can," the young driver said.

"Anytime I want to make a run they have coal for me. Those people in Ohio can't get enough coal. It's just like gold."

The nationwide United Mine Workers strike has brought boom times to the part of the Eastern Kentucky coalfields that stretches from Hazard in Perry County northward to Campton in Wolfe County.

Drivers say they are making several extra runs a week and twice their normal incomes. There are reports of truckers from other parts of Kentucky, Ohio, Indiana and as far away as North

See STRIKE
Back page, col. 5, this section

column six

Perfect cars, conditions yield flawed mileage rates

By HARRY ANDERSON
© L.A. Times-Washington Post Service

ANN ARBOR, Mich. — At the cavernous Environmental Protection Agency building in Ann Arbor, cars drive the morning rush hour through downtown Los Angeles.

Like their Southern California counterparts, the vehicles crawl along in heavy traffic, covering a congested route on the freeway and surface streets at an average speed of 19.6 mph.

Unlike the real thing, however, professional drivers operate all the cars on dynamometers — laboratory treadmill devices that simulate driving conditions. Some other real-life factors are also left out — including hills, jackrabbit starts, rough roads and cold temperatures.

The EPA uses the Los Angeles rush hour driving pattern to test new cars for pollution control and fuel economy in city driving. It is these Los Angeles driving tests conducted in a Michigan laboratory that are the basis of the EPA's increasingly controversial gasoline mileage ratings.

The agency has been publishing new car fuel economy estimates based on such simulated driving tests since the 1973 models were introduced. The automobile industry has also made extensive use of them in its advertising.

The trouble is, nobody believes that the EPA mileage numbers reflect the kind of fuel economy normal drivers achieve. And nobody — not even the EPA — is satisfied with the numbers.

"We have begun to study just how good our estimates are," says Eric O. Stork, the EPA's deputy assistant administrator for mobile source air pollution control. "From the very first, we have always represented these numbers as estimates; that is the nature of all test data. They are good, but they certainly aren't perfect."

Recent studies by the EPA itself suggest that the fuel economy achieved by typical drivers is often 7 to 16 percent below the agency's test results. The studies also found cars that get the highest mileage in EPA tests — usually small, subcompact models — frequently suffer the largest reduction in actual driving results.

Such studies confirmed what the EPA already suspected. The agency has been criticized by dissatisfied car buyers. Stork says he signs about 10 letters a week to members of Congress in response to angry constituents who are upset with EPA mileage numbers compared with actual performance.

The agency intends to be more vocal in informing the public that the numbers are meant to be used only to compare relative fuel economy of various cars — not as an exact measurement of gasoline mileage.

However, EPA officials do suggest that beginning next year a method may be used to lower the test figures and bring them more in line with the results obtained in normal driving.

"We will be somewhat closer to mean (typical) fuel economy, but we will still not be perfect," says Stork. "There is no way to reduce the infinite variation in the way people use cars or the conditions in which they drive."

EPA will hold a series of public hearings next month in several cities to test reaction to several proposed

See EPA
Back page, col. 1, this section

Senate panel finds no Torrijos link to drug trade

By RICHARD PYLE
Associated Press

WASHINGTON — Panamanian leader Omar Torrijos knew that officials of his government were engaged in drug trafficking, but there is "no conclusive evidence" that Torrijos was involved, the Senate intelligence committee said yesterday.

The committee said it found that reports linking Gen. Torrijos to the drug market were "largely secondhand and of varying reliability."

The committee report was presented to the Senate as debate on the Panama Canal treaties continued in a 10-hour closed-door session. The session, which set a record for length, is to continue today.

Senate leaders voted to release an unclassified version of the report, committee sources said.

Sen. Birch Bayh, D-Ind., chairman of the panel, told the Senate that reliable intelligence showed that Torrijos knew about drug trafficking by government officials "and did not take sufficient action" to stop his brother, Moises, from becoming involved.

But he added that the committee's investigation of Torrijos "has turned up no conclusive evidence that could be used in a court of law."

Bayh also said the panel found no evidence that drug intelligence activities affected the final terms of the Panama Canal treaties, which would turn control of the canal over to Panama by the year 2000.

But Sen. Bob Dole, R-Kan., a treaty opponent, said that the "sanitized" version of the committee report indicated that Torrijos knew of drug trafficking and that the general's credibility was at issue.

The Senate discussion focused on widely reported allegations that Torrijos and members of his family have engaged in illicit narcotics trade — charges that some treaty foes hope will be effective in blocking ratification.

But some pro-treaty senators, who contend that the drug question is a peripheral issue where the treaties are concerned, predicted that the strategy would fail.

Sen. George McGovern, D-S.D., said the secret session "may have been the biggest waste of time during the 15 years I have been in the Senate."

He added: "Its only value was to demonstrate that the opponents of the Panama Canal treaties have run out of arguments and now are resorting to side

See PANEL
Back page, col. 4, this section

Inside today

Who will win the 50th Oscars?

Woody Allen scored a personal triumph yesterday when he was nominated for three Academy Awards — as writer, director and star of "Annie Hall." Two films received 11 nominations each — "The Turning Point" and "Julia" — and "Star Wars" received 10 nominations. In Accent, Page C 5.

Vol. 246, No. 53

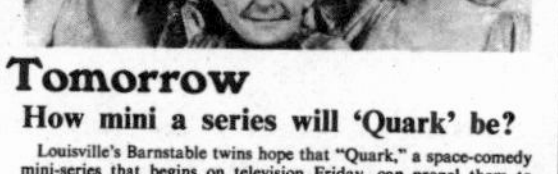

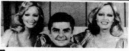

Tomorrow

How mini a series will 'Quark' be?

Louisville's Barnstable twins hope that "Quark," a space-comedy mini-series that begins on television Friday, can propel them to commercial network success a la "Charlie's Angels." TV critic Tom Dorsey reviews the premiere in Accent tomorrow.

Bill setting population quota for schools passed by House

By RICHARD WILSON
Courier-Journal Staff Writer

FRANKFORT, Ky. — A bill that supporters said would eliminate discrimination against rural Kentuckians in professional-school admissions passed in the House of Representatives yesterday on a 65-23 vote.

The vote indicated that HB 118, originally pushed by Eastern Kentucky legislators, picked up support from House members throughout the state. (Other legislative stories, Pages B 6 and 7).

If the bill becomes law, it will drastically alter admissions procedures to the state's medical, dental and law schools by requiring entry to be closely tied to each congressional district's population.

The schools that would be affected if the bill becomes law are the medical and dental schools at the University of Kentucky and the University of Louisville, and the law schools at UK, U of L, and Northern Kentucky University.

Admissions committees at these schools now rely heavily on applicants' undergraduate grades, test scores on en-

See QUOTA
Back page, col. 5, this section

Today the editor-publisher of *The Courier-Journal*, Barry Bingham, Jr., evidences the same dedication to excellence in journalism and the same courageous and progressive spirit instilled in the paper during its first half-century by "Marse Henry" Watterson. "Quality" and "commitment" are two important journalistic concepts at the newspaper. Staff members are sought who have a high level of intelligence, three to five years experience, special expertise or training in special news subject areas, a high sense of ethics, a questioning mind, and potential for outstanding writing and editing.[4]

The Courier-Journal has been called "an institution" by the present Chairman of the Board, Barry Bingham, Sr., who sees the paper as greater than any individual who works for it; the paper has a kind of "institutional greatness far more enduring than the men and women who serve it." Now owned by the Bingham family, the newspaper is, indeed, a "public trust," as Bingham Sr.'s father (Judge Robert Worth Bingham) once called it, and now "his son and grandson are pledged to the same view, and dedicated to serving it with unflagging enthusiasm."[5]

The Courier-Journal's daily circulation is slightly more than 200,000 and on Sundays it reaches nearly 350,000. About 85 percent of its circulation goes to subscribers. The reporters and editors on the paper (exclusive of the sports and editorial page writers) number 135, some 95 of whom are writers. There are no permanent foreign correspondents, but the paper sends special writers abroad from time to time. In addition, the paper makes use of three wire services—the AP, the New York Times News Service, and the Los Angeles-Washington Post News Service. *The Courier-Journal* also gets the AP Wirephoto service and also uses many photographs from free-lance photographers.[6]

Some 60 percent of a typical copy of the newspaper is given over to advertising, probably a common figure among American dailies. It is estimated that about 13 percent of the total space goes for local and state news, about 5 percent for business news, about 6 percent for sports, about 4 percent for national news, and about 2 percent for international news, and the other 10 percent for an assortment of material such as editorials, news analysis, letters, travel, reviews, and public service. The paper publishes four editions Monday through Saturday, and three on Sunday. It uses color printing on one or two news pages at least two or three times a week, especially in some photos, in charts, maps and special layouts and drawings.

Editors of *The Courier-Journal* say that the paper is aimed at "solid citizens and self-improvement seekers—those with large appetites for news and interpretation." The paper considers every reporter an "investigative" reporter, and sufficient time is allowed for pursuit of the complete story if the subject warrants it. Three reporters are full-time on investigative work at all times.

The newspaper considers itself—and is considered by its readers—as very "liberal," and generally espousing a Democratic point of view. As to its basic edi-

[4] Questionnaire sent authors by Stanley L. Slusher, assistant managing editor, and Robert T. Barnard, opinion page editor, April 24, 1978. Hereafter cited as: Slusher-Barnard questionnaire.

[5] "A Public Trust," by Barry Bingham, in *Mirror of a Century*, p. 2.

[6] Slusher-Barnard questionnaire.

torial policy, it might be stated by four important questions: Is it news? Is it in good taste? Is it accurate and fair? Is it written understandably? As for its stands in controversial areas, the newspaper has recently come out in favor of gun control legislation, right of women to control their own bodies, of school busing if necessary to achieve desegregation. *The Courier-Journal* considers itself primarily a "regional" newspaper and prides itself on the thoroughness and sophistication and general quality with which it represents its region. Its editors believe the newspaper is a good example of newspaper quality largely because of "an extremely strong commitment of news resources to covering the entire state of Kentucky and Southern Indiana, linking readers throughout the region."[7]

With a notable record as an award-winning newspaper, *The Courier-Journal* has received seven Pulitzer Prizes—in 1918, 1926, 1956, 1967, 1969, 1976, and 1978. In addition to this important achievement, the newspaper has garnered many prizes and awards from such groups as the following: Sigma Delta Chi, American Bar Association, National Conference of Christians and Jews, National Association of Real Estate Editors, National Council for the Advancement of Education Writing, Executive Council of the Episcopal Church in New York, the Penney-Missouri Awards Committee, the National Sportscasters and Sportswriters Association, the Religious Public Relations Council, and the University of Kentucky School of Journalism.

The Courier-Journal today has an ombudsman, a kind of readers' representative with the newspaper's executives. This position began in 1967 and gives the readers somebody at the paper they can always talk to and know that their complaints are being taken care of. *The Courier-Journal* was the U.S.'s first paper to put somebody into this kind of job; today the ombudsman at the paper handles about 3,000 complaints and other reader suggestions every year. In 1977 the Circulation Department of the paper also created an ombudsman to whom complaints about newspaper delivery are carried.

Although the newspaper places greatest emphasis on objective news reporting, it also believes that opinion (analysis and debate) is crucial to a quality newspaper. On its editorial pages the reader will find several kinds of opinion: editorials, and opinion of others from outside the newspaper. An important opinion section is the Letters to the Editor. And there are also editorial cartoons,[8] essays by people in the Louisville area (run under the heading "Your Turn"), and nationally syndicated columnists.

The Courier-Journal is highly computerized and automated in its editing and printing. Editors on the desk do much of their work by typing onto computer keyboards instead of writing on paper, but their basic job is exactly the same as it always has been—to make sure that stories are well-written, accurate, and clear, and to arrange the pages sensibly and attractively. The reporters put their stories directly into the computer through a machine called an OCR (optical character reader) which "reads" the words and translates them into computer language. When the editor wants to look at the story, he sits at his com-

---

[7] *Ibid.*

[8] *The Courier-Journal* has a regular cartoonist, Hugh Haynie, whose cartoons also appear in dozens of other American newspapers.

puter screen (VDT) and calls for the story; corrections can be made by typing onto the keyboard and showing the computer exactly where to make the change. When the editors are finished with the stories, they punch a certain key and the stories are sent to the composing room where the words are turned into type. *The Courier-Journal* is printed by offset, and its presses have an average speed of 57,000 copies an hour.

The modern "new technology" and newspaper production at *The Courier-Journal* is dramatically different from that of the little ancestral paper, printing in 1868 from "hot type" in crowded quarters. Outstanding journalists through the years, led by strong and dedicated executives, have forged the newspaper into the editorial and technological power it is today.

Some names should be mentioned in the paper's colorful history. First, there was the flamboyant "Marse Henry" Watterson, the last of the great personal editors in the U.S., who guided the paper during its first half-century. Then came Judge Robert Worth Bingham, the grandfather of the present editor, who controlled the paper until 1933 when he left to become Ambassador to the Court of St. James. In 1936 a triumvirate took over management of the paper—Barry Bingham (Robert Worth Bingham's son), Mark Ethridge, and Lisle Baker Jr. They remained in control for nearly 30 years, until Ethridge retired in 1963 and Baker in 1968. This left Bingham, who is now principal owner and board chairman. His son, Barry Jr., is editor and publisher, and Michael J. Davies is managing editor.

The journalists who are producing the newspaper today are aware of the illustrious history of their journal, and they are determined that *The Courier-Journal* press forward constantly and not rest on its laurels. And, in the tradition of "Marse Henry" Watterson, they are turning out a newspaper that excels in most areas of modern journalism and easily deserves a place among the world's great dailies.

The Miami Herald

(UNITED STATES)

"THE HERALD makes a conscientious effort to do a thorough job of covering and monitoring its own area, and is the dominant newspaper in South Florida. But it also feels that, in its responsibility to give people full information so they can make sound decisions, it must strive to present first-rate national and international reporting."[1]

[1] Letter to John Merrill from Lee Hills, dated Feb. 24, 1978.

Chilly

Sunny, windy and cold today, partly cloudy and a little warmer Thursday. High near 60. (Details, Page 2A.)

TUESDAY'S TEMPERATURES

The Miami Herald

Wednesday, February 22, 1978   Florida's Complete Newspaper   100 Pages   68th Year — No. 84

A Latin American Edition is Published Daily

Copyright 1978 The Miami Herald

Treasury Won't Let Buck Stop, Requests New Dollar

WASHINGTON — (AP) — The Treasury Department, which two years ago resurrected the $2 bill, now wants to bring back a shrunken — and mostly copper — version of the once-popular silver dollar.

The department also told Congress that it has rejected proposals to eliminate the half-dollar and that it wants to keep the penny indefinitely.

The reason behind the proposed shift to copper dollar coins is economic. The proposed coin will cost between 2 and 3 cents to produce and will last at least 15 years. In comparison, a paper dollar costs only 1.7 cents to produce but wears out quickly.

The Treasury would continue to produce dollar bills if the dollar coin proposal is passed.

"It is anticipated that the new dollar coin, sized between the quarter and half-dollar, would be more acceptable to the general public than the present dollar coin," Treasury Undersecretary Bette B. Anderson said.

Vending machine operators want a dollar coin because it would allow them to sell products costing more than a dollar. Some members of Congress have expressed fears that it also would allow vendors to raise prices.

Terry Markberry, special projects officer for the Treasury, said that if Congress approves the new

dollar coin this year, the government can produce 250 million of them for distribution early next year.

The administration is hoping a one-dollar coin would supplement the $2 bill, which has had trouble catching on in two years of production.

As for the half dollar, the Treasury had said last year it wanted to get rid of this coin because it was unpopular. But Anderson indicated Tuesday that she would like the issue settled separately.

The Ford Administration had wanted to eliminate the penny too,

but Treasury Secretary Michael Blumenthal wants it retained.

The chairmen of the congressional banking committees also want the penny retained because they think merchants would round prices off to the highest nickel, adding to inflation.

Anderson wrote, "The recommendation of the department is that the one-cent coin be retained as part of the U.S. coinage system."

She said copper prices have remained low and that the U.S. Mint has enough room to make pennies into the mid-1980s.

New Coin, Center, Would Feature Liberty Head, Symbolic Cap on Stick
... its size would place it between quarter and Kennedy half-dollar
— Associated Press

Lori Emmons, 19, of Syracuse, N.Y., Is a Bundled and Lonely Figure on the Beach
... says she's going to find it embarrassing going home after two weeks with no tan
— MICHAEL STEINBACHER / Miami Herald Staff

Chile Asked To Question 2 in Slaying

By HARRY F. ROSENTHAL
Associated Press

WASHINGTON — U.S. officials disclosed Tuesday that they are seeking to question two Chilean military men about the murder of former Chilean ambassador Orlando Letelier, killed in a bomb explosion on a Washington street in 1976.

Letelier died when a remote-control bomb exploded in his car as he and Ronne Moffitt, Mrs. Moffitt's husband, Michael, drove along Embassy Row to their jobs at the Institute for Policy Studies, a liberal think-tank where they worked. Mrs. Moffitt also was killed in the blast.

Since then, a grand jury and the FBI have been looking into the murders.

THE GRAND JURY has questioned more than a score of Cuban exiles, most of them from Miami. U.S. officials have said privately that they believe both Cuban exiles and Chilean agents were involved in the slaying, but no charges have been filed.

The alleged connection of the two Chilean military men to the case was disclosed when the United States asked the Chilean government to question the two about the assassination.

"At least one of these men met with one of the persons believed to be responsible" for the murders, said the U.S. request to the Chilean courts.

Attached to the request was a list of questions to be put to the two men, Juan Williams Rose, 28, and Alejandro Romeral Jara, 27.

The list of questions was not made public. The documents did not identify "the persons believed to be responsible."

THE REQUEST was addressed to the Supreme Court of Chile and was signed by William B. Bryant, chief judge of the U.S. District Court for the District of Columbia.

Letelier and Mrs. Moffitt, 25,

Turn to Page 3A Col. 1

Israeli Cabinet Reported Split On Settlements

By MARCUS ELIASON
Associated Press

TEL AVIV — The Israeli cabinet is divided over whether to press on with Jewish settlement on occupied Arab land; a split apparently widened by U.S. censure of the settlements in recent months, sources reported Tuesday.

Attached to the request was a list of questions to be put to the two rival camps have been taking shape lately — one is led by Defense Minister Ezer Weizman, who wants to freeze settlement projects, and the other by Agriculture Minister Ariel Sharon, who is calling for construction of many new outposts in the territories.

Weizman has considerable support among the 19 ministers in the cabinet, some of whom were shak-

Turn to Page 3A Col. 1

BACKGROUND REPORT

Little More Sun, Lots More Chills: That's What's in Wind for Area

By ROBERT LISS
Herald Staff Writer

A cold front accompanied by gusty winds and clear skies will threaten crops and chill people in the Sunshine State this morning. It will continue causing problems for farmers and tourists at least through Friday, forecasters say.

The chill air that blasted into the Miami area with strong winds near midnight Tuesday will bring temperatures early this morning down to the low 40s in South Florida, and into the mid-30s in the north.

WITH WINDS at 20-25 miles an hour and gusty, scant relief from the cold is expected this afternoon. High temperatures will range from the low 40s in the north of the state to the low 60s in the south, and the wind will make it seem considerably cooler.

"The rain and clouds are finally clearing away," said forecaster Allen Cummings, "but with this bitter

cold, you can't really say the weather's improving."

The cold spell will hang on through Thursday, but the wind is expected to die down late today, said Cummings. Diminished winds will cause more problems for farmers.

"When there is a strong wind, it stirs up the air in the groves and fields," he said. "When there's little wind, the cold settles to the ground, tonight is the night the farmers will really have to worry."

THE COLD spell is caused by a cold air mass that has hovered over the Midwest and Southeast for about a week, breaking cold records but remaining stationary.

That cold air was pulled into South Florida by the back winds of a low-pressure area that crossed the peninsula Tuesday. By Tuesday afternoon, the back winds cleared most of the rain that drenched South Florida since Friday and made way for the cold air to enter Miami.

Today's Chuckle

"Why are you so late getting home from school?" asked the mother. "The bus driver broke down," replied the boy.

FONDA   BANCROFT   KEATON   MACLAINE   MASON   ALLEN   BURTON   DREYFUSS   MASTROIANNI   TRAVOLTA

Sorry, Artoo Detoo — You Won't Be Best Actor

HOLLYWOOD — (AP) — Two dramas about relations between women, Julia and The Turning Point, scored top honors in the 50th annual Motion Picture Academy nominations Tuesday, beating a pair of highly popular space epics.

Twentieth Century-Fox was the big winner in the Oscar sweepstakes, with 11 nominations apiece for Julia and The Turning Point and 10 for the biggest box-office hit of all time, Star Wars.

Another film of intergalactic travel, Close Encounters of the Third Kind, followed with eight nominations.

As expected, the race for best actress proved to be the strongest. The nominees: Anne Bancroft, The Turning Point; Jane Fonda, Julia; Diane Keaton, Annie Hall; Shirley MacLaine, The Turning Point; and Marsha Mason, The Goodbye Girl.

SURPRISINGLY, Keaton was named for a comedy rather than her heavy dramatics in Looking for Mr. Goodbar.

Keaton's director and co-star in Annie Hall, Woody Allen, was nominated for best actor, along with Richard Burton, Equus; Richard Dreyfuss, The Goodbye Girl; Marcello Mastroianni, A Special Day; and John Travolta, Saturday Night Fever.

The winners will be announced at a nationally televised awards ceremony April 3.

The nominees for best picture of 1977: Annie Hall, The Turning Point, Julia, Star Wars and The Turning Point.

A surprising omission was Close Encounters of the Third Kind.

Other major nominees:

Supporting Actor — Mikhail Baryshnikov, The Turning Point; Peter Firth, Equus; Alec Guinness, Star Wars; Jason Robards, Julia;

and Maximilian Schell, Julia.

SUPPORTING Actress — Leslie Browne, The Turning Point; Quinn Cummings, The Goodbye Girl; Melinda Dillon, Close Encounters of the Third Kind; Vanessa Redgrave, Julia; Tuesday Weld, Looking for Mr. Goodbar.

Direction — Woody Allen, Annie Hall; Steven Spielberg, Close Encounters; Fred Zinnemann, Julia; George Lucas, Star Wars; Herbert Ross, The Turning Point.

Foreign Language Film — Iphigenia (Greece); Madame Rosa (France); Operation Thunderbolt (Israel); A Special Day (Italy); That Obscure Object of Desire (Spain).

Original Song — Candle on the Water from Pete's Dragon; Nobody Does It Better from The Spy Who Loved Me; Waltz from The Slipper and the Rose; Somebody's Wait-

ing for You from The Rescuers; and the title song from You Light Up My Life.

ORIGINAL screenplay — Woody Allen and Marshall Brickman, Annie Hall; Neil Simon, The Goodbye Girl; Robert Benton, The Late Show; George Lucas, Star Wars; and Arthur Laurents, The Turning Point.

Screenplay Adaptation — Peter Shaffer, Equus; Gavin Lambert and Lewis John Carlino, I Never Promised You a Rose Garden; Alvin Sargent, Julia; Larry Geibart, Oh, God!; Louis Bunuel and Jean-Claude Carriere, That Obscure Object of Desire.

Woody Allen was the big winner of nominations, scoring for his performance, direction and writing of Annie Hall. Orson Welles was the only other person in academy history to be nominated in all three categories — for Citizen Kane in 1941.

These words from Lee Hills, chairman of the board of Knight-Ridder News-papers, Inc. and publisher of *The Miami Herald,* describe one of the most in-novative and successful of the world's great newspapers.

Beginning intensive coverage of Latin America in the late 1940's, the *Herald* has no close rival among U.S. newspapers in consistent and thorough reporting of that region. In January, 1946, the International Edition of the *Herald* was launched, circulating today in 23 Latin American countries. The paper's staff of Latin American experts, based in Miami, provides readers with insightful reports on the vast region sprawling to the south. One result of these efforts is that the *Herald* has won the prestigious Maria Moors Cabot Award (for contributing to inter-American understanding) five times, a record for U.S. newspapers.

In naming the *Herald* one of the ten best dailies in the U.S. in 1974, *Time* magazine not only praised its Latin American coverage but gave it high marks for its "hell-for-leather legwork" in all areas of news coverage, which the maga-zine said had resulted in its being "the strongest link in the Knight [now Knight-Ridder] newspaper chain."[2] Two years later, in a piece called "Dixie's Best Dailies," *Time* again lauded the *Herald* for its consistently good journalism and especially for its notable Latin American coverage.[3]

The Miami Herald was founded on December 10, 1910 by Col. Frank B. Shutts in a two-story building on South Miami Ave. at a time when Miami was a dusty little town of some 5,000. Today the newspaper is situated in one of the largest, most modernistic and beautiful buildings in Florida, overlooking Bis-cayne Bay. Its total daily circulation is some 480,000 (slightly above 600,000 on Sundays).[4] About 70 percent of the newspaper's copies go to subscribers, the other 30 percent sold on the street, in hotels, and other public places.

Some 350 persons are on the staff of the *Herald,* 210 of them writers and editors. The *Herald* participates in the Knight-Ridder Washington Bureau (staff of 23) and also has its own correspondent there. Reporters are also sent from Miami to Washington frequently. The newspaper also has two full-time re-porters in the state capital at Tallahassee, and augments them with two to four others during legislative sessions. No other U.S. daily has so consistently cov-ered Latin America since World War II. The *Herald's* full-time correspondents are based in Miami but travel extensively throughout Latin America and else-where. In the last few years the paper's staffers have reported from Canada, Europe, the Soviet Union, Asia, Africa, and most extensively, from Central and South America and the Caribbean.[5]

In addition to full-time staffers, the paper has twelve regular foreign stringers (part-time correspondents), and dozens of others which it uses oc-casionally. They are located in Canada, Europe, Israel, Latin America and the Caribbean. Among the distinguished foreign correspondents who have worked for the *Herald* these are particularly well-known: William Montalbaño, Don Bohning, William Long, Bom Bonafede, and Al Burt.

---

[2] *Time,* Jan. 21, 1974, p. 59.
[3] *Time,* Sept. 27, 1976, p. 65.
[4] Questionnaire from Robert D. Ingle, managing editor, to authors, dated Feb. 24, 1978.
[5] Ingle questionnaire.

Journalists working for the *Herald* are usually recruited from other newspapers or they work through the newspaper's extensive state bureau system. For the city, state, and national reporters, the newspaper normally requires five years' experience. The present staff includes four Nieman fellows, four Stanford fellows and one Alfred B. Sloan fellow. The *Herald* maintains a strong college intern program, recruiting from major American schools of journalism such as Columbia, Northwestern, Missouri, Kansas, Nebraska, Michigan, Florida, and Ohio State.

Five news wire services are taken by the *Herald:* the AP, UPI, Knight-Ridder News Service, Los Angeles Times-Washington Post News Service, and the London Observer Foreign Service. In addition, the paper gets the syndicated services of King Features, United Features, Universal, Register & Tribune, Field, NEA, and numerous minor syndicates. The *Herald* ranks in the top four of U.S. dailies in total lines of news content, with some 31 million lines daily and Sunday. Of its non-advertising space, a typical issue of the *Herald* allots the following space to these categories: international news, 8 percent; national news, 17 percent; local/state news, 10 percent; analysis/editorials, 6 percent; features/entertainment, 23 percent; sports, 7 percent; travel/leisure, 4 percent, and business, 11 percent. Approximately 70 percent of each issue is given over to advertising, an allocation rather typical of American newspapers.

The Miami Herald uses computer-generated cold type composition in its printing. All editing is done on VDTs; local copy is typed and entered through OCRs; bureau reporters write on VDTs and file to the central office. The newspaper uses color several days a week, mainly in photographs, graphics, and advertising. The *Herald* is one of the U.S. leaders in use of multicolor for both editorial and advertising material. For many years the *Herald* has been among the leaders in the industry in new technology, being among the earliest to computerize typesetting (in the early 1960's), among the first to use extensive full color, and one of the first six large metropolitan dailies to install a VDT editing system.[6]

Robert Ingle, *Herald* managing editor, says that his newspaper is aimed at a general readership, trying to stimulate public interest in the problems, solutions and progress of the community, state and nation. It tries to be innovative; for example, the *Herald* publishes a Spanish-language daily section reaching some 550,000 Miamians who consider English only a second language. Begun in 1976, *El Miami Herald* has its roots in the early 1960's when the first waves of exiles from Cuba began coming to the U.S. Frank Soler is editor of this special section of the *Herald.*

Then there is the English-language International Edition ("Newspaper of The Americas") of the *Herald,* with some 15,000 daily circulation (Sundays, nearly 18,000) in some 23 Latin American countries. This air edition to Latin America took its present name (International Edition) on January 9, 1977. It first began back on January 9, 1946, as the "Air Express Clipper Edition," and was the idea of Lee Hills, then managing editor of the *Herald,* and some of his associates. In a statement in 1946, Hills announced: "Our primary objective is

---

[6] Ingle questionnaire.

to provide up-to-the-minute news coverage of the United States and the world
for the large English-speaking population of the South. . . ."[7] What Hills, now
Herald publisher, said then still holds today; what the *Herald-Tribune* (Paris)
tries to do for English-speaking readers in Europe, the *Herald* tries to do with its
International Edition in Latin America.

What about the newspaper's editorial policy today? Lee Hills calls the
Herald's editorial stands "vigorously independent." He notes that over the years
the paper has consistently shown that it is not afraid to take stands without
regard to whether the majority approves. An example of this is the fact that the
Herald opposed American involvement in Vietnam as far back as 1954, fully a
decade before other major papers became concerned. The *Herald*'s publisher
also is proud of the fact that the paper has been a leader in protecting First
Amendment press freedom rights.[8]

Robert Ingle, managing editor, calls the paper "fiscally conservative but
socially progressive." He stresses that the paper publishes news that is relevant,
important and interesting to readers. "We are proud," he writes, "of the completeness of our coverage, and of our close relationship with our readers." In arriving at editorial decisions, the *Herald* tries to determine what best serves the
public's interest—using the classic utilitarian guide of "whatever does the greatest good for the greatest number."[9]

The editorial pages of the *Herald* have always had a high priority. According to Hills, the paper is often critical of government, including officials whose
candidacies the *Herald* has supported, and it never hesitates to take issue with
the Establishment. At the same time, says Hills, the *Herald* has formed a close
bond with its readers, and it stands up for them. The paper has been an innovator on its editorial page, and began its "op-ed" page on July 1, 1958—long before
The New York Times and many other newspapers discovered such pages. And,
for more than 20 years the *Herald* has published a Sunday opinion and analysis
section called "Viewpoint."[10] A good example of the discursive forum provided
by this "Viewpoint" section came in 1978 when Anwar Sadat and Menachem
Begin wrote for it exclusive essays concerning their ideas about Middle East
peace possibilities.[11]

The Miami Herald gives special attention to the selection and promotion of
editors. Today's editors are building on a tradition of excellence going back
through the years to the paper's founding. The executive editor is John Mc-
Mullan; the editor is Jim Hampton, and the managing editor is Robert D. Ingle.
The assistant managing editors are Pete Weitzel (news) and Janet Chusmir
(features). The executive city editor is Heath Meriwether, and the executive
news editor is Jerry Ceppos. Graphics editor is Robert Mellis.

The *Herald* is an award-winning newspaper. Under Lee Hills' leadership
the paper won a Pulitzer Prize in 1950 for cleaning up organized crime in South

[7] *The Miami Herald*, Jan. 9, 1977.
[8] Hills Letter.
[9] Ingle questionnaire.
[10] Hills Letter.
[11] *The Miami Herald* (Viewpoints; Section E), Jan. 29 and Feb. 5, 1978.

Florida. And in 1967 reporter Gene Miller won a Pulitzer for local reporting and another one in 1975, also for local reporting. Dozens of awards have been garnered by the *Herald;* they are too numerous to name here, but a few will be mentioned (since 1968) to show the diversity of the newspaper's quality:

Pulitzer Prizes, George Polk Memorial Awards, Sigma Delta Chi Distinguished Service Awards, Tom Wallace Awards (for Latin American Coverage); Maria Moors Cabot Awards (for contributions to inter-American understanding); J.C. Penney-University of Missouri Awards (for best women's pages); Jerusalem Liberation Awards; APME Public Service Awards; Overseas Press Club Awards; Inter-American Press Association Awards; Ernie Pyle Memorial Awards; National Press Club Awards; American Bar Association Awards, and National Press Photographers Association Awards.

The Miami Herald has come a long way since its founding by Frank Shutts in 1910 to reach its present status as a progressive, award-winning, and highly respected daily. It was Shutts and his managing editor, Frank B. Stoneman,[12] who established a solid journalistic foundation for the paper. John S. Knight of the Knight Newspapers bought the *Herald* on October 15, 1937, and John Pennekamp was made managing editor, and later editorial page editor. Pennekamp became a man of great influence at the *Herald* and was known by the 1940's as "Mr. Miami Herald."[13]

The newspaper moved into a new office building in 1941, and the next year Lee Hills, the present publisher of the paper, joined its staff and took over its newsroom. He, probably more than any other person, is responsible for building a strong writing and editing staff and infusing in it a high morale. Under Hills the *Herald* became known as a paper that encouraged individual style and original writing, while maintaining a tradition of sound straight reporting.

In 1951 Hills was made executive editor of the paper—and also of another Knight newspaper, *The Detroit Free Press.* Hills selected as managing editor of the *Herald* George Beebe who had been on the paper's staff since 1944. In 1952 the circulation of the *Herald* has passed 200,000 for the first time and was reaching about 235,000 readers on Sunday. In 1958 Don Shoemaker succeeded Pennekamp as editorial page editor. Pennekamp retained his title of associate editor and continued to write a column until 1960 when he left the paper.

The *Herald* moved into its new modernistic plant on Biscayne Bay in 1963; at the time the building was the largest in Florida and provided the *Herald* staff with what was probably the best newspaper facility in the United States. It was a building definitely built for the future and still today is one of the premier newspaper plants in the U.S.—producing what is certainly one of the country's outstanding journalistic products.

---

[12] Stoneman became editor-in-chief and remained in this position until his death in 1941.
[13] For a good history of the *Herald,* see Nixon Smiley, *Knights of the Fourth Estate: The Story of the Miami Herald* (Miami: E. A. Seemann, Publishers, Inc., 1974).

Le Monde

(FRANCE)

FRANCE'S *Le Monde* ("The World") is far more than the nation's most prosperous and fastest expanding daily. With its unrelenting serious, highly intellectual approach, it also represents the epitome of quality journalism and thereby occupies a position high among the world's best elite newspapers.

Dull in appearance, *Le Monde* has earned the respect of serious press critics everywhere for its depth coverage, thoughtful opinion, and uncompromising concern for spiritual and intellectual values. In France, the paper is required reading for the intellectual and the influential, "for anybody wishing to stay informed on the significance of events in France, not to mention other parts of the world."[1] One informed French professor observes, "I don't think anyone who has responsibilities in government, business, unions . . . can do without *Le Monde* however much he or she might hate it."[2]

Along with Zurich's *Neue Zürcher Zeitung* and Frankfurt's *Frankfurter Allgemeine*, *Le Monde* ranks as one of the world's most serious dailies. It concentrates on world news and commentary, supplemented by weighty political and economic analysis. A tabloid in size, it eschews any resemblance to the sensational content and flamboyant style of such journals which publish in small-sheet form. It is the only paper which appears more gray and austere than Switzerland's *Neue Zürcher Zeitung*. It keeps its pages, headlines and type small and its ideas large. Normally 36 pages in length, its six picture-less columns appear almost monotonous. But amid the tiny seven-point type, with eight-point (the regular body type of most newspapers) for specially emphasized stories, the reader can find more complete information than in any other French newspaper. *Le Monde* even uses footnotes in some stories; these are set in six-point type.

Pictures are spurned because the paper believes a good verbal description is more valuable and less detracting to reader concentration on a subject. Jacques Sauvageot, the paper's administrative director, says the practice of not printing pictures got started because *Le Monde* had the oldest presses in Paris, and "they simply couldn't print satisfactory photographs."[3] But Hubert Beuve-Méry, the paper's founder and managing director until his retirement in 1969, preferred to credit the policy to a preference for good verbal reporting over visual materials:

[1] "As Le Monde Turns," *Time* (December 26, 1969), p. 36.
[2] Claude-Jean Bertrand, professor, Université de Droit d'Economie de Sciences Sociales de Paris, Paris, in letter to J. Merrill, dated March 1, 1978.
[3] Herbert Lottman, "The Newspaper deGaulle Has to Read," *Harper's* (January, 1967), p. 63.

TRENTE-CINQUIÈME ANNÉE — N° 10 284   38 PAGES   DERNIÈRE ÉDITION   MERCREDI 22 FÉVRIER 1978

La contre-offensive éthiopienne aurait repris dans l'Ogaden

LIRE PAGE 3

Le Monde

Fondateur : Hubert Beuve-Méry   Directeur : Jacques Fauvet

1,60 F

Algérie, 1,30 DA; Maroc, 1,60 dir.; Tunisie, 130 m.; Allemagne, 1 DM; Autriche, 12 sch.; Belgique, 13 fr.; Canada, $ 0,75; Danemark, 3,50 kr.; Espagne, 35 pes.; Grande-Bretagne, 20 p.; Grèce, 20 dr.; Iran, 50 ris.; Italie, 350 L; Liban, 250 p.; Luxembourg, 13 fr.; Norvège, 3 kr.; Pays-Bas, 1,25 fl.; Portugal, 17 esc.; Suède, 2,80 kr.; Suisse, 1 fr.; U.S.A., 80 cts; Yougoslavie, 10 din.

Tarif des abonnements page 6

2, RUE DES ITALIENS
75427 PARIS — CEDEX 09
C.C.P. 4267-23 Paris
Télex Paris n° 650572
Tél. : 246-73-23

BULLETIN DU JOUR

La conférence de Belgrade en échec ?

La conférence de Belgrade sur la sécurité et la coopération en Europe s'achemine vers un échec à peine camouflé. Elle ne se maintient en état de survie que par la respiration artificielle. Son programme de travail étant épuisé lundi soir, elle a décidé de le prolonger de deux jours. Une autre prolongation n'est pas exclue, mais aucun indice de réanimation n'apparaît.

Après les réponses de M. Brejnev à envoyées à des messages qui lui avaient adressé M. Giscard d'Estaing et le maréchal Tito, aucune relance n'est en vue. Le président de la République, dans une lettre du 15 février, avait essayé d'intéresser le chef de l'État soviétique au projet français de compromis. La réponse serait un accusé de réception courtois, mais sans engagement aucune ouverture. La correspondance Tito-Brejnev aurait la même signification.

En présence de cet échec, M. Brenner (Suisse) a suggéré de se contenter du « minimum minimorum » : l'adoption d'un document « court et sobre », où les trente-cinq participants exprimeraient leur attachement à l'acte final d'Helsinki et à la réaffirmation de la continuité de la C.S.C.E. Ainsi les timbrés chantent : « Marchons ! Marchons ! », en restant sur place.

La réunion de Belgrade avait pour objet, s'il n'est pas prématuré d'en parler au passé, d'examiner la mise en œuvre des décisions d'Helsinki et d'établissant un bilan et en exprimant des intentions pour l'avenir. Or la Belgrade ne fera l'objet d'aucune formulation précise. Un seul point acquis : les Trente-Cinq se retrouveront à Madrid dans deux ans.

L'idée de la C.S.C.E. remontait au temps où M. Molotov était ministre des affaires étrangères. Le Kremlin voulait faire entériner dans une grande conférence Est-Ouest la nouvelle carte de l'Europe et l'existence de deux Allemagnes. Les Occidentaux n'acceptèrent, après la conclusion d'un « modus vivendi » entre Bonn et Berlin-Est, que si les Soviétiques s'engageaient à assouplir les contacts humains entre les deux parties de l'Europe. Aussi, toute la négociation d'Helsinki porta sur les droits de l'homme. Le Kremlin, après avoir empoché ses dividendes au moment même où tous les États d'un côté et de l'autre de l'Atlantique à l'Oural « acceptaient à la mise table, s'était promis de prendre des engagements humanitaires centrigrants. Curieusement, ce sont pourtant les Soviétiques qui provoquèrent de perpétuer la C.S.C.E. mais ils ne craviérent quand ils s'apercevraient qu'elle permettrait le respect des droits de l'homme à l'Est sous surveillance internationale. Aussi comprend-on qu'ils n'aient eu de cesse de minimiser et d'écourter la réunion de Belgrade.

Moins logique et l'attitude occidentale. La France mise à part, qui a joint ses efforts à ceux des autres pour faire adopter un document à la fois significatif sur le fond et réaliste, les Occidentaux n'ont fait aucun effort de conciliation. Visiblement, ils prendraient aisément leur parti d'un échec, et ils tiennent seulement à ce que celui-ci apparaisse clairement comme imputable aux Soviétiques.

Le fil tenu et fragile tissé à Helsinki risque ainsi d'être brisé. La détente recevra un coup particulièrement préjudiciable aux Européens de l'Ouest et aux démocraties populaires. Les relations des superpuissances se situant à un autre niveau. Reste le rendez-vous de Madrid en 1980, mais pour quoi faire ? Et d'ailleurs, du côté français au moins, qui n'est plus certain que cette nouvelle conférence ait jamais lieu.

Nouvelle « expérience » en Tchécoslovaquie

Le système de planification va être rénové

De notre correspondant en Europe centrale

Vienne. — Dix ans après le « printemps de Prague », les dirigeants tchécoslovaques viennent d'annoncer, par l'intermédiaire de M. Leopold Ler, ministre des finances, qu'ils allaient tenter une nouvelle « expérience » économique. Il s'agit de refondre dans un ensemble logique le système de planification.

L'expérience sera menée dans quelque cent cinquante entreprises industrielles, neuf organisations du commerce extérieur et vingt et un centres de recherche, comptant au total un peu moins de cinq cent mille travailleurs, et représentant une production annuelle d'une valeur que de 85 milliards de couronnes, soit un sixième du revenu national.

M. Ler a soigneusement évité d'employer le mot de « réforme ». Ce n'est pas assurément un hasard. Les éléments dogmatiques qui dominent la direction du parti tchécoslovaque ont une telle phobie de tout ce qui pourrait rappeler, de près ou de loin, les événements de 1968, qu'il est des termes qu'il vaut mieux éviter. Surtout lorsque cela ne s'impose pas : l'expérience annoncée aujourd'hui n'a, de fait, que peu de rapport avec celle qui fut jugé inoffensif par le président de la commission d'étude dans la dernière année du réformisme, en janvier 1968 (par Mota Šik et ses amis.

C'est au mois d'octobre de l'année dernière, au cours d'une conférence sur la responsabilité de l'économie à Gottwaldow, que M. Ler révéla, semble-t-il, pour la première fois, les intentions du parti et du gouvernement. Les idées qu'il développa alors, beaucoup plus en qualité de président de la commission gouvernementale pour les questions de gestion et de planification qu'en tant que ministre des finances, sont à peu près les mêmes que celles qu'il vient d'exposer aujourd'hui, de fait, que peu de réformistes d'avant 1968 tels que qui, représentées par MM. Husak et Bilak, s'opposaient en parti à toutes idées, parmi lesquels M. Lenart, le parti bratislavien du parti slovaque d'un retour prudent aux réformes d'avant 1968. La hardiesse de M. Lenart en ce domaine s'explique sans doute par le fait que, en tant que chef du gouvernement dans les dernières années du régime d'Antonin Novotny, il assuma la responsabilité de l'introduction...

CRÉATION D'UN COMMISSARIAT À L'ÉNERGIE SOLAIRE

Le conseil des ministres du mercredi 22 février doit décider la création d'un commissariat à l'énergie solaire, dont le principe avait été annoncé par le président de la République, dans une interview qu'il avait accordée au « Monde » (« le Monde » du 26 janvier). Cette création extrastatutaire la disparition de la délégation aux énergies nouvelles, dirigée par M. Jean-Claude Colli.

... la réduction du nombre de ces réformes.

L'impossibilité d'aboutir à un accord conduisait, comme souvent en pareil cas, à la création d'une commission d'études dont la perspective fut confiée à M. Ler, en sentiellement pour la raison que, n'étant pas une personnalité politique de premier plan, il fut jugé inoffensif par les adversaires des réformes. C'est un résultat exactement le contraire : elle respecte les principes du centralisme démocratique ; elle doit favoriser la participation des membres à la gestion de l'économie (on ne précise pas comment) ; elle doit en outre obéir aux principes scientifiques.

Une expression de la lutte des classes

De quoi s'agit-il ? La nouvelle « expérience » se fonde sur cinq principes : elle doit être contraignante vis-à-vis de l'entreprise, mais donnant-donnant, elle doit respecter les principes du socialisme, trouver une expression de la lutte des classes ; elle doit renforcer le rôle du parti (le réformistes d'avant 1968 voulaient exactement le contraire) ; elle respecte les principes du centralisme démocratique ; elle doit favoriser la participation des membres à la gestion de l'économie (on ne précise pas comment) ; elle doit en outre obéir aux principes scientifiques.

MANUEL LUCBERT.

(Lire la suite page 4.)

Épreuve pour le gouvernement belge

Le pacte intercommunautaire risque d'être remis en question

De nouvelles difficultés sont apparues lundi 20 février, en Belgique, lors de la mise au point des modalités d'application du « pacte d'Egmont ». Les signataires de cet accord intercommunautaire, qui définit les rapports entre les communautés linguistiques et les régions, donnent des interprétations différentes. Ces divergences pourraient menacer la cohésion du gouvernement de M. Tindemans.

De notre correspondant

Bruxelles. — « Le cheval a refusé l'obstacle, la situation est sérieuse. » C'est en ces termes que M. Tindemans, premier ministre, déçu et irrité, a commenté l'échec des négociations autour du château de Bruyendover, les Flamands et les francophones chargés de préparer l'application du pacte d'Egmont.

A l'origine, vendredi soir, 17 février, une rencontre devait cependant être une simple formalité. Les négociateurs des partis de la coalition majoritaire — chrétien, socialiste, Volksunie (flamande) et Front des francophones bruxellois (F.D.F.) — devaient simplement approuver et signer les textes du « compromis historique » élaboré en mai et juin 1977 au palais d'Egmont et rédigés pendant la marathon des négociations du château du Stuyvenberg, fin janvier. Cependant, comme le premier ministre l'a admis lui-même, la pâte qui règle le nouveau statut des Bruxellois, notamment sur le plan régional, avait été conclu dans la hâte.

Quand il s'est agi, ces derniers jours, de faire la toilette à définitive des textes, les négociateurs ont constaté avec une certaine stupeur qu'ils n'avaient pas, en mai 1977 puis en janvier dernier, compris les mêmes choses. Le procès-verbal de quarante-cinq pages préparé par les deux délégations issues de la réforme d'un francophone et « autre néerlandophone ») n'a donc pas été signé. Très demain aucun des traducteurs de ce pacte ne pas avoir rectifié le désaccord aux suffisamment d'exactitude. Mme Spaak, présidente du F.D.F., jusqu'alors sur de vue, mais à rappelé que le climat des difficiles négociations avait été marqué par la confusion.

Toutes les dispositions du pacte peuvent encore être remises en cause. Un des points de désaccord est le budget culturel des Flamands dans la capitale. Bien que le gouvernement ait fixé à 15 % de la population bruxelloise, les Flamands réclament un minimum garanti de 20 % du budget, dans chacune des dix-neuf communes de l'agglomération. Les francophones s'y opposent. Mme Spaak a déclaré, lundi soir, que ses négociations nouvelles concessions aux néerlandophones mais elle estime que les négociateurs doivent faire preuve d'imagination.

Dans certains milieux, on allait jusqu'à évoquer, lundi, la possibilité d'une crise gouvernementale. La dislocation de la majorité serait alors provoquée non seulement par les tiraillements dans le château d'Egmont, mais aussi par différentes autres causes. Le ministre des postes et des affaires bruxelloises des S.P., M. Defosset, ancien président du P.D.F., fait actuellement l'objet d'une violente campagne à la suite de la découverte d'irrégularités dans son département. L'affaire a entraîné la démission du chef de son cabinet. L'après M. De..., vice-premier ministre, chargé de la défense nationale, M. Vanden Boeynants, renonce-t-il de donner, lui aussi, sa démission si ses collègues socialistes continuaient à s'opposer à l'achat de nouvelles fusées Hawk-Hellip, pour un montant de 4 milliards (600 millions de francs français). La Belgique a besoin de ces missiles pour remplir ses engagements envers l'O.T.A.N., mais les socialistes (le Monde du 20 février) demandent que la situation économique et financière du pays ne permet pas une telle dépense.

PIERRE DE VOS.

Et le 20 mars ?

par MICHEL MOUSEL (*)

C'est dans ces vieilles casseroles qu'on fait les meilleures soupes. Tel était le bon choix proposé au menu du chef à Verdun-sur-le-Doubs. Recette publicitaire, mais non gastronomique : la quincaillerie rouillée de la matière traditionnelle n'atttire guère à la clientèle. Mais, à l'auberge d'en face, on paraît moins occupé à le servir qu'à aménager ses cuisines.

Cuisine : le mot qu'on aurait pu pouvoir éviter depuis quarante jours de changement. Et pourtant, c'est lui qu'a glissé le débat, à peine ouvert au fond, à l'intérieur de la gauche. Où sera-t-on donc qui doit changer ? Le mode d'emploi de la machine économique ou la machine elle-même ? Le degré d'importance ou de cohérence à l'égard du président de la République ou la monarchie républicaine de 1958 ? La répartition du pouvoir entre ceux qui nous gouverneront ou son exercice professionnellement candidats à l'exercer ou la réforme ?

... lui-même ? C'est la politique ou la politique ?

Quand chacun a chiffré son programme commun, et, quand on lance des appels solennels au président pour qu'il renonce à faire la tasse, quand la question du débat-devient du second plan dans la polit de charge, quand la distribution des portefeuilles prend le pas sur celle du programme commun, chacun ne peut que ressentir une profonde amertume. Parce que l'aspect de spectacle politique télévisé qui recouvrait l'uniformisation de la vie politique. Réservé aux « quatre grands », même si le devant se répéter à longueur de temps d'antenne, il ne cesse de restreindre le champ d'intérêt du débat. Et, surtout, on est un droit de se demander si le succès d'égalité formelle obtenu par le P.C.F. et le P.S. sur tels ordres du jour n'est pas l'accepter de jouer le jeu qui suppose qu'il existe un trirla les citoyens en minaux débiles et irresponsables.

Pendant que la droite s'énerve par tous les moyens à rallier le spectre de l'insécurité « aux changer pour autant les intentions d'un vote de la gauche ange », sa marchère, en complit dans une troublante grandeur et hésite même à réagir lorsque les libertés sont menacées aux de l'extrême. Quel mal entendu ! Ce n'est pas ainsi que l'on va motiver la nouvelle majorité autour du programme qu'elle l'a signé. On a beau réclamer des voix ou leur demander, bien, au nom du programme, comme ne que sans les mêmes. Pour ignorer de la crise du gouvernement en place et n'exercées pas seulement l'avenir de la société en général, mais aussi dans un aveuglement à qui ne va guère au-delà du rideau de fumée qui noie sous les lumières froides de la télévision la réalité qui s'attache au vote nul.

(Lire la suite, page 9.)

(*) Secrétaire national du P.S.U.

La faiblesse du dollar s'accroît

Le franc a perdu 5 % sur le deutschemark en trois semaines

Déjà très éprouvé la semaine précédente, le dollar a été victime d'un nouvel accès de faiblesse dans la journée du lundi 20 février, touchant ses taux historiques à Francfort, et surtout à Zurich, où le franc suisse a été très vivement recherché contre toutes les monnaies, y compris le deutschemark. Mardi 21 février, la dollar se redressait légèrement, dans la confusion à Francfort, à Paris, où le dollar a dérivé du franc par rapport à toutes les monnaies fortes se poursuivait, avec un déplacement à près du 2,8 francs et un franc suisse à 2,6250 francs. En trois semaines, le franc a ainsi perdu 5 % sur le deutschemark et 9 % sur le franc suisse.

La nouvelle attaque lancée contre le dollar après cinq semaines de répit traduit la défiance croissante des milieux financiers internationaux quant à la capacité des dirigeants américains de résoudre les problèmes qui se posent aux États-Unis : l'énorme déficit de la balance commerciale, poursuite de l'inflation, blocage au Congrès de la loi sur l'énergie.

De plus, les cambistes font état de rumeurs persistantes suivant lesquelles les banques centrales ouest-allemandes, nipponnes et helvétiques soutiennent mieux pouvoir soutenir la chute le mark, notamment le franc suisse, sur leur devise très ...table e...a, qui bas tous les records, même vis-à-vis du deutschemark. Prises dans cette tourmente, les monnaies « faibles » ont tendance à accompagner le dollar dans sa descente.

Tel est le cas de la lire italienne, de la livre anglaise et, dans une moindre mesure, du franc français, qui a regagné une partie du terrain perdu sur le mark à la suite de l'entrée en vigueur, à partir d'un franc à 2,25 deutschemark pour par rapport aux monnaies fortes, telle évolution ne gonfle guère le coût de notre facture de pétrole, libellée en dollars, mais elle consacre la dévalorisation de notre monnaie par rapport à celles de nos partenaires européens, avec lesquels nous effectuons plus de 35 % de nos échanges. Cet effet pervers des fluctuations monétaires, bien connu des économistes. — **F. R.**

Un chef-d'œuvre inconnu de Racine : « la Thébaïde »

Jocaste et ses enfants

Oui, le hasard fait bien les choses. Quand la nation est saisie par perplexités politiques, tombe du ciel un « OVNI » de poésie ; la première tragédie de Racine, *la Thébaïde*. On jam, non identifié puisqu'on ne la quelque peu oublié de poésie, aérolithe ou pas, est un fortifiant souverain, à l'heure des demandes ...blique. Qui plus est, ce chef-d'œuvre inconnu du théâtre avec un soin si chaleureux que cette soirée va faire le bonheur de tout le monde.

la Thébaïde n'est jamais joué, même par la maison qui de décembre dont l'ouvrage, la Comédie-Française : je me demande si, depuis deux-trois siècles ? Handicap, après cela, défini cela on l'a pas dit, à 13 h le 21 décembre, jour anniversaire de la naissance de Racine. C'est tout la poésie, qui aiment Racine, il-

... sent chez eux *la Thébaïde* et trouvent là cela très beau. Le toujours dit son seul studio Racine, les Barthes, les Mauron, les Goldmann, ne réfèrent souvent, dans leur livres, à *la Thébaïde*, parce qu'il y a des choses, et sur des sujets brûlants, que Racine n'a dites que si, là N'importe : ceux qui aiment Racine, et *la Thébaïde* est exclue. Racine commence à Andromaque.

Quel de plus méchant que des doux matins à l'aveuglette et qui traversant les siècles ? Handicap, après cela, défini cela on l'a pas dit, et peut beaucoup de mal à rendre la beauté ... dans leur fraîcheur.

MICHEL COURNOT.

(Lire la suite page 21.)

AU JOUR LE JOUR

QUARANTE JOURS

Après quarante jours de navigations errantes, Noé retrouva un monde silencieux et dépeuplé. Le voyageur moderne est moins tragique. La France que le retrouve, après quarante tours est tellement semblable à celle que l'homme a quittée que le désert, les dialogues s'enchaînent si exactement, les conflits et les querelles se poursuivent avec tant de continuité que l'on la retrouve si n'être jamais parti.

Et c'est en vain que, d'un horizon à l'autre, le cherche la colombe porteuse du rameau d'olivier.

ROBERT ESCARPIT.

"We believe our reports are clear and can hardly be helped by the kind of pictures usually presented by the newspapers."[4] Today's director, Jacques Fauvet, has followed the picture-less practices of his predecessor.

Although *Le Monde* appears less stern than in the past—it now contains daily cartoons and advertisements with pictures and has carried a comic strip— it remains the paper to which the serious reader goes to be informed. And largely because of its commitment to a serious, in-depth scholarly approach to news and information, its readership has been rising steadily. Many habitual readers of *Le Monde* say their allegiance to its intellectualism is a kind of addiction that has produced a world-wide body of elite readers, most of whom are in positions of leadership and influence. *Le Monde* is highly conscious of its audience's needs and tastes. It formerly aimed at mature elite adults—professors, diplomats, civil servants—revelling in this snob appeal. But it hasn't remained content with this sophisticated clientele; in recent years it has gone after—and captured—the intellectually-inclined high school and university student. More recently, it has begun working on the third generation—youth just beginning to reach adulthood. The paper's experience has been that such readers, once addicted to *Le Monde*'s intellectualism, remain faithful even when they leave France to reside elsewhere.

The paper cannot rest content with merely making a general bid for the intellectually-oriented. It wants to know all about its readers and "does more market research than any American paper."[5] It constantly studies distribution patterns and trends. It has commissioned the French Institute of Public Opinion to survey the structure of its reading public. From several studies, the management of *Le Monde* has concluded its readers are young (28 percent are under 25 years of age and half under 35), highly educated (half have a university education), either a manager or a professional, middle-class, frequently women (40 percent), and, interestingly, more often a resident of the provinces than of Paris. This last finding both helps to establish its reputation as a national paper and reflects that it actually is a national paper. The paper's reader, the findings also showed, is actively interested in public affairs and cultural activities. He is characteristically a member of the elite, capable of forming opinion and institutional policy. *Le Monde*'s typical reader spends an hour with his paper and finds it honest, accurate and complete, in short, a highly credible news source.[6]

Le Monde, in the form it is known today, represents a relatively late newcomer to the French newspaper world. The paper got its start after the Nazi occupation of Paris had ended in 1944. The new government under General de Gaulle wanted a newspaper which would be respected both at home and abroad. DeGaulle realized a new press would help France quickly re-establish itself as an important European nation. Some even said he was hoping for a highly respected paper which would reflect his own views and purposes. By this time, the conservative pre-war *Le Temps* newspaper had largely been discredited be-

[4] Hubert Beuve-Méry, Director, *Le Monde,* in letter to J. Merrill dated September 23, 1965.
[5] Milton Viorst, *"Le Monde:* Very Serious, Very Successful," *Columbia Journalism Review* (September/October, 1974), p. 44.
[6] *Ibid.,* p. 45f.

cause of its political policies and associations with big industry. So six Resistance editors representing different French political parties, with the blessings of deGaulle, banded together to produce a London *Times* type of paper for France.[7]

Hubert Beuve-Méry was chosen as the new director of *Le Monde*. He accepted the position with the proviso that *Le Monde* would be guaranteed independence and freedom from any public or private subsidies. Then, with the help of a 200,000 franc initial loan from the government, he put together a group of journalists into an employee-ownership arrangement for the new paper. He had inherited the *Le Temps* building, presses, even much of its staff. With this staff and equipment, he put out the first issue of *Le Monde* in December, 1944. Thus, many of *Le Temps'* characteristics—its neo-Gothic nameplate (logotype) design, its basic typeface and its ultraserious tone—were carried forward into *Le Monde*.

A front-page article of the first issue informed the reader of the new paper's goals:

> Its main ambition is to assure the reader of clear, real information, fast and complete. But in our times one cannot be satisfied with merely observing and describing. . . . What is needed is a revolution—a revolution by law—in order to triumph; a revolution that will restore, by the union and creative effort of all the French that are worthy of this name (*Le Monde*), French grandeur and freedom.[8]

Within a year, *Le Monde* was successful, with a circulation of at least 150,000 and a reputation as an independent and reliable newspaper. It had begun selling outside France, and was clearly established as a journal directed to an intelligent, well-educated and liberal audience.

At first *Le Monde* was criticized by the Left as a thinly disguised organ of the trusts. The Right, especially highly placed Army officers, attacked the paper and Beuve-Méry as "crypto-Communist" during the fighting in Indo-China and Algeria—in both issues *Le Monde* was ahead of the public in calling for negotiated settlements. At one point terrorists exploded a bomb near the *Le Monde* building, and copies of the paper were confiscated several times in Algeria. The paper favored de Gaulle's efforts to end the Algerian crisis. It also supported his return to power in the December, 1958, referendum, making it clear it agreed with his aims but often disliked his means.

Le Monde's progress to an undisputed place of leadership among Europe's elite dailies owes much to Hubert Beuve-Méry, its founder and directing editor for 25 years. He was the strong and vital force behind *Le Monde* as it struggled for political and financial independence. "Beuve," as his staff called him, had been born in Paris of poor parents in 1902. In 1928, at the age of 26, he went to Prague, where he taught at the French Institute, becoming a few years later the Prague correspondent for the great pre-World War II serious Paris daily, *Le Temps*. He resigned in 1939 when his political opinions did not agree with those

[7] Kenneth Olson, *The History Makers: The Press of Europe from its Beginnings through 1965* (Baton Rouge: Louisiana State University Press, 1966), p. 193.
[8] *Le Monde* (December 19, 1944), p. 1.

of the *Le Temps* editors. In World War II, Beuve-Méry served first in the French Army and later in the Resistance, where, working for the underground, he took the pen name "Sirius," an alias under which he wrote a stinging column for years.

Beuve-Méry supervised *Le Monde* closely. He believed ardently in complete economic, political and moral independence for his paper and he put that belief into practice. He instilled his high regard for the press in his staff. Each morning, he would hold an hour-long "standing" conference with his top editors (they actually stood up; the practice continues even today). "We're in a hurry to get to work, there isn't time to sit," he would explain. There was good give-and-take on major issues and full discussion of general suggestions. He also inspired staff loyalty. Once, in 1951, when he felt *Le Monde*'s political independence was threatened by administrative compromises, he resigned. His entire staff refused to work for his proposed successor, and Beuve-Méry was restored when the administration retracted. Although he often lacked tact—Françoise Giroud, editor-in-chief of the competing *L'Express,* once said he was "as gracious as a cactus"—Beuve-Méry was known for his integrity, accuracy, lucidity and utter lack of selfish ambition. Born in humble circumstances, he never became softened by luxury; to the end, he lived in a modest apartment and drove an economy-class Citroën. But under his wise soft-spoken guidance, *Le Monde* became one of the best newspapers in the world.[9]

Beuve-Méry's successor was his editor-in-chief, Jacques Fauvet, a man with many of Beuve-Méry's convictions. Like Beuve-Méry, Fauvet was noted for "his sharp intellect and his aloofness from all of France's political and social factions."[10] Fauvet had authored a half-dozen books on France's domestic politics, including a definitive two-volume history of the French Communist Party, background that has proven invaluable to him as *Le Monde*'s director. Although both Beuve-Méry and Fauvet came out of liberal Catholic backgrounds and their journalistic principles are similar, the latter differs in two important ways. Whereas Beuve-Méry held unrelentingly to an austere format and cared little for reader appeal. Fauvet is more sensitive to interesting layout techniques and has allowed several conservative innovations. But the principal difference lies in Fauvet's greater sympathy for causes.

In contrast to Beuve-Méry's firm insistence on complete political independence for *Le Monde,* Fauvet listened to student demonstrators in the 1968 rebellion and gave their cause generous space in the paper. Under him, *Le Monde* "clearly favors the Parti Socialiste, although it can be critical of it and does open its pages to all kinds of 'Libres Opinions' and regular articles by anti-socialists."[11] But the paper's news stories have remained unbiased and reliable. Although it reportedly has been torn by internal strife between a group of young Leftist journalists allied with Fauvet and an older guard insisting on complete political independence recently, it must be noted that *Le Monde* did not take any open position in the recent legislative elections campaign. Yet it openly cam-

[9] "As *Le Monde* Turns," *op. cit.,* p. 36.
[10] "Successful Sobriety," *Time* (January 5, 1970), p. 43.
[11] Bertrand letter to Merrill, March 1, 1978.

paigned for Mr. Mitterand in the Presidential elections of 1974. Although *Le Monde* may appear to be Left-leaning at this juncture, it remains far from being in the Leftist camp; it has had more clashes with the Communist daily *L'Humanité* than any other publication.[12]

The recent accusations placing *Le Monde* with the Left represent a repetition of an old phenomenon. Over the years, the paper has been damned by conservatives, conformist Roman Catholics, Communists, European Federalists, and the United States' State Department. But it continues pursuing an independent attitude, refusing to be tied to any political philosophy, desiring rather to be honest, frank and as objective as possible, letting "the chips fall where they may." As Professor Bertrand indicates, although *Le Monde* was meant to be a kind of semi-governmental Voice of France, "it has never supported any government longer than a few weeks."[13]

Giving *Le Monde* a political label is made difficult, too, because of the great diversity of its contributors. In general, it may be considered liberal, somewhat left-of-center and internationalist. As in the days of Beuve-Méry, so today under Fauvet, it seeks to reconcile liberty with justice. In the process, it is blunt and forceful as it looks for the significance beyond the event. Early in 1978, for example, it commented on the influence of the U.S. television program "Holocaust" (about treatment of Jews under Nazis) by stressing the program's effect on the millions who watched a people being liquidated. But it warned against illusions that the program might have permanent political influence with the observation: "Hitler is not dead in Uganda; systematic killings today in Cambodia and elsewhere do not elicit the indignant outcry of nations any more than they did before. There is nothing worse than being a deaf mute."[14]

It was Beuve-Méry's insight and insistence on complete editorial independence that led to *Le Monde*'s unique ownership arrangement and its financial success. At his direction, the paper was set up as a limited liability company (S.A.R.L.) with nine associate owners. Beuve-Méry and an archivist owned 20 percent each, the remainder of the associates less. They were all convinced the paper should be run as a public service and not for profit. When in 1950, two of the owners found they could not go along with the paper's opposition to the North Atlantic Treaty, they withdrew. The next year, after Beuve-Méry had resigned over the issue of owner interference in *Le Monde*'s contents, he was reinstated and newsmen were allowed to become part of SARL. The journalists then formed the "Société des rédacteurs du *Monde*" and became the first working journalists to own a major share in an important French national daily. Because French law makes necessary a 75 percent vote in all extraordinary decisions in SARL, the journalists, with their 28 percent ownership share, could have decisive influence on *Le Monde*'s contents.[15]

In 1968, the ownership arrangement was revised to allow participation by

[12] Christopher Henze, Paris, in letter to H. Fischer, March 15, 1978.
[13] Claude-Jean Bertrand, "A Newspaper Owned by Working Journalists," *St. Louis Journalism Review*, IV:22 (May, 1976), pp. 9–10.
[14] "Atlas World Press Review," *Atlas* (July, 1978), p. 8.
[15] Claude-Jean Bertrand, *op. cit.*

other *Le Monde* staff members. Stockholders unanimously decided holdings of the paper would be divided as follows: Association of *Le Monde* Journalists, 40 percent of the capital; founding and co-opting partners, 40 percent; management, 11 percent; administrative staff, 5 percent; and clerical staff, 4 percent. A board was established to advise management on financial policies. Participation in the plan is not compulsory, but anyone who has worked on *Le Monde* staff for one year may take part. Two persons who have had major influence on *Le Monde* during the past decade were appointed at this time: Jacques Fauvet as managing director and Jacques Sauvageot as administrative director.[16]

Largely because of this ownership policy and the efficiency and pride it has inspired in its staff, *Le Monde* remains Paris' one solvent newspaper today. Amid French print journalism's myriad headaches—among them rising cost of newsprint, competition from television, less reading, unions and overstaffing—*Le Monde*'s profits have been dwindling, too, but not like those of competing newspapers. Recently, its best support has come from advertising and a hike in the sale price of the paper. Advertising volume has risen steeply to the point where *Le Monde* has been forced to increase its size and pad its serious content with special sections on tourism, restaurants and the like to keep within the 40 percent maximum space allowed advertising. Raising the price of the paper brought down the proportion of advertising revenue from 73 percent in 1970 to 66 percent in 1976.[17] Although the circulation of the French popular press has been suffering, *Le Monde*'s benefits from both its ownership policies and the type of intellectual readers it attracts. Its circulation has risen rather steadily from 167,000 copies daily in 1960 to 515,000 in 1977. During the same period, circulation of the popular *France-Soir* fell from 1,115,000 to 712,000. An official French government source attributes this success to the fact that *Le Monde* is the only paper "to have adjusted to social, economic and cultural changes in France."[18]

While *Le Monde* excels as a national newspaper, it provides top-rate international coverage as well. Over 25 percent of its editorial matter is devoted to foreign affairs. It has divided its foreign bureaus by continents and into three major divisions: Africa-Asia; Europe-America; and diplomatic-international affairs. It keeps 23 full-time correspondents located in key large and middle-sized cities and has stringers in at least 17 other locations. The paper also sends specialists and special envoys to the "trouble spots" of the world or to cover special events. The reportage and analytical commentary of this far-flung network of international correspondence is supplemented by input from four international press agencies: Reuters, AP, UPI and, naturally, Agence France Presse.[19]

Fauvet and his *Le Monde* staff take great pains to get the most objective story possible. They constantly seek more than one account of an event and

---

[16] Jean Schwoebel, *Newsroom Democracy: The Case for Independence of the Press*, Monograph (Iowa City: Iowa Center for Communication Study, 1976), pp. 41–43.
[17] Bertrand, *op. cit.* Also Bertrand Letter to Merrill.
[18] "Survey of the Daily Press in France," *France*, publication of French Embassy, New York (August–September, 1977), p. 5.
[19] Brochure, "Le Monde," *Le Monde*, Paris (October 6, 1977), pp. 8–9.

input from as many sources as possible, before writing. Often, they will publish several versions of a story. If they are wrong, they publicly acknowledge the error and try to rectify it.[20] Although spot reporting does not stand as *Le Monde's* greatest strength, the staff has at times scored "scoops," such as getting the Kurdish point-of-view in their uprising against Iraq.

However, *Le Monde's* real forte lies in its critical analysis and insightful commentary. As Director Fauvet explains: "We provide texts and documents when they're relevant but, more important, we try to provide the most complete reporting and analysis of the news that's possible."[21] The analyses are forthright and penetrating. Often, the mix of facts which permit objectivity and valid interpretation of an event and *Le Monde* opinion commentary become so blended it is difficult to distinguish between the two. Bernard Lauzanne, the paper's co-editor, admits to this tendency, says the editors consciously seek to control excessive opinion, but at the same time encourage writers to be both industrious and thoughtful. Fauvet says the cross-over of his journalists between fact and enlightened commentary is allowed because it provides readers better bases on which to make their own judgments:

> Life is never neutral, nor is judgment. . . . A journalist can escape from his obsessions and his prejudices, but not from his training, the values he has received from his teachers, his mileu, his experiences. *Le Monde* does its best to establish an event in all its truth, or at least what appears to be the truth, to create an authentic document, but it's not an easy task, given imperfect sources and contradictory versions. *Le Monde* then makes judgments, often severe, sometimes categorical; but it also believes it has that right because, at the same time, it gives its readers all the elements of information possible for them to make their own judgments, as well.[22]

Le Monde makes serious effort to keep commentary and event separate by placing comments tagged onto news stories and official statements in bold type and between parentheses. These comments, loaded with insight, often slyly cut down prevailing stereotypes, inaccuracies and false images and ideas.

For several years, *Le Monde* has carried regular daily supplements on economics, science-technology, books, the arts and leisure, with the focus differing each day. Circulation increased significantly when these supplements were introduced. But the editors flex these categories according to their relevancy. Within the typical daily issue of *Le Monde,* the reader may expect to find, in addition to the special supplement, several pages of foreign news (usually grouped by geographical region), several each on politics and economics, and at least one each on society, religion, culture, and the entertainment arts. Only a few advertisements break the gray, serious appearance of these pages; most advertisements are grouped in a section of their own. Normally, just over one-third of the total space is taken up by advertising, about half the advertising-to-news ratio of American papers. But the advertisements *Le Monde* accepts do bring in over 60 percent of the paper's total revenue.

[20] Jacques Fauvet, *Le Monde* (October 6, 1977), pp. 1–2.
[21] Viorst, *op. cit.,* p. 45.
[22] *Ibid.,* p. 46.

For a newspaper with such wide influence and coverage, *Le Monde* keeps a relatively small staff. As of September, 1977, there were 183 writers, reporters and editors, plus the overseas correspondents, stringers and a hundred or so occasional writers, 131 administrative and advertising staff and 35 technicians. The editor-in-chief is André Fontaine, a distinguished *Le Monde* writer on foreign affairs. He was named Editor-in-chief of the Year 1976 by the *Atlas: World Press Review* of New York. Most of the editorial staff is comparatively young, yet experienced, with one-third of them ranging between 31 and 40 years of age. Nearly three-fourths (135 of 183) is well educated, holding degrees in fields such as law, economics, philosophy and literature. All are intellectually curious. Staff morale is high. Writers have great freedom; copy is not changed to fit policy. The political views of staff members run the range from Right to Left, with most leaning towards the Left. *Le Monde* practices the procedure of looking for young journalists with promise, giving them experience, then assigning them to apprenticeships in a special area in addition to their regular reporting duties. This process at least partially accounts for the paper's informative reports and commentary on special topics, such as the Common Market, French military policy and provincial planning.

Le Monde publishes several similar editions each day six days each week (a Sunday-Monday issue is printed on Saturdays). Most French readers in the provinces get their paper after the Parisians do. The latter get it in the afternoon, and those in the provinces the morning of the following day, but dated so they will not get the impression they are receiving yesterday's paper. *Le Monde*'s offices are still where they have been for years—in the old Napoleon III building on Rue des Italiens, but the paper is printed in a modern plant in the Paris suburb of Saint-Denis. In addition to *Le Monde,* the plant publishes a weekly digest of its most important articles, plus three monthlies: *Le Monde Diplomatique, Le Monde des Philatélistes,* and *Les Dossiers et Documents du Monde.* In April, 1969, *Le Monde* began publishing an English language edition of its French Paris daily. Erudite and scholarly and virtually advertisement-free, this version quickly built up a wide circulation, especially among American and British professors, students, Francophiles, diplomats, government officials, businessmen, journalists and artists who seek "to understand France and Europe from within."[23]

Throughout its 34-year history under two masterful "directeurs"—Beuve-Méry and Fauvet—*Le Monde* has represented the best in quality journalism—thorough coverage, reliable reportage, incisive analysis, editorial independence, courage and such austere seriousness that even its appearance is sombre. Between its adherence to these strong journalistic principles and its financial soundness rooted in ownership by its staff, it has gained strength steadily while the remainder of the French press has been failing. This head-and-shoulders-above-the-competition position has made *Le Monde* somewhat arrogant at times and provides it with what co-editor Lauzanne terms "Our principal danger . . . temptation to become complacent."[24] While *Le Monde* cannot

[23] "Inside France," *Time* (May 16, 1969), p. 60.
[24] Viorst, *op. cit.,* p. 48.

provide the full information of a New York *Times* or the aggressive investigation of a Washington *Post,* even its critics—and it has always had its share of them—generally agree it is "undisputably the best daily in France." In the eye of those more favorably disposed, *Le Monde* is also undeniably one of Europe's—and even the world's—finest elite newspapers.

Neue Zürcher Zeitung

(SWITZERLAND)

AUTHORITATIVE COMMENTATORS everywhere agree that Switzerland's German-language daily *Neue Zürcher Zeitung* holds a unique place among the world's elite journals. Unanimously, they praise the *NZZ,* as it is often called, for its "no-nonsense" seriousness and thoroughness. Few newspapers—if any—have been as instrumental in shaping a nation's freedom and democratic policies as has the *NZZ.* Few quality journals—if any—provide readers with such perspective of world news as does the *NZZ.* Yet it is only the rare paper that, at the same time, is as mindful as the *NZZ* of local news and developments. Few papers—if any—can match the careful, clear writing, objectivity and fairness of the *NZZ.* In rankings of the world's top elite newspapers by journalism professionals and educators, the *Neue Zürcher Zeitung* has always rated in the top ten, frequently as one of the top three of the world's best quality major newspapers.

Why is the *Neue Zürcher Zeitung* regarded so highly in so many informed critics' circles and among so many thoughtful, reflective readers both within and outside Switzerland? Certainly the paper's circulation, size and financial stability, while adequate, are not impressive. Certainly, too, with its sombre, plain pictureless front page and "all-business" ultraserious, almost pictureless inside pages, the *NZZ*'s appearance is not as aesthetically enticing to readers as are many quality papers. Although the paper covers news better than any Swiss paper—well over 50,000 news items each year—it does not match the complete news coverage of several other of the world's quality dailies.

The answer to the question "Why?" lies in *NZZ*'s quality, in the kind of information it presents. Perhaps no other paper in the world so masterfully gives background to a running account of the world's news, places items in context and produces such a comprehensible picture of the contemporary scene as does *NZZ.* For the paper, the term "quality journalism" means assuming responsibility for giving its readers news and information in perspective so they can make informed decisions. This requires, in the eyes of *NZZ* editors, that the facts be examined, given background, arranged, placed in relationship with one another and interpreted objectively. They say: "The idea is to help readers to form a picture of the world and age they live in, to be conscious of the existing situation and to be in a position to form an opinion."[1]

As a result of this approach, *Neue Zürcher Zeitung* holds a unique place among the world's elite journals. It has all the attributes of a quality paper, but it has developed in a very special, very Swiss manner. From its lofty pinnacle in neutral and freedom-loving Switzerland, the *NZZ* views all the world with an intellectual detachment that has no equal among the world's quality papers. It has always avoided "scoops" and sensationalism. It digs for background material and checks and double-checks for accuracy. It has a proclivity for pushing "hot" wire stories to inside pages to make room for a long interpretive piece by one of its own correspondents. Its long reports sometimes ramble across whole pages, broken only by an occasional one- or two-column crosshead. The casual reader will be put off by its heavy, coldly intellectual pages. But the motivated reader finds in its contents not a mere daily newspaper but a kind of leisurely textbook on contemporary society complete with the situation and its setting.

To achieve its lofty standing as probably the most serious, the most individual, the most responsible and the most cosmopolitan of all the world's elite newspapers, the *NZZ* breaks many of journalism's contemporary rules and principles and simply excels in others. It eschews the gaudy gimmicks of its less prestigious cousins with much larger circulations. Sensationalism is simply not in the paper's vocabulary: to be sensational would be an affront to the paper's traditions and an insult to its readers. In its thoroughness, it out-does its contemporaries. Correspondents are respected for their conclusions and the copydesk does little to tamper with their written products. Story length is a matter of the correspondents' needs, judgment and conscience. Editors and correspondents view their tasks professionally as they seek to make *NZZ* an all-inclusive, trustworthy daily encyclopedia of current events. *NZZ*'s journalistic practices, it could be said, are shaped by the paper's main interest which, according to editor-in-chief Dr. Fred Luchsinger, is "to inform as responsibly as we can; what the influence of such information may be is not a matter which regards us primarily."[2]

According to Dr. Luchsinger, *Neue Zürcher Zeitung* addresses itself mainly to "those readers who *want* to think and assimilate, rather than those who merely react to assorted stimuli. We regard our newspaper as a vehicle of public thought and assimilation."[3] This policy has automatically selected the paper's readership and has served to keep its circulation more confined than many papers of reknown. Total daily circulation of *NZZ* has never been extensive; today it hovers at 110,000, with 85 percent receiving it by subscription.[4] A 1977 read-

---

[1] Brochure, "Characteristics of the *Neue Zürcher Zeitung*," (Zurich: *Neue Zürcher Zeitung*, n.d.)

[2] Letter, Dr. Fred Luchsinger to J. Merrill, dated July 26, 1965.

[3] Fred Luchsinger, "A Modern Newspaper—Nearly 200 Years Old," in brochure *The Neue Zürcher Zeitung Speaks for Itself* (Zurich: *Neue Zürcher Zeitung*, 1977), p. 5.

[4] Eric Mettler, foreign editor, *Neue Zürcher Zeitung*, in response to questionnaire, dated October 4, 1978.

Mittwoch, 22. Februar 1978   Der Zürcher Zeitung 199. Jahrgang   Umfang 56 Seiten Nr. 44

Neue Zürcher Zeitung

und schweizerisches Handelsblatt

Briefadresse von Redaktion, Verlag und Druckerei:
Postfach, CH-8021 Zürich, Telefon (01) 32 71 00, Telex 52 157
Auslandvertrieb: Postfach 660, CH-8021 Zürich
Annoncenabteilung: Postfach 215, CH-8021 Zürich, Telex 54 675
Abonnementspreise auf Seite 4

Schweiz
70 Rp.

hFr. 25.—   Dr. 29.—   S 10.—
eKr. 3.—   C 0.30   Esc. 18.—
DM 1.—   Lit. 400.—   sKr. 2.50
fFr. 2.50   hfl. 1.25   Pts. 20.—

Zähe Regierungskrise in Rom

Arbeit der Experten am Programm

Von unserem Korrespondenten

T. W. Rom, 21. Februar

Die italienische Regierungskrise schleppt sich mühsam unter öffentlichem Desinteresse durch eine weitere Woche. Nachdem am vergangenen Freitag vor allem mit Intervention des christlich-demokratischen Führers Moro ein Aufschub erreicht und damit eine Verhärtung vermieden worden war, sollen auf dem Wege einer Bereinigung des Programms die Standpunkte von KPI und Democrazia cristiana einander angenähert werden. Zu diesem Zwecke sind die Experten unter den Augen der Parteichefs am Werk. Der designierte Ministerpräsident *Andreotti* hofft mittels einer programmatischen Einigung seiner eigenen Partei die Uebereinkunft mit den Kommunisten schmackhafter machen zu können und wartet mit *zwersichtlichen Kommentaren* und Prognosen auf. Der republikanische Chef *La Malfa* wirkt als Vermittler zwischen den Fronten. Die KPI verlangt jedoch, dass programmatische und politische Verständigung Hand in Hand gehen, und scheint zurzeit nicht gewillt, Abstriche an ihrem Sachprogramm zu machen. Zusammen mit Sozialisten, Sozialdemokraten und Republikanern verlangt die KPI weiterhin eine *klar ausgehandelte Mehrheit*, und das bedeutet zum einen von den Partnern unterzeichnete Vertrauensmotion in Parlament.

Ringen um Sachfragen

Am Montag beschäftigten sich die Experten mit dem Staatshaushalt, um die Ausgaben zu reduzieren und die Einnahmen zu erhöhen. Für Mittwoch stehen *wirtschaftliche und soziale Fragen* an. Heute geht es um Vermittlung in den alten Streitfragen der von der Linke geforderten Entmilitarisierung und Syndikalisierung der Polizei, ausserdem um strittige Bestimmungen der «Legge Reale» zum verstärkten Kampf gegen den Terrorismus. Der Republikaner Mammi, Präsident der Kommission für Inneres der Kammer, bemüht sich zurzeit um eine Auflockerung der Gegensätze. Doch fast in allen wichtigen Fragen klaffen noch *Kontraste*, so dass es zurzeit schwierig scheint, im Aufwind des Programms die Front zwischen den beiden grossen Parteien zu überbrücken.

Tagesinformation

Schweizer Vorstoss in Belgrad

Der schweizerische Delegierte Brunner hat an der KSZE-Nachfolgekonferenz in Belgrad vorgeschlagen, ein «kurzes und nüchternes» Schlussdokument zu verabschieden. Soll wenigstens vermieden werden, einen Konferenzversuch zu veröffentlichen, der allein die sowjetischen Vorstellungen berücksichtigt.   Seite 1

Beruhigung um den Dollar

Die bis Montag anhaltende Talfahrt des Dollars ist am Dienstag zum Stillstand gekommen; die Situation bleibt weiterhin labil.   Seite 15

Neuer Anlauf zu einem Umweltschutzgesetz

Am Dienstag präsentierte Bundesrat Hürlimann einen zweiten Versuch zu einem Bundesgesetz über den Schutz der Umwelt, nachdem der erste Entwurf von 1974 vor allem bei den Kantonen auf Widerstand gestossen war. Das Gesetz ist relativ kurz gehalten und visiert vor allem eine Rahmengesetzgebung.   Seite 29

Vereitelte Gefangenenbefreiung

Im Bezirksgebäude Zürich ist dank der Aufmerksamkeit eines Beirksbeamten die Befreiung eines israelischen Gefangenen verhindert worden.   Seite 41

Luszczek Weltmeister im 15-km-Lauf

Der Pole Josef Luszczek, bereits über die 30-km-Distanz an dritter Stelle, hat in den Nordischen Skiweltmeisterschaften den 15-km-Lauf 2.25 Sekunden vor dem Russen Evgenij Beljaew und Olaf Sekunden vor dem Finnen Juha Mieto zu seinen Gunsten entschieden. Die Schweizer klassierten sich schlecht.   Seite 45

Inhaltsübersicht

Schwindende Hoffnung auf ein substantielles KSZE-Dokument

Der Schweizer Vorstoss am Belgrader Folgetreffen

Für ein «kurzes und nüchternes» Ende

Von unserem Korrespondenten

R. St. Belgrad, 21. Februar

Der vom schweizerischen Delegierten *Edouard Brunner* in die Diskussion geworfene Vorschlag, man möge das Belgrader Folgetreffen mit einem kurzen und nüchternen Dokument beenden, hat bei den übrigen Delegationen zunächst *eine gewisse Ueberraschung* ausgelöst. Im Laufe des Dienstags mehrten sich jedoch die zustimmenden Aeusserungen. Einige Delegationen finden den Zeitpunkt für einen solchen Vorstoss *verfrüht*, weil nach ihrer Ansicht die jetzt Hoffnung auf ein substantielles Dokument noch nicht aufzugeben ist. Bei der Beurteilung des Timings der schweizerischen Intervention muss aber auch in Betracht gezogen werden, dass der sowjetische Delegationschef *Woronzow* abermals seine absolute Ablehnung gegenüber allem vom Westen wie von den Neutralen und Blockfreien vertretenen substantiellen Inhalten des Schlussdokumentes vorgebracht hatte. Es sollte verhindert werden, dass man in der Debatte plötzlich auf den sowjetischen Vorschlag zur Verhandlungsgrundlage einschwenke.

Sowjetisches Nein gegen neue westliche Formulierung

In der Beurteilung, dass alle Möglichkeiten ausgeschöpft waren, stimmten die andern *neutralen* Staaten naben — mit Ausnahme Jugoslawiens — der Schweiz zu. Die *neutralen* deutschen Delegierten und der schweizerische Vorschlag fanden im wesentlichen — mit kontroverser Ansicht der desrepublik Deutschland — den von der Schweiz vorgeschobenen Weg ebenfalls als ein einzig noch gangbaren. Die Sowjetunion und ihre Alliierten würden in dem Vorgehen kaum

widersetzen. Der amerikanische Delegationschef *Goldberg* wird das Plenum noch einmal zur Redaktion eines Dokumentes aufrufen, in dem eine Vorschläge enthalten sind, die im Laufe des Herbstes eingebracht wurden und die auf eine Vertiefung der Zusammenarbeit abzielen. In diesem Sinne sollten *15 westliche Länder* einen 17 Seiten langen Dokumententwurf ein. Er soll zeigen, dass die Schlussdokument nach westlichen Vorstellungen hätte aussehen *können*; dass er als Verhandlungsgrundlage in Betracht gezogen würde, stand unter den gegebenen Verhältnissen nicht mehr zur Diskussion. Woronzow lehnte ihn sofort als unakzeptabel ab.

Ein Produkt der Resignation

Für alle, auch für die Initianten der «kurzen und nüchternen» Lösung, steht ausser Zweifel, dass sie nur ein *Ersatz für das eigentlich angestrebte* ist. Der Vorstoss ist mithin das Produkt einer Resignation. Im Kreise der Neutralen und Blockfreien haben bereits Diskussionen über die Gestaltung dieses kurzen Papiers begonnen. Jugoslawien und Malta, die sich besonders stark verochten haben, dass die westlichen Vorgehen entäuscht zeigten, konnten für die Mitarbeit gewonnen werden, was bedeutet, dass auch für die Einsicht reift, dass die Basis für einen anderen Ausweg schmal geworden ist.

Die Meinungen, wie in einem kurzen Schlussdokument verankert werden soll, gehen zunächst auseinander. Uebereinstimmung herrscht darüber (und zwar nicht nur im Kreise der N+N-Staaten, sondern unter allen Teilnehmern), dass es eine Bekräftigung des Willens zur Durchführung der Schlussakte von Helsinki enthalten soll. Ferner will man die *Kontinuität sichern*, anderseits dass das Treffen in Madrid vom 1980 und anderseits *X* verschiedene Expertentreffen. Was die politische Wertung des Belgrader Treffens angeht, wird man versuchen, wenigstens andeutungsweise auszudrücken, dass in verschiedenen Teilen Europas die Verwirklichung *unterschiedlich* geschätzt wird.

Folgen der knappen Mehrheit für die Antiterrorgesetze im Bundestag

Gestörtes Verhältnis in der Bonner Koalition

Unsicherheit und Verdächtigungen

Von unserem Korrespondenten

Mr. Bonn, 21. Februar

Die Abstimmung über neue Gesetzesparagraphen zur Bekämpfung des Terrorismus im Deutschen Bundestag hat eine Koalition nur mit der denkbar *knappsten* Mehrheit von einer Stimme gewonnen; eine Stimme weniger als vorausberechnet, und der SPD-Abgeordnete und Porzellanfabrikant Rosenthal die falsche Stimmkarte verwendet hat. Die Folge davon ist, dass das Verhältnis in beiden Koalitionspartner SPD und FDP politisch und vor allem psychologisch schwieriger geworden und von Unsicherheit und Verdächtigungen belastet ist. Etwas zu betont hat der FDP-Vorsitzende *Genscher* am Wochenende die Frage der Regierungsmehrheit als internes Problem der SPD hingestellt, obwohl die FDP nach Ansicht des selbst-vertretenden SPD-Vorsitzenden *Koschnick* am «Dissidenten-Problem» in der SPD-Fraktion — vier Abgeordnete stimmten gegen die Gesetzesnovellierung — indirekt ebenfalls mitschuldig sei. Grenscher der Stimmkartensperregesetz eine von der FDP als Gefahrensignal für die Koalition bezeichnete «wechselnde Mehrheit» drohte (das bedeutet, dass Koalitionsabgeordnete mit der Opposition gegen die Regierung stimmen oder der Opposition der Regierung eine kleine Minderheit in deren eigenen Reihen zur Mehrheit verhilft), waren auch liberale Abgeordnete beteiligt.

Ob es im Bundesrat (Länderkammer) zu einem Eingriff gegen die Antiterrorgesetze, welche die Opposition als unzureichend ablehnt, kommt, hängt von den sozialliberalen und *sozialländischen Politikern* ab, die entweder die CDU/FDP-Koalition vertreten. Genscher erklärte, es könne nicht die Sache dieser *Länderkoalitionen* sein, Schwierigkeiten der SPD zu lösen, die Feststellung müsse den Landesregierungen allein überlassen bleiben, dass im wesentlichen als Gensches Aufgabe über die Aufgabe dieser Länderkoalition im Bundesrat. Sein Hinweis auf die Schwierigkeiten der SPD ist vor dem Hintergrund als Kritik verstanden worden: Man glaubt hier bereits an die Möglichkeit eines *Absatzbewegung* der Liberalen in Richtung eines Koalitionswechsels für 1980, der vorläufig allerdings erst noch vom Ausgang der kommenden Landtagswahlen abhängig ist. Die Distanzierung

der FDP von den Schwierigkeiten der SPD deutet *Koschnick* als den Versuch dieser Partei, für die Landtagswahlen Profil zu gewinnen.

Verschleierte Kritik

Genscher hat am Montag versucht, Erklärung abzugeben, worin seine Kritik an der SPD sei nur durch die Sorge um den scharfen Fortbestand der Koalition bis 1980. Seine Zusicherung, die Liberalen würden alles tun, um den Bestand der Regierungsprogramm zu sichern, zeigt jedoch in erster Linie, wie *eingeengt* der Spielraum für öffentliche Meinungsäusserungen der Koalitionspartner noch ist, wenn man es verhindern wollen, dass nicht jedes Wort gleich im Hinblick auf Koalitionstreue oder die Frage genommen wird. Das hat bereits dazu beigetragen, dass erst jetzt eine Atmosphäre der Unsicherheit entstanden ist.

Verschiebung des FDP-Parteitags

Die FDP hat daher in die Situation dass sie noch nicht weiss, wie man am sinnvollsten entscheiden sollte. Die Parteiführung hat am Montag ihren Parteitag, der in diesem Jahres in Nürnberg stattfinden *Parteitag* auf den November nach Mainz zu verschieben, offiziell aus Gründen der Parteinaitungen, aber auch um das Ergebnis der diesjährigen Landtagswahlen — vor allem die wichtige in Hessen im Oktober — abzuwarten. Genscher liess die FDP will ihre Koalitionsaussagen erst nach den Wahlen in Niedersachsen und Hamburg machen. Das Gespräch über eine CDU, deren Vorsitzender Dregger, wie vor früheren Wahlen, der FDP ein grosszügiges Koalitionsangebot gemacht hat, verläuft noch ergebnislos.

Hauchdünne Mehrheit

Für die SPD ist die Situation ebenfalls unangenehm, für den misslicher Satz des Fraktionsführers *Herbert Wehner* in der Debatte zu den Antiterrorgesetzen belegte, dass es immer hat noch mit äusserster Anstrengung gelungen war, die Zahl der Nein-Stimmen in der eigenen Fraktion knapp unter der kritischen Grenze zu halten. Tatsächlich sind bei den 249 Stimmen, die nötig ist, um einen allfälligen Einspruch des Bundesrates im Bundestag zu überstimmen — vom Dissidenten hart bleiben, die Koalition nur erreichen, wenn alle anderen Abgeordneten anwesend sind (das letztemal waren zwei krank, einer im Ausland,

Aufruf der französischen KP zu einer linken Wahlallianz

Paris, 21. Febr. (Reuter) Der französische Kommunistenführer Marchais hat die Sozialistische Partei am Montag abend aufgefordert, an Verhandlungstisch zurückzukehren, das sie keine andere Wahl habe. In einer Fernsehdebatte mit Justizminister *Peyrefitte*, drei Wochen vor den Wahlen zur Nationalversammlung, erklärte Marchais, falls die Sozialistische Partei nicht zu der Allianz mit den Kommunisten und einer gemeinsamen Politik zurückkehre, werde sie in die «Arme der regierenden Rechten» laufen. Er sei sicher, dass eine Einigung zwischen den beiden Parteien erzielt werden könne, die es ihnen ermögliche, die Regierungsparteien bei den Wahlen zu schlagen und eine linksgerichtete Regierung *unter Einschluss der Kommunisten* zu bilden. Nach jüngsten Meinungsumfragen wäre ein Sieg der Linken bei den Wahlen am 12. und 19. März möglich, falls sich Sozialisten, Kommunisten und Radikale auf ein *gemeinsames Programm* einigen würden. Die Allianz der drei Parteien war im vergangenen September an dem Versuch zerbrochen, ihr gemeinsames Programm von 1972 zu erneuern und zu aktualisieren.

4285 Kandidaten für 491 Sitze

Paris, 21. Febr. (afp/Reuter) Beim ersten Wahlgang am 12. März in Frankreich bewerben sich laut einer Mitteilung des Pariser Innenministeriums 4285 Kandidaten um die 491 Sitze in der Nationalversammlung. Davon sind 4231 im «Mutterland» und 54 in den Uebersee-departementen eingeschrieben. Damit entfallen auf einen Parlamentssitz in Durchschnitt etwa *neun Kandidaten*.

und einer stimmte falsch). Da die vier trotz dem — vom rechten Flügel als ungehörig empfundenen — Entgegenkommen der Gesamtfraktion bei ihrer Ablehnung blieben, befürchtet man bei Teilen der SPD, dass andere Motive als die Sorge um das Gesetz massgebend waren: etwa ein *genereller Aerger* über den Kurs der Regierung, der ihnen nicht mehr «sozialdemokratisch» sei. Eine Trotzhaltung, die sich um eine *Regensierungs* in der Politik der Opposition genährt würde? Das SPD-Präsidium musste vor Diensttag zur Kenntnis nehmen, dass die Regierungsfähigkeit der SPD in Frage gestellt werden, aber zugleich auch erklärt, dass «Sozivoten» das Ansehen und der Erfolg der Koalition gefährden.

Weitere Meinungsdifferenzen

Die Ungehaltenheit bei der SPD und die sorgende Kritik der FDP sind nicht nach verschieden ausgefallen, weil sie sich bei der Abstimmung vom vergangenen Donnerstag nicht um ein Ausnahmefall handelte. Als Ausnahme von einem Vorgang, der den Zusammenhalt der Koalition gefährden könnte, wenn er sich wiederholt. Weitere *Meinungsverschiedenheiten* zwischen den beiden Koalitionsparteien und innerhalb der beiden Parteien sind voraussehbar. Die neue Rentenanpassungsgesetz dürfte nicht ungeteilten Beifall finden, zumal schon der Gewerkschaftsbund seine Opposition angemeldet hat. Ein geplantes Meldegesetz zur polizeilichen Registrierung verstösst chen weitere Kontroversen. Und schon im Bundestag für die Einführung der Neutronenbombe — an Entgegennahmen der Gewerkschaften — geplant. Aussenminister Genscher dringt auf eine realistische Beurteilung und scheint mit seinen Argumenten auf eine vorzeitige Rücksichtnahme und Vorwug greift. Die Bundesregierung muss aber ihre Argumente gegen die Neutronenbombe abgeben können. Offenbar hat die Regierung noch nicht endgültig gefunden, obwohl, wie Regierungssprecher Bölling am Montag erklärte, die Konsultationen innerhalb der Allianz noch beginnen sind. Zumindest wird die Bundesrepublik darauf dringen, dass die Neutronenbombe als Verhandlungsgegenstand in der Abrüstungsverhandlungen einbezogen wird.

Was der FDP Sorge um Unterstützung verwalten. In der SPD-Fraktion und in der Parteiführung der Sozialdemokraten selbst bestehen aber noch erhebliche *Widerstände*. Dabei bereitet man dem vor allem seinen Beschluss des Hamburger Parteitags vom vergangenen November ab. Die Regierung und die Partei, so ist unternehmen, um eine Stationierung der Neutronenbombe in der Bundesrepublik zu verhindern. Dieses Beispiel zeigt, dass es im Augenblick der FDP gelingt, ihren linken Flügel zum Stillhalten zu verpflichten; bei der SPD bleiben die dagegen die Gegensätze zwischen der Regierungspolitik und der Parteibasis für die Regierung und den Bundeskanzler ein dauernder «Störfaktor».

ership study revealed that an average of 226,000 actually read *NZZ* daily,. 66 percent of whom are men (the percentage of men in the Swiss population is only 44 percent). Most of the readers represent the wealthy and upper middle income class urban dwellers in the 30-to-49-year-old age bracket. The bulk are executives or officials (including those in high position in government), industrialists, craft tradesmen and housewives. One other important readership classification is "Students," with over six percent of all the readers.[5] Clearly *NZZ* is intended for—and read by—the educated, the better-to-do, the influential and the opinion-makers. It is a paper for the "thinking" person, important in democratic Switzerland where each citizen must constantly be well-informed so he or she can discuss, decide and vote upon issues intelligently.

Politically, the *NZZ* has always been nominally independent, but historically it has advocated Swiss liberalism. It holds "a fundamental commitment to the principles of a liberal social order within a democratic, federalist, constitutional state, an open society capable of reform and regeneration."[6] This makes the paper's political point-of-view "liberal-conservative" (in the European meaning of the term),[7] which is not the same as the American interpretation of the term. In the interest of serving the democratic principles to which it has pledged its allegiance, the *NZZ* has been strongly anti-Communist and anti-socialist, a good friend of the United States (but not afraid to criticize excesses), an opponent of Britain's Labour Government, a supporter of German re-armament, a proponent of free capitalism, a skeptic about the possibilities of permanent coexistence.

Although not a party publication, the *NZZ* is unabashedly partisan and historically has held views parallel to those of Switzerland's Radical (Freisinnig-Demokratische) Party. As editor Luchsinger puts it: "We freely admit to being a journal of opinion—not one which permits no other opinions to appear in its pages, but one which does not obscure its own orientation nor change it from case to case."[8] The positions the paper takes—here again it puts the events of history in a framework—are and have always been based mainly "on the fact that it has maintained a clear line in past decades and has taken an unequivocal stand against totalitarianisms of all shades."[9]

In its approximately 200-year history—it is now one of Switzerland's oldest papers—*Neue Zürcher Zeitung* has often led the battle for freedom and the democratic way of life. Born during a time of authoritarian restraints in the Swiss Federation, *NZZ* was founded in 1780 "as the heir to a succession of journals that went right back into the seventeenth century."[10] Until 1821, it was known as the *Zürcher Zeitung*. The early issues had four pages in octavo format and came out twice weekly, on Wednesdays and Saturdays. Its publisher and

---

[5] Brochure, "Readership Data According to the AG für Werbemittleforschung," (Zurich: *Neue Zürcher Zeitung*, 1977).

[6] Luchsinger, *op. cit.*, p. 5.

[7] Mettler questionnaire.

[8] Luchsinger, *op. cit.*, p. 5.

[9] *Ibid.*

[10] John Sandford, *The Mass Media in German-Speaking Countries* (London: Oswald Wolff Publishers, Ltd., 1976), p. 157.

printer was a firm known as Orell, Gessner, Füssli and Company, forerunner of the present-day well-known Zurich publishing house Orell Füssli and Company. The first issue of *Zürcher Zeitung* published a statement that still serves as a guideline to *NZZ* editors: "It will not be possible for us, as so many other papers do, to report the news of the world before it happens."[11] The new paper heralded a new era of quality journalism in Switzerland, and was the first newspaper (the London *Times* followed eight years later) "to unite the hitherto largely separated realms of information, comment, entertainment and advertisement—the staple contents of today's press."[12]

At its outset, the new paper was forced by official restraints to content itself with being purely a journal of information. But public resentment was growing against the feudal reign of the patrician families who controlled the Swiss cantons and soon *Zürcher Zeitung* was leading the revolution for change. The paper's fearless editor, Paul Usteri led a group of intellectuals who "advocated changes in the constitution to bring a more democratic government and recognition of the rights of men."[13] By 1798, a full-blown revolt had come and with it a brief five-year period of press freedom until Napoleon, by then the country's conqueror, again imposed strict supervision of all Swiss papers.

But the freedom-loving Swiss were not to be put down for long, and the dauntless Paul Usteri mounted a campaign that resulted in the lifting of press censorship in 1829. About this time, the *Neue Zürcher Zeitung* began to play an increasingly prominent role in the public affairs of Zurich and elsewhere in Switzerland. It led the struggle, too, for national regeneration in the 1830s and championed the development of the country's loose confederation of states into a strong federalist nation.

In 1868, a joint stock company was formed which purchased *NZZ* from its original owners for a sum of 100,000 Swiss francs. Until that time, the paper's circulation had always been low, but under the new ownership, sales began to pick up. Today, the paper is published by a corporation called "Aktiengesellschaft für die *Neue Züercher Zeitung*," which is made up of 500 residents of Zurich who hold the company's 1,800 registered shares worth about 1,000 Swiss francs each. Their voting power is limited to a maximum of 30 shares per stockholder. Payments for the welfare of the paper's personnel has been about 20 times that paid to shareholders; yet the shareholders have received an annual average of 10 percent on their holdings since 1968.[14]

In December, 1869, the *NZZ* became the first Swiss paper to come out with two editions daily. In general, the last half of the nineteenth century was prosperous for the Swiss press. For the *NZZ*, circulation climbed steeply from 1,400 copies daily in 1860 to 5,800 in 1880 to 11,900 in 1900. In order to keep pace with Zurich's economic development and growing reader hunger for information, the paper increased to three editions daily in 1894. Then came the twen-

[11] *The Neue Zürcher Zeitung Speaks for Itself, op. cit.,* p. 6.
[12] Sandford, *op. cit.,* p. 6.
[13] Kenneth E. Olson, *The History Makers: The Press of Europe from its Beginnings through 1965* (Baton Rouge: Louisiana State University Press, 1966), p. 217.
[14] *The Neue Zürcher Zeitung Speaks for Itself, op. cit.,* p. 7.

tieth century, and in both World Wars the Swiss press found itself divided in its allegiance as the nation struggled to remain neutral. However, *NZZ* circulation zoomed upward in the first half of the century, going from less than 12,000 in 1900 to 38,200 in 1920 to 62,600 in 1940.[15] The sharp upward swing in circulation has continued steadily to the present. Over the past century, too, the paper's reputation as a quality daily has kept pace with its ever-rising circulation.

As early as 1930, the paper warned of the Nazi threat, bemoaning the rise of Hitler and offering detailed analyses of what was happening in Germany. And after the war began, the *NZZ* continued to warn of the totalitarian peril and provided what was probably the most objective and thorough analysis of German activities until the war was over. During the war, the Germans repeatedly threatened to invade and occupy Switzerland unless the *NZZ* and other Swiss papers stopped reporting on Germany in such a critical (i.e. truthful) manner. Under the able direction of Willy Bretscher, who was then fairly new in the editor's position, the *NZZ* continued to speak as Germany's conscience, withstanding numerous pressures from the Nazis. The *NZZ* was banned in Germany from 1934 onwards because the paper had reported that it was Goering, not the Communists, who had set fire to the Reichstag. However, the German Government subscribed to 200 copies of the *NZZ* each day for its own information. Although the paper was firmly established as a great newspaper before World War II, its reputation abroad was further fostered by its insightful analysis of the months of Nazi preparation for the war, by the wealth of its information and its wartime comments. Since 1945, its prestige has been ever greater, due largely to its ever-increasing coverage and analysis of the world during the "cold war."

The *NZZ* has had a series of outstanding editors. Those who occupied the editorial chair for the longest periods, all men who gained wide recognition, include Dr. Peter Felber (1849–1868), Professor G. Vogt (1878–1885), Dr. Walter Bissengger (1888–1915) and Dr. Albert Meyer (1915–1929). Two of its post-World War II "greats" have been Urs Schwartz and Willy Bretscher, the latter perhaps the journal's most illustrious editor. The present editor-in-chief is Dr. Fred Luchsinger, who took office in 1968 after having served as *NZZ*'s foreign editor. The paper's present director in charge of publishing and printing is Fritz Huber.

The *Neue Zürcher Zeitung*'s international reputation comes in large measure from its outstanding corps of foreign correspondents. A steady flow of up-to-date material comes to the *NZZ* Zurich headquarters from a network of 24 full-time correspondents stationed in 33 of the world's strategic capital and news-making cities. In several cities, the paper keeps two reporters, one expert in the field of politics and the other in economics. The work of these overseas correspondents is supplemented by 18 regular contributors, dozens of part-time reporters and news analysts all over the world, and a half-dozen wire services. Most of the foreign correspondents have doctoral degrees in history, law, economics or literature and they invariably are specialists in the areas they report and write about. They are, in addition to their advanced academic training and

---

[15] *Ibid.*, p. 16.

experience in journalistic excellence, people with " a rapid grasp of events and careful, thoughtful judgment . . . with a sense for the essential."[16] Although *NZZ* professes to be disinterested in receiving awards, most of the foreign journalists have distinguished themselves.

The volume and quality of international news and views this staff presents to *NZZ* readers is phenomenal. One International Press Institute study has indicated that the *NZZ* carries nearly twice as much foreign news as its nearest competitor among 23 newspapers from eight leading countries of the world, and the ratio of foreign material to non-advertising text was one-third higher in *NZZ* than in its nearest competitor.[17] But it is the quality of *NZZ*'s international news that attracts most of its readers. Because of the paper's analyses, many of its thoughtful readers feel they can understand, even anticipate the conditions that suddenly thrust an area into the world's spotlight. The very quality of an analysis in *NZZ* gives readers the assurance that the article has had the attention of some of the keenest minds and the best writers in Europe.

Because of its thoroughness and objectivity in covering and analyzing foreign news, the paper's international reputation has increased. Foreign sales of *NZZ's* foreign edition account for over 20 percent of the total circulation; some 20,000 copies go all over the world every day, mostly to businessmen and politicians. Over 1,000 copies go to Communist countries, with some 300 reaching U.S.S.R. officials. The paper has gained such prestige overseas because each issue may contain "as many as a hundred items of foreign news alone, often in the form of informative essays that are both highly literate and thoroughly researched."[18]

In addition to its consuming interest in overseas news and its special foreign edition, since 1951 the *NZZ* has published a monthly English-language news magazine called the *Swiss Review of World Affairs*. It reflects the depth and scope of *NZZ's* international coverage. Printed on high-grade airmail-weight paper, the journal finds its presitge increasing all over the world. Each issue offers remarks on recent world events called "Comments from the *NZZ*," plus "Swiss Kaleidoscope," a roundup of domestic Swiss developments. The magazine's stated goal is "to help provide some of the foundations on which leaders in politics, business and industry . . . make their decisions."[19] In a larger sense, it helps build cultural bridges between Europe, the United States and other overseas areas. Today, *Swiss Review,* originally requested by American friends of *NZZ*, goes to nearly every country in the world, but is most widely read by North Americans, who comprise over 60 percent of its readership.

Although *Neue Zürcher Zeitung* has distinguished itself in reporting and interpreting the international political and economic scene, it remains a paper very much rooted in Switzerland. Its sub-title is "Swiss Trade Journal," an indicator of its special interest in Swiss economic and financial news. Its thoroughness extends to coverage of every Swiss canton and village. It is the

[16] *The Neue Zürcher Zeitung Speaks for Itself, op. cit.,* p. 13.
[17] *The Flow of the News* (Zurich: International Press Institute, 1953) pp. 249–250.
[18] Sandford, *op. cit.,* p. 214.
[19] *The Neue Zürcher Zeitung Speaks for Itself, op. cit.,* p. 22.

only German-language Swiss paper which keeps reporters in the French- and Italian-speaking sectors of the country. Its coverage of the city and canton of Zurich is particularly noteworthy. It reports from the legislatures and courts on municipal, cantonal and federal levels with precision and objectivity. It now carries a regular section entitled "Canton Zurich" and a feature page called "Around Zurich." Eight full-time reporters are assigned to the federal capital and more than forty, many of them full-time, cover events in Winterthur, Canton Zurich's second largest city and in the other 169 townships in the canton.[20]

Despite its thorough, in-depth reporting and serious appearance, the NZZ can hardly be considered dull. On the contrary, it is most readable paper, full of life, variety and color. Even the local Swiss news is presented in a way that will attract the foreign reader who has little personal interest in such matters. Another characteristic makes the NZZ interesting—its provision of numerous supplements. The supplement "Wochenende" appears in each Sunday edition (unlike most European papers, NZZ publishes seven times each week). Each weekend, the editors develop their own special themes and provide richly illustrated articles on a broad range of subjects which complement NZZ's rich political, economic and cultural reports. Six other supplements are presented once each week: "Literatur und Kunst" gives the reader insight into the major works and personalities in all artistic fields; "Forschung" covers latest scientific and medical research and developments; "Technik" informs the reader in layman's terms about diverse technological advances; "Tourismus" offers articles on travel and vacationing everywhere, but especially in Switzerland; and "Film" and "Radio und Fernsehen" reflect on the mass media and evaluate specific films and broadcasts. Every two weeks, there are supplements on Aviation, on Motoring and on Woman and Society. Finally, there are periodic supplements: one on Corporate Management is published four times a year, another on Advertising thrice yearly, and on Fashion bi-annually.[21]

The NZZ's attention to background, analysis and placing news developments in a framework meaningful to its readers means that its editors do not draw the sharp, distinctive line between analysis and straight news found, for example, in American quality papers. Dr. Luchsinger explains that it is NZZ's view that news and background are inseparable and that the main task of the paper's correspondents "is to explain the facts which, of course, does not mean to give their subjective views on them."[22] Because NZZ reporters must explain the facts, they are left at their posts for relatively long periods of time so they can become fully knowledgable about both the event and all its related background in an area. What is more, reporters are not "under the gun" to produce stories regularly, a policy which gives them freedom to sift until the truth in its setting is sufficiently clear for accurate, thorough reporting.[23] The paper does encourage full investigation by its reporters, but "not in the 'Watergate' sense";

[20] Ibid., p. 10.
[21] Ibid., pp. 14–15.
[22] Luchsinger letter to Merrill, loc. cit.
[23] "Characteristics of the Neue Zürcher Zeitung," op. cit.

nor does it seek to "specialize in disclosures" which might produce juicy, but superficial stories.[24]

One may wonder how *NZZ*'s mixture of reporting the facts and providing the story's context can avoid falling into dangerous journalistic pits of pure subjectivism and tedentiousness. Willy Bretscher, a former editor-in-chief of *NZZ*, once described why his paper can dodge the pitfalls without much problem:

> The solution of this problem is comparatively simple. It lies first of all in the professional and human qualities of the reporters, in their integrity and independence; it consists furthermore in the fact that these reporters fulfill their task as citizens of a small neutral nation which has no irons of its own in the fire of international politics, which pursues no specific policies which could come into conflict with the aims of other nations but whose national interests are linked to the highest interests of all other peoples, with the interest of mankind in the preservation of the peace, in the moral and material reconstruction of the world in the protection of freedom and human rights.[25]

While the *Neue Zürcher Zeitung* prides itself in its objective reporting and analysis, it does not claim to be neutral in its opinions and views. Instead, it unashamedly seeks to shape Swiss opinion in conformity with its own position of Liberalism based on the principles of free order, a democratic state and an open society. It recognizes the validity of other views. As Dr. Luchsinger explains, the *NZZ* does not find its drive for objectivity and its being a journal of opinion a contradiction:

> To observe the realities as precisely and soberly as possible by no means makes it impossible to have one's own standpoint and opinion—just as "to have an opinion" must not mean to narrow one's view or close one's eyes to anything that does not fit one's preconceptions or to relinguish one's standards of quality in making judgments. To objectively and correctly analyze and comment upon questions of international affairs cannot and must not mean to give up one's basic orientation in the evaluation of questions concerning one's own home ground.[26]

In appearance, the *NZZ* is most distinctive. Its format is small, measuring just 19 by 13 inches. The paper's typical length on weekdays is 24 to 28 pages. Its headlines are very little larger than its small typeface—mere labels giving the general theme of each article. Its four wide columns are broken only by a rare picture (except in the supplements), giving it its gray, ultraserious appearance. Each issue is divided into several sections—on politics, on economics, on internal Swiss news and on Zurich, plus, of course, the special supplements. Within the sections, there are also sub-sections and special pages, covering subject areas such as the *feuilleton*. Color is employed only in a few advertisements. Although one source notes that the *NZZ* is "fat with advertising,"[27] the advertisements are not obtrusive; they never shift the spotlight away from the news to themselves.

[24] Mettler questionnaire.
[25] Information sent by Willy Bretscher, *Neue Zürcher Zeitung*, to J. Merrill, August, 1965.
[26] Luchsinger, "A Modern Newspaper—Nearly 200 Years Old," *op. cit.*, p. 5.
[27] Olson, *op. cit.*, p. 227.

At present, *NZZ* employs some 700 people: 100 on the editorial staff, 250 in printing and distribution, and 350 in administrative and secretarial positions. In addition, there are about 130 street vendors. Mostly women are employed for delivery of the paper, but the editorial staff is predominantly male. The paper's input from its correspondents and other sources is put together with up-to-date facilities in a modern five-story building at Falkenstrasse 11 in Zurich. The staff uses video display terminals for the composition and correction of editorial text and advertisements. The paper is in process of installing computer-controlled photo-composition equipment.[28]

From its 1780 beginnings as a modest local sheet, the *Neue Zürcher Zeitung*, following its formula of undiluted quality, has developed into one of the world's best newspapers, and in many ways, easily *the* best. The paper's philosophy of "accuracy, wide scope and thoughtfulness"[29] have made it "widely regarded as the world's most serious and thorough newspaper."[30] Not only is it the best informed newspaper in Switzerland, but also it has world impact highly disproportionate to its size. In spite of its conservative and sober physical and editorial practices, it is progressive and forward-looking. As one of the world's most prestigious and influential papers, it sets a high-standard model for all newspapers seeking to climb the steep and rigorous path to uncompromising quality. It is an elite journal among elite papers, not content to rest on past achievements, for it recognizes that the world, becoming ever more complex, frustrating and dangerous, must be clearly explained to readers so they can reach informed, life-shaping decisions. Little wonder, then, that an ever-increasing chorus of informed critics are proclaiming *Neue Zürcher Zeitung* as "quite simply, the best newspaper in the world."[31]

———————

THE NEW YORK TIMES

(UNITED STATES)

IN SEVERAL RESPECTS, the *New York Times* ranks as the best or near-best newspaper in the United States. Certainly the biggest in total operations among American elite papers, it places, with 854,000 copies daily, along with the *New York News* and the Los Angeles *Times,* among the nation's top three in circula-

[28] Mettler questionnaire.
[29] Norbert Muhlen, "PRESS—An Encyclopedia with Three Deadlines a Day," *The Reporter* (July 23, 1959), pp. 38–9.
[30] Sandford, *op. cit.*, p. 163.
[31] Sandford, *op. cit.*, p. 213.

"All the News
That's Fit to Print"

The New York Times

LATE CITY EDITION

Weather: Partly sunny, cold today; fair, cold tonight. Fair tomorrow. Temperature range: today 17-28; yesterday 21-34. Details, page D18.

VOL.CXXVII..No.43,859   Copyright © 1978 The New York Times   NEW YORK, WEDNESDAY, FEBRUARY 22, 1978   25 cents beyond 50-mile zone from New York City. Higher in air delivery cities.   20 CENTS

BLUMENTHAL PRESSES ALBANY FOR A PLEDGE ON NEW YORK CITY AID

SEEKS A GROWTH COMMITMENT

Goldin Tells a House Banking Panel City May Have to Default in July —P.B.A. Decides to Go It Alone

By STEVEN R. WEISMAN
Special to The New York Times

ALBANY, Feb. 21—Treasury Secretary W. Michael Blumenthal pressed Governor Carey and the legislative leaders today to commit themselves to state aid to New York City that would grow in the years ahead beyond the $200 million they have already agreed upon for next year.

The new request from Mr. Blumenthal was conveyed in a round of private meetings, where it was described as a prerequisite before President Carter could recommend a program of continued Federal financing assistance when the current Federal seasonal-loan program expires June 30.

The request for agreement on "growth" did not meet with any immediate resistance from the Democratic or Republican legislative leaders, but some fiscal aides said they were less than certain that Republicans, in particular, would agree to it without extracting some like commitment for nonurban areas. An aide to the Senate majority leader, Warren M. Anderson, a Republican from Binghamton, said Mr. Anderson wanted to wait before committing himself outright to a "growth" package of aid.

While the Treasury chief was in Albany, New York City's Comptroller, Harrison J. Goldin, was in Washington, where he told a House banking subcommittee that unless Federal assistance was continued, the city would be short $269 million in July and would have to default on its obligations. [Page A16.]

Police to Negotiate Alone

And in New York City itself, the Patrolman's Benevolent Association said it had decided to negotiate alone with the city for a new contract rather than join a coalition of other municipal unions in bargaining. [Page A16.]

At a news conference after his meetings at the Capitol, Mr. Blumenthal would not say that he had asked for a commitment on growth. He said only that he had asked for specific information on New Governor Carey's original proposal for aid to the city would recur in subsequent years. But aides to the legislative leaders who met with the Secretary confirmed that he had asked for the new assurances before he presents his own proposals for New York City next month.

"I was encouraged by the general assurances that I got," Mr. Blumenthal said. "I am encouraged by this visit that there seems to be a great deal of common determination here to really make a concerted effort for New York City. That's a prerequisite before getting anything approved in Congress."

Aides to Mr. Anderson and Assembly Speaker Stanley Steingut, a Brooklyn Democrat, also voiced the feeling that the New York City rescue package seemed to be evolving. They were obviously pleased that Mr. Blumenthal made the unusual choice of traveling to the Capitol to meet with them—aboard a commercial flight.

The leaders had originally planned to

Continued on Page A16, Column 4

Treasury Secretary W. Michael Blumenthal, center, with Governor Carey and Lieut. Gov. Mary Anne Krupsak in Albany   Associated Press

Senate Report Asserts Torrijos Ignored Drug Dealing by Brother

By ADAM CLYMER
Special to The New York Times

WASHINGTON, Feb. 21—A Senate Intelligence Committee report asserted today that Panama's head of Government, Brig. Gen. Omar Torrijos Herrera, was aware of narcotics dealings by his brother and other Government officials but said charges that General Torrijos himself had been involved were "second-hand and of varying reliability."

An edited version of the committee report, with passages deleted, was released by the Senate without a dissenting vote. Meanwhile, the Justice Department made public a three-count Federal indictment accusing Moisés Torrijos Herrera, the General's brother, of smuggling 155 pounds of heroin into the United States in 1971.

The indictment, which was returned May 16, 1972, was ordered unsealed today by Federal District Judge Jack B. Weinstein in New York.

Issue Raised by Treaty Foes

The drug issue, which was debated by the full Senate in closed session today, has been raised by opponents of the proposed Panama Canal treaties, under which control of the Panama Canal would be turned over to Panama in the year 2000. The opponents of the treaties contend that the drug case illustrated the immorality and unreliability of the Torrijos Government, and argue that such a regime will not stand by its commitments.

Charges of narcotics trafficking involving the Panamanian leadership have been circulating for several months, but a number of law enforcement sources have scoffed at the reliability of the accusers. The 20-page committee report, issued without its supporting evidence, neither accuses General Torrijos nor exonerates him of dealing in drugs, but it treats the subject seriously. The report asserts flatly that the narcotics issue did not

Continued on Page A4, Column 3

A School Board Spurns Job Aid Limited to Poor

By ARI L. GOLDMAN

In what some residents are calling a "middle-class revolt," a Queens school district has refused to participate in a Federal jobs program because the program would have benefited only poor children, most of whom are bused into the community, and not its middle-income youngsters.

In a recent 5-to-4 vote, Community School Board 26, whose jurisdiction comprises several affluent communities in eastern Queens, rejected as much as $40,000 in Federal funds that would have created part-time jobs for economically disadvantaged youths. Most of the youngsters who would have been eligible for the program live outside of the district and are now bused in for the purposes of school integration.

The spurning of the Federal aid, believed to be the first such action by a local school board, has created a controversy that has split the School Board 26's district, which takes in the communities of Douglaston, Bayside and Little Neck. The youngsters who are bused in come from low-income areas in St. Albans, Hollis and Queens Village.

The proposed program, under the Federal Youth Employment Act, was to create jobs to clean, maintain and restore Alley Park, 500 acres of woodlands and

Continued on Page B5, Column 5

INSIDE

Soviet Buys More in Germany
West Germany, with the know-how and the goods the Russians want, is now the Soviet Union's biggest capitalist trading partner. Page D1.

Woody Allen Up for 3 Oscars
Woody Allen was nominated for Oscars for acting in, directing and writing "Annie Hall." "Julia" and "The Turning Point" got 11 nominations. Page C15.

CALL THIS TOLL-FREE NUMBER FOR HOME DELIVERY OF THE NEW YORK TIMES. PHONE: 800-631-2500. IN NEW JERSEY: 800-932-0300.—ADVT.

NEW CONGRESSMEN FROM NEW YORK, S. William Green, left, and Robert Garcia, walk to their Capitol offices after swearing-in ceremony. Page B5.   The New York Times/Benson Tuttle

Coal Operators Refuse to Accept Pact as Model

Companies Demanding Binding Arbitration

By BEN A. FRANKLIN
Special to The New York Times

WASHINGTON, Feb. 22—The nation's major coal companies this morning rejected as a model for a strike settlement the contract announced Monday between the United Mine Workers and the Pittsburg and Midway Coal Company, an independent mine operator.

Union officials had hoped that the contract would be a pattern-setting one that would bring about an end to the 79-day miners' strike.

The coal concerns demanded binding arbitration instead, a legislative resolution that President Carter and Congressional leaders have called the least likely formula to resolve the longest strike in American coal labor history.

The rejection after midnight of the Pittsburg and Midway formula was accompanied by a proposal by the Bituminous-Coal Operators Association that the union and the bargaining arm of the major coal concerns resort to binding arbitration of their differences by a three-member board of arbitrators. The association suggested that one be appointed by the union, one by the coal-industry and a third by the Secretary of Labor.

Friday Meeting Proposed

Under the companies' proposal, the arbitrators would convene on Friday and report their findings by March 11. The companies proposed that the 160,000 striking miners return to work while the arbitrators came up with recommendations.

The coal operators' proposal was a hard-line response to efforts by union and Federal mediation officials to present the more liberal Pittsburg and Midway settlement Monday as a model for an industrywide agreement. Kenneth Dawes, the union official chiefly responsible for the separate agreement, said this morning that the major coal operators "can go straight to hell."

The companies' response to hopes yesterday that the separate settlement could serve as a model for an agreement came against an overwhelming reaction from Congress that the Carter Administration could not hope to obtain legislation for mandatory binding arbitration of the coal dispute.

Coal shortages in Ohio, Indiana, Michigan and Pennsylvania, where Gov. Milton J. Shapp asked yesterday for Federal declaration of any energy emergency,

Continued on Page A14, Column 1

HIGH COURT CLEARS WAY FOR OIL DRILLING OFF COAST OF JERSEY

EXPLORATION TO BEGIN SOON

Justices Refuse to Hear Appeals From Long Island Interests on Offshore Leases

By STEVEN RATTNER
Special to The New York Times

WASHINGTON, Feb. 21—The Supreme Court today removed the last legal barrier to exploration for oil and natural gas off the New Jersey coast, clearing the way for drilling to begin within a few weeks.

Although the Federal Government sold exploration rights to the Continental Shelf area along New Jersey and Delaware more

In other actions, the Supreme Court agreed to hear cases on the treatment of pension funds as securities, and on imports based on Japanese television sets, Pages D1 and D9.

than 18 months ago, legal challenges have kept the issue in the courts since then and blocked exploration. In today's decision, the high court refused to hear appeals from Suffolk County, L.I., and a citizens group based in Montauk.

"I am delighted by the decision," said Interior Secretary Cecil D. Andrus. "The requirements that we have in place for maximum oil-spill development of tracts leased in the Baltimore Canyon area will assure a high degree of protection for the coastal region."

Shoreline Protection Promised

In a statement issued this afternoon, Governor Byrne said he had definitely asked that "every effort will be made to protect the New Jersey shoreline."

He added, however, that the Supreme Court's action "gives a greater sense of urgency to the need for passage of Federal Outer Continental Shelf legislation."

The exploration effort would be the first off the East Coast and would likely be followed by similar efforts off Cape Cod and Georgia. Although the oil companies believe that the area is promising, there is no certainty that either gas or oil will be found in quantities large enough for commercial exploitation.

The United States Geological Survey estimates that reserves in the area could total 400 million to 1.4 billion barrels of

Continued on Page A21, Column 1

ETHIOPIA SENDS U.S. PROMISE ON SOMALIA

Pledges Not to Invade—American Envoy May Soon Be Received

By GRAHAM HOVEY
Special to The New York Times

WASHINGTON, Feb. 21—The White House said today that the head of Ethiopia's military Government had sent "personal assurances" to President Carter that Ethiopian forces "would not invade neighboring Somalia nor interfere in the internal affairs of any adjoining countries."

The assurances given by the Ethiopian leader, Lieut. Col. Mengistu Haile Mariam, were conveyed by David L. Aaron, deputy assistant for national security, who headed a special Presidential mission to Addis Ababa over the weekend. Administration officials have expressed concern that if the Ethiopian forces, aided by Cuba and the Soviet Union, succeeded in regaining control of the Ogaden region of eastern Ethiopia, they would invade northern Somalia.

Previously, assurances had been received from the Soviet Union that Somalia would not be invaded.

The White House also said today that the Ethiopian Government had sent word that it would soon agree to receive a new United States ambassador to provide "better channels of communication" between the two countries.

The United States has not had an ambassador in Addis Ababa since Arthur Hummell left in June 1976. However, there is a small Embassy staff there headed by a career diplomat, Richard Mathesron.

Ethiopia had not had an ambassador in Washington for about 30 months when Ayalew Mandefro was named to the post last November. But Mr. Ayalew resigned

Continued on Page A3, Column 1

North Carolina's Leaders Worried By Blemishes on the State's Image

By WAYNE KING
Special to The New York Times

RALEIGH, N.C.—North Carolina, which long prided itself on being the most progressive and enlightened state in the South, now finds itself staggering under the same avalanche of national and international criticism that plunged the racist regimes of the Deep South in the 1950's and 60's.

"Whatever happens to me," said Gov. James B. Hunt Jr. at a news conference recently, "I'm concerned about North Carolina, our image, our good name."

The Governor, elected as a New South liberal, was speaking specifically about notoriety surrounding the case of the so-called Wilmington 10, nine black activists (the 10th has been paroled) who have fired an international furor with their contention that they are political prisoners—railroaded into jail for their civil rights activities.

Amnesty International, the London-based human rights organization that was awarded the 1977 Nobel Peace Prize, has lent its name to their cause, listing them among 18 so-called "prisoners of conscience" incarcerated in the United States.

Added to the list are black activist, convicted of burning a horse stable in 1972, are also on the list, meaning that North Carolina accounts for 11 of the 18 prisoners on Amnesty International's American list.

Other Current Situations

While Governor Hunt is most concerned with the Wilmington case and similar cases on which there has been a possibly more damaging long-term decline in the state's progressive image in the eyes of activists who have viewed it since World War II.

Against that backdrop, there are other, current situations that have, rightly or wrongly, hurt the state's reputation, among them the following:

¶ Joan Little, the young black woman who was acquitted in 1975 in the ice-pick slaying of her jailer in a celebrated case, has fled the North Carolina prison where she was serving a term for burglary and her allegations that she fears for her health and safety if she is extradited from New York have been given wide currency.

¶ The J. P. Stevens Company, the giant textile company that has extensive installations in the state, including seven plants at Roanoke Rapids, has become a symbol of corporate intransigence in

Continued on Page A12, Column 1

Egyptian Says Commandos Struck After 'Unnecessary' Cypriot Delay

By CHRISTOPHER S. WREN
Special to The New York Times

CAIRO, Feb. 21—The commander of the Egyptian commandos force that became involved in a battle with Cypriot troops when it tried to storm a hijacked plane in Cyprus on Sunday said today that he had begun his assault because the negotiations with the hijackers were being "unnecessarily prolonged."

[In Nicosia, the capital of Cyprus, President Spyros Kyprianou urged President Anwar el-Sadat of Egypt to meet with him to try to repair the shattered relations between the two countries resulting from the clash.]

Brig. Gen. Nabil Shukry, who heads Egypt's commando units, said that after his plane landed at the airport at Larnaca he waited for an hour and a half to let Cypriot authorities persuade the two gunmen to release their 12 hostages.

"When I found out that the negotiations were unnecessarily prolonged," General Shukry said, "I decided to go ahead with my orders. My men stormed the Cypriot plane and released the hostages after the gunmen surrendered."

Brig. Gen. Nabil Shukry in Cairo   Associated Press

"If the Cypriot force had not intervened, the rescue attempt could have been fulfilled without any bloodshed," the commando leader said in an Arabic-language interview on Cairo radio and television this evening. The fighting between the two sides cost the Egyptians 15 killed and 17 wounded in a strike force of just over 70 commandos.

The Cypriots have asserted that the

Continued on Page A6, Column 1

tion. *Time* magazine terms it the nation's best newspaper, "though pressed by the Washington *Post*," and calls it "the platinum bar by which editors across the country measure their own papers."[1] Although in recent years it has cut down on full texts of speeches and documents, the *Times* does publish the total transcripts of most presidential press conferences and thus comes closest of all American dailies to being a newspaper of record.[2]

In a nation where no true national daily flourishes, the prestigious *New York Times* comes closest to the claim of being nationally read. A 1963 West Coast edition failed because most American newspaper advertising is local and out-of-state circulation does not seem to attract advertisers. But, despite that and the paper's pre-occupation with the populous metropolitan East Coast, over one-fourth of its readers live more than 100 miles from New York. The *Times* manages to have readers in 10,651 towns in every state and in nearly all countries. Because of its thoroughness, it is highly respected in the nation's colleges and universities, found in practically every academic library and widely read by college presidents, professors and students. Its thick Sunday edition (circulation, 1.46 million) sometimes containing 400 pages and weighing four pounds, finds its way into pace-setting homes across the face of the nation, with at least one-third of the copies going outside New York City. Many of the paper's readers are influential; for example, President Jimmy Carter carefully reads one of the 86 copies which reach the White House each day.[3] Nor does the *Times* influence end at the nation's borders; its prestigious leadership audience around the world has long helped to make it not only a great American daily, but also a key member of the world's elite press.

Much of the *Times'* prestige rests on its excellent in-depth coverage—the best in the nation—of national and international issues and political events. For an important event, its accurate and comprehensive coverage may extend to several pages, include all the main texts and offer numerous sidebar stories. The *Times'* long-established policy of actively encouraging probing reporters and investigative digging leads to such thoroughness. The paper takes itself seriously and has a right to the pride, almost arrogance, it sometimes exhibits.

Reportage of the international scene has always been one of the *Times'* strongest suits. Already in the early 1920's, publisher Adolph Ochs determined to make his paper's foreign coverage the world's best. By 1924, the *Times* was carrying so much foreign news that its own radio station began to receive press messages direct, first from Europe and shortly thereafter from other parts of the world.[4] However, some feel such accolades are unjustified. One journalism critic has called the paper's foreign coverage "over-rated" and scores its writing, accuracy and objectivity in reporting foreign affairs.[5] But Ochs' successors have continued to press towards his goal until today many experts consider the *Times* foreign coverage unrivalled.

[1] "The Kingdom and the Cabbage," *Time* (August 15, 1977), p. 73.
[2] *Ibid.*
[3] "The Kingdom and the Cabbage," *op. cit.*, p. 73.
[4] John Hohenberg, *Foreign Correspondence: The Great Reporters and Their Times* (New York: Columbia University Press, 1964), p. 267.
[5] George Lichtheim, "Reflections on the *New York Times*," *Commentary* (September, 1965), p. 33.

The excellence of the *Times* international coverage must not, in fact, be put down. Press critic John Lofton, appraising the paper's 1963 coverage of the Berlin crisis noted that it stood alone among American papers in its attempts to put the situation in perspective by reporting "events suggesting the possibility of negotiation" and "diplomatic efforts to avert a military clash."[6] A. T. Steele, in his 1966 book on China, called the paper's coverage of that country "pre-eminent in the field."[7] The paper's list of outstanding overseas correspondents is lengthy, and includes, to mention a few, such prominent journalistic names as Max Frankel, Harrison Salisbury, A. M. Rosenthal, C. L. Sulzberger, Clifton Daniel, Arnaldo Cortesi, Walter Duranty, Seymour Topping, Hedrick Smith, Clarence Streit, Wickham Steed, Frank Kluckhohn, Wythe Williams, George Barrett, Herbert Matthews, Henry Lieberman and Tad Szulc.[8] David Halberstam received a Pulitzer Prize for his Vietnam coverage in 1964 and Sydney Schanberg's reports from Cambodia won a Pulitzer in 1976. *Time* editors believe James Markham should have gotten yet another Pulitzer for his recent reporting on war-torn Beirut.[9]

The quality and completeness of the *Times'* international coverage is directly traceable to eyewitness reporting by its large foreign staff. Thirty-two full-time correspondents work out of 23 bureaus located in the world's strategic centers and another 25 part-timers complete the paper's world-wide coverage network. In addition, the *New York Times* may be the only newspaper to take all five major international wire services—AP, UPI, Reuters, TASS and AFP.[10]

Although the arch-rival Washington *Post* has outshone the *Times* in thorough coverage of Washington politics on several occasions in recent years, generally speaking the *Times* still has better total national coverage. During the 1940's and 1950's under Arthur Krock and in the 1950's and 1960's under James Reston, the *Times* coverage of Washington excelled. It was also the first paper to start publishing the Pentagon Papers. Later, the *Post*'s revelations of government tricks began to scoop the *Times*. In the past few years, the tables have begun to turn again as the *Times* beat the *Post* on investigations of Central Intelligence Agency drug experimentation and domestic spying, revelations that led to the appointment of the Rockefeller Commission on the CIA. The *Times* keeps 20 reporters at the national capital, considerably less than the *Post*'s 33.

Despite its comprehensive reportage of national and international news, the *Times* remains a paper rooted in New York. The news of the city, its boroughs and the peri-urban vicinity often gets as much prominence as national and international developments, and certainly more emphasis than news from the rest of the nation, except Washington. Recently, insiders even claimed the paper gave more attention to Manhattan than the city's four other boroughs, support-

[6] John Lofton, "The Press Manages the News," *Progressive* (June, 1963), p. 18.
[7] A. T. Steele, The American People and China (New York: McGraw-Hill, 1966), p. 143.
[8] Franklin Whitehouse, Corporate Communications Department, The New York Times Company, in answer to questionnaire, February 17, 1978.
[9] "The Kingdom and the Cabbage," *op. cit.,* p. 74.
[10] *Times* bureaus are located in Athens, Bangkok, Beirut, Belgrade, Bonn, Buenos Aires, Cairo, Hong Kong, Jerusalem, Johannesburg, London, Madrid, Montreal, Moscow, Nairobi, New Delhi, Ottawa, Paris, Rio de Janeiro, Rome, Tokyo, Vienna and the United Nations.

ing their arguments with the observation that the *Times* keeps just one reporter among Queens' two million inhabitants and none among the Bronx's one and one-half million. However, since Sydney Schanberg has taken over as metropolitan editor, the *Times'* local coverage has improved and increased. One source sums up the paper's local accent with the conclusion: "The *New York Times* is first and foremost a paper for New Yorkers."[11]

The *New York Times* got its start towards greatness on September 18, 1851, after journalist Henry J. Raymond, a Republican politician, and two financiers, George Jones and Edward Wesley, saw the need for another inexpensive newspaper for the city's populace, which then numbered only a half-million. At first, the *Times* was a rather crudely printed four-page broadsheet paper selling at one cent a copy. But Raymond as editor and Jones as business manager edited it well, packed its front page with foreign and local news and soon improved its technical production quality. Circulation expenses forced the paper to increase its subscription price to two cents after a year. According to journalism historian Frank Luther Mott, the *Times* may be considered the "culmination and highest achievement" of the inexpensive newspaper movement which began with the New York *Sun* and other papers in the early 1830's.[12] From the first, editor Raymond determined to make his paper appeal to a highly intelligent audience, one which would, like Greeley's *Tribune*, take a high moral tone. But, as the late Dr. Mott has said, the *Times*, in addition to its moral tone and conservatism, was predominantly a *news*-paper, presenting the reader a well-balanced and heavy diet of news—especially foreign news.[13] Thus, Raymond set the basic pattern for the *Times* to follow throughout its history.

The paper went through a period of decline between 1884 and 1896, mostly because Joseph Pulitzer had brought techniques to newspapering which made the *Times* appear stodgy and old-fashioned. Editor Raymond had died in 1869, and his successors were unable to fight successfully the forces which were undermining the *Times*. In spite of the paper's general quality and high moral standards, it has fallen into bad financial straits. Jones died in 1891, and Charles Miller and associates bought the paper from the Jones family in 1893. But the new owners were unable to stem the paper's financial slide. By 1896, the *Times* was losing at least a thousand dollars a week, staff morale was low, and closedown seemed certain unless a rejuvenation took place. Circulation had dropped to a mere 9,000, far below the morning New York *Journal's* 300,000.[14]

Then, out of the Tennessee hills came Adolph Simon Ochs, not yet 40, to set in motion the greatest newspaper miracle the country had seen as he brought new life to the faltering *Times*. Ochas realized he was taking on a stupendous task, for he wrote his wife in March, 1896, "Here I am in New York ready to negotiate for the leading and most influential newspaper in America— the supreme gall of a country newspaperman burdened with debt."[15] But Ochs

---

[11] "World Press: The *New York Times*," Dispatch of the London *Times* (October, 1975).
[12] F. L. Mott, *American Journalism, 1690–1960* (New York: Macmillan, 1962), p. 280.
[13] *Ibid.*
[14] Roger Kahn, "The House of Adolph Ochs," *The Saturday Evening Post* (October 9, 1965), p. 47.
[15] *Ibid.*

had exactly what the paper needed: an intuitive business sense, faith, and imagination. While retaining the *Times'* emphasis on sobriety and reliability, Ochs went even further than in the past to stress news. He eliminated the short fiction stories, comic strips and gossip columns the paper had been carrying, increased business news significantly, and started a weekly book section. He instituted a Sunday magazine and chose the slogan—"All the News That's Fit to Print"—still used by the paper. By 1898, when he had brought circulation back to 25,000, he had cut the price of the paper from three cents to a penny. Within three years, the *Times* was back on a firm financial footing with a circulation of 102,000.

One of Ochs' best journalistic moves was to hire sharp-minded Carr Van Anda from the *Sun* to be his managing editor. Van Anda quickly established the principle of sparing no expense to get and print the news—a goal that has endured to the present. Like Ochs, Van Anda believed in "hard" news, thoroughly and accurately presented. A tireless worker, he often stayed in the office all night, and he was present when, at 1:20 A.M. on April 15, 1912, the first garbled message that the *Titanic* had hit an iceberg and might be sinking came in. Van Anda deduced that the *Titanic* had sunk, went all out on his hunch and reported the sinking in every possible respect, even though the ship's owners did not confirm that the ship had actually gone down until the evening of the 16th of April. Although publishing the story involved great risk on Van Anda's part and his "deductive journalism" may have shocked many, it remains as one of the great against-a-deadline news coverage feats in all journalism.

During World War I, the *Times* excelled in depth news coverage. It printed a full eight-page text of the Versailles Treaty. It maintained its tradition of thorough coverage throughout the 'twenties and 'thirties, presenting long, accurate stories, many of which other papers either ignored or merely summarized. When, in 1935, Ochs died of a cerebral hemorrhage, his son-in-law, Arthur Hays Sulzberger took over as publisher until he became the New York Times Company's board chairman in 1961. Sulzberger was followed by another son-in-law, Orvil Dryfoos, who died unexpectedly in 1963. In his short span as publisher, Dryfoos faced two crises. His 1962 West Coast edition failed and later that year the *Times* was hit by a 114-day strike of printing unions that left the paper's staff demoralized.

Then Arthur Hays Sulzberger's son, Arthur Ochs Sulzberger (or "Punch" as he is widely called), when he was just 37 years old, became the youngest publisher the *Times* ever had. "Punch" has made many changes in the newspaper, not all of them popular with his key staff members. He shifted top executives and their job titles around. He brought up from the ranks men and women whose names have since become a trademark synonymous with the greatness of the *Times:* the late Lester Markel from Sunday editorship and James ("Scotty") Reston from the Washington bureau to associate editorships, and Harrison Salisbury from a distinguished foreign correspondent role to become "national editor," a post now held by David Jones. Clifton Daniel was made managing editor until he retired in 1977, when Seymour Topping, also a famous foreign correspondent, took that position. Tom Wicker moved first to the position of Washington bureau chief and is now an associate editor and columnist. "Punch" Sulzberger made most of these changes between 1962 and 1964.[16] Today, Sulzberger's executive editor is A. M. Rosenthal, his managing editor Seymour Topping and his editorial page editor Max Frankel.[17]

As publisher of the *Times* and chairman and president of its parent organization, the New York Times Company, "Punch" Sulzberger keeps a watchful, benevolent, yet disciplinary fatherly eye on the *Times*. Late each night, he studies the early morning city edition for the next day, making notes and clipping items that will help him improve his paper. A neat, orderly person, "Punch" appears to have fun being publisher. He sometimes writes letters to the *Times* under a pseudonym. He tackles tasks with enthusiasm—and a smile. His attitude towards his work and position is well summed up in his observation: "The idea that a publisher sits up here and issues directives, wields great power and smites people to their knees is a lot of baloney. But it's a lot of fun. It's the best job in the world."[18]

Sulzberger keeps his paper great by encouraging dynamism, change and improvement. Under him, the *Times* has undergone a number of marked innovations in style, content and technical developments, especially in the past three years.

In response to a dropoff in the number of people who buy newspapers daily, the levelling off of population growth in the country and research indicating people want a paper that is useful for more than just the news, the *Times* has, since 1976, been introducing special insert sections for different days of the week. In April, 1976, it added "Weekend," a Friday guide for leisure and cultural activities around New York. "Weekend" was so successful that seven months later the paper added "Living," a 20-page insert on Wednesdays, and then "Home" on Thursdays. "Living" is packed with enthusiastic articles on food, the culinary arts and gourmet eating, with ads to match. "Home" deals with interior decoration and gardening. In January, 1978, the *Times* started a flashy "Sports Monday" section. Late in 1978, the paper added a fifth section on Tuesdays to cover science, education and medicine news. These new sections have already changed and moved the *Times* forward. The paper has developed a new advertising slogan, "More than Just the News." The new additions have turned the *Times* into a four-section paper. Circulation surged in 16 months from 821,000 to 854,000 daily and approximately 35,000 more people buy the paper on days it contains a special section.[19]

Improvement has not ended with the addition of these new sections. Beginning on May 17, 1978, the *Times* began publishing "Business Day," which is "a new, expanded and redesigned business, financial and economic section,"[20] made necessary by the introduction of the other new sections to fill

[16] See Gay Talese, "The Kingdoms, the Powers and the Glories of the *New York Times*," *Esquire* (November, 1966), pp. 91ff. for an excellent description of the *Times* and its personalities.
[17] Whitehouse questionnaire.
[18] "The Private Life of A. Sock," *Time* (August 15, 1977), pp. 78–9.
[19] "Newspapers' New Lifestyle," *Media Decisions* (April, 1978), p. 71, and "The Kingdom and the Cabbage," *op. cit.*, p. 73.
[20] "The *Times* to Publish 'Business Day,' a New Section, Starting May 17," *New York Times* (April 14, 1978).

out a four-section paper. "Business Day" (published daily except Saturdays) gives full coverage of business and financial news and related feature material, a daily business news summary, increased coverage of the communications industry (now the nation's largest), investment and banking interests and especially the fashion and apparel trades, of which New York City is the capital. *Times'* executive editor A. M. Rosenthal says readers are, in effect, now getting three publications each day, "a newspaper with the country's most complete coverage of national, international, cultural, sports and other news. . . . 'magazines within a newspaper' (in the recently developed special sections). . . . And the new, comprehensive 'Business Day'."[21]

Another Sulzberger-inspired innovation took place on September 6, 1976, when the *Times* switched from an eight-column-per-page format to one of six columns for news and nine for advertisements. The change has increased advertising space without seriously affecting "news hole"-to-ad ratio (which stands at 70 percent advertisements, 30 percent news), and has resulted in improved makeup and a more readable product. But, as some critics note, "often the choice and play of pictures leaves much to be desired," and much of the paper's news writing remains "stilted, wordy and dull," although, of late, some reporters and feature writers are bringing a refreshing vigor to the paper's pages.

Even the usually-predictable editor and op-ed pages have been changed and brightened. The former editorial page editor, John Oakes was made senior editor in 1976, and Max Frankel, who had moved previously from the Washington bureau chief post to that of Sunday editor, took Oakes' place. Frankel has initiated a number of features, among them "Topics," a collection of brief, bright commentaries, which have expanded the paper's range of subject matter and have made its opinion pieces more punchy.[22] Other improvements include "Editorial Notebook" (often made up of anonymous articles by the editorial board), freer interchange between letter writers and editorial writers, and occasional use of illustrations in the editorial columns. Frankel believes it is "the duty of the editorial page to help the reader fairly analyze public controversy, even if the reader's conclusion may differ from that of the editorial."[23] In 1977, the editorial page received 57,128 letters.

Change has also extended to the *Sunday Times*. Since 1976, the well-known *Sunday Times Magazine* has been "printed on premium-grade paper, providing advertisers with superior color reproduction and readers with a more attractive product."[24] The *Magazine* section got a new editor in 1976 in the person of Edward Klein, a former assistant managing editor of *Newsweek*. In April, 1977, the *Sunday Times* introduced a newly-renovated "Book Review."[25]

For all these changes, executive editor A. M. Rosenthal has been hyping up his editorial staff. To do so, he has installed energetic, loyal and experienced younger-middle-aged personnel into his key editorial positions, among them Hedrick Smith, Sydney Schanberg, Robert Semple, Allan Siegal and Terrence

[21] *Ibid.*
[22] "The Kingdom and the Cabbage," *op. cit.,* p. 74.
[23] Whitehouse questionnaire.
[24] "Year of Change and Growth," 1976 Report, The New York Times Company, p. 26.
[25] *Ibid.*

Smith. He has ended the paper's newsroom seniority system and has improved working relations by re-organizing the newsroom. In 1976, the daily and Sunday news staffs were merged under a single editorial management team. While Rosenthal rules his stable of over 400 writers and reporters (there are 485 in all when overseas correspondents and Washington reporters are included) in the *Times'* 1.3 acre newsroom with a firm, but fatherly hand, congratulating reporters for a good job and railing at them for failures; he allows them increased writing freedom whenever they demonstrate creativity with words like, "If you're half-way talented, we practically kiss your feet. You can do anything you want."[26] In recent years, Rosenthal has gradually been shifting away from emphasis on fast-breaking stories to more thoughtful, descriptive articles on social trends, controversies, new ideas and white collar crime.

Simultaneous with its makeup and content changes, the *Times* has been improving its production facilities. As of the end of 1978, it planned to have about 180 video display terminals in place in the newsroom for writing and editing, with an all-electronic newsroom soon to come. The mode of composition is in process of being switched from hot metal to photo-composition. In October, 1976, a new offset printing and distribution plant was opened at Carlstadt, New Jersey. Laser scanning and microwave transmission of page images are also due for early installation.[27]

The *New York Times* is published by the New York Times Company, a corporation which controls nine smaller dailies and four weeklies in North Carolina and Florida, six magazines, two broadcasting stations (WREC-TV in Memphis and WQXR-AM/FM in New York City), three book publishers (Arno Press, Cambridge Book Company and New York Times Book Company), and part of three Canadian paper mills. It also operates the New York Times News Service, the Information Bank, and enjoys part-ownership of the *International Herald Tribune* (with the Washington Post Company and Whitney Communications Corporation), published in Paris. Until 1978, the Company had regularly been achieving a steady, strong improvement in earnings each year. In recent years, the *Times* has been one of few New York papers to show a profit, and at times it has been the only city paper to report an increase in circulation. The 1976 Report of the Company, after indicating the paper had earned 64 cents a share in 1976 as compared with only 29 cents in 1975, modestly indicated the *Times* "appears to be meeting with success."[28]

A 1978 strike by the Pressman's Union closed down the *New York Times* and its rival, the *Daily News*, for 88 days (The *Post* was closed down for a shorter period because its owner, Rupert Murdock made a separate agreement with the pressmen). The strike, which began on August 9th, was partially a result of the newspapers' moves to modernize; the pressmen feared loss of their jobs and wanted security as well as a raise in pay. The strike was settled when the 1,508 printing pressmen were all guaranteed lifetime jobs, with the number

---

[26] "The Kingdom and the Cabbage," *op. cit.*, p. 80.
[27] Whitehouse questionnaire.
[28] "Year of Change and Growth," *op. cit.*, p. 3.

of job roles gradually being reduced through retirements, other attrition and publishers' incentives.

The strike already has proven costly to the papers, their staffs and readers. The strike cost the papers an estimated $150 million in lost advertising and circulation revenues and the 10,000 employees of the *Times* and the *Daily News* some $60 million in lost wages. The toll of the strike on readers, on the cultural and entertainment life of the city and on business is considerably harder to estimate. Some former readers may have shifted their media loyalties away from newspapers never to return, as happened after the 114-day strike in 1962–3, when some 400,000 New Yorkers lost the newspaper habit.[29] During 1978, the *Times* suffered several heavy losses that are certain to affect its fiscal balances— the costly 88-day strike, a $350,000 settlement for female employees claiming sex discrimination and heavy $5000-a-day fines during the period its reporter, Myron Farber, was jailed for refusing to surrender his files on a New Jersey murder case.

One measure of a paper's greatness is the degree of recognition given it by fellow professionals. That measure, in the case of the *New York Times,* would place it above all other newspapers, certainly in the United States. Altogether, as of early 1978, the *Times* and its writers had won 42 coveted Pulitzer Prizes, more than any other newspaper. Individual Pulitzers went to Sydney Schanberg and Red Smith in 1976, to Hedrick Smith in 1974, to Max Frankel in 1973, to Harold Schonberg in 1971, to Ada Huxtable in 1970, to J. Anthony Lukas in 1968, to David Halberstam in 1964 and to Anthony Lewis in 1963. Among Pulitzers the paper as an entity has received is the one it won in 1972 for its work on the Pentagon Papers.[30]

The *Times'* list of distinguishing marks that make it special goes on and on. The sheer volume of words and information it processes daily staggers the imagination. From nearly two million words that flow into its newsroom daily from an amazing range of sources, the paper's staff culls and writes 70 pages—some 152,000 words—of information, enough that publisher Sulzberger once remarked: "Anybody who claims to read the entire paper every day is either the world's fastest reader or the world's biggest liar."[31] The writing and production effort of the *Times* comes from a highly qualified staff; most (but not all) reporters and editors have had experience on other papers and hold baccalaureate degrees or higher.[32] Since even the *Times* cannot keep a reporter on the spot everywhere, the paper employs a staff or nearly two dozen regional reporters who send in their stories from all over the country. It continues to upgrade investigative reporting by keeping such reporters in many fields—politics to finance to general assignment—and by not insisting they produce a story every day.[33] Although in the past it has editorially supported eight Democrats and four Repub-

[29] "Ready to Roll," *Time* (November 13, 1978), pp. 62–7 and "New York Feasts on its Newspapers," *Christian Science Monitor* (November 7, 1978), p. 4.
[30] Whitehouse questionnaire.
[31] "The Kingdom and the Cabbage," *op. cit.,* p. 73.
[32] Whitehouse questionnaire.
[33] *Ibid.*

licans for President, it maintains political independence. In all its writing and reporting, it excels in accuracy and comprehensiveness, even, sometimes, to the detriment of easy readability.

While most commentators speak of the *Times'* size, thoroughness and complete coverage, there is no doubt that the general quality of its journalism ranks with the world's best. While it is not as careful in its typography as *Pravda,* not as unpretentiously interesting in its prose as the London *Times,* not as well documented as *Le Monde* and not as scholarly and serious as Switzerland's *Neue Zürcher Zeitung* or West Germany's *Frankfurter Allgemeine,* it does go further in combining the worthy characteristics of all these great papers than any other daily.

The *Times* as a newspaper defies classification; it forms a kind of composite of the best in all journalism. Consequently, even though it aims primarily at "upscale readers in educational attainments, income and employment,"[34] there is material for all audiences. If one were forced to characterize the *Times* in a single word, one would probably have to say "thoroughness." Of the thoroughness of the *Times,* Robert Natson of the Portland *Oregonian* once said, "The *New York Times* is unique in its field. Both in completeness and authority it sets a high standard. Newspaper editors, as well as other readers, find in it a great resource. As nearly as a newspaper can be, it is a history of one day in the world of events."[35] But the paper's thoroughness is merely a wavecap in a sea of outstanding characteristics that make the *Times* one of the world's finest newspapers. In the innovative changes it has made recently and in publisher Sulzberger's plans for still further improvements, it is obvious the *New York Times* intends to stay at or near the top of the list of the world's greatest elite dailies.

L'Osservatore Romano

(THE VATICAN)

THE VATICAN's *L'Osservatore Romano* (The Roman Observer) rivals the influence of Milan's prestigious *Corriere della Sera.* Yet the two are about as different as two papers could be. *L'Osservatore* gains its influence because it represents, at least semi-officially, the voice of the Pope. It brings a special perspective to news events because it sees them not in terms of deadlines, but through the perspective of the history of the Christian Church. Thus, even

---

[34] Whitehouse questionnaire, *loc. cit.*
[35] *Editor and Publisher* (May 29, 1965), p. 8.

L'OSSERVATORE ROMANO

GIORNALE QUOTIDIANO ✠ POLITICO RELIGIOSO

UNICUIQUE SUUM — NON PRAEVALEBUNT

Anno CXVIII · N. 43 (35.726) — CITTÀ DEL VATICANO — Mercoledì 22 Febbraio 1978 ✱

Kyprianu auspica un incontro con il Presidente dell'Egitto

Il Governo del Cairo ha disposto il richiamo da Nicosia della propria rappresentanza diplomatica - Il ritorno in patria del commando egiziano

IL CAIRO, 21.

Risposta negativa di Mosca agli appelli per Belgrado

Erano stati formulati dai Presidenti della Jugoslavia e della Francia, al fine di superare le difficoltà per la redazione del documento finale della conferenza europea

BELGRADO, 21.

Colloqui a Londra tra Owen e Sithole

LONDRA, 21.

Accordo fra l'Argentina e il Cile sulla vertenza del Canale di Beagle

E' stato firmato dai Presidenti delle due Nazioni

BUENOS AIRES, 21.

Il Ministro della difesa cecoslovacco a Mosca

PRAGA, 21.

Khaled invita i Paesi arabi a fornire aiuti alla Somalia

Il Sovrano saudita ha inoltrato la richiesta per il tramite della Lega araba - Un'iniziativa di Nimeiry

IL CAIRO, 21.

Nimeiry a Riad

RIAD, 21.

Elezioni generali domenica in Colombia

BOGOTÀ, 21.

Colloqui tra Brezhnev e Assad

MOSCA, 21.

Inizio in Australia della nuova legislatura

SYDNEY, 21.

Ondate di maltempo in Romania e Germania

BUCAREST, 21.

UN ALTRO ATTACCO ALLA LIBERTA' DI STAMPA

Un attentato al «Gazzettino» di Venezia ha provocato la morte di una guardia giurata

L'azione terroristica è stata rivendicata da « Ordine nuovo » - Primi sviluppi delle indagini

VENEZIA, 21.

Commenti della stampa internazionale

LONDRA, 21.

La situazione economica europea esaminata dai Ministri della CEE

Sono stati riscontrati progressi nella lotta all'inflazione, mentre rimane insufficiente il tasso di crescita dell'economia comunitaria

BRUXELLES, 21.

La strategia militare americana nel Golfo Persico e nel Pacifico

Il Segretario alla difesa Brown considera vitale la salvaguardia delle fonti e delle rotte petrolifere - Esclusa la possibilità di un conflitto terrestre con la Cina

WASHINGTON, 21.

La ripresa della missione di Atherton

TEL AVIV, 21.

«Libro bianco» britannico sui problemi della difesa

Aumento in termini solo monetari degli stanziamenti - Allarme per il crescente rafforzamento del Patto di Varsavia

LONDRA, 21.

though its small circulation has been shrinking, *L'Osservatore* carries national and international influence disproportionate to its size.

Observers disagree about *L'Osservatore*'s status with the Vatican. It was founded, say some, as the official Vatican organ in 1861.[1] But others think it is "unofficial," and the paper calls itself "unofficial." However, there is no doubt it reflects the Pope's thinking. One of Italy's leading journalism historians, Ignazio Weiss considers it an official journal in all articles pertaining to the Vatican and unofficial in the remainder of its contents. A 1975 official publication of the Vatican declares the paper's primary goal is to give "faithful reflection of the thought of the Pope."[2] But the same publication notes that *L'Osservatore* is also concerned with political, social and cultural matters and notes that it continually strives to promote truth, justice, true liberty, honest teaching and human dignity. Actually, the Vatican has an official paper called *Acta Sedis Apostolicae* (Acts of the Apostolic See), a kind of papal counterpart to the United States' *Congressional Record*. Although many have tried to classify *L'Osservatore*'s resultant status by appellations such as "the Vatican newspaper," "the Pope's own paper" and an "official unofficial paper," perhaps the best designation is "semi-official," or that of the Italians themselves, "the paper of the Pope."

L'Osservatore's editor until recently, Raimundo Manzini did not think of his paper as an official voice of the Pope. Instead, with the exception of the daily column "Nostre Informazioni" (Our News), which listed papal audiences, major nominations and appointments, Manzini perceived it to have reporting and opinion functions. On the other hand, Count Giuseppe Dalla Torre, who preceded Manzini as editor, regarded it as official: "a Catholic newspaper in which the Holy See publishes its official bulletins. Nothing else."[3] Since Catholics are not required to accept its views and the argument about *L'Osservatore* status can never be neatly resolved, it is sufficient to say it is "the paper of the Vatican" and the most reliable means of ascertaining the thinking of those closest to the Pope.

In 1861, the Church was being pressured by anti-clericals to give up Papal lands to the new Italian state. Pope Pius IX desired a literary voice to aid the Vatican cause in this struggle. In Romagna, two Catholic zealots, one a lawyer and the other a journalist, had been in conflict with the Piedmontese authorities who had replaced papal rule there. Consequently, the Pope was easily persuaded to let Nicola Zanchini and Giuseppe Bastia found *L'Osservatore Romano* and to name them the paper's first directors. It was then, as now, to be a political-religious newspaper. The name *L'Osservatore Romano* was taken over from a newspaper which had ceased publication some ten years earlier. The purpose of the new paper was to

> . . . refute the calumnies being launched against Rome and the Roman Pontificate, to record everything worthy of note that happened during the day in Rome,

[1] Kenneth E. Olson, *The History Makers: The Press of Europe from Its Beginnings through 1965* (Baton Rouge: Louisiana State University Press, 1966), p. 236.

[2] "L'Osservatore Romano," in *Vaticano E Roma Cristiana* (Vatican City: Tipografia Poliglotta Vaticana, 1975), p. 365. The authors are grateful to Father James Trautwein, Vicar, St. John's Episcopal Church, Bowling Green, Ohio, for his translation of this work.

[3] *America* (July 27, 1961), p. 541.

to recall the unshaken principles that are the basis of Catholicism, to instruct in the duties the people have toward their country and to urge and promote the reverence owed to the Pontiff and Ruler.[4]

The official backing of the paper was kept secret, the reason perhaps being to keep the paper free from censorship of the Vatican itself or to give the Vatican a voice without Vatican officials knowing it was a voice.[5] The two editors were given as much freedom as possible by the government and by the Church, which at this time were almost one and the same. Although the Vatican officially owned the paper, it was necessary to disguise ownership by allowing it to remain with the Ministry of the Interior. The editors were, in effect, subsidized.

Before long, *L'Osservatore Romano,* still in the hands of private individuals faithful and devoted to the Pope, faced economic difficulties. It was restored to economic health after Augusto di Baviera, secretary of the papal editorial staff, became editor. After 1840, the paper was the only journal in the hands of the Holy See. In 1890, Pope Leo XIII bought *L'Osservatore,* paying off all mortgages and other debts. The Pope appointed Giambattista Casoni, a zealous Catholic as editor, and a new relationship of the paper to the Holy See began. Casoni described it this way: "The Pope said to me: 'Everybody has his paper, the Holy See must also have its own. I have called upon you to take the direction of the paper. . . . Be independent of everybody; you are answerable only to me and my secretary of state.'"[6] Casoni and his successors considered it their role to defend the Papacy, to expound the Roman solution to problems and to be faithful chroniclers of major events. They saw themselves as liberal protagonists of the Holy See in doctrinal and social affairs, often called upon to take a balancing position between Church and State.[7]

During World War I and immediately after, *L'Osservatore* echoed Papal views in the preparation of the Concordat (the Lateran Pact whereby Vatican City was set up as an independent state). In 1929, after the Pact was signed, the paper was moved from its quarters in Rome to a new printing plant within Vatican City. The move was designed to keep the paper safe from ever more destructive and vicious groups of Fascists and to make it more directly responsible to the Pope. Although it was still regarded as the official voice of the Vatican to the outside, the paper became less combative in the area of politics and more concerned with religion and defense of the Church's rights.[8]

However, *L'Osservatore* was far from silent on political matters. As the only Italian paper operating with substantial freedom from Fascist control, it became a window for Italians to judge the gains and designs of Fascists' moves everywhere. *L'Osservatore* condemned the invasion of Finland by Russia as an act of wanton aggression and a warning to all the world that Soviet expansionist plans

[4] Andrea Lazzarini, *L'Osservatore Romano,* centennial edition, (July 1, 1961), p. 7. See also: Lazzarini, "The True Story and the Origin of 'L'Osservatore Romano'," *Catholic Press Annual* (1962), p. 12.

[5] *Ibid.*

[6] George Seldes, *The Vatican: Yesterday, Today and Tomorrow* (New York: Harper and Row, 1934), p. 242.

[7] "L'Osservatore Romano," *op. cit.,* p. 367.

[8] "Newspapers of the World—VII," London *Times* (March 4, 1965).

were being unmasked. Its warnings of the implications of German invasion of Poland without declaring war were not nearly as forceful, but the event was reported with a note of sadness even though the editors were aware even this would antagonize Mussolini and his friend Hitler.[9]

A clash between the *L'Osservatore* and the Fascists was bound to occur since Mussolini's party increasingly attacked the Church and advocated social changes which the Vatican newspaper could not permit to pass unchallenged. Leader in the paper's running fight with the Fascists was Count Giuseppe Dalla Torre, probably the most famous of the nine men who have edited the *L'Osservatore*. Dalla Torre had joined the paper as a fiery young Catholic journalist from Padua, and it ended in 1960 when he retired at the age of 75 with the title of director emeritus. He died in October, 1967. Dalla Torre was a persistent thorn in Mussolini's side, and never permitted the paper to refer to him as "Il Duce." The paper was constantly harassed by the Fascists and Dalla Torre was threatened with arrest for lack of cooperation; the editor boldly answered by referring to Hitler as an "antichrist."[10]

When Hitler came to Rome in May, 1938, Pius XI left his summer residence at Castel Gandolfo to avoid contact with him. *L'Osservatore*'s typical between-the-lines comment was that the Pope preferred the air of Castel Gandolfo to that of Rome. The paper then proceeded to completely ignore Hitler's visit. It was in 1939, the year the former Cardinal Pacelli became Pope Pius XII, that the Fascists began beating newspaper delivery men in the streets of Rome. Priests found reading the paper were also beaten, and newspaper sales in the streets were prohibited at the beginning of 1940. When Italy entered the war in June, 1940, the mailing of the Vatican paper was halted for three months. An announcement appeared in the paper saying that it would halt publication. For some reason, the beatings stopped and mailed copies began getting through; the paper never really missed publication.[11]

During the course of the Second World War the Vatican paper was the only daily which printed a daily column impartially reporting war news. The circulation zoomed to some 350,000 as Italians were eager to read Allied communiques. *L'Osservatore* became Mussolini's greatest irritant within Italy. Dalla Torre was once waylaid outside St. Peter's by Fascists and barely escaped injury. For weeks thereafter he made his way home through a route entirely inside the 108-acre Vatican State. When Rome was liberated by Allied armies toward the end of the war, *L'Osservatore Romano* carried the news on the last page, while headlining a religious ceremony on page one. A writer on Vatican affairs explained: "I don't think the editor . . . intended to snub the conquerors of Rome. It was just his tactful way of reminding his readers that wars are won and lost, empires crumble, regimes rise and fall, but the Church goes on forever because her power is spiritual and not material."[12] In all the crises of the two

[9] Denis Gwynn, *The Vatican and the War in Europe* (London: Burns, Oates & Washbourne, Ltd., 1940), p. 204.

[10] *Time* (April 18, 1960), p. 98.

[11] Don Sharkey, *White Smoke Over the Vatican* (Milwaukee: Bureau Publishing Company, 1943), p. 105.

[12] Irving R. Levine, *Main Street, Italy* (New York: Doubleday, 1963), p. 360.

world wars and subsequent rebuilding of the society, the paper stood firmly for justice, concord and peace and against Fascism, Socialism and Communism.

In 1960, after he had served *L'Osservatore* 40 years and seven years before his death, Dalla Torre retired at the age of 75 with the title of director emeritus. His place was taken by Raimondo Manzini, who had edited Bologna's influential Catholic daily, *L'Avvenire* for 30 years. Upon becoming *L'Osservatore*'s editor, Manzini said, "I don't want this to be a paper read only by priests, a sort of bulletin of the Holy See."[13] He immediately improved the paper's layout, ran livelier pictures, added new general interest features and otherwise made it a more readable product. During his eight-year stay at *L'Osservatore,* Manzini more than doubled the staff and placed correspondents in many regions of Italy. Although the paper has no official full-time overseas correspondents, Manzini encouraged leading ecclesiastics, friends and admirers to serve as stringers in foreign capitals and, in general, tried to increase the paper's foreign coverage.[14] Among those overseas correspondents who served in an outstanding manner were names such as Guitton, Maritain, Ratzinger, Waldheim, Emmanuel, Congar, Del Noce, Mohrmann and DeLubac. On January 6, 1978, Valerio Volpini, a professor, writer and married layman with a family of three children became *L'Osservatore*'s new editor-in-chief.[15]

Volpini is *L'Osservatore*'s eighth director (as its editors-in-chief are called). Those who preceded him were: Zanchini and Bastia, 1861–1866; Augusto Baviera, 1866–1884; Cesare Crispolti, 1884–1890; Giovan Casoni, 1890–1900; Giuseppe Angelini, 1900–1919; Giuseppe Dalla Torre di Sanguinetto, 1920–1960; and Raimondo Manzini, 1960–1978.

Each Pope has dealt with *L'Osservatore* differently. Pope Benedict XV controlled the paper closely; each morning he would mark passages he approved and disapproved and sometimes he would follow up with handwritten instructions to the editor. Pius X and XI also sent written directives on occasion. For the paper's 75th anniversary, Piux XI called a world Catholic Press Eposition, which was termed "very successful." Leo XII had a more modest aim for the paper: "If it cannot always be first with the news, it would be nice for it not to be always last."[16] John XXIII instructed the paper to stop calling him by his exalted titles and to refer to him simply as the Pope or the Pontiff.[17] Under Pope Paul VI, *L'Osservatore Romano* was administratively restructured in 1972 into four divisions: distribution, editorial, administration and technical.[18]

Before he became Pope, Paul VI had been Vatican state secretary and, in that position, had received criticisms lodged against *L'Osservatore.* In 1961, two years before he was elected Pope, he made this lucid statement about the paper's policies and practices:

> We have little in comparison with other big papers, but what we have is good. . . . Our news perhaps is too dignified, too polished, too quiet; readers are not

[13] *Newsweek* (July 10, 1961), p. 41.
[14] "L'Osservatore Romano," *op cit.,* p. 367.
[15] Virgilio Levi, deputy editor-in-chief, *L'Osservatore,* in response to questionnaire, dated October 16, 1978.
[16] *Catholic Digest* (January, 1961), pp. 48–50.
[17] *Time* (April 18, 1960), p. 96.
[18] "L'Osservatore Romano," *op. cit.,* p. 367.

thrilled. It is a serious newspaper. . . . The emphasis is on editorials rather than on news. It doesn't want to give news, but it wants to create thought. It is not enough for it to relate events; it wants to comment on events. . . . In this paper the journalist is an interpreter, a teacher, a guide. . . . The paper appeals more to specialized people—to the politicians, to scholars, to devout persons and not to the mass of the readers. . . . No other paper can see more, can tell more or can give a better orientation towards educating people to truth and charity. It is the "paper of the the Pope." [19]

L'Osservatore regularly carries just one column entitled "Nostre Infor-mazioni" reserved officially for the Holy See, but any other official pronounce-ments of the Pope will appear verbatim in the rest of its pages. The remainder of the paper is normally divided about equally between religious, political and cul-tural news and information. It does give considerable space to religious ceremo-nies, texts of papal speeches and pronouncements by other Church dignitaries. But it also engages regularly in commentary and opinion. Ever since the edi-torship of Dalla Torre, who relished a fight with Communists or Socialists, it has had a tendency to avoid highly controversial political issues. However, it has often been at the center of strong polemics and it is unafraid, when necessary, to face powerful opposition in the name of truth and justice. It always strives for objectivity, equilibrium and serenity.[20]

L'Osservatore's 50,000 or more readers (80 percent subscription, 20 percent street sales) usually receive an eight-page, seven-column broadsheet-size paper. The front page may contain a picture or two; more often, masses of grey print highlighted only by clear black headlines in upper case type greet the reader. The nameplate, in block type, is accompanied by selected details of the paper's location and subscritpion price. Multi-column headlines surrounded by ample white space represent an attempt at modern horizontal makeup. Ten-point italic type is often used as body type for as much as a third of the front page. The ini-tial page may have as few as four stories (features and special articles of analysis often run long) to as many as two dozen. The front page typically contains the "Nostri Informazioni" column, a major item of news about the Holy See or a pronouncement by its officials, and a number of international news items. Sometimes these articles will be purely political; at other times, they will contain obvious religious overtones.

Page two reports the ecumenical scene plus giving international news, usually related to need for benevolence. Sometimes the appeal for assistance is direct. Frequently a short sermon or homily occupies part of this page. Articles on art and literature appear on the third page. Page four usually carries a major analysis or feature article, liturgical calendars, Vatican radio schedules and news about the Church. The fifth page contains a major essay and other short news items. The page invariably also presents a "News in Brief" column. Page six carries the paper's editorial, often a guest commentary and occasionally a reader letter. The editorials normally discuss religious questions or humanitar-

[19] G. B. Montini, "The Difficulties of 'L'Osservatore Romano'," *L'Osservatore Romano*, centennial edi-tion (July 1, 1961), p. 11.
[20] "L'Osservatore Romano," *op. cit.*, p. 368.

ian issues. The seventh page often offers a feature on a special topic, such as
community life or economics, carryovers from previous pages and a wide range
of advertisements. Since the ratio of advertisements to total space in the paper is
low and since there is a limited circulation, one may presume that the Vatican
must subsidize some of the paper's production costs. The back page offers a
hodge-podge of Italian state news and some European items. Usually there are
few pictures in the paper; however, the editors make room for a full page of pictures to highlight a special event or occasion important to the Vatican.

L'Osservatore Romano engages a total staff of 130 people, 80 assigned to
technical duties, 30 to editorial functions and 20 in an administrative capacity.
For its staff members, it seeks out personnel who have a good theological, philosophical, literary, linguistic, scientific and general cultural background. The
paper's contents are a composite of the writing and reportorial work of its editorial staff, the stories sent by its overseas stringers and the input of five news
agencies: ANSA. AFP, AP, UPI and Reuters.[21]

L'Osservatore is published six times each week in Italian from its printing
plant in Via del Pellegrino. A more comprehensive companion paper called *L'Osservatore della Domenica* (The Sunday Observer) fills in on Sundays. Over the
past 20 years, *L'Osservatore Romano* has spawned six vigorious weekly editions.
The first weekly edition—in Italian—started in 1947. Two years later, in 1949, a
French edition was begun under the supervision of the man who became Pope
Paul VI. It was organized to serve France, Belgium, Switzerland, Canada and
the Near East. The Spanish weekly started in Buenos Aires in 1951 under the
sponsorship of a society called "Petrus" in order to bring Latin American Catholics closer to the Vatican. Until 1969, material for this edition was prepared in
Rome, sent by air to Buenos Aires, and printed there for distribution in Spanish-
speaking Latin American countries, mainly Argentina, Uruguay, Chile, Bolivia,
and Paraguay. Now this edition is printed at the Vatican. Meantime, the English
version began in Rome in 1968. Shortly thereafter, the weekly issued from the
Vatican in two additional languages: Portuguese in 1969 and German in 1970.

All seven *L'Osservatore* newspapers—the parent daily and its six weekly
satellites—have a single goal, that of faithful reflection of the thoughts of the
Pope and concern with religious, political, social and cultural affairs deemed important to their readers. The weeklies simply offer the essentials of the daily's
contents in a more succinct, compact form.

Throughout its existence, *L'Osservatore Romano* has presented its news
and opinion with a serenity and a sense of history one would expect from an
organ published in the shadow of St. Peter's. "According to *L'Osservatore Romano*" is a phrase newspapers often use to describe the Vatican's word and the
paper's pen has been called "the papal sword." Its influence far outstrips its
modest circulation. Leading churchmen around the world take the paper; also
many other opinion and political leaders read it, since they are anxious to know
what the Vatican and the Church, neutrals in world affairs, are thinking and
saying. *L'Osservatore* is widely quoted throughout the world—from the pulpit,

[21] Levi questionnaire.

from the press and from radio and television. By these means, and aided by its weekly editions in six languages, its opinions diffuse throughout the world. Thus, although—or perhaps, because—its circulation is restricted and its contents are very serious, balanced and "objectively presented in accordance with Christian moral law,"[22] *L'Osservatore Romano* has a distinctive prestige all its own among the world's great dailies.

El País

(SPAIN)

ONLY SIX MONTHS AFTER the death of General Francisco Franco, on May 4, 1976, the daily newspaper *El País* appeared on the newsstands of Madrid for the first time. It was almost immediately a success. By the middle of 1978 it had become one of the largest, and in many ways the most influential, newspaper in Spain. It was obvious that the reading public was more than ready to back a newspaper dedicated to a wide and thorough news coverage and to democratic ideals and an independent editorial policy.

El País (The Country) is considered an "intellectual umbrella," as one American correspondent called it,[1] for the Socialists, liberals, and Christian Democrats who desire Western-style democracy and have felt slighted by Spain's generally conservative daily press. *El País* is a clean-cut, attractive newspaper, combining makeup characteristics of the staid *Le Monde* of Paris and the best of the West German newspaper design techniques. It is a tabloid, running about 24 pages during the week and about twice that on Sundays. Its general orientation is liberal-left and the impact of the French *Le Monde* is obvious on its editorial policy.

Its Sunday supplement magazine, *El País Semanal,* running about 48 pages in color, is well designed and printed. It contains excellent features—on politics, on culture, literature, economics, etc. In one issue (May 29, 1977), for example, it carried a long article with pictures on the British royal family, several political stories, a cultural article, several profiles of important people, an article about letters to the editor of the *London Times,* an article about the 1977 book fair, another about political authors in Spain, another on motorcycling, a feature on photography, a travel article, and another on gardening. The supplement is a far more serious magazine that most U.S. Sunday supplements.

[22] Levi questionnaire.
[1] Joe Gandelman (of the *Christian Science Monitor*), "Spanish liberals gain a voice in the press," *Christian Science Monitor,* May 12, 1976, p. 14.

EL PAIS

DIRECTOR: JUAN LUIS CEBRIAN
DIARIO INDEPENDIENTE DE LA MAÑANA
MADRID, MIERCOLES 22 DE FEBRERO DE 1978
Redacción, Administración y Talleres: Miguel Yuste, 40. Madrid-17 / Teléfono 754 38 00 / Precio: 18 pesetas. Ediciones urgentes: 20 pesetas / Año III. Número 560

Cuarenta y un ex ministros permanecen en los consejos de las empresas públicas

Un total de 41 ex ministros continúan ocupando puestos en las empresas estatales disfrutando de sustanciosas remuneraciones y demás *prebendas* derivadas del cargo, sin perjuicio de seguir percibiendo las 60.000 pesetas de *jubilación posministerial* asignadas con carácter vitalicio. Esta presencia dificulta, en opinión de los expertos, el desarrollo de la labor de los profesionales encargados de la gestión de las sociedades y deberá ser uno de los puntos esenciales a considerar en el futuro Estatuto de la Empresa Pública, comprometido en los pactos de la Moncloa.

El Estado tiene en estos momentos, directa o indirectamente, participación en unas trescientas empresas. Los ministros de Hacienda, Industria, Economía y Transporte fundamentalmente tienen capacidad para designar presidentes y consejeros de estas sociedades, y han utilizado esta atribución frecuentemente para premiar lealtades y servicios prestados a compañeros o predecesores en el Gabinete y demás escalones de la Administración, así como a *notables* del Régimen. **Páginas 42 y 43**

Ha muerto el boxeador Rubio Melero

A la una y cuarto de esta madrugada ha muerto el boxeador Juan Jesús Rubio Melero, a consecuencia de un paro cardíaco. El púgil había sido internado en la residencia sanitaria Francisco Franco, el pasado viernes, tras sufrir una lesión de tronconecéfalo y edema agudo de pulmón en su pelea contra el campeón de España de los pesos medios, y la intervención quirúrgica que se le practicó no pudo evitar que permaneciera en coma profundo hasta el fatal desenlace.

Rubio Melero tenía veintitrés años y su muerte aviva la polémica sobre el boxeo profesional.

Página 37
Editorial en **página 6**

La decisión del Comité de Liberación no fue unánime

El Consejo de Ministros de la OUA discutirá el tema de Canarias

El Consejo de Ministros de la Organización para la Unidad Africana (OUA), reunido desde el lunes en Trípoli, decidió ayer discutir todas las recomendaciones formuladas por su Comité de Liberación, entre las cuales se incluye una referente a las islas Canarias. La recomendación relativa al archipiélago español pide al Gobierno de Madrid que permita la entrada en las islas de una comisión investigadora africana y solicita a los países miembros de la OUA que presten «apoyo logístico» al movimiento separatista que dirige el abogado Antonio Cubillo desde Argel.

Una decisión semejante fue ya analizada en la reunión del Consejo de Ministros de la organización africana el año pasado en Libreville (Gabón). A la propuesta, el Gobierno español respondió entonces con una negativa rotunda a permitir la entrada de una comisión investigadora y el caso no pasó a mayores.

Por otra parte, las recomendaciones del Comité de Liberación no son vinculantes, y hay algunas, como la del reconocimiento del Polisario como interlocutor válido —adoptada hace más de año y medio—, que todavía no han sido aprobadas por el Consejo ministerial.

El ministro mauritano de Asuntos Exteriores, Hamdi Ould Mouknass, precisó ayer en Trípoli, de otro lado, que su país sobre Canarias adoptada por el Comité de Liberación no había sido unánime, y que su país, entre otros, había opuesto reservas a la consideración de Canarias como un enclave colonial y a la cuestión del apoyo al MPAIAC.

Las recomendaciones del Comité de Liberación y el discurso pronunciado el lunes por el dirigente libio Muamar el Gadafi han suscitado, por otra parte, la extrañeza de Portugal, cuya soberanía sobre el archipiélago de Madera también fue puesta en duda.

El ministro portugués de Asuntos Exteriores, el democristiano Sa Machado, declaró ayer que el coronel Gadafi desconocía la naturaleza de la revolución portuguesa, uno de cuyos principales logros fue precisamente la descolonización del antiguo imperio lusitano.

Petición del PSOE

Entretanto, el grupo parlamentario socialista ha pedido al general Gutiérrez Mellado que comparezca ante la Comisión de Defensa del Congreso para que informe de la situación militar de las islas, cuyas guarniciones visitó recientemente el vicepresidente primero del Gobierno.

Por la mañana, el ministro de Asuntos Exteriores, Marcelino Oreja, había recibido en su despacho al embajador de Libia en España, señor Fawzi, aunque la Oficina de Información Diplomática explicó más tarde que el encuentro se inscribía en el marco de «contactos más amplios».

De otro lado, un representante del Frente Polisario en Madrid declaró a EL PAIS que el futuro del archipiélago «es algo que el pueblo canario debe decidir».

Aprovechando aparentemente el respaldo obtenido por el MPAIAC en el Comité de Liberación de la OUA, miembros del movimiento separatista habían intentado «reventar», el lunes por la noche, un mitin de los partidos de la izquierda canaria contra el acuerdo de pesca con Marruecos, recientemente ratificado por el Congreso.

Los diversos oradores del acto abandonaron en ocasiones el motivo principal de la reunión para pronunciarse sobre la decisión de Trípoli y contra los *reventadores*. «Hace un año eran los fascistas quienes no nos dejaban hablar; los que lo hacen hoy son igualmente fascistas», afirmó Antonio Martino, del PSP.

Páginas 2 y 3

Movilización general en Somalia. Centenares de ciudadanos somalíes recorrieron ayer las calles de Mogadiscio tras varios días de manifestaciones en apoyo de la decisión de su Gobierno de implantar el estado de emergencia y decretar una movilización general. La decisión del presidente Siad Barre tiene como objetivo prevenir una eventual invasión etíope, apoyada por soviéticos y cubanos, después del derrumbe de la resistencia somalí en la discutida región del Ogaden. Sin embargo, dirigentes soviéticos y el propio Fidel Castro habían dado garantías a Estados Unidos de que las tropas etíopes no atravesarán la frontera de su vecino.

No fue votada la enmienda a la totalidad del PCE

Aprobada casi la mitad del proyecto de elecciones municipales

La Comisión de Interior del Congreso de Diputados aprobó ayer algunos artículos del proyecto de ley de elecciones municipales —casi la mitad—, tras un debate sobre la filosofía general del proyecto, oportunidad proporcionada por la defensa de una enmienda a la totalidad del PCE. Finalmente no fue puesta a votación, pero los comunistas reiteraron que el proyecto lleva al bipartidismo.

Entre los temas importantes aprobados figura el número de concejales a elegir en función de la cifra de habitantes, tema en que se adoptó una solución intermedia entre las distintas propuestas existentes parecida a la propugnada por el PSOE. Igualmente se aprobó —en voto en contra del PCE, minoría catalana y grupo mixto— que las coaliciones hayan de efectuarse a nivel provincial. Fue suprimida la fianza de las 5.000 pesetas por candidato.

Hubo una propuesta comunista para utilizar, en vez de la regla D'Hont, la fórmula del *resto mayor*. Entre los argumentos aducidos figuraba que en las elecciones del 15 de junio habría producido los siguientes resultados en escaños: UCD, 123; PSOE, 103; PCE, 33; AP, 30, y PSP, 16. La fórmula fue rechazada. **Páginas 8 y 9**

Absuelto el primer acusado de ocupación ilegal de vivienda

Marcelino Castillo, protagonista del primer juicio civil celebrado en Madrid contra una familia de ocupantes de viviendas vacías, ha sido absuelto por el Juzgado de Instrucción número 16, en base a sus circunstancias económicas y sociales —una familia con seis hijos— y a que no se ha podido demostrar que el señor Castillo fuera el autor material de *la patada a la puerta*. Sin embargo, el presidente de la Asociación de Vecinos de La Ventilla, José Carlos Alía, ha sido condenado a un mes y un día de arresto mayor, 10.000 pesetas de multa y a pagar la mitad de las costas del juicio.

Los abogados defensores han manifestado su decisión de recurrir al Tribunal Supremo.

Página 21

El País insists that it is an "independent newspaper." Its editor lays strong emphasis on a determination to break away from the "old school" of Spanish journalism and to be in the vanguard of a new breed of opinionmakers. The paper has an excellent staff of writers and editors (111 in 1978), with young leadership—the average age of the various department heads being 32.

According to Juan Luis Cebrián, the *director* or editor-in-chief, the newspaper is aimed at Spain's upper-middle classes—professionals and intellectuals, leaders of the working class, students, women, and young people. He says that *El País* encourages investigative reporting by giving its journalists freedom to "track down information" whenever possible, and he maintains that the paper "puts special emphasis on conflicts of a national nature, and on problems of social importance." The paper, says Cebrián, tries to present all sides of issues on its editorial page. The editor-in-chief stresses that the paper especially crusades for democratic government, freedom of expression, and integration of Spain into the European Economic Community. The newspaper, says Cebrián, is totally dedicated to "neutral and objective reporting and to the presentation of the full spectrum of political opinion." He has referred to *El País* as "the first independent, democratic newspaper in Spain in forty years."[2]

Cebrián says that *El País* is the first truly national newspaper in Spain, not only in terms of circulation, but in terms of its interest scope and appeal, and the variety of opinions expressed in its columns.[3] When the newspaper began in 1976 there were 500 shareholders, among them more than 100 university professors, most of them political liberals. No single group or individual held more than 7 percent of the shares.[4]

The newspaper today has more than 1,000 shareholders, including a large percentage of employees. It has about 350 staff members, some 120 of them writers and editors. Its national (Madrid) reporting staff numbers about 60, and its international staff about a dozen—stationed in Caracas, Moscow, Lisbon, Brussels, Paris, Bonn, Rome, Washington, and London.[5] The newspaper prefers its staff of writers and editors to have degrees in journalism and some experience on daily newspapers. A knowledge of foreign languages is also considered very important for staff members, according to the paper's editor-in-chief.

El País subscribes to nine European news wire services and to the New York Times News Service. It also receives services of EFE (Spanish News Agency) and Europa Press. In 1978 the paper's daily circulation was slightly more than 200,000, with about 250,000 on Sundays. About 98 percent of the circulation is through street sales. Cebrián estimated in 1978 that some 10 percent of the total space was given over to international news in a typical issue of the paper; about 20 percent to national news and about 8 percent to local news. He said about 30 percent of a typical issue's space was used for advertising.

In 1976, its first year of publication, the newspaper received the following

[2] Questionnaire to J. Merrill from Juan Luis Cebrián, *El País* director, Jan. 25, 1978. Hereafter referred to as Cebrián questionnaire.
[3] Harry Debelius (from Madrid) in *The New York Times*, May 11, 1976.
[4] *Herald-Tribune* (Paris), May 9, 1976.
[5] Cebrián questionnaire.

honors: The Premio Reseña, Radio Central Popularity Award, Velocity Magazine Award, El Vigia Port Award; and in 1977, the European Quality Award, the Laus Award, Affiche Award, Tanit Award, and the Alpha Award. It has also been quoted widely and lauded in the press all over the world for its vigor, courage, good writing, news coverage, and overall excellence.

The idea for the newspaper which was to become *El País* actually was formulated five years prior to the newspaper's birth. In 1971, José Ortega Spottorno, son of the famous philosopher José Ortega y Gasset, began to nurture the idea of a truly liberal, independent newspaper—one based on the model of various other European dailies. Ortega, in 1972, founded the company which would become the publisher of *El País*—Promotora de Informaciones S.A. (PRISA).[6] The founding capital was only 500,000 Spanish pesetas (about $9,000). After a few months of campaigning for this idealistic venture, the company's capital reached 15 million pesetas.

At the time the various Spanish governmental agencies were totally opposed to the idea of an independent newspaper, believing it would be dangerous to Franco. In 1973 the government demanded that the young company increase its capital by almost ten times—from 15 million to 150 million pesetas. In only ten months this sum was met by new stockholders.

During Franco's first of two grave illnesses, in the fall of 1974, things began to look more hopeful for the prospective newspaper of PRISA. By then it was increasingly obvious that the General was mortally ill, and that it was only a matter of time until the system of government in Spain would be changed. So, after much discussion, debate, and planning—in the autumn of 1975, almost simultaneously with the death of Franco—the new newspaper was approved by the government for publication.

In December, 1975, Juan Luis Cebrián, at that time only 31 years of age, but with more than 15 years in Spanish journalism, was named editor-in-chief of *El País*. In only a few weeks a staff was formed, largely young journalists of high professional quality and independence. By the following February the new building at Miguel Yuste 40 was ready for occupancy. Even before the presses had arrived, the journalists were already busy with experimental issues. Soon the presses—Harris Marinoni offset, capable of printing 50,000 copies an hour—arrived and were installed.

The first issue of the newspaper hit the streets of Madrid on schedule, on May 4, 1976, launching *El País* into what was then the rather gloomy world of Spanish journalism. The paper was an immediate hit, and the circulation rose rapidly from day to day.

The young newspaper predicted the outcome of the general elections of June, 1977, with almost 100 percent accuracy, thereby reinforcing its credibility with the readers. During this period it was interesting to see *El País* on the desks of government officials, and foreign papers began to cite the newspaper as a reputable source of information. By June, 1977, the circulation had risen to more than 200,000, and was growing steadily.

[6] Cebrián in 1978 listed José Ortega Spottorno as "the founder" of *El País;* he is also president of the board of PRISA.

Today the newspaper is in a strong economic position, so that it has independence from government and strong pressure groups. The paper owns its five-story building. National bureaus have been opened in Barcelona, Bilbao, Valencia and Seville, and there are foreign correspondents representing *El País* in numerous countries of Europe, Africa, and America.[7]

A standard copy of *El País* today has 48 pages. The sections are, in this order: International, National, Regions, City, Cultural and Society, Sports, and Economy. The two pages between International and National news are given over to Opinion pieces and editorials, letters to the editor, and reprints of opinions in other publications. The major article on these two pages is an in-depth analysis. On Sundays the paper contains the color supplement (*El País Semanal*) as well as an insert on "The Arts."

In 1979 the paper was still dedicated to its founding ideals: political independence at the service of the new Spanish democracy, and the incorporation of Spain in the European Economic Community.

The long-term goals of the daily *El País* can best be expressed in the words of Jesús de Polanco, the newspaper's managing editor: "We never thought of just making *a* newspaper, but rather *the* newspaper. Now we are working toward making it not just *the* newspaper of Madrid, but an institution."

Pravda

(U.S.S.R.)

PRAVDA (TRUTH), the official organ of the Soviet Union's controlling Communist Party, sets the pace for Russia's press system and for serious, *prestige* papers elsewhere in the world. Standing at the apex of the Soviet Union's press, it takes the lead in shaping the nation's journalistic policies. As the press organ of the Central Committee of the CPSU, it shapes and disseminates official Party doctrine throughout the entire union. With its present circulation of some 10.7 million copies, it takes the lead in circulation in the nation (with the possible exception of the U.S.S.R. youth daily, *Komsomolskaya Pravda*, which claims 11 million issues daily), and in the world (here, with the possible exception of Japan's *Asahi Shimbun*). Without a doubt, it is the calmest, most businesslike, most influential and most authoritative daily in the U.S.S.R. and perhaps in the world. And, with the possible exceptions of China's *Renmin Ribao* or Vatican City's *L'Osservatore Romano*, there is an official quality and prestige associated with *Pravda* unparalleled elsewhere.

[7] Cebrián questionnaire.

Пролетарии всех стран, соединяйтесь!

Коммунистическая партия Советского Союза

ПРАВДА

Газета основана
5 мая 1912 года
В. И. ЛЕНИНЫМ

Орган Центрального Комитета КПСС

№ 53 (21753) • Среда, 22 февраля 1978 года • Цена 3 коп.

ГОРДОСТЬ И СЛАВА НАРОДА

Советский народ торжественно отмечает 60-летний юбилей своих доблестных Вооружённых Сил. Это большой праздник...

НАГРАДЫ РОДИНЫ

УКАЗ
ПРЕЗИДИУМА ВЕРХОВНОГО СОВЕТА СССР
О награждении
Героя Советского Союза
Маршала Советского Союза
Москаленко К. С. орденом
Ленина в второй медалью
«Золотая Звезда»

Председатель Президиума
Верховного Совета СССР
Л. БРЕЖНЕВ.

Секретарь Президиума
Верховного Совета СССР
М. ГЕОРГАДЗЕ.
Москва, Кремль,
21 февраля 1978 г.

УКАЗ
ПРЕЗИДИУМА ВЕРХОВНОГО
СОВЕТА СССР
О присвоении звания
Героя Советского Союза
с вручением
ордена Ленина
и медали «Золотая Звезда»

Москва, Кремль,
21 февраля 1978 г.
(Окончание на 2-й стр.)

ВСЕ — НА СУББОТНИК!

Широкое распространение получил почин ряда предприятий Москвы — провести 21 апреля коммунистический субботник, посвящённый 108-й годовщине со дня рождения В. И. Ленина...

(ТАСС).

Направленный трудовой темп с первого дня третьего года десятилетки вои коллектива Всесоюзного ударного комсомольского...
Фото Н. Петрова.

Один из 150.000

РОЖДЕНО СОРЕВНОВАНИЕМ

Московский завод «Калибр». Его продукция — контрольно-измерительные приборы — известна всюду...

Н. ИГУНИН.
Корреспондент журнала
«Социалистическое
соревнование».
Москва.

СОВЕТСКО-СИРИЙСКИЕ ПЕРЕГОВОРЫ

21 февраля в Кремле начались советско-сирийские переговоры. С советской стороны переговоры ведут Генеральный секретарь ЦК КПСС, Председатель Президиума Верховного Совета СССР Л. И. Брежнев...

(ТАСС).

Во время переговоров.
Фото М. Скурихина.

В ДРУЖЕСТВЕННОЙ ОБСТАНОВКЕ

ИНИЦИАТОР ВЕРЕН СЕБЕ

ЦК(ЧИКИ) (Тульская область).
21. (Корр. «Правды» В. Шевцов).
«Прогнулся бойцы» — персонаж...

Речь товарища
Л. И. БРЕЖНЕВА

Дорогой товарищ Хафез Асад!
Уважаемые сирийские друзья!
Товарищи!
...

(Окончание на 2-й стр.)

От Центрального Комитета КПСС
и Совета Министров СССР

20 февраля 1978 года на шахте «Карагандинская» произошла авария — взрыв метана...

ЦЕНТРАЛЬНЫЙ
КОМИТЕТ КПСС

СОВЕТ
МИНИСТРОВ
СССР

A spacious seven-story building in Pravda Street in the quiet north-western corner of Moscow serves as *Pravda*'s headquarters. In this building and in the sprawling printing plant which adjoins it, the Publishing House of "Pravda," owned and operated by the State in behalf of the Soviet people, publishes *Pravda* and five other important all-Union journals—*Komsomalskaya Pravda, Sovetskaya Rossiya, Agricultural Life, Sovetskaya Kultura* and *Socialist Industry*—plus some 35 other periodicals, including the popular satirical fortnightly *Krokodil*. About one-third of *Pravda*'s nearly 11 million copies issue late each night seven days a week from this center; the rest emanate from some 40 other printing plants located around the Soviet Union.[1] Matrices are flown from Moscow to ten of these dispersed printing centers; material is sent by teletype to the other 30. Since about two-thirds of *Pravda*'s circulation is outside of Moscow, these satellite printing plants make it possible for nearly all readers to get their *Pravda* on the same day, even in the remote parts of the vast nation. Some 90 percent of *Pravda*'s readers have a subscription to the paper; the rest are sold in kiosks.

The paper's estimated 50 million readers all over the U.S.S.R. can buy the six-page *Pravda* each morning (except Mondays, when it contains just four pages) for three kopecks (under five U.S. cents).[2] Readers get their *Pravda* for such a small sum because the paper is heavily subsidized by the State; thus a paper like *Pravda* can publish without having to worry about costs. For the small sum they pay, readers get a product that typifies the best in Soviet journalism—a serious, up-beat, well-written, attractively made up and well printed newspaper. The paper that subscribers open to read contains well-written special features on cultural subjects, interpretive articles on science written by outstanding scientists, pieces on literature by the nation's leading literary figures, a variety of letters from readers, and the Soviet Union's most authoritative articles dealing with Party theory and programs. Of late, there are a few more news items about events which affect Soviet life and policies than in the past. But if the reader is searching for sensationalism, interesting pictures or light entertainment, he will be disappointed. After a visit to *Pravda*'s editorial offices, *Christian Science Monitor* correspondent David Willis reported on the paper's seriousness:

> There is no advertising, no crime, no comics, no travel tips, no crossword, no personality columns, no law court reports, no inside gossip from the Kremlin, no late bulletins, no list of international sports results. There also is no pessimism, no despair, no problem that cannot be solved.[3]

Pravda started as an underground paper in St. Petersburg on May 5, 1912, and has been issued regularly now for about two-thirds of a century.[4] According to the International Organization of Journalists, it was founded by V. I. Lenin

[1] Alexei Burmistenko, foreign editor, *Journalist* Magazine, in letter to H. Fisher, dated April 28, 1978.
[2] David K. Willis, "How *Pravda* is Published: Contrasts with the West," *Christian Science Monitor* (March 17, 1978), p. 5.
[3] Willis, *op. cit.*
[4] "B.A.," a member of *Pravda* staff, in response to questionnaire, dated January 29, 1978. (Source provided only his initials.)

"in accordance with the decision taken by the Prague Party Conference acting at the workers' requests to have their own daily newspaper and its publication was financed from workers' voluntary contributions."[5] At first, the tabloid-size *Pravda* had just three staff members—Lenin and two others, with Lenin acting as manager. During its first five or six years until the Bolshevik Revolution succeeded, *Pravda* was often suppressed by the Tsarist Government. Each time it would reappear under a different name.[6] In 1918, it moved to Moscow to become the Party's principal journal. During those early pre-October Revolution years, Lenin wrote some 500 articles for his fledgling paper. Since the Revolution, *Pravda* has grown steadily and rapidly.

During its growth, *Pravda* has had among its editors some renowned Party leaders, such as Molotov, Suslov and Shepilov. Other Party leaders have been among its most prolific contributors.[7] During the Khrushchev era, it was guided by one of its most capable editors, Pavel A. Satyukov, who did much to build up the paper's circulation and prestige. When Khrushchev fell from power, Satyukov was replaced by another capable editor, Alexei Rumyantsev, who had edited *Kommunist* (the Party's ideological journal), and who had held other important positions in Soviet journalism. During his short editorship, Rumyantsev editorialized under his own name for greater freedom of thought for scientists, writers, and other intellectuals. He was replaced in 1965 by Mikhail Zimyanin, Soviet deputy foreign minister, who took a harder line against the United States, especially in regard to Vietnam. He also stopped agitation for more freedom for intellectuals; rather he stressed the need for a unity of thought and support of Party policy by the intellectual community—at least in public expressions.

In March, 1976, when Zimyanin became Secretary of the Central Committee of the Communist Party of the Soviet Union, Victor Afanasyev, a well-known Soviet philosopher and associate member of the Academy of Sciences of the U.S.S.R., became *Pravda*'s editor-in-chief.[8] Afanasyev has written numerous articles on theoretical Marxism-Communism.

The former editor-in-chief of *Pravda*, Mikhail Zimyanin recently described in an interview the paper's role in the Soviet society: "*Pravda* plays its part in all of the Party's political, organizational and educational work and is an invaluable link between the Party and the masses, a means of directly approaching the masses."[9] He went on to explain that the paper works within the context of the Party's effort for "world peace, democracy and socialism." These purposes are consistent with Lenin's definitions of the role of the press in the Marxist society. He declared, "A newspaper is not only a collective propagandist and a collective agitator, it is also a collective organizer" and he also said the Soviet newspaper must act as a forum for the millions.[10] Lenin indicated further that these two

[5] Sepp Horlamus (ed.), *Mass Media in C.M.E.A. Countries* (Prague: International Organization of Journalists, 1976), p. 211.
[6] Kenneth E. Olson, *The History Makers: The Press in Europe from its Beginnings through 1965* (Baton Rouge: Louisiana State University Press, 1966), p. 322.
[7] Horlamus, *op. cit.*, p. 211.
[8] "B.A.," *loc. cit.*
[9] "In the Interests of Peace, Democracy and Socialism," (interview with Mikhail Zimyanin), *World Marxist Review*, 17:8 (August, 1974), p. 136.
[10] *Ibid.*, p. 139.

expressions of the press—as organizer and as a forum—are really two aspects of the unity of the Party with the masses, a unity which also gives the Soviet press its prestige and its power.

In serving these purposes, *Pravda* and its sister Soviet newspapers find themselves in constant tension. They must, on the one hand, serve the Party and the nation, and in this service they have no alternative but to support the official goals and views. On the other hand, they are the government's instruments to test public reaction, to report criticism and thereby reveal and help rectify flaws in the Soviet political order. In this tension, the press is free only to serve official purposes.[11]

Pravda functions to carry out its broad commissions in several specific ways. First, it explains Marxist theory and the Communist philosophy to its readers. It gives special attention to the ideological work carried out by the Party organizations. Under column titles such as "Problems of Theory," "Helping the Propagandist," and "Problems of Social Life," it explains the Party's theory.[12] It expends considerable effort towards giving a full picture of important developments in world affairs and to the Soviet definition of and efforts towards international peace. At the same time, *Pravda* serves as ". . . a tribune of public opinion expressing the views and aspirations of millions throughout the country."[13] It accomplishes this by means of its numerous letters to its editors. And the paper also believes it must "bring to the masses a profound understanding of the processes of our times through Marxist-Leninist analysis so readers will become more conscious of their social duties and activities."[14]

Everything *Pravda* publishes is in harmony with its goals and basic functions. All party ideological articles get priority in its pages and many are beamed across the U.S.S.R. by Radio Moscow or transmitted to regional and local papers by the Soviet news agency TASS. Its main editorial, which reiterates the Party's purposes or explains its actions is wired or broadcast in full to all major papers each day. As the "guardian of the Party line," *Pravda* takes a position on all questions of public life, and the other Soviet media follow its lead. In short, the voice of *Pravda* is heard regularly throughout the whole land and, since it is one of the most-often quoted papers of the world, its influence is international. Its reputation for giving the "official line" on all important matters makes it essential reading for all patriotic Soviet citizens.

Because of its international prestige, its interest in promulgating Lenin's idea of a just, democratic peace and its role of interpreter of world developments, *Pravda* has always demonstrated a consuming interest in international affairs. Thus, it covers a broad spectrum of international life in its articles; it popularizes Soviet foreign policy by its selection and slanting of materials; and it helps to unite the socialist community by featuring it in its pages. The paper also continues to link its international and domestic coverage, believing that "at-

[11] Mark Hopkins, "Media, Party and Society in Russia," in Alan Wells (ed.), *Mass Communication: A World View* (Palo Alto: National Press Books, 1974), p. 56.
[12] Horlamus, *op. cit.*, p. 211.
[13] "In the Interests of Peace, Democracy and Socialism," *op. cit.*, p. 139.
[14] *Ibid.*

tainment of our social and economic objectives (at home) is directly linked with the successful conduct of our foreign policy."[15]

As evidence of *Pravda*'s concern for the international scene and its belief that international and home affairs are interdependent, the paper keeps a staff of 50 correspondents abroad in 42 countries and 60 in the Soviet Union. It subscribes to TASS and other news services and receives hundreds of newspapers and magazines. In addition, "it gets adequate help from research institutes and contributions from Party leaders, statesmen, scientists, international affairs experts and rank-and-file workers."[16] Contributions come regularly, too, from leaders, politicians, scientists and Communist party workers in other socialist countries. Although the Central Committee keeps a watchful eye on what this staff writes, according to *Pravda*'s present editor-in-chief, Victor Afanasyev, it is not true that every article must be cleared in advance.[17]

Pravda's writers have a degree of freedom because they are trusted members of the Party, because they have a deeply ingrained sense of responsibility in regards to the U.S.S.R.'s role in international affairs and because they are well-educated and experienced journalists. They are graduates of Moscow University's special School of Journalism or from the journalism departments of a number of other universities spread across the nation. Although these university departments have not had high standards of professional preparation, as students the journalists did receive excellent instruction in courses covering the theory of Marxism-Leninism, history of the Communist Party and of the workers' movement, and in the political and economic decisions of the congresses and Central Committees.[18] Furthermore, *Pravda*'s journalists are members of the U.S.S.R. Union of Journalists, a voluntary organization of media professionals whose purpose is to assist the Party in the following ways:

> The U.S.S.R. Union of Journalists considers it its honourable duty to actively propagate the great thoughts of scientific communism, Soviet patriotism and socialist internationalism, to promote friendship among the nations of the U.S.S.R., to promote brotherly relations with the socialist countries, to promote friendship among all nations, to participate in an unceasing struggle for peace, democracy and progress, against hostile bourgeois ideology, against colonialism and imperialism.[19]

Further evidence of the Party's trust in and recognition of the excellent work of *Pravda* may be found in the fact that it has been awarded two Lenin Orders and the Order of October Revolution.[20]

An editorial collegium named by the Central Committee of the Communist Party manages *Pravda*'s operations and oversees its contents. Two main editorial sections, domestic and foreign, occupy the *Pravda* building, with each divided into many departments. The foreign section is on the third floor and the

[15] "In the Interests of Peace, Democracy and Socialism," *op. cit.,* p. 140.
[16] *Ibid.,* p. 144.
[17] Willis, *op. cit.*
[18] Antony Buzek, *How the Communist Press Works* (New York: Frederick A. Praeger, 1964), p. 247.
[19] "Statutes of the U.S.S.R. Union of Journalists," in Horlamus, *op. cit.,* p. 246.
[20] Horlamus, *op. cit.,* p. 211.

home section occupies the fourth floor. These editorial sections are broken up into several large and airy rooms in which staff members work in smaller, specialized groups or singly.[21]

Pravda's foreign section is composed of five departments. Most of its material comes from the paper's foreign correspondents. However, TASS, which has exchange agreements with numerous other national agencies, provides some of the other input from sources outside Russia.

About 150 people work in the home section. Most home section staffers are specialists with university or technical school educations and are ideologically committed to the Party. In addition to this Moscow staff, *Pravda* has an extensive network of correspondents scattered throughout the Soviet Union; these correspondents work with local contributors in their areas in addition to sending in their own news items and *feuilletons*. About 50 of this staff are women; some 15 of them are writers whose journalistic abilities are particularly appreciated by the paper's executives.

The readers' letters department, so vital to every Soviet paper, forms an essential part of *Pravda*'s home section. The 1,200 or more letters which *Pravda* now receives daily perform a major criticism feedback function for the society. The letters section provides readers opportunity to get complaints "off their chests," to criticize the system, to clarify questions about political and ideological problems or the international situation, to call to account erring officials and to praise the achievements of someone who has excelled. Some of the letters are printed in the special reader's column called "The Echo." In recent years, *Pravda* has been publishing more critical letters than in the past. Writers increasingly have been using this "escape valve" to stress their felt need for better consumer goods, to lash out against public wrongs, to attack minor bureaucracy and to discuss other facets of Soviet life not mentioned in print a decade or so ago. A reader's letter frequently stimulates a broader discussion on moral, philosophical, literary or economic themes.

Pravda tries to respond in some way to all letters it receives—by letter replies where publication is not possible and by further investigation where that is necessary. The subjects of these letters run from very serious questions about domestic and international affairs to extremely personal matters. In addition to the letters, *Pravda* receives many of its readers who want to come to its offices to discuss problems and to ask questions in person.

While the pattern may vary from day to day, the following page-by-page account of one day's recent issue provides insight into *Pravda*'s makeup and contents.[22] Page one carried an instructional editorial, information about Soviet cosmonauts, a farm report, a brief story about President Leonid Brezhnev's presentation of an award, an overseas item on the arms race, and an interview with the Ethiopian foreign minister. There were photographs showing Moscow residents welcoming spring. Page two presented feature and Party articles. Page three gave the people's comments and criticisms. The fourth page covered foreign and East European news. The fifth page carried commentary attacking

[21] Buzek, *op. cit.*, p. 315.
[22] Willis, *op. cit.* Mr. Willis examined the March 6, 1978 issue of *Pravda*.

Israel for invading south Lebanon and explaining the U.S.S.R.'s campaign against the U.S. neutron bomb. The back page offered weather charts and information and theater, television, radio, sport and chess schedules.

Pravda's main interest does not lie in reporting news events, but in promoting, in the words of editor Afanasyev, "the will, the policies, and the interests of a huge party and a huge country."[23] For *Pravda,* correct interpretation of the significance of the event supersedes the facts of the event itself. Because the paper sees itself as a front-line defense against the inroads of bourgeois capitalism, readers are given long serious discussions of the Party's interpretation of developments and relationships within Russia and on the international scene. Primarily for this reason, the outlines of each edition are fixed as much as three months in advance, even down to plans for the front page. Only a news event of earth-shaking significance could subvert these arrangements. However, in recent years, there has been a tendency to publish more news events, and unnecessary delays in printing late news are now less frequent.

Because *Pravda* represents the latest "inside" thinking of the Communist Party, its pages are closely watched by diplomats, scholars and the press around the world "to catch the slightest policy nuances."[24] At the same time, the paper serves, along with TASS and Radio Moscow broadcasts, as an excellent barometer to read Party reaction to developments in the rest of the world. Western diplomats, for example, carefully assessed *Pravda*'s reaction to the Chinese treaty with Japan and U.S. recognition of China late in 1978. In Soviet support of revolutionaries in Africa and backing of Cuban intervention, the editorials of *Pravda* have provided key clues to Soviet options and intentions.[25]

Recently, *Pravda* has been the Soviet instrument employed to prod the United States to show its hand on American wishes vis-a-vis a new strategic arms agreement (SALT) and to tip the West on Soviet views of the consequences of failure to achieve a solution. In March, 1978, a series of *Pravda* commentaries warned that the time for crucial decision in Soviet-American relations is approaching, and the outcome of the talks would determine future detente. The articles, written by Georgy Arbatov, head of Moscow's U.S.A. and Canada Institute, clearly implied the alternatives—a new accord could bring further Soviet-American cooperation and failure would worsen relations—and signalled impatiently that President Carter should overcome his ambiguity and speed new talks.[26]

Pravda proceeds carefully, soberly and calmly to serve an ever-growing readership as it extends its influence ever deeper into the hinterlands of the Soviet Union and ever farther throughout the world. The paper must be commended for printing the truth as it sees the truth and for loyalty to the principles of the Party it represents. The seriousness of its articles and the responsibility it takes towards its readers serve as good examples to daily journals everywhere.

[23] Quoted in Willis, *op. cit.*

[24] Willis, *op. cit.,*

[25] Elizabeth Pond, "Soviet Media Message: No Angola Pullout," *Christian Science Monitor* (January 8, 1976), p. 5.

[26] "*Pravda* Prods U.S. on Arms and Detente," *Christian Science Monitor* (March 29, 1978), p. 22.

Its prestige and influence as a prestige journal are probably not surpassed anywhere. In spite of its existence as the official organ of the ruling party in a controlled society—a position that makes it "enslaved" from the Western point-of-view—*Pravda* deserves a firm place among the world's elite newspapers.

Die Presse

(AUSTRIA)

IN THE NINETEENTH AND twentieth centuries, the city of Vienna dominated the lives of some 50 million inhabitants of the expansive Austro-Hungarian Empire. World War I changed all that and reduced Austria to a small nation so that today Vienna is an anomaly, "in effect a capital city designed for an empire eight or nine times as big as the country it finds itself in today."[1] Perhaps, proportionately speaking, Vienna remains as influential now as in the days of great empire, since one out of five of Austria's seven and one-half million citizens live in it. Hence, it should not be surprising that the Viennese press overwhelmingly dominates the country and accounts for nearly three-fourths of Austria's daily newspaper circulation.

Actually, two mass appeal dailies claim the capital's biggest readership: the left-of-center and popular *Neue Kronen-Zeitung* with 725,000 daily readers and over a million on Sundays ranks as Europe's largest-selling paper and its rival right-wing *Kurier* circulates another 430,000 copies on weekdays and 620,000 on Sundays. Together, these two papers account for 85 percent of the Viennese readers and 60 percent of all those in the nation.[2] But neither of them can claim the long tradition of the *Wiener Zeitung,* which got its start in 1703 as the twice-weekly *Der Postalische Mercurius* and today is the world's oldest extant newspaper.[3] However, none of these three nor Vienna's other three newspapers can compete with the high quality of the daily *Die Presse.*

For several reasons, *Die Presse* stands as Austria's best elite paper. Even though its readership is concentrated in Vienna, it is read all over the nation (and outside), making it the nation's nearest approach to a national newspaper. Because of its able corps of foreign correspondents, it is the country's—and one of Europe's—best informed papers on international affairs. With a primary appeal to intellectuals, businessmen and the upper middle income classes, it offers

[1] John Sandford, *The Mass Media of the German-Speaking Countries* (London: Oswald Wolf Publishers, Ltd., 1976), p. 132.
[2] *Ibid.,* p. 137.
[3] Sandford, *op. cit.,* pp. 132–3.

Preis 5 Schilling
DM 1.—, Lit 400, sfr 1,30, Din. T.—,
hfr 12,—, hfl 1,—, F 1,70, Ptas 25,—
Redaktion und Verlag:
1191 Wien, Muthgasse 2,
Pressehaus
Postfach 199, Telephon 36 52 90
Abonn.-Bestellung: Tel. 65 69 03
FS 07-4110, 07-5406
Telegramm: Wienpresse
Verlagspostamt: 1190 Wien, P. b. b.

Die Presse

Unabhängige Zeitung für Österreich

Jahrgang 1978 / Nr. 8975
Wien, Mittwoch, den 22. Februar 1978
Gegründet 1848

Der große Horizont

Kreisky zu Larnaka: Staatssouveränität hat unbedingten Vorrang

Eigenbericht der „Presse"

WIEN (bm). „Kein souveräner Staat kann einem anderen Staat erlauben, seine Souveränität zu kränken", betonte Bundeskanzler Kreisky am Dienstag, von der „Presse" über den völkerrechtlichen Aspekt der blutigen Vorfälle von Larnaka befragt. „Wenn man damit irgendwo anfängt, kann man nicht wissen, wo es aufhört." Also absolute Priorität der Souveränität? Kreisky: „Ja freilich, es es mir galt oder nicht." Man könne und dürfe von diesem Prinzip nicht abgehen. Freilich sei das in der Beurteilung von Larnaka „nur eine Seite", aber über die anderen Aspekte wolle er, der Bundeskanzler, keinen Kommentar abgeben. Auch die Aktionen des deutschen Militärischen Abschirmdienstes (MAD) in Österreich seien eine Souveränitätsverletzung gewesen. „Eine reine formlose Entschuldigung aus Bonn ist, soviel ich weiß, schon da", sagte Kreisky.

„Alternativ-Universität" in Polen nahm Arbeit auf

WARSCHAU (reuter). Regimekritische polnische Akademiker und Intellektuelle haben nach Angaben aus Dissidentenkreisen am Montagabend eine Serie von Vorlesungen begonnen, die als Alternative zu den offiziellen Universitätskursen gedacht sind. In einer Privatwohnung in Warschau wurde zum Thema „Konservatismus als Ideologie" vorgetragen. Der Plan einer Alternativuniversität ist seit voriger Woche bekannt.

Funkbild: „Die Presse"/ap

WIEDER NEUES FLÜCHTLINGSELEND IN AFRIKA
Mit dem Vordringen der äthiopisch-kubanisch-sowjetischen Truppen kommt in der Ogadenschlacht auch ein neuer Flüchtlingsstrom in Bewegung. Die vorwiegend somalische Bevölkerung zieht ostwärts

---

VOR ENTSCHEIDUNG ÜBER GRAZER BÜRGERMEISTER

SP-Offert an Hasiba Götz ausgebootet?

Eigenbericht der „Presse"

GRAZ (hws). Sensationelle Wende in der steirischen Landeshauptstadt: Die SP hat auf ihren Anspruch auf den Bürgermeistersessel verzichtet und würde den VP-Spitzenkandidaten Hasiba „unter gewissen Bedingungen" wählen. Diese Kehrtwendung der Sozialisten hat bei einer Grazer Parteien zu hektischen Verhandlungen geführt. Wird Hasiba das Angebot annehmen — oder doch wieder eine Koalition mit FP-Bürgermeister Götz eingehen?

Das sozialistische Angebot kam für alle Beteiligten überraschend. Denn bisher hatte SP-Vizebürgermeister Stoiser in allen Gesprächen darauf gepocht, seine Fraktion müsse die stärkste Partei den Bürgermeistersessel beanspruchen. Am Montagabend machte Stoiser dann Franz Hasiba auf und übereichte ihm folgendes Vorschlag: Die SPÖ würde Hasiba zum Stadtoberhaupt, wenn die der VP wirklich Hasiba und keinen anderen Kandidaten präsentiert; in der Kompetenzverteilung würde eine gravierende Änderung eintritt; und — als entscheidende Bedingung — sich die VP verpflichtet, während der fünfjährigen Legislaturperiode die Sozialisten nie mit einer anderen Fraktion zu überstimmen.

Ist es kein Koalitionsangebot", wurde am Dienstag der „Presse" von Stoisers Büro versichert. Doch in der Praxis könnte in Hinkunft keine Entscheidung mehr gegen den Willen der SPÖ fallen. Eine maßliche Verlockung für

Hasiba liegt im Grazer Statut: Wird er Bürgermeister, steht der VP auch noch einer der drei Vizebürgermeister zu.

Die SPÖ ließ das Angebot am Dienstag „einengen"; für die Landes-SPÖ vor Landesparteichef Sebastian anwesend. Die Sozialisten erwarten, daß Hasiba heute, Mittwoch, das Angebot ablehnt oder annimmt. Dazu wird es jedoch nicht kommen: Nach einer sofort stattfinenden Besprechung bei der Landeshauptmann Niederl werden jetzt erst die VP-Gremien befragt.

Beobachter halten es für durchaus denkbar, daß FP-Bürgermeister Götz den Sozialisten doch noch zuvorkommt: Er verhandelt heute nachmittag mit der Volkspartei. Der Wahlsieger könnte einerseits der VP zum zusätzlich gewonnenen Stadtratsmandat anbieten, anderseits eine unwahrscheinliche Variante ebenfalls Hasiba zum Bürgermeister machen — als Preis für eine neuerliche „Bürgerkoalition" in Graz.

Neuer Denkprozeß in Belgrad

Schweiz für Schluß ohne Worte

Von unserer Korrespondentin CHRISTINE VON KOHL.

BELGRAD. In der nachträglichen Beurteilung fanden sich alle Schattierungen von „Mut" bis „Ruthanasie": Dem Schweizer Delegierten bei der Belgrader KSZE-Nachfolgekonferenz, Brunner, war es am späten Montagnachmittag gelungen, das Plenum aus der resignierenden Apathie herauszureißen. Brunner erklärte, daß es unmöglich geworden sei, zum öffentlichen Umständigkeit, ein Schlußdokument im westlichen oder ein Schlußdokument im östlichen Sinn zu produzieren, nur noch eine dritte logische Variante gebe, nämlich einen Text mit „politischer Abschlußerklärung in Erfüllung der Schlußakte und der Fixierung des Nachfolgetreffens in Madrid und unser Uneinigkeit.

Er hatte damit gesagt, was seit Wochen in den Couloirs der Konferenz „laut gedacht", aber offiziell von niemandem ausgesprochen worden war. Die überwiegende Mehrheit der westlichen und neutralen Staaten wollte zumindest formal an einem „substantiellen Abschlußdokument" festhalten. Niemand wollte jenen den Schwarzen Peter haben und die Initiative für ein Abschlußdokument ergreifen.

Die Reaktion auf die Schweizer Äußerung konnte nicht widersprüchlicher sein. Manche nannten die

Schweizer Franken über Acht-Schilling-Marke

WIEN/FRANKFURT (ap). Sowohl Finanzminister Androsch als auch Notenbankpräsident Koren versicherten am Dienstag, es werde trotz der neuerlichen Kursturnisse des Dollars keine Änderung der österreichischen Hartwährungspolitik geben. Koren sprach sich für eine abwartende Haltung" aus. Allerdings notierten sowohl Schweizer Franken als auch DM in Wien höher als an den Vortagen: Mit einem Devisen-Mittelkurs von 802,70 Schilling für 100 Franken durchbrach die Schweizer Währung erstmals die 800-Schilling-Marke. Für 100 DM betrug der Kurs 719,15 Schilling Am Dienstag, Der Dollar hatt sich hingegen auf den Devisenmärkten etwas gefestigt: In Wien lautete der Mittelkurs auf 14,9775 nach 14,6850 Schilling, in Frankfurt auf 2,0425 Schilling, nach 2,0405 DM.
Seite 5

Diplomatische Beziehungen Budapest – Vatikan?

ROM (dpa). Die Aufnahme diplomatischer Beziehungen zwischen Ungarn und dem Vatikan erwartet der ungarische Botschafter in Italien, René Palásti. Vor Journalisten sagte der Botschafter am Dienstag in Rom, die Treffen zwischen beiden Partnern entwickelten sich schon zu einer „Annäherungspapier" bezeichnet. Sie wollten damit die Berücksichtigung der bisherigen Diskussionen und Vorschläge von allen Seiten ein letztes Mal dokumentieren, was ihre Vorstellungen seien.

Nach der Tragödie von Zypern: Kyprianou will Sadat treffen

NIKOSIA (ap/afp). Nachdem sich die 15 Geiseln am Bord der von zwei arabischen Terroristen gekaperten Maschine zu befreien und mit Waffengewalt daran gehindert haben, versuchte Kyprianou, den Präsidenten Ägyptens im Gefolge der Geiselbefreiungstragödie von Larnaka am Sonntag derart zugespitzt hatten, daß einen einen Geschäftsträger in Nikosia einberief und die zyprische Regierung aufforderte, ihren Verlreter ebenfalls abzuziehen, versuchte Präsident Kyprianou, die Lage zu entspannen. Er erklärte sich am Dienstag zu einem Treffen mit Präsident Sadat bereit, um die schweren Differenzen beizulegen. Auf einer Pressekonferenz erklärte der zyprische Staatschef, seine Regierung wolle alles daransetzen, die freundschaftlichen Beziehungen zu Ägypten wiederherzustellen. Gleichzeitig forderte er die Araber und die verschiedenen Befreiungsorganisationen auf, Zypern nicht mehr zum Schauplatz ihrer Konflikte und zum Austragungsort ihrer Meinungsverschiedenheiten zu machen. Er appellierte an die Araber, die Kairo in der Region nicht weiter zu überziehen.

Sadat hatte nach wie vor bei seiner Darstellung der mißglückten Geiselbefreiungsaktion am Sonntag, bei der 15 ägyptische Kämpfer nach einem Gefecht mit der Nationalgarde getötet worden waren.

Insgesamt 70 Soldaten — hätte versucht,

sich die 15 Geiseln an Bord der von zwei arabischen Terroristen gekaperten Maschine zu befreien und mit Waffengewalt daran gehindert haben.

In Begleitung von Staatsminister Butrus Ghali traten in der Nacht auf Dienstag die überlebenden Mitglieder des Kommandokodos, die Leichen der fünfzehn Gefallenen sowie auch der Leiche des Landes verwiesene ägyptische Militärattache in Kairo ein, wo von einem gesamten Kabinett empfangen wurden. Indessen besteht Kairo halt vor die Ermordung der beiden Mörder des Al-Ahram-Verlegers Sebai ausgelöst worden sind. Zypern hat dem bereits abgelehnt und will am Montag den Prozeß gegen die Verbrecher eröffnen.

Der PLO hat indessen erklärt, die beiden Attentäter hätten auf eigene Faust gehandelt, gehörten keiner Organisation an, und seien für ihre Tat zu verurteilen.

Der Sekretär des ermordeten ägyptischen Kulturpolitikers Sebai, Hussein Rizk, erklärte nach seiner Rückkehr in Kairo, die Geiselnehmer seien „äußerst dumm und unausgeglichen gewesen". Die beiden Mörder hätten sich zwar nach Beginn der Befreiungsaktion ergeben, seien aber mit Stichrig und zum gesamten Schauplatz der ägyptischen Aktion ergeben, aber die Maschine von den Spezialtruppen erreicht worden sei.

Graz oder die Option für morgen

VON HANS WERNER SCHEIDL

Die Zeit des Abschieds für Friedrich Peter dürfte gekommen sein. Wenn der freiheitliche Parteivorstand morgen, Donnerstag, seine zweitätige Klausur beginnt, dann steht mehr auf der Tagesordnung, als die offizielle Einladung verrät: „Politischer Bericht des Bundesparteiobmannes." Pikanterweise erst beim Punkt „Allfälliges" dürfte das Thema angefaßt werden: Wie verabschiedet man Friedrich Peter ehrenvoll?

Denn am 14. September könnte der damit der ohne 37jährige Eisenbahnerschn mit Attnang-Puchheim seinen zwanzigsten Jahrestag als Parteiführer feiern. Ein einsamer Rekord in der Zweiten Republik. Dieses zwanzigjährige Ehejubiläum mit der FPÖ, die Volkszumal nennt die „Porzellan-Hochzeit", könnte aber noch dem Stichtag in Scherben gehen. Dann nämlich, wenn die Vorstandsmehrheit beschließen sollte, den 15. ordentlichen Bundesparteitag auf Frühsommer vorzuverlegen.

Dabei ist noch keineswegs hundertprozentig ausgemacht, wer Peter

beerben wird. Heute, Mittwoch, könnten sich in Graz die Ungewißheiten über den Bürgermeisterssel entscheiden. Sollte Alexander Götz trotz der dramatischen Wendung dennoch als Sieger hervorgehen, dann wäre der Druck seiner Parteifreunde groß, der Peter Graz aus zu führen. Daggen können es der Peter noch sein letzter treuer Kampfgefährte Tassilo Broesigke mit Argumenten an: Auch Peter dürfte Jahrestag die FPÖ als Linzer Landesgeordneter. Wird aber heute Götz zweidrigdig in eine „Verliererkoalition" ausgebootet, wäre der sofort für Wien frei.

Doch die beiden FP-Routiniers dürften beim letzten Kampf — daher auch bestimmen, ob nicht ohne Raffinement. Sie wissen, daß Götz nur dann kandidieren würde, sollten ihn alle Länder bestimmen, sollte er der einzige Auswege und der einzige Kandidat bleiben. Sollte aber auch nur ein Landeschef zu erkennen geben, auch er wäre einen möglichen, so würde er sich unter Umständen zur Kandidatur bereit, so könnte Götz ablehnen. Das

wissen die beiden klauen Kampfgeführten sehr genau und taktieren geschickt: Vielleicht gelingt es doch noch, den Oberösterreicher Schender so zu einer derartigen Aussage zu bewegen. Dann wäre das Spiel nicht nur wieder völlig offen, sondern schon halb gewonnen. Denn wer sagt zu diesem Fall, daß Schender auch tatsächlich Obmann wird? Vor die Frage wie Alexander Peter-Schender gestellt, könnte mancher Delegierter — es bedenklich werden, und plötzlich würde Peter als Phönix aus der Asche steigen. Stark verengt zwar, aber immerhin.

Für die Vorstandssitzung dürften aus derlei Sandkastenspiele allerdings sich nicht zu, denn nach, aus derlei Sandkastenspiele allerdings sich nicht zu. Die Stimmung innerhalb der Partei und sind sich wahrscheinlich auch bewußt, daß ihre Entscheidung auch ein Vorgang des Problems wäre eine Entscheidung für die Zukunft stehen wird. Peter hat die Partei fast zwanzig Jahre geführt, er hat sich unzählige Verdienste erworben; doch die politischen Umstände haben sich gewandelt, wie man immerhin.

Parteien mit absoluten Mehrheiten im Lande, eine Koalition ist nicht notwendig. Und die Jahre 1970/71, als Minderheitskanzler Kreisky die Freiheitlichen brauchte, bei Peter oben geschickt zur Aufwertung benützt. Doch auch die zuklemmaßigen Bilanz muß man sehen: Mit 338.110 Stimmen in ganze Österreich begann tatsächlich Obmann werden? Vor die Frage wie Alexander Peter-Schender gestellt, davon 249.444.

Was der FPÖ jetzt not tut, ist ein Obmann, der seinen Allein durch seine bisherigen Handeln ein glaubwürdiger Garant dafür ist, daß Kreisky aus jenen Verlust der absoluten Mehrheit auch wirklich gibt. Welche es sich nicht so sehr um den Kreisky handelt als um jenen mehr anderen zu helfen wissen, wie voll es dann ein kleiner Lann ohne Schutzmaßnahmen schaffen? Daß der Freiheitliche Beispiel der großen Dimelsmächte USA und EG macht eben Schulz, Mit eingehen Zollerwägungen wird nur mehr gesteigert. Mindestgreise, Importquoten oder Selbstbeschränkungen begannen ihrerseits jetzt die Druck: Wahn das führen soll, läßt sich noch schwer absehen. Es ist allzuleicht noch nicht so lange her, daß allgemeiner Protektionismus die Welt in die Krise stürzte. Erst Textilien, dann Stahl. Wer wird die nächste schutzsuchende Branche sein?

Schlechtes Beispiel

r.n.f. — Schlecht ausgelastete Werke, Kurzarbeit und hohe Verluste bei den Stahlfirmen haben jetzt auch die österreichische Regierung in die Krise gezwungen. Marktstörenden Billigimporten will sie künftig ebenso einen Riegel vorschieben wie die meisten anderen Staaten auch. Aber zwei darbender Industrie werden der natürlichen Marktkräfte nun, oft geprießenen freien Handel auch eine Abfuge erteilt. Damit mehr aber Österreich einer der kleinen selbst keineswegs allein und gemeiner Protektionismus die Weltwirtschaft schützt.

---

some of the best financial and business news and information pages in the European Common Market area. And it continues to hold to the traditions of political independence and press freedom under which it was born.

When *Der Postalische Mercurius* became Austria's first daily in 1714, every publication had to be approved by the authorities. Ten years later, *Mercurius* was made the government's official organ. Press freedom was unheard of in Austria-Hungary until Joseph II came to the throne and in 1781 abolished censorship and established a brief period of press freedom. But the grace period for the press lasted just nine years. When Joseph died, his successor, Leopold II, re-established censorship, especially of news from France. Official censorship continued through the period of Napoleonic occupation until the overthrow of Francis II and his powerful minister, Prince Clemens von Metternich in March, 1848. Then the parliament abolished censorship and established a new liberal press law. In a short time, 206 papers (90 of which were dailies)—most of them bold spokesmen for press freedom—mushroomed into existence.[4]

The most important of these new papers was *Die Presse,* founded July 3, 1848, by August Zang. A small daily with three wide columns per page, it heralded the birth of modern journalism in Austria. From the beginning, it was cosmopolitan and literate, giving emphasis to non-governmental and objectively reported news. The first issue also gave background interpretation of what was transpiring in government and carried an editorial explaining why a press must be indpendent across the bottom of the first page.

Zang, who had been a professor of medicine at Wurzburg, was inspired to found *Die Presse* by the success of Emile Girardin's *La Presse* in Paris. Like Girardin, Zang wanted to produce a paper priced low enough that the masses could purchase it and be exposed to more liberal ideas. Under Zang's leadership, *Die Presse* stressed home, national and foreign news and downplayed political comment. As the paper's circulation grew, it broke the advertising monopoly held until then by the official *Wiener Zeitung.*

Die Presse became Austria's best newspaper. It went through a tumultuous decade in the 1850's when authoritarianism returned, but in 1862 a new press law eliminated press censorship once more and also punishment for errant editors. Despite the roller-coaster now-throttled, now-free period, *Die Presse,* as the country's leading voice for democracy, thrived. Circulation was 13,000 in 1851; 17,000 by 1853; 23,000 by 1854; and 28,000 by 1859.

In September, 1864, *Die Presse* in effect became *Neue Freie Presse.* Two of the chief editors, Theodor Friedlander and Michael Ettienne, and the bulk of the *Die Presse* staff left *Die Presse* to found the new paper. As *Neue Freie Presse* directors, Friedlander and Ettienne made few changes in policy or format. But, contentwise, they improved on the excellence of *Die Presse* and made the new paper both the best the nation had had and one of international repute. *Neue Freie Presse*'s extensive foreign and national news were very well written and the paper's commentary and backgrounding were excellent. Its *feuilletons* were especially noteworthy, with contributions of noted writers, such as Speidel, Hof-

[4] Kenneth E. Olson, *The History Makers: The Press of Europe from its Beginnings through 1965* (Baton Rouge: Louisiana State U. Press, 1966), pp. 194–7.

mannsthal, Herzl, Spitzer, Sweig and Polgar.[5] It stimulated interest in cultural affairs and exercised such a strong influence on Austrian internal affairs that one important Austrian official remarked, "It is nearly imposible to govern against *Die Neue Freie Presse.*" Although it started with a circulation of just 4,000 in 1864, it was claiming 35,000 readers in 1873 and over 100,000 by 1910. Its staff of 600 included some 100 foreign correspondents, one reason for its outstanding external news coverage.

In 1879, after the death of Friedlander in 1872 and Ettienne seven years later, Moriz Benedikt took over as editor of *Neue Freie Presse*. He actually ran the paper until he became its publisher in 1920. He modernized the plant, extended coverage, emphasized interviews and hired better-educated staffers. He became one of the dozen most powerful men in Austria, often compared to Northcliffe of Britain and Hearst of the United States.

After World War I, when provinces were pressing for independence from the Austrian national government, *Neue Freie Presse* lost much of its influence and its circulation. Soon, it faced serious financial difficulties. However, it kept up its general quality, and largely on the basis of its excellent *feuilleton* articles it was regarded, along with Paris' *Le Temps* and *Journal des Debats,* the best in Europe. It still was strong in fiction, theater, music, culture and economics. The period between the two world wars might be called the paper's "literary" era, as this area of its contents took precedence over its general news coverage during that time. In 1934, its circulation for both its morning and evening editions was around 34,000. Then, in 1939, as the Nazis took over the Austrian press, the *Neue Freie Presse* and the *Neues Wiener Tagblatt* were merged into a pro-Hitler propagandistic mouthpiece.

After the war, on January 26, 1946, the paper reappeared under its old name, *Die Presse*. Its director was Dr. Ernst Molden, a strong-minded Swedish immigrant who held the reins until 1953. Molden continued the paper's finest traditions and principles, but left the strong stamp of his own personality on it as well. He upgraded content by using articles contributed by leading governmental figures, university professors and experts from various fields. Under Molden, the paper became Austria's best-known serious, independent and outspoken newspaper and the daily respected by people in responsible positions.

In 1953, Ernst Molden's son Fritz became publisher of *Die Presse*. Four years later, in 1957, the younger Molden, to balance his serious journal, brought out the popular Viennese picture paper *Express*. Fritz Molden's first chief editor was Milan Dubrovic, who was later succeeded in that post by Dr. Otto Shulmeister. Since 1976, Schulmeister has been publisher of *Die Presse* and his chief editor is Dr. Thomas Chorherr, a long-time assistant chief editor.

Today, *Die Presse* is owned by an association known as "Verein der Freunde der Freien Burgerlichen Presse in Osterreich." It is published from a 16-story building named "Presse-Haus" located in a suburb of Vienna. A staff of 193 produces the paper, of whom 65 have writing and editorial responsibilities, 70 technical duties and 58 administrative positions. Most of the highly-qualified staff hold university degrees; the paper seeks workers who have had university

5 Olson, *op. cit.,* p. 201.

training. Together, the staff publishes some 65,000 copies of *Die Presse* each work weekday morning Monday through Thursdays and about 80,000 for its Friday and Saturday/Sunday issues. Subscribers comprise 72 percent of this circulation, with the remaining 28 percent sold in kiosks and other street-front outlets.[6]

Like most Austrian papers, *Die Presse* is well organized. Though not a thick paper (it averages 10–12 pages on weekdays and some 32–36 pages on weekends), it is packed with information. Its makeup is attractive, orderly and conservative, regarded as more Anglo-Saxon than German in appearance by at least one source.[7] Its pages are full size—also unusual for Austria. Under a band of blue color across the top of its front page, the paper runs its nameplate flanked by basic information about itself on the left and the latest weather report in brief on the right. The serious-appearing initial page contains a mixture of the day's leading national and international news and a leader editorial by the paper's staff in the lower half. A box outlined in blue provides a clue to two or three key stories inside the paper. Generally, there is a single photograph placed in the upper right-hand quadrant. In general, the page has a vertical appearance. Headlines are small and adroit use of empty space contributes to an attractive, orderly page.

Inside, each page is headed with a title which gives the reader direction to its contents. Page two, "Politik," offers national and international political news and a cartoon. Page three, "Kommentar und Reportage," carries two or three major by-lined commentaries or background articles. A page on culture ("Kultur"), which stresses art and literature and letters to the editor and another chronicling ("Chronik") information important to Austrians follow. There is a page of sports news and two or more containing economic and financial news and information. After an advertising section, the back page carries general stories, often of a human interest nature, about less important national and international events. Inside pages generally contain two or three well-composed, aesthetically pleasing photographs. Friday's issues carry a color cultural magazine supplement and color is also used to enhance editorials and advertisements. About 40 percent of the paper's total space is devoted to advertising, allowing the editors to pack considerable meaty content into a relatively thin newspaper.

Die Presse specializes in special pages and inserts, some of which appear regularly and others on an occasional basis. Friday and Saturday/Sunday issues regularly contain a large number of special pages on fashion, modern living, homemaking and leisure time. A regular weekend supplement named "Spectrum" carries reviews, essays and high quality, well-written articles designed to appeal to the paper's generally well-educated readers. On the last weekend of each month, there are special sections on health and on new books. Other in-

---

[6] Thomas Chorherr, chief editor, *Die Presse*, in response to questionnaire, May 4, 1978. The authors are also grateful to Dr. Benno Signitzer, professor, University of Salzburg and Mr. Franz Froehlich for their assistance in providing information about *Die Presse*.

[7] Sandford, *op. cit.*, p. 214.

serts feature household management, management and marketing, and portraits of various professional groups.

Ever since its founding, *Die Presse* has had a reputation for being well informed on international affairs. A large percentage of its space is reserved for accounts of international news and interpretation of their significance—a symbol
of Austrian interest, because of the country's history, location and size, in the
outside world. The paper has a good foreign staff, with full-time correspondents
in Bonn and Washington, D.C. and 18 more part-timers in as many strategic
centers.[8] It also gets information from three wire agencies—APA, UPI and
AP—and AP Wirephoto services. The paper sometimes shares in exchange and
joint publication of stories with *La Stampa* of Italy, *Le Monde* of France, *Die
Welt* of Germany and other leading quality European dailies.

Die Presse makes its principal appeal to intellectuals of the upper middle
class. It considers itself a "genuine medium for decision-makers." About 50 percent of its readers represent the upper-middle income classes and 40 percent
have completed degrees in higher education. An estimated 25 percent are in
decision-making positions. Because *Die Presse* editors consider their paper Austria's best decision-maker's medium, they emphasize analysis and interpretation, especially in financial and consumer affairs areas. They take pride in the
quality and thoughtfulness of the paper's articles. The paper seeks to develop
strong reader-to-newspaper relationships. When a survey sample of Austria's
populace was asked which medium they would miss most if it was not available,
59 percent said *"Die Presse."*

Die Presse is part of an association of 14 leading European dailies called
TEAM, an acronym for "Top European Advertising Media." The group has
organized to cooperate in providing outlets for international advertisers in influential national papers such as *Die Presse* and a means for placing local businesses
in contact with the media of other countries. TEAM-associated newspapers, like
Die Presse, generally seek to appeal to the socially and economically elite who
are the big spenders and who exercise strong influence in business, policy-making and professional circles.

The paper's ownership association and its editorial staff have established a
code of standards for *Die Presse.* It outlines the paper's principles and sets forth
policies. Under the code, the paper pledges itself to support of parliamentary democracy, social justice, the individual responsibility and freedom of the private
citizen, right to own property and freedom of initiative. It aims to defend human
freedoms and human rights in the context of the democratic society. Staff
pledges to respect these policies and to suppress its personal opinions in the interests of objectivity and in support of the papers's policies.

The high principles for which it stands are everywhere evident in *Die
Presse.* Its articles and commentary support free enterprise, the rule of law, personal initiative, individualism and courage. Politically, it exercises middle-of-the

[8] Thomas Chorherr, in response to questionnaire, *loc. cit.* Part-time staffers are presently located in
Bern, Paris, Brussels, Tokyo, Rome, Milan, Madrid, Stockholm, Rotterdam, Cairo, London, Berlin,
Moscow, Belgrade, Munich, Jerusalem, Geneva and Amman.

road liberal views and it strongly defends press freedom. Its news is objective and it does an excellent job of providing background and interpretation of critical issues. Its seriousness, orderliness and neatness compare favorably with similar values in the best elite European dailies. In 1973, the University of Missouri School of Journalism recognized this all-round excellence of *Die Presse* by naming it Newspaper of the Year—a title it justly deserves since it stands on a par with Europe's better dailies and exhibits a generous quantity of those traits characteristic of the world's elite journals.

Rand Daily Mail

(SOUTH AFRICA)

IN RECENT YEARS, South Africa's press, long the continent's freest, has been experiencing such accelerated governmental intimidation and restriction that some now claim "press freedom has disappeared."[1] More than any other paper, the English-language *Rand Daily Mail* has distinguished itself with brave, outspoken resistance against these advancing encroachments by the government. Although the paper has been hauled into court, fined, and censored and has had its reporters arrested and detained, it continues to hold tenaciously to the principles on which it stands: "Non-racialism, an end to apartheid injustices and maintenance of the rule of law."[2]

Despite the mounting restrictions and tensions—or, perhaps because of them—the paper continues to produce high-quality award-winning journalism. Recently, for example, the Checkers Prize for Consumer Affairs journalism went to *Rand Daily Mail* correspondent Vita Palestrant for her exposé of large-scale exploitation of South African consumers, mostly blacks.[3] Throughout its history, the paper has made a name for itself through its investigative reporting and its interest in the total South African public—blacks, coloreds, whites and Afrikaaners.

Because of the history and politics of South Africa, the press there has always been divided into three groups: the Afrikaans, the English-language and the non-European. Although the Afrikaans papers have always been pro-government, there is no official or government-owned daily. The Afrikaaner papers have always been more interested in political partisanship than in straight news

[1] Peter Galliner, "Director's Report to 1978 IPI Assembly," *IPI Report* 27:4 (April/May, 1978), p. 22.
[2] Benjamin Pogrund, deputy editor, and Trevor Bisseker, assistant editor, *Rand Daily Mail*, in response to questionnaire, March 3, 1978.
[3] "Consumers' Ally," *IPI Report*, 27:10 (November, 1978), p. 3.

RAND
Daily Mail
JOHANNESBURG, WEDNESDAY, FEBRUARY 22, 1978.
Price: 12c

'EVE'
NOT IN
STYLE

DON'T miss EVE's
super Winter '78 fa-
shion supplement to-
morrow. Seventeen
pages of great styles
for the coming season,
plus advice from the
fashion boffins on how
to plan a wardrobe. Ac-
tress Gayle Hurmiciutt
models some of the
styles.

It's in the
'Mail' tomorrow

France says no
FRANCE yesterday re-
jected the Rhodesian in-
ternal settlement plan and
called for the Organisation of
African Unity is almost certain to follow suit.
PAGE 2

No rush yet
JOHANNESBURG's liem-
sing department did brisk
business issuing motor
vehicle licences yesterday
— but the last-minute
rush is not on yet.
PAGE 3

Strike talks
A DISPUTE over working
conditions, which led to
about 1 000 workers in
KwaZulu going on strike,
could be resolved through
negotiations.
PAGE 2

Walvis clash
WESTERN negotiators on
South West Africa are be-
lieved to have clashed with
Swapo over Walvis Bay.
PAGE 2

A soppy dog
WHO is a big soppy dog,
very sympathetic and the
world's worst joke teller?
According to Pam Schuck-
it's her husband, South
African racing ace Jody.
PAGE 3

NPSL plan
PLANS for a spectacular
24-team league were an-
nounced by the National
Professional Soccer Lea-
gue yesterday.
BACK PAGE

Kevin says 'no'
SPRINGBOK rugby lock
Kevin de Klerk has turned
down a R1 700- a - month
job offer and will be available for Transvaal this
season.
BACK PAGE

TV highlights
● 6.40 Mysteries of the
Deep
● 7.40 The Tony Randall
Show
PAGE 1

Wall St sags
Gold $181.45
($182.25)
PAGE 13
RDM 100 203.5
(204.7)
PAGE 14

Weather	Page 2
Consumer Mail	5
The World	7
PlayMail	8, 9
Flair	9
Leaders	10
Inside Mail	11
Business Mail	12-14
Stocks	14
Property Mail	15
Turf Mail	24
Social Mail	25, 26
Appointments	16-20
Bridge	20
Crosswords	20
Engagements	20
Radio	22
Car Specials	23
Comics	21-23
Classified	21-23
Auctions	25
Legal	26

Your 'Mail'
Phone the "Mail" 28-1500
ext 234 between 8 am and
4.30 pm for delivery com-
plaints.

Big attack launched on SA business

By RICHARD WALKER

NEW YORK

A MULTI-PRONGED assault on big
business links with South Africa
was launched in the United States
yesterday.

These include a prominent senator's
call for "active discouragement" of investment in South Africa, and a flood of allegations by American specialists before the
United Nations.

Senator Dick Clark, chairman of the Senate's
Africa Panel, has publicly called on the Carter
Administration to take the Western lead and
hit South Africa with all the investment curbs
Sweden supports.

"Financial support of
apartheid should no longer
be tolerated," Sen Clark
said in a prominent article
in the New York Times.

The almost R2 000-mil-
lion South Africa received
in US bank loans in 1976
roughly matched the for-
eign exchange the Republic
needed to cover defence
and fu oil imports, he
said.

Among Sen Clark's pro-
posals were:

● Ending all official in-
vestment support, includ-
ing a stop on all loan and
insurance guarantees, and
the withdrawal of the commercial attache.

● Denying tax credits to
US firms paying taxes in
South Africa that back any
of the Republic's strategic
projects. Barriculas or tor-
der developments, or who
fail to enforce a code of
fair labour practices to be
introduced by the US Gov-
ernment.

The proposals were "mo-
derate, pragmatic and constructive," he claimed. If
they failed to budge South
Africa, "then stronger
measures may be called
for in the future.

Dodge
In another move, Profes-
sor Anne Seidman of the
University of Massachusetts
has told the UN Apartheid
Committee that the same
techniques used to leap-
frog sanctions on Rhodesia
were being used to dodge
the arms embargo against
South Africa.

A booklet she distribut-
ed, "Linkage Charts"
claims to expose in detail
how American technologi-
cal material is pumped into
South Africa through third
nation licensing deals.

Prof Seidman has criti-
cised big business for providing South Africa with
the loss on which to build
its military strength.

Mr Quaciquist, from the
Centre for International
Policy in Washington, said
the IMF was a specialised
UN agency, but through its
generous loans was "en-
couraging selfreliance in
South Africa by reducing
the domestic, political and
economic costs" of its policies.

Prof Seidman, Mr Gu-
arinquist, and a Washington-
based consultant, Mr James
Morrell, now plan to pool
their information on sanc-
tion areas of South African
policy.

They will prepare "depth
research" papers for a special meeting in May.

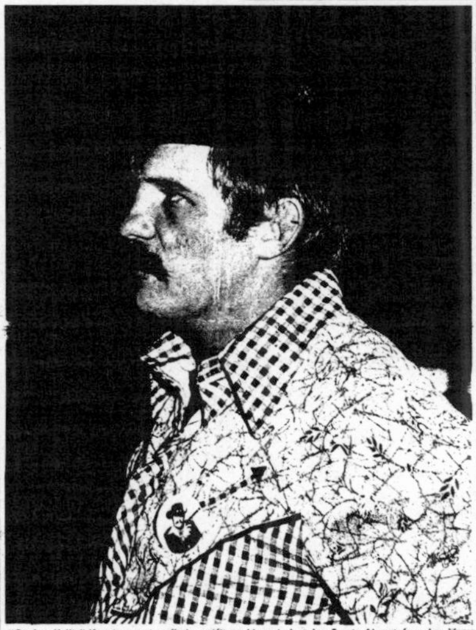

"Cowboy Kallie" Knoetze sports a flashy outfit on his arrival at Jan Smuts Airport from Las Vegas
yesterday after watching the Ali - Spinks world heavyweight title fight. Knoetze's next fight will
be in America on May 27.
● See Back Page

Currency probe on abattoir firm

By HUGH MURRAY
Political Correspondent
CAPE TOWN. — The
Commercial Branch is in-
vestigating allegations that
the consulting engineers
to the controversial City
Deep and Cato Ridge abat-
toirs have been sending
money out of the country
illegally.

They are also looking
into claims by Mr Rupert
Lorimer, MP for Orange
Grove, that certain key
evidence was withheld
from a commission of in-
quiry into the massive cost
escalations on the two
slaughterhouse projects.

The firm involved,
Swerdlow, Cohen, Baur and
Associates, has been sub-
jected to a Reserve Bank
probe and the relevant
papers have now been sent
on to the police.

Mr Stanley Ernest Co-
hen, senior partner of the
firm, was reluctant to
comment, but he confirmed
yesterday that inspectors
from the Reserve Bank
had conducted a probe.

"I have nothing to hide
and therefore I'm not the
least bit worried," he said.

Mr Cohen was the un-
successful National Party
candidate for Johannes-
burg North in the last
election.

The currency investiga-
tion was initiated by the
Minister of Finance, Senator Owen Horwood, after
he received a dossier
from Mr Lorimer.

According to the Com-
mercial Branch, the other
matter relating to the
Commission of Inquiry
was referred to it directly
by the Minister of Justice,
Mr J T Kruger.

This development is sig-
nificant because the report
of the Investigation of Inquiry — giving a clean bill
of health to SCRA — was
tabled in Parliament only
three weeks ago.

The alleged exchange
control contraventions involve a SCRA director, a
Mr C Smith, now living in
Israel. There appears to be
some doubt about his sta-
tus within the company
and the authorities are
checking to see whether a
large amount of money
sent to him by SCRA was
used for the purpose giv-
en by SCRA in its transfer
application to the Reserve
Bank.

Prison count
THE SENATE. — South
Africa's prison population
amounted to a daily aver-
age of 100 802 people last
year, the Minister of Prisons, Mr J T Kruger, dis-
closed yesterday. In reply
to a question put by Mrs
H Suzman (PFP, Houghton)
Mr Kruger said the daily
average of convicted
prisoners comprised a
daily average of 4 481
whites, 74 613 Blacks, 621
Asians and 21 169 colour-
eds. — Sapa.

Breakfast Quip

"There were plural rea-
sons for the be-lo-
vuts poll."

Political Correspondent
THE ASSEMBLY. — The
Post Office has paid out
R19 700 to the widow of
a man who died from in-
juries sustained in a collision with an ostrich on a
road while riding from his
cycles.

It has also donated a
South African postman's
cap to the West German
postal administration.

These items of expendi-
ture were revealed in the
report of the Adminis-
trator-general into the
Accounts
of the postal administra-
tion for the 1976/77 fin-
ancial year.

The Post Office paid
compensation for perso-
nal injuries and for da-
mage to private property
totalling R37 614 in
1977 as against the
1975/76 financial year
and R14 900 more than
the previous year.

It also paid R67 287 in
2 133 cases where regist-
ered articles were not received by the addressees,
R8 394 by parcels not
received, R5 963 for pay-
ments in respect of mis-
sing "cash on delivery"
and R1 372 for deposit-
ers whose savings bank
books had been lost or
stolen or where fraudu-
lent withdrawals had
been made.

R10 700 to bike crash widow

All-race bid by city restaurants

By BOB HITCHCOCK
Race Relations
Correspondent
THE first applications for
multiracial restaurant permits in Johannesburg's
central business district
will be lodged within the
next few days.

Among a dozen appli-
cants for permits to ad-
mit all races to their un-
licensed restaurants are
five of the city's leading
stores—Edgars, Garlicks,
Greatermans, John Orrs
store-Edgars.

In a few weeks at least
nine applications for multi-

racial custom will be lodged by licensed restaurants
in the city.

These will include the
East African Pavilion and
the Phoenix.

Applications will be
machine-by the attorneys
acting for each of the applicants.

All applications will be
supported and coordinat-
ed by the influential Central Business District Association of Johannesburg,
the organisation behind
a campaign to give the
city centre an international image.

The association's chair-
man, Mr Nigel Mandy, re-
cently saw the Cabinet
Ministers concerned with
the applications — the
Minister of Community
Development, Mr Marais
Steyn, and the Deputy
Minister of Plural Rela-
tions and Development, Dr
W L Vosloo.

A number of other own-
ers and managers of cen-
tral city restaurants are
believed to be keen to apply for permits and are
waiting to see the results
of the present applica-
tions.

Mudge cuts Nat SWA majority

By DAVID FORSEY
Staff Africa Bureau
WINDHOEK.—A Nation-
al Party member of the
South West African Legis-
lative Assembly yesterday
crossed the floor to join
Mr Dirk Mudge's Repub-
lic Party, cutting the NP's
majority in the all-white
assembly to two.

Announcing his switch
yesterday, Mr Nico Jan-
sen, the Keetmanshoop re-
presentative, said the NP
leaders were leading the
party into a cul-de-sac.

He said they were too
negative.

In the assembly yester-
day, Mr Mudge gave no-
tice of a motion urging
the members to support
the establishment of an
independent SWA repub-
lic with a democratic system of government that
would promote a common
loyalty among all the residents and would safeguard
the rights of all population
groups.

Terror at mission

By JUSTIN NYOKA
SALISBURY. — A group
of nationalist guerrillas ter-
rorised hundreds of black
schoolchildren at the Goko-
mere Roman Catholic Mis-
sion near Fort Victoria, in
southeastern Rhodesia.

Combined Operations
Headquarters in Salisbury
announced the raid yesterday, but did not say when
it took place.

Church sources said the
children went through a
night of terror, in which
two of them were shot by
a guerilla, who was executed on the spot.

The children, and the
staff of priests, teachers
and nuns, were summoned
to a meeting for lecture
in communists when the
guerillas took over the mission.

The guerillas lectured
to the children and staff
for most of the night.

One guerilla, said to
have been belligously
drunk, shot down two children, after an argument.
He was immediately exe-

cuted by his companions.
One of the children died.

Soon after the shooting
incident Rhodesian Secu-
rity Forces arrived and the
terrorist group took refuge
in the mission.

Combined Operations
Headquarters said in the
gun battle that followed,
one guerilla was killed by
Security Forces and three
pupils were injured by
guerilla fire.

According to Combined
Operations Headquarters,
innocent black victims of
the Rhodesia conflict now
number more than 1 600.

A communique from
Combined Operations Head-
quarters last night said a
Rhodesian soldier, Private
Clemence Nyanga, 26, of
the Drungwe district, had
been killed during a con-
tact in action, reports
Sapa.

The communique said
three tribesmen had been
murdered by terrorists in
the operational area, and
that Security Forces had
killed three terrorists, and
eight terrorist collaborators.

A jam at 4.55p.m. can cost you the deal!

Typek Bond ensures jam-free copying.

Absolute consistency means a
great deal when it comes to office
copying. Each sheet, each ream, each
lot of paper fed into your machine must be
standard. Otherwise, it misfeeds, skips
sheets, or worse still, jams.

That's why it's so reassuring to use
Typek Bond Rotary Precision Cut Paper,
for printing, plain paper copying,
duplicating, typing.

And because it's moisture-proof
wrapped, there's no waviness. Because it's
Rotary Precision Cut, it never varies. In size
squareness, long grain direction. Any way
at all. And because it never varies, it does
not cause jams. Jams that can mean a
great deal, when they cost you
the deal.

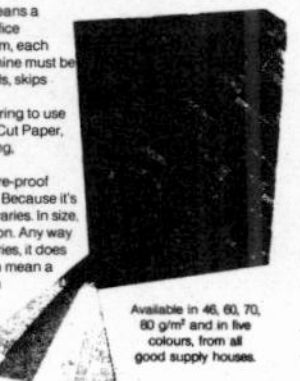

Available in 46, 60, 70,
80 g/m² and in five
colours, from all
good supply houses.

Make Typek Bond your only paper and prove how many ways it saves.

I'd accept new policy — Sybrand

By HELEN ZILLE
Political Reporter
MR SYBRAND van Nie-
kerk, Administrator of the
Transvaal, said yester-
day he would have to op-
tion but to accept a non-
racial open casinos in
Pretoria if the Govern-
ment decided on this
policy.

But he described the
suggestion that the Gov-
ernment was on the point
of changing its permit
policy for admitting
people of all races to
theatres as "irrelevant and
'academic' because such a

policy change was "im-
probable".

Mr van Niekerk—who
in recent weeks has
emerged as an arch-oppo-
nent of open theatres—
made his remarks at a
time when the Govern-
ment is preparing to an-
nounce a broad new policy
for all races to share
theatre and other enter-
tainment facilities.

This was reportedly con-
firmed yesterday by the
Minister of Plural Rela-
tions and Development,
Dr Connie Mulder, who is
chairman of the "permit
committee" investigating

and preparing the guide-
line

Dr Mulder said the idea
was to establish a broad
policy to implement the
policy laid down by the
Prime Minister, Mr Vor-
ster, that where facilities
could not be duplicated,
they should be shared.

Mr Van Niekerk said the
Government would not al-
ter its present policy towards the opera house
without consulting the executive committee of the

3-month call-up is over

CAPE TOWN. — Three-
month call-ups of Citizen
Force and commando sol-
diers will cease from
March 1 unless military
needs dictated otherwise,
a spokesman for the De-
fence Force confirmed yesterday.

Part-time soldiers will
revert to attending short
annual training camps of
not more than 30 days, reports Sapa.

In April last year the
Chief of Staff (Personnel),
Rear-Admiral R A Ed-
wards, said the extending
of national service to two
years was a "trade-off" for
shorter Citizen Force
camps. This would cause
less disruption to the economy.

Dominee is bell-tower baritone

Own Correspondent
CAPE TOWN. — The Rev-
Piet Oot du Toit of the
Three Anchor Bay Dutch
Reformed Church says
he's not much of a singer.
But hundreds of people in
Sea Point stopped to listen
to the sound of his bari-
tone on Sunday evening.

It all happened acci-
dentally switched to the
microphone over the pul-
pit. As a result Sea Point
was treated to a hi-fi ren-
dition of several hymns.

"My son, Piet, came run-
ning to tell my wife that
I was broadcasting all over
Sea Point, and I wasn't
even singing in tune," said
Mr du Toit.

The broadcast lasted 15
minutes and a crowd ga-

thered outside the church.
"You could hear the
singing — mainly my sing-
ing — with a little back-
ground of the choir and
the organ, all over Sea
Point," said Mr du Toit.

The State President's
wife, Mrs Diederichs, told
Mr Du Toit that she had
heard some of the Sea
Point broadcast, at the
Presidential home at
Westbrook.

"There was a north-west
wind blowing," Mr Du Toit
said.

"It must have sounded
quite funny, because
when you think nobody
is listening you tend to
sing rather apprehensibly
stopping every now and
again. The problem is I
really can't sing very
well when the wind's
blowing," he said.

● TO PAGE 2

and Cabinet members are usually well represented on their boards of directors. With one exception, papers for Africans, coloreds and Asians have been owned by whites. The English-language newspapers were intended for the large English-speaking audience in the big cities; however, many educated Africans and coloreds and Asians have been members of the English dailies' audiences. Until recently, all these press divisions enjoyed considerable freedom and protection under South African press law. There was no content-controlling government news agency. All three sections have been privately owned and economically independent.

The *Rand Daily Mail* made its entry into South African journalism on September 22, 1902, just after the Boer War. Founded by H. Freeman Cohen, it quickly provided competition against the *Star,* which had come to Johannesburg by ox-wagon from Grahamstown in 1887. The *Daily Mail's* first editor was Edgar Wallace, who had been a British officer in the Boer War, but was better known as a prodigious popular novelist. The third great Johannesburg English-language paper, the *Sunday Times* was founded in 1906 and, as Professor Hachten observes, it "has always held a unique position in South African journalism; for years it returned a profit of 7,000 percent to stockholders on the original investment."[4] The *Sunday Times* made this annual gain despite the fact that it rented all production from the *Rand Daily Mail.*

The founding of Johannesburg's "big three" English dailies reflects another step in the development of two competitive newspaper chains which have dominated English-language South African journalism ever since. The Argus Printing and Publishing Company got its start by buying Cape Town's *Cape Argus* in 1881. Then it acquired the Johannesburg *Star* in 1889. In the early 1900's, it added several other South African dailies. Argus has become the country's biggest chain, with control of eight newspapers and several leading periodicals. *Rand Daily Mail's* owner, the South African Associated Newspapers (SAAN) began by acquiring the *Cape Times* in 1876. It has added the *Sunday Times* and three other papers to provide a counterpoise to the larger Argus group. The association of SAAN newspapers has shared staff and materials among its members. The *Rand Daily Mail* and *Sunday Times,* in particular, have provided the rest with "numerous innovations such as imaginative makeup, ample illustrations and photographs, and breezy features."[5] For a time during the 1930's and 1940's, Argus and SAAN newspapers so dominated South African journalism that, as it came to power in 1948, the Nationalist Party· could with some validity accuse the two groups of monopolizing the press. But those charges ceased as the Afrikaans press gained circulation and advertising strength.

During its history, the *Daily Mail* has been blessed by a succession of noteworthy editors. Founding editor Edgar Wallace gathered the finest group of journalists in South Africa for his new charge. From 1904–1921, Ralph Ward-Jackson, an ex-cavalry officer, edited the paper with distinction. Laurence Gandar gave outstanding service to the *Mail* and to freedom of the press during his

---

[4] William A. Hachten, *Muffled Drums: The News Media in Africa* (Ames: Iowa State University Press, 1971), p. 240.

[5] Hachten, *op. cit.,* p. 241.

1957–1966 editorship. His successor, Raymond Louw was highly respected in the world press for his handling of the paper during the increased governmental pressures of the 1966–1977 period. And today's editor, Allister Sparks, up from the paper's lower ranks, has already distinguished himself with a Pringle Award for an article on three African cities.[6]

Although not South Africa's largest newspaper—the Johannesburg *Star* has a larger circulation—the *Rand Daily Mail* has made its mark as the nation's outstanding quality newspaper in other ways. As spokesman for the small Progressive Party, which opposes governmental policies, the *Daily Mail* has been the voice of liberal dissent. In its editorials and news columns, it has persistently opposed the ruling Nationalist Party. Of all South Africa's English-language dailies, it has identified most closely with the social and economic problems of the Africans. It has strongly protested arrest and detention laws and has probed poor housing, educational, transportation and penal arrangements for the blacks and the minorities of the nation. It is read the most widely of all the English-language papers by the blacks of South Africa.

For its non-partisan efforts, the *Rand Daily Mail* had had to face a rising tide of apartheid government opposition and oppression, especially during the past decade and a half. Like its English-language counterparts, the *Daily Mail* is founded on libertarian principles and believes firmly in press freedom. But in the 'sixties the government began to make inroads into press freedom, so much so that early in the 1970's South African Trevor Brown was observing: "The press may oppose; it may not expose."[7] In 1969, the government passed a law which gave a newly-created Bureau of State Security power to prevent information they felt prejudicial to public security from being used in the nation's courts. The country's Newspaper Press Union (NPU) queried this move and the South African Society of Journalists (SASJ) protested by saying "As long as this law remains in force, never again will the public of South Africa have any means of knowing how much information is being suppressed and whether the Government . . . is acting genuinely in the interests of the State. . . ."[8] At the time, the *Mail* was being tried for violating the Prisons Act by failing to verify information in its June and July, 1965, exposé of South African prison conditions. During the investigations leading to the trial, security forces raided the *Mail* four times and editor Laurence Gandar had his passport withdrawn. The court decided in favor of the Government and fined SAAN $420, editor Gandar $280, and reporter Benjamin Pogrund, the author of the article, was given a suspended jail sentence.

The trial and the new regulations were merely means to make the press more subservient to the interests of the government. In his remarks to the court at the trial, the State's senior counselor declared the press must not attack government officials or cause stirs and must serve the interests of the country and

[6] "The Birth of a Great Newspaper," *Rand Daily Mail,* Special 75th Anniversary Supplement (September 22, 1977), pp. 2–3.
[7] Trevor Brown, "Free Press Fair Game for South Africa's Government," *Journalism Quarterly,* 48:1 (Spring, 1971), p. 120.
[8] *Rand Daily Mail* (July 9, 1969).

not of small sections of extremists (such as oppressed prisoners). *Rand Daily Mail's* editor Gandar responded with a front page editorial which boldly pointed out that, without press freedom to print news and the right to expose malpractice, "democracy will die."[9] The implications of the governmental actions and trial for the *Daily Mail* and the entire South African press were succinctly spelled out at the time by Sean McBride, Secretary-General of the International Commission of Jurists:

> The *Rand Daily Mail* has criticized the policies of the South African government and dared to publish information which displeases the authorities, hence it must be silenced. Instead of suppressing it openly, an attempt is being made to prosecute it out of existence. In this manner, the *Rand Daily Mail* will be effectively silenced and the rest of the South African press will be intimidated into subservience. In our view, it is the freedom of the press in South Africa which is now at stake in the Gandar trial.

Since that 1969 decision, governmental strictures on the press, and especially on the *Mail*, have increased. In 1972, *Mail* reporter Benjamin Pogrund was given another suspended jail sentence for possessing banned publications.[10] Early in 1973, the Ministry of Information threatened to propose new legislation to deal with papers that stirred racial friction. Late the same year, Prime Minister John Vorster issued a public ultimatum to the press to put its house in order and there was "no doubt that his chief target is the *Rand Daily Mail,* the country's biggest morning paper."[11]

In February, 1974, the Vorster government filed a new law which made liable to one year imprisonment anyone who publishes a declaration or speech by anyone banned from public appearance—an extension of its apartheid laws. In response, NPU created a Press Council with power to fine newspapers guilty of racial incitement up to $9,000. The South African Society of Journalists (SASJ) vigorously protested this attempt to impose self-censorship and many of the English-language newspapers rejected the NPU action.[12]

The Vorster government's response, coming after a long period of silence, was to introduce a code of rigorous discipline on the press and a government-administered Press Council with power to suspend publication, then to shelve its action for a year in 1977 to allow the press time to prepare its own code. That move left the press divided and extremely apprehensive. Journalists feared strong pressures for self-censorship would arise. *Mail* editor Raymond Louw declared the new move presented "real danger that the government will just keep on forcing concessions out of the press and might still bring in the Bill next year."[13] This new threat to the press came on top of 75 laws already regulating the press, the jailing of numerous reporters—especially black—for writing on the uprisings and riots, the seizure of Chief Gatsha Buthelezi's news-

[9] Laurence Gandar, "A Free Press," *Rand Daily Mail* (July 12, 1969), p. 1.
[10] "South Africa," *IPI Report,* 22:1 (January, 1973), p. 7.
[11] "Vorster's Vague Ultimatum," *IPI Report,* 23:1 (January, 1974), p. 1.
[12] "South Africa," *IPI Report,* 24:1 (January, 1975), pp. 15–17.
[13] "Press Split in South Africa over 'Year's Grace'," *IPI Report,* 26:3 (March, 1977), p. 1.

paper, and a tightening of defense laws to enable the government to censor information about internal disorder.

Before the year 1977 had ended, the government made several further moves to harass the press and leave it wondering when a full-scale assault on press freedom would be launched. As a result of his pictures of the June 16, 1976, Soweto riots, the *Mail*'s black photographer Peter Magubane was jailed in August and held in solitary confinement until Christmas. Other *Daily Mail* journalists detained for covering Soweto were blacks Nat Serache, Willie Nkosi, Jan Tugwana and a white British citizen, Patrick Weech.[14] In October, Minister of Justice James Kruger called for an immediate meeting of the industry's Press Council to make judgment on its complaint that the *Mail* front page report of the death of Steve Biko while under police detention had been picked up by the foreign press. Although the Minister absented himself from this "trial of national importance," he charged the *Mail* had published a faulty headline and the government had been dealt serious damage by the overseas transmissions. Under duress from the government, the Council punished the paper by making it put out a front page retraction. Four days later, the Minister, at another snap hearing, lunged out at and threatened closedown of the African newspapr, *The World* for its editorial comment on his handling of the Biko case.[15]

Before the year was over, further blows came which made press freedom in South Africa mere sham. *World*'s editor Percy Qoboza and *Weekend World*'s news editor Aggrey Klaaste were arrested and their papers closed down for their exposure of the Biko affair. Next, Donald Woods, editor of the East London *Daily Dispatch* was banned for five years under the Suppression of Communism Act. In all, nine black journalists were detained without trial for covering the Soweto disturbances. Some additional 150 black journalists lost their rights when dozens of their union organizations were banned, and 28 were arrested for walking a picket line.[16]

In mid-1978, a number of black journalists were still being detained and others had fled the country. The *Mail*'s Jan Tugwana was still being held. Unfortunately, public opinion has not reacted against the suppression. *Natal Witness* editor Richard Steyn recently noted: ". . . a growing number of English-speaking people are coming to believe the propaganda of those in office . . . who equate disclosure, which is the only real weapon the newspapers have, with anti-South African sentiments."[17]

Despite the resistance to government domination put up by the *Rand Daily Mail* and others, some feel the newspapers do not—possibly cannot—fully challenge official moves. In 1971, Brown criticized papers for allowing freedom to remain a consideration secondary to commercial and financial self-interest by

[14] Peter Galliner, "Annual Review of World Press Freedom, 1976," Booklet, International Press Institute, 1977, pp. 20–22.
[15] Raymond Louw, "Africa's Freest Press Fears New Offensive," *IPI Reports*, 26:10 (November, 1977), p. 2.
[16] "World Press Freedom Review of 1977," *IPI Report*, 27:1 (January, 1978), p. 8.
[17] "Another South African Journalist Flees; Editor Queries 'Duty' of Press," *IPI Report*, 27:7 (August, 1978), p. 4.

writing, "It is difficult to avoid the conclusion that management is concerned more with material self-interest than morality."[18] Although they have protested the government's encroachments, the owners have found themselves powerless and, in fact, are now being used by the government to restrict press freedom.

Its stand in the 1960's as the most effective white voice against apartheid cost the *Daily Mail* loss of readers. Circulation dropped from around 125,000 in 1961 to only 111,000 in 1968. Even though about 8,000 blacks now subscribe and an undetermined number buy it on the streets, its circulation has climbed only slowly in the 1970's to 138,000 at present, the distribution of which may be categorized as follows: subscriptions, 12 percent; street sales, 40 percent; and agents and cafes, 48 percent.[19]

The *Rand Daily Mail*, owned and published by SAAN, has a total staff of 874. Of that number, 370 technicians and an administrative staff of 380 serve the *Daily Mail* and two sister Sunday papers. An editorial staff of 124 works exclusively for the *Daily Mail*. The editor is Allister Sparks. His deputy is Benjamin Pogrund, a former *Mail* reporter, and Trevor Bisseker serves as assistant editor. Five reporters are on full-time duty at the nation's capital and another eight serve on teams of full-time correspondents in London, Salisbury and Windhoek. Twenty stringers report from Europe, Australia, New Zealand, Israel, Zambia, Kenya, Washington and New York. The paper also receives the releases of four wire services, four syndication services, and the UPI wirephoto input.[20] At least three overseas reporters have attained distinction: Billy Ward-Jackson, Raymond Heard and Stanley Uys. Since South African universities have been slow to recognize their responsibilities for training journalists and most papers have only a cursory in-service training program, the *Daily Mail* trains its own young journalists. The qualifications and experience demanded depend on the job category being filled.

The *Rand Daily Mail*'s staff each day presents an attractive, high-quality product averaging some 26–30 pages in length. The paper's contents by category on a typical day would be composed of these percentages: international news, 5 percent; national, 7; local, 5; features and analyses, 7; editorials, 2; sports, 7; business, 6; home, 3; syndicates (cross-words, comics, etc.) and schedules (eg., radio), 3; and advertising, 55 percent.

The front page is headed by the paper's nameplate in color. Stories are made up into a variety of forms and patterns across the 10-column broadsheet, some of them stretching horizontally across four or five columns, others running vertically down a single column. The left-hand column typically contains a promotion for a coming feature, "Quick Mail" capsules of the paper's stories for the day and their page location, and "Inside," a listing of additional contents. Typically, too, the front page contains predominantly South African news, one or two color pictures and a large advertisement in the lower right-hand corner of the page.

[18] Brown, *op. cit.*, p. 125.

[19] Pogrund and Bisseker questionnaire.

[20] *Ibid.* The paper receives the S.A. *Press Association, UPI, AP* and *Reuters* wires and syndicated materials from *The Observer*, the *Telegraph, Financial Times* and *Gemini*.

International, national and local news are normally found on pages two to seven. The paper's regular columns, pages or sections are entitled "Mail," such as "Consumer Mail," "Business Mail," "Property Mail," "Play Mail," "Racing Mail," and "Sports Mail." Numerous features and investigative pieces are scattered throughout, both within the regular columns and between them. Use of excellent visuals—large action photographs, cartoons and maps—and striking layout effectively entice the reader. Throughout, the paper's news, features and editorials treat all South Africans as people and their selection and slant make its stand against apartheid obvious.

The *Mail* employs up-to-date technology. Video display terminals have just been installed for writing and editing stories. Composition is carried out with a mixture of hot and cold type and litho offset computer-controlled presses. The paper pioneered in South Africa in employing full-color news photography and advertising. With rare exceptions, a large full-color photograph graces the front page and there are usually six or more major full-color advertisements scattered throughout the paper. Color tones and registration are pleasant and accurate.

The paper and its staff have received an enviable number of awards and citations which testify to the quality of its content and makeup. In 1966, after its courageous reporting of gruesome conditions in government prisons, the paper was awarded the American Newspaper Publishers Association World Press Achievement Award for "contribution to human betterment and freedom." In 1968, it received the Stellenbosch Farmers' Winery Award, South Africa's main award for journalism, for enterprising works in the field. Three years later (1971) it took the SASJ's Pringle Award for outstanding services to journalism, an award it again captured in 1977. In 1972, it won, for the fifth time, the Frewin Trophy, the nation's principal award for newspaper technical production. Meantime, individual *Mail* journalists have received many awards: Laurence Gandar, the Institute of Journalists' gold medal (1965) for service to journalism; Mervyn Rees and Chris Day for drug investigation (1969); Lin Menge and Wilmar Utting for an exposé of slums (1971); Bob Hitchcock for a series on Zambia (1973); Howard Preece, financial reporter of the year (1975); and Peter Magubane for photographic coverage of the Soweto riots and Adam Payne for industrial reporting (1976).[21]

Without a doubt, the *Rand Daily Mail* has been and continues to be South Africa's most courageous and enterprising English-language daily. It remains the country's liveliest and most liberal daily, with a genuine interest in serious news, excellent international coverage, forthright reporting amidst South Africa's confusing ethnic and political relationships and in the face of increasing pressures from its apartheid government. It aims to publish as boldly and as completely as possible "while remaining within the confines of the law and good taste."[22] When it sometimes appears oblique or too cautious and tactful, critics must bear in mind that the *Mail* must continually "walk the fine line" between "serving the public interest and ensuring the paper's survival."[23] For courage,

[21] Pogrund and Bisseker questionnaire.
[22] *Ibid.*
[23] Pogrund and Bisseker questionnaire.

public service, quality journalism and defense of libertarian principles under such conditions, the *Rand Daily Mail* justly deserves a place among the world's elite dailies. As Donald Trelford, editor of London's *Observer* observed on the occasion of the *Mail*'s 75th anniversary in 1977, because of its outstanding contribution to human rights, the causes it has championed and the multi-racial character of its readership, "The *Rand Daily Mail* is a source of pride to newspapermen throughout the world."[24]

Renmin Ribao

(CHINA)

ONE OF THE WORLD'S most unusual and unorthodox dailies, if one judges by the usual standards of quality journalism, is China's *Renmin Ribao (People's Daily)*. It has no reporters of its own, sometimes takes two months to write an editorial, buries world-shaking events in its back page briefs, contains almost no advertising, and still sells for the equivalent of two and one-half U.S. cents. While the paper probably contributes little to "a world community of reason," there can be no doubt that it ranks as one of the world's most widely read serious journals and serves as the ultimate voice of authority for China's more than 800,000,000 people.

Perhaps in some ways *Renmin Ribao* should not be considered at all in this book. In many respects, it is more a governmental bulletin board or organ of political agitation and propaganda than a newspaper. It constitutes a classical example of the restricted or managed paper of the closed or restricted society discussed in the introductory sections of this book. As the voice of the Central Committee of the ruling Chinese Communist Party, it provides "must" reading for all who wish to be informed on Party matters, be they officials, Party leaders or diplomats or interested "China-watchers" outside the Bamboo Curtain. *People's Daily* does not represent the State, as *Izvestia* does the U.S.S.R.; rather, it is similar to *Pravda* in that it serves Party interests. Since a more moderate government has taken over in China, *Renmin Ribao,* while remaining the firm guardian of Party interests, has become less directly and openly supportive of the Party.

To grasp fully why *Renmin Ribao* behaves as it does, one must understand those elements in Communist ideology which affect the press. According to Dr. Alan P. Liu, "The structure and operation of the Chinese Communist press are

[24] "Tributes to the *Mail* from Around the World," *Rand Daily Mail* Special 75th Anniversary Supplement, *op. cit.,* p. 2.

人民日报
RENMIN RIBAO
1978年2月22日 星期三
农历戊午年正月十六 第10820号

文艺到山村

广西壮族自治区金秀瑶族自治县公社队，坚持文艺为工农兵服务的方向，常年在深山瑶寨巡回演出。这件党的好政策，受到社员群众的欢迎。

新华社记者摄

坚决把"四人邦"颠倒了的干部路线是非纠正过来
安徽采取果断措施全面落实干部政策

充分发挥老干部的骨干作用，积极培养选拔青年干部，妥善安排知识分子干部，调动百分之九十五以上干部的积极性，迅速发展全省社会主义革命和建设的大好形势

本报讯 中共安徽省委遵循党的十一大路线，以揭批"四人邦"为纲，把"四人邦"颠倒了的干部路线是非纠正过来，认真落实党的干部政策，实行按劳分配，把在十次、十一次路线斗争中受受冲的干部充实到各级领导班子中来，分发挥他们的骨干作用。同时，坚持在职训分子干部，正确对待知识分子干部，迅速发展了全省社会主义革命和建设的大好形势。

张广厚又获世界水平的重要成果

（在函数理论研究中不畏艰难勇往直前）

新华社北京二月二十一日电 我国青年数学家张广厚在函数理论的研究中，最近取得重要的具有世界水平的新的重要成果。

四川研制成功群众欢迎的电子新产品

新华社成都二月二十一日电 不久前，科技人员在四川中江县的千坊地区测定了一个井位，解决了三表之间的相互关系，井场的社员们欢欣雀跃。

一坐五万吨级干船坞建成

落实政策是做好备耕工作的重要环节
——中共昌潍地委书记魏坚毅谈落实农村经济政策

新华社济南二月二十一日电 山东省潍坊地区最近，经过一年来扎实的调查，提高一认识到搞好农业生产备耕工作的重要意义。

（下转第四版）

（下转第四版）

substantially determined by two elements . . . the Leninist (or Soviet) and the Maoist conceptions of mass persuasion and the press."[1] Lenin believed—and pushed for—a press fully integrated in the structure of the Communist Party and its government, dependent on the Party and supportive of it. To Lenin, it naturally followed that the contents of the press should reflect the political or economic tasks of the Party in each stage of national development. Chairman Mao Tse-tung built on these concepts; he added three strategical concepts of his own. China's political system, under him, united four classes in a "people's democratic dictatorship," and allowed the existence of a non-party press in China, thus accounting for China's numerous local newspapers. Mao believed in mass mobilization and the rights of mass organizations to publish their own papers. Thirdly, Mao felt so strongly journalists' first duties were to carry out revolution in the name of the Party that he opposed a professional role for them. Whereas in the Soviet Union reporters and editors are politicians first and journalists second, in China they are almost entirely political representatives for the Party. Thus, journalism exists in China to educate, to propagandize and to mobilize the masses to Party objectives. In 1948, Mao told a group of Chinese newspaper editors:

> You comrades are newspapermen. Your job is to educate the masses to know their own interests, their own tasks and the Party's general and specific policies. Teach the people to know the truth and arouse them to fight for their own emancipation.

The achievement of these goals places objective reporting of factual information—so important to Western journalism—in a secondary role. As a result, any "negative news" about the Party, any sex or crime does not appear in the Chinese papers. There is little room for criticism of the Party; sporadic criticism of individuals or failures in some aspect of the Party's program appears only in the local press. Nor is there much information about personnel changes in the Party, administration or army, about political meetings or discussions or economic statistics above the district level. All such "hard" facts appear in the local communications medium—the wall posters or *dazibaos* (formerly known as *tat-zepao*), which make it possible to address the public without use of the regular mass media of print and radio.[2] This avenue makes it possible for the Party both to observe the Chinese Constitution of 1975, which guarantees freedom of the press as long as the socialist system, the laws and the leadership of the Party are not contradicted or infringed, and to use *Renmin Ribao* fully as a tool for wide propagation of official Party ideology and opinions.

Although it is not China's largest newspaper, *Renmin Ribao* probably comes as close to being a national newspaper as can be found in the nation. Its exact official circulation figures are unpublished and difficult to determine, but it is known the paper sells well over six million copies each day. One well-in-

[1] Alan P. L. Liu, "Communist China," in *The Asian Newspapers' Reluctant Revolution*, edited by John A. Lent (Ames: The Iowa State University Press, 1971), p. 43.

[2] Helmut Opletal, "Four Observations on Chinese Mass Media," *The Asian Messenger*, (Autumn/Winter, 1977), pp. 38–9.

267

formed source indicates circulation hovers around the eight million mark, which would be about one copy for each 100 Chinese citizens. Certainly *Renmin Ribao*'s growth has been remarkable in the past decade; whereas circulation figures were about two million in 1968, today estimates have tripled or quadrupled. Also, "the paper is now printed in 17 other cities instead of nine and six cities instead of three get pages by facsimile."[3] However, because of the great distances in China, poor transportation facilities and high illiteracy, the paper does not penetrate the provinces extensively. But it appears safe to say the influence of *Renmin Ribao* is felt throughout the land and that copies filter to opinion leaders on a national scale.

In fact, *Renmin Ribao*'s circulation figures belie actual readership. Issues of the paper are posted at most city intersections in glass-encased "holders" and read aloud in cities and on farms and communes. The official news agency Hsin-hua (New China News Agency) disperses its articles widely. Editorials are frequently read over the People's Broadcasting Station (Radio Peking), which reaches many villages and communes by wired speaker systems. What is more, the paper's important stories and editorials are repeated in China's numerous regional dailies, which are found in every province, autonomous region and municipality in China and whose circulation ranges from 200,000 up to 900,000.

Despite *Renmin Ribao*'s large circulation and nation-wide influence in behalf of the Party, it is not China's largest circulation daily. Best estimates now place readership of the daily eight-page tabloid-size *Reference News (Tsan-kao Hsiao-hsi* or *Cankao Xiaoxi)* somewhere between nine and ten million each day—to say nothing of the extra ten or so who read copies second-hand or have stories read to them from it. Published six times each week, *Reference News* comes closest in China to being a daily newspaper in the normal usage of the term. Its content consists primarily of current world events excerpted from the international press, plus a special column on scientific news, in which Peking has particular interest. Its coverage of breaking news stories is generally unbiased; "The presentation of world affairs is generally balanced and stresses factual information. . . ."[4] While *Reference News* items are rarely distorted or expurgated, bias does occur in the selection of stories included—for two reasons. First, as one China-watcher points out, "There is a limit on how much you (can) put into eight tabloid pages."[5] Secondly, there is the natural inclination to reflect the Party slant of the moment. Presently, for example, stories are rather anti-Soviet.

The Soviet writer Fyodor Kovtov has called *Reference News* China's "closed press" as contrasted with the "open press" exemplified by *People's Daily* and other publications. While *Reference News* prints no Party speeches, no proclamations by Chinese governmental leaders and no lengthy editorials glorifying socialism in the country, it is closed in the sense that, at least until recently, it has only been available to Party and government cadre. The ordinary Chinese

[3] Robert L. White, II, "Second Journey to China," *Mexico Ledger,* Mexico, Missouri, 1977.
[4] Opletal, *op. cit.,* p. 39.
[5] Chang Kuo-sin, "World News Read only by China's Selected Few," *IPI Report,* 25:2 (February, 1976), p. 2.

individual cannot subscribe. As is the case with local papers, foreigners cannot obtain copies, but they can buy *Renmin Ribao*. Even today, the masthead of *Reference News* carries the line, "An internal publication; preserve with care." Since the remainder of the Chinese press, including *People's Daily* carried almost no news of the outside world, *Reference News* was originally designed to keep the trusted Party cadre and official leadership informed on news unfit for the public press as it took place in the world outside China. Chinese writers are now calling *Reference News* a "semi-open" press, possibly because "almost anyone can read (it) now, if he wants to," and more literate Chinese are reading it both for its foreign articles and because "it now publishes more and more information on internal events."[6] One authority suggests the leaders of China's closed society may allow the open reporting of international and even a certain amount of internal news as a kind of safety valve; since people hunger for news, it is better to satisfy them in a controlled way than to encourage clandestine listening to foreign broadcasts by shutting off news of the outside world entirely.

People's Daily or *Renmin Ribao*, as it is now referred to in the romanization promoted in the People's Republic of China (under the Wade-Giles form it was called *Jen-min Jih-pao*), was supposedly founded in the caves of Yenan province in 1948, but that paper was really the *Liberation Daily*, the important Party paper in Shanghai. Instead *Renmin Ribao* got its start in the Hopei province towards the end of the civil war in 1948 as the main Party paper, and it was moved to Peking the next year. Under Chairman Mao, it became the tool Lenin believed a newspaper should be, "collective propagandist, collective agitator and collective organizer, totally integrated with the Communist Party and government." In China, the press was organized from national to local levels in correspondence with the territorial-administrative divisions of government, with the Department of Propaganda in charge.[7]

Whenever the Party or government makes a new move or takes a position on an international issue, the *Renmin Ribao* has been—and continues to be—the first apologist. In that role, it has dealt almost exclusively with the "big" national and international issues, giving about 60 percent of its space to the former and 40 percent to the latter. Local news have been left to the provincial newspapers, which have increased in number phenomenally from an estimated 200 to over 1,500 during the 'fifties and 'sixties as the government agitated for agricultural cooperatives and people's communes. The main news in *Renmin Ribao* has been largely concerned domestically with national progress and internationally with unfavorable aspects of events related to its ideological foes, whether the west or the other Communist nations. During the 'sixties, for example, it lashed out repeatedly against "U.S. imperialism in Vietnam." Since 1965, its attacks on the Soviet Union have become increasingly vitriolic.

During the late 1960's and until 1976, the *People's Daily*, like all Chinese propaganda and media organizations, came under the nearly unchallenged control of the so-called "Gang of Four." From about 1973 to 1976, when Yao Wenyuan was the de facto propaganda director of the Party and Chang Chun-chiao

---

[6] Opletal, *op. cit.*, p. 39.
[7] Rita A. Ropp, "China Press Takes Orders," *Grassroots Editor* (Fall, 1976), p. 9.

the politburo member responsible for propaganda and ideology, the paper particularly reflected the factional views of the Gang of Four. After the purge of the Gang in October, 1976, the new, more moderate regime under Chairman Hua Ku-feng has experimented with the content and format of the paper. Attempts have been made to make it more representative of the broad spectrum of opinion in the Party.

Today, as it has been in the past, *Renmin Ribao* is housed in a four-story unimpressive building on Peking's Wang Fu Ching street. It is partly concealed by a low brick wall on which hang display boxes containing the paper's latest editions. Until recently, Liberation Army soldiers armed with automatic rifles and fixed bayonets barred the entrance of anyone lacking official clearance.[8] Now that moderates have assumed power, the guards—and the formality— remain, but they are no longer armed.

Inside, a staff of 1,000 produces *Renmin Ribao*'s typical morning six-page issues seven days a week. An editorial staff of 400, up from 300 during Maoist days, writes and edits the paper. Its two pages of domestic and foreign news is supplied by the New China News Agency (NCNA), which has staff stationed in about 70 foreign countries. The NCNA, in addition to supplying news, is "the mouth and ear of the people, the Party and the Government," responsible for "control" over news, and it maintains close identification with Peking's foreign affairs establishment.[9] Because of NCNA. *Renmin Ribao* has no local reporters of its own and just two foreign correspondents, one in Tokyo and the other in London. One Party official explained this phenomenon by saying: "There is no point in having our own correspondents in China because we are doing the same work. So dealing with news is simple for us because all our news come from NCNA."[10]

Four of the pages of *Renmin Ribao* are filled with features on Chinese life, much from amateur contributors from schools, hospitals, factories, communes, the Army and other institutions.[11] As Chinese officials explain, "Most articles are written collectively. We are the Party organ—the paper of the Central Committee . . . (so) they must be the views of the Party."[12]

On a typical day, the first page of *People's Daily* contains important news and commentaries. Page two carries economic news. The third page has articles related to the political sphere, to art and to literature. The fourth is theoretically oriented, dealing with academic topics designed to propagate the Party and Communistic views. The final two pages relate to the international scene.

According to visiting journalists, the editorial is divided into five sections: domestic news, international news, the Propagation of Theory Department, Arts and Literature, and the Mass Work Department. The last deals with readers' letters, suggestions and visitors. Since the moderates have taken over, the new

[8] "Inside People's Daily," *Time* (March 12, 1973), p. 62.
[9] "Keeping News in the National Interest," *Time* (March 12, 1975), p. 31.
[10] Derek Ingram, "Inside Peking: The *People's Daily*," *Commonwealth Press Union Quarterly*, (April, 1973).
[11] John Burns, "China's 'Newspaper' with No Reporters," *The Christian Science Monitor* (October 24, 1974), p. 3.
[12] Ingram, *op. cit.*

editor-in-chief of *Renmin Ribao* has been Hu Chi-wei, who was assistant editor in the 1950's and has worked on the paper ever since.[13] Under the Gang of Four, the editorial role was more tenuous and there was high turnover of leadership, to preserve the principle of collective leadership. Previous editors have either disappeared from public view or have been sent to Communist indoctrination camps for re-education.

Renmin Ribao editors work long—sometimes an entire month—and diligently on editorials. For important national and international subjects, the leader-writing process begins with a list of subjects the Central Committee instructs the paper to cover. Then, since editorials always appear in triplicate, writers of *Renmin Ribao* meet with representatives from *Red Flag* and the *Liberation Army Daily* to agree on a draft for an editorial. That copy then goes to the Central Committee for approval or suggested revisions. When the leader finally appears, it carries the imprimatur of the politburo of the Party. On less important domestic issues, *Renmin Ribao* frequently "goes it alone" and takes less time.[14] While Chairman Mao used to write some of the editorials, to date Chairman Hua has yet to write one.

Editors of *Renmin Ribao* are appointed by the Party's Central Committee. None of the paper's staff nor that of other dailies may be a member of the Politburo or the Central Committee, but they sometimes sit in on the Committee's deliberations. Since *Renmin Ribao* plays such a vital role in the Party's ideology and work, half of the editorial staff are Party members, as compared with about three percent for other papers.[15]

Although *Renmin Ribao* has an editorial staff of about 400, only about one-third of them are at the paper's headquarters to produce copy at any given time. Another one-third is doing investigation at the grass-roots level for full-page features, generally eulogizing the work of the Party or the satisfaction of the citizens. To some, their work comprises the heart of the paper. In a report on education, for example, dozens of the paper's staff will fan out to educational institutions all over the country, then converge and collectively produce a feature page. The final third of *Renmin Ribao*'s staff will be at the special May 7th school for its staff, where, for a full year, cadres study Marxism while doing manual labor.

The equipment at the paper's headquarters is outdated and very much of the work of production is still done by painstaking handwork techniques. The handwritten copy of the editors is laboriously set by girls who must deal with up to 6,000 different characters. About 140 printers are employed to set about 2,000 characters for each edition. "Reproductions of the pages are then sent by facsimile to three machining centers and by matrices to eleven other printing shops."[16] Although editors hope to go offset soon, the paper is still printed on a 1952 model East German letterpress unit staffed by teams of six men and women. The old press is capable of running off an average of 40,000 four-page

[13] "Moderates Take Over in China," *IPI Report*, 26:4 (April, 1977), p. 2.
[14] "Read All About It," *The Economist* (November 18, 1972), p. 23.
[15] *Ibid.*
[16] "China's Barefoot Journalist," *Media* (July, 1975).

papers an hour. *Renmin Ribao*'s average six pages daily makes necessary a second run and with circulation now reaching an estimated 1.6 million for Peking alone, press runs are long. Post Office employees are responsible for the stuffing and mailing of subscriptions. Matrices (all editions are the same throughout the country) are either delivered by plane or by electronic fascimile transmission to the other 17 cities in which the paper is printed.

The average pay for *Renmin Ribao* editorial staff is 80 yuans (about $40.) per month. The editor-in-chief, at 290 yuan a month (over $145.), receives the best salary, while the lowest monthly pay amounts to only 40 yuan, or just over $20. Everyone works three shifts, for it is necessary to operate 24-hour days to produce the paper. Work weeks are six days long.

Editors of the paper admit to two persistent problems: tardy delivery and dullness. Although technically it is a morning paper, one Chinese official explains, "Sometimes the *People's Daily* is a morning paper, and sometimes it is an afternoon paper." Although readers complain, the daily 3 A.M. deadline is ignored if late-breaking events occur. China's as yet under-developed transportation, so vital to the production and delivery of the paper, also often contributes to the paper's tardiness. Editors also admit their stories are frequently long and dull and cause reader frustration. But they are caught with the dilemma of having to present lengthy, philosophical apologetic materials in behalf of Communism and the Party in brief, interesting form. Speaking to this problem, one official of *Renmin Ribao* explained: "We can only solve it by a process of struggle, improvement and reform, followed by more struggle, improvement and reform. The trouble is that all correspondents would like to write long articles."[17]

More than 90 percent of *Renmin Ribao*'s copies are sold on subscription. The few copies sold at newsstands go for about two and one-half U.S. cents. Three of the five yuan received from sale of a copy go into production costs, another to costs of distribution and the remainder to the government for redistribution as "development money."[18] Distribution is handled by the Post Office. Cost of the paper to subscribers is 18 yuan a week, of which 25 percent goes to the Post Office for delivery. Although paid advertisements are few, the paper has operated with comfortable profits. For the past several years, surpluses have run at about 45 million yuan (some $22.5 million) annually. The excess is, of course, turned over to the State. When there is need for new equipment—as has been the case of the request for offset presses—appeal is made to the Government.

People's Daily has always received letters to its editors, but until recently only a few were ever published. Several enthusiastic responses were published, for example, when the paper called for a new, lively writing style in 1972. Since the Gang of Four has been deposed, more reader opinions have been printed. One January, 1977, issue carried nine letters openly criticizing either the former regime or the newspaper's style and contents. Shortly after that step, Pan Fei, deputy editor-in-chief of the paper commented: "Although we are a party paper . . . it does not mean we have no freedom of the press. We publish letters cri-

[17] Burns, *op. cit.*, p. 3.
[18] "China's Barefoot Journalist," *op. cit.*

ticizing the government. Sometimes names are signed to the letters."[19] A "Letters to the Editor" column has been published sporadically ever since.

Since the moderates have come to power, *Renmin Ribao* has instituted other changes which reflect greater freedom from Party domination. Fewer polemical articles have been published. There has been increased emphasis on the "investigation reports" of the situation in local areas. Whereas the upper right hand corner formerly carried a quotation from Chairman Mao, Marx, Engels, Lenin or Stalin, beginning in 1977 this space has been used for quotations from a wide range of sources, photographs and even brief news articles. Occasionally an issue will carry cartoons on the front page—an obvious attempt to appeal to reader requests for less dullness and heady theorizing about Party philosophy and actions.

Since it came to power in 1976, the present moderate government has taken significant steps towards modernization and opening its doors to the outside world. Extreme leftist publications have been closed down. Chairman Hua Kuo-feng has felt secure enough to travel across Asia and Europe to establish new diplomatic ties. Japan and China have signed a pact which will provide open relationships. The once-closed nation appears increasingly open to ideas and artifacts from the outside, to overseas trade, even to the movement of journalists inside the country. Recently, a hundred writers and editors were told the official Party policy now allows greater freedom of expression and that Chairman Hua wishes to implement the principles of "letting a hundred flowers blossom and a hundred schools of thought contend."

In his 1971 book, *800,000,000: The Real China*, Ross Terrill illustrated graphically the wide influence of *Renmin Ribao* as he told how drivers and governmental aides alike offered political views direct from the paper and how China-watchers consider its pages an invaluable source on developments within the great nation of China.[20] Although it is certain *Renmin Ribao* has made and is continuing to make a strong impact on the Chinese society and to provide outsiders insights into China's thinking and change, it is equally certain the paper has been and remains loyal to the Central Committee and the Party, skillfully using information to support their views and causes. It should prove interesting to observe what impact China's new openness and modernization will have on the contents, format and style of this serious, high-quality newspaper, still with ways often strange to the Western sense, as it continues to serve as China's outstanding journalistic voice.

[19] White, *op. cit.*
[20] Ross Terrill, *800,000,000: The Real China* (New York: Delta, 1971), pp. 40–41.

The Scotsman

(SCOTLAND)

DIGNIFIED. AUTHORITATIVE. IMPARTIAL. Honest. Enlightened. Distinctive. Patriotic, yet constructively critical. Enterprising. Acute judgment. Progressive spirit. Independent. Prestigious.

Every one of these descriptors has been used to characterize Edinburgh's stately *Scotsman* newspaper by journalists and civic leaders in a position to know. What is more, these compliments have not been given once, but frequently over the paper's more-than-160-year history, indicating the high quality standards it has held since its inception and continues to maintain today.

When *The Scotsman* celebrated its centenary as a daily in 1955, people from the former Prime Minister of Great Britain on down took advantage of the occasion to laud the paper. Winston Churchill wrote of the paper: "It represents the highest traditions of British journalism. . . ." Lord Bilsland, then President of the Scottish Council for Development and Industry, praised its "honesty, patriotism and constructive criticism." The High Chancellor of Great Britain, Lord Kilmuir remarked about *The Scotsman*'s long-standing "authority, independence and literary distinction." Scotland's Secretary of State cited its freedom from bias and good reporting. Others have praised its spirit of independence, sense of responsbility to the Scottish people and enlightened commentary on public affairs.[1]

Even rival newspapermen have registered their admiration for *The Scotsman*. On the occasion of its one hundredth year observance, Sir William Haley, then editor of the *Times* of London called The Scotsman "distinctive." Mr. A. Wadsworth, editor of the *Manchester Guardian* noted his rival's tradition of independence and forthrightness. The *Observer*'s editor, David Astor, remarked about the great respect attributed to *The Scotsman* the world over and its skilled and careful presentation of news. Calling *The Scotsman* "as national as the kilt," John Gordon, editor-in-chief of the *Sunday Express* wrote: "Its independence, its integrity and its judgment on all matters . . . made it great newspaper." The most generous of rival praise for *The Scotsman* came from Sir Linton Andrews, editor of the *Yorkshire Post* and vice-chairman of the British Press Council:

As one of its constant readers for half the century, I appreciate the scholarly care and integrity in its editing, the soundness of its reporting, and the weight of its influence. Nor can I, as a journalist, fail to acknowledge its outstanding technical

[1] All these comments and observations are taken from "Scotland's National Newspaper: 1817–1955," *The Scotsman*, Edinburgh, 1955.

enterprise. . . . The public spirit we need for the best working of democracy has its champions. While papers of national standing and influence like *The Scotsman* keep to their historic character we need not despair of our method of government. It is a fine thing for the Highlands and Lowlands alike that this great paper keeps their just interests to the forefront in Britain's political agenda. . . .[2]

The *Scotsman*'s plaudits extend beyond the British Isles. In 1963, the University of Missouri School of Journalism awarded the paper its Honor Medal, a recognition given only to a very few foreign elite newspapers, citing the paper for its "editorial independence, good writing, and usually acute judgment of events, men and situations." Similar statements praising *The Scotsman* continue to the present moment.

Little wonder, then, that *The Scotsman* has sometimes been labelled the "London *Times* of Scotland." Like the *Times*, *The Scotsman* is a national paper. Its owner, newspaper magnate Lord Thomson declared in 1967: ". . . it is one of the most vigorous national newspapers I know. . . ."[3] Like the *Times*, too, it combines dignity, a progressive spirit and prestige with stability, responsibility and reliability.

From its founding as a weekly in 1817, *The Scotsman* has been committed to the highest standards of quality journalism. At its birth, it "at once proclaimed itself as a journal devoted to liberal institutions."[4] The paper was started because its founders were convinced that the Edinburgh press of the times was spiritless, timid about reporting political matters and entirely too dependent on government. The first issues were smuggled like contraband goods into the hands of timid readers by clerks and porters. *The Scotsman* quickly became recognized by the public as an authoritative, independent voice on topical affairs.

The Scotsman was the product, not of journalists or of a media magnate, but of concerned citizens with limited financial resources. The seven original shareholders included William Ritchie, a Supreme Court solicitor; John Ritchie, a haberdasher; Charles Maclaren, a Customs clerk; John M'Donald, a silk manufacturer; John Robertson, a bookseller; A. Abernathy, a printer; and John M'Diarmid, a banker. None was wealthy. Their stated aim was to launch a weekly which "by uniting original discussion with a history of passing events shall maintain the character of a political and literary journal."[5] Under its scrolled masthead, the first issue carried the maxim: "This is not the cause of faction, or of party, or of any individual, but the common interest of every man in Britain."

While all seven contributed to the paper's contents, William Ritchie and Charles Maclaren became joint editors. Ritchie devoted himself to the literary side of the paper and Maclaren to the political. Their abilities and personalities complemented each other. Maclaren was a scholarly man of science, always

[2] "Scotland's National Newspaper: 1817–1955," *loc. cit.*

[3] Magnus Magnussen et al, *The Glorious Privilege: The History of the Scotsman* (London, Thomas Nelson & Sons, Ltd., 1967), Foreword.

[4] *Ibid.*, p. 3.

[5] Pamphlet, "The First Stage: Early Finance and Administration," *The Scotsman*, Edinburgh.

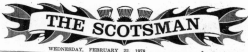

THE SCOTSMAN

No. 42,020

WEDNESDAY, FEBRUARY 22, 1978

3 a.m. news

PRICE 10p

Deadly blow to job plans feared

By TOM JAMES, Our Political Correspondent

Britain fears a deepening of the world trade recession which will deal a deadly blow to the Government's efforts to create more jobs.

The fears were voiced by a sombre Prime Minister at yesterday's meeting of the Government, Labour Party and TUC liaison committee.

Mr Callaghan envisages a growth of protectionism among the industrialised nations rather than the expanding role they agreed at the last economic summit.

He thinks France will lead the rush to bring down the economic shutters, but he is afraid that the United States will not be far behind.

The Prime Minister has already been in contact with President Carter on the subject of world expansion and there are signs that he is seeking an early meeting.

Mr Callaghan is scheduled to visit Washington for a NATO heads of Government meeting at the end of May. On June 2 he plans to attend the United Nations disarmament conference in New York, and he has June 1 free for a bilateral meeting with President Carter, if desired.

But the way things look at the moment, the Prime Minister may seek an even earlier meeting with the US President. Decision time on world rade will be within the next few months, he told yesterday's liaison committee meeting.

Intervention

The Prime Minister's essentially gloomy mood was underlined when he contradicted Mr Denis Healey, the Chancellor of the Exchequer. Mr Healey was well launched on an optimistic review of job prospects, stating that more people were in work in Britain today than at any time in her history and more job vacancies existed than at any time in the past three years.

Mrs Barbara Castle asked Mr Healey to spell out his growth target for next year but Mr Callaghan intervened to prevent him answering. If published it would enable people to make certain conclusions about the Budget, he said.

Only slightly deterred, Mr Healey spoke about Britain's efforts to cajole other European countries to improve their growth rates, reflate and expand world trade.

It was then the Prime Minister said he took a more gloomy view of the world outlook than the Chancellor. The decision time on world trade would be in the next few months, resulting in either more protection or decisions to expand.

Mr Callaghan made it clear which way he thought the decisions would go. The French would start with import controls and the US was in danger of bringing out measures certain to hamper world trade.

Shorter hours

The Prime Minister told the committee he was deeply concerned about this prospect. Mr Healey, seeing the way the wind was blowing, agreed with the Prime Minister's assessment that the French would be at the head of the queue for protectionism.

And he gave a hint that Britain's patience with Japan over her protectionist laws is rapidly coming to an end. The Japanese seemed to expect to be able to import nothing but export everything to the rest of the world, he said.

The UK is now likely to press even harder than before for the EEC to erect barriers to Japanese trade in Europe.

If the Prime Minister's pessimistic prophecies occur, then it will certainly show up in the prospects for increased employment in the UK.

"The world recession which has thrown nearly 17 million out of work in the OECD countries, will get worse this year unless there is a faster rate of growth among Western industrialised countries. We depend upon it very much for our exports and increase in jobs," Mr Callaghan said in the Commons after the meeting.

But Mrs Margaret Thatcher said Britain needed new incentives to encourage workers to increase productivity and brighten Britain's performance. A Tory Government would give the greatest priority to tax cuts, profitability and competition.

The scale of the employment problem was spelled out by Mr Albert Booth, the Employment Minister, who presented the liaison committee with a paper on the jobs situation.

The number of people seeking work will continue to increase by an estimated 170,000 a year over the next four years, Mr Booth told the meeting. So the Government have to create many more jobs to absorb the increase in the labour force as well as catch up with unemployment.

After reviewing the measures the Government were already taking, Mr Booth could point only to actual new job creation as a way out of the unemployment trough. The trend towards shorter working hours and earlier retirement was likely to continue in the period ahead. But the Government did not regard them as desirable ways of dealing with the problem.

A general reduction in retirement age would be costly and reduce the resources available to pay the additional pensions. Work-sharing also carried high risks of reducing Britain's competitive position.

"We shall not master unemployment until we work our way out of world recession through a concerted effort to get economic activity moving again," said Mr Booth.

Mrs Thatcher said yesterday that the Conservatives could create a million more jobs in the next few years.

Tax pledge

"Our best hope of reducing unemployment is by increasing our competitiveness, and therefore our sales, she told the Engineering Employers Federation in London. A 1 per cent increase in our share of world trade would represent 400,000 extra jobs.

"Mr Healey has talked of a million jobs being provided in the next few years. It could happen—but not his way. It could happen by raising profits, cutting taxes and bureaucracy, freeing the labour market, encouraging managers, raising investment, and getting more value out of existing investment," she said.

Mrs Thatcher said that the top priority of the next Conservative Government—"which may not come until next year"—would be to cut direct taxes so that hard work, responsibility and success could be properly rewarded.

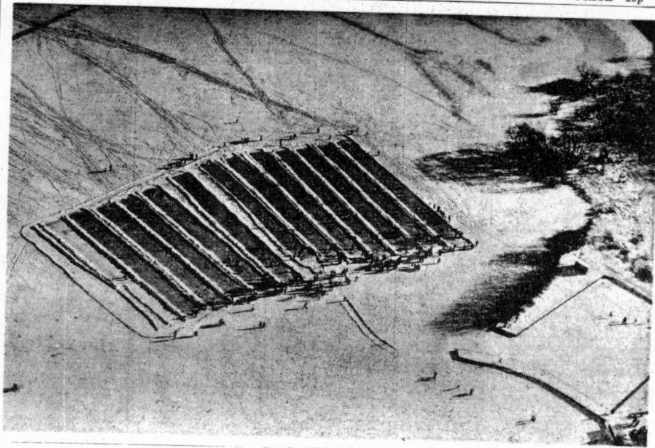

The surface of Loch Leven, normally dotted with trout-fishers' boats, preesnts a very different pattern during the cold spell. Curlers from Loch Leven Province prepared these 12 sheets for weekend matches.

On Friday, Glenfarg Club won the Province Bonspiel and on Saturday the Blairhill Trophy was won by Kinross Club. For both events it was the first time since 1959 that they had been played outdoors.

The Royal Caledonian Curling Club announced yesterday that it would not be possible to play the Grand Match tomorrow, as had been hoped, on the Lake of Menteith. There are only five inches of ice and six are needed for safety. The forecast for the weekend does not suggest that the required depth of ice will be achieved and so all the planning that has already been done looks like being lost. Over 200 of the 300 sheets required have already been marked out for the match which was last played in 1963.

Fewer unemployed—but figures are illusory

By MAURICE BAGGOTT, Our Industrial Correspondent

Scottish unemployment figures showed a sharp drop last month, taking totals below the crucial 200,000 level, but after seasonal adjustment the fall is less than 1000.

With the figures showing no real overall trend, both sides of industry are now looking to the Chancellor for measures to reduce unemployment, as there is still no sign of increasing business activity.

Although the overall drop of 6840 on the register is a higher percentage drop than that in the rest of the UK — where unemployment fell by nearly 40,000, to 1,508,000 — the Scottish figures are distorted to some extent by Christmas school-leavers in Scotland finding jobs, whereas elsewhere in Britain there is now only a summer leaving date.

A total of 2468 school-leavers found jobs during the month, but there are still 12,650 on the register. The Christians leaving date added 7300 young people to the register and the latest figures show that two-thirds of these school-leavers are still without a job.

'APPALLING'

Against that there are 844 vacancies for school leavers, a slight increase on last month. In the adult vacancy figures there has been an increase of 1459, to 17,145, the highest figure for well over a year.

This is one aspect which is particularly worrying the Scottish Council (Development and Industry). Their new chairman, Mr Peter Balfour, said yesterday: "The figures are quite appalling, but do not reflect the shortage of skilled people needed by many Scottish firms. This is a major problem which needs to be looked at urgently. An increased supply of skilled labour would open up many other opportunities for employment."

One surprise in the figures was the relatively big fall in female unemployment of 1123, which suggests at least a stabilisation in the lighter consumer oriented industries.

Total unemployment, however, remains at 196,789 or 8.9 per cent of the Scottish working population and the drop, though welcome, can give little comfort to the Government in the face of the tough electoral challenges expected this year.

Unemployment in Strathclyde is 10.5 per cent, against 11 per cent last month, and in the main central belt the lowest unemployment percentage figure is Central Region, with 7.6 per cent. Lothian is 7.2 per cent, Fife 8.3 per cent and Tayside 8.1 per cent.

REFLATION PLEA

The Western Isles, with 12.4 per cent, is the highest in Scotland, while in the other regions Grampian has 5 per cent, Highland 10 per cent, Borders 5 per cent, Dumfries and Galloway 8.6 per cent, Orkney 5 per cent and Shetland 3.5 per cent.

The STUC welcomed the slight fall in the figures, but said that but for specific Government employment and training schemes the unemployment totals would show 56,500 more on the register. The situation still left 12,500 school-leavers who had not found their first job.

In a statement, the STUC said: "The Government must accord increasing importance to the task of reducing unemployment. There is some leeway in the economy for the Chancellor to inject substantial reflation."

The unions also urged Britain to act jointly with other developed countries to reverse deflationary policies which had led to the present high levels of unemployment.

The CBI in Scotland urged the Chancellor to seize the opportunity to give the economy a shot in the arm by creating the incentives for people to work harder and increase employment. They particularly want more emphasis on help for small firms.

A spokesman said: "The drop in the figures is welcome, but sadly we do not think there is a major trend towards dramatic improvement of employment in the manufacturing industries.

"If the Chancellor provides the incentives and creates the right climate for small firms to grow, the increased employment from this sector alone would make a substantial dent in the unemployment figures."

The SNP senior vice-chairman, Mrs Margo MacDonald, said the decrease in unemployment was unimpressive and was still a 143 per cent increase since 1974. She added: "Every objective survey of current trends shows that real unemployment will increase in Scotland in the foreseeable future."

The Liberal Party spokesman on employment, Mr Charles Brodie, called for Budget stimulus for the economy but urged the Government to give the Scottish Assembly greater economic and taxation powers and more responsibility for dealing with the employment situation in Scotland.

Mr Teddy Taylor, Conservative spokesman on Scottish affairs, said the reduction in unemployment was certainly welcome but the figures showed that 6000 of the 6840 was the normal seasonal variation. The real improvement was only 900.

"In short, there has only been a marginal change in a frightening total, which is the highest since the 1930s," he said. "The figures would be a lot higher if it were not for the temporary measures, of which temporary employment subsidy is the most important. It demonstrates the extent to which the total would soar if we are forced by the EEC to scrap such temporary measures."

LATEST NEWS

Climber swept to death

A climber died yesterday in an avalanche which swept him from the slopes of Carn Mhor Dearg, the 4000-feet peak just north of Ben Nevis.

Police last night named the dead man as Mr Jason Hunnisset (19), of 133 London Road, Deal, Kent, who had been working as a temporary climbing instructor in the area.

Mr Hunnisset was in a party of climbers coming down the mountain after they had been ridge walking. He was swept down the mountainside by an avalanche of hundreds of tons of snow.

One of the party, Mr Terry Small, (30), an instructor at Loch Eil Centre, watched helplessly as Mr Hunnisset was hurled down 1200 feet.

Mr Small said later: "We realised that there was a risk of avalanching so we decided to come down a gentle slope rather than a difficult route. We were strung out across the slope when suddenly I heard a crack like gunfire.

"There was absolutely nothing we could do. Jason was swept off his feet." The member of the party nearest to Mr Hunnisset, who was in front, was Mr Small's brother-in-law, Mr David Meadows, of Nottingham. He ran across the slope and only just missed the edge of the avalanche.

After spotting a rucksack in the snow they began to dig and when Mr Hunnisset was found Mr Small gave him the kiss of life and massaged his heart for about 15 minutes.

At the time of the accident there were 12 other climbers on the mountain and some helped carry Mr Hunnisset's body down.

The party's cries for help were heard by members of a Welsh mountain rescue team, out training on the mountainside, as they rested in the Charles Inglis Clark hut on the south face of Carn Mhor Dearg. They joined in the search.

A police Sno-cat was sent to join the search, but within minutes of its arival Mr Hunnisset's body was found.

SECOND CANAL DEATH

The Forth and Clyde Canal yesterday claimed its second victim this week when an eight-year-old boy drowned at Clydebank.

William Gabriel, of 7 Strauss Avenue, Linvale, Clydebank, was on his way home from school and began crossing the canal when he fell into the icy water.

Police sergeant Gavin Bremner dived in and pulled the boy to the edge, but William, one of a family of six and the only son, was found to be dead. On Monday a four-year-old boy drowned when he fell through ice on the canal at Old Kilpatrick.

900 WALK OUT AT LEYLAND PLANT

A strike involving about 900 members of the Amalgamated Union of Engineering Workers began yesterday at the Leyland body plant at Cowley.

The men stopped work after shop stewards claimed that management had carried out repairs to an assembly line during the men's lunch break. The strikers are to meet tomorrow.

VENICE BLAST KILLS

VENICE, Tuesday. — A time bomb exploded here early today outside an office of the newspaper "Il Gazzettino," killing a watchman, police said.

An unidentified telephone caller later claimed that the outlawed neo-Fascist group "New Order" had been responsible. — Reuter.

Police may seek ban on Front march

The Metropolitan Police Commissioner, Sir David McNee, may call for a ban on Saturday's National Front march through Ilford, Essex, rather than mount one of the biggest anti-riot control operations in Britain.

A four-man delegation from Redbridge Community Relations Council at Ilford, who went to Scotland Yard last night, said the Commissioner had told them that he would make the decision within the next 48 hours.

Mr Ian Haig, Redbridge Community Relations Officer, said: "If the march goes ahead, I understand the police will be using almost a quarter of the Metropolitan force—5000 out of 22,000 men. This is totally absurd."

Another of the delegation, Councillor John Hogben, leader of the Labour group on Conservative-controlled Redbridge Council, said: "I believe that there will be large-scale disorder if the march goes ahead."

The Socialist Workers' Party have already called on "anti-Nazis" in London to gather at Ilford on Saturday to stop the march.

The Anti-Nazi League have predicted an "explosive mixture" of Right and Left-wing street demonstrations. They are planning their own two-mile counter-march with the Redbridge Against Racism and Fascism Organisation.

Jewish taxi drivers are also planning a "cab-cade" during the march which takes in the Barkingside district with its huge Jewish community.

Fifty thousand posters and 25,000 leaflets inviting support for the counter-demonstration are being distributed throughout London.

Redbridge Borough's 60-member council will debate the threat at a meeting tomorrow night. Councillors will be asked to support a motion calling on the Police Commissioner to advise the Home Secretary, Mr Merlyn Rees, that the Front's march should be banned in the interests of public order.

Callaghan attack—Page 7

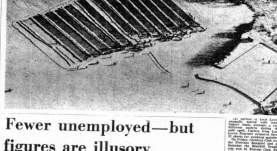

eminently honest, fair and courteous. He was a slow, laborious writer, but his work was simple, clear, sharp, occasionally even abrupt. Ritchie, on the other hand, was an ardent liberal, thoroughly honest, with a warm spirit, but his straightforwardness sometimes got him into trouble. He was a quick, fluent, voluminous writer who sometimes had to help Maclaren meet writing deadlines. Thus:

> While Ritchie was the chief founder of The Scotsman in that his energy was the force that ensured its existence, it was Charles Maclaren who formed the paper's character, and gave to it the personality that justified its existence.[6]

In its early years, The Scotsman demonstrated those characteristics which have continued to mark it as an elite newspaper. It criticized the privileged and excessive ways of government and of the Tory party. It denounced Scotland's landowner-only voting system. It reported on parliamentary speeches and public demonstrations. It lambasted the Reform Bill and gave the working class some overdue praise. Despite the fact that it sprang from Evangelical tradition, it favored equal political rights for the Catholics. Its early reporting was accurate, detailed and forthright, covering a wide range of subjects and events. At the same time, it quickly gained a reputation for the excellence of its book reviews and literary criticism.

When the Newspaper Stamp Duty was abolished in 1855, The Scotsman went daily.[7] The first issue was a small eight-sheet tabloid-sized paper costing only a penny. Again its efforts were dominated by strong, independent men. John Ritchie had become sole proprietor of the paper in 1849. Alexander Russel was editor and John Ritchie Findlay his assistant. Again, as in the case of Ritchie and Maclaren earlier, their skills and personalities complemented one another. Both were energetic, "but where Russel was enthusiastic Findlay was cool, and where Russel was full of views, Findlay was full of ideas for the paper."[8] Russel had a passion for worthy causes, whereas Findlay was more objective. The combination was ideal for maintaining The Scotsman's reputation as a fair, independent, impartial paper. Through the ensuing years, Findlay, in his dual role of manager and editor, reorganized procedures in the printing office and wrote some powerful feature articles. Russel, meanwhile, impressed his character and his robust, humorous writing style on the paper as it gained in authority and prestige. By 1865, it was selling 17,000 copies daily and flourishing financially.

In 1857, energetic 18-year-old James Law joined The Scotsman's staff as business manager. He devoted his career to improving the production and selling capacities of the paper and initiating a long string of distinguishing technical "firsts." In 1865, because the paper's circulation was confined to Edinburgh and its immediate surroundings, Law got the railways to agree to

---

[6] The Glorious Privilege, op. cit., p. 13.

[7] Between 1855 and 1860, the paper was called The Daily Scotsman to distinguish it from the weekly Scotsman, which continued. In 1960, after the daily became well established, the word "Daily" was dropped from the title.

[8] The Glorious Privilege, op. cit., p. 33.

cooperative delivery and fixed charges for distribution of papers. Then he established a network of retail newsagents to distribute the papers direct to readers all over the country. Within a few months, the list of agents grew from eighty to over a thousand. As a result, circulation zoomed. Within a year, sales of *The Scotsman* rose by 10,000; by 1887, circulation topped the 60,000 mark—the largest of any morning paper then published outside London.[9]

In the early days of telegraphy, *The Scotsman* pioneered again by leasing a special telegraph wire for the paper's exclusive use between London and Edinburgh. Then, in 1868, it became the first newspaper outside London to open an office in Fleet Street. It became (1872) the first paper in Scotland to use a rotary printing press, a Walter capable of printing 12,000 eight-page sheets on both sides per hour from a continuous web. The same year, it became the first to run a special newspaper train to speed morning delivery of 12,000 copies to Glasgow. Later in its career, *The Scotsman* became the first European journal to own and operate a machine which sent photographs by wire (1928), the first to send pictures and words on a single line (1931), the first to operate a mobile van containing picture telegraph and teletype equipment (1947) and the first British newspaper to print pictures using a Vario-Klischograph. Because of these twentieth century developments, the paper has often been congratulated on the excellence of its photographs.[10]

On the editorial side, many developments took place. In 1868, Charles Cooper, a respected, experienced and thorough journalist, joined the staff. Under Cooper's leadership, the paper established a regular "London Letter," based on factual information which brought the opinions of many of the nation's leaders to the readers. It pioneered in treating book reviews as news, giving notice every Monday of books shortly after their publication—an innovation in Britain. It gave greater depth to foreign news and instituted discursive features on international problems, thus giving it an unusual tone for a paper printed outside London. Late in the nineteenth century, *The Scotsman* supported the liberal views of Gladstone, Irish Home Rule and delegation of Parliament's power to local bodies. Cooper did much to sustain *The Scotsman*'s reputation as an independent paper championing the interests of the public. However, in one case he allowed his personal biases to color his editorial judgment. He properly championed the cause of the underdog dissenting Free Church against the United Free Church; unfortunately his bitter dislike of the leader of the latter resulted in caustic, vitriolic charges in the paper which led to vandalism and destruction of churches and slowed union of the two bodies.

Under the editorship of John Croal (1906–1924), *The Scotsman* again was the political conscience of the people. Under his fiery, demanding leadership, the paper weathered World War I.

The first crisis which faced George Waters when he became editor was the general strike of 1926. Waters had to use devious means to publish and deliver his paper. Next, he masterfully championed the Scottish Home Rule movement and further established *The Scotsman*'s role as a national paper, action for

---

[9] *Ibid.*, p. 41.

[10] Pamphlet, "The Record of The Scotsman," *The Scotsman*, North Bridge, Edinburgh.

which he was abusively criticized by some. Waters introduced several innovations, among them a picture page and a column called "A Scotsman's Log."
Waters was knighted during World War II and the paper cited for "cooperation
in the great and almost sacred task of leading and steadying public opinion in
times of national stress and crisis."[11]

After the war, under the editorship of James Watson, the paper continued
on its high-quality course. But rising costs, slumping circulation and heavy taxation put *The Scotsman* into debt, a state from which its new owner, the late
Lord (Roy) Thomson had to extricate it. Thomson, a Canadian of Scottish de-
scent, bought the paper in 1953. Thomson's financial wizardry soon bailed *The
Scotsman* out and all worries about its independence were quickly forgotten.
Today, Thomson Regional Newspapers, Ltd., a corporation, owns *The Scotsman*.

Thomson kept *The Scotsman*'s policies and staff very much the same as
they had been. In 1956, he hired Alastair Dunnett from a Kemsley paper in
Glasgow to edit *The Scotsman*. Together, they agreed to replace the front page
of advertisements with news. When they did so in 1957, they ran into opposition, but, nevertheless, sales increased dramatically almost immediately. Dunnett's impact on the paper was quiet, but effective. He accepted *The Scotsman*
for what it was—conservative in that it believed in private enterprise—and infused it with a liberal, adventurous spirit. He insisted on excellent, thoughtful
writing, well-selected news and intelligent features. Because he created an entirely new spirit in the paper, its circulation rose steadily from a low of 54,000 in
1956 to over 70,000 by the end of 1965. Under Dunnett's editorship, the paper
won the award for being Best Designed Newspaper in 1959, a feat it repeated in
1963.

Dunnett remained as Editor until 1972, when Eric B. MacKay took over the
post. To the present moment, MacKay has maintained the paper's independent
spirit, high quality, patriotism, balance, thoughtful editorial approach, impartiality, fairness and interest in a wide range of subjects. Under him, the paper
stands firmly against apartheid and for open government and freedom of
speech. Under him, too, circulation has slowly, but steadily built to nearly
90,000 daily, some seventy percent of which are delivered to homes with most of
the remainder representing street sales.[12]

The Scotsman has its main office in Edinburgh with branch offices in London, Glasgow, Aberdeen, Inverness, Dundee, Falkirk and the Borders. It publishes four daily editions which presently are produced by computer-set hot
metal composition, but shortly will be done by photo-composition. The separate
editions go to England, the Highlands, Borders and East and West Scotland,
thereby assuring each area its own local news as well as national and world coverage.

Early in 1978, a staff of 553 was employed by *The Scotsman*, 153 of them
engaged in writing and editing tasks, 186 technical and 214 administrative. For
its editorial work, the paper seeks university trained personnel with analytical
minds and preferably with journalistic experience. It has a full-time staff of 92
journalists and seven photographers within Scotland itself and 15 in London.

[11] *The Glorious Privilege, op. cit.*, p. 129.
[12] Eric B. MacKay, Editor, *The Scotsman* in reply to questionnaire dated February 18, 1978.

Many freelance correspondents from all over Scotland also contribute to the paper.[13] The efforts of this reportorial team are reflected in *The Scotsman*'s thorough coverage of home (Scottish) and national news.

Although *The Scotsman*'s reportage of international news has been excellent, its coverage of overseas events is somewhat more limited than that of many quality newspapers its size. At present, it has but one foreign correspondent—stationed in Brussels—and four stringers located in Rhodesia, Zambia, Italy and Washington, D.C. Their reports are supplemented by the four wire services the paper takes: Deutsche Presse Agentur, Reuters, Associated Press and Extel. In addition, the paper receives the *Times* Foreign News Service. *The Scotsman* claims at least one distinguished foreign correspondent: Neal Ascherson, who reports on eastern Europe.[14]

A typical weekday edition of *The Scotsman* runs between 22 and 32 pages, with Sunday papers going to at least four main sections. There is a fairly predictable distribution of materials. Except for the occasional important international news story, the front page normally carries the top news of Britain and Scotland. Page two, typically carrying stock exchange quotations, and pages three and four, the Financial and Business Section, all reflect the paper's interest in business enterprise. In fact, the paper's primary appeal is to the business, professional and intellectual community—businessmen, lawyers, doctors and teachers—and, because of the current atmosphere in Scotland, to the politically conscious. Home and national news occupy the next several pages, and there are excellent background features was well as news. There is a page of foreign news and one of editorial commentary and reader feedback entitled "Points of View." Feature pages and several pages of classified and retail advertisements follow. Sports news is found on the last two or three pages. The back page carries announcements, a TV and Radio Guide and a crossword puzzle.

On several days of the week, *The Scotsman* carries an extra four- or six-page section; for example, Monday's extra pages focus on books and book reviews, Friday's on the home, and on Saturdays there is the "Weekend Scotsman." The last typically contains articles on travel and fashion, a section on fiction and a children's story. One of the paper's many strengths is it attention to well-written, highly-informative feature articles.

In general, the paper uses pictures well, spotting an average of two or three per page. White space is employed effectively, but the eight-column paper appears sober and plain. Front page ads are kept to a minimum. In general, the paper is serious and contains little entertainment; for example, there are no comics or advice to the lovelorn columns and very few cartoons.

In the editor's room at *The Scotsman* hangs a wall plaque which has served as a constant reminder to staff of the high vision and noble goals of the paper. Its quotation from the original prospectus of *The Scotsman* reads:

> The conductors pledge themselves for impartiality, firmness, and independence. . . . their first desire is to be honest, the second to be useful. . . . the great requisites for the task are only good sense, courage and industry.[15]

[13] MacKay Questionnaire.
[14] *Ibid.*
[15] *The Glorious Privilege*, p. 39.

Sustaining highest quality standards once the excitement of achieving them has subsided is difficult at best in any field of endeavour. In the journalistic world, with its numerous demands and temptations to be satisfied with something less than the best, keeping up a high quality across time is doubly difficult. But the stately and prestigious *Scotsman* has managed to maintain its excellent reputation for independence, impartiality, fairness, accuracy, patriotism, constructive criticism, responsibility to the public and wide interests for over 160 years. And today, it continues to hold its own among the front ranks of the world's great newspapers with typical Scottish reserve, not boasting, but with quiet, honest determination giving its readers each day the highest possible quality *Scotsman*.

La Stampa

(ITALY)

ITALY HAS A LIMITED national press and few quality dailies. Italian readers tend to take the newspaper from their own city and show little interest in reading another from elsewhere. Also, same-day delivery is difficult because of Italy's length and difficult terrain, particularly when a paper is located at the northern or southern extremity of the country. At the same time, much of the press is filled with political intrigue to satisfy Italian love for political argumentation and with sensation and scandal. As a result, only a few Italian dailies, most of them morning papers, can claim to be serious, responsible elite newspapers with national or wide regional appeal. It so happens these same quality papers lead Italy's circulation race: *Corriere della Sera* (Milan), with 523,000; *La Stampa* (Turin), with 362,000; *Il Messaggero* (Rome), with 233,000; *Il Resto del Carlino* (Bologna), with 197,000; and *La Nazione* (Florence), with 194,000.

Perhaps Italy's quality press is best exemplified by either Turin's *La Stampa* (The Press) or Milan's *Corriere della Sera*. Their serious journalistic approach, progressive outlook and intellectual tone place them among the best in world journalism. *La Stampa*, in particular, has managed quite effectively to combine a strong provincial orientation with nation-wide authority and prestige.

La Stampa is especially popular in northern Italy. It is no exaggeration that practically everybody in Turin reads *La Stampa*. At the same time, "*La Stampa* is one of the few Italian newspapers which can reasonably claim national standing."[1] Along with *Corriere della Sera*, it is one of just two Italian journals with

---

[1] "World Press, II," Dispatch of the London *Times* (October, 1975).

Anno 112 - Numero 44

Edizione teletrasmessa

LA STAMPA

* Mercoledì 22 Febbraio 1978 *

REDAZIONE, AMMINISTRAZIONE, TIPOGRAFIA: 10126 TORINO, VIA MARENCO N. 32, Centralino tel. 65.651 ...

A PAGINA 18

Corno d'Africa
Stati Uniti ed Etiopia ristabiliscono le relazioni diplomatiche. Successo della missione di Aaron
di Furio Colombo

A PAGINA 19

Le nuove "131"
La Fiat presenterà al Salone di Ginevra la rinnovata "Mirafiori" e l'inedita "Supermirafiori"
di Ferruccio Bernabò

Non si discute più, il disordine ha proprio vinto?

Si aggravano le tensioni dalle medie all'università

La libertà è scesa a licenza, la tolleranza a permissività - La crisi della scuola è gravissima crisi di comportamenti e di valori del Paese - Manca la volontà di costruire

La crisi di governo ritarda gli interventi per l'economia

Il costo della vita + 1,27 in febbraio

Carli giudica debole il piano di Andreotti

Se non si espande il reddito in misura maggiore di quanto programmato, si possono perdere 70 mila posti di lavoro nel 1978

La scuola non è dei violenti

Venezia, 21 febbraio.

Giovanni Trovati

A Venezia i docenti si ribellano

(Dal nostro inviato speciale)

Venezia, 21 febbraio.

Giuliano Marchesini

Renato Romanelli

Il Piemonte "tiene" nella crisi

Emilio Pucci

Il movimento in crisi
Assemblea caotica a Milano

Milano, 21 febbraio.

Marzio Fabbri

Riemergono i problemi non risolti a luglio

Ora al centro della crisi il sindacato della polizia

Roma, 21 febbraio.

Luca Giurato

(Continua a pagina 2 in settima colonna)

La Malfa su laici e socialisti
"Siamo lontani ma discutiamo,,

Caro Direttore,

Ugo La Malfa
presidente del pri

L'ordigno, ad alto potenziale, devasta l'ingresso di Ca' Faccanon

Venezia: bomba al Gazzettino, un morto Ordine nuovo, Br rivendicano l'attentato

(Dal nostro corrispondente)

Venezia, 21 febbraio.

Franco Battagliarin

international circulation. It has a large office in Rome and is staffed by some of Italy's best political commentators. Ever conscious of the need to reach a wide readership, *La Stampa* was the first Italian newspaper to resort to facsimile printing in Rome, thus making it possible for the capital and the south to see a reasonably late edition with the other morning papers.

The paper is part of the industrial and financial empire of the Agnelli family, which also owns the Fiat automobile company. *La Stampa,* in fact, was bought in 1952 to become a business partner with Fiat. However, the ownership puts no checkrein on the paper. Its editors have always acted independently and have put their own stamp on *La Stampa.* Nor is there attempt to hide the connection between the paper and Fiat. Late in 1977, the Libyan Government bought shares in Fiat, and its representatives now sit on the Fiat Board of Directors. Despite the wealth of its parent and business partner, *La Stampa* has experienced its share of financial difficulties. Industrial strife in the mid-'seventies threw the paper into deep deficits from which it has not yet fully recovered.

Journalism in Italy goes back to the Renaissance, when men known as "gazzettanti" or "corrieri" circulated handwritten newsletters containing shipping and other news which sold for the price of a small coin called a "gazzetta." Then, under foreign dominance, the press was suppressed for 165 years. A long struggle for political freedom followed, and Italians from the country's numerous independent states united in revolt under the leadership of Piedmont king Victor Emmanuel and his prime minister Cavour. The decade of the 1860's, known as the "decade of resistance," finally brought liberation and unity to the country.

During the years of resistance, the press could only flourish in Piedmont, where Victor Emmanuel and Cavour had maintained press freedom. Consequently, two of Italy's strongest voices for liberation were born in Turin. The earlier of the two, *Gazetta del Popolo,* was the stronger at first. Then, in 1867, *Gazetta Piedmontese* was founded, the other strong voice for independence, and the paper which later, as *La Stampa,* was destined to become one of Italy's truly great newspapers. Cavour himself played a role in the development of *Gazetta Piedmontese* by assisting Guglielmo Stefani in establishing Italy's first news agency, *Agenzia Stefani* so the Piedmont papers could have access to foreign news. Thus, from its inception the newspaper *La Stampa* had much wider interests and appeal than its native Piedmont.[2]

Most of *La Stampa*'s early prestige and broad outlook must be credited to two remarkable early editors, Luigi Roux and Alfredo Frassati. Both were active, outstanding political leaders who held seats in the Senate during the years Italian unity was being fashioned.[3] In 1895, they bought the old *Gazetta* and renamed it *La Stampa.* Together they developed the progressive tradition the paper now holds and made it one of the main liberal voices of the country. Together, too, they established the credibility and wide appeal of their paper by full and clear presentation of cabled news.

[2] Kenneth E. Olson, *The History Makers: The Press of Europe from its Beginnings through 1965* (Baton Rouge: Louisiana State University Press, 1966), pp. 232–5.
[3] "World Press, II."

From 1901 on, Frassati edited the paper alone and continued improvements in all departments. Later, he bought *La Stampa* but continued as its editor. When Mussolini and his Fascists came to power in 1925, Frassati refused to sign a Fascist card and realized his days with *La Stampa* were over.[4] So he sold the paper in 1926, and it re-opened with a Fascist staff. During his period with *La Stampa*, Frassati had established it as a high quality newspaper—a position it continues to hold today.

Once Italy was again free after World War II, new papers appeared to take over from the Fascist sheets. Old, once-great independents were restored, but to distinguish them from pre-war papers which perforce had a Fascist tint, the word "new" was added to their titles. Thus, for a while *La Stampa* became *La Nuova Stampa* and *Corriere della Sera* was *Nuovo Corriere della Sera*. Numerous parties flourished after the long dominance of the monolithic Fascist system, giving rise to a number of party papers. Because these papers were completely devoted to political causes, some of the dailies which remained independent, among them *La Nuova Stampa* in Turin, *Nuovo Corriere della Sera* in Milan and *Il Messaggero* and *Il Tempo* in Rome, were able to gain larger followings by means of broad news coverage, especially of national and foreign news.[5] At first *La Nuovo Stampa*, like its newspaper counterparts, faced a newsprint shortage and was limited to a single sheet on both sides. By 1948, however, conditions had improved to the point where four pages were allowed.

In 1948, Dr. Giulio de Benedetti took over as editor of the paper and quickly established for himself a special niche in Italian journalism. He managed to retain the best traditions of *La Stampa* while at the same time imprinting his own image vividly on the character of the paper. He insisted on clear, precise writing and on changes in the paper's makeup. Whereas *La Stampa*, like most Italian newspapers, had used wordy, pompous prose and had displayed a bleak, dull, tightly-printed appearance, under de Benedetti it became attractive, well-ordered and easier to read. Dr. de Benedetti's own political and journalistic philosophy became clearly manifest, too, in the paper's pages. He prided himself on being an editor who both directed the editorial functions of his paper but who also took an interest in its technical and circulation activities. *La Stampa* was his life, and even in his seventies just prior to his retirement, he would often remain until three or four A.M. to supervise page makeup in the composing room and to help with details related to preparing the paper for delivery. Without a doubt, Dr. de Benedetti contributed heavily to *La Stampa*'s greatness, both in his editorial policies and in practical matters of craftsmanship.

Before taking over his editorial duties with *La Stampa*, its present editor, Arrigo Levi had had a brilliant career as a foreign correspondent and as a television commentator. Both Levi and his friend and predecessor in the position, Alberto Ronchey, have insisted on consistency and on a clear, non-rhetorical style. They have tried—and have largely succeeded—in overcoming the heavy rhetoric which continues to blight much of Italian journalism. Levi is continuing *La*

---

[4] The period of *La Stampa* in Mussolini's early days is discussed in Adolf Dresler, *Geschichte der italienschen Presse* (Berlin: Oldenbourg, 1938), Pt. 3, pp. 48, 118.
[5] Olson, *op. cit.*, p. 243.

Stampa's emphasis on good international coverage, on maintaining its independence and keeping up its traditional high quality. He is a sensitive person, deeply committed to the principles of journalistic freedom and integrity.

Much of *La Stampa*'s reputation has come from its concern with Italian social problems. Probably no other paper in the country gives as much emphasis to economic and social changes or need for change. Its concern for economic matters is natural, since Turin is in the heart of the bustling industrial north. Along with Milan to the east, Turin also has the most cosmopolitan outlook of the country. On foreign news, *La Stampa* continues the foresight of its founders; its overseas news is about the best in the country. Its local and regional coverage is thorough, one reason why the citizens of Milan and the rest of Piedmont are very proud of the paper and insist it is the best in the entire country. Other than that of Milan's *Corriere della Sera,* its "third page," a special and varied display of serious essays and other assorted articles of quality, stands without a peer in Italian journalism where this cultural-literary page is a national institution. And it carries more sports news and pictures than any other general newspaper in Italy.

Politically, *La Stampa* is to the left of center, lay and anti-Communist. Its reporters and commentators have given support to the center-left Government program of internal reforms which the latter has felt necessary to keep in step with the country's radical social transformation. Frequently, the paper has agreed on social issues with the Socialist Party, but it maintains independence from any direct ties with the party. Basically, the paper's general attitude continues the liberal orientation it has held since its inception, definitely anti-Fascist and just as vigorously anti-Communist. In short, it is "liberal" in the old European, and perhaps the truest, sense of the term. It is not a slave to doctrinaire politics of any type. Rather, it is its own master and plays each policy decision in a way it thinks is called for at the time under the special circumstances which prevail.

In recent years, *La Stampa* has in two types of situations demonstrated its independence and fearlessness in the face of opposition. The first incidents tested the paper's resistance to economic pressures. Late in 1974, editor Arrigo Levi and two *La Stampa* writers were accused of mocking Colonel Qaddafi of Libya in a satirical article. As a result, Libya and an Arab committee threatened economic blockade against Fiat, *La Stampa*'s owner, unless the editor and writers were dismissed. The paper and Fiat Chairman Giovanni Agnelli refused to comply; for their actions, they received the unanimous support of the entire Italian press.[6] Later, in December, 1976, when the Libyan Government became a co-owner of the paper by buying shares from the parent Fiat motor company, the threat of interference arose again. This time, *La Stampa* journalists declared openly they would resist any overt interference in their paper's editorial policies and expressed their determination to defend the paper's independence. At the time of the purchase, editor Levi wrote an Agnetti-approved editorial expressing

[6] "IPI in Action: Italy," *IPI Report,* 23:2 (February, 1974), p. 7.

concern that Fiat's new owner-partner was a state "most irresponsible in our irresponsible age."[7] To date, no interference by Libya has occurred.

Just a year later, on November 29, 1977, a Red Brigade terrorist gunman cut down and killed *La Stampa's* deputy editor, Carlos Casalegno in broad daylight. Casalegno, who had been with the paper for 61 years, had been a Resistance fighter in World War II and was a fearless defender of democracy as Italy's only valid form of government.[8] Again, the paper did not flinch from its opposition to Fascism and its defense of democratic views.

La Stampa carries a daily letters-from-readers section, a rarity in Italy. Letters of all types appear—from those about people in difficulty requesting help to those from well-educated persons discussing serious philosophical questions. Although letters to the editor are quite common in most quality newspapers of the world, *La Stampa* can be said to have pioneered in this area of Italian journalism. These letters to the editor provide both yet another reason why the paper's circulation saturates Turin and its environs and a typical example of the paper's progressive, flexible policies which have placed it among the great dailies of Italy and of the world.

In appearance, *La Stampa* is serious, gray, even somewhat somber. What few pictures the paper carries are usually small and person-centered rather than action-oriented. Typically, the front page will have a single picture one column wide. Vacant space is fully used, lending to the solemn appearance. The standard-size broadsheet pages employ nine columns, making the paper look larger than normal. The stories tend to run vertically down the page, although some are blocked in three to six column widths, particularly near the bottom of the page. This arrangement seems confusing at first, but once the reader becomes accustomed to the practice, he finds it pleasing and effective for concentrating on a story. Usually each story will have a major headline in heavy, black block letters and a sub-head in lighter type just above it. The body of the story itself is printed in lower case letters, with heavy black type used for stories the editors wish to emphasize. The front page carries no advertising. In the upper left hand and right hand corners near the nameplate, there are brief announcements of special features or stories inside the issue. The nameplate and the masthead are blended into one at the top of the front page, and include details about the paper's publisher, sales, offices and prices. The unique method of dating the paper goes back to its founding; for example, the February 22, 1978, issue is labeled "Year 112, Number 44." The front page features numerous stories, many of which are carried over to page two or to the back pages. Many of the stories carry reporter by-lines.

La Stampa's front page is made up mostly of Italian news, with some key international news stories. The editorial article leads the front page and often fills the two left-hand columns. Page two continues page one stories, contains a

[7] Patricia Clough, "*La Stampa* Journalists Say they are Prepared to Resist any Attempt by Government of Libya to Interfere in Editorial Policies of their Newspaper," *IPI Report*, 26:2 (February, 1977), p. 6.
[8] "Red Gangs Claim First Dead Editor, 61-year-old Anti-Fascist," *IPI Report*, 26:11 (December, 1977), p. 16.

feature article or two and carries a single large advertisement. Advertisements constitute a smaller percentage of the paper's contents than most quality dailies. Usually there is a single full-page ad, plus numerous smaller ones and a full page of classifieds. The third or cultural page, already alluded to, often carries a single book advertisement in addition to its excellent feature articles. There is a page or two of Turin city news and another two-to-three pages of "Dall'Interno" news from around Italy. Financial and agricultural news make up another page. A full page of foreign news and background stories reflects the paper's interest in international affairs. Finally, in addition to at least two pages of sports news and pictures near the back, there are two pages set aside for entertainment and the arts, one for a listing of cinema, music and theater programs and a second giving radio and television schedules and short features on the radio, TV, film and musical worlds.

La Stampa is published every day except Mondays. A typical week-day edition runs from 18 to 20 pages in length. The paper also has an evening edition called Stampa Sera (Evening Press), which comes out on Mondays but not on Sundays. It carries more sports news and pictures than any other Italian general newspaper.

The pride of the people of Turin and northern Italy in their newspaper is well justified. For, in La Stampa they have a serious, progressive, politically independent, well-written and attractive high quality newspaper that is one of Italy's most highly respected dailies. Because it can speak fearlessly with authority and prestige all over the country and stands at the pinnacle of Italian serious journalism, as well as providing good international coverage, La Stampa must also rank among the world's great newspapers.

St. Louis Post-Dispatch

(UNITED STATES)

CONTRARY TO MANY COUNTRIES where cities of the interior are provincial and isolated, St. Louis, Missouri, in the center of the nation is one of America's most sophisticated, cosmopolitan, culturally and intellectually wide-awake cities. The state's most prestigious daily, the St. Louis Post-Dispatch contributes significantly to the city's progressive spirit. The newspaper has grown with the city and has infused its progressive spirit and its concern for human rights and freedom into the city's citizens and its many readers throughout mid-America and in important places everywhere.

That the St. Louis Post-Dispatch ranks among the best of United States

On Today's Editorial Page
Who Benefits From Tax Breaks?
Editorial
The Downward Crime Rate
Editorial

ST. LOUIS POST-DISPATCH

FINAL
★ ★ ★
2:30 P.M. New York Stocks
Pages 6F and 7F

Vol. 100, No. 52   ©Copyright 1978, St. Louis Post-Dispatch   WEDNESDAY, FEBRUARY 22, 1978   15¢ / Suggested Home Delivery $3.30 a Month

Disruption Of 40% Of City Classes Reported

By ERIC L. ZOECKLER
Of the Post-Dispatch Staff

More than four of every 10 St. Louis public school classrooms are more than occasionally disrupted by a few students whose actions range from petty offenses such as talking out in class to physical violence.

And outside the classroom—in hallways, restrooms and on playgrounds—disruptive behavior is worse, according to a survey disclosed Tuesday by the St. Louis Teachers Association.

Overall, more than three-quarters of the teachers surveyed said that disruptive student behavior, including fighting, classroom profanity, back talk and property destruction, was more than an occasional problem in their schools.

The results of the survey, said Thom Downey, president of the association, might explain why standardized test scores and other evidence show that students are learning less these days.

"A large number of teachers are reporting that less than four students per class are disrupting the education that's desired by all the rest of the students," Downey said.

"While some would lead you to believe the amount of disruption is to be tolerated in a large urban district, there appears no consistent disciplinary code for teachers to adequately handle the problems facing them."

More than 36 percent of the teachers said that disruptive students also were doing poorly academically. Chief causes of disruptive behavior, teachers said, were poor home environment, poor parental attitude toward education, peer pressure and lack of motivation.

The survey indicated that problems grow worse in the higher grades. Elementary schools were most commonly troubled by playground misbehavior and fighting. Senior high school teachers said 18 types of incidents were more than occasional problems. Included were chronic absenteeism, property destruction, smoking violations and use of drugs and alcohol.

Property destruction was cited as a more than occasional problem in junior and senior high schools, while weapon possession occurred less often, still occasionally, all levels of school, including elementary grades.

Violent threats were reported to be considerably less of a problem than other types of disruptive behavior. About 11 percent of teachers believed physical threats against other students were more than an occasional problem. About 6 percent said threats against teachers were more than an occasional problem.

Teachers indicated that several problems needed immediate attention by school officials. These problems coming to class unprepared, swearing and talking back to teachers, cutting classes and rough-housing in class.

In senior high schools, teachers thought smoking violations, property destruction, use of drugs and alcohol and trespassing needed the most attention, the survey suggested.

More than 90 percent of the teachers said that troublemakers should be identified early and placed in corrective programs and that schools should establish stronger and more consistent disciplinary measures to curb disruptive behavior.

But Downey said that School Board policies showed that the city system was moving away, rather than closer to,

See DISRUPTION, Page 14

Mines Urge Binding Arbitration

WASHINGTON (AP) — The coal industry today called for voluntary binding arbitration in the coal strike, but a spokesman for the United Mine Workers said the union was likely to reject it.

The industry said binding arbitration was "preferable to the loss which the economy is now suffering." It urged UMW members to return to the mines while a three-member arbitration board would try to settle the record 79-day strike.

A Carter administration official close to the talks who declined to be identified said the call for arbitration was "an interesting proposal." It said he hoped the UMW would consider the proposal seriously.

However, the union spokesman said the proposal was unlikely to meet with UMW approval.

Meanwhile, the White House announced that Secretary of Labor F. Ray Marshall was to meet with the UMW negotiators this afternoon to consider the industry's suggestion for binding arbitration. Marshall will meet with industry representatives this evening. Officials said it was hoped these talks might lead to resumption of face-to-face negotiations.

The industry issued its arbitration proposal in a letter to UMW President Arnold Miller several hours after Miller and his bargainers met separately with UMW and industry bargainers.

"The secretary met with both sides ... and he has received the positions of the parties and he's assessing them," said Labor Department spokesman John Leslie.

Privately, officials indicated the two sides remained far apart.

The White House called the resumption of talks Tuesday "somewhat encouraging," but presidential press secretary Jody Powell cautioned, "Whether it's possible through these discussions to make progress remains to be seen."

One administration official, who asked not to be named, said the tentative agreement reached Monday between the union and a major independent producer, Pittsburg and Midway Coal Mining Co., would "figure in a major way" in the talks.

The call for voluntary arbitration was issued early this morning by Joseph P.

See COAL, Page 14

BURNING BRIGHT: Despite an appeal by Union Electric Co. to reduce electricity consumption, much of downtown St. Louis remained brightly lit Tuesday night. In the foreground is the General American Life Insurance Co. Building, and in the background, the illuminated dome of the Old Courthouse. (Post-Dispatch Photo by Jim Forbes)

Power Slashed In Sauget Plant, Forcing 200 Zinc Worker Layoffs

By ERIC L. ZOECKLER
Of the Post-Dispatch Staff

Dwindling coal supplies forced Union Electric Co. today to cut off 80 percent of the power supplied to AMAX Zinc Co. Inc., in the St. Clair County community of Sauget. As a result nearly two-thirds of the company's 360 employees have been laid off.

The electrolytic zinc plant was forced to halt production when the St. Louis-based utility exercised a special contract clause.

An estimated 200 of the plant's 360 employees were expected to be laid off indefinitely because of the cutback, a spokesman said.

The 20 percent of available electricity "will be just enough to keep the plant alive," said Chuck McCullough, public

SOME MAJOR INDUSTRIES would be hit by proposed production cuts in Kansas City. Page 1G

THE POWER PINCH in Terre Haute, Ind., is felt by nearly everyone. Page 1G

relations manager. "There won't be enough to produce zinc."

"Our plant operates on three shifts a day for seven days a week and the curtailment will affect about 200 production workers," said Jim Gorman, plant manager.

Gorman said he did not know how long the cutback would last. The plant has faced other curtailments during summer heat waves when use of air conditioning strained electric supplies, Gorman said. But these plant interruptions have never

lasted longer than one day, he said.

The firm has an agreement with Union Electric, approved by the Illinois Commerce Commission and Atomic Workers Union detailing the order in which persons are laid off during an electrical cutback, Gorman said, but he said he preferred not to divulge details.

The plant was the only Union Electric industrial customer with a special "interruptible" contract that allowed UE to curtail power to the plant in emergency situations in return for the AMAX paying cheaper rates.

A Union Electric spokesman said the company exercised the contract clause effective today, when the utility asked customers to cut back on electric usage in light of dwindling coal stockpiles caused by the nationwide coal strike.

See LAYOFFS, Page 14

Poor Security At Art Museum Angers Police

By SALLY BIXBY DEFTY
and ROBERT W. DUFFY
Of the Post-Dispatch Staff

St. Louis Chief of Police Eugene J. Camp has sternly criticized the St. Louis Art Museum's security arrangements in the aftermath of the second burglary at the Museum in less than a month.

In the second theft, which occurred Monday night, a thief or thieves took three bronze sculptures by Auguste Rodin. On Jan. 29, the first break-in at the Museum in recent memory — a bronze by the American artist Frederic Remington and three other sculptures were taken by three thieves who smashed through a window on the north side of the building.

"I am thoroughly disgusted," Camp said. "One right on the heels of another."

He said Museum officials "should set up an internal security program that works. I am sending out for a burglary prevention unit out there and it is up to them to avail themselves of it. We can't be their nursemaids."

The chief said he had instructed all officers writing reports at night on incidents in Forest Park to put the report-writing while parked at the Museum.

But he added that if Museum officials "don't even know it when they've had a burglary — if they don't know enough to put the lights on — what kind of organization is that?"

The gallery lights were not turned on Monday night after the break-in was discovered. Museum spokesmen said that was why no one knew the sculptures were missing until Tuesday morning — at least 12 hours after the theft.

Security equipment monitored the break-in as having happened at 8:24 p.m. Police were notified at 8:28 p.m. and arrived at the Museum at 8:37.

The thief or thieves broke a panel in a glass door at the east wing of the Museum — a door that had been blocked off before the recent renovation of that wing. The alarm was set off. The thief or thieves then went up the east stairway, through Galleries 207, 209 and 212 and into Gallery 213, from which the Rodins

were stolen, a Museum spokesman said.

Newly installed electronic monitoring equipment picked up the movement through the galleries. But the thieves were in the Museum only 60 seconds, a spokesman said.

When a thorough investigation was finally made on Tuesday morning, the three Rodin sculptures, valued together at about $45,000 were discovered missing. Previously, police reports stated only that an "attempt" had been made to break into the Museum.

Museum director James N. Wood refused Tuesday to say whether guards have a checklist of works in the galleries under their supervision. But a source close to the Museum said flatly that the guards lacked such information.

Other questions left unanswered by the Museum were:

—Did the guards attempt to catch the

See MUSEUM, Page 4

Ham In A Jam Again; Powell To The Rescue

By JAMES DEAKIN
A Washington Correspondent
of the Post-Dispatch

WASHINGTON—The White House is upset about the latest reports on the social life of presidential assistant Hamilton Jordan.

As a result, press secretary Jody Powell's briefing for reporters Tuesday was not amiable. Powell denounced a Washington Post story on Jordan as inaccurate and vicious. He accused the press of trying to put him in a bad light when he tried to set the record straight. He was angry.

A short time later, Powell telephoned a Post-Dispatch reporter and criticized him for 45 minutes for a question that the reporter had asked at the briefing. He

See JORDAN, Page 7

wednesday

national

NIXON'S DARK IMPULSES: H. R. Haldeman, the doorkeeper to the Oval Office in the Nixon administration, gives his insight into the former president. Nixon was a man with a light side and a dark side, and Haldeman saw his own role as building up the light and minimizing the dark, Haldeman writes in the third installment of excerpts from his book, "The Ends of Power." Page 3F

H.R. HALDEMAN
THE ENDS OF POWER

Chance Of Snow

ROGUES' GALLERY

Official forecast for St. Louis and vicinity: Cloudy tonight with chance of snow; low in the teens; tomorrow cloudy with high in the 30s; Friday through Sunday partly cloudy and turning colder with highs in the 30s; clear and cold over the weekend; lows in the teens.

Other Weather Information on Page 3A

local

SENATE PASSES DRUG EXEMPTION: The Missouri Senate today approved 22 to 0 a bill to exempt prescription drugs, insulin and prosthetic devices from the state sales tax. A similar bill has been passed by the House. In previous sessions, similar proposals have been defeated in the Senate.

features

AUSTRIAN CUISINE: From bacon dumplings to Sachertortes, a culinary tour of Austria is a triumph of taste. Page 1D

THE GREAT BOOKIE: Mortimer Adler is still advocating reading, and with pen in hand, making margin notes. Page 3H

sports

BLUE CHIPPER: The Blues made just enough mistakes to drop a 5-4 decision to the Pittsburgh Penguins Tuesday night at the Checkerdome, but there was one bright spot. Tony Currie, playing his first National Hockey League game, scored a goal on his first NHL shot. Page 1E

MAY DAY: Joe May is a personality, not an announcer. And, based on his sports work for WIBV radio in Belleville, he's a busy personality. Page 1E

inside

72 Pages

Business	5–7F
Classified Advertising	6–14E–3G
Editorials	2F
Everyday	1–10H
Food Section	1–4D
Her Line	5H
Metro Report	6B
News Analysis	3F
Obituaries	6E
People	6A
Reviews	4F
St. Louis	1F
Sports	1–4E
State Capital	3B
TV–Radio	8H
Vital Statistics	3G

Severed Roots

Adopted Children Challenge Laws That Hide Their Origins

By GEORGE E. CURRY
Of the Post-Dispatch Staff

As a result of last year's television dramatization of Alex Haley's "Roots," many Americans have successfully traced their ancestry back for generations. But for adopted persons, attempts to trace their roots often have been an unsuccessful and frustrating experience.

Mrs. Janet Kendall of Spanish Lake knows that frustration well.

"Every day of my life I wonder about my past," Mrs. Kendall said. "It goes through my whole existence. I carry a void around with me everywhere I go.

"When my mother told me I was adopted, I was 4 years old. I felt like an alien in an alien world. I felt a sense of rejection and confusion. Didn't my natural mother love me? Or did she give me up out of love? If the latter is the case, then why can't I return to thank her?"

One reason Mrs. Kendall cannot return to thank her natural mother is that the adoption laws of this country are designed to sever those old ties. In all but four states, adoption records that would disclose the adoptee's biological parents are

sealed by state law and cannot be opened without a court order.

These laws, as well as the belief that mothers who gave up their children at birth are entitled to lifelong privacy, are coming under increasing attack by adoptees, many of whom have formed their own organizations.

While agreeing that adoption records should remain sealed during their childhood, many adoptees argue that upon reaching adulthood, their records should be open to

The adoption issue poses a difficult question: In the mother's right to privacy more important than an adoptee's basic right to know his family origins? The reply in that question is likely to be emotional and deeply personal. And it affects each person in the adoptive triangle — the adoptee, the adoptive parents and natural parents.

That such an issue can be discussed so freely today underscores the changing nature of American

See ROOTS, Page 12

ROOT SEARCH: Marie McLeod (standing) and Denise Schroeder, founding members of Adoptees' Liberty Movement Association chapter. (Wayne Crosslin Photo)

quality newspapers does not come by accident. From its beginnings, it has been associated with a family of newspaper publishing "greats," the Pultizers. A liberal paper, it has always advocated political independence, intellectual freedom and social justice. Besides receiving national acclaim for its national and regional news, it has built up a reputation for excellence in its foreign coverage. Its editorial pages and investigative pieces rank among the nation's best. Evidence of the newspaper's excellence in every department is reflected in the long list of awards it has received.

The *Post-Dispatch*'s rich one-hundred-year heritage is based on its founding in 1878 by one of America's greatest publishers, Joseph Pulitzer.* A German-speaking immigrant from Hungary, Pulitzer arrived in St. Louis in October, 1865, coatless, friendless and penniless. In 1868, he became a reporter for the German-language newspaper, the *Westliche Post*. A year later, he was elected to the Missouri House of Representatives and in 1875, he became a member of the Missouri Constitutional Convention. On December 10, 1878, Pulitzer bought the bankrupt *St. Louis Dispatch,* merging it two days later with the *Post* to form the *Post and Dispatch*. In its first edition, Pulitzer announced:

> The *Post and Dispatch* will serve no party but the people; will follow no causes but its own convictions; will not support the "Administration" but will criticize it; will oppose all frauds and shams wherever and whatever they are; will advocate principles and ideas rather than prejudices or partisanship.
>
> These ideas and principles are precisely the same as those upon which our Government was originally founded, and to which we owe our country's marvelous growth and development. They are the same that made a Republic possible and without which a real Republic is impossible.
>
> They are the ideas of a true, genuine, real Democracy.[1]

The next year, the paper's name was changed to its present title, the *Post-Dispatch*. The paper was a success from the start. Pulitzer quickly instilled a liberal spirit into his paper, a spirit which has guided its development to the present. His paper pressed for civic improvements such as street paving and cleanup of refuse. It also crusaded against excesses—tax evasion by the wealthy, extortion and commercialized gambling. Because of such actions, circulation rose rapidly and the increase, combined with growing advertising revenue, led to a larger-size and financially sound newspaper. When Joseph Pulitzer retired in 1907 at the age of 60, he left these journalistic commandments which, chipped in granite on a plaque for all to see, still form the "Platform" for the *Post-Dispatch*:

> I know that my retirement will make no difference in its (the *Post-Dispatch*'s) cardinal principles, that it will always fight for progress and reform, never tolerate injustice or corruption, always fight demagogues of all parties, never belong to any party, always oppose privileged classes and public plunderers, never lack sympathy with the poor, always remain devoted to the public welfare, never be

---

* Because it was temporarily closed down by a strike, the *Post-Dispatch* was unable to publish on the date of its 100th anniversary, December 10, 1978.

[1] *The Story of the St. Louis Post-Dispatch,* Eleventh Edition (St. Louis: The Pultizer Publishing Company, 1973), p. 2.

satisfied with merely printing news, always be drastically independent, never be afraid to attack wrong, whether by predatory plutocracy or predatory poverty.[2]

Joseph Pulitzer II came to the *Post-Dispatch* in 1906, but he did not take over as director of it and the New York *Herald,* which his father had bought in 1883, until the founder died in 1911. In 1912, the second Pulitzer became president of the Pulitzer Publishing Company. Like his father, he stressed the news operation of the *Post-Dispatch.* His memoranda to his staff, called "the yellow peril," were filled with gentle, but firm suggestions and pointed questions urging better journalism in all departments. In addition to his criticisms and suggestions, the second Pulitzer did considerable writing and editing himself, all of which increased the paper's concern for careful news reporting and sharp editorial commentary.

From its beginnings, the afternoon *Post-Dispatch* has always valued intellectual freedom. No staff member has ever been required to write an editorial which went against his beliefs. The paper has always considered political independence important, too. Through the years, its support for Republican and Democratic candidates has been about evenly divided.

Like his father, Joseph Pulitzer II was keenly aware of the importance of public opinion as a force in democratic society. Consequently, he stressed "professional standards that assured superior public service from the *Post-Dispatch* in informing and persuading its readers."[3] During his 43 years, the paper won distinction for its reporting, especially of overseas events, its pungent editorials, its investigation of civic problems and its attention to cultural subjects.

After the death of his father in 1955, Joseph Pulitzer III assumed the post of editor. He has continued along the principles laid down by his grandfather and under his guidance the paper has continued its quality and award-winning performance.

Through the years, the *Post-Dispatch* has built up its reputation for thorough and high quality news coverage. Especially under Joseph Pulitzer II, the paper expanded its horizons and its interpretation of world affairs. In 1912, it scored an outstanding news beat when reporter Carlos Hurd was able to provide the first comprehensive eyewitness account of the sinking of the Titanic. Its coverage of World War II and other wars and peace conferences has been outstanding, partly because it has reported overseas economic and sociologic conditions as well as the foreign events. In recent years Richard Dudman, chief Washington correspondent, has made many trips to Asia. While covering developments in Cambodia in 1970, he was taken prisoner by guerrilla forces. He used his 40 days of captivity to study tactics of his captors and to study some of the guerrilla leaders, gathering material for a series of revealing articles. In 1977, as the first American reporter to tour Vietnam after the Communist victory, he wrote a series of articles that was published in newspapers all over the world.

To achieve its commendable overseas coverage, the *Post-Dispatch,* unlike

[2] *The Story of the St. Louis Dispatch, op. cit.,* Frontispiece.
[3] *Ibid.,* p. 6.

much of the quality press, does not keep a large staff of alert correspondents in strategic spots. It has but a single full-time correspondent who covers Ireland's continuing civic troubles. Instead, it resorts to assigning reporters to critical areas, changing as the focus of significant world events shifts and supplements their work with the seven wire services and numerous syndicated sources it receives.[4] As one example of this practice, Marquis Childs became a trans-Atlantic commuter in the 1950's as he reported European developments. Later, he covered southern Asia and the Middle East in a similar manner. In 1959, too, a reporter-photographer team produced a series which documented political and economic conditions in a changing Africa.

In 1963, another reporter-photographer team travelled through countries bordering Red China to report on "Asia's Frontiers of Freedom." In 1967 a reporter and photographer spent two months in the Soviet Union gathering material for a series of illustrated articles on the 50th anniversary of the Russian revolution. In 1969 two reporters and a photographer were sent to Alaska to study the economic, ecological and ethnic issues raised by the discovery of oil there. In 1976 Pulitzer himself made a 15-day trip to the People's Republic of China with William Woo, editor of the *Post-Dispatch* editorial page, who then wrote a series of articles on life behind the Bamboo Curtain. The year 1977 brought other in-depth articles by reporters who had spent some time at a foreign scene: Robert Joiner wrote a series of articles on Africa; Paul Wagman reported on the intricacies of the Panama Canal treaty dispute as seen by Americans and Panamanians in Panama. In addition, James Deakin, the *Post-Dispatch* White House correspondent, usually covers the President on all foreign trips.

Important names in the paper's foreign correspondence, besides those already mentioned, stand out, such as Clair Kenamore, Charles Ross, Raymond Brandt and Julius Klyman in the period between the two world wars. During and after World War II, foreign stories carried such distinguished *Post-Dispatch* by-lines as Richard Stokes, Theodore Wagner, Virginia Irwin, Sam Armstrong, E. A. Graham, Jr., Ralph Coghlan, Thomas Phillips, George Hall, Donald Grant, Tom Yarbrough and Thomas Ottenad.

Joseph Pulitzer, the present publisher, has expanded the paper's Washington bureau to seven members, making it one of the largest in the nation's capital. There, its reporters have helped the *Post-Dispatch* become one of the first newspapers to obtain the Pentagon Papers. This bureau keeps the paper's readers well posted on all important legislative and administrative moves. Managing editor Evart Graham, Jr. considers the paper's Washington bureau one of the principal factors which make it one of the world's leading quality dailies.[5]

The *Post-Dispatch* stands on solid journalistic principles. It seeks solutions through negotiation of national and international disputes. It shows concern for those everywhere whose liberty and equality are denied. It supports aspirations for better housing, education and medical assistance. It backs minority groups

---

[4] Evarts A. Graham, Managing Editor, *St. Louis Post-Dispatch,* in letter, questionnaire and accompanying information to H. Fisher, January 27, 1978. Much of the material in this profile is drawn from Mr. Graham's useful information.

[5] Graham letter.

and demonstrations against social ills. It is deeply dedicated to human dignity and liberty. It is conservative in its zealous protection of liberties guaranteed by the Constitution and the Bill of Rights. In typical liberal fashion, it favors all efforts at human betterment, whether in the United Nations, peace movements, social welfarism, civil rights legislation or investigation of excesses.

From the time the United States intervened in Vietnam, the *Post-Dispatch* criticized the action, pointing out the danger of escalation, the folly of interference, the perpetuation of atrocities and the deterrence such a militaristic policy provided against moves to world peace. In August, 1965, for example, when Max Freedman and the Manchester *Guardian* criticized Martin Luther King for meddling in Vietnam, the *Post-Dispatch,* in an editorial entitled "The Prize for Absurdity," strongly defended King's right to interfere.

Comparison is often made between the *Post-Dispatch* and England's *Guardian.* Both papers are highly literate, hard-hitting liberal dailies which make it their business to puncture pomposity and to indicate rational solutions to human problems. Both shun emotionalism, detest bigotry in any form, and lash out against extremists wherever they are found. Both prod and agitate their readers into grappling with important issues of the day.

The *Post-Disptach*'s present daily circulation is around 257,000, with 450,000 for its thick Sunday edition. Two-thirds of the copies sell by subscription, the remainder being street sales. About 175 persons are on the writing and editing staff. Many of its staff members have advanced (graduate) degrees. Most of the staff has had experience on other newspapers before joining the *Post-Dispatch.* The staff works in the paper's main building at 900 North 12th Boulevard in St. Louis, where editorial, business and printing facilities cover an entire city block. Two-thirds of the paper's press capacity is in an auxiliary printing plant in suburban Maryland Heights. Negatives of complete pages are transmitted by electrical impulse over leased telephone lines from downtown to the suburban plant.

The *Post-Dispatch* was the first big metropolitan newspaper in the United States to switch from letterpress to offset printing to get improved legibility and sharpened color reproduction. Virtually all news and classified advertising content of the paper is processed by electronic editing terminals. The *Post-Dispatch* also prints its main competitor, the morning *Globe-Democrat,* which is about as conservative as the *Post-Dispatch* is liberal.

The *Post-Dispatch* presents a highly attractive appearance. Under its bold nameplate banner in Bodoni capitals, one finds a horizontal makeup consisting of several leading national and local stories and, occasionally, one from an overseas source. One to several color photographs grace the front page, as well as a box in the lower right-hand section containing brief "teasers" to leading national, business and sports stories inside, a page index of other inside materials and a brief weather capsule accompanied by a small cartoon. Frequently, an investigative story or feature by-lined by a staff member commences on the front page. In general, the front page has a clean, uncluttered, sprightly appearance.

The paper is made up of several sections. Weekday issues may run from 44 to 60 pages in length, while the thicker Sunday edition normally contains anywhere from 120 to 160 pages plus three magazine sections—"Parade," "Sunday Pictures," and a weekly television schedule booklet. The first section of the daily usually contains most of the national and international news, which comprise three and two percent of the total space respectively. Special pages of news by category, for example on "People" or "Religion," are headed by a lead story encased in a box. Although order of the sections is flexible, frequently the second section is devoted to classified or retail advertising, sometimes indexed for the reader's convenience. As is typical of American dailies, about two-thirds of the total space consists of advertising. Other sections are devoted to sports, business and the economy, local news, editorial and news analyses. A cultural section entitled "Everyday" followed by the name of the day appears regularly. It usually contains news and features on culture and the arts, music, theater and the cinema, television and radio, plus a syndicated editorial and advice columns by Art Buchwald, Ann Landers, Dr. Thostesen and others. This section usually ends with a full page of color comics and cartoons. Color for pictures and special effects is used daily except on Saturdays, and the paper's peers regard the *Post-Dispatch* color about the best in the industry.

Although the news coverage of the *Post-Dispatch* is good, what really distinguishes it are its articles of interpretation, background and perspective as well as its vigorous, well-written editorials. Eight staff members are engaged full-time in investigative reporting, with others assigned to help out from time to time. The paper's in-depth reporting and thorough analytical articles are some of the best found anywhere in the newspaper industry. The opposite-editorial page for many years has provided an example of the founder's request: "Never be satisified with merely printing news." This is especially true of the Sunday edition, where two whole pages are given over to interpretive reporting and discussions of basic issues in the news. These pages, under the direction of the managing editor, are called the "dignity" pages by the staff. The reporting of governmental affairs and politics continues as one of the *Post-Dispatch*'s major concerns. Specialists on the newspaper staff provide material in various fields, including education, science, the arts, environment and consumer affairs. They are generally recognized as among the best such pages in the country. The late President Harry Truman, with whom the paper often differed, said, "The Sunday editorial title section of the *Post-Dispatch* is one of the finest things I read. As matter of fact, it is the first thing I read on Sunday morning."

The *Post-Dispatch*'s editorial page is distinctive also. While many American newspapers have abandoned provocative editorials, the *Post-Dispatch* continues to express frank and forceful opinions in a dignified manner. Perhaps this page, more than any other, has given the paper its special place in American journalism. It takes up disagreeable subjects and fights for unpopular causes. Although the editorials generally represent a liberal position, the spirit is independent. The page's editorial cartoon has a long reputation of ranking among the best. Two of the truly great editorial cartoonists of the United States have been *Post-Dispatch* staffers, the late Daniel Fitzpatrick until 1958 and Bill Mauldin until 1962.

Working with editor Joseph Pulitzer III, grandson of the paper's founder, is a staff of highly capable writers and editors. Evarts A. Graham, Jr., who joined the *Post-Disptach* staff in 1941 and distinguished himself after World War II with a series of in-depth stories on Germany's future, has been managing editor since 1968. Editor of the editorial pages is William F. Woo. The editorial section of the paper is supported by a large technical and administrative staff.

One significant indicator of the *Post-Dispatch*'s continuing excellence as one of the world's leading elite newspapers may be found in its impressive list of awards and achievements. The paper has received America's most coveted journalistic award, the Pulitzer Prize, five times for its outstanding accomplishments. In addition, ten individual staff members have received Pulitzer Prizes for outstanding service in specialized fields.

Besides the Pultizer Prizes, the *Post-Dispatch* has won numerous citations for its excellent journalism. In 1932 and again in 1975, it received coveted Honor Awards from the University of Missouri School of Journalism. Seven of its staff members have also received these highly valued Missouri honor awards. In 1968, the American Bar Association cited the paper for "its contribution to public understanding of the nation's legal and judicial systems," an award given because of Irving Dilliard's excellent six article series on the U.S. Supreme Court. Other awards received from a wide range of organizations including citizens' councils, business and industrial groups, professional newspaper and journalistic societies and universities indicate the high quality nature of *Post-Dispatch* performance.

Accolades for the paper have also come from national leaders. The late Adlai Stevenson said: "My views on the *Post-Dispatch* are simple: I regard it as one of the best papers on earth. I have read it all my life and, as long as I live, I intend to go on reading it." Pierre Salinger, press secretary to the late President Kennedy, wrote during the Kennedy administration: "Ever since I have been associated with the President I know that he has read the *St. Louis Post-Dispatch* and has paid particular attention to the views expressed by that newspaper." And the American author, John Gunther, once called the *Post-Dispatch* "the most effective liberal newspaper in the United States."

Finally, as perhaps the best tribute of all to its excellence, rivals have repeatedly given the *Post-Dispatch* a high standing among the great quality newspapers. *Newsweek* has noted: "The *Post-Dispatch* has won more crusades, perhaps, than any other American daily." The *Saturday Evening Post* was even more laudatory: "In any professional ranking of present-day American newspapers, the *Post-Dispatch* must head somewhere up among the first five." *Time* magazine has termed it "one of the world's ten greatest newspapers," a ranking borne out by several other studies.[6]

The *St. Louis Post-Dispatch* stands high today among the world's dailies because it continues to emulate the Platform of Principles laid down by its founder, the first Joseph Pulitzer. Daily, in each issue, its dedicated staff earnestly tries to carry out Joseph Pulitzer's 1955 pledge based on the Platform when he took over the paper's editorship:

[6]*The Story of the St. Louis Post-Dispatch, op. cit.,* pp. 54–5.

With all the moral strength, the intellectual strength, the professional strength at our command, we will continue to labor as public servants. Not only will we report the day's news, but we will illuminate dark places, and, with a deep sense of responsibility, interpret these troubled times.[7]

The Statesman

(INDIA)

FROM THE DIGNIFIED white four-story structure in Chowinghee Square, Calcutta, is published one of Asia's most distinguished and courageous dailies—*The Statesman*. The headquarters of the paper is in Calcutta, with Cushrow R. Irani as managing director, but an edition of the paper is also published in New Delhi, the national capital. Publisher of the paper is The Statesman Limited, a corportation.[1] Editor is S. Nihal Singh.

C. R. Irani feels that there are several factors which make *The Statesman* one of the world's leading quality newspapers.[2] He puts it this way:

> One of the qualities for which *The Statesman* has always been known is the courage of its convictions. This was particularly so during the recent Indian Emergency.[3] Besides, *The Statesman* has always believed in giving a fair coverage to all points of view, even those with which the newspaper violently disagrees. Thirdly, *The Statesman* has been known for setting a standard in responsible reporting and journalism.

Since its founding in 1875 *The Statesman* has prided itself and impressed readers in India and abroad with its reportorial accuracy, its political and social insights, and its editorial courage. It has always aimed especially at the segment of Indian society which might be described as intellectuals or opinion-leaders. The newspaper is an independent liberal newspaper, one that has always fought for press freedom and the achievement of maximum individual human rights in India. Staff members of *The Statesman* are determined to publish everything significant on the local, national, and international levels. This is achieved, mainly, say its staffers, through extreme care in news judgment and careful editing.

---

[7] *Ibid.*, p. 1.
[1] Private Limited Company made Public by virtue of Section 43A of the Indian Companies Act of 1956.
[2] Questionnaire and letter to the authors from C. R. Irani (Calcutta), dated March 31, 1978; hereafter: Irani Questionnaire.
[3] The "Emergency" in India was proclaimed by Prime Minister Indira Gandhi in June, 1975, and it ended in 1977 when she and her Congress Party ousted by a victory at the polls by the Janata Party.

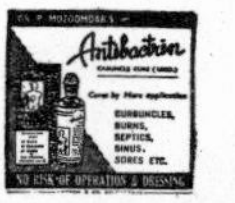
Antibactrin
BURBUNCLES, BURNS, SEPTICS, SINUS, SORES ETC.
NO RISK OF OPERATION & DRESSING

LATE CITY EDITION

THE STATESMAN

REG. NO. D-(C)-87
REG. NO. M-8905

DELHI, WEDNESDAY, FEBRUARY 22, 1978

35 Paise

for 22 Ct. GOLD & DIAMOND JEWELLERY
KHANNA JEWELLERS (P) LTD.
BANK STREET, KAROL BAGH N. DELHI-5 Ph: 567619, 568451

NO INCREASE IN FARES & FREIGHT

Dandavate's Surplus Railway Budget

PASSENGERS TO GET MORE AMENITIES

FROM OUR SPECIAL REPRESENTATIVE

NEW DELHI, TUESDAY—WHILE RAILWAY FARES AND FREIGHT RATES HAVE BEEN LEFT UNTOUCHED COMMUTERS HAVE BEEN GIVEN SEVERAL CONCESSIONS AND PROMISED FURTHER AMENITIES IN THE RAILWAY BUDGET FOR 1978-79 PRESENTED IN THE LOK SABHA TODAY BY MR MADHU DANDAVATE.

PRESENTING THE SECOND SUCCESSIVE SURPLUS BUDGET, MR DANDAVATE ANNOUNCED THAT FROM APRIL LONG-DISTANCE SECOND CLASS PASSENGERS WOULD HAVE TO PAY A FLAT RS 5 AS SLEEPER CHARGES IRRESPECTIVE OF THE NUMBER OF NIGHTS INVOLVED. THE RAILWAYS ALSO INTEND TO PROVIDE FOOD PACKETS, "JANATA KHANA", COSTING ONLY ONE RUPEE ON ALL MAJOR LONG-DISTANCE TRAINS.

Among the other concessions and proposals were reduction in the surcharge on super-fast Express trains from Rs 1.50 to one rupee for second class passengers, cut in reservation charges for second class sitting and sleeping accommodation from 50 paise to 25 paise, cushioned comfort for second class travellers, and extension of hill concessions.

Referring to the steps taken to ensure safe rail travel, the Railway Minister pointed out that about Rs 1 lakh was being spent every day on patrolling arrangements which included deployment of 11.000 men of the Railway Protection Force and 14.000 gangmen.

After the introduction of these and other measures several cases of suspected sabotage were detected in time and accidents averted. The situation had "taken a turn for the better during the last two months."

Referring to the efforts to achieve the ultimate objective of providing one class of travel, Mr Dandavate said all long-distance trains in the next two or three years would have second class three-tier coaches with padded cushions and improved amenities on the pattern of Gitanjali Express.

Linked with this was the proposal not to increase first class air-conditioned accommodation and in fact, to progressively phase it out. Besides more cushioned seats in more trains he also announced that passenger capacity in the existing long-distance trains would be increased to accommodate 200 to 300 additional passengers.

The Budget for 1978-79 estimated gross traffic receipts at Rs 2.220 crores or Rs 88 crores more than the revised estimates for the current financial year. The working expenses were estimated at Rs 1.701 crores, Rs 90 crores more than that for the current year. The surplus for 1977-78 was expected to be Rs 89 32 crores, Rs 57 crores higher than what had been anticipated.

The coming financial year was expected to yield a net surplus of Rs 65.43 crores, after allowing for additional expenditure on staff and increased provision for depreciation and pension funds.

CAPITAL STRUCTURE

The expected surplus in the next financial year would, the Railway Minister hoped, help to reduce the Railways' indebtedness to the General Revenues from Rs 368.68 crores at the end of March to Rs 345 37 crores by March next.

Disclosing his intention to explore ways to overcome the adverse effects of indebtedness, Mr Dandavate said he was considering an in-depth study of the Railways capital structure by a committee. A high-power committee had already been appointed to examine some of the issues connected with social burdens which the Minister thought ought to be borne by the general revenues.

Of the Rs 170 crores accounted for by "social burdens" during the current year Rs 69 crores went to commodities carried below cost and Rs 21 crores to the working of uneconomic branch lines. The balance represents the loss incurred on short distance and suburban passenger traffic.

For the staff there was good news in the announcement that about 500 Class III posts would be upgraded to class II, the quota for promotion of Class II officers to Class I would rise from 33.3% to 40% and the grades and working conditions of loco running staff would be improved.

(Text of Railway Minister's speech—page 7)

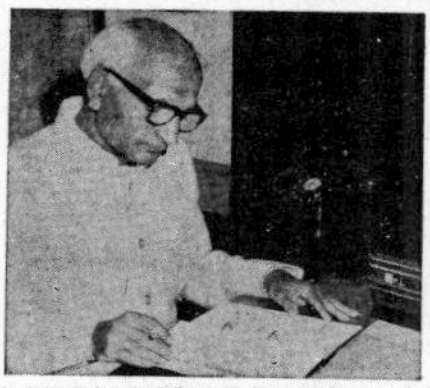

The Union Minister for Railways, Mr Madhu Dandavate, giving finishing touches to the Railway Budget for 1978-79 just before presenting it to Parliament on Tuesday.

ONLY WOMEN FOR BOOKING OFFICES

From Our Special Representative

NEW DELHI, Tuesday.—Mr Madhu Dandavate is obviously firm in his belief that women were less prone to be corrupt than men.

He announced in the Lok Sabha today that henceforth only women would be employed as reservation or booking clerks and supervisers in the major railway booking offices.

A beginning in this "anti-corruption drive" was to be made in metropolitan cities.

Computerization of passenger reservation in the four major cities was also being considered to check malpractices, he said.

RAILWAY BUDGET AT A GLANCE

(Figures in crores of rupees)

	Actuals 1976-77	Budget Estimates 1977-78	Revised Estimates 1977-78	Budget Estimates 1978-79
Gross Traffic Receipts	2036.11	2110.24	2131.61	2219.86
Ordinary Revenue Working Expenses (Net) that is after taking credit for recoveries	1548.96	1648.74	1611.06	1700.90
Appropriation to Depreciation Reserve Fund from Revenue	135.00	140.00	140.00	145.00
Appropriation to Pension Fund	35.00	40.00	40.00	50.00
Net Miscellaneous Expenditure (including cost of works charged to Revenue)	20.86	23.68	24.16	25.71
TOTAL:	1739.82	1852.42	1815.22	1921.61
Net Railway Revenue	296.29	257.82	316.39	298.25
Dividend to General Revenues	209 05	225.32	227.07	232.82
Net Surplus(+)/ Shortfall(—)	+87.24	+32.50	+89.32	+65.43
Operating Ratio	84.4%	86.6%	84%	85.4%

Congress To Move Amendment

From Our Special Representative

NEW DELHI, Tuesday.—A move for scrapping both the Preventive Detention Law and the Maintenance of Internal Security Act will be made by the Congress in the present session of Parliament.

The executive of the Congress Parliamentary Party at its meeting here today decided to move an amendment to the Motion of Thanks to the President (for his Address to the joint session of Parliament) when it is taken up by the Lok Sabha, to this effect.

The executive noted with concern the Government move "to perpetuate and codify as permanent law the Preventive Detention Act in the Code of Criminal Procedure". It felt that codification would amount to violation of the Janata Party's pledge to revoke MISA.

The executive said that the Government has not disclosed how it proposed to curb inflationary trends and tackle the problem of unemployment, bring about a suitable climate for industrial relationship and promote production and growth.

The Government had not taken adequate steps to bring under control lawlessness. The executive regretted that the President's Address was "significantly silent" on the communal riots.

It regretted that the Address did not take note of the peaceful agitation of teachers and industrial workers and the "anarchic conditions" prevailing in universities.

It appointed a six-member committee to report on Centre-State relations. The members of the committee are: Mr C Subramaniam, Professor D P Chattopadhyaya, Mr Vyalar Ravi, Mr Hitendra Desai, Dr V A Seyid Muhammad and Mr Dwendranath Dwivedi. Mr Dwivedi will be the convener of the committee.

The executive expressed the view that the Centre should not be weak, but at the same time, the Centre should not be strong at the cost of the States.

A list was released by Mr Amjad Ali, CPP Secretary, showing that 90 Lok Sabha members (out of a total of 142 Congress members) and 77 Rajya Sabha members (out of a total of 140) were with Mr Reddy's party.

PANDEMONIUM IN LOK SABHA

INCIDENT OF INSULT TO JAGJIVAN RAM

Pandemonium prevailed in the Lok Sabha for over 15 minutes on Tuesday when several members agitatedly demanded an immediate discussion on the insult heaped on the Defence Minister, Mr Jagjivan Ram, and the Harijans in the country as a whole, reports Samachar.

As soon as the House assembled for the day a number of ruling party members started shouting that the action of some persons who performed "suddhi ceremony (purification)" with Ganga water on the statute of Dr Sampoornanand which was unveiled by Mr Jagjivan Ram in Varanasi last month, was a serious matter and the House should discuss it.

The Speaker, Mr K. S. Hegde, assured the members that he would try to give the time for discussion on this issue on Wednesday. He would also request the Home Minister, Mr Charan Singh, to be present in the House.

Mr Kenwar Lal Gupta said that the entire House should condemn the insult meted out to the national leader. He thought that the Congress Party was behind this incident.

The leader of the Opposition Mr Y. B. Chavan, immediately retorted by saying that his party had nothing to do with this incident. He, however, condemned the incident.

U.S.A., RUSSIA SUSPEND INDIAN OCEAN TALKS

BERN, Feb 21.—The U.S.-Soviet negotiations over arms limitation in the Indian Ocean have been suspended, a U.S. Embassy communiqué said here today, reports AFP.

The talks had begun on December 6 last year and then halted. They were again resumed this month.

The communiqué did not indicate when the negotiations would be resumed. The talks had been frank and useful and would constitute the basis for future work on the question, the communiqué said.

The U.S. negotiators were led by the U.S. Disarmament Chief, Mr Paul Warnke. The Soviet Ambassador Mr Lev Isaakovitch Mendelevich, headed the Soviet team.

Samachar adds from New York: The USA is planning to strengthen its strategic forces in Asia and upgrade its fleet in the Pacific, the Defence Secretary, Mr Harold Brown, disclosed in a policy speech he made to the World Affairs Council at Los Angeles last night.

ECONOMIC DEVELOPMENT

Mr Brown said this was being done because of "uncertainties" that the U.S. forces face in the area.

According to officials, these "uncertainties" include possible changes for better or worse in Chinese-Soviet relations, hostilities between North and South Korea, fear that Vietnam "might undertake adventuristic policy actions against non-Communist neighbours and consequences of the faltering economic development in less development countries in the region".

The USA believes that the present Super-Power tranquillity may be affected for any of these reasons and that it must strengthen its forces in the region.

"The situation in Asia is more favourable to our interests than in the past," said Mr Brown. "We want to ensure that this environment continues."

"In the next five years we will be strengthening our forces in the region by the introduction of several advanced weapon systems: trident nuclear missiles for our submarine fleet, cruise missiles for B-52s, F-14 fighters for our carriers, F-15s for Air Force squadrons, the aerial warning and control system and other improvements.

"We will maintain the size of our Pacific fleet and modernize and increase it to the extent our shipbuilding schedules permit."

4 P.A.C. MEN KILLED IN ACCIDENT

LUCKNOW, Feb 21.—Four PAC men were killed and five injured when a U.P. State Road Transport bus hit a stationary PAC truck last night about 50 km from here on the Lucknow-Kanpur road, according to an official spokesman, reports Samachar.

The truck was unloading goods when the accident occurred.

The U.P. Transport Minister, Mr Abid Ali Ansari, who visited the place announced a grant of Rs 1,000 to the dependants of each of those killed and Rs 500 each to those injured in the accident.

The injured have been admitted to hospital.

STONES THROWN AT RAJ NARAIN

NAGPUR, Feb 21.—An attempt was made today to disturb an election meeting addressed by the Union Minister for Health and Family Welfare, Mr Raj Narain at Katol near here, by some people, reports Samachar.

Some stones and chappals were also thrown at him, but they fell short of the target. Anti-Raj Narain slogans were also raised for a while.

Karnataka Results On February 26

From Our Special Representative

NEW DELHI, Tuesday.—The first set of results to be announced for the ensuing Assembly elections in five States and one Union Territory will come from Karnataka, the Chief Election Commissioner, Mr S. L. Shakdher, said today.

He told a Press conference that the results from Karnataka would start coming from February 26 and will be completed on February 27, for the new Ministry must take over on February 28.

For the other States, counting would begin on February 27 and be completed on February 28. Only in Meghalaya and Arunachal Pradesh, this would be taken up and completed between March 1 and 3.

Mr Shakdher said that the number of polling booths had been increased by at least 25%, to ensure that no one had to walk more than 1.5 km to reach a polling booth. Steps had also been taken to have polling booths located near the places of residence of Harijans and other backward classes to free them from fear and intimidation.

Formerly there used to be a booth for every 900—1,200 voters. Now there would be one for every 750—1,000 voters.

The last two elections—for the Lok Sabha and the State Assemblies in 1977—had been held in peaceful conditions. He had no doubt that the ensuing elections would also be held in conditions of complete peace and freedom.

Asked about some incidents in Maharashtra and Karnataka, he said he had directed the formation of constituency committees by Returning Officers and to invite representatives of political parties and request them to review the law and order situation and see that the code of conduct was implemented and law and order maintained.

It was the first time that polling in the five States and one Union Territory would be held on one day. This would mean creation of additional administrative facilities and "to do this we will seek the help of both civilian and police personnel".

(See also page 5)

CHINA MAY INVITE DESAI

TOKYO, Feb 21.—A Chinese goodwill delegation headed by Mr Wang Ping-nan, President of the Chinese People's Association for Friendship with Foreign Countries, left Peking yesterday for visits to Pakistan, Bangladesh and India, reports AP.

Japan's Kyodo news service, said in a despatch from Peking that Mr Wang was reported to be carrying a Chinese Government invitation for Mr Desai to visit China.

The Chinese delegation's visit to India follows Mr Desai's remarks in Calcutta early this month that "I am always ready and willing to meet any Chinese leader" because "we believe in negotiations; we do not believe in wars".

The New China News Agency quoted Mr Wang as saying at the airport before his departure that the Chinese people had a long-standing traditional friendship with the peoples of Pakistan, Bangladesh and India.

"Our aim is to promote this friendship and learn from the people of these three countries. We hope that the visits will make due contribution in deepening mutual understanding and friendship between the Peoples of China and the three countries."

CHINESE TEAM'S TALKS IN CALCUTTA

From Our Calcutta Office

FEB 21.—A Chinese trade delegation, now in India, attended a meeting organized by the State Trading Corporation in Calcutta today to get a first-hand knowledge of the shellac industry. Representatives of the Shellac Export Promotion Council, Indian Lac Research Institute and Directorate of Lac Development were present.

The delegation was given details about the various aspects of Indian lac and its uses. It was pointed out that India was in a position to meet the lac requirements of China not only in quantity but also in quality.

The delegation gave the impression that China had a large consumption base for lac. The first consignment of Indian shellac was exported through the State Trading Corporation in August last year. Another export order for 600 tonnes is pending.

FOUR CHANGES IN HOCKEY TEAM

The Indian Hockey Federation has decided to include Ashok Kumar, Baldev Singh, Virinder Singh and Sayed Ali in the national team for the World Cup. They replace Gurdishpal Singh, Mehboob Khan, Charanjit and Prabhakaran.

(Details on back page)

'Detention Ordered By Dhawan'

From Our Special Representative

NEW DELHI, Tuesday.—Mr Harideo Joshi, former Chief Minister of Rajasthan, today told the Shah Commission that he took action against two officials, an advocate and the latter's teacher wife, following a specific direction from Mr R. K. Dhawan.

"You told me what to do; my job was to note down your directions; and as for the action taken by me, you were in a position to know everything", he told Mr Dhawan, as the latter cross-examined him.

Mr Dhawan's direction conveyed over the telephone was that one of the two officers should be compulsorily retired, the other suspended, the advocate detained and the advocate's wife removed from her job in a Government school.

The ground was ostensibly that they had Ananda Margi connexions, although the true reason was different.

'AN ORDER'

"Your message was a direction, and you told me to carry it out", Mr Joshi told Mr Dhawan.

Earlier, answering Mr Karl Khandalawala, counsel for the Commission, Mr Joshi said he regarded Mr Dhawan's message as "an order emanating from Mrs Gandhi herself".

He added: "There is no higher constitutional authority than the Prime Minister for a Chief Minister". And how could the latter flout the former's orders?

Besides, he said, there were other compulsions on him to carry out that direction. There was the Emergency. Also, the Home Ministry had sent a note virtually admonishing the State Government for being slack in detaining RSS and Ananda Marg members. There was a report that MLAs were themselves complaining to that effect and that some of them had done so to the then Prime Minister. "So I felt there was no option except to take necessary action."

'NECESSARY ACTION'

Mr Joshi had a point to make about the "necessary action". It meant that officials had to take, according to the law, whatever action was called for.

In other words, he suggested, no blame could attach to him for the action taken.

He supported that position by saying that in cases where he wanted specific action, he suggested the action and always wrote: "for compliance, and report".

You were not much concerned about the fate of the people involved? Mr Khandalawala asked him.

Mr Joshi: My job was to carry out the Prime Minister's orders.

Mr Khandalawala: You were not interested in what happened to these?

Mr Joshi: I was not interested in any person.

It emerged from today's testimony that the IAS officer who was asked to be compulsorily retired (but was sent on long leave) had objected to trucks of the State Electricity Board being used for carrying people for a Congress rally in Delhi on June 20, 1975. A week later, he was asked to go on leave.

Mr Joshi incidentally denied that he had any hand in the despatch of 58 trucks of the Board packed with workers for the Delhi rally. He had not known about it. "I had no reason to send those trucks of the Electricity Board; I could have procured private trucks" he added.

Mr Dhawan denied that he had conveyed any direction to Mr

(Continued on page 7 col 8)

Koirala Acquitted Of Treason In Bomb Case

KATHMANDU, Feb 21.—A special tribunal today acquitted the former Prime Minister of Nepal, Mr B. P. Koirala, of the charge of treason in what is known as the Dharan Bomb case, reports Samachar.

Hearing in the case began yesterday and the judgment came shortly before the tribunal rose for the day after defence lawyers had completed their arguments.

The former Prime Minister is facing charges of treason in five more cases and a sedition charge in another. All the cases will be heard by the tribunal, which will be in session until Monday.

Cases against Mr Ganesh Mansingh will also be heard by the tribunal. It will hear two cases of treason against Mr Koirala tomorrow.

The special tribunal said in its findings that the prosecution had relied mainly upon the confession of the co-accused, Bom Bahadur, from whose possession a bomb was alleged to have been seized.

The tribunal stated that the confession could not be an independent evidence to prove the guilt. So Mr Koirala was acquitted of the charge of conspiracy and collecting arms for rebellion.

The tribunal, however, stated that this was a reference judgment subject to confirmation by the Supreme Court.

Mr Koirala was brought to the tribunal in a covered jeep and was present throughout the sitting today. Also present in court were his two nieces.

FAIR TRIAL

Three lawyers of Mr Koirala argued in the case today. Mr Kusum Shrestha told the tribunal that the prosecution had not been able to prove criminal intent and action on the part of Mr Koirala. He said Mr Koirala had not spoken against constitutional monarchy which was the achievement of the revolution of 1950.

Counsel also read out Articles 10 and 11 of the Declaration of Human Rights which, he said, had been incorporated in some of the judgments of the Supreme Court of Nepal about fair trial principles. In the present case, Mr Koirala had been denied these principles of fair trial.

Another lawyer, Mr K. P. Bhandari, told the tribunal that the prosecution had been launched with the "vindictive" attitude of the Government without even elementary facts and evidence.

The call of Mr Koirala for revolution was in accordance with the right of defence of the people. Until it violated the legal provisions of the law of the land, Mr Koirala could not be vexed for the trial.

Further, the lawyer argued, the jurisdiction of the tribunal did not go beyond the country. In the prosecution charge it was alleged that the conspiracy was hatched in Forbesganj, India. The jurisdiction of the tribunal could not be extended to that area.

'India-Vietnam Talks On Friday

From Our Special Representative

NEW DELHI, Tuesday.—The Vietnamese Prime Minister, Mr Pham Van Dong, who arrives here on Friday on a week's visit, is due to have two rounds of talks with Mr Desai.

Mr Pham, one of the leaders of the Vietnamese liberation struggle, is coming to India for the first time and Indian leaders are naturally looking forward to their first direct exchange of views with him.

The emphasis at his talks with Mr Desai on Friday and Saturday will be on bilateral cooperation. Vietnam now engaged in massive reconstruction, has sought Indian assistance for some of the projects.

An Indian delegation headed by the Minister of State for External Affairs, Mr S. Kundu, which visited Hanoi recently, has worked out the details of some aspects of cooperation between the two countries. India has also promised a Rs 30-crore credit.

The Vietnamese Prime Minister is interested in extending cooperation to the spheres of agriculture and cattle-breeding, to which India has already committed her support.

The visiting Prime Minister's 25-member delegation includes one of the country's senior scientists, whose task will be to identify the areas in pure science and technology in which India can assist.

The External Affairs Minister, Mr Atal Bihari Vajpayee is expected to give Mr Pham the Indian view of developments in the region as also on international affairs.

Mr Pham will address members of Parliament in the Central Hall of Parliament House.

Before he leaves for Colombo Mr Pham will sign agreements on bilateral cooperation. He will also visit Haryana, Agra, Bombay and Tamil Nadu. He will address a Press conference on Saturday.

TODAY'S WEATHER IN DELHI

Sunny day becoming cloudy at times; rise in night temperature.

The maximum temperature in New Delhi (S'jang) on Tuesday was 22-6 degrees C (72.7 degrees F), 2 degrees C below normal and the minimum 9.6 degrees C (49-3 degrees F), 1 degree C below normal.

The maximum relative humidity was 83% and the minimum 37%.

Sun sets today at 6.16 p.m.; rises tomorrow at 6-53 a.m. Moon rises today at 6-46 p.m.; sets at 6-08 a.m. Full Moon tomorrow.

Lighting up time 6-46 p.m.

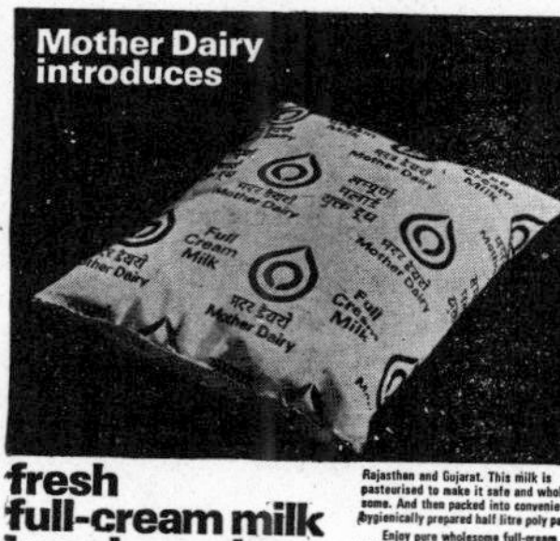
Mother Dairy introduces
Full Cream Milk
Mother Dairy

fresh full-cream milk in poly packs.

Now taste the goodness of pure, wholesome full-cream milk. A new high fat content of over 6.0% guaranteed. Available in hygienically packed half litre poly packs.

Mother Dairy obtains the best quality milk directly from farmer organisations in Punjab, Haryana, Uttar Pradesh, Rajasthan and Gujarat. This milk is pasteurised to make it safe and wholesome. And then packed into convenient hygienically prepared half litre poly packs.

Enjoy pure wholesome full-cream milk in a number of ways. Drink it straight, prepare the most wholesome curd, paneer and khoya. Not to mention the pleasure of good home-made butter, cream and lassi.

Available in Delhi in convenient half litre poly packs at:
Empire Stores
Steak House
Modern Bazaar
Morning Stores and
at selected Mother Dairy Milk Booths

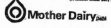

Mother Dairy Delhi

According to Irani, *The Statesman* takes great care not to publish unsubstantiated accusations, libellous reports and commercial promotion campaigns disguised as news reports. Also, emphasizes the managing director, the paper is very careful "not to publish anything that would be considered encouragement of the prurient taste."[4] Rather, *Statesman* journalists are interested in investigative reporting and are encouraged to do in-depth background stories, and to look analytically at specific problems—especially assessing their impact on social development of Calcutta and India generally.

Perhaps out of step with most of the great dailies of the world, *The Statesman*—in its editorial organization and technical aspects—is produced along lines which its director terms "old-fashioned." There are no VDT terminals in its offices, no wall-to-wall carpets and glittering equipment; there is no color printing, few pictures are used in its pages, and the Linotype machine is still king.

In spite of the "traditional" technical character of the paper, it is forward-looking and vigorous in its editorial operations. It has always been highly respected in academic and government cricles and has long been heralded as a good standard for aspiring journalists in India. Since 1968 it has garnered many prizes and awards, among them the Government of India National Award for Excellence in Printing and Designing (which it won for 11 years in the period 1955 through 1977).

Today there are nearly 2,000 persons on the staff of the newspaper, approximately 175 of them journalists (reporters, editors, and photographers). There are nine correspondents in New Delhi, and one full-time foreign correspondent—stationed in London. In addition, *The Statesman* has six part-timers writing from the U.K., the United States, Sri Lanka, and Nepal. Although the paper does not require its journalists to have university degrees, it does require a high proficiency in English grammar and expression, a broad general education, an intellectual curiosity, and considerable in-house training.[5]

The Statesman gets most of its national and international news from Samachar, the national Indian news agency.[6] Foreign news agencies in late 1978 were channeled through Samachar; so it might be said that the newspaper receives dispatches from Reuters (Britain), the Associated Press (U.S.), Agence France-Presse, Deutsche Presse Agentur (West Germany), and TASS (Soviet Union). The newspapers also has a long-standing arrangement with *The Times* of London to use any of the material printed in it except for specifically copyrighted articles. *The Statesman* also receives the Associated Press Photo Service from the United States.

Circulation of the newspaper hovers around 220,000 copies for the daily editions and around 250,000 for the Sunday editions. More than 99 percent of the copies are "street-sales," with only a little over one-half of 1 percent going

[4] Irani questionnaire.
[5] Irani questionnaire. Also talks with staff, summer, 1977, in Calcutta (by Merrill).
[6] During the "Emergency" in India the two English news agencies—the Press Trust of India and the United News of India—as well as the two Hindi language agencies were forcibly merged into Samachar. According to Irani in 1978, these agencies are in the process of reverting to their original status.

directly to subscribers. A rough breakdown of a typical edition's total space allocation follows: International news, 5 percent; national news, 8 percent; local/state news, 10 percent; news analysis and editorials, 6 percent; features/entertainment, 3 percent; sports, 3 percent; and advertising, 60 percent.

As for the newspaper's basic editorial policy or guidelines, there are five main principles followed. The paper will (1) uphold the concept of the Rule of Law and the principles of democratic government (2) support and defend humanist causes and oppose any form of tyranny or oppression, (3) support all sound and democratic plans for India's economic advancement, showing due regard for the part played by private enterprise in national development, (4) foster goodwill between India and other countries, especially those which cherish values of free and democratic institutions and representative government, and (5) seek by these and all other means to promote a free, united, peaceful, prosperous and democratic republic.

It is *The Statesman*'s basic policy to take stands in its leading articles (editorials); however, the main article on the editorial page does not always reflect editorial policy. In addition, the paper encourages people to criticize the editorial stands through letters to the editor. In these letters, for example, the topical issues on which views of both sides are aired—for instance, the merits and demerits of the Indian Emergency and the rightness or wrongness of the Israeli and Arab stands in the Middle East.[7]

Now, in conclusion, let us take a brief look at the history of the newspaper. *The Statesman* was founded in 1875 by Robert Knight and was directly descended from, and merged with, *The Friend of India* which was started 58 years earlier.[8] On Knight's death in 1890, his sons, Paul and Robert, succeeded to the ownership of the newspaper and by their business ability, far-sighted enterprise and hard work made it the most prosperous newspaper in the eastern part of India. In 1922 they formed the company, The Statesman Limited, which owns the newspaper.[9]

The Statesman has been associated with numerous noteworthy and pioneering achievements in the journalistic history of India. It was the first newspaper to sell for one anna, at a time when four annas was the accepted newspaper price, and it maintained this price for 67 years. It was the first Indian newspaper to publish simultaneously from two centers (Calcutta and Delhi), more than 800 miles apart, and thus to have a more extensive geographical coverage, probably, than any newspaper in the world. *The Statesman* was also the first newspaper in India to introduce mechanical typesetting and to print from a rotary press.

The newspaper has a unique ownership pattern. Until 1963 it was owned by a British family which zealously guarded its independence even against pressures from the British administration in India prior to 1947. In 1963 the ownership was transferred to 19 handpicked corporations in India pledged to continue

---

[7] Irani questionnaire.

[8] In 1934 the popular Calcutta journal, *The Englishman* was also merged in *The Statesman*.

[9] Much of this historical data was obtained from *A Brief History of The Statesman* (Calcutta: Statesman Ltd., 1947) and from information from C. R. Irani; Letter, Feb. 22, 1978).

safeguarding the paper's integrity and reputation. Under pressures and threats from Mrs. Gandhi's Government, both before and during the Emergency,[10] several of these corporations transferred their holdings to public charitable trusts. Others sold their holdings to the staff. More than 27 percent of the Company is now owned by the staff of *The Statesman*.

India, as one of the largest and most populous countries on earth, certainly faces monumental problems. Development, in all segments of society, is imperative. And one social institution—the press—is particularly important in this area. And within the press are several distinguished leaders, among them being *The Statesman*, a newspaper which sees its responsibility in this area and is determined to meet it head-on.

Süddeutsche Zeitung

(WEST GERMANY)

IN CONTRAST TO THE UNITED STATES which can claim no truly national newspaper, West Germany can boast of several. At least three quality German dailies are generally considered to be national in scope—Bonn's *Die Welt*, Frankfurt's *Frankfurter Allgemeine Zeitung* and Munich's *Süddeutsche Zeitung*. In the 1960's another daily which had been a local paper, the *Frankfurter Rundschau* extended its circulation and its influence so dramatically it is sometimes now considered the country's fourth national daily.

The largest of these quality Germany national dailies is the liberal, left-of-center *Süddeutsche Zeitung* (South German Newspaper). Because the *Süddeutsche Zeitung* escapes the strong conservative biases of *Die Welt*, the somber gravity of *Frankfurter Allgemeine* and the left-wing slant of the *Rundschau*, one source calls it "arguably the best daily in the country."[1] Its circulation slightly exceeds that of *Frankfurter Allgemeine*, making it the nation's largest quality daily. A thick paper, it usually contains 40 to 50 or more pages per day during the week and its much-thicker weekend edition, *Süddeutsche Zeitung am Wochenende* usually weighs in at nearly a kilogram or more.

---

[10] During the Emergency Mrs. Gandhi veered sharply toward authoritarian government—in the name of national stability and security—and imposed great restrictions on the Indian press. For an excellent record of this period and the years leading up to it, see an incisive book by a journalist who was caught in the middle of it—Kuldip Nayar, *The Judgement: Inside Story of the Emergency in India* (New Delhi: Vikas Publishing House, Ltd., 1977).

[1] John Sandford, *The Mass Media of the German-Speaking Countries* (London: Oswald Wolf Publishers, Ltd., 1976), p. 211.

Süddeutsche Zeitung

MÜNCHNER NEUESTE NACHRICHTEN AUS POLITIK · KULTUR · WIRTSCHAFT · SPORT

S. 10; Lit. 500; Din. 12; Dr. 25; sfr. 1,30;
fr. 3.00; Pts. 55 (I. C. 60); Esc. 25; ø 35; hfl. 14;
bfr. 20; hfl. 1,35; dkr. 3,50; skr. 3; nkr. 3,25

| 34. Jahrgang | München, Mittwoch, 22. Februar 1978 | B 6558 A | Nummer 44/8.W./80 Pfennig |

Das Streiflicht

(SZ) Es war im Jahre 1976, da hatte der Winter in Bayern zu so schreckliche Ergebnissen geführt, daß den armen Leuten im Lande nur noch der verwerfliche Hilferuf an die Obrigkeit übrigblieb. *Eine Naturkatastrophe* habe sich ereignet, formulierten damals ein paar Hauptbetroffene (Lißbekälner und Händler) in ihrer Bittadresse an den Landtag, und sie legten ein Tremolo zwischen die Zeilen, das im Falle einer Sintflut oder eines Tornados nur schwer noch zu steigern gewesen wäre. In der Tat war ja auch was Schreckliches passiert: Kein Schnee war gefallen — die schönste Tragödie, was auch München Boulevardzeitungen gerne bestätigten. Zu überbieten ist so ein unglaubliches Vorkommnis höchstens noch durch die Tatsache, daß in anderen Wintern doch Schnee fällt. Dabei handelt es sich dann um eine *Schnee-Katastrophe* (München-Abenteilung 1977) oder gar um einen *Schnee-Notstand*, wie ihn das gleiche Blatt soeben ausgerufen hat: auch den Verfassungsartikel, der die Auflagenentwicklung von Straßenverkaufsblättern von einer besonderen Art Schlagzeilen abhängig sein läßt.

Freilich kommt sowas ja nicht von allein, hängt vielmehr sehr mit jener sonderbaren Art zusammen, in der wir alle uns ausgewählt haben, mit Naturereignissen zu leben. Jahrtausende hindurch soll die Sache so vor sich gegangen sein, daß der Mensch das Wetter in der Regel so laufen ließ, wie es kam, je der richtigen Erkenntnis, daß er doch nicht viel dagegen machen konnte. Wenn es also besonders heiß war dräußen, setzte man sich einfach in den Schatten, und wenn es regnete, galt das zu dringlicheren Klagen nur Anlaß, von wo aus man das rettende Haus schrecken vom Himmel fielen. Diese Plagen fanden dann auch Eingang in die Literatur, genaue wie andere Jahrunderterreignisse, wie Dürre, Eiszeiten, Überschwemmungen, (Mün-chen ihre Existenzgrundlage raubten. Dafür war das Wort Katastrophe dem auch erfunden sich dann um eine Schwee-Katastrophe (München-Abteilung 1977) oder gar um einen ten jehn Jahre hinaus unsere Autodichter belastet und der zu den katastrophalen Ergebnissen führt, daß sich jemand beim Wegräumen einen Muskelkater holt oder gar seine Arbeitsstelle mit hathündiger Verzögerung erreicht.

Man könnte man sich über Außergewöhnliches ja auch freuen, über die Möglichkeit zum Beispiel, mitten in der Hochzivilisation mal in einem Hauch von weißem Dschungel seine Überlebensfähigkeit zu testen. Aber das geht leider nicht, weil ja irgend etwas vielleicht noch so funktionieren könnte wie vorgeschrieben: Weshalb denn auch der Winter, wenn er einen Fahrplan durcheinanderbringt, oder einen schuldhaften Studenplan oder, um Gottes willen, die Bundesligaterminliste, zumindest einen strengen Tadel verdient. Auf längere Sicht wird uns wohl ohnehin nichts anderes übrigbleiben, als die Jahreszeiten auf dem Verordnungswege abzuschaffen.

IG Druck läßt Arbeitgeber im unklaren

Ergebnis der Gewerkschaftsberatung über mögliche Urabstimmungen geheimgehalten

Stuttgart (dpa) — Gegenseitige öffentliche Appelle der Arbeitgeber- und Gewerkschaftseite zur Vermeidung eines offenen Arbeitskampfes kennzeichneten am Dienstag die weiter angespannte Lage des Tarifstreits um die Einführung neuer Techniken im Druck- und Verlagswesen der Bundesrepublik. Hauptverstand der IG Druck und Papier hält in Stuttgart Beratungen, ohne sie jedoch bekannt zu geben. IG-Druck-Chef Leonhard Mahlein erklärte das: "Wenn die Unternehmer nicht in letzter Minute einlenken, dann werden wieder neue Verleger-kampfmaßnahmen eingeleitet." In rund der Hälfte der 70 saschen Tageszeitungen erschien nach Verlegerangaben am Dienstag eine Anzeige der Arbeitgeberverbände, mit einem Appell an die IG Druck, keine kampfmaßnahmen zuzurufen, da die Arbeitgeber sich noch gezwungen sähen mit Aussperrungen zu kontern.

Es wird damit gerechnet, daß die Gewerkschaftsspitze auf dem Wege zu einem bundeseinheitlichen Tarifvertrag jetzt zum konkreten Fahrplan über Urabstimmungen in Schwerpunktbetrieben mit dem Ziel künftiger konkreter Streiks durchzusetzen. Bis zum Dienstag tag der IG Druck keine positive Äußerung zu ihrer Aufforderung an 120 Betrieben vor, in konkrete Verhandlungen einzutreten.

Gleichzeitig mit dem Ablauf der von IG-Druck und Papier gesetzten Frist, innerhalb derer die 120 von der IG Druck ausgesuchten Unternehmen der Druck- und Verlagsindustrie zum Abschluß von Firmentarifverträgen über die Einführung neuer Techniken aufgefordert werden sollten, ist in zahlreichen deutschen Zeitungen eine zum Bundesverband Druck, dem Bundesverband Deutscher Zeitungsverleger und dem

Verband Deutscher Zeitschriftenverleger unterzeichnete Anzeige gedruckt worden, in der von Schwerpunktstreiks gewarnt wird.

Nach der Ablehnung der Arbeitgeberverbände, wieder Verhandlungen aufzunehmen, heißt es in der Anzeige: "Rufen Sie nicht zu Punktstreiks auf! Gefährden Sie die Arbeitsplätze unserer technischen Mitarbeiter nicht! Zwingen Sie die Arbeitgeber nicht zum äußersten Mittel, der Notwehr! Zwingen Sie uns nicht zur Aussperrung! Wir appellieren an den Vernunft der Gewerkschaftsführer, nehmen Sie doch endlich den gemeinsamen Tarifvertrag an." Ein Arbeitskampf in der gegenwärtigen Situation wird von den Arbeitgebern als "der überflüssigste Streit der deutschen Tarifgeschichte" bezeichnet, der allem schade.

Der Verlag der Hessischen/Niedersächsischen Allgemeinen (HNA) in Kassel, (Fortsetzung auf Seite 4, Spalte 4)

Stahlkocher demonstrieren an der Saar

fl. Neunkirchen (Eigener Bericht) Mit einem Sternmarsch durch die Hüttenstadt Neunkirchen haben am Dienstag etwa 5000 saarländische Stahlarbeiter für die Erhaltung ihrer Arbeitsplätze demonstriert. Von den Klängen des Neunkircher Eisenwerkes aus zogen sie mit Spruchbändern und -plakaten durch die Innenstadt zu einer großen Sportshalle, wo später eine nichtöffentliche Betriebsversammlung stattfand. In Flugblättern und in Gesprächen kritisierten die demonstrierenden Stahlarbeiter das vor einigen Tagen kataststrophale Sanierungskonzept für die saarländische Stahlindustrie unter Führung des luxemburgischen Arbed-Konzerns. Es sieht bis 1983 den Abbau von nahezu 9000 Arbeitsplätzen in der saarländischen Stahlindustrie sowie unter anderem die Stillegung

des Hochofenwerkes im Neunkircher Eisenwerk vor.

An der Demonstration nahmen Landtags- und Bundestagsabgeordnete aller Parteien sowie die Oberbürgermeister von Saarbrücken und Neunkirchen, Lafontaine und Neuber (beide SPD), teil.

Die Schlichtungsverhandlungen für die 560 000 Beschäftigten in der Metallindustrie von Nordwürttemberg/Nordbaden sind am Dienstag in der fünften Runde fortgesetzt worden. Den Auftakt dieser Runde bildete ein getrennte Gespräche des Schlichters mit den Tarifpartnern. Unter dem Vorsitz des früheren baden-württembergischen Ministerpräsidenten Filbin für rund eine Million Beschäftigte der nordrhein-westfälischen Metallindustrie unter Vorsitz des Präsidenten des Arbeitsgerichtshofs für den Verbrauchern, Otto Blume, in Krefeld fortgesetzt worden.

SPD-Präsidium mahnt Fraktion zur Einigkeit

Die nicht genannten Abgeordneten Coppik, Hansen, Lattmann und Meinike werden erinnert: Wir sind 1976 nicht gewählt worden, um 1978 daran mitzuwirken, daß unsere Bundesrepublik von rechts regiert wird

Von unserer Bonner Redaktion

dr. **Bonn, 21. Februar** — Das Präsidium der Sozialdemokratischen Partei hat sich am Dienstag zum erstenmal in dieser Deutlichkeit gegen "Sonderoten" von SPD-Abgeordneten gewandt. Mit einem indirekten Tadel für die nicht namentlich genannten Abgeordneten Coppik, Hansen, Lattmann und Meinike erklärte die SPD-Führungsspitze: "Wir sind im Herbst 1976 nicht gewählt werden, um Anfang 1978 — wenn auch ohne Absicht — daran mitzuwirken, daß unsere Bundesrepublik von rechts regiert wird." Zugleich wurde bekannt, daß führende Politiker von SPD und FDP übereingekommen sind, in naher Zukunft strittige Abstimmungen, bei denen die Mehrheit der Koalition nicht gesichert ist, zu vermeiden.

Aus diesem Grund wird das Bundeskreiz-setz, mit dem eine strengere Hotelmeldepflicht und die zentralisierte Speicherung persönlicher Daten eingeführt werden soll, vor der Osterpause dem Parlament nicht mehr zugeleitet werden. Die Vorlage des Bundesinnenministeriums hatte schon einmal auf der Tagesordnung des Kabinetts gestanden, war dort aber abgesetzt worden und wird jetzt nochmals in Beratungen mit anderen Ressorts und den Ländern geändert. Sie sie im Kabinett kommt, soll sie mit den Fraktionen abgestimmt werden.

Landesverbände werden eingeschaltet

Dabei will man testen, ob es wiederum starke Widerstände in der SPD-Fraktion gibt. Dies wird jedoch nicht vor Mitte April geschehen. In der Zwischenzeit sollen vor allem die Landesverbände mit den Abgeordneten, die ihrer deutmal nicht mit der Mehrheit gestimmt haben, Gespräche führen und versuchen, sie umzustimmen, an ihnen soll, wie sich am führenden SPD-Mitglied äußerte, "Seelenmassage" vorgenommen werden.

Ebenfalls erst später wird die Novellierung des Gesetzes über das Bundeskriminalamt (BKA), die dem BKA mehr Kompetenzen einräumen soll, im Parlament eingebracht. Das Paket der Gesetze zur wirksameren Bekämpfung des Terrorismus wird damit zeitlich stärker gestreckt als noch gegenüber der bisherigen Absicht gemeldet werden. Die Rentengesetzgebung, die allerdings in der SPD-Fraktion nicht so umstritten ist, soll allein stehen und gleichfalls erst im Sommer im Bundestag behandelt.

Das SPD-Präsidium, unter Leitung des Parteivorsitzenden Willy Brandt, mahnte in einer hierauf mit der Erklärung hinaus, daß in der Anti-Terrorsetzgebung jetzt eine Regierungsfähigkeit nicht im Zweifelt gerate. "Die sozial-liberale Koalition darf nicht unnötigen Belastungen ausgesetzt werden", hieß es in einem Communiqué des SPD-Präsidiums.

Ferner wurde betont, die Führungsspitze habe zur Kenntnis genommen, daß die Abgeordneten, die nicht mit der Fraktion gestimmt hätten, "die Regierungsfähigkeit der SPD nicht in Frage

stellen" wollten. Gleichwohl sollen Sonderroten-unterbleiben, "die das Ansehen und den Erfolg der sozial-liberalen Koalition gefährden". Die Bezirke und Unterbezirke der Partei werden aufgefordert, darauf zu achten, daß über die Vorlagen zur inneren Sicherheit objektiv berichtet und so diskutiert werde, daß die Zielsetzungen und Interessen der Partei klar blieben.

Die Rückwirkungen der Auseinandersetzungen innerhalb der SPD-Bundestagsfraktion um die Anti-Terror-Gesetzgebung auf die FDP bildeten auch Anstoß der SPD-Fraktionsvorsitzenden Herbert Wehner "Anlaß zur Sorge". Vor der Fraktion erklärte Wehner nach Angaben aus Fraktionskreisen zugleich, Disziplinarmaßnahmen gegen die "Dissidenten" hätten nach seiner Auffassung wenig Sinn.

Zur CDU/CSU hieß es in dem Communiqué, die Opposition sei jetzt beim Anti-Terrorismuspaket wiederum über das "Neinsagen" nicht hinausgewachsen. Sie sei abermals in einem ihrer machtpolitischen Manöver steckengeblieben.

In der SPD ist inzwischen untersucht worden, ob es sich bei den "Neinsagern" um eine organisierte Gruppe handelt, die mitgliedermäßig von außen gesteuert wird. Anhaltspunkte dafür hat

(Fortsetzung auf Seite 2, Spalte 2)

WIE HELDEN *wurden am Dienstagmorgen in Kairo die Überlebenden des ägyptischen Sonderkommandos nach ihrem mißglückten Einsatz in Larnaka begrüßt. Kriegsminister Gamasi rief aus: "Ihr habt einen ehrenhaften Kampf für Ägyptens Ehre, Würde und Stolz geführt." Die Soldaten erhielten hohe Auszeichnungen, die kaum mehr erschütten 15 toten.* AGYPTENS *Präsident Sadat war "aus gesundheitlichen Gründen" an dem Empfang durch das gesamte ägyptische Kabinett verhindert. (Bericht seite 2)* Funkbild: AP

Neue Geldquellen zur Rentensanierung

Freiwillig Versicherte sollen regelmäßig zahlen / Versicherungspflicht ab 350 Mark

Von unserer Bonner Redaktion

for. **Bonn, 21. Februar** — Von den Maßnahmen zur Konsolidierung der gesetzlichen Rentenversicherung werden nicht nur Rentner und Pflichtversicherte, sondern auch die freiwillig Versicherten betroffen sein. Nach dem jetzt bekanntgewordenen Entwurf des 21. Rentenanpassungsgesetzes sollen freiwillig Versicherte künftig nur noch dann zum Abschluß ihrer dynamische Anpassung ihrer späteren Rentenbezüge haben, wenn sie regelmäßig Beiträge entrichten. 100 Millionen Mark zusätzlicher Beitragsaufkommen erwartet die Bundesregierung von der geplanten Regelung, von 1979 an schon Monatseinkommen von 350 Mark an der Versicherungspflicht zu unterwerfen.

Die beiden geplanten Bestimmungen gehören zu den Maßnahmen, die nach dem Wort von Bundesarbeitsminister Ehrenberg im Rentensystem zu einer höheren Beitragsgerechtigkeit führen sollen. Die Ausgestaltung der freiwilligen Versicherung ist nach dem Wortlaut des Gesetzentwurfs mit dem Umlageverfahren und mit der Dynamisierung der Rentenleistungen nicht vereinbar, weil bisher regelmäßige Beiträge nicht entrichtet werden müssen. Als problematisch, daß freiwillig Versicherte die Höhe ihrer Beiträge derzeit selbst bestimmen könnten.

Durch das 21. Rentenanpassungsgesetz sollen die freiwillig Versicherten indessen nicht verpflichtet werden, Beiträge in einer bestimmten Zahl oder in einem bestimmten Umfang zu entrichten. Es sollen vielmehr dynamische Leistungen aus künftigen freiwilligen Beiträgen nur dann gezahlt werden, wenn sie für einen zusammenhängenden Zeitraum von drei Kalenderjahren entrichtet sind, von denen jedes mindestens in Höhe von wenigstens zwölf Mindestbeiträgen belegt ist.

Bei geplanten Neuregelung von versicherungsfreien Beschäftigungsverhältnissen, nach der 1979 schon ein Monatseinkommen von 350 statt von 430 Mark versicherungspflichtig sein wird,

hat nach dem Wortlaut des Gesetzentwurfs ebenso die Auslagen soziale Sicherung das betroffen, den Personenkreis zum Ziel. Von dieser Bestimmung werden vor allem teilzeitbeschäftigte Frauen erfaßt sein. Diese zusätzliche Heranzuziehung von Niedrigeinkommen dient deshalb auch Rentnern der Versicherung zur Altersversorgung wird der Meinung von Experten wird diese geplante Regelung zuzunehmen zur Erhöhung der Schwerarbeitsquote führen.

Gleichzeitig nennt der Gesetzentwurf die Zahl der Gesamtrentenkommens, die von 1982 an voraussichtlich zur Berechnung der Krankenversicherungsbeiträge der Rentner herangezogen werden sollen. Danach gehören zu den Bezügen, die der Rente vorgleichbar sind, die Leistungen der betrieblichen Altersversorgung, Versorgungsbezüge nach beamtenrechtlichen Vorschriften sowie Leistungen öffentlich-rechtlicher und berufsständischer Versorgungseinrichtungen. Nicht erfaßt werden sollen dagegen Einnahmen, die auch bei den aktiven Arbeitnehmern nicht zur Beitragsbemessung herangezogen werden. Dazu zählen unter anderem Renten aus der Unfallversicherung, Leistungen nach dem Bundesversorgungsgesetz sowie Einkünfte aus Vermietung und Verpachtung und aus Kapitalvermögen.

Der Entwurf des 21. Rentenanpassungsgesetzes liegt dem Kabinett am 8. März vor. Beschlossen werden soll es nach dem Willen des Sozialbeirat schon noch vor der Sommerpause. Am vergangenen Freitag ist das Ergebnis 5,5; bei der Sitzung waren indessen zwei Mitglieder nicht entschied sind, von denen jedes mit Beitragsein in Bonn um den Rahmen beim CDU-Politikern Kohl, Geißler und Katzer auch Rudolf Mickels (IG Bergbau), Walter Quartier (DAG), Rudolf Kleine (Reichsbund) und Karl Weishäupl (VdK) sprachen.

Sie lesen heute

Leitartikel und Kommentare
Heute: Genschers verhaltene Flucht nach vorn
Von Robert Leicht . . . . Seite 4
Der Schatz am Ufer des Trombetas
Aluminium-Produktion:
Eine brasilische Geschäft mit rotem Kies
Von Manfred v. Conta, Rio de Janeiro . Seite 3
Hochschulzugang
Die wichtigsten Regelungen
im neuen Staatsvertrag . . . . . Seite 8
Fernsehen und Hörfunk . . . Seiten 12 und 16
Forschung · Wissenschaft · Technik . Seite 24
Feuilleton . . . . Seiten 25 und 27
Roman . . . . Seite 29
Theater und Kino

FDP-Minister Karry plädiert für Lohnstop

fl. **Wiesbaden** (Eigener Bericht) Angesichts des amerikanischen Verfalls des amerikanischen Dollar und der sich dadurch verschlechternden Wettbewerbslage der deutschen Exportindustrie hat der hessische Wirtschaftsminister Heinz Herbert Karry (FDP) die Tarifparteien aufgefordert, für die laufenden Tarifverhandlungen auszusetzen; Karry plädierte damit indirekt für einen befristeten Lohnstop. Bundeswirtschaftsminister Lambsdorff soll bei seinen Bemühungen unterstützt werden, die konzertierte Aktion unverzüglich wieder zusammenzurufen. Der FDP-Minister befürchtet durch Einkommensbesserungen der Arbeitnehmer eine weitere Schwächung der deutschen Industrie. Karry erinnerte an die Gewerkschaften in England, wo die Bergarbeiter ihre Lohnforderungen von 90 auf zehn Prozent zurückgenommen hätten, und an Norwegen, wo der eingebrochene Vertrauen habe, müsse man Einsicht verlangen. Gleichzeitig forderte der hessische Wirtschaftsminister in der deutschen Industrie auf, durch Dollarvorkäufe erzielten Preissenkungen bei Importen voll an die Verbraucher weiterzugeben.

Kommunale Arbeitgeber lehnen Gewerkschafts-Forderungen ab

Wuppertal (ddp) Die gewerkschaftlichen Forderungen für den öffentlichen Dienst sind nach Auffassung der Kommunalen Arbeitgeber "auch nicht ansatzweise erfüllbar". Das erklärte der Wuppertaler Oberstadtdirektor Rolf Krumsiek, nachdem die Mitgliederversammlung der Vereinigung Kommunaler Arbeitgeberverbände (VKA) unter seinem Vorsitz im Wuppertaler Rathaus ihre Marschroute für die am 28. Februar beginnenden Lohnrunde im öffentlichen Dienst abgesteckt hatte.

Bull für Grundrecht auf Datenschutz

Dortmund (dpa) Für die Einführung eines Grundrechts auf Datenschutz in das Grundgesetz hat sich der Datenschutzbeauftragte des Bundes, Professor Hans Peter Bull, ausgesprochen. In der Westfälischen Rundschau erklärte Bull, er halte einen entsprechenden Vorschlag des nordrhein-westfälischen Innenministers Burkhard Hirsch (FDP) "im Prinzip für gut". Ein solches Grundrecht könne bewirken, daß der "hohe Rang des Datenschutzes" für die ohnehin schon bestehenden Grundrechte klargestellt werde. Nach Ansicht Bulls wäre dies auch ein allgemein abgesichert werde. Nach schutz verstand Bull zugleich als "spezielle Form von Rechtsschutz".

Bürger beklagen schlechte Behandlung bei Behörden

Bonn (dpa) Genau 1013mal klingelte am Dienstag auf dem DGB-Beamtentag das Telefon bei den Bürger-Telefon, unter denen die Sorgen und Nöte über den eigenen Umgang mit Behörden zu erzählen. DGB-Vorstandsmitglied Gerhard Schmidt sagte am Ende: "Der Umgang mit den Ampelphasen des öffentlichen Dienstes ging mit Menschen haben, scheint eine entsprechende Verschlechterung beizubehalten." Nach seiner Schilderung bezogen sich die Klagen überwiegend auf unhöfliche Behandlung von Beamte und auf "hilflose Herumirrander" in den Behörden.

Aktienkurse behauptet

München (SZ) An der Dienstagsbörse hielten sich Geschäft und Kursveränderungen noch in engen Grenzen. Nach freundlicher Eröffnung gingen die Anfangsgewinne im Verlauf teilweise wieder verloren. Der SZ-Aktienindex war mit 140,73 wenig verändert. Der Rentenmarkt lag weiter freundlich. (Berichte Seite 21, Kurse Seite 22)

Vom Westen her Milderung

München (SZ) Tiefausläufer reichen vielfach über Deutschland ein westlicher Luft über Vorhersage: Vom Westen Durchzug von Wolkenfeldern und gebietsweise etwas Niederschlag, dann milder. Vom Süden, Tagestemperaturen in Gefrierpunktnähe, nachts milder; im Osten zum Teil strenger Frost. (SZ-Wetterbericht Seite 3.)

Süddeutsche Zeitung (SZ) rightly prides itself in its objectivity, its independence and its liberal views. The Bavarian Broadcasting Service has described it as "the paper for the intelligensia of German left-wing Liberalism."[2] Shortly before his death in 1970, the SZ's editor-in-chief described his paper's attitudes as "Loyal to the government in power, but at the same time critical and awake, in general situated somewhat left-of-centre—open-minded and tolerant, but never indifferent."[3] When the paper is described as liberal, the reference is not to political party allegiance, but to its general world-view. The paper's earnest attempts to avoid bias and narrow-minded dogmatism are evident in its objective reporting of the news and in its presentation of conflicting views in its editorial pages.

The SZ's goals and operating principles are clearly defined in its "Editorial Statutes" ("Redaktionsstatut"), a set of internal regulations set down to guide its own journalists. The document describes the paper as a political daily, very much involved in reporting and interpretation of political news, but one which eschews all connections with political parties. It is to be economically free, to serve the public interest, to seek to provide complete information and the truth. It pledges the paper's obedience to the basic laws of Germany, a free and democratic society, avoidance of allegiance to radical groups and views and support liberal social aims. In the document, journalists are encouraged to shape the paper in accord with these ideals.[4]

Like the remainder of Germany's quality newspapers, *Süddeutsche Zeitung* came into being shortly after the defeat of the Nazis. Until 1949, any Germans desiring to start a publication had to acquire a license. The licensing system had been devised to screen Nazis out of the press and the process contributed to the creation of a strong free press simultaneously with the development of a democratic form of government in the country.

Three German partners—Edmund Goldschagg, Dr. Franz Joseph Schöningh and August Schwingenstein joined together into an organization they called "Süddeutscher Verlag GmBH," applied for and received the first license issued by the U.S. occupation forces in Bavaria to found a newspaper. On October 6, 1945, they published the first issue of *Süddeutsche Zeitung* on a war-damaged press in Munich that had belonged to the Knorr and Kirth Company, publishers of *Münchner Neueste Nachrichten*. In their first issue, the publishers described their humble start: "We begin on a small platform with restricted means and thus reflect the general situation."[5] Because newsprint was difficult to obtain, SZ at first published just twice a week, later three times and finally, in 1949, began coming out on a daily basis.

The new paper and its founders flourished. The old press was restored and renovated. Within a year, the company took on a fourth licensee, Werner Friedmann. By 1948, Hans Durrmeier, formerly the commercial director of *Münchner*

[2] Brochure, "A World-Famous Newspaper and Its Publishers," (Munich: Süddeutsche Verlag GmBH, 1977), p. 4.
[3] *Ibid*.
[4] "Redaktionsstatut für die *Süddeutsche Zeitung*" (Munich: Süddeutsche Verlag GmBH, 1971).
[5] "A World-Famous Newspaper and its Publishers," *op. cit.*, p. 2.

Neueste Nachrichten, became *SZ's* publishing director and, three years later, the paper's manager. By the end of its fifth year, the company had a staff of 1,774 and a business volume of about 30 million D.M. annually. Meantime, *SZ* was establishing a reputation for itself as a high-quality journal. In 1946, it began publishing the short articles entitled "Streiflicht" ("Spotlight") for which it has become famous. Very quickly, too, the paper became known for its clear expression of news and ideas and for its courageous stand on touchy issues. As a result, circulation increased steadily.

After five years, Süddeutscher Verlag GmBH founded a book publishing company and became a corporation. But, unlike some German publishers, Süddeutscher Verlag did not try to buy up newspapers and other media to gain control; instead, it expanded by entering into partnerships with other firms such as Bayerische Staatszeitung GmBH and the Europa-Fachpresse-Verlag. Through the years, it has continued to diversify and grow. In 1962, it bought an offset printing firm; in 1964, it acquired shares in one of Germany's best book publishing companies; and in 1965, its first shares in the Stuttgarter Nachrichten Verlagsgesellschaft. Today, it holds 25 percent of the shares in this last organization.[6] Because of inflation, skyrocketing costs of newsprint and labor and a recession, the *SZ*, like most German papers, has been facing financial difficulties in the 1970's. Its losses were heaviest in the mid-1970's. For some of the German papers, the solution to the crisis has been merger with other publications; *SZ* has not chosen that route.

Süddeutsche Zeitung's current daily circulation hovers around 310,000, with 80 percent of the copies sold by subscription and the balance in street sales.[7] In recent years, as the country's largest circulation newspaper, it has consistently led its nearest competitor, the *Frankfurter Allgemeine* by 10-to-20,000 sales. In the second quarter of 1975, for example, it sold an average of 296,274 copies each day, while its Frankfurt competitor's sales averaged 286,239 per day.[8] During the past decade, *SZ's* total daily sales have increased by about 50 percent.

Although its circulation penetrates southern Germany most heavily, the *SZ* does reach many influential readers throughout the remainder of Germany. An estimated three-fourths of all the paper's readers live in Bavaria. Outside of Germany, the national issue is distributed to 77 countries. Within Europe, its diffuses across the continent after being delivered by air to 23 European cities and by surface to 45 rail and post connections.

The *Süddeutsche Zeitung* presents its readers a wide range of news and other information. In all, each day there are about two pages of international news, another two of national news, three to four of state news, a page of news analysis and editorials, two of features and entertainment items and five or six of business information. The amount of sports stories and information varies from seven or eight pages on Monday to a mere page daily for the remainder of the

[6] *Ibid.,* p. 3.
[7] Horst Schneider, Information Department, *Süddeutsche Zeitung,* in response to questionnaire, dated January 13, 1978.
[8] Pamphlet, "Süddeutsche Zeitung," (*Süddeutsche Zeitung,* 1975).

work week. Once a week, there is a four-to-six page section on travel and leisure.[9]

Süddeutsche Zeitung maintains a lively involvement in reporting foreign affairs. While not as well informed on world affairs as some of the other elite papers, it still has very good foreign coverage. One indicator of the paper's interest beyond Germany's borders is its staff of 14 full-time correspondents stationed in Paris, London, Rome, Tel Aviv, Cairo, New Delhi, Nairobi, Washington, Madrid, Rio de Janeiro, Tokyo, Belgrade, Moscow and Vienna. Approximately an additional 30 part-time stringers report from diverse sectors of the world. The paper gets further foreign input from its three wire services: AP, DDP and DPA.[10]

The paper is a serious, but pleasant-appearing journal. Under its front-page nameplate, it announces in heavy type its specializations: political news, culture, business and sports. Its five wide columns, use of paragraphs of heavy type to highlight the essentials of leading stories, well distributed white space and index to stories within the paper all combine to make SZ appear orderly, business-like, yet attractive to readers. The short leader "Das Streiflicht" always appears at the top of the front page's left-hand column. A lone picture usually occupies a prominent place with its own cutline; as is generally true elsewhere in SZ, the pictures are usually not related to other stories the page carries. Front page items normally cover national and international political news of significance.

Page two usually presents the weather report in detail. The paper's Third Page has traditionally been reserved for special in-depth reports of general interest or for cultural features. The fourth page has been the paper's editorial opinion page since 1965. Every day, it carries opinions of the editorial staff, correspondents and other contributors, a cartoon and a press review. After more pages of general news and background features, there is a page covering art, literature, the theater and films. A page on radio and television schedules and commentary follows. The *feuilleton* pages are next; on Fridays and weekends, this is a particularly rich section. A continuing serial story constitutes one feature of this section. Several pages of local news and five-to-six more of business and economic news and information come next. After several pages of advertisements, sports occupy the last page or more. In general, SZ is less clearly organized than either the highly predictable *Frankfurter Allgemeine* or *Die Welt.*[11]

Süddeutsche Zeitung offers numerous permanent, regular and occasional supplements to benefit its readers. Twice each week on a permanent basis, it offers "Regionalanzeiger," covering news and items of interest to eight rural districts where its circulation is heaviest. The other permanent supplement, "Münchner Stadtanzeiger," giving detailed coverage of local Munich and vicinity events, is inserted only in papers destined for the city and its environs. Two supplements which appear on a regular weekly basis cover "Man and Technol-

[9] Schneider questionnaire.

[10] *Ibid.*

[11] The authors are grateful to Bernd Golke, Bowling Green State University student from Germany, for his assistance in translating and reviewing materials about *Süddeutsche Zeitung* in German.

ogy" and "Contemporary Design." Occasional supplements feature a rainbow variety of subjects, among them architecture, books, fashions, recordings, gifts, gardening, youth, careers, arts and food.

The paper's archives, one of Europe's largest, provide one clue to *Süddeutsche Zeitung*'s success. About 150 German and foreign newspapers and magazines are regularly read, analyzed, evaluated, clipped and filed. The archive entries, many on microfilm include over ten million clippings under 80,000 titles. Some 13 million photographs, some going back to the beginnings of photography, are also stored in the files. "Bilderdienst der Süddeutschen Zeitung," SZ's photo service department, also lends the pictures to newspapers, magazines, book publishers and television companies all over the world by means of radio-photograph.[12]

Compared with many other elite newspapers, SZ carries a modest quantity of advertising. Its percentage of advertising in relation to the paper's total space volume amounts to about 45 percent from Monday through Friday, with an additional 10 percent advertising in weekend editions. The paper holds membership in the Top European Advertising Media (TEAM) group of 16 newspapers in 11 countries which stimulates increased international advertising and introduces local advertisers to a means of selling their products more widely.

Süddeutscher Verlag GmBH has a total staff of 1,800 personnel. Working for the paper itself are 500 technicians, 20 in administration, and 150 on the writing and editorial staff.[13] Part of the editorial staff is stationed outside Munich; in addition to foreign correspondents, 16 editors are located in seven branch offices (Bonn, Berlin, Dusseldorf, Frankfurt, Stuttgart, Ausburg and Nuremberg), and a staff of 60 reporters, ten of them in the national capital, cover political, cultural, economic and sports stories across all of West Germany. Dr. Hans Heigert serves as *Süddeutsche Zeitung*'s current chief editor. Süddeutscher Verlag publication is guided by an editorial management team of six members. The team is chaired by Dr. Heigert and Hugo Deiring acts as its manager. Other team members are Immanuel Birnbaum, Dr. Hans Schuster, Dr. Franz Thoma and chief correspondent Hans Ulrich Kempski.[14]

Although SZ has few definitive directives regarding its staff qualifications, it searches for—and gets—highly qualified personnel. Remarking about the general high caliber of German reporters and editors, one source noted in 1971 that "An estimated 45 editorial employees of the *Süddeutsche Zeitung* alone hold Ph.Ds."[15] The same source observed that German journalists are generally young, idealistic, independent, assertive self-starters holding doctorates in political science and other disciplines from leading universities. Although the paper does not keep a record of citations its staff members have received, a large number of the regular staff and contributors have been awarded prizes and have gotten recognition by the public of their high quality work.

At least part of *Süddeutsche Zeitung*'s success and genius may be attributed

[12] "A World-Famous Newspaper and its Publishers," *op. cit.,* p. 17.
[13] Schneider questionnaire.
[14] "A World-Famous Newspaper and its Publishers," *op. cit.,* pp. 4–5 and 19.
[15] M. L. Stein, "West Germany's Adversary Press," *Saturday Review* (May 8, 1971), p. 48.

to the cooperation of its staff in preparing the paper for publication. It reaches decisions about what to publish and what to exclude by discussion. To begin the conference process, editor-in-chief Heigert and a small group of his deputies— the group is called the "Ressortleiter" in German—meet at 11:00 A.M. to discuss mainly opinion articles. A half hour after this pre-conference, the chief editor, all editorial desks and administrators meet to share their plans for the next issue, to hammer out cooperatively what the issue actually will include and to discuss what should be included in future issues. Everyone has an equal voice in these free-wheeling discussions and the meetings may take considerable time to reach a majority decision on the day's contents for the paper. Action is by discussion and consensus, never by formal vote. The process contributes significantly to the staff's cooperative spirit and pride in SZ.

The paper publishes four editions late each day so its readers will have their papers early the next morning. The national edition is "put to bed" first at 6:30 P.M. Two Bavarian editions go to press in the early evening hours and the last, the Munich city edition, moves to the printing room shortly before midnight.[16] Composition is partly in hot type and partly photo-composition. SZ uses color for special headlines, to head special sections, for borders and occasionally for advertisements. The paper is planning to procure video display terminals for writing and editing in the near future.

Süddeutsche Zeitung's staff regards its journalistic responsibilities seriously. As the quality German weekly *Die Zeit* once observed, SZ is ". . . not afraid of anything or anybody and (is) responsible from the first page down to the last. . . ." When its rival national daily, *Die Welt* became too involved in character-damaging accusations, SZ rose up and admonished *Die Welt* publicly for failing to uphold honest, high quality journalism.[17] Besides exhibiting courage and a strong sense of responsibility, SZ is noted for its thoroughness, accuracy and reliability. It is especially good at providing an array of stories and articles related to the main event.

The testimonials of some of the world's leading publications leave little doubt that *Süddeutsche Zeitung* stands high in the ranks of West Germany's best quality newspapers and among the world's top elite dailies. *Time* magazine has called it "one of Germany's best dailies," and the German weekly *Stern* magazine goes a step further to call SZ "Germany's best daily newspaper." London's *Times* witness confirms that of *Stern*: ". . . the best in West German journalism." Sweden's *Dagens Nyheter* extends SZ's recognition as a high quality paper beyond Germany by calling it ". . . a German *Manchester Guardian*: open, fresh, reliable—and, last but not least, well written. . . ." And *Die Zeit's* testimonial places it firmly among the world's elite: "Among the daily papers that really count, the *Süddeutsche Zeitung* is at the top, in some respects even at the very top."[18]

16 "A World-Famous Newspaper and its Publishers," *op. cit.*, p. 10.
17 Adolph Schalk, "Putting the Starch in the German Press," *Saturday Review* (March 25, 1972), pp. 80–81.
18 "A World-Famous Newspaper and its Publishers," *op. cit.*, back cover page.

The Straits Times

(SINGAPORE)

ONE MORNING IN JULY, 1845, Robert Carr Woods, anxious to put out the first copy of his newspaper that was to make its appearance that day, unlocked the door of a little office at No. 7 Commercial Square (now Raffles Place) in Singapore. Today, some 135 years later, that modest single-sheet weekly, *The Straits Times,*[1] has become an ultra-modern daily serving not only Singapore and Southeast Asia, but making its influence felt from New York to Tokyo.

It has expanded, diversified and opened up new fields of endeavor. Headquartered today in an ever-expanding modern facility in Times House, 390 Kim Seng Road, the newspaper is part of the Times Publishing Organization which comprises 22 companies which publish seven newspapers and 12 magazines and serve international publishers as commercial printers and book distributors.

The Straits Times has come a long way from that day in 1845 when it appeared as a small, hand-printed page. Singapore was then a town of only 40,000 people with no more than 500 of them literate in any language. But the paper provided a needed service to the commercial interests of the thriving seaport and slowly, but constantly, gained in circulation. It was not, however, until January, 1858, that *The Straits Times* became a daily.

The newspaper had a hearty and dedicated staff determined to see that the journal was a real *daily*—and not a sporadic paper as were so many "dailies" at the time. Not even when fire destroyed the newspaper offices in 1869 did the paper miss an edition. In fact, the day after the fire, a friendly printer came to the rescue and made sure the *Straits Times* appeared on schedule—complete with a fiery editorial lambasting the local fire brigade.

As the present century began, Alexander William Still was editor of the newspaper. A man of forceful personality, Still was actively concerned with local problems, constantly urging the Malay, Chinese and Indian communities to speak up. He passionately advocated higher education for all.[2] During the "Roaring Twenties," *The Straits Times* took on a more modern look; its makeup became more sprightly, it was enlarged to 20 pages, and for the first time featured drawings and photographs. The paper's reporting staff swelled to a record four persons. (It has 80 today.)

---

[1] The full name was *Straits Times and Singapore Journal of Commerce.*

[2] Much of the historical data used in this sketch of *The Straits Times* came from information sent the authors by Mrs. Chen Li Jen, editorial manager of the newspaper, with a letter dated Aug. 3, 1978.

In the 1930's the paper faced a serious crisis, and had to reduce its price from 10 cents to 5 cents. In those days 10 cents bought a pork chop or three pounds of rice. Within a year, the paper's circulation soared from 6,000 to 15,000. Then the War came, and with it the Japanese Occupation. During the period many of the newspaper's staff were interned. On September 7, 1945, *The Straits Times* re-emerged as a morning tabloid. It was printed on a simple flatbed press by loyal staffers who had headed straight for the press offices upon their release from the Japanese prison camps.

During the postwar period *The Straits Times* was delivered by road every day to Malaya, and by February of 1952 the paper's readers in Malaya were getting their copies airfreighted to them. In 1956 *Straits Times* executives decided to print a separate edition in Kuala Lumpur (now the capital of Malaysia) in addition to the main Singapore edition. This new edition was begun because the circulation had reached 80,000 and transport was beginning to be too costly. The newspaper's circulation has continued a steady growth and today the average daily sales are well over 180,000. And from its original one page a week, the paper has grown to a typical 30 pages every day.

Today's editor-director of *The Straits Times* is Peter H. L. Lim, who was named to the position in September, 1978, on the retirement of T. S. Khoo. Joining the newspaper in 1948 as a subeditor, Khoo became a kind of institution there, rising to direct the editorial activities of the paper. Even though he retired as director in 1978, he continues as editorial adviser and consultant and a member of the board of directors for the Straits Times Press Ltd.

Peter Lim, the new editorial head of the newspaper, joined the *Straits Times* in 1957 as a reporter and has held the posts of subeditor, film critic, and motoring correspondent. In August, 1969, he became chief subeditor of the newspaper, and in February, 1970, was promoted to executive editor. Then in 1975 he was appointed chief editor of the Times Organization's (New Nation Publishing Ltd.) newspapers. The present executive editor of the *Straits Times* is Bob T. G. Ng.

In 1979 the *Straits Times* had a writing-editing staff of nearly 100 and a technical staff of some 200. On its national staff (reporters and correspondents) were 40, and it had two foreign correspondents—one in London and one in Washington, D.C. In addition, it had stringers and part-time correspondents in New York, Tokyo, Jakarta, Manila, Hong Kong, Brussels, and Sydney.[3]

The newspaper receives four wire services—Reuters, Associated Press, United Press International, and Agence France-Presse. Its total daily circulation is about 185,000, about 90 percent of which goes to subscribers. On Sundays, the circulation is close to 200,000.

The Straits Times has a distinctive "British look" in its makeup, using its main story in the upper left part of the page and making use of underlinings, borders and other typographical gimmicks often found in Britain. It is a cleancut paper, easy to read, and averaging about 15–16 pages of advertising in its typical 30-page daily edition.

---

[3] Questionnaire from T. S. Khoo to J. Merrill, dated April 13, 1978.

The Straits Times

Estd. 1845

WEDNESDAY, FEBRUARY 22, 1978   25 CENTS   M.C.(P) No. 214/1/78

'Ties will be restored only if Arab gunmen are handed over to Cairo'

ANGRY EGYPT RECALLS ITS ENVOY

CAIRO, Tuesday

EGYPT has summoned its diplomatic mission from Nicosia, asked Cyprus to close down its legation in Cairo and pointed accusing fingers at Moscow and Damascus in the political sequel to a bloody battle at Larnaca airport between Egyptian and Greek Cypriot troops.

The Egyptian commando force, which was hit by Cypriot fire, arrived in Cairo early today, carrying its 15 dead and 11 wounded, and was given a heroes' welcome by Prime Minister Mamdouh Salem and his entire Cabinet.

The government said Egyptian-Cypriot relations, which it broke off in effect, could be restored only if two Palestinian gunmen who killed prominent Egyptian journalist Youssef Sibai in Nicosia on Saturday, were handed over for trial in Cairo.

A four-hour emergency Cabinet session, summoned to deal with the first crisis ever in Egyptian-Cypriot relations, charged the Nicosia Government was taking a markedly hostile attitude toward Egypt and Egyptian citizens."

Pullout

The Cabinet, therefore, decided to "withdraw the Egyptian diplomatic mission, as well as Egyptian technical and commercial officers in Cyprus" and asked the Cypriot Government to recall its legation staff from Cairo.

The Cabinet also said: "All forms of Egyptian-Cypriot relations should be reconsidered."

Cyprus thus became the fifth country in the Middle East to become involved in a quarrel with Cairo following President Anwar Sadat's historic peace trip to Israel in November.

Shortly after the trip, Cairo broke off relations with the radical Arab states — Syria, Iraq, Libya, Algeria and South Yemen — because they declined.

■ See Back Page—Col. 6

Call to outlaw hostage-taking

GENEVA, Tues. — Any taking of hostages, even by a liberation movement, should be outlawed by international convention, France proposed at the United Nations here yesterday.

French delegate Mr. Regis de Gouttes made the proposal at a session of experts from the United Nations special committee preparing for an international convention against hostage-taking.

Mr. de Gouttes said the convention should state that hostage-taking "is banned, everywhere, under any circumstance".

He said that "no circumstances justifies hostage-taking, whatever the justice of the cause in whose name it is committed".

This viewpoint is opposed by Algeria but supported by many Third World countries. Algeria is expected to propose complete freedom of action for liberation movements. — AFP.

Dow Jones

NEW YORK, Tues. — The Dow Jones industrial average was off 2.11 to 749.48 shortly before 11 a.m. today. It lost more than 10 points last week and has been in a slide for the past seven sessions. — UPI.

Cyprus plea to Sadat: Let us heal the rift

CYPRUS, Tues.

PRESIDENT Spyros Kyprianou said today he was prepared to meet Egyptian President Anwar Sadat to heal the rift caused by the bloody shootout between Egyptian and Cypriot forces at Larnaca airport on Monday night.

Mr Kyprianou said his government would do its best to restore friendly relations with Cairo and he appealed to Arab leaders not to turn Cyprus into an arena for settling Middle East conflicts.

He said he had not yet received any official word from the Egyptians on their decision to have envoys from both countries recalled from Cairo and Nicosia.

"I would like to appeal to Mr. Sadat to do his best to calm down the atmosphere in his country ... and to try, both of us, to restore the old relations and the old friendship," he told a news conference.

Consultations

In reply to reporters' questions, the Cypriot President said he had no direct communications from Mr. Sadat since Sunday's "tragic events," but that "a lot would be prepared to meet Mr. Sadat if the latter would be prepared to respond."

Such a summit meeting, Mr Kyprianou added, should be well prepared in advance. "This preliminary work," he said, "already is being done."

This was an apparent reference to the meeting in Nicosia yesterday with Mr. Butros Ghali, Egyptian Minister of State for Foreign Affairs.

Mr. Ghali, who said the consultations would continue, returned to Cairo last night aboard an Egyptian C-130 Hercules which carried the 57 surviving commandos following their abortive shooted raid on a Cyprus Airways jetliner.

Mr Kyprianou said he had not received any renewed Egyptian request for extradition of the two terrorists. But, in any event, this would not be possible under Cypriot law since the assassination of Mr Youssef Sibai, editor-in-chief of Al Ahram, occurred in Cyprus. the President explained. — AFP.

Five killed

MANILA, Tues. — Five people were killed and 13 others injured when a passenger mini-bus fell into a precipice in the central Philippine province of Cebu on Sunday, police said today. — Reutr.

Thai PM honoured

Rebels grab mayor and colonel

ZAMBOANGA CITY, Tuesday

MUSLIM guerillas abducted an armed force's colonel, a town mayor and a Muslim priest on the southern Philippine island of Jolo, a released woman captive said today.

The kidnapping occurred on Thursday near the capital town of Jolo, 180 km west of this major seaport city and 800 km south of Manila.

Motive for the kidnapping, the second to be reported from the south since last month, has not yet been established.

The victims were identified as Col Simeon Peres, manager of the Sulu Electrical Cooperative, acting Jolo mayor Tibing Assail and the high priest, Imam Yacob Jami.

Intercepted

Mrs Maslinglap Ali, a Muslim employee of the cooperative, said she was seized along with the three men but was released later by the captors, believed to be members of the Libyan-backed Moro National Liberation Front.

Mrs Ali said her group was intercepted while en route to Indanan township, outside Jolo town, to attend some rural electrification projects and to negotiate for the surrender of rebels, according to Provincial Gov Quirino Kajandal. —AFP.

Oil discovery confirmed

MANILA, Tues. — An American oil exploration company announced tonight that tests had confirmed the Philippines first oil discovery off Palawan island 144 km south-west of Manila with a production rate of 9,940 barrels a day.

The announcement was made by Cities Service Company, with headquarters in Tulsa, Oklahoma, which had been engaged in oil exploration in a common area called the Nido Complex. — UPI.

Blast at Bangkok's police arsenal

BANGKOK, Tues. — A predawn explosion at the Bangkok police arsenal touched off a fire that rased the single-story building this morning.

Policemen on guard at the time of the explosion scampered to safety. No one was reported injured in the blaze.

A spokesman for the police department said investigators believe a chemical reaction might have caused the explosion. No evidence of criminal activity has been found so far, the policeman said.

The arsenal was used to store weapons seized during police investigations and included ballistic, automatic weapons, hand grenades, ammunition and plastic explosives. — UPI.

US to beef up Pacific forces

LOS ANGELES, Tuesday

AMERICAN Defence Secretary Harold Brown said yesterday the US will strengthen its forces in the Pacific area with advanced weapons in the next five years as insurance against "major uncertainties which could threaten future peace."

Mr. Brown said this in a prepared speech aimed at assuring Americans and friendly Asian governments that "we are and will remain a major force in the Pacific."

He told the Los Angeles World Affairs Council that "the attention we have given to the strategic balance, to the North Atlantic alliance, and to the Middle East has not been at the expense of our posture in Asia."

Mr. Brown said "the situation in Asia is more favourable to our interests than in the past" and that the United States plans to keep supporting their forces in the Western Pacific "to ensure that this environment continues".

Among other measures, he said, "in the next five years we will be strengthening our forces in the region by the introduction of several advanced weapon systems."

"We will maintain the size of our Pacific fleet and modernise and increase it to the extent that our shipbuilding schedules permit," he said.

MR. BROWN ... Insurance against uncertainties.

Japan to send survey team

TOKYO, Tues. — Japan said today it would send a survey mission to Thailand, Malaysia and Singapore on Thursday for preliminary studies on a project to lay a submarine cable to link these three nations.

The seven-member mission will inspect proposed cable-laying route, collect data, and exchange views with the respective governments, and the three-week visit before starting a full-scale ocean survey. — Reuter.

Anxiety

The US forces Los Angeles area conferences in Honolulu with top US military commanders for the Pacific to discuss the planned withdrawal of ground troops from South Korea and matters bearing on US deployments in the Asia-Pacific region.

After acknowledging that the Korean troop withdrawals, which will start late this year, has caused anxiety in the Pacific area.

But he said the South Koreans "are able and willing to defend their own country" and he said help from the US in improving and modernisation of their military equipment.

Elsewhere in Asia, Mr. Brown said, the situation has changed dramatically" over the past 10 years with the bitter split between Russia and China, "the improvement of US-Chinese relations and the strong development of Japan and other noncommunist countries.

But he cautioned that the current equilibrium in Asia "is not necessarily permanent."

He noted that Soviet strength in Asia and the Pacific is growing and that "the changes of funding, mental strategic significance in Sino-Soviet relations are possible. — AP.

The weather

UP TO NOON TODAY: No rain, according to the Singapore Meteorological Service.

Causeway

PHILIPPINES President Ferdinand Marcos is assisted by his wife Imelda as he invests visiting Thai Premier Kriangsak Chamanand (right) with the Order of Sikatuna, at the official residence of Gen Gabriela Silang, a government award usually given to the wives of visiting dignitaries.

Gen. Kriangsak is in Manila during a tour of Asean states. He arrived on Monday from Indonesia. He will visit the Philippine Military Academy in the northern mountain city of Baguio and return to Manila tomorrow in time to depart for Kuala Lumpur. — UPI picture.

DOCUMENT PROCESSING DIVISION

Birds ground airliner

DUBAI, Tues. — An Egyptian airliner with 91 passengers and crew aboard made a forced landing after hitting a flock of birds near take-off last night, Sharjan airport sources said today.

The Boeing 707 engine and body were badly damaged, the sources said. — Reuter.

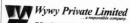
LATEST

Army takes over Tabriz

TEHERAN, Tues. — The Iranian army took over the northern city of Tabriz for one day and Iraqis each evening to enforce a curfew after ant-Government riots which ravaged the wel-known resort, a local official said today.

Tanks and soldiers paraded through the city. Newspapers reported at least 100 people were injured in two days of rioting which began on Saturday between demonstrators including many religious zealots and security forces. Some theatres were looted and burned. — AP.

At present the newspaper gives about 20 percent of its nonadvertising space to international news, a large proportion. It is obvious that the paper prides itself on providing news in perspective, in depth analyses and comment that explain political, social and economic events, changes and trends.[4]

Editors use video terminals instead of typewriters, and in most respects the paper has the most modern equipment including computerized systems. One editor says the computer gives him 100 percent more control over his work. The Times organization is expanding its plant by building a new Press Block to house the 24-hour seven-day-a-week operations of all the newspapers; in addition, new office buildings are being constructed.[5]

The Straits Times attempts to be a general newspaper, not trying to appeal to any one segment but rather to the whole Singapore public—and to readers in nearby Malaysia. It encourages investigative reporting, but according to editorial adviser T. S. Khoo, the newspaper is "rather careful about getting into 'sensitive' areas like religion and race." The word that best describes the paper's editorial policy is *decency*, for the editors see the publication as a "family paper."[6]

Khoo feels that *The Straits Times* should be considered a great newspaper in a world context because it "provides a better than average coverage of events that happen outside of Singapore—keeping the readers well-informed of what's going on in the rest of the world." Although the paper is rather small when compared to many of the great dailies of the world, it does show that a smaller paper in a small nation can rise above mediocrity. This, certainly, the *Straits Times* has done.

Svenska Dagbladet

(SWEDEN)

SWEDEN'S EIGHT MILLION PEOPLE are among the most avid newspaper readers in the world—some 411 papers per thousand of population. But, because of spiralling costs and stiff competition, until a decade ago newspapers were dying and readers' choices were becoming fewer and fewer. To correct the trend, the Swedes coolly and rationally worked out a press subsidy system which aided the economically-losing, and often better-quality, newspapers. Today, the paper that tops the list for subsidies is also one of Sweden's most serious and responsible quality dailies—Stockholm's *Svenska Dagbladet* (Swedish Daily Paper).

[4] Sample copies of *The Straits Times* were sent the authors by T. S. Khoo. Also: Khoo Questionnaire.
[5] Booklet entitled "The Times Organisation and the Daily Best Seller" sent the authors by Mrs. Chen Li Jen, editorial manager of the Times Publishing Co.; with letter dated July 3, 1978.
[6] Khoo questionnaire.

Prenumerera på
Företagsekonomi
Lås bla.
C. F. Pokorny
Sven-Erik Johansson
Tel. 031-42 22 40
Linnégatan 36 A
41 304 Göteborg

Sopstrejk hot från Transport
"Vill hjälpa LO"

Vi vill få fart på den centrala uppgörelsen och hjälpa LO. Det är ett av motiven till att vi strejkvarslar för 1500 renhållningsarbetare.

Transportordföranden Hans Ericson har åter påtagit sig huvudrollen i en avtalsrörelse.

Den här gången lägger han strejkvarsel för 1 500 renhållningsarbetare från den 2 mars.

Om varslet träder i kraft berörs flera städer i Sverige. Värst väntas situationen bli i Stockholm, Jönköping och vissa förorter till Göteborg, I Stockholm exempelvis sköts sophämtningen till 87 procent av medlemmar i Transport. De renhållningsarbetare som är anställda av kommunen berörs inte av varslet.

Hans Ericson säger att LO inte informerats om tisdagens beslut.

— Transport anser att en medlingskommission bör tillsättas i de centrala förhandlingarna mellan SAF och LO/PTK. Vi vill även ha medling för vårt förbund för att klara bättre löner åt renhållningsarbetarna, säger Hans Ericson.

— Det här kommer förrvara den centrala avtalsrörelsen, säger SAF:s förhandlingschef, Lars-Gunnar Albåge.

Se sidan 27

Hans Ericson, Transport, i ny huvudroll.

SJ-Peterson avgår
Blir ny TSV-chef

SJ-chefen Lars Peterson lämnar sin tjänst vid utgången av juni och blir ny chef för trafiksäkerhetsverket (TSV) efter Per-Olov Tjällgren. Ny SJ-chef utnämns redan om några dagar.

Lars Peterson, som varit chef för SJ i nio år, avgår på egen begäran mot bakgrund av trafikpolitiska beskeiut som fått på senare tid. Den avgörande frågan var att regeringen gick emot SJ:s planer på stora inskränkningar i trafiken från och med sommaren. Lars Peterson var med bara på statssekreterarnivå med att utforma 1963 års trafikpolitiska beslut, som bl.a. innebar att SJ skulle bära av en nya kostnader — en princip som lagat bakom många konflikter mellan SJ och regeringen.

Lars Peterson väntas bli ny chef för trafiksäkerhetsverket.

Se sidan 4

Norge pressar Fälldin
Hotar sälja oljan till Västtyskland

Det brådskar om Sverige och statsminister Thorbjörn Fälldin vill ha ett norskt oljeavtal. Norske industriministern Bjartmar Gjerde menar att svenskarna snart måste komma med industriprojekt som de båda länderna kan diskutera.

— Vi är beredda att gå mycket längre med oljesamarbetet, men då får också svenskarna gå längre. De måste komma med förslag om industriprojekt så att vi får något att förhandla om.

Det säger norske industriministern Bjartmar Gjerde i en intervju med SvD.

Samtal om svenskt köp av norsk olja har pågått i flera år.

Kan Sverige komma med projekt som intresserar norrmännen kan vi i blixt få ett oljeavtal med Norge som inte bara inbegriper köp av olja utan även svensk prospektering på de norska oljefälten.

— Men hittills har svenskarna inte kommit med något konkret, säger Gjerde och dröjer inte att det finns andra som är intresserade, t. ex. Västtyskland.

Den svenska regeringen har dock vid samtal med norrmännen under Nordiska rådets session i Oslo utlovat att förslagen skall komma.

Statsminister Thorbjörn Fälldin bekräftar att Sverige gjort en sådan markering.

Se sidan 4

Falska aktier gav fängelse

Det blev ett års fängelse för den 65-årige civilekonomen från Malmö som åtalats för medhjälp till försök till grov urkundsförfalskning. Han medverkade i förfalskningen av 5 000 Saab-Scania aktiebrev, a.k. femfärer, till ett nominellt värde av ca 2,5 milj. kr. I fängelsedomen inger domstolen med synlig avsmak av aktieskurken även ansvar för rättsfylleri.

Det var 15 november i fjol som västtysk polis vid husransakan på ett trygsheri och i en bostad i Hamburg påträffade ca 5 000 änno ej helt färdigställda aktiebrev.

Polack ny skidkung

En ny skidkung inträdde på tisdagens längdåkartävlan vid VM i Lahtis. Sensationsmannen Josef Luszczek dröde ned det 15 km. I distansloppet åkte guldet i förbundskakylterna var vikt för ryssarna, och slog hela skidvärlden med häpnad.

Se sista sidan

"Kyligt" byggmoral

— Det verkar som om byggmoralen varit mycket låg.

Det säger hälsovårdsinspektör Karl Gustav Åström i Kvikom i Jämtland sedan en hel del innevånare i kommunen klagat på kalla lägenheter i ny-byggda radhus och andra fastigheter.

I flera av de nybyggda husen har det uppmätta minusgrader (eskorderi var minus 17 grader). Folk fick sitta i ytterkläderna för att inte frysa.

"Falsk bild i TV-program"

Programmet Studio 6 om narkotikaproblemen förra tisdagen var oklämpligt och missvisande, anser en rad organisationer som ägnar sig åt narkomanvård. På tisdagskvällen pressibelärade en organisation, behandlingsgruppen i City som noterar under socialförvaltningen i Stockholm, en protestskrivelse till samhällsredaktionen på TV 2.

Grupperna anser att programmet gav en falsk och ensidig bild av narkotikaproblemen, och inte fillnulashapen som "socialpornografi". Bl.a. vändes hur en narkoman ger sig själv en injektion, något som nanas kunna skapa ångest hos många människor och i.o.m. kunna leda till återfall i narkomani.

Visste redan allt om Borås

Den kampanj som startade i Dagens Nyheter med "Borås 356 år" och som syftar till att tvätta bort stämpeln av Borås som tråkviämne uppgift. Kampanjen med dragit i gång på alvar på tisdagen vann och det inga vidare och 100-tal deltagare.

Uppstakten blev dock mindre lyckad. Arrangörerna hade hyptit in 150 journalister från hela Norden. En panel med fäterrildare firm kommunen, vet och-fackel satt berodd att svara på frågor.

I stället för de 150 inbjudna journalisterna kom sju — de flesta från lokala massmedia som redan här i väldigare med hand och deltaglandena i Borås.

vädret

Ytliga vädret fortsätter i Svealand och Norrland. I Götaland kan ett soldande med snöfall passera åt väster. Temperaturen något lägre sanerade i elder längst kad ligga.

BRIDGE sid. 13
OFFICIELLT sid. 13
SKOLMATEN sid 13

Del I, sid. 1—18,
del II, sid. 19—38.

Något att drömma om i vinterkylan:

Allt fler tar kanotsemester

Kanoting har blivit den moderna tidens cykelsemester. I smart nog varje kommun finns ett kanotcenter där du kan hyra kanot och i praktiket taget vacenda del av landet finns förslag och beskrivningar på olika turer lämpade för paddling.

Kanoting är alternativet till segling och motorbåtsfärder. Kanoting utgör så betydligt billigare och du får resenären närmare naturen! med kanot kan man ta sig fram praktiskt taget var som helst.

Men SvD-tema i dag handlar också om mycket annat som är friluftslivet till sjöss: nya modeller som skall ge ny fart åt småbåtsindustrin, om långfärdssegling, om färden till havs vintertid, om matlagning ombord.

SvD-tema innjuder även till en tävling om bästa matrecept till sjöss.

Se sidorna 19—25

Kanoting har blivit ett alternativ till segling och motorbåtsfärder.

Svårare få strimlade lån

En uppstramning av eller kanske t. o. m. totalstopp för systemet med strimlade lån förbereds nu inom budgetdepartementet. Ett förslag i någon form kommer troligen i samband med skattepropositionen i höst.

Strimlade lån innebär att en byggmästare säljer en lägenhet i ett flerfamiljshus på samma villkor som de vore vilor. I stället får att ta upp ett enda lån på hela huset kan man då "strimla" skulden i lika många personliga lån, som det finns lägenhetsinnehavare. De som äger lägenheterna kan därigenom göra samma skatteavdrag för låneräntor och reparationer som villaägare.

Ännu 1974—75 förekom systemet sparsamt, men nu sprids det snabbt även ungefär Stockholm.

Se sidan 4

Hyresgäster i kö för husköp

Den här veckan avgörs det: skall hyresgästerna i nio hus på Östermalm och radhusyrare i Bredäng och Bagarmossen få köpa de hus de bor i?

Husen ägs nu av två kommunala bostadsföretag, Svenska Bostäder och Familjebostäder.

i var ett av vallöftena från Stockholms borgerliga "regering". Nu sätts vallöftena på prov.

Det företagens styrelser är det numera borgerliga majoritet. Att få köpa de hus man bodde

STORSTOCKHOLM
Se sidan 10

| ... | brännpunkt | kultur | scenen | marginalen | idag |

Sjukt läge

Regleringarna och subventionssystemet i bostadspolitiken har skapat en sjuk marknad. Men de har också direkt motverkat sitt eget syfte. I stället för att stimulera bostadsbyggandet motverkar de detta. Det är nödvändigt med ett nytt finansieringssystem.

Se sidan 2.

Oattraktivt

Att vara politiker blir mindre attraktivt — i alla fall om man samtidigt har rätt så normalt privatliv, skriver Gunnar Heckscher. Dagens politiker skall vara lätt att identifiera sig med och samtidigt begripa det mesta i livet.

Se sidan 3

Bokrean

Det blir samre men på filmproduktion utanför Sveriges Radio säger Mats Lönnerblad, Urban Andersson utvärder inför bokrean, professor Lars Folkesson recenserar Cohens verk om jordbrukets historia och Under Strecket får vi veta vad USA betytt för 24 framstående svenskar... *Se sidan 8*

Kåkteater

En ny kvinnopjäs, som gjort succé ute i Europa får sin Sverigepremiär — i fängelserna! Det är Pionjärteatern, som tar upp den engelska författaren Pam Gems pjäs Lyan. Regissör är Lars-Erik Liedholm, som skall resa på turné i USA för att nå ut "om teater på käken".

Se sidan 9

Talar ut

Kar de Mumma talar ut i dagens SvD, exklusivt för Marginalen. Anfägen får vi veta hur det egentligen var med vinterna förr. Kerstin Hallert berättar om chimpanser i kulturlivet och deras revir.

Se sidan 12

Ny vårdform

Bryt din gamla identitet och träna din förmåga att klara konflikter utan våld av alkohol eller narkotika och utan att ta till våld. Så är den behandlingsmetod som tillämpas både av narkomaner, alkoholister och kriminella inom det alternativa samhället Synanon i USA.

Se sidan 18

At least partially because of the subsidies it has received in the 'seventies, the *Svenska Dagbladet* has attracted the most interest and the most new readers of any Swedish paper. While maintaining the high quality for which it is known—it is often considered *The Times* of Sweden—it has brightened its appearance, broadened its appeal and increased its independence from party affiliation during the past decade. As a result, it has become the nation's most authoritative independent moderate voice.

Although 146 newapapers were being published in Sweden in 1976, only 13, among them the *Svenska Dagbladet,* appeared daily. Sixty-four were six-day-a-week papers, but they were mostly provincial journals with regional distribution. The number of dailies which could be called *rikspress* or national papers is small. Stockholm has just four papers with nationwide distribution and relatively good coverage throughout the country. Two non-subscribed evening papers, *Expressen* (1976 circulation: 574,000) and *Aftonbladet* (477,000) lead the competition, probably because of their highly efficient delivery systems. The two leading morning dailies—*Dagens Nyheter* (452,000) and *Svenska Dagbladet* (180,000)—are not as widely distributed, but also have subscribers throughout the country.[1] While the *Svenska Dagbladet* is the smallest of these Stockholm national newspapers, its influence extends widely to all parties and to opinion-leaders throughout the nation.

Founded in 1884 as a conservative voice, *Svenska Dagbladet* was in one economic crisis after another until 1897, when a new regime took over. During the next two decades, it established itself as the journal for the educated classes. "With the turn of the century, under the editorship of C. G. Tengwall the paper was enlarged, made more newsworthy, given more interesting makeup, and dressed up with more illustrations than any other Swedish paper."[2] During this period, it proclaimed itself primarily as a cultural organ and gave a new dimension to Swedish journalism by stressing the arts and sciences. Outstanding intellectuals as the author Verner von Heidenstam and the literary critic Oscar Levertin contributed articles to the paper and it was soon known throughout Scandinavia as a journal of concern and reasonableness. One of its primary characteristics right up to the present has been its devotion to cultural matters. It has, however, also taken a special pride in a thorough coverage of business and economic news.[3]

Until 1973 *Svenska Dagbladet* was owned by a foundation, formed in 1940, in a way that attracted international interest. It was considered very effective as a guarantee against financial transactions which might endanger the freedom of the paper. All profits went back into the paper for all types of improvement—including the building of a beautiful and functional new 14-story plant

[1] Karl Erik Gustafsson and and Stig Hadenius, *Swedish Press Policy* (Stockholm: Stellan Stal Tryck, 1976), pp. 9–10 and 116–18.
[2] Kenneth E. Olson, *The History Makers: The Press of Europe from its Beginnings through 1965* (Baton Rouge: Laouisianas State University Press, 1966), p. 39.
[3] Karl Axel Tunberger, former chief political editor and presently leader writer on international affairs, *Svenska Dagbladet,* in letter to H. Fisher, June 8, 1978. Much of the information in this profile about *Svenska Dagbladet*'s present operation comes from Mr. Tunberger.

near central Stockholm (at Marieberg), completed in 1952. Making up the foundation are representatives of various segments of Swedish society—industry, the Church, the armed forces and educational and industrial institutions. The editor alone decides what will go into the paper as long as he largely follows the main lines established when the foundation was formed.

The foundation is still there as the guarantee of editorial continuity, but the forms of ownership have been changed. The main reason was that towards the middle of the 'sixties, the *Svenska Dagbladet,* both from the circulation and the economic point of view, began to decline. In 1973, *Svenska Dagbladet* was taken over by an organization formed in such a way that a number of well-known Swedish firms and companies guaranteed certain sums annually according to a share system which has worked well. Non-interference on the part of the shareholders in editorial policy was, of course, made a pre-condition.

Most Swedish newspapers have stagnated or suffered severe circulation and economic setbacks in recent years. Even Stockholm's biggest morning paper, *Dagens Nyheter,* which is by far the most important advertisement organ in the city, has suffered heavy losses and the tendency has been the same all over the country. Many papers, in fact, failed in the late 'sixties. At first the Swedes provided help to papers in distress by giving concessions for telecommunications and telephone charges and other forms of indirect aid. But that was insufficient. So, to correct fully for such losses and to save more newspapers from "going under," and to guarantee competing press voices, the Swedish government passed its Press Support and Advertisement Tax Bill in 1971.[4]

The bill provides a system of subsidy unique in Europe and is now being considered by other countries in the continent. Under the Bill, funds are gathered from a six percent tax on all forms of newspaper advertising over a designated level. The money goes to the national treasury, then is distributed by the Press Support Board to papers which are losing in market penetration.[5] Any paper with less than 40 percent of the households in its area is eligible for the subsidies. This procedure has served to help the runner-up papers in more-than-one-daily cities and to encourage new dailies, thus preserving competition. Since the subsidies were started, no Swedish daily has had to go out of business.

The *Svenska Dagbladet,* together with Malmo's *Arbetet,* tops the list of recipients for subsidy. In 1976, these two papers were receiving 19.5 million Swedish kroner each in direct aid annually—the maximum allowable. Although there is theoretical danger these government-supported grants could lead to curtailment of press freedom, to date government interference has not even been hinted. Contrary to many other conservative papers, the *Svenska Dagbladet* has supported the subsidies, indicating they "undoubtedly will mean increased competition between newspapers, while their abolishment would have led to less and less competition as the number of monopoly papers became even greater."[6] Because of the subsidies and its "new look" editorially, the *Svenska Dagbladet* has been the only Swedish daily to increase its circulation steadily, as it has

---

[4] Olof Wahlgren, "Press Subsidies: Swedish Case," *IPI Report,* 23:2 (February, 1974), pp. 1–2.
[5] Anthony Smith, "Europe's Changing Newspapers," *Atlas* (February, 1978), p. 27.
[6] Einar Östgaard, "Swedish Press Subsidies go up 40 Percent," *IPI Report,* 25:8 (August, 1976), p. 11.

gone from about 170,000 in 1968 to about 180,000 today, a decade later. In spite of its substantial aid, however, it is still badly "in the red" and will need continued monetary infusions to remain competitive and healthy.

Since its inception, the *Svenska Dagbladet* has always been a paper with conservative views. Generally speaking, in the 1800's Swedish papers were intimately related to political parties or factions. *Aftonbladet,* for example, was the voice of liberal opposition to Karl XIV Johan. *Dagens Nyheter* was likewise of liberal opinion and closely related to Sweden's largest political party, the Farmers' Party. In its earliest days, *Svenska Dagbladet* was no exception, for it, along with the *Sydvenska Dagbladet,* sympathized with the Conservative Party.[7] If *Svenska Dagbladet* has any party sympathies today, they are with the Moderate Party (formerly the Conservative Party), but any ties are purely informal and non-financial. It has, in fact, on several occasions deviated drastically from the Party. Moderate conservatism is perhaps the best way of describing its political line. Its devotion to democracy was demonstrated during World War II, when it played a leading role in opposing the Nazis. Since the war, it has supported Swedish neutrality, but military preparedness. It is generally pro-Western in its stance.

Svenska Dagbladet is one of Sweden's most respected papers. Its readership reflects its informed, progressive and flexible character; in addition to reaching high government officials, intellectuals and industrial and financial leaders, *Svenska Dagbladet* is read by the politically influential in all parties. *Svenska Dagbladet* is the main and highly respected critic of the Social Democratic Party, which governed Sweden from 1932 to 1976, but members of that party often contribute articles. Circulationwise, it is one of very few morning dailies which reaches to all parts of the country.

One reason why *Svenska Dagbladet* has been labeled "The Times of Sweden" is that, like *The Times* of London, it has traditionally carried advertisements on its front page. While its London counterpart eliminated this practice in the late 'sixties, *Svenska Dagbladet* did not go over to carrying news on the front page until September 1, 1970—probably the last of the world's important papers to do so. Until that time, the third page had been the "display window" of the paper. Like *The Times* of London, the *Svenska Dagbladet* handled news and interpretation in a serious and dignified manner, though recently its makeup has been more lively than *The Times* and several other serious elite newspapers.

Svenska Dagbladet's main and longstanding editorial policy is to present good international coverage, both in news and commentary. This is perhaps its strongest area. Principal international news stories, along with national news, are featured on the front page, and there is an excellent full page of foreign news, often with several related pictures, on the inside, usually on page six. The paper also carries numerous features and background stories on the international scene. It comments on world affairs in its leader pages. To provide its readers such effective international coverage and commentary, it receives the London *Times* News Service as well as that of the *New York Times*. In addition,

[7] Gustafsson and Hadenius, *op. cit.,* pp. 33–4 and 39.

it has news-exchange agreements with Copenhagen's *Berlingske Tidende* and Oslo's *Aftenposten;* its Scandinavian coverage is thus greatly enhanced, supplementing its excellent world coverage. It has eleven foreign correspondents stationed in Washington, New York, Bonn, Paris, London, Moscow, Rome, Vienna, Copenhagen, Helsinki and Oslo.

The national news also receives thorough coverage and treatment in *Svenska Dagbladet.* One page carries Scandinavian news, another more local, Stockholm-oriented events and information. The paper regularly features several "Persons of the Day" stories of Swedish personalities. One of its greatest strengths is its business news section. Business and economic news and features, usually totalling three to five pages, head the second major section of the paper. Editorials both by the paper's leader writers and guest commentators appear inside the front page, and there is a highly appealing and heavily-used letters-to-the-editor column entitled "Dagens Debatt."

As it has always been, the *Svenska Dagbladet* continues to provide one of Sweden's best newspaper outlets for articles on education, science, art, literature and theology. There is a regular page for culture, another for literature and books, another to cover music, film and the theater and still another for feature materials on the radio and television fields. One page is devoted to weddings, promotions, retirements and deaths. In addition, there are numerous feature articles, some of them occupying a full page, on various culturally-related subjects.

Although its stress is on serious news, *Svenska Dagbladet* contains more entertainment materials than many of the more somber quality papers. Sports news may cover as many of five pages of the typical 30–42 page daily. There is a daily full-page guide to radio and television programs. A half-page of cartoons is carried daily. There is space for bridge plays, crossword puzzles, cinema and other entertainment guides, lottery results, cartoons and similar material with entertainment values.

The front page of *Svenska Dagbladet* gives an attractive, bright appearance. Print is always interspersed with clear, descriptive photographs, sometimes as many as eight in number on a page. Front page color is used to outline stories and for advertisements on the inside. Good use is made of white space between stories and around the paper's nameplate. Part of the attractiveness of the front page stems from the "teasers" to inside-page stories which run down the right-hand column and across the bottom—briefs which give sneak previews of the full story's contents. Many of the news stories are placed in boxes composed of short vertical columns, giving the paper a broad horizontal appearance. Many of the paper's numerous advertisements are grouped on pages separate from the news pages. Pictures are used liberally throughout both sections of the paper. Business news, sports, comics and advertisements usually make up the paper's section.

Gustav von Platen, who succeeded Sven Gerentz as editor-in-chief in 1974, has continued to brighten the paper's appeals. But its quality has not diminished, for the *Svenska Dagbladet*'s writing and editorial staff of some 210 members, at least half of whom have university degrees, has continued to produce three editions each day. Their efforts daily provide the paper's Swedish readers—mostly intellectuals and opinion-leaders whose influence counts—with excellent foreign, national, business and economic coverage, incisive commentary and, especially, enriching cultural information. Such high-quality journalism enables the *Svenska Dagbladet* to hold its own in comprehensiveness and enlightenment with the best papers of Scandinavia and all Europe.

The Sydney Morning Herald

(AUSTRALIA)

AUSTRALIA—THAT FASCINATING "down under" continent where the press is virtually free from governmental control, where the newspaper is a pervasive medium, and where the people are news-hungry, often for the sensational—harbors some of the world's finest serious dailies. Although competition from *The Age* of Melbourne and a few others is keen, *The Sydney Morning Herald,* the nation's oldest metropolitan daily, is among the top contenders—if, indeed, not the top—for the position of the leading quality newspaper.

The Sydney Morning Herald's claim to this prominence is backed at least by its serious, dignified appearance and approach to journalism, by its objective reporting, by its reasoned lead and feature articles, by its watchful eye on government and by its success as a business. Like much of the Australian press, the *Herald* has been shaped by British origins. Consequently, in a way, it appears to be a composite of England's *Times* and *Daily Mail,* combining the traditional serious and comprehensive news and views presentation of the former with the appeals to a larger audience found in the latter. In its makeup, too, it reflects British quality daily patterns—few pictures on the front page, little art, and unadorned columns with simple label heads. Until 1944, also in British tradition, its front page contained only classified advertisements.

The Sydney Herald got its start as a weekly on April 18, 1831, some 28 years after Australia's oldest paper, the *Sydney Gazette* was founded as a government-censored weekly, edited and printed by a convict.[1] Like its counterparts in the American colonies, the *Gazette* was published "By Authority of the British Crown." The *Herald* became a daily in October, 1840, and added "Morning" to its name two years later. For ten years, after the *Gazette* folded in 1842, it was the New South Wales colony's only newspaper. Like the *Gazette* and other early Australian journals, it struggled hard for full press freedom until in-

---

[1] W. Sprague Holden, "Australia," in *The Asian Newspapers' Reluctant Revolution,* edited by John A. Lent (Ames, Iowa: Iowa State University Press, 1971), p. 119.

LATE EDITION

DEFORMITY FEAR OVER DRUG

—Page 2

TELEPHONE 2 0944
No. 43,739

The Sydney Morning Herald

FIRST PUBLISHED 1831

WEDNESDAY, FEBRUARY 22, 1978

42 PAGES
13 CENTS*

TODAY

The last great liner

James Cunningham looks at the ultimate symbol of a more glamorous age — the QE 2, which arrives in Melbourne today. Page 7.

Education's toughest job?

Colin Allison talks to the multi-cultural consultant for Sydney's western region. Page 7.

The new federalism

Cutting the strings from Federal grants to the States. Part III of Ross Gittins's report. Page 7.

TOMORROW

The spoilt industry

Mining companies begin moves against Aboriginal land rights. A report from Stewart Harris.

Personalities

The Look! line-up includes radio man Bill Dowsett, the top French cartoonist (a woman) and Lone Koppel Winther of the Australian Opera.

Report on Christmas Day trouble

Jail had no plan to fight riot

An internal report by the Department of Corrective Services on the Christmas Day riot at Long Bay jail says that there was no battle plan at the jail to meet such a situation.

And there was an inadequate amount of riot gear, including respirators, and confusion on how supplies of gas could be obtained if needed.

The report says it appeared that junior officers had no basic ideas as to what to do if they were asked to be part of a riot squad.

And there was no permanent roster of experienced senior officers.

There was no experienced officer operating the switchboard. The officer on duty was unable to contact the Deputy Commissioner who was in his home throughout the afternoon.

The department's legal officer, Mr K. Maughan, the director of special security units, Mr I. Sanders, and the chief psychologist, Mrs I. Manoutowf, were directed in January to inquire into the disturbance.

They interviewed prison officers and prisoners who were present during the riot at the Central Industrial Prison, at Long Bay.

Their report has not been made officially available to the press or the public.

The Christmas Day disturbance led to demands by prison officers to reopen Bathurst Jail and build a new maximum security jail.

Since then the Commissioner of Corrective Services, Mr W. McGeechan, has been replaced. His negotiations with prisoners at Parramatta Jail on January 5 brought the call for his replacement to a head.

Mr McGeechan is mentioned only briefly in the department's report, although he was called to Long Bay to help quell the disturbance.

The report says the police were not informed about the riot until the next morning.

Prisoners were able to contact the media by using the chaplain's phone, which has a direct line.

They were able to enter the jail clinic through an unbarred window and take drugs. The clinic has since been moved.

The prisoners also made alcohol from yeast obtained illegally from the bakehouse. The refrigerator containing the yeast has since been moved to the main gate area. The officer in charge of the bakehouse now gets his yeast from there and personally places it in the dough.

The report says the disturbances started when two prison officers tried to separate two fighting prisoners.

Other prisoners later organised a sit-in to lodge a number of complaints.

The report gives details of prisoners taking prison officers hostage, lighting fires and causing damage.

It says when the Commissioner and the Deputy Commissioner later arrived, all available officers assembled at the gate and riot equipment was issued from the armoury to a number of them.

The report noted that a number of No 3 wing prisoners had earlier asked to be locked in their cells and took no part in the destruction of furniture and the taking of hostages.

QE2 HEADS FOR DATE WITH SYDNEY

The Queen Elizabeth 2 crossing Bass Strait yesterday.

Burnoff fire rages out of control

From Joseph Glascott at Smiggin Holes

A large bushfire in Kosciusko National Park, started as a deliberate burnoff 14 days ago, jumped the Murray River into Victoria and was burning yesterday through valuable timber forests.

The fire, in hot and windy weather, was burning on a 30 km front in the Snowy Mountains of NSW and on a 15 km front in Victoria.

By last night it had burnt out 12,000 hectares in the Kosciusko National Park, and was within two kilometres of private grazing properties on its western front in Victoria.

In NSW on its northern front it was within three kilometres of private property in the Khancoban district and about 10 km from private land on its southern front.

In the south-east it jumped the Alpine Way south of Geehi.

But these were small fronts of the fire and bushfire authorities believe the fire could be controlled before private properties are damaged.

A huge pall of smoke hung over Mt Kosciusko yesterday.

Ash and cinders were falling on the resort area of Charlotte Pass on the northern side of the Alps.

Mr Len Moorse, fire controller for the Hume-Snowy Bushfire Prevention Scheme in the area, said last night: "It will be a big job to get the fire under control but I'm confident we will contain it soon.

"We have bulldozers, fire tankers and men with hand tools on the job.

"The main damage so far is to the park.

"No installations are threatened, but the Victorians are concerned about their forests."

COLUMN 8

THE HEAT got to a lot of us yesterday. A Chester Hill woman complained that when she got to the Social Security office at 4.20 it was closed because, according to a sign on the door, it was too hot. A Blacktown reader had a similar experience at the employment office. Perhaps a summertime siesta rule is the answer?

QE2 pulls into Sydney Harbour on Friday morning. The liner is due to cross the Heads at 6 am and berth at Circular Quay an hour later. Transport Commission spokesman said it's impossible to lay on a special passenger ferry for escort because of peak traffic. Readers will be able to get a close look at the Queen, however, from the Manly and Mosman ferries, which run every half-hour. James Cunningham tells you more about QE2 on Page 7 today.

CONCRETE mixer drivers ferried water in the bushfires. One of them took on a smaller job this week. A Volkswagen stopped for a city traffic light beside a big Farley & Lewers truck. Seeing the car's engine afire, the truckie leapt out and extinguished it with his truck's water hose. Before anyone could thank him he was off, with a wave to the cars backed up behind and a polite "Sorry I kept you waiting."

THE RSL is inviting former war correspondents and photographers — for the first time ever — to lead the Sydney Anzac Day parade. "These blokes have been overlooked," says Bob Leonard, who originated the idea. "They ran more risks getting their stories through than the average soldier." Mr Leonard can be reached by phone at 290 9909, and by mail at the Bank of NSW Sydney office.

FOR the first time in its 60 years, the Imperial Services Club, Sydney, has appointed a life member. He is Major-General A. C. Murchison, former Inspector-General of the Reserve and commander of the 2nd Division, CMF, and a former club president.

CHATSWOOD reader S. T. Pollitt is wondering if he should call a TV repairman, an electrician, a vacuum cleaner fixer or all three. His television, he says, works only on one socket in the house, and only if he plugs in a vacuum cleaner next to it first. No, the TV does not suck up dirt and the cleaner does **not** *give a picture.*

Call to mark farm roofs

By the Land Editor

NSW farmers have been asked by the State Emergency Services to paint the name of their properties on the roofs of farm buildings.

According to the director of SES, Air Vice-Marshal W. E. Townsend, the easy identification of properties may save lives in bush fires or floods.

Pilots flying mercy missions had often reported great difficulty in finding the right homestead, he said.

Smoke was a problem in bush fires, and in floods, wide expanses of water often covered roads or other landmarks used by pilots to identify specific properties from maps.

TODAY'S WEATHER

Metropolitan: Mild southerly winds. Max Temps: City 25, Liverpool 27.

NSW: Sultry with thunderstorms in NE. Milder SW to S winds elsewhere.

Details, Page 39.

LATE NEWS

Telecom has $99m profit

The Australian Telecommunications Commission made a profit of $99 million in the last half of 1977, a rise of 6 per cent on the profit for the last half of 1976.

Announcing this yesterday Telecom's chairman, Mr R. D. Somervaille, said the profit was made despite the freeze on basic telephone rents and call charges.

The trading result was after $184 million had been set aside for depreciation and $155 million paid to the Federal Government and Telecom bondholders as interest on past borrowings.

Telecom does not pay tax.

The figures pointed to the result for the full year [to June 30, 1978] being about 6 per cent up on the $164 million profit in the year ended June 30, 1977.

The result reflected the gains in productivity made from new technologies and decentralised management. Telecom's cost-containment program and the stimulus given to traffic through selective marketing, particularly of night rates for STD.

Govt will bear down on inflation

From PETER BOWERS, Political Correspondent

CANBERRA. — The Federal Government totally rejected yesterday any short-term action to stimulate the economy to reduce record postwar unemployment.

In reaffirming rigorous restraint of Government spending, the Government laid the groundwork for a tough 1978-79 Budget next August.

An unyielding hard line in Government management of the economy was the central theme of the speech by the Governor-General, Sir Zelman Cowen, at the formal opening of the 31st Commonwealth Parliament.

The speech, written in the Prime Minister's office, set out the Government's legislative program and overall strategy for the next three years.

It emphasised the Government's resolve to continue to bear down on inflation.

Unprecedented security was imposed outside Parliament House after last week's bomb outrage at the Sydney Hilton Hotel. Inside Parliament, security was kept to a discreet police presence to avoid marring the ceremonial opening.

However the Senate chamber, where the ceremony took place, had been under tight security for 24 hours. Before the ceremony bomb squads throughly checked the red carpeted chamber.

In his speech, Sir Zelman said the Government had been returned to power with a majority surpassed only once before.

Its resolve had been strengthened by this decisive expression of the people's conviction that the basic direction of the Government's policies reflected their aspirations and interests.

Heading the Government's priorities were:

To build on the progress made in the last two years, defeat inflation and unemployment and restore full economic health to the country;

To promote vigorously the development of Australia's resources and enlarge external trade;

To maintain policies which had halted the excessive growth in government bureaucracy and expenditure, and to continue the pursuit of greater efficiency and responsiveness by the public sector.

Sir Zelman said the Government's economic policy would continue to be based on four points:

Rigorous restraint of government spending to provide for longer-term expansion in the private sector.

A monetary policy which would enable a sustained growth in economic activity and continue to bear down upon inflation, thus laying the only sound foundation for further reduction in interest rates.

Advocacy before the Conciliation and Arbitration Commission of wage restraint so that inflation could be further reduced and job opportunities expanded.

Firm action to support Australia's external economic position, including an active and continuing program of government borrowing overseas.

A busy program outlined by Sir Zelman included legislation to proclaim an Australian fishing zone covering all living marine resources out to 200 nautical miles.

He said the Government planned to implement a deposits insurance scheme to strengthen permanent building societies and protect the funds of depositors.

Measures would be taken to strengthen the Federal Bureau of Narcotics in its fight against illegal drug trafficking and to co-ordinate international measures more closely.

Report of speech — Page 11.

Half-way point in 96-day cruise

The British liner Queen Elizabeth 2 arrives this morning in Melbourne, half-way point of its 96-day Pacific Orient cruise.

Aboard are passengers from Europe, the United States and South America who have paid fares ranging up to $133,000.

Sixty Victorians will be on board this afternoon as the ship slides out of Port Phillip Bay on the way to Sydney. It is due at Sydney Heads at 6 am on Friday (see Column 8).

In Sydney a further 200 will join the liner — billed as the world's most stylish holiday resort.

One of the Melbourne passengers is a 57-year-old retired airline head, Mr Alan Rea, of Caulfield, who sailed on the final voyages of the Queen Elizabeth 1 and the Queen Mary.

He has paid $3,200 for a 23-day cruise to Hong Kong via Port Moresby, Bali, Singapore and Manila.

"I am a ship nut from way back," he said yesterday.

"I am wrapped in ships and have travelled on many of the great liners.

"Having been on the other two Queens I always hoped I would be able to go on the QE2, but little did I think she would be coming to Melbourne to pick me up.

"It's got a touch of magic about it."

Page 7: Last of great liners.

Relief for Sydney

A weak southerly change moved across the City late last night bringing the temperatures slightly down, much to the relief of Sydney residents.

Earlier, after a hot and humid day the temperatures had hovered around the 26 deg mark, about 5 deg above average.

The Weather Bureau did not expect that temperatures would fall below 19 deg during the early morning hours.

Yesterday, the temperatures reached 29 deg in the City, 32 at Liverpool and 36 at Richmond.

A Weather Bureau spokesman said temperatures in the City were up to 12 deg higher than normal for February and at night had been consistently about four deg higher.

Temperatures dropped during scattered storms in the metropolitan area yesterday afternoon. Hail fell at Broadway. But the storms lasted only briefly and the sticky conditions returned.

The bureau expects a cooler, partly cloudy day today. Forecast temperatures are 25 deg in the City and 27 deg at Liverpool.

On other pages

Tides, sun, moon

FORT DENISON: High 8.55 am (1.7 metres), 9.23 pm (1.4 metres). Low 2.34 am (0.3 metres), 3.20 pm (0.2 metres).

SUN: Rises 6.36, sets 7.41.

MOON: Rises 6.59 pm, sets 5.35 am.

State Government changes its mind on coal

The State Cabinet reversed yesterday a decision made by the Minister for Mines and Energy, Mr Hills, on the development of the Warkworth coal deposits near Singleton.

Mr Hills threw the NSW mining industry into turmoil last October by announcing that the lease to develop the Warkworth deposits, containing more than 800 million tonnes of coal, would be granted to the State Electricity Commission.

Yesterday, Cabinet decided that Coal and Allied Industries Ltd should be given the right to mine 406 million tonnes from the deposits.

The Cabinet also decided that a further 134 million tonnes of coal under the Hunter River, on the river flats and in adjacent locations should not be developed until a thorough environmental inquiry had been carried out.

Mr Hills

Mr Hills, in a statement after the Cabinet meeting, did not say what would be done with the balance of the deposits. It is understood that the development of these deposits — about 300 million tonnes — will be decided after talks between the Government and the SEC.

The Government's decision on the future of the rich Warkworth coal deposits was accompanied by the announcement of new investment guidelines for the mineral industry in NSW.

(See Front Page, Section 2)

When he announced last October that the SEC would develop the Warkworth deposits, Mr Hills said that the Government had taken this step to conserve Australian equity in the deposits.

At the time, CAIL had been the subject of a $88 million joint takeover bid by the UK-controlled Conzinc Riotinto of Australia Ltd and Howard Smith Ltd.

CAIL had already committed $11 million towards proving up the Warkworth prospect.

Several days later the Premier, Mr Wran, said the parties could still achieve "a fair resolution of a totally unsatisfactory situation" if they were prepared to talk.

Extensive negotiations between a Cabinet sub-committee and representatives of CAIL followed.

The Leader of the Opposition, Mr Coleman, said yesterday that the Cabinet decision represented another example of the Government backing off from a wrong and hasty decision.

Mr Hills had obviously blundered into an area in what was nothing more than a further attempt at grabbing control of the State's energy resources.

In announcing the Cabinet decision yesterday, Mr Hills said approval had been given to the allocation of 406 million tonnes of coal deposits in the Warkworth area to CAIL. The company would be invited to apply for the rights to mine the deposit.

"The area which the company will be invited to mine comprises 56 million tonnes located north of the Hunter River and 350 million tonnes south of the river," he said.

Although details on the projected costs of mining the 406 million tonnes were not available yesterday, virtually all of the deposits are capable of being mined by open-cut methods.

Mr Hills said: "It is my belief that the allocation will satisfy the needs of CAIL for the next 50 years."

In a prepared statement, the Government said that the basic objective of its investment guidelines was to promote the growth of the minerals industry, consistent with the interests of NSW in the ownership and development of the State's natural resources.

In his statement, Mr Coleman said the Cabinet decision would allow private enterprise to get on with its business.

"The damage caused by Mr Hills's futile exercise in his attempted socialisation of energy resources is considerable, particularly to NSW reputation as a suitable site for industrial and mining development," he said.

Mr Coleman said he believed the guidelines were adequate, although they left several questions unanswered.

There was no indication of policy in relation to port facilities such as coal loaders, how road or rail transport would be increased to cater for the extra volume of coal and other minerals and ores being mined, or of the royalties or taxes to be levied by the State on new deposits.

This made the costing of mining developments difficult for the companies involved.

Two hurt in factory fire

Two firemen were treated at hospital last night after fighting a fire at a Lane Cove factory.

One man was overcome by smoke. The other received burns to his left eye.

The fire severely damaged a large section of the roof and ceiling of the two-storey Philips Electronic building in Mars Road.

Policemen injured

Two police officers were injured in a struggle with an accused man in Wollongong Court of Petty Sessions yesterday.

Maxwell Cecil Folkes, 29, of no fixed address, charged with stealing a safe, attempted to strike Detective Sergeant D. Driver in court.

Five policemen struggled with the man and he was overpowered.

Folkes was remanded in custody to February 28.

Dollar slips

The dollar was devalued further yesterday by a reduction from 88.7 to 88.5 in the trade-weighted index of value. But in US dollar terms it appreciated from $US1.1370 to $US1.1407.

Details in Finance, Front Page, Section 2.

Turn behind the Financial news for —

Personal notices: P23

Classified index: P23

Printed and published by John Fairfax and Sons Ltd. of Jones Street, Broadway. Postal address: Box 506, GPO, Sydney, 2001. Registered for posting as a newspaper—Category B. * Recommended and maximum price only. Interstate by air extra.

dependence in 1901, and since then has championed freedom under the Australian government.

One feature of the Australian press has been ownership by more than one individual. *The Sydney Morning Herald* provides a prime example of this tendency. The paper claims co-founders—John Fairfax and Charles Kemp.[2] The proprietors started with two reporters and did not hire an official editor until 1854, when it had a full-time staff of seven or eight, including a chief of staff, a shorthand writer, a music critic, commercial, police and law reporters and an all-around man.[3] In 1853, Fairfax bought Kemp's share and guided the paper's destinies until his death in 1877. The Fairfax family has continued in control ever since.

In 1953, John Fairfax and Sons Pty., Ltd. took over control of most of Sir Hugh Denison's Associated Newspapers, continuing *The Sun,* an afternoon tabloid and combining its own *Sunday Herald,* founded in 1949, with the *Sunday Sun,* thus making the *Morning Herald* part of a newspaper group. Three years later, the family company became a public corporation, John Fairfax, Ltd., with the Fairfax family retaining half ownership of the company's shares. Shortly thereafter, in 1958, John Fairfax Ltd. financed an independent group to acquire interests in Sydney's Truth and Sportsman, Ltd. publications named *Truths, Daily Mirror* and *Sunday Mirror.* The *Daily Mirror* was sold in 1960 to News Ltd. of Adelaide.[4] Then, in the mid-sixties, the company acquired the *Canberra Times* and made it a first class newspaper. In 1967, it purchased a considerable share of *The Age* of Melbourne. In 1969, it initiated a sister paper, the *Canberra News.*[5]

Today, the holding company, John Fairfax and Sons Ltd. regularly publishes *The Sydney Morning Herald,* the *Sun,* the *Sun-Herald,* the periodicals of Associated Newspapers and a weekly called *The Financial Review.* The Fairfax group's operation is proving to be profitable. Despite a printer's strike late in 1976, it showed a 20 percent increase in profits in the 1976–77 fiscal year over that of 1975–76, from A$5.8 million to A$7 million.[6]

Nearly all of Australia's metropolitan newspapers are owned by four "public companies" or corporations designated by the word "Limited"—John Fairfax Ltd., the Melbourne-based *Herald* and *Weekly Times,* Australian Consolidated Press, and Rupert Murdock's News Ltd. In addition to owning newspapers, these groups control or own radio and television stations, book publishing firms, printing plants, record companies, newsprint mills and numerous magazines. Yet, their powerful proprietorships are benign. Although there is competition both in morning and evening papers only in Sydney and Melbourne, there appears to be little ownership bias in their papers or evidence that lust for power

[2] Completed questionnaire and letter from G. H. Wilkinson, Editorial Manager of the *Sydney Morning Herald,* dated April 20, 1978.

[3] Henry Mayer, *The Press in Australia* (Melbourne: Landsdowne Press, 1968), p. 188.

[4] W. Sprague Holden, *Australia Goes to Press* (Detroit: Wayne State State University Press, 1961), p. 236.

[5] Holden, "Australia," in Lent (ed.), *op. cit.,* pp. 126–7.

[6] "The Press 'Down Under'," *IPI Report* (December, 1977), pp. 6–7.

destroys emphasis on effective work. Within groups, each paper is encouraged to have its own "personality." Despite some quarrels, the groups demonstrate restraint and fair play most of the time. In fact, competition among the groups is so keen that sometimes one group will purchase a paper first to keep a competitor from growing. For example, the serious, virtuous *Sydney Morning Herald* shares ownership and a production plant with the *Sun,* a rag which delights in "keyhole peeping" and sensation. The Fairfax group purchased the *Sun* to keep it from Consolidated Press, and the *Herald*'s excellence appears little affected by its "tarnished" companion.[7]

In remaining a high-quality, serious, dignified, albeit sometimes a trifle dull and staid newspaper, the *Sydney Morning Herald* has remained faithful to founder John Fairfax's desire to make it a first-class paper. Today, it sees itself, as it did when it marked its centennial in 1931, as a special type of Australian paper with unique qualities:

> The aim of the *Herald* is to provide a full, comprehensive, and responsible service to the minority whose tastes require it, while also giving it, in substance and form, suitable to the vast numbers of modern newspaper readers who demand a "popular" press. . . .[8]

Following this formula, the paper has made itself acceptable to a large segment of Australians, and its present circulation of about 275,000 is quite substantial for the country. In many ways, its general appeal and serious demeanor remind one of Denmark's influential conservative *Berlingske Tidende.*

Although the *Sydney Morning Herald* does not give the proportional stress to international news given in such papers as the *Neue Zürcher Zeitung* of Switzerland or *The Guardian* of England, it does provide good foreign coverage. The work of six full-time correspondents located in London, Washington, New York, Tokyo, Peking, Port Moresby and Jakarta is supplemented by that of ten stringers placed in other strategic spots.[9] Additional coverage comes from the *Australian Associated Press* (AAP), a cooperatively-owned news service in which the *Herald* holds stock, which receives world news round-the-clock from its staff of 80 and has close links with Reuters. In addition, the paper takes the syndicated services of the New York *Times* and three London dailies, the *Express,* the *Daily Mirror* and the *Sunday Times.* Overseas stories appear scattered throughout the paper. Sources usually are not given, since the AAP is the only wire service source and the *Herald*'s own staff provides nearly all the remaining stories. The paper's New York and London coverage is especially strong and its general presentation of foreign news compares favorably with the best in Australia.

Perhaps the *Herald*'s most significant strength lies in its watchfulness over government and its challenges to official complacency and partisanship. As early as the 1880's, its rival paper, *The Bulletin* conceded the *Herald* was the

[7] Holden, "Australia," *op. cit.,* p. 128.
[8] "A Century of Journalism: The Sydney Morning Herald and Its Record of Australian Life, 1831–1931," (Sydney, 1931), p. 761.
[9] Wilkinson questionnaire.

only Sydney paper "which even pretends to report in detail the debates in the Legislature."[10] In World War II, its exposés for patriotic reasons led to the downfall of the Menzies Government and the subsequent advent of the Curtin Labour Government, which it supported for some time in spite of repeated criticisms by non-Labour forces. Mr. W. O. Fairfax defended those actions of his paper by writing:

> We have been unsparingly critical of all political parties; if more so of Labour, no doubt it is a matter of opinion whether we are impartial or partisan. If we have at any time been partisan during the 25 years for which I have been responsible then it has been through my stupidity rather than through my ill will.[11]

During the Suez crisis, the *Herald* was condemning the British and French attack at a time when nearly all the Australian press was supporting or at least condoning it.[12] Today, it keeps six reporters at Canberra to keep a watchful eye on government.

The *Herald* has also stood up against local government strictures. In 1953, a Sydney City Council Disclosure of Allegations Bill was introduced to penalize corporate bodies and individuals who failed to comply with court orders to disclose information. One day after the bill became law, the local courts ordered the *Herald* to disclose the names of city council members allegedly guilty of graft. The paper refused and a subsequent Supreme Court decision vindicated its stand.[13]

For the purposes of keeping a watchful eye on government and for investigating other social problems, the paper maintains a team of senior investigative reporters appropriately named "The *Herald* Investigation Team." That team spearheads another qualitative activity which has helped the paper gain the reputation of being "a gadfly to complacency"—the use of well-reasoned lead articles and short well-researched features and series of articles. Reporters and correspondents frequently get their own credit lines for these pithy, interesting pieces.

Perhaps partly because it is a successful business itself and certainly because of its appeals to the better-informed middle classes, the *Herald* stresses economics, finance and business. An entire section is devoted to Finance and Business. Its success in this and other specialized fields is assured by the assigning of personnel to cover a single area; consequently, the paper has, among others, an economics writer and an industrial editor.

The *Herald* encourages comment and feedback. Fully half of the editorial page is consigned to letters to the editor. The remainder of the page is made up of locally-written editorials (leaders), usually by the paper's staff, which are incisive, lively and highly readable.

To compete for the popular tastes, the *Herald*'s news columns likewise feature police activities, accidents, and it does not "pass up cheesecake qua cheesecake, or neglect wholly the . . . three angles of sexual triangles."[14] But its cov-

[10] Holden, *Australia Goes to Press*, p. 55.
[11] W. O. Fairfax, in letter to Editor of *Guardian*, January 29, 1954.
[12] Holden, *Australia Goes to Press*, p. 55.
[13] Mayer, *op. cit.*, p. 185.
[14] Holden, *op. cit.*, p. 161.

erage of ethnic affairs, medical, church, court and other civic news, to say nothing of its international/national news lift it above its more raffish competitors. Its literary articles and book reviews are especially good and its criticism of the arts in general is considered the best in Australia.

To assist the objectivity and quality of their reporting and writing, *Sydney Morning Herald* staffers can avail themselves of one of the best newspaper library-morgues found anywhere. Most of its staff of 18 hold university degrees. On the shelves are well over 50,000 reference works. Stories are indexed, filed chronologically and cross-referenced so news personnel can quickly trace the development of events. The morgue's microfilms of the paper go back to the first issue in 1831.

The John Fairfax Ltd. group employs about 2,800 personnel, 170 of which are on the editorial staff of the *Herald*. The paper has no managing director, but is run by the editor-in-chief, currently David W. Bowman. The editor in charge of the leader pages and the book section and the news editor are co-equals in authority. Both are responsible to the editorial manager, currently Mr. G. H. Wilkinson. Individual reporters are often assigned permanent beats (or "rounds" as they are called in Australia), and given appropriate titles to mark their specialties, such as "Civic Reporter," "Ethnic Affairs Reporter," "Medical correspondent," and "Industrial Editor." Reporters and writers often receive name by-line credits for their stories and features.

To qualify as a full member of the *Sydney Morning Herald* staff, news editorial personnel must have had "high school plus a three-year cadetship in journalism or a university degree plus a one-year cadetship."[15] Under the unique Australian cadet system of training journalists, a fledgling begins an up-to-three-year apprenticeship with simple tasks under the supervision of experienced, working journalists. Assignments become increasingly difficult until the cadet has had practical experience in a wide variety of news situations.

One of the persons who during recent years has been most influential at the *Sydney Morning Herald* has been Rupert Henderson. He was managing director until 1964 and presently is a member of the board. Former board chairman, Sir Warwick Fairfax, has said that Henderson, who has been with the paper about a half century, "is entitled to be regarded as the outstanding newspaperman of his generation." The present managing director, Mr. G. H. Wilkinson has already established himself in a class with Henderson. The senior staff members of the *Herald* are all outstanding Australian newspapermen— competent, literate, cosmopolitan and experienced.

Undoubtedly the most dignified of Australian newspapers in its makeup, the *Herald* spreads its contents with great reserve and care. As is the case with several leading British quality papers, the *Herald*'s main front page story is positioned in the upper-left corner and a large picture normally appears at the page's top center. Its broadsheet pages are wider than most European and American newspapers, making it possible to carry eleven narrow columns rather than the usual six or eight. "Column 8" occupies the extreme right-hand column of the front page. This nationally popular column combines sophisticated commentary with gossipy items and symbolizes the urbanity of the *Herald*. The front page

[15] Wilkinson questionnaire.

also features a "Late News" box and a unique "Today–Tomorrow" column heralding articles in the current issue on the upcoming one. Color is used discreetly to emphasize headlines or to highlight special news or events. Numerous pictures are displayed inside the *Herald*. Graphic presentation is attractive and good use is made of white space.

The *Herald* is published in an up-to-date plant at Broadway and Wattle Streets in Sydney. At this writing, conversion to photo-composition and a video display terminal input system employing 160 VDT positions for writing and editing is in process.[16]

When all its qualities are considered, the *Sydney Morning Herald*'s claim to high ranking among Australia's finest elite newspapers is well substantiated. Among its principal qualifications is "its reputation for nearly 150 years of fair, objective reporting and reasoned, subjective leading articles."[17] Beyond that, it can claim Australia's oldest tradition of serious journalism, a dignified appearance, strong appeals to the nation's better-educated intellectuals without forgetting popular tastes, an excellent staff of well-qualified journalists and financial stability. Such qualities of excellence combine to make the *Herald* not just a leading quality Australian paper, but also one of the great newspapers of the world.

The Times

(ENGLAND)

ONE AUTHORITY RECENTLY WROTE of the London *Times*, "It is much more than a newspaper; it is a national institution."[1] Across its nearly 200-year span of history, *The Times*, one of Britain's oldest newspapers, has managed to gain and hold a highly respected image of reliability, civility and dignity. It has been a "newspaper of record," *the* paper to read for nearly everyone, but especially for the influential opinion-maker of government, nobility, ruling class and business and financial circles. It has ever stood in the highest journalistic circles of the world as the paper which most readily comes to mind when thoughts turn to quality newspaper journalism.

Great Britain has more national dailies—those read from coast to coast—than any other nation in the world. Each of its top quality national newspapers has a distinguishing character of its own. The *Daily Telegraph* has traditionally

---

16 Wilkinson questionnaire.

17 *Ibid.*

1 Peter Hebblethwaite, "Man Behind *The Times*," *America*, (March 17, 1973), p. 239.

Wednesday February 22 1978
No 60,243
Price fifteen pence

THE TIMES

British Leyland and public money: Bernard Levin, page 16

Mr Callaghan defends neutron bomb for Nato

The Prime Minister, defending Nato's retention of the neutron bomb, accused the Soviet Union yesterday of using propaganda to prevent discussion about even more destructive weapons being developed, including the Russian SS 20 missile.

New Soviet missile 'more dangerous'

By Hugh Noyes
Parliamentary Correspondent
Westminster

Mr Callaghan in the Commons yesterday struck back at what he described as the Russian propaganda campaign aimed at having the neutron bomb outlawed from the Nato armoury.

The bomb is considered to be the most destructive weapon so far developed in the West, with the reputation of being able to destroy people while leaving property undamaged.

But the Prime Minister, setting the scene for the important speech he will be making on June 2 in New York at the United Nations world disarmament conference, told Labour MPs who were urging him to denounce the neutron bomb that it was a fearful weapon but no more fearful than the SS 20 now being developed by the Russians.

He agreed with Mr Winston Churchill, Tory MP for Stretford and a defence spokesman, that the SS 20 had a destructive potential thousands of times greater than that of the nuclear neutron bomb.

Then, emphasizing that he wanted to ensure that his next words were on record, Mr Callaghan continued: "The neutron bomb and its serious effects are being used by the Soviet Union as propaganda to prevent discussion of some of the other weapons being developed.

"Mr Brezhnev in particular has insisted on focusing propaganda on the neutron bomb whenever there are discussions in the United Nations or elsewhere on how we are to deal with some of the other weapons now being developed and on which research is taking place."

Mr Callaghan said a formidable prospect faced the world on that matter. He did not want to see the world destroyed by terror, nor did he want the West to succumb to blackmail by someone else's terror. That was the spirit in which he urged Labour MPs to approach the matter.

The SS 20 was far more dangerous than the neutron bomb. That was why he did not wish attention to be focused on a single weapon. There were weapons on both sides that must enter into a comprehensive disarmament discussion.

Mr Callaghan told the Commons that the practical programme he wanted to put forward as quickly as possible included a curb on the accumulation and development of nuclear weapons by international agreement; a treaty to assure the world that those who renounced nuclear weapons would not have them used against them; an extension of confidence-building measures now operational in Europe to other parts of the world; and a comprehensive test ban treaty.

Our Defence Correspondent writes: The SS 20 is an intermediate range ballistic missile which the Russians began to deploy in the western Soviet Union last year.

Its three independent warheads can travel an estimated 3,000 miles: not enough to reach the United States but enough to offer the Russians a wide choice of targets in Western Europe.

Nato countries have watched the development of the SS 20 with some concern over the past few years, partly because it poses a new threat to Western European countries, partly because it is mobile.

That obviously makes it more difficult to destroy. One argument put forward by the West Germans in favour of the Cruise missile is that it could provide a means of striking back at the new range of Russian weapons like the SS 20 and the Backfire bomber.

Parliamentary report, page 14

Jobless total is down for fifth month in a row

By Caroline Atkinson

For the fifth successive month the underlying level of unemployment in Britain fell in February to a seasonally-adjusted total of 1,350,200—5.8 per cent of the workforce. The fall of 10,800 in adult jobless was foreshadowed by Mr Healey last week when he speculated that unemployment might now have peaked.

Officials are still cautious on this score, however, as the steady though slight falls in the jobless total over the last five months are somewhat puzzling. Since they have come at a time when output is still flat.

But another sign that the labour market is picking up comes from the official February figures for vacancies, also published yesterday by the Department of Employment.

These show that there was a further rise of 6,900 in job vacancies notified to employment offices—to 185,200 this month. There was also a sharp rise in notified vacancies in January, the fifth consecutive monthly increase.

The total on the unemployment register stood at 1,445,863 this month, including school-leavers. When the jobless in Northern Ireland are added, the figure rises to 1,508,674, or 6.3 per cent of the labour force. Unemployment is higher in Northern Ireland than in the rest of the United Kingdom, and the gap has been widening.

There are still many school-leavers who have been unable to find work, although the numbers have fallen from the peak reached last summer. This month 46,634 school-leavers were on the register, a fall of 10,791 from January.

About 90 per cent of those who left school in the past academic year have found jobs. The rate at which these first-time job-seekers have left the dole queue is about the same as last year, although the actual number without work is higher. At this time last year there were 39,400 jobless school-leavers in Britain.

There has been a fall of 28,000 in the underlying level of unemployment since last September when it reached 1,378,000. Although this could signal the turning point, the figure is too small to be a reliable guide.

There was a period last year when the dole queue appeared to be stabilizing, but it was followed by sharp rises in unemployed during the summer which more than outweighed the earlier falls.

The apparent halt in the rising trend of unemployment has confounded most predictions. It is unusual for the number of jobs to increase, oh for unemployment to decline before production picks up. All indications of output in the economy

Continued on page 21, col 6

Racehorses being exercised on the beach at Filey, North Yorkshire, because their training grounds are frozen.

Thaw brings flood threat to West Country

By Staff Reporters

A mass of warm air moved into the snowbound West Country yesterday and brought dangers of extensive flooding. It also brought dense fog that curtailed helicopter rescue flights. Plans to fly fodder to thousands of cattle and poultry and other animals had to be postponed.

The South West Water Authority gave a warning that with the rise in temperature many rivers were dangerously high. There were severe flooding in the tarns of Kingsbridge and Totness, in south Devon.

Mr Howell, minister responsible for coordinating assistance to the beleaguered counties, said in Taunton that the Army would be moved into Somerset to help clear the roads. In north Devon five hug esnowploughs were brought in. One was flown from Switzerland. The Ministry of Defence said that two Army snow vehicles, normally used in freezing Arctic conditions and insulated to withstand extreme cold, would be used.

The Minister said that local authorities in the South-west would have to pay only the product of a penny rate towards emergency operations.

Mr Howell said later that the Wessex Water Authority was preparing for floods and a warning system was in operation. Levels in reservoirs were being dropped to meet any possible threat.

Electricity workers were taken into Devon yesterday to restore power supplies, but the local electricity authority said power might not berestored to isolated areas until the end of the week.

Villages and hamlets on high ground on Dartmoor, Exmoor and Bodmin Moor and other parts of north Devon and north Somerset were still cut off, as also was Okehampton, with a population of about 5,000.

The RAF battled through bad visibility to bring emergency supplies to Lynton and Lynmouth, overlooking the Bristol Channel. Food, drugs, oxygen cylindersand other essentials were takento the area.

In one mission a woman was lifted by helicopter from Lynton to Barnstaple with a broken thigh.

A premature baby boy weighing 1lb 13oz was struggling for life last night after a four-hour Land-Rover journey through snow to hospital in Taunton.

The child was driven from a hospital in Wells, Somerset, when fog prevented a naval helicopter from making the journey. Condition of the boy, who was put into an incubator, was later said to be fair.

The coroner's officer in Exeter, Mr Robert Sampson, said that at least five middle-aged or elderly men had died in the previous three days in the Exeter area after heart attacks while shovelling snow.

There were fears for the safety of Mr Martin Wibmer, aged 74, who left his home in Hatton, near Weston-super-Mare, on Sunday. The police said: "When he left home he was well wrapped up, but we are now very concerned for his safety."

A man was found dead in a snowdrift near Midsomer Norton, Avon.

Police and emergency services launched a big operation to try to find motorists who might still be trapped in their cars in the aftermath of the blizzards.

At least one driver is missing. Mr Glen Biss, of Milborne Port, Somerset, vanished four days ago in his Austin Princess car.

Police again appealed to sightseers to stay away from the area and not hamper rescue work.

The man found dead in his car near Port Talbot, West Glamorgan, on Monday was identified yesterday as Mr Jack Harrison, aged 52, of Stoke-on-Trent.

More than 200 people remained stranded at the village of Newton, near Porthcawl.

In the Vale of Glamorgan helicopters searched for people in distress, and farmers dug out live sheep and newly born lambs from huge snowdrifts. But there were fears of huge losses of animals.

There were heavy snowfalls in Scotland yesterday and the AA reported 11 main roads blocked, mostly in the North and the Borders. The main A9 route to the North was blocked at Blair Atholl and Kingussie.

Forecast, page 2

Paper that plans tomorrow's news today

From Michael Binyon
Moscow, Feb 21

Tomorrow *Pravda* will devote three columns on its front page to the talks between President Assad of Syria and President Brezhnev. Whether the talks go well or badly is immaterial: the space was planned yesterday before the Syrian leader had even arrived in this country.

To a Western journalist such management of the news seems extraordinary, but in no sense is *Pravda* a Western newspaper.

"Our aim is propaganda", said Mr Viktor Afanasyev, the Editor-in-Chief, "the propaganda of our party and state. We do not hide this. We are clearly a party newspaper". Propaganda in Soviet society, of course, has positive connotations.

As the central organ of the Communist Party of the Soviet Union, founded and first edited by Lenin, *Pravda* is the most highly regarded and authoritative newspaper in the Soviet Union. It is also the largest selling newspaper in the world, with 10,700,000 copies sold each day and an estimated total readership of 50 million people.

"We work under the leadership of the Central Committee", Mr Afanasyev told a group of foreign journalists.

"There is a mistaken idea in the West that all our material has to be approved. It is not so.

"The Central Committee trusts us and we make the paper so that it answers the needs of the party and country, conforming to party policy. In the West there are great newspapers, but they express the interests of very limited circles. We express the will and policy of our huge party and huge country. No other paper can claim to speak on behalf of so many people."

Certainly *Pravda* serves a huge area. It is printed in 45 towns in the Soviet Union, 29 of them receiving the plates by telegraph and those in the Far East by satellite. The first edition, serving small cities and the provinces, goes to press at 6 pm; the deadline for Moscow and other main cities is 11 pm. But *Pravda* works well ahead even of this early deadline: up to 60 per cent of the material is planned in advance, and the bulk of the work each day is for the edition two days ahead.

The paper maintains 60 correspondents within the Soviet Union and 50 abroad, a generous proportion for a daily

Continued on page 7, col 2

Mr Callaghan and Mrs Thatcher in new exchange on immigration

By Our Political Staff

Immigration and race relations were again the subject of angry exchanges yesterday between Mrs Thatcher, Leader of the Opposition, Mr William Whitelaw, chief Conservative spokesman on home affairs, and Mr Callaghan, the Prime Minister.

Mrs Thatcher described criticism of herself by Mr Rees, Home Secretary, on Monday night, reported in later editions of *The Times* yesterday, as "absolute nonsense". Mr Callaghan, in a message to the Labour candidate in the Ilford North by-election, said some Tory leaders were preaching a doctrine that would cause conflict and confrontation.

Mr Whitelaw, who was speaking at Newbury Park, Ilford, said that like all other Conservatives he deeply resented the charge made by Mr Rees that Mrs Thatcher was making racial hatred respectable. It was a manufactured, artificial and thoroughly unjustified charge.

"I believe that he has made a grave error in lending the authority of his great office to make respectable the chorus of misleading abuse we have lately been hearing on this subject", Mr Whitelaw said.

He recalled that last April, speaking in Flint, East, Mr Rees had urged Mrs Thatcher to speak out on immigration because silence would be harmful to race relations. Now, for some reason, he had changed his tone.

"Perhaps he is using a speech of this sort as a smokescreen for his own failures in office", Mr Whitelaw said. "The truth is that his actions reveal a damaging lack of initiative based on almost shattering complacency, whether over crime, immigration or child pornography."

Mr Whitelaw said that at a time of rising crime, violence and vandalism people in London were crying out for more police protection. Mr Rees sat idly by in the Home Office while the number of officers in the Metropolitan Police fell in 1977, largely due to dissatisfaction with status, pay and conditions.

Mrs Thatcher defended her past statements on immigration during a visit to the by-election constituency. She said she stood by all that she had said in her answers on television, during a radio programme, and what she said to the Young Conservatives at Harrogate.

Mr Callaghan said Labour was working to preserve Britain's tolerant society, which was just and fair towards all people regardless of creed or colour. "We shall not allow that tolerance to be taken advantage of by vandals and thugs."

He said that hooliganism in the streets or elsewhere would be firmly dealt with by the courts in the interests of all.

Another attack on Mr Rees was made by Mr William Shelton, Conservative MP for Streatham, who played a leading part in the campaign for the election of Mrs Thatcher as leader of the party. He said that Mr Rees's "disgraceful speech" on Monday was unworthy of his high office. "I question whether he remains fit to be Home Secretary".

"We must have a year's moratorium on all immigration, except on exceptional compassionate grounds", Mr Shelton said.

Labour accused, page 2

Leader of Egyptian raid 'thought negotiations taking too long'

From David Watts
Cairo, Feb 21

The leader of the Egyptian raid on Larnaca airport said tonight he regarded the operation as a complete success in spite of the heavy loss of life. Fifteen Egyptian commandos were killed and 17 wounded; seven Cypriots were also injured. The Egyptian dead are to be buried tomorrow with full military honours.

Explaining the gap between the arrival of the Egyptian Air Force Hercules transport and the beginning of the operation, Brigadier Nabil Shukri said he had given the Cypriots 90 minutes to negotiate with the two gunmen before sending his men into action.

"When I found that the negotiations were prolonged unnecessarily, I decided to go ahead with my orders", he said. It was clear the two gunmen were not responding to the Cypriots' suggestions "since they took such a long time".

Answering a question he admitted he did not know the outcome of the negotiations

The brigadier's account did nothing to clear up the basic point at issue between Cyprus and Egypt: whether the Egyptians received permission to land an armed group of troops on Cypriot soil.

Mr Moneim de Sawy, the Minister of Information, did nothing to clear up the question last night when he was asked.

"Of course", he said, "What would be in the airplane? Some pastries? Some sandwiches? It was very clear that there would be people in the airplane."

The Egyptian request for the extradition of the two men still stands, but it is hard to see how it can be satisfied now that the men are to go on trial in Cyprus.

The Egyptians fear that, as has happened with countries in a far better position to resist extremist pressure, honour will be satisfied for the Cypriots by a trial and subsequent expulsion of the men to a country prepared to take them.

The Egyptians say it is important for them to find out who was behind the men and whether they represent part of a larger rejectionist plot

'Restore ties' plea: President Kyprianou, urging Arab leaders to leave Cyprus out of their conflicts, today appealed to President Sadat to work with him on restoring the close relationship which prevailed between their countries before the airport battle.

"We do not wish Cyprus to be turned into an arena for the settlement of Arab disputes", he said in Nicosia.—Reuter.

Cypriot permission: Mr Costas Ashiotis, the Cyprus High Commissioner in London, said the Cypriot authorities at Larnaca airport had given permission for the Egyptian C130 Hercules to remain on the tarmac while negotiations continued with the hijackers (Our Foreign Staff writes).

The aircraft was not ordered to take off, nor was it asked to remain. The only instruction was a firm one that the Egyptians should not interfere in any way with the talks taking place with the hijackers.

Mr Ashiotis said that, after it was discovered the Hercules had arrived full of commandos and not an Egyptian government minister as the Cypriots had been led to believe, the commandos had been asked to remain inside the plane.

"Left to die": Mr Youssef Sibai, editor-in-chief of the Egyptian newspaper *Al-Ahram*, lay dying and neglected under a white tablecloth in the corridor of the hotel where he was shot on Saturday, a newspaper report in Nicosia said today.

Mr Richard Cowell, a businessman attending a wedding reception in the hotel, was quoted by the *Cyprus Mail* as saying he decided on impulse to look at the body 30 minutes after Mr Sibai was shot.

"I felt his pulse", he said. "It was weak and his hand was hot and feverish. I knew he was not dead. Blood was thick around the wounds. He was still alive.

"He was dying, but no one seemed to give him a thought."

Mr Sibai was shot in front of a bookshop in one of the hotel corridors. A member of the hotel staff covered his body with the white tablecloth, assuming he had been killed outright.—UPI.

Mr Begin to take top ministers on US visit

From Michael Knipe
Jerusalem, Feb 21

Mr Begin, the Israeli Prime Minister, disclosed today that he will take both Mr Dyan, his Foreign Minister, and Mr Weizman, his Defence Minister, when he goes to Washington next month for talks with President Carter on the Middle East peace negotiations.

Mr Begin spent nearly two hours this evening with Mr Alfred Atherton, Assistant Secretary of State, who is mediating between the Israeli and Egyptian Governments. The American envoy leaves tomorrow for Cairo.

The legality of Israeli settlements in the occupied Arab territories is sure to be raised in Washington. The Israeli Cabinet is divided on the issue, with some ministers, led by Mr Weizman, arguing for a long halt in settlement development to foster peace negotiations.

Mr Ariel Sharon, the minister in charge of settlement development, believes development should continue as a security measure. The Cabinet is to continue its settlement debate on Sunday, when a decision is expected.

Britain wants more top jobs in EEC

Mr Christopher Tugendhat, one of the two British EEC Commissioners, has upset Whitehall by promoting a Frenchmen to an important Brussels post, ignoring advice from the Treasury and the Bank of England. The Government feels that Britain is not getting its fair share of the top EEC jobs and that neither Mr Tugendhat nor Mr Roy Jenkins, the President of the Commission, is doing much to put matters right. Mr Tugendhat believes he chose the best man for the post Page 6

Chancellor's denial

Mr Healey, Chancellor of the Exchequer, defending the use of discretionary sanctions against companies in breach of pay policy guidelines, denied that the Government intended to apply pressure on employers to break contracts. "That would be unlawful", he said. Page 4

More Ulster arrests as victims are buried

The grief and anger felt throughout Northern Ireland at the La Mon House bombing was given public expression as the first two of the 12 victims were buried. Meanwhile 13 more people were arrested in another security operation in Belfast. Of the 20 republicans arrested after the bombing eight were freed Page 2

More constituencies

The number of parliamentary constituencies in Northern Ireland should be increased from 12 to 17, the all-party Speaker's conference has recommended. It says, however, that the boundary commission should have powers to vary that number to 16 or 18 Page 6

Bank severs pact

A blow to industrial relations in banking was dealt when Midland Bank announced the unilateral termination of a procedural agreement with the National Union of Bank Employees. The decision centres on an inter-union row and Nube immediately condemned the bank and warned of possible industrial action Page 21

Australia bars blind girl

A Nottingham family has been refused permission to settle in Australia because one of the children is blind. The Immigration Minister said he could not approve the family's entry because of the long-term cost of providing the girl, now aged 12, with a blind invalid pension Page 8

Secret drug debate

The United States Senate went into secret session to discuss allegations that General Torrijos, the Panamanian leader, had been involved in drug smuggling. The White House fears that the debate, instigated by opponents of the Panama Canal treaties, could imperil their ratification, for which a two-thirds majority is required Page 7

Fund is KGB target

A KGB campaign to destroy the fund set up by Alexander Solzhenitsyn to help the families of political prisoners in the Soviet Union is being extended to the West. Mrs Natalia Solzhenitsyn, the fund's president, says KGB agents in Switzerland are trying to unearth names and details Page 8

S Africa may open theatres to blacks

Recommendations are soon to be put before the South African Cabinet that opera houses, theatres and other places of entertainment hitherto open to whites only should allow in all races. It is expected that such places would do this by applying for "international status" Page 7

Football results

Gillingham 1, Chester 0.
Preston 3, Oxford Utd 2.

Trade outlook: The Prime Minister has been in touch with President Carter about ways of stimulating world trade 2

Hairdressing: Women supporting a Bill for compulsory registration of hairdressers tell of horrifying results from their visits to salons 4

Madrid: Strike wave worsens throughout Spain, making an estimated 100,000 workers idle 6

been on the right, appealing to the conservative middle class, *The Guardian* has
been at the opposite end of the spectrum, on the moralistic left, appealing to the
young intelligensia. London's third, but best-known elite paper, *The Times* has
always been considered the Establishment paper, a daily to read to keep up
with the affairs of empire.

In the past decade, under the able, progressive editorship of William Rees-
Mogg, *The Times* has maintained its distinctive role as a national Establishment
paper, while taking the lead in finding a new role for Britain. It moved to more
intellectual debate in its correspondence columns and on its op-ed page. It extended its influence to the opinion-leaders of western Europe by reporting European as well as British elections, government and law. It became more lively
and controversial, a better-balanced journal. The new policy generated payoffs:
one-third of the influential of Britain and Europe whose names appear in the *International Who's Who* recently said they read *The Times* regularly, while another third read it "from time to time."

Unfortunately, in the past decade, *The Times* new look has been over-
shadowed by financial problems, eclipsed by production strife and finally halted
completely on November 30, 1978, for an indefinite period by an impasse between the paper's managers and its trade union workers.*

During the fierce circulation battles of the sixties and seventies between
Britain's national dailies, the big papers, such as *The Times,* were forced to
spend millions on TV and other advertising and on public relations to keep up
with the competition. The battle was reminiscent of the 1930's when newspapers almost destroyed themselves financially to win the promotional race. Recently, the situation was rendered especially critical because, while promotional
expenses mounted, the number of potential purchasers of national dailies was
decreasing. To add to *The Times* and other newspapers' woes, continued inflation has sent the costs of newsprint and production soaring.

The circulation battle has been complicated by labor unrest. Printers who
fear that new automation processes will make them redundant have engaged in
a series of strikes and slowdowns at the precise times when *The Times* needed a
circulation increase to make ends meet. As a result, during the past decade *The
Times* and its counterpart *The Sunday Times* have occasionally been at the
point of near closure. That problem so threatened the financial security of Britain's 200 news agents and 30,000 shopkeepers who retail the papers that they
marched on Fleet Street in protest against non-delivery. In the process, *The
Times* suffered financially. Circulation fell from near 450,000 in the sixties to
284,000 in early 1978. Already in 1968, the paper's losses reached a staggering
£2 million sterling. At the end of 1971, the paper announced, almost with pride
that it had lost only £1.2 million for the year. Its more recent deficit has been
about £600,000 annually.

---

* As *The World's Great Dailies* went to press, prospects were bright for an early settlement of the
ten-month-old strike. In an exclusive interview with the *Christian Science Monitor*, *Times* editor
William Rees-Mogg explained the significant progress made during his paper's latest talks with the
seven unions and 60 bargaining units involved in the shutdown and expressed confidence his paper
will be back in publication shortly.

In 1978, the fury of the bitter dispute between the newspapers and their production workers mounted, causing staggering circulation and financial losses. Then the Thomson Organization, Ltd., owners of *The Times* since 1959, forced a showdown by giving unions until November 30th to reform work procedures and allow introduction of new technology or the paper would close down. In turn, *The Times* would increase wages and worker benefits. But the workers refused to negotiate at all unless management revoked its threat of suspension.[2] The deadline came and the paper's publication was suspended in spite of a last-ditch effort by the House of Commons to prevent the stoppage, but Kenneth Lord Thomson, the president of *Times* Newspapers, said there was no intention of closing permanently.[3]

The production strife even affected editorial staff freedom. For example, *The Times* and *The Sunday Times* were closed briefly in 1977 because the editors wanted to print the full truth about the situation. Earlier, the printers' union had used tough tactics to stop *The Times*' publication of stories about union featherbedding in the newspaper industry, first demanding deletion of the stories, then when that failed, seeking insertion of their disclaimer on each story. But *The Times* editors stuck by their guns and published the original articles in full. Commenting on the dispute, Rees-Mogg made the kind of statement that has characterized *The Times*' independent spirit for two centuries: "*The Times* will not allow either censorship by subtraction from, or censorship by addition to, copy."[4]

The Times began in 1785 as a small sheet called *The Daily Universal Register*. After three years, its founder and editor, John Walter, changed its name to *The Times*. Walter wanted his paper to be "a register of the times, a faithful recorder of all species of intelligence and independent of any party," but, because of his financial problems, the paper fell far short, even stooping at times to government-subsidized and edited news and to sensational scandal.[5]

Then, at the beginning of the nineteenth century, John Walter II, the founder's son took over the paper and gave it a new journalistic direction. He desired that it should serve Britain's rapidly rising middle class and become something more than it had been. With his editor, Thomas Barnes, who was to take over the editorial reins in 1819 and move on to fame, Walter developed *The Times* into an important organ of public opinion and political influence. Under Barnes, *The Times* won its reputation as the "Thunderer." Barnes, a great liberal and one of England's most powerful men, responsible for many reforms, developed *The Times* into a strong independent paper, a leader in influence and circulation. He perfected a technique that has served the paper well—continuing contact with the right people. In 1815, the circulation was 5,000; six years later it had doubled.

---

[2] "Showdown on Fleet Street," *Time* (December 4, 1978), p. 77. Compare: "*The Times* (London) at Closing Date," *Christian Science Monitor* (December 1, 1978), p. 4.
[3] "Last-Ditch Commons Move to Avert *Times* Suspension," *The Times* (November 30, 1978), p. 1.
[4] "Printers Stop *The Times* for a Day," *IPI Report*, 26:2 (February, 1977), p. 5.
[5] Kenneth E. Olson, *The History Makers: The Press of Europe from its Beginnings through 1965* (Baton Rouge: Louisiana State University Press, 1966), p. 12.

By the time the great John T. Delane took over as editor in 1841, *The Times* had become the semi-official spokesman for the government itself, irrespective of what party was in power. Under Delane the paper improved its position, and it was said that there was no state secret safe from its hardworking reporters. By mid-century, *The Times* was the largest and most influential daily in the world. Abraham Lincoln once said he knew of nothing, with the possible exception of the Mississippi River, more powerful than *The Times*.[6] Disraeli spoke of two British ambassadors in every world capital—one sent by the Queen and one by *The Times*. In 1856 the British Government learned of the Russian acceptance of peace proposals ending the Crimean War by reading *The Times*.

Delane himself did very little writing, but he stamped his ideas on the whole paper. He made the decisions on everything that went into its columns. He had a flair for turning colorless articles into journalistic masterpieces. More than any of his predecessors, he understood the impact of a newspaper on political thinking and used *The Times* skillfully in this area. Governmental leaders, foreign and domestic, sought his friendship. Although Delane is generally praised and considered the greatest of all British editors, some feel he has been overrated. For example, Brian Inglis, writing in London's *Spectator* accused Delane of "getting infatuated with ministers and doing exactly what they told him." What is probably worse, Delane is said on occasion to have permitted the ministers to write editorials for the paper.[7]

The Times made some notable contributions during the nineteenth century. Probably the greatest of these was the paper's infusion into British journalism of the idea that a newspaper was independent, responsible to public opinion and not to government. *The Times* expanded its national coverage greatly, introduced important production equipment and employed the world's first war correspondent, William Howard Russell, whose critical reports of British management of the Crimean War helped bring down the Cabinet in 1855 and led to a needed Army reorganization. Although Russell's reports angered the Army and Government, little could be done about *The Times* since it had developed such a powerful following among opinion leaders throughout the country. The paper scored another first during the Crimean War by collecting funds for charitable purposes—in this case, money for British wounded in the war. The reporting of the Crimean War boosted circulation from 50,000 to 70,000. Without a doubt the second and third quarters of the nineteenth century were the Golden Age of *The Times*.

The age of Delane lasted from 1841–1887, but the drive of the great editor slackened during his last years, and with it the great period of *The Times*. In 1877 Delane was succeeded as editor by Thomas Chenery, who was followed by George E. Buckle in 1884. From 1848 John Walter III was publisher; when he died in 1894, he was succeeded by Arthur Walter.

In 1908, *The Times*, which had been suffering financially and was about to go under, was purchased and rescued from its economic slump by Alfred Harmsworth (Lord Northcliffe). Arthur Walter died in 1910 and was succeeded

[6] John Hohenberg, *Foreign Correspondence* (New York: Columbia University Press, 1964), p. 62.
[7] "The Thunderer," *The Spectator*, London (July 10, 1959), p. 23.

by his son, John Walter IV, as chairman of The Times Publishing Company. For the new owner, Lord Northcliffe, the purchase of the influential paper was the fulfillment of a long ambition. Northcliffe was ambitious, and he had strong views about journalism; he thought of news as "what someone somewhere wants to suppress, and all else is advertising."[8] But Northcliffe did not fit well with *The Times,* and for the first time he was frustrated by a journalistic failure. He even brought in Geoffrey Dawson as editor to try to get some order into *The Times,* but he really was his own editor, meddling in every department just as he had been doing on his *Daily Mail* and the *Mirror.* Lord Northcliffe died in 1922, and it is generally thought that because of his tendency to personally supervise everything and his affinity for sensation, he would have ruined the paper's reputation had he lived much longer. To his favor, it must be said that he did make some much-needed organizational changes, increased efficiency in certain departments and kept the paper financially solvent.

In 1919, editor Geoffrey Dawson left *The Times* after a dispute with Northcliffe, and Henry W. Steed took over the post. On Northcliffe's death, *The Times'* ownership passed into the hands of John Jacob Astor who, in association with John Walter IV, set up a Trust to run the paper. Dawson returned to the paper as editor and remained until 1941. He was followed by R. M. B. Ward and then W. F. Carey. In 1952 Sir William Haley became editor of *The Times* and by 1966 had given the paper new life and had brought back to it much of the prestige it had enjoyed in pre-Northcliffe days.

Haley came to *The Times* from the British Broadcasting Company where he was director-general; he moved to the editorship of the paper at the right time, for the image of the old "Thunderer" was in need of repair. It was often referred to as the "Whimperer" and its circulation had dropped to 230,000. Under Haley, *The Times* grew steadily, although its financial condition was not always what its owners would wish. Haley did not abandon the paper's traditional values, but he did change it, brightening somewhat both its physical appearance and its contents. As editor, he consistently attempted to give the paper more spirit, but he also insisted on its traditional emphases on accuracy, truth and careful reporting. Often referred to as "the doyen of London editors," he made some cosmetic changes, such as introducing photographs, simplifying the nameplate, taking advertisements off the front page. Perhaps his most important change was to instill a new vitality into the editorials, many of which he wrote himself. British journalist and critic Henry Fairlie called *The Times* editorials perhaps the most articulate editorializing in either Britain or the United States which were at their best when Haley wrote them. Fairlie said the leaders had "a primitive force, which sweeps one through them, even when one disagrees with what they say, and leaves one feeling six inches taller."[9]

Haley, who actually began his career as a telephone copytaker on *The Times* in 1920, gave the paper a new vigor, edge and first-class news reporting. Under him, *The Times* gave few by-lines and insisted on a large degree of anonymity, but certain of its staffers, such as Louis Heren (now deputy editor) be-

---

[8] Smith, *op. cit.,* p. 208.
[9] Henry Fairlie, "Anglo-American Differences," *Encounter,* 26:6 (June, 1966), p. 83.

came recognized leaders in British journalism. Haley probably did more than any previous editor to improve the quality of his paper's foreign coverage. An American content analysis of British papers in 1966 showed that *The Times* devoted 20.8 percent of its news space to foreign news, and a year before another study showed its foreign news took up 19.65 percent of its non-advertisement space.[10]

Some called Haley "a latter-day Victorian." He certainly was relentless, with a boundless appetite for work and a strong streak of puritanism that came out in his biting Profumo leader, "It *is* a moral issue." But he was no reactionary in his journalistic philosophy. In a speech he gave in 1965, he declared:

> For a newspaper to have a sense of responsibility did not mean it should blindly accept that authority was always right, however well-meaning. Responsibility was not a hesitation to be revolutionary, a preference for the official over the unofficial or for accepted ideas over those seemingly unacceptable. It was an honest searching for truth. . . . The press should be part of the general educational process that is going on all the time.[11]

Under Haley, *The Times* remained a paper of the Establishment, but definitely independent and not the Conservative spokesman it sometimes had been accused of being. Haley left his editorial chair in 1967 to become editor of *The Encyclopaedia Britannica,* but his influence on the paper continues.

Late in 1966, Lord Thomson purchased 85 percent of *The Times* stock, with the remaining 15 percent retained by Gavin Astor, whose family had owned the paper since 1912. Though some feared *The Times* would lose much of its old freedom and quality as part of Roy Thomson's press empire, that did not happen. Thomson promised at the time he became owner, "all my life I have believed in the independence of editors, and the new editor-in-chief (Denis Hamilton) has been guaranteed absolute freedom from interference."[12] Thomson lived up to his word. He applied himself to keeping *The Times* a quality journal, while encouraging his staff to make it more widely appealing. He successfully merged *The Times* and *The Sunday Times,* action for which he has been commended since the papers had been similiar editorially- and philosophically-speaking, for years. Under Thomson's ownership, circulation eventually rose to well over 400,000 in the late 1960's.

When Thomson came to *The Times,* Denis Hamilton became the paper's editor-in-chief. As the former editor of *The Sunday Times,* Hamilton was interested in the values *The Times* upheld, and he set about to increase coverage, enlarge the paper's scope and size, and get more correspondents. Hamilton strongly supported the merger of *The Sunday Times* and *The Times,* foresight which the passing of time has proven wise. He has staunchly defended the paper's editorial freedom and prerogatives in its battle with the printers' unions.[13]

[10] Jim A. Hart, "Foreign News in U.S. and English Daily Papers: A Comparison," *Journalism Quarterly,* 43:3 (Autumn, 1966), p. 444.
[11] London *Times* (November 30, 1965).
[12] "Thomson Takes *The Times,*" *Time* (October 7, 1966), p. 61. Compare, "Thomson Acquires *Times* of London," *Editor & Publisher* (October 8, 1966), p. 11.
[13] "Britain's Battling Press," *Time* (December 2, 1974), p. 64.

By their actions and policies, Thomson and Hamilton indeed did improve coverage and secure greater editorial independence.

In 1967, a truly competent, colorful and remarkable man, William Rees-Mogg became editor of *The Times*. While at Oxford, he reputedly read himself to sleep with *The Financial Times*. His humor and his ability to turn a clever phrase add zest to his views, as for instance, his wry remark on *The Times* as an Establishment paper: "We were founded about four years before the French Revolution—an event of which we strongly disapproved."[14] A patrician with a taste for good living, he has also exercised good leadership, making policy decisions and trusting the details to his staff. Once the basic approach to a story was decided—a decision in which he participated—Rees-Mogg believed that, for the sake of high morale, a team approach was best: "It is preferable to gather a smallish team, small enough to be in continuous touch with each, and each having substantial independence in his own area. . . ."[15] Politically, Rees-Mogg is a liberal Tory, who has fought—often unsuccessfully—for the Conservative Party. And he is a firm, though unobtrusive Roman Catholic who has tried to infuse his paper with simple, non-denominational values. As he explains, "The paper is Christian rather than non-Christian as a collective entity, and this colors its judgment."[16]

As a progressive editor, Rees-Mogg tried to continue his newspaper's tradition of being the voice of the British people when a clear national function could be performed by speaking out. However, he wished *The Times* to be independent, unburdened with national responsibility. He has been an untiring seeker after truth in the time-tested methods of sifting and evaluating all materials objectively. He has shunned emotional language because it could not help in the discovery and presentation of the truth. He has insisted on quality writing and reporting; hence, under him, *The Times* remained serious and austere. He declared his editorial policy to be: "Ruthless in publishing important matters; considerate of privacy on trivial matters," and on arriving at editorial decisions based on that policy, his attitude was, "When in doubt, apply historic criteria: Will this still seem important in a year's or a century's time?"[17]

Under Rees-Mogg, *The Times* has aimed at readers who wanted serious and thorough coverage of national, economic and international affairs. Its contents confirmed that goal. Peering out from its gray front-page visage marked by but a single picture, *The Times'* initial page each day presented an average of 22 stories, mixed about half-and-half national and international. On an average day, one could find another three or four pages of "Home News," a page for Parliament and news of national government, two or three pages of "Overseas News," plus a page of news from western Europe, and four to six of financial and business stories and information. The paper's editors have indicated the breakdown for these three types of news in relationship to all space in the typical 28–32 page paper was as follows: international news, over 10 percent; na-

[14] Hebblethwaite, *op. cit.*, p. 239.
[15] *Ibid.*, p. 240.
[16] *Ibid.*, p. 239.
[17] William Rees-Mogg, Editor, *The Times*, in response to questionnaire, dated February 14, 1978.

tional, nearly 14 percent; and business, about 19.5 percent. A staff of 250 journalists covered all aspects of the national news.[18]

The paper has excelled in regular feature columns such as "Bureaucracy in Britain." Its special features have been numerous. In terms of breadth and depth of criticism, *The Times* Literary Supplement has stood unchallenged. High caliber reviews of current books in Russian, French, Italian and German have been given space commensurate with that accorded reviews of books in English. Regularly, one page has provided a guide to entertainment in London, another information on the courts, science, obituaries and important social events. Advertising has taken up about one-third of the total space, with half- or full-page color advertisements appearing twice each week. The personals which once graced the front page (*The Times* was the last London paper to abandon the practice) were moved to the back, but readers still have found them as surprising, readable, humorous and lively as in the past.

Under Rees-Mogg and earlier under Hamilton, foreign coverage was increased and strengthened. Both reported western Europe thoroughly. A network of 20 full-time foreign correspondents and 40 part-timers was distributed worldwide. The work of these reporters was supplemented by wire services from six sources—Reuters, AP, UPI, PA, Extel and AFP—plus the New York *Times* Syndicated Service. Foreign editorship was for a number of years under the direction of Louis Heren, who earlier had been a Washington correspondent for *The Times* for ten years.

The editorial staff has enjoyed latitude in its service with *The Times* under Hamilton and Rees-Mogg. Louis Heren, first the paper's well-known Washington correspondent, then its foreign editor and more recently its deputy editor, observed of his own experience with *The Times:* "I was never told what to do and in accordance with the tradition of *The Times*, my copy was never rewritten."[19] In a book entitled *Growing Up Poor on The Times* he has recently published, Heren reflects further on the freedom he and his colleagues enjoyed and notes that, in a very real way, the editorial staff felt the paper belonged to them and not to the proprietors. This freedom has generated a strong sense of responsibility towards *The Times*, so much so that there has never been a question about editorial staff loyalties during the recent labor disputes and subsequent suspension of the paper.

The leader and op-ed pages have always been *The Times'* greatest strengths. But under Rees-Mogg, the editorials became more incisive, more forceful, more controversial than ever before. They became highly polished and deceptively sharp, took sides, but remained eminently fair because the editors tried to understand all sides of issues before writing. Some of them have been written by journalist, broadcaster and economics expert Rees-Mogg himself. The op-ed pages have delighted in intellectual debates. The famous correspondence columns, long one of the most popular aspects of the paper, also thrived and improved under Rees-Mogg.

Many observers have felt that Rees-Mogg, by his innovations, was moving

[18] *Ibid.*

[19] Louis Heren, *"Fleet Street and the Free Press," Saturday Review* (June, 11, 1977), p. 24.

The Times to the left, away from being a paper of the Establishment and a paper of record. Nothing could be further from the truth. As Rees-Mogg himself explains, the paper was simply following the "healthy non-conformism" of previous editors, and has been saying the same thing it always has, but in a different way. In fact, Rees-Mogg has talked considerably about his paper's anti-totalitarianism stance, which at its base has opposed anti-democratic principles and has stood on independence and social democratic principles. Rees-Mogg himself once described *The Times* position this way: "We stand to the left in terms of welfare; to the right in resisting state power."[20]

Throughout its history, *The Times* has been recognized for its thoughtful and interpretive articles, for its calm and rational discourses, and for its selective, but thorough news coverage. Under Rees-Mogg, the paper continued, as it had in the past, to stand "for the provision of trustworthy information and reasonable comment."[21] In the past, too, the paper has often shown remarkable foresight in seeing the future importance of an event or a speech; it has recognized the importance of "ideas" long before "newsworthy" activities emerged from them. A good example of this "intuitive reporting" occurred when *The Times* became the only newspaper to publish in full Dean Acheson's speech outlining the Marshall Plan weeks before the plan was officially announced. With typical wryness, Rees-Mogg upheld the importance of such foresight to *The Times* under his editorial care: "We are only unique in that we invented the idea."[22]

As its editor, Rees-Mogg helped *The Times* retain its finest values; at the same time, he made his paper more progressive, questioning, energetic and intelligent. At present, the bitter labor-management dispute is denying the public the benefits of the excellent journal Rees-Mogg and his staff have made of *The Times*. British readers, with a touch of the stoic endurance that got them through the grim days of World War II, mourn the temporary loss of their paper, but await its return. Their attitude is epitomized by a Sheffield reader's letter to the paper upon its suspension: "A day without *The Times* is a desolate day, but if you must leave us for a time in order to put your house in order, so be it. We will be waiting when you return."[23]

Meantime, management insists the paper's suspension is only temporary. On the occasion of its last issue before suspension, issue number 60,472, it apologized to its readers for the break and editorialized, "It is quite certain that *The Times* will return."[24] When it does return, thanks to Rees-Mogg and his staff, *The Times* will possess the potential to assume with renewed vigor its place of undisputed leadership both among Britain's quality national dailies and in the world of elite journalism at large.

[20] Rees-Mogg questionnaire.
[21] Rees-Mogg questionnaire.
[22] *Ibid.*
[23] "Showdown on Fleet Street," *op. cit.*
[24] "There Will Be an Interval," London *Times* (November 30, 1978), p. 17.

The Times of India

(INDIA)

A VISITOR EMERGING FROM the Victoria Terminal in the Westernized seaport city of Bombay cannot fail to notice the massive oriental-looking edifice of *The Times of India*. He will see clusters of people looking through the glass panels at the roaring rotary presses bringing out a newspaper which has become a kind of national institution in India. If he could peer down the corridor of time he would marvel at the stupendous expansion and progress made by this newspaper since its beginnings some 140 years ago.

Published today in three Indian cities—Bombay, New Delhi, and Ahmedabad—but with its main offices in Bombay, *The Times of India* is the oldest of the English-language dailies of the country[1] and the one with the largest circulation. It was founded in 1838 by a group of Bombay businessmen.

From its early days as a struggling little weekly and daily (it began daily publication in 1851) the newspaper has taken pride in its comprehensive news coverage and dignified expression of editorial opinion. Its circulation daily (and also on Sundays) stands at 375,000. From the beginning the newspaper has been aimed primarily at the English educated intelligentsia, including businessmen, executives in the corporate sector, leaders in the academic world, government officials, and other leaders of public opinion.

The editor of *The Times of India*, Girilal Jain, believes that such factors as objective reporting, the ability to view various sides of a question with fairness and responsibility, the quality of writing, the scope and depth of news coverage have led the paper down the path of quality journalism through the years and account for its reputation at home and abroad.[2]

The newspaper is a champion of freedom and integrity in India, the well-being of all segments of Indian society, international amity, civil liberties; and it opposes vigorously tyranny and bureaucratic corruption, high-handedness and bungling in government. At least these noble guidelines are put forth as the paper's by its editor, Girilal Jain, who sees *The Times of India* as a "liberal journal," supporting private enterprise without advocating a policy of laissez-faire or being opposed to the public sector as such. It is a journal which avoids publishing anything which, in its view, would incite regionalism, castism and communalism. For example, in case of a riot it does not name the communities in-

---

[1] Actually the paper took its present name, *The Times of India,* in May, 1861, having been known earlier as *The Bombay Times*.
[2] Letter and questionnaire from Girilal Jain, editor, to authors, dated April 3, 1978.

REGD. NO. D. (C) 198
Published from New Delhi, Bombay and Ahmedabad.
ESTABLISHED 1838
AIR SURCHARGE — Rajasthan, Patna, Gauhati & beyond: 10 paise
Ahmedabad, Calcutta & beyond by rail;   10 paise
Kochmandu, Southern States & beyond Calcutta by air; 10 paise

THE TIMES OF INDIA

Rail fares, freight rate unchanged

New deal for the staff

Concession, amenities for second class travel

By Our Special Correspondent

NEW DELHI, February 21.

NO change in passenger fares or freight rates have been proposed in the railway budget, which was presented to Parliament today by the Railway Minister, Mr Madhu Dandavate. This is the second year in succession that the rates have remained unchanged.

Indeed, a series of minor concessions to second class travellers have been announced, and passenger amenities are going to be improved substantially to even away traffic from the first to the second class. The railways are also going ahead with several new lines, including the first leg of the West Coast Konkan railway. Safety measures are being strengthened to prevent sabotage, and the employment conditions

of staff are being improved in a number of ways.

The new emphasis on the common man rather than the money-making aspect of budgeting is in keeping with the Janata Party's philosophy. Mr Dandavate has been able to avoid any revision in fares and freight rates thanks to buoyant revenue, which will yield an estimated surplus of Rs. 89.2 crores in the current financial year, and Rs. 65.43 crores in 1978-79. Revenue earning goods traffic is expected to reach 214 million tonnes this year to 222 million tonnes next year.

The sleeper charge for second class passengers will henceforth be a flat Rs. 3 per journey, regardless on the number of nights spent on board. Till now the charge has been Rs. 5 for the first night and Rs. 3 to Rs. 5 for subsequent nights.

The surcharge on super-fast express trains for second class passengers has been cut from Rs. 1.05 together for certain trains no longer regarded as super-fast.

The full concession, hitherto available for only nine months of the year (July to March), will now be available throughout the year, and should promote tourism.

In response to the public demand for cheap food while trains all orders will be for three standard

major long-distance trains. Food packets will be supplied at just Re. 1 each, and will be of three varieties to suit the differing tastes of people from different parts of the country. Normal catering arrangements will continue.

To improve the lot of the ordinary traveller, all second class coaches in fast trains will be equipped with cushioned seats as well as berths. A new prototype coach is being developed with six toilets instead of four, more fans and better water supply arrangements. Twelve double decker coaches are expected to be produced this year, and will be pressed into service from April 1978.

At the same time it has been decided to stop making any more first class air-conditioned coaches, and to phase out this class progressively. Mr Dandavate said it was the sum of the railways ultimately to have only one predominant type of accommodation, and within a few years the improved second-class amenities should attract passengers who travelled first class at present. Selected stations are also going to be provided with superior facilities such as toilets, lighting and refreshment rooms, at a cost of Rs. 5 crores.

It is proposed to increase the accommodation on long-distance trains to the tune of 200 to 300 seats per train by rationalising the types of coaches in service. At present 14 different kinds of coaches are in service, but in future almost all orders will be for three standard

Continued on Page 5 column 1

The Railway Minister, Mr. Madhu Dandavate, giving last-minute touches to the Railway Budget at Parliament House on Tuesday. — TOI photograph

Janata meal at Re 1 per packet

NEW DELHI, February 21 (Samachar): The railways have decided to supply "Janata khana" (snacks) on all major long-distance trains at Re. 1 per food packet.

Announcing this in the budget speech, the Railway Minister, Mr Madhu Dandavate, said this was being done in response to the demand of the travelling public for supply of food at cheaper rates.

Bihar CM's order irks ministers

By Our Correspondent

PATNA, February 21: There is resentment among cabinet ministers of Bihar at an order reported to have been issued by the Chief Minister, Mr Karpoori Thakur, directing ministers not to use government planes without his approval of that of the Finance Minister.

While Mr Thakur's colleagues do not mind obtaining his permission for using the aircraft, they dislike the idea of seeking the approval of the Finance Minister with regard to them in cash.

Both the Chief Minister and the Finance Minister have gone to the southern states for electioneering, accompanied by the Education Minister. They are using a nine-seat plane. They are expected back on February 24.

Of the five government planes, only three are at present in flying condition. Two of the smaller planes have been grounded.

According to official sources, the nine-seat aircraft has been hired by the Janata Party, which will pay for its use by the Chief Minister

and others. Its operational costs are less than those of the other aircraft. The cost works out to Rs. 7.50 per 1.6 km. It was purchased in April last at a cost of about Rs. 65 lakhs. Another plane has been employed by it. However, a number of technical hands have been employed to maintain the planes.

According to official sources, the expenditure on the aircraft has already crossed the budget allocation of Rs. 16.11 lakhs during the current financial year.

Haryana civic poll this year

ROHTAK, February 21 (Samachar): Mr Mannohar Singh the Revenue and Local Self-Government, said yesterday that elections to civic bodies would be conducted by March 1978.

Addressing a public meeting, he said preliminary arrangements were being made for these elections. The government was taking steps to check the rise in the prices of essential commodities.

He appealed to the people to enthusiastically cooperate with the government in maintaining peace and making arrangements for solving the economic crisis. He said the attitude of the Janata government would be regarded as a role model for others to follow. Mr Singh further said that work on the Jawaharlal Nehru canal scheme would be completed by May 1978, and Hisar and Shajpur canal of Rohtak district.

Quorum bell rings for Bill to raise marriage age

By Our Special Correspondent

NEW DELHI, February 21. AFTER a somewhat lackadaisical debate, the Lok Sabha today approved the Law Sabha today seeking to raise the age of marriage from 18 to 21 for boys and from 15 to 18 for girls.

Even though the measure is of vital social significance, the attendance in the House was poor. At one stage, only 23 members were present. Just as the Bill was about to be put to the vote, a Congress member drew the attention of the Chair (Dr Sushila Nayar) to the absence of a quorum. The quorum-bell was rung and a few more members trooped in to

give the House a slightly better, though far from substantial, look.

Introducing the Bill, the Health Minister, Mr Raj Narain, said Mohammad Shah Qureshi, would have to raise marriage in the measure not for the fact that he had hurled angry epithets at a Janata member.

Mr Qureshi had sprung to the defence of Mr B. Venkataraman (Congress) who was arguing that the amendment sponsored by the Law Minister, Mr Shanti Bhushan, was identical with the one moved earlier by him. Since his amendment had been negatived by the House, Mr Qureshi argued, the Law Minister's amendment could not now be taken up.

Mr Shanti Bhushan joined issue with the Congress member and explained that his amendment was very much different. The House agreed.

Although almost all the members who took part in the debate welcomed the Bill, they gave divergent figures as the proper age of marriage. Mr O. P. Tyagi (J) thought 25 was the right age for both boys and girls. Mr A. Suntam Sahib from Kerala suggested that the age of marriage for girls should also be raised at 21. Mr Ram Kishan (J) wanted it to be 21 for boys and 25 for girls and pleaded that widows and widowers should be debarred from remarrying.

Mr O. V. Alagesan (C), though supporting the measure, pointed out that Rama and Sita were married when he was 16 and she was 13. He prompted the Law Minister to refer to his own case and the case of the Minister of State, Mr Nihal Singh.

Mr Shanti Bhushan said he was married at 29 and Mr Nanmagh at 12. "And look at the difference: I have four children and he has one."

One of the arguments by the Law Minister in favour of the Bill was that late marriage would help control the growth of population.

Miss Maniben Patel (J), perhaps her maiden speech in the Lok Sabha, remarked that late love was not check child marriage, while two other members championed the cause of their sex.

Mrs Bibha Goswami (CPI-M) pleaded for the promotion of the status of women, while Mrs Parvati Krishnan (CPI) urged compulsory registration of marriages.

Several members argued the case for educating the people and making them socially conscious. Mr P. G. Mavalankar (Ind) thought a combination of publicity and social education would be necessary.

China may invite Desai

PEKING, February 21 (Reuter): Diplomatic sources said here last night that the Chinese government may invite the Prime Minister, Mr Morarji Desai, to visit China.

They said Mr Wang Ping-nan, president of the Chinese People's Association for Friendship with Foreign Countries, is taking the invitation of the Chinese government to Mr Desai.

Blacks reject parity in interim govt

SALISBURY, February 21 (AFP). THE three Black delegations participating in the constitutional settlement talks have rejected the proposal of the Prime Minister, Mr Ian Smith, for an interim government with equal number of Black and White members.

Blacks delegates believed the proposal would mean the country would still be run by Whites, sources close to the talks said yesterday.

The talks between the government and delegations from the United African National Council (UNAC), the African National Council (ANC) faction led by the Rev. Ndabaningi

Sithole and the Zimbabwe United People's Organisation (ZUDOP) have centred on the structure of the government during the transition to majority rule.

The Black delegations were said to favour equal representation in the transition government for both of the three nationalist movements and the White minority, giving Blacks a majority.

Mr Smith proposed a two-tier government with an executive council of equal number of Black and White members. The chairman would alternate between the two colours.

The executive council would consist of the heads of the Black delegations and three White members, including the Prime Minister who would be the chairman, they added.

The Council of ministers would be composed of equal numbers of Black and White members, and the executive man would be appointed by the Prime Minister, the sources said.

Mr Smith also proposed that the existing Parliament of 50 White and 16 Black seats should continue during the transition, but the Black members could increase their representation until the power Parliament was elected.

Negotiations are continuing.

Ashok, Baldev, Virender, S. Ali back in team

By A Staff Reporter

NEW DELHI, February 21. ASHOK KUMAR and Baldev Singh will after all play for India. They and two other Olympians, Virender Singh and Syed Ali, have been chosen for the World Cup at Buenos Aires.

This was stated by Mr M. A. M. Ramaswamy, President of the Indian Hockey Federation on his return from Lahore, where the decision was taken at a meeting attended by selection committee chairman Louis Cornelius, coach Gnesh, manager Kartar Singh, vice-president R. P. Keio and assistant secretary, Sathyaswaryan.

The I.H.F. chief explained that the decision was taken at national interests after the views of four star class against Pakistan during which the team had to have a penalty corner expert successfully hit. It was also felt that Ashok Kumar would add to the incisiveness of the forward line. Syed Ali was the most outstanding centre-half in the test series against Pakistan in which he scored four goals. He and Baldev Singh were the players to figure in and Mr Keio wanted at a centre-half to replace him to be included.

Prabhakaran, Charanjit Kumar, Mahinoo Khan and Gurbhajan Singh have been dropped from the team to make way for the newcomers. Mr Ramaswamy said. He also met Dr. Shunder, Union Education Minister, who welcomed the decision and reiterated the need to clear the way to select an India team. He said the all-India Council of Sports had suggested that a panel of five, including two selectors and coach Gnesh be set up to discuss the charge of conspiracy and collecting arms for rebellion.

Koirala acquitted in one of six treason cases

KATHMANDU, February 21 (Samachar): The special tribunal today acquitted the former Prime Minister of Nepal, Mr B. P. Koirala, in one of the six charges of treason, while hearing of the other five cases continued.

The judgment came shortly before the tribunal rose for the day after defence lawyers had completed their arguments.

The former prime minister is facing charges of treason in five more cases and sedition charge in another, all of which will be heard by the special tribunal which will be in session till Monday.

Cases against Mr Ganesh Man Singh will also be heard by the tribunal.

It will hear two cases of treason against Mr Koirala tomorrow.

The special tribunal said in its findings that the prosecution had relied mainly on the confession of the co-accused, Bom Bahadur, from whose possession a bomb was alleged to have been seized.

The tribunal stated that the confession could not be independent evidence to prove the guilt. So Mr Koirala is acquitted of the charge of conspiracy and collecting arms for rebellion.

The tribunal, however, added that the judgment was subject to confirmation by the supreme court.

Statute amendment proposed to ensure right of life, liberty

NEW DELHI, February 21.

THE Janata government proposes to amend Article 359 of the Constitution to ensure that the right of life and liberty given to the citizen under Article 21 are not "capable of" suspension under any circumstances and under any kind of emergency.

Announcing this in the Lok Sabha today, the Law Minister, Mr Shanti Bhushan, hoped that all sections of the House would extend their support to the measures which would be part of the proposed Bill to rectify the distortions made by the 42nd Constitution Amendment Act.

The minister was replying to questions on the appointment of Mr Justice Y. V. Chandrachud as the next Chief Justice of India and, the controversy over the views held by him in the habeas corpus case during the emergency.

Mr Kanwar Lal Gupta said he was in a dilemma since the appointment of Mr Justice Chandrachud. There was a conflict between reason and sentiment. While he was not opposing the decision already taken on the basis of "reason," he wondered what the government was going to do to restore the faith in the Supreme Court because of the judgment in the habeas corpus case.

MAJORITY OPINION

As regards the consultations held with judges of the Supreme Court and the chief justices of the high courts on the new appointment, Mr Shanti Bhushan said that an "overwhelming opinion" expressed by them was that the ... seniormost judge should be the ... successor to Mr Justice M. H. Beg.

Asked whether the government had any proposal to limit the term of the Chief Justice of India to three years as was being done in the case of the Chief of Staff of the Army (irrespective of the age), Mr Shanti Bhushan replied in the negative.

A long time ago, Mr Shanti Bhushan recalled, the Law Commission headed by Mr C. Setalvad, former Attorney-General, had recommended a term of five to seven years for the Chief Justice of India. The Constitution, however, had provided that the retirement age of Supreme Court judges should be 65 whatever might be the term.

Mr Shanti Bhushan said another question that the government did not suggest any specific method to the judges of the Supreme Court and the chief justices of the high courts in the matter. The government simply posed the controversy to them and asked for their views to help the government take a decision.

Raj Narain's meeting disturbed

NAGPUR, February 21 (Samachar): An attempt was made today to disturb an election meeting addressed by the Union Minister for Health and Family Welfare, Mr Raj Narain at Katol, near here. A few shoes and chappals were thrown and the dais.

The Law Minister denied that the Janata Party had politicalised the appointment of the Chief Justice of India by disputing the decision in working committee and other forums. The present appointment, he declared, had been made in accordance with the provisions of the Constitution. In future also the government would strictly act in accordance with the Constitution.

Closer ties with Vietnam envisaged

By Our Special Correspondent

NEW DELHI, February 21: Three agreements will be signed with Vietnam during the week-long visit of the Prime Minister of Vietnam, Mr Pham Van Dong, beginning February 24, Under one agreement India will provide over Rs. 20-crore credit to Vietnam.

The agreements will relate to cooperation in the fields of economy and trade, science and technology and agricultural research.

The Indian credit will be extended, in cooperation with the Indian banking system, to finance import by Vietnam of machinery and equipment, and services to help rehabilitate its transport.

Mr Dong and Mr Morarji Desai will exchange views on a wide range of bilateral and international issues, such as Vietnam-India relations, which India wants to be developed into closer and broad-based negotiations between the two neighbours, will figure on the visit on February 24 and 25.

Mr Dong's major engagements in the Capital include an address to members of Parliament and a visit to Rajghat and Gandhi Smriti, presentation of a civic address at Red Fort, and a press conference.

Apart from the Agra tour Mr Desai will host the distinguished visitor on February 24 at Rashtrapati Bhavan. Mr Dong will have breakfast with Mr Desai on February 25 and see over the Pusa Institute of Agricultural Research. Later he will fly to Calcutta.

He will visit Taj Mahal on Febru-ary 27 and fly the same afternoon to Bombay, where he will visit the Indian Council of World Affairs in Bombay. He will also be visiting a petroleum refinery, Bhakra Nangal Atomic Energy establishment at Trombay.

Jagjivan Ram mauls newsmen

By Our Special Correspondent

BANGALORE, February 21. UNLIKE some other Janata leaders who speak confidently about the success of the party in the forthcoming elections, the Defence Minister, Mr Jagjivan Ram, today took stock of the state, preferred to be cautiously optimistic.

Asked whether he was sure that the Janata Party would win, he said: "We always content elections to win don't we?"

At the same time Mr Jagjivan Ram did not accept the "assumption" that the Janata Party has won the coalition government it failed to get absolute majority, it would build coalitions for those who had done best on the other side of the assembly elections, he said: "Why do you want to present Mr Gandhi who, Mr Waterloo?" After "what he had done to the Congress, you

there any doubt that she had not created her Waterloo?"

Asked whether he had been an Press statement that "the next government with the Janata leaders using its helicopter in the election campaign, Mr Jagjivan Ram said the Janata Party had not used any Indian Air Force helicopter or aircraft for electioneering. "We have only a private party, IAF helicopters could be used for party work on his visits to UP as the Prime Minister. Even as a Congressman he had travelled the helicopter, he said. Political parties managed to get funds and faithful travel of their leaders.

The Anti-Defection Bill would need agreement and consensus among all parties to be passed by Parliament. He was probably referring to the Janata Party did not want majority in the Rajya Sabha.

Mentioning that he would mean defection of any person left his party and joined another for personal reasons. If a minister gave up his ministership and got nothing in return by crossing over to another party, it would not be defection.

mailah, former Union Minister denied on the Congress ticket from the Lok Sabha, to the Janata Party was an isolated case. The Janata Party had already taken notice of it in its executive meeting.

Mr Jagjivan Ram did not think that Mr S. Nijalingappa's resignation from the Janata Party, protest against the defectors being given the party ticket would have any affect on the prospects of the party since at the Chitradurga constituency he was not working against the Janata candidate.

Asked if he had been effective in policy-making in the Janata government, he said he refuse to answer personal questions.

Would the Congress for Democracy be revived? He shot back: "Why does it question arise?" Then he asked when the Janata Sangh would be revived?

In reply to another question, he said he had not made any assessment of the role of the RSS. It was not a political body.

Continued on page 5 column 6

Urban Ceiling Act gets low priority in Rajasthan

By Our Special Correspondent

JAIPUR, February 21. ENFORCEMENT of the Urban Land Ceiling Act is being scaled down by the Rajasthan government's priorities. The urban land department that it cannot make for lack of adequate staff to implement it optimally. The director, Mr J. M. Khan, who nearly brought the work of starving out "surplus lands" to fruition, being transferred to the secretariat.

The view that this will not lead to a devaluation of the importance of the scheme seems correct to how things are taking shape.

As an economy measure, the scale of the work up to appreciable cut in the staff strength.

The urban lands department was engaged in identifying urban "surplus areas" in Jaipur, Jodhpur, Bikaner, Ajmer and Kota. Declarations were obtained from those who owned land in excess of the permissible limits and the processing of the cases was under way.

The department was hopeful of acquiring sizable chunks of land in these towns particularly from the owners of the former rulers and from the extensive holdings of the government's leading industrialists who hail from this state. The surplus land was to be used for building dwellings for weaker sections of society and for renting places of public utility and recreation.

The department was also charged with the work of creating urban agglomerations of 1,500 to 2,000 metres around the bigger cities and bringing within the ambit of the urban land under master plan.

The work of the department had, however, slowed down considerably as the letter passes for lack of guidelines from the Centre. This was perhaps expected after the change in the government. But when the guidelines finally arrived in December last, they gave more than enough time from the provisions of the Act that the "surplus land" would be available. After the winding up of the urban

the committee to finalise the teams.

The Law Minister denied that the Janata Party...

LIC Bonus Act struck down

NEW DELHI, February 21 (Samachar): The Supreme Court today struck down the LIC Bonus (Modification of Settlement) Act enacted during the emergency, nullifying bonus settlement between the management and employees.

As a result of the judgment, about 50,000 class three and four employees of LIC will become entitled to bonus for 1976 and 1977.

(Details on page 5)

3 Margis remanded in Bangkok

BANGKOK, February 21 (Reuter): Two Australians and an American, held as members of the Anand Marga, were often charged in a Bangkok court today and remanded in custody in connection with an attempt on the life of the Indian Ambassador here.

During a remand hearing, the court extended their detention until March next to enable the police investigation to be completed, the court sources said.

The three foreigners were seen at the apprehended in a flat here last month. An Indian was also held but released on bail.

volved and does not as a rule apportion blame on its own; rather, it awaits judicial or official findings in such cases.

The Times of India scrupulously avoids gossip, invasion of privacy, character assassination, unsubstantiated charges, unverified news, obscenity, salacious reports, nude pictures, and anything it considers in bad taste. It attempts to give special coverage to the problems of the weaker and disadvantaged sections of society like the Harijans, and it espouses the cause of minorities, religious as well as linguistic.

According to editor Jain, the paper is independent and non-partisan and places special emphasis on promoting secular issues and democratic values. It seeks to present various points of view. In foreign relations the paper supports the country's policy of non-alignment and respect for human rights, and is critical of suppression of basic freedoms anywhere and under whatever circumstances.[3]

The Times of India is owned by Bennett, Coleman & Co., Ltd., a public corporation. It has a staff of about 4,000, some 200 of this number being in news-editorial positions. Of the writers and editors, a little over half of them work in Bombay, with 64 in Delhi, and 27 in Ahmedabad. The newspaper has three full-time foreign correspondents—in Washington, London, and Katmandu. In addition, there are part-time correspondents for the paper in Hong Kong, Kuala Lumpur, Sydney, and Colombo. Two of the most distinguished foreign correspondents to serve the paper in recent years are M. V. Kamath (in Washington), and B. K. Joshi (in London). *The Times of India* puts a premium on university educated staff members and, in addition, requires at least five years' experience on a metropolitan daily for its beginning journalists.

In addition to receiving the news services of the Indian national news agency, Samachar (which has a linkup with the big international news agencies), *The Times of India* gets the services of the *New York Times*, the Indian News Feature Alliance, and the Public Opinion Trends (POT) from New Delhi. For its photographs from abroad, it receives the services of the Associated Press (London), and the United Press International (New York).

A typical issue of the newspaper contains about 70 percent advertising (varying with number of pages—from about 50 percent for a 12-page edition to 70 percent for a 20-page edition). International news takes up about 4 percent of the total edition, national news about 12 percent, and local/state news about 5 percent. The paper still uses Linotype machines for its typesetting and letterpress for its printing; it has not gotten into the VDT-computer-offset technology. No color printing is used by the newspaper. One picture is normally used on the front page, and a few more are scattered throughout the other pages.[4]

The Times of India has won several first and second prizes in competitions held by the Ministry of Information and Broadcasting and by the All-India Master Printers Conference, and it has also garnered many lesser honors and commendations. The paper has also received plaudits from journalistic groups in other countries, and it is usually found in libraries and governmental offices

[3] Jain questionnaire.
[4] Jain questionnaire and sample copies of paper sent authors.

around the world as a premier representative of the Indian press. The paper is more than a journalistic institution in India; it has become a general social institution. It has led in collecting relief funds whenever there has been any disaster like a flood, cyclone, famine, earthquake, or war. The Armed Forces Family Welfare Fund, organized and collected by the newspaper, has been used to provide allowances to widows for the education of their children and for the rehabilitation of the wounded and disabled.

The newspaper is the only one east of Suez which brings out an Index for the paper. And its reference department is the only one of its type in India; it provides comprehensive and prompt reference service to the newspaper's own departments and also to students, Indian and foreign, engaged in research.

Now that we have had an overview of the newspaper as it is today, it might be well to take a brief look into the past to see how the paper which is *The Times of India* evolved.

Begun as a small commercial newspaper in 1838 and published on Wednesday and Saturday, *The Bombay Times and Journal of Commerce* (as it was then called) was edited by Dr. J. E. Brenan. A retired doctor from Dublin, Brenan combined his editorial work with that of being secretary of the Bombay Chamber of Commerce. Explaining the objective of the newspaper, the editor said that it would provide its readers "the earliest possible intelligence upon all subjects of politics, science and literature and changes and promotions in the civil, military and naval services."[5]

Production of a newspaper was not easy a century and a half ago. Four years after the *Times* was founded it had to bring compositors and pressmen from England. The association of Indians as shareholders with the journal began as early as 1850; and it was in 1851 that the paper was converted into a daily. In the next few years *The Bombay Times* absorbed other Bombay papers such as *The Bombay Standard* and *The Telegraph and Courier*.

On May 18, 1861, the paper changed its name to *The Times of India*, and announced in the day's editorial: "The purely local title we have hitherto bourne, has hardly done justice to our circulation, which extends to every part of India, while the overland summary of the 'Bombay Times' is a paper with which people are familiar in every part of the world."

Managers and editors changed. Journalism, however, in those days was an avocation of amateurs and part-timers of little or no training or experience. This was true at the *Times*, at least, until Thomas Jeweel Bennett, a trained journalist, became editor. As its sole proprietor sometime later, he brought from London F. M. Coleman, a printer with considerable daily newspaper experience—hence the present name of the publisher of *The Times of India*: "Bennett, Coleman and Co., Ltd."

In the ensuing years the newspaper has had many great editors and managers who have persistently guided it on its road to quality, focusing always on the characteristics which the present editor has enthroned: freedom, fairness, objectivity, good writing, depth of coverage, and a generally constructive tone.

[5] Historical data here is largely from notes sent J. Merrill by Ram S. Kolatker, reference officer of *The Times of India*, March 4, 1978.

La Vanguardia Española

(SPAIN)

THE GREAT CATALAN NEWSPAPER, La Vanguardia Española (The Spanish
Vanguard), was founded in 1881 by Carlos Godó, assisted by his brother Barto-
lomé. The brothers set up their printing plant on the calle Pelayo at Number 28,
where it is still found today in the center of Barcelona. The paper grew rapidly
in importance until it was, by 1918, the daily with the largest circulation in all of
Spain. It is still the country's largest (if Madrid's ABC does not count its Seville
edition), with its influence now going far beyond the borders of Cataluña into all
of Spain and beyond.

Although the paper's main offices are in the heart of Barcelona, there are
other important printing plants on the city's outskirts where other publications
are printed—such as the newsmagazine Gaceta Ilustrada, the humor magazine
La Codorniz, the historical magazine Historia y Vida, and the sports dailies El
Mundo Deportivo and Dicen.

A standard-format daily, La Vanguardia has an average circulation of
280,000 on weekdays and some 330,000 on Sundays. An average weekday edition has 86 pages and the Sunday edition has 96. On Sundays a rotogravure
color supplement of up to 16 pages is published.[1]

The newspaper is privately-owned, the sole owner being the Count of Godó,
the heir of the dynasty of the founders, and its political philosophy is liberal. La
Vanguardia maintains an editorial staff in Madrid in order to obtain direct news
and commentary from the nation's capital.[2] It is the Spanish daily having the
largest number of permanent correspondents abroad; and, in addition, it sends
special correspondents to other countries when considered advisable.

In 1978 the newspaper's permanent correspondents and their assignments
were these: New York (Angel Zúñiga); London (Luis Foix); Paris (Tomás Al-
coverro); Bonn (Valentín Popescu); Brussels (Andrés Garrigó); Rome (Javier M.
de Padilla); Vienna and Eastern socialist countries (Ricardo Estarriol); Oslo and
Scandinavia and Finland (José Coll Barot); Maghreb countries (Alberto
Míguez); Middle East, with permanent office in Tel Aviv (Pedro Sánchez
Querirolo), and in Buenos Aires (Oriol de Montsant).

La Vanguardia also has its own correspondents in all the capital cities of

---

[1] Letter to J. Merrill from Horacio Sáenz Guerrero, director of La Vanguardia, dated June 21, 1978.

[2] One of the most popular writers from Madrid is Ramón Pi whose insightful political articles appear in
Vanguardia almost every day. (Information from Prof. Esteban López-Escobar F., University of Na-
varra, May 17, 1978.)

Editora: T. I. S. A.
REDACCION Y ADMINISTRACION
Pelayo, 28 (1)
TELEFONOS
301 - 54 - 54
(20 LINEAS)
«Telex»: 54.530 y 54.781
DEPOSITO LEGAL
B. 6.389 — 1958

LA VANGUARDIA
ESPAÑOLA

PRECIO DE ESTE EJEMPLAR: 18 pesetas
Sobretasa aérea: 2 pesetas

Director: Horacio Sáenz Guerrero

MIERCOLES, 22 de febrero 1978

PRECIOS DE SUSCRIPCION

Barcelona. Un mes	496'—
Provincias. Trimestre	1.486'—
Provincias. Trimestre por avión	1.824'—
Extranjero	3.153'—
Portugal, Andorra, Gibraltar, Filipinas, México, Venezuela y Paraguay. Trim.	1.524'—
Rep. Dominicana, Cuba, Costa Rica y Chile. Trimestre	2.903'—

También Mauritania reconoce la españolidad de Canarias

Ofensiva diplomática de España contra la propuesta de la OUA

Madrid, 21. ("La Vanguardia".) — Mientras en Trípoli continúa reunido el Consejo de Ministros de la Organización para la Unidad Africana. —OUA— y sigue sin saberse si tomará en cuenta la propuesta de su Comité de Liberación sobre Canarias o, por el contrario, trasladará su decisión a un próximo encuentro en Jartum, Madrid está moviendo los hilos diplomáticos a todos los niveles.

El ministro español de Asuntos Exteriores recibió hoy al embajador libio en Madrid, sin que trascendiera si el embajador había sido llamado o por el contrario, había acudido al palacio de Santa Cruz por propia iniciativa. Por la tarde, la diplomacia española recibía una noticia que enjugaba los sinsabores de los últimos días: Mauritania, a través de su Embajada en Madrid, reconocía oficialmente la inapelable españolidad de las islas Canarias.

Dentro del contexto canario no puede olvidarse la defensa del archipiélago. Sobre este tema podrían haber tratado el Rey y el ministro de Defensa, teniente general Gutiérrez Mellado, en el curso de una audiencia real que mantuvo el vicepresidente primero del Gobierno con don Juan Carlos. La audiencia era posterior en horas a la solicitud del grupo socialista del Congreso a la Mesa de la Comisión de Defensa para que el teniente general Gutiérrez Mellado informe sobre la situación y planificación de la defensa militar de Canarias.

Gestiones diplomáticas

Aunque la oficina de información diplomática del Ministerio de Asuntos Exteriores se mostraba remisa a emitir información suficiente sobre el problema diplomático planteado por la decisión del Comité de Liberación de la OUA, nuestra redacción pudo saber en círculos del palacio de Santa Cruz la concreción del planteamiento diplomático del tema de Canarias cerca de las cancillerías africanas. También supo que las gestiones diplomáticas se están intensificando en torno a los «grandes» de la política mundial.

Las gestiones que la diplomacia española ha llevado a cabo se pueden resumir en los siguientes puntos:

- Explicación del verdadero carácter del archipiélago en las cancillerías africanas, y en la propia OUA, saliendo al paso de las tergiversaciones del MPAIAC.
- Disociación del tema de Canarias del conflicto del Sahara, aunque algunos sectores políticos españoles traten de relacionarlos, poniendo de manifiesto su distinto origen en el tiempo y la manipulación de que es objeto el primero en favor de quienes mantienen determinadas posturas sobre el segundo.
- Tratamiento del tema de Canarias fuera del marco mogrebí, por ser su planteamiento por la OUA algo que trasciende de aquel marco geográfico situándolo en un contexto africano.
- Distinta óptica en el enfoque de las gestiones sobre el archipiélago en función del específico carácter de cada interlocutor africano a la vista de su orientación política.
- Gestiones al más alto nivel cuando vínculos personales lo hacían posible o se trataba de personalidades políticas cuyos países estaban directamente afectados por el tratamiento del tema de Canarias, en particular por ser sede de reuniones de la OUA o de algunos de sus órganos.
- Presión indirecta sobre los miembros de la organización a través de terceros países extracontinentales, que, por su ideología o influencia, pudieran influir positivamente sobre la conducta de aquéllos.
- A algunos de estos países extracontinentales se les ha hecho ver la negativa incidencia que, sobre el

(Continúa en la página siguiente)

Nueva York: El descenso del dólar, cada vez más preocupante

La caída de esta moneda en los mercados internacionales se atribuye a la preocupación por la larga huelga de los mineros norteamericanos

El "goteo" en la depreciación del dólar es noticia diaria. Sólo en aquellos países que como Alemania se dedican a sostener la divisa norteamericana a base de compras masivas de dólares, esta moneda consigue mantenerse precariamente en sus cotizaciones. Para muchos analistas no existe un sincero deseo por parte de Washington de tomar medidas capaces de apuntalar su moneda, por cuanto esa depreciación favorece indiscutiblemente la capacidad exportadora estadounidense en detrimento de sus rivales comerciales. El riesgo que se corre con esta actitud es sin embargo doble: el da una guerra comercial proteccionista entre las distintas economías mundiales y también el encarecimiento de los precios del petróleo como consecuencia de las aspiraciones de los países productores de percibir sus ingresos petrolíferos en una moneda más estable. En uno y otro caso las consecuencias serían una reducción drástica del comercio mundial y un incremento de la inflación.

Nueva York, 21. — (Crónica de nuestro redactor.) — La enfermedad del dólar es la nota más preocupante en la gráfica económica nacional y, por supuesto, internacional. Una nueva caída en las bolsas internacionales, llegando a su más baja cotización en los tiempos últimos, es el mejor barómetro para indicar el estado de esta economía.

En Francfort, pese a los esfuerzos de los bancos alemanes para equilibrar el cambio, en Zurich, Bélgica y Japón, el dólar sigue adelgazando considerablemente, atacado de una anemia que puede tener derivaciones muy sensibles en un momento en que la economía mundial del mundo libre se siente aquejada también por la incertidumbre de los tiempos.

La ilusión de una recuperación mundial puede venirse abajo, si continúa el descenso por la pendiente peligrosa reflejada, no menos, en lòs interrogantes de la bolsa neoyorquina, el Wall Street imperial que determina también la precaria salud de la moneda. Si las exportaciones norteamericanas pueden resultar más baratas con los cambios, la idea del proteccionismo pudiera albergarse de nuevo en Europa, como sueñan aquí muchas voces para alzar barreras contra las exportaciones japonesas que desequilibran en favor de Japón, y con números dramáticos, la balanza de pagos norteamericana.

MAS DE SETENTA DIAS

Un dólar débil puede también dar ánimos para que los países petroleros eleven el precio de los crudos, dando otro empujón hacia arriba a la inflación mundial. Es de suma importancia la declaración del secretario de Defensa norteamericano, Harold Brown, señalando que la seguridad en el Medio Oriente y de las zonas productoras de petróleo del golfo Pérsico, son tan vitales para Estados Unidos como lo es la seguridad de la Organización del Atlántico Norte o de los aliados asiáticos.

La caída del dólar en los mercados internacionales se atribuye a la preocupación por la huelga de los mineros de este país, que lleva ya más de setenta días. Aunque hoy, por vez primera, existe cierta esperanza que la mayor huelga carbonífera en Estados Unidos pudiera resolverse, la pelota está todavía indecisa en el tejado. Mientras tanto, los efectos de la huelga, quien quiera tenga razón para continuarla, se ha extendido ya a varios estados del Medio Oeste, con paro en algunas industrias, cortes de electricidad y calefacción inevitables, en uno de los inviernos más crudos de los últimos tiempos. Los mineros siguen en sus trece de no acceder a la vuelta al trabajo de no lograr sus reivindicaciones. Tampoco estamos en tiempos pasados donde el obrero era ampliamente explotado. Falta saber si a la larga, no se irá a desbaratar el sistema.

Lo peor del caso es que el presidente Carter se ha mostrado harto indeciso, en un conflicto en el que tenía que haber mediado mucho antes. Invocar la ley Taft-Hartley, que congela la huelga por ochenta días, para negociar de-

Angel ZUÑIGA

(Continúa en la página siguiente)

La política educativa, ante las Cortes

Cavero basa su programa en reformas continuadas y en un pacto escolar entre todos los partidos

Madrid, 21. — El ministro de Educación, don Iñigo Cavero, expuso hoy ante el Congreso y el Parlamento las líneas de política educativa del Gobierno, a la vez que anunció los nueve proyectos de ley que presentará a las Cortes antes de las vacaciones para reformar diversos aspectos de la enseñanza.

De estos proyectos destaca el establecimiento de un bachillerato general con integración del primer grado de la formación profesional y revalorizando ésta, suprimiendo el artículo de la Ley General de Educación que le da un cierto carácter discriminatorio y al mismo tiempo ampliando sus contenidos.

El ministro trazó un amplio esquema de reformas dentro del sistema educativo, poniendo de relieve que esta reforma hay que ir haciendola paulatinamente. El punto de partida es lograr un compromiso entre todas las fuerzas políticas, porque no conviene suscitar una batalla escolar que sería en estos momentos de un gran coste social para el país. Constató que entre los distintos grupos parlamentarios se mantienen discrepancias en algunos puntos, pero que había un amplio campo en el que se pueden establecer una convergencia de criterios, sobre todo asumiendo como principios básicos la libertad, la justicia, la igualdad, la generalidad y el respeto al pluralismo y la concepción de que la finalidad de la educación es el pleno desarrollo de la personalidad humana en el respeto a los principios democráticos de convivencia.

El ministro puso de relieve la dificultad para llegar a un pacto escolar, pero dijo que este tipo de reuniones podían dar lugar a dialogar en torno a ese pacto, que se puede basar sobre los siguientes principios: evitar la tentación de elaborar un nuevo sistema educativo, sustituyendo de forma global y total el ya existente; tener previsto que nuestro esquema operativo esté en condiciones de adaptarse eficazmente a reformas parciales pero continuadas, que progresivamente sería preciso afrontar.

El ministro dijo que el sistema educativo actual se caracteriza por una escolarización total en el nivel obligatorio, si bien existen centros inadecuados para una escolarización correcta; insuficiente escolarización en la preescolar con un fuerte peso de enseñanza no gratuita; enseñanza secundaria general y profesional escasamente generalizada y de baja calidad y alto índice de mortalidad del sistema educativo, con abandono, repeticiones, etc.

(Continúa en la página siguiente)

Barcelona: Jardines y una escuela en el solar de la Modelo

Transcurrirán más de dos años antes del traslado total de la prisión provincial

El Ayuntamiento de Barcelona convertirá los actuales terrenos ocupados por la cárcel Modelo en jardines y zona de equipamiento para el barrio. Las dos terceras partes de las dos hectáreas en las que actualmente se levanta la prisión será destinadas a jardines públicos. El resto, a equipamiento, siendo segura la construcción de una escuela de E.G.B. para los niños de la izquierda del Ensanche, zona urbana que carece de colegios públicos y, especialmente, de centros escolares de E.G.B.

En principio, los técnicos municipales de la delegación de Urbanismo han valorado estas dos hectáreas en 60 millones de pesetas. El Ministerio de Justicia está estudiando esta oferta, aunque no parece que vayan a surgir serias dificultades en torno a estos contactos entre el Ayuntamiento y el Estado. Sin embargo, deberán transcurrir alrededor de dos años y medio para que la ciudad pueda efectivamente disfrutar de los terrenos de la calle Entenza. Este es el plazo fijado aproximadamente para que se lleven a término los proyectos y la construcción del nuevo centro penitenciario, donde quiera que éste vaya a levantarse. *(Información en pág. 21.)*

45 millones de pesetas en pérdidas en el incendio del Pazo de Meirás

El edificio no podrá ser habitable hasta dentro de un año

La Coruña, 21. — Hasta dentro de un año no podrá ser habitado de nuevo el Pazo de Meirás, tras el incendio que ha afectado a un tercio de su superficie y edificio, valorándose las pérdidas en una estimación provisional en 45 millones de pesetas, de los 150 millones en què está valorado el Pazo.

No se conoce aún la decisión de la familia Franco sobre si va a restaurar los grandes deterioros de la estructura del Pazo. En cualquier caso, después de las visitas realizadas y los informes pertinentes que le han sido facilitados, la Señora de Meirás y su familia tienen previsto abandonar hoy La Coruña.

Ha quedado confirmado que el motivo del siniestro ha sido un cortocircuito, porque la instalación eléctrica no se hallaba en buenas condiciones y un equipo técnico que lo revisó hace pocos años así lo había advertido en un informe, hasta el punto de que en algunes zones del edificio se habían verificado reparaciones. En la inspección ocular verificada con motivo del siniestro se han podido observar esos deterioros, con el cobre de los cables al aire, lo que debido a la gran humeded en invierno de dicho paraje, podría producir por sí solo cualquier cortocircuito. — Pyresa.

En 1977

La balanza española por cuenta corriente mejoró en 1.780 millones de dólares

El Banco de España ha dado a conocer las cifras provisionales de la balanza de pagos española en 1977. Según estas cifras el déficit de la balanza de mercancías se redujo en 1.256 millones de dólares respecto a la cifra de 1976. La balanza de servicios registró un superávit de 2.418 millones, manteniéndose casi idéntico el saldo de la balanza de transferencias. Con ello el déficit de la balanza por cuenta corriente se situó en 2.512 millones de dólares que significan 1.780 millones menos que en 1976. Este hecho constituye, sin duda, el logro más importante de la política económica española, en un año presidido por una profunda crisis. Por su parte, las reservas de divisas se incrementaron en 1.145 millones de dólares, frente a un descenso en el año anterior de 944 millones.

(Más información en pág. 34)

Paulo VI, ligeramente indispuesto

Ciudad del Vaticano, 21. — El Papa se halla ligeramente indispuesto, víctima de un resfriado, pero su estado de salud no es preocupante.

Así lo informaron hoy fuentes vaticanas, que afirmaron que la tradicional audiencia, que el Pontífice celebra cada miércoles, no se vería suspendida mañana.

Paulo VI participó durante toda la última semana en unos ejercicios espirituales dirigidos por el padre jesuita Carlo Martini.

El Papa, a causa de un ligero resfriado, no pudo asistir el sábado a la ceremonia final de su retiro espiritual, teniendo que ser el cardenal secretario de Estado, Jean Villot, el que leyó la carta de agradecimiento al padre Martini.

A pesar de no sentirse en buenas condiciones, Paulo VI rezó el domingo el «Angelus», en el curso del cual se refirió a la violencia que hoy impera en el mundo.

Recientemetne, se filtraron informaciones según las cuales la salud del Pontífice había empeorado, aunque el Vaticano desmintió categóricamente las mismas.

Paulo VI tiene en la actualidad 80 años y sufre de un agudo proceso de artrosis, debido a su avanzada edad. Efe.

the Spanish provinces and has a network of "collaborators" (stringers, contributors) second to none in Spanish-speaking countries.[3]

The newspaper is a member of the prestigious TEAM (Top European Advertising Media), an association of 16 leading daily newspapers read by people of influence in Europe.[4]

A copy of La Vanguardia is organized in sections; usually they appear in this way: the first two pages carrying general news, then a "Tribuna" section including editorials, contributed essays from colaboradores, and letters to the editor; then a Political Section, followed by sections in this order—"España," International, Culture, Barcelona, Cataluña, Religion, Economics, Local Events, Sports, Automobile Market, Brief Notices, Entertainment and Weather, and Latest News. And, from time to time (e.g. on Thursdays), there will be a section on Books.[5]

The present director of La Vanguardia is Horacio Sáenz Guerrero, a highly respected journalist who became head of the editorial side of the paper in 1969. He was born in Logroño, his father being chief editor of the daily Nueva Rioja there. Soon his family moved to Barcelona, his father died, and Horacio had to go to work. He joined the staff of La Vanguardia where, in the ensuing years he has held all positions on the newspaper.[6]

Other important directors of La Vanguardia since its founding have been Miguel de los Santos Oliver, who was the right arm of the first Count of Godó and was famed for his intellectual and independent character; Luis de Galinsoga, who made significant innovations in the news operation of the daily; Manuel Aznar, whose friendship and teaching had a special impact on the present director; and Xavier de Echarri who brought to the paper his valuable experience as director of Arriba and correspondent for ABC, both of Madrid.

Several other staff members of La Vanguardia should be mentioned. The local news editor is Miguel Martín, who has done much to increase the local prestige of the newspaper. Jaime Arias is the national news editor; he has contributed greatly in making the paper an important force in documentation. Javier Comín, the makeup editor, has continued the paper's tradition of having an orderly and attractive physical appearance. Santiago García produces one of the best sports sections in Spain as sports editor. The paper has long been noted for its full coverage of athletic events in Spain and abroad. And then there is Lorenzo Gomís, editor for "editorial coordination." In effect, he is what would be

---

[3] Some of the most important of these colaboradores are Augusto Assia, Jaume Miratvilles, Guillermo Díaz-Plaja, Néstor Luján, Indro Montanelli, Baltasar Porcel, Julián Marías, Miguel Masriera, Joan Fuster, Sebastián Juan Arbó, José Luis Aranguren, and Jorge Edwards. (López-Escobar Information).
[4] Other members: Die Presse, Vienna; Daily Telegraph, London; Her Laatste Nieuws, Brussels; Corriere della Sera, Milan; Le Soir, Brussels; Il Messaggero, Rome; Berlingske Tidende, Copenhagen; NRC Handelsblad, Rotterdam-Amsterdam; Die Welt, Bonn; Aftenposten, Oslo; Frankfurter Allgemeine Zeitung, Frankfurt; Süddeutsche Zeitung, Munich; Neue Zürcher Zeitung, Zurich. Of all the TEAM members, according to a recent survey, La Vanguardia is the daily with the highest advertising average; a crucial element of this fact is that the paper is published in the richest city in Spain.
[5] Lopez-Escobar information.
[6] Pedro J. Ramirez, "La Vanguardia Española: El Diario Catalán más Poderoso," La Actualidad Española, 21.XI, 1974, p. 46.

a managing editor in the United States; he supervises the various editors, correspondents, and stringers.[7]

Carlos Godó Valla, the second Count of Godó, is actually the publisher of *La Vanguardia* and titular head of its publishing company, TISA. Manager of TISA and probably the person most active presently in changes and renovations going on within the newspaper is Javier Godó M. This young man, 37 years old in 1979, is a dynamic executive, trained basically in technical affairs, but knowledgeable and interested in all aspects of journalism. He is especially dedicated to press freedom and diversification of the mass media.

However, setting the journalistic tone for the newspaper is the director and veteran journalist, Horacio Sáenz Guerrero. He is a firm believer in quality journalism and puts much stress on writing style, accuracy, a broad general education, and a sense of ethics for his staff members. He believes that his newspaper is, indeed, among the great dailies of the world. Here is the way he puts it:[8]

> Personally, I think that a great newspaper is one which offers its readers more and better information than its competing colleagues, always on the basis of rigorous objectivity and with an aim of well-defined impartiality for the benefit of the interests of the whole community.

Just what does an issue of *La Vanguardia* look like? Let us look briefly at the issue of Wednesday, February 22, 1978. This was an edition of 30 pages. The front page (the cover page) is really not the first news page; rather it carries pictures and brief cutlines only. The *real* Page One is actually page 3 and is mainly concerned with foreign and national affairs. Page 4 continues the foreign and national news. Pages 5 and 6 form the "Tribuna" (editorial page), carrying a long editorial and an essay, and a number of letters from readers. A political section ("Política") follows on pages 7, 8, and 9. Pages 10 and 11 are full-page advertisements.

A national news section ("España"), comes next on pages 12, 13, and 14; this is followed by a well-edited world news section ("Internacional") on pp. 15, 16, 17, and 18, being broken by only a very few small advertisements. Then comes a "Cultura" page of news, pictures, and features about the arts—on page 19. A full-page advertisement is on page 20. Beginning on page 21 and running for five pages is the local (city) news section—"Barcelona." This is followed by three pages of news from the home province—"Cataluña." Then advertisements and a feature on bicycling complete the edition.

The entire edition is crammed with news and features and is very attractively laid out. On most days there would also be a very complete and well-edited sports section, a part of the paper for which the staff and the public have a high regard. Any reader looking through *La Vanguardia* will see at once that it is a "news" paper, filled with a variety of serious news from all parts of the world and presented in a neat and pleasing manner.

"In my view," the director, Sáenz Guerrero, says, "*La Vanguardia* is a great

[7] *Ibid.*, p. 50.
[8] Sáenz Guerrero letter.

newspaper—and this is so acknowledged by its readers—because its long-standing tradition of independence and earnestness is fully confirmed by everyday experience."

The morale among *La Vanguardia* staff members is high; this can be felt at once by a visitor to its editorial offices. All the reporters and editors appear to have a real love for their newspaper and what it is trying to do in their community, in Spain, and in Europe. Perhaps best personifying the pride its staff has in the newspaper is the director, Sáenz Guerrero himself. He summarizes with these words the spirit and basic value of the newspaper:

> In the democratic Spain of the present time, *La Vanguardia* is always the leading one among many other important newspapers in our country, precisely because its essential purpose is to properly inform its readers and to emit serious-minded, responsible and if necessary courageous editorial judgments, defending the supreme interests of the country and its citizens.

To what better policy than that expressed in these words above could any journalist or editor be dedicated?

The Wall Street Journal

(UNITED STATES)

SINCE ITS FIRST EDITION on July 8, 1889, *The Wall Street Journal,* with main offices in New York City, has been a successful and highly respected journalistic institution. Owner and publisher of the daily, which through the years has offered premier news and analysis of the financial world, is Dow Jones & Co., Inc. Although the daily still provides the sophisticated reader a thorough and insightful look at the world of finance and business, it has increasingly become what might be called a "general" newspaper as it has infused a wealth of serious nonfinancial news and interpretation into its pages.

Headquarters for this truly national newspaper, which publishes four different regional editions[1] across the country, is at 22 Cortlandt St. in New York City. The daily circulation of the paper is about 1.5 million (one of the U.S.'s largest), some 85 percent of which goes to subscribers. In the United States the paper is printed in ten plants around the country, using facsimile transmission via satellite[2] to locations in South Brunswick, N.J.; Orlando, Florida, and River-

[1] Eastern, Midwest, Southwest, and Western editions average 32–48 pages and carry basically the same news, with advertising varying.
[2] Images of the paper are sent from the mother plant in Massachusetts, bouncing signals off a satellite 22,300 miles over the Galapagos Islands; these signals are received in plants in New Jersey, Florida and California where pictures of each page are created from which the papers are printed.

THE WALL STREET JOURNAL

VOL. CXCI NO. 36 ★★★   EASTERN EDITION   WEDNESDAY, FEBRUARY 22, 1978   PRINCETON, NEW JERSEY   25 CENTS

Stalled Locomotive

Japan's Growth Lags, Cutting Hopes That It Can Aid Rest of World

Many Doubt Nation Can Lift GNP 7%, Help U.S. Pare Its Serious Trade Deficit

Over 18,000 Business Failures

By MIKE THARP
Staff Reporter of THE WALL STREET JOURNAL

TOKYO—Thirteen months ago, Japanese Prime Minister Takeo Fukuda called 1977 "the year of the economy."

Last month, he called 1978 "the year of the economy."

The prime minister wasn't accidentally reading a year-old speech. Things haven't developed the way I had hoped," he conceded recently. "This year will be another year of the economy. We must put our economy again on the track of stable growth."

In April, Japan will enter its fifth fiscal year since the 1973 oil crisis abruptly halted the nation's once-flourishing economic growth. Real gross national product—the output of goods and services adjusted for inflation—dropped 0.2% in the year ending March 31, 1975, and the recovery since then has been slow and painful. Real GNP rose 3.4% in fiscal 1976 and 5.7% in fiscal 1977, and the increase in the year ending at the close of next month is estimated at 5.3%.

For many nations, Japan's growth rates in the past two years would be greeted as a hearty rebound from the recession. The United States, for example, posted real growth of only about 4.9% in calendar 1977, and West Germany managed about 2.4%. But for Japan, accustomed to a decade or more of double-digit gains, the slower growth has seemed like stagnation.

Misled by Successes?

"The American public that sees Sony and Datsun and Toyota as conspicuous success stories thinks the Japanese economy is booming," a Japanese government official says. "This image is buttressed by our accumulation of huge trade surpluses. But the fact is we are in one of the most serious economic phases we have faced in 30 years."

The seriousness of Japan's economic problems was demonstrated Monday, when Eidai Co. and four of its major affiliates sought court protection under the bankruptcy laws; the Eidai group, Japan's largest plywood maker, has liabilities estimated at the equivalent of more than $756 million (see story on page 18). Moreover, the filing is unusual only in its size. Last year, more than 18,000 Japanese companies failed. And a recent survey by Sanwa Bank indicated that one out of 10 concerns listed on various stock exchanges is "virtually bankrupt."

The largest has world-wide repercussions. It indicates that, at least for a while, Japan isn't likely to be much help in pulling other capitalist nations out of the international recession—the "locomotive" role widely assigned to Japan, West Germany and the U.S. at the London economic summit meeting last May. Japan's relatively slow growth is particularly important because, for various reasons, the other two alleged "locomotives" also have been behaving more like cabooses.

Moreover, Japan's economic sluggishness will affect the trade accord negotiated here last month with the U.S. Under that agreement, which the U.S. hopes will help alleviate the current imbalance of trade between the two countries, Japan reemphasized its intention to take "all reasonable and appropriate measures" to reach 7% real growth in the fiscal year beginning April 1. Since the pact was signed, however, the Japanese government has carefully avoided calling that 7% projection a promise; instead, the 7% figure is termed a "policy target."

Attack on Surplus

The agreement also stipulated that Japan's surplus in its current account—its merchandise trade plus so-called invisible items such as travel expenditures, interest and dividend payments, and transportation bills—will be "considerably reduced." The reduction would be achieved by expansion of domestic demand, by the effects of the appreciation of the Japanese yen and by improved access of foreign goods to the Japanese market. However, many analysts believe that, mostly because of persistently slack demand in Japan, the surpluses will remain large. Daiwa Securities Co., for example, estimates the current-account surplus in fiscal 1978 at the equivalent of $9.1 billion and the trade surplus at $18.4 billion.

Such figures wouldn't represent much improvement over the comparable calendar-1977 totals of $11 billion and $17.5 billion. And if Japan can't achieve some of the goals outlined in the U.S. accord, analysts say, trade friction will become abrasive again. In fact, the Japanese see the threat of rising foreign protectionism hanging over their industry like a samurai sword.

In an effort to escape this danger, Mr. Fukuda and his government have embarked on an ambitious program to stimulate the economy. "We are determined to realize" the 7% growth goal, the prime minister says.

Private Forecasts Lower

But, as many Japanese say, that will be "very difficult"—meaning, impossible. Scarcely anyone outside the white and gray government buildings in central Tokyo—and even few people inside them—believes that Japan will grow 7% in its next fiscal year. Most private research organizations peg real growth at 4% to 5%. One, the Japan Economic Research Center, projects a 4.4% rate, for instance.

"The main reason for the difference between the government's forecast and ours is that we see a much lower rate of growth in the private sector," Hisao Kanamori, the center's president, says.

And Japan's problem does seem to lie in

Please Turn to Page 18, Column 1

What's News—

Business and Finance

THE SUPREME COURT refused to interfere with development of mid-Atlantic offshore oil-gas leases sold in August 1976, apparently removing the bidders' final impediment. Separately, the Interior Department set March 28 to sell oil-gas leases offshore four southeastern states.

Zenith won high court review of its arguments that the U.S. should impose special penalty duties on electronic imports from Japan that are exempted from that nation's commodity tax. Justices also will consider whether private pension funds are securities and thus subject to antifraud provisions of securities law.

A program to help states calculate taxes owed by multistate companies is constitutional, Justices affirmed, rejecting a challenge by some big concerns. And they left standing a lower court's contempt finding against J. P. Stevens for violating decrees involving union activity.

(Story on Pages 2, 3, 4, 5 and Back Page)

Economic growth in 1977's final quarter was revised downward to an estimated 4% annual pace from 4.2%. That was a further slowing from 5.1%, 6.2% and 7.5% gains previously.

(Story on Page 3)

Zinc prices were cut 1.5 cents a pound by Asarco in response to mounting inventories.

(Story on Page 3)

Western Pacific's railroad unit is to be sold to a new company formed by the subsidiary's operating management. It will pay $11.6 million and assume debts totaling $103 million as of year-end.

(Story on Page 10)

American Motors expects an accord within several months on some type of combination with a foreign auto maker.

(Story on Page 7)

Protectionism barriers against growing imports to halt the loss of U.S. jobs were urged by the AFL-CIO.

(Story on Page 2)

Terms for McDermott's proposed acquisition of the 51% of Babcock & Wilcox it doesn't already own were sweetened a bit, raising the payout for one stock to be swapped.

(Story on Page 4)

The oil cartel's output is declining more than expected because of the world oil glut. Last month, Saudi Arabia's production fell to near a two-year low.

(Story on Page 5)

A Cities Service unit completed tests on a well 27 miles off Palawan Island in the Philippines that flowed oil from four intervals.

(Story on Page 5)

Quaker Oats appears likely to win dismissal from the FTC's "shared-monopoly" charge against it and three other breakfast cereal makers.

(Story on Page 4)

Peter Paul would be acquired by Cadbury Schweppes for $27.50 a share under a $58.2 million agreement.

(Story on Page 4)

Harvey Hubbell agreed to a $54 million acquisition of Ohio Brass, offering convertible preferred or $73 cash for each Ohio Brass share.

(Story on Page 4)

Royal Crown Cola officers said the company will move more heavily into the restaurant business to make itself less susceptible to buffeting by Coca-Cola and PepsiCo.

(Story on Page 6)

Bache Group's net skidded 93% in its Jan. 31 second quarter to $191,000, or three cents a share.

(Story on Page 6)

Commodity regulators urged Congress to keep their beleaguered agency, the Commodity Futures Trading Commission, in operation for six more years and to strengthen its enforcement powers.

(Story on Page 2)

Markets—

Stocks: Volume 21,890,000 shares. Dow Jones industrials 749.31, off 3.38; transportation 203.81, off 0.83; utilities 102.84, off 0.68.

Bonds: Dow Jones 20 bonds 89.56, up 0.24.

Commodities: Dow Jones futures 358.16, up 1.43; spot index 346.58, off 0.50.

TODAY'S INDEX

(index listing)

World-Wide

SENATORS HEARD drug-dealing allegations involving Panama's leaders.

In a secret session, Sen. Birch Bayh (D., Ind.), chairman of the Select Intelligence Committee, delivered a report that corroborated earlier press accounts that linked Panamanian officials, including a brother of Panamanian leader Gen. Omar Torrijos, to illegal traffic in drugs. Bayh said the panel found evidence that Gen. Torrijos knowingly tolerated the activities. But the report said that evidence wasn't conclusive enough to stand up in court. The panel's findings also confirmed that the general's brother was indicted by a U.S. grand jury in 1972 on drug charges, but avoided arrest after the State Department alerted Gen. Torrijos.

Foes of the Panama Canal treaties hope the report impedes the ratification effort. But supporters dismissed the allegations, contending they weren't relevant.

BEGIN PROPOSED immediate resumption of peace talks with Egypt.

The Israeli prime minister said that in his meeting with U.S. envoy Alfred Atherton he suggested that the military committee of the peace talks meet in Cairo and the political committee resume negotiations in Jerusalem. He said he also suggested that he and Egyptian President Sadat confer again in Ismailia on the Suez Canal. Atherton will convey the suggestion to Egyptian officials in Cairo later as he continues his shuttle diplomacy.

Begin said he expected Atherton to return by the weekend with Egyptian counterproposals on a declaration of principles to serve as a guide in the peace discussions. But he said there had been no change in the Israeli positions.

The Israeli cabinet adjourned its debate on whether to press on with Jewish settlements on occupied Arab lands, a key issue hindering the resumption of the talks. The special cabinet meetings, which began Monday, will resume Sunday. Sources said two rival camps emerged in the debate—one led by Defense Minister Ezer Weizman, who wants to freeze settlement plans, and the other by Agriculture Minister Ariel Sharon, who is calling for new outposts.

In Washington, Secretary of State Cyrus Vance told a House committee that the administration wouldn't accept any effort to dismantle its proposed package of fighter planes for Egypt, Saudi Arabia and Israel. Asked about the possibility that Congress would approve planes only for Israel, Vance said such a move would "further distort" the balance of power in the region.

Cypriot President Kyprianou offered to meet President Sadat to try to head the rift caused by an abortive Egyptian commando raid to capture two Arab terrorists in Cyprus. Egypt suspended relations with Cyprus over the incident, in which 15 of the commandos were killed in a shootout with Cypriot forces. Kyprianou also appealed to Arab leaders not to turn Cyprus into an arena for settling Mideast conflicts.

Ethiopia has assured President Carter that it doesn't intend to send troops into Somalia or interfere in the internal affairs of its neighbors, White House Press Secretary Jody Powell said. He said the assurances were conveyed by the U.S. special emissary to Ethiopia, David Aaron, in a meeting with Carter. Aaron also said Ethiopia was willing to receive a new U.S. ambassador soon.

Attorney General Bell told the Senate Judiciary Committee that he would make available "anything and everything we want" about the controversial firing of David Marston as U.S. attorney in Philadelphia. The ouster of Marston, a Republican, was brought up by GOP committee members at the hearings on the nomination of Benjamin Civiletti to be Deputy Attorney General.

The House voted to give states $250 million to fill potholes and make other repairs to storm-ravaged roads. The measure, which now goes to a Senate committee, provides that no state receive more than 1% of the funds but that each state get at least $500,000.

The Supreme Court agreed to review a lower-court decision that National Labor Relations Board jurisdiction over Catholic school teachers unconstitutionally interferes with religious freedom. The lower court said the NLRB couldn't force the Roman Catholic Bishop of Chicago and the Diocese of Fort Wayne-South Bend, Ind. to bargain collectively with lay teachers in two parochial schools in Chicago and five in northern Indiana.

Chile has been asked to question two military men about the 1976 slaying of former Chilean ambassador Orlando Letelier in a bomb explosion on a Washington street. U.S. officials said. A U.S. request to Chile's supreme court said that at least one of the two men "met with one of the persons believed responsible" for the assassination.

Three black leaders rejected Rhodesian Prime Minister Ian Smith's proposal that he head a transitional government designed to lead the way to full black majority rule. The black leaders reportedly told Smith that his proposal to chair the executive council of the transitional government was tantamount to a continuation of white minority rule.

Iranian army troops took over the northern city of Tabriz amid reports that the death toll from rioting last weekend rose to at least nine persons. Newspapers said 10 persons were arrested on suspicion of being part of the Islamic Marxist underground movement that is officially blamed for the riots in which hundreds of shops, banks and theaters were burned or looted.

Business Failures

Annual Rate per 10,000 Businesses
Source: Dun & Bradstreet

1974   1975   1976   1977

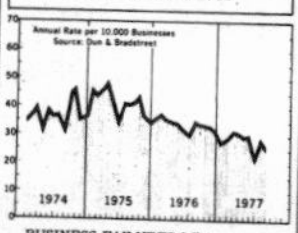

BUSINESS FAILURES fell to a seasonally adjusted rate of 27 per 10,000 in September from 28.7 in August, Dun & Bradstreet Inc. reports.

A Fish Story: How Bell Landed Contract To Sell Iran Copters

Code Names Played a Part; Snapper Asserts the Pike Was Impressed at a Party

By JERRY LANDAUER
Staff Reporter of THE WALL STREET JOURNAL

WASHINGTON — Corporate executives who went fishing for an arms contract in Iran some years ago had to know their snapper and their trout from their pike or their "Grouse."

Those were among the code words devised by the Bell Helicopter subsidiary of Textron Inc. to keep competitors from divining the sales strategy that landed a Bell-made order for helicopters from the Iranian armed forces in 1973. Afterward, Textron paid fees totaling $2.9 million to Air Taxi Co., a sales agency in Iran that was partly owned by an influential government official, Gen. Mohammed Khatemi, the late chief of the Imperial Iranian Air Force.

Questions about this payment have already delayed Senate confirmation of G. William Miller, Textron's chairman, to head the Federal Reserve Board. Now the coded communications between Bell Helicopter's headquarters in Fort Worth and Air Taxi Co., in Tehran are surfacing just as the Senate Banking Committee is scheduled to meet again today to consider Mr. Miller's nomination.

Nothing in these messages, nor in depositions of Bell Helicopter executives taken by the committee staff, contradicts Mr. Miller's repeated contention that he has paid month that he didn't know about Gen. Khatemi's financial interest in Air Taxi. Mr. Miller testified that he wouldn't have approved the payments to Air Taxi if government officials or military officers were known to have been intended beneficiaries.

Further Questioning of Miller?

But the communications between Bell and Air Taxi raise fresh questions about Gen. Khatemi's help in reeling in the big contract, and some Senators want to recall Mr. Miller for further testimony before voting on his nomination.

In any case, Bell's coded records show fascinating glimpses of how the company and the Iranian general cooperated in arranging a big helicopter deal.

A Bell code book accorded unique status to Gen. Khatemi (who died in a glider accident in 1975). Of all the Iranian functionaries concerned in the messages, he alone was known by a number—"No. 1." All the others were named after fish, including the likes of Trout, Salmon and Perch, or of Iran, who would chase the ultimate decision about equipping his armed forces. His Imperial Majesty was dubbed "Pike."

Bell's intensive sales campaign began soon after the company hired Air Taxi as its sales representative in 1968. "We want ... (the) sale and you must sell our proposal," Fort Worth insisted in one early telex to A. H. Zanganeh, manager of Air Taxi. "You may be the only snapper. A subsequent message urged, "so let's not leave anything to chance."

Snapper's best contact by far in the Iranian hierarchy was Gen. Khatemi, his secret business associate. Early in the sales campaign the general gave a party for the Bells and members of their families to soften them up for their business of landing a great interest in the film," Snapper gloated later.

'Play a Very Low Key'

At times, in fact, Gen. Khatemi appeared to take command of Bell's sales campaign. In April 1971, Fort Worth informed Air Taxi that a three-man sales team was en route to Tehran. Mr. Zanganeh cabled back to arrange a meeting with the air-force commander. "Gen. Khatemi gave very important and useful guidance and advice for future sales of the Huey Cobra" helicopter, Mr. Zanganeh observed in a memo for his files. "The Bell Helicopter team were very impressed."

Essentially, Gen. Khatemi advised Bell to avoid publicity splashes that could alert competitors, and, if Mr. Zanganeh's notes are accurate, the general regarded himself as the superior salesman. The general believes that "Bell should play a very low key and only coordinate and adhere to public/instructions which would be given to them," Snapper's notes say.

Similar advice to Bell Helicopter, according to Mr. Zanganeh's files, came from Gen. Hassan Toufanian, the Shah's chief procurement officer, known as "Salmon," and from Gen. Toufanian's key civilian aide, "Trout." Then as the sales campaign developed "Grouper" appeared at "Sea," meaning in Iran. Grouper (apparently a misspelling of grouper) was the code name for the Iranian company that produced transport helicopters under license from Bell.

The Italian concern had previously sold more than 100 aircraft to the Iranian government. But in the summer of 1971 Gen. Khatemi seemed eager to knock Grouper out of the water and increase the month's "Bass" (Bell Helicopter) purchases of the water and permit "Bass" (Bell Helicopter) alone.

Please Turn to Page 21, Column 2

Tax Report

A Special Summary and Forecast Of Federal and State Tax Developments

IF THE FIGURES DON'T LIE does that mean President Carter does?

Carter says his tax-relief plan would cut taxes for "96% of all American taxpayers." It also will offset the effects of increased Social Security taxes and inflation, he says. But some experts say it won't. "Carter's claim that 96% of the people will have lower taxes isn't true at all—unless you ignore inflation," says Michael Evans, president of Chase Econometrics, an economic-analysis firm. Inflation pushes up wages, lifting people into higher brackets.

Inflation makes Carter's "tax cut" vanish: The federal tax burden on personal income jumps by $15.2 billion next year due to Social Security tax increases; inflation adds $9 billion, Evans says. That's a total increase in tax burden of $24.2 billion, and Carter's plan provides only $19.3 billion of relief. So, overall, federal taxes on personal income increase $5.9 billion next year.

"We've had plump tax cuts for the last 15 years," asserts Gerard Brannon, economics professor at Georgetown University. "We ought to stop letting the politicians get away with this cheap talk."

HOW CARGILL CORP. BEAT Buffalo, N.Y., out of $996,600.

Cargill refused to pay property taxes on three grain elevators for the five years before it abandoned them. The city acquired the property at its own tax sale but can't get as much from selling the property as Cargill owed in taxes. So the city tried to collect from Cargill.

But New York State's highest court recently told Buffalo it can't collect. State law compelled the city to bid on the property at the tax sale and state law deems the delinquent taxes to have been paid when Buffalo acquired the property at the tax sale, the court said. "The law isn't a very good state," unhappily puns Stanley Moskal, a city assistant corporation counsel.

Cargill tried to get taxes lowered on the elevators before abandoning them, a spokesman says. "We won (the case). We're gratified," he declares. "In terms of New York law, the city can't collect."

THE ONLY WAY to reap the benefits of a joint return is to file one.

Seems simple enough. But it isn't if you haven't filed returns for years. That was the case with Joseph and Evelyn. They didn't file for five years. When the Internal Revenue Service caught up with them, it computed their delinquent taxes at rates for married people filing separate returns. That resulted in more tax for the couple than if the IRS had used joint-return rates.

The couple complained to the Tax Court that the IRS should have to use joint rates. But the court disagreed. The tax code "clearly predicates the benefits of joint-return rates on the filing of a joint return," the court asserted. The pair hadn't filed joint returns and thus they weren't barred from getting the benefits, the court concluded.

A tip for nonfilers who get caught: Don't wait for the IRS. If joint rates are better, file a joint return before the IRS sends a deficiency notice. Some cases indicate delinquents can get joint-return benefits this way, Research Institute of America says.

YOU GOTTA REST OR SLEEP, it seems, to deduct a meal eaten alone after a long work day. When some sales people worked a 14-hour day, they stopped to eat on the way home. The IRS says their meals aren't deductible. If they had been away from home overnight, or had to stop to "sleep or rest" during the long work day, the meals may have been deductible, the IRS noted.

WRECK, THEN LEASE: This building are demolished so the land they occupy can be leased. If the building is demolished before a lease is signed, the entire wrecking costs usually can be deducted at once. But if a lease is signed before demolition, the wrecking costs may have to be written off over the life of the lease, Touche Ross & Co., a CPA firm, relates. If a 50-year lease is involved, only 1/50th can be written off each year.

HE'S EASY: An "inadequate personality" merits a demanding IRS agent.

Agent Smith asked Joe for his business records. Joe handed them over. But later he sued to get the records back and told the IRS from using them against him. Joe was "incapable than the average person" in handling the confrontation with the agent: he is a "passive person with an inadequate personality," a psychologist averred. Joe "panicked, became mentally confused and wanted very much to reduce the stress and tension" the agent's presence caused.

Joe is "authority bound," and under stress "reacts pretty much to what a person tells him to do," a U.S. district court found. So the IRS must return the records because Joe couldn't have given them to Agent Smith "freely and voluntarily," the court held. If the IRS can try to get them again with a proper court order, the court added.

As for Joe, he and wife Blanche were indicted on criminal charges while the issue of their business records was in litigation.

BRIEFS: Property tax relief, mostly for the poor and elderly, was enacted in some form or another by 22 states last year...The Accountable Association recently known as the AAA) is giving away a pamphlet on automobile income tax deductions... Bless the stranders: Tax on 1.5 billion packs of butts provided $11.7 million of revenue to the state in the month of December alone.

—SANFORD L. JACOBS

Seeking a Solution

Carter Faces Problems No Matter What Step He Takes in Coal Strike

Compulsory-Arbitration Use Might Fail; Taking Over Mines Would Lose Time

Defiance of Taft-Hartley?

By URBAN C. LEHNER
and GEORGE GETSCHOW
Staff Reporters of THE WALL STREET JOURNAL

Bobby Jeffrey, a bearded 26-year-old miner from Carey, W.Va., has a message to send the President. "Carter can't make me mine coal, or nobody else around here," Mr. Jeffrey proclaims.

A lot of other miners share Mr. Jeffrey's defiant sentiments, and therein lies a particularly knotty problem for President Carter. With the 78-day coal strike forcing widespread power curtailments and threatening widespread layoffs, Mr. Carter is under mounting pressure to get the mines producing again. The President is thinking about a number of possible drastic steps, but there are serious doubts that any of them would work.

Negotiations between the 160,000 striking members of the 277,000-member United Mine Workers union and the 130-member Bituminous Coal Operators Association are deadlocked, despite public pressure from the President and the personal mediation of Labor Secretary Ray Marshall.

Yesterday, the BCOA did say it was willing to sit down with the union for further face-to-face talks, and Secretary Marshall resumed separate discussions with both sides. But the industry group rejected adopting as the basis for an industry-wide settlement the agreement worked out between the UMW and a company that isn't part of the BCOA, Gulf Oil Corp.'s Pittsburg & Midway Coal Mining Co. subsidiary.

Unsatisfactory Alternatives

And it's highly problematic whether renewed talks between the union and the BCOA would produce a settlement, whether rank-and-file miners would approve it if reached, and if they did, whether the process could move fast enough to get coal out of the ground before layoffs and brown-outs become serious.

Thus, by the end of this week or nearly next week, the administration may be forced to choose among a number of unappealing alternatives for getting coal production resumed.

The administration could ask a federal court for an injunction under the Taft-Hartley Act ordering the miners back to work. But the "conventional wisdom" in administration councils, according to a top aide, is that such an order "wouldn't be obeyed in any substantial measure."

Mr. Carter is also considering more drastic steps—asking Congress for power to impose compulsory arbitration on the parties or even for power to seize the mines temporarily in hopes that the miners would return to work for the government while the companies and the union worked out a contract. "None of the options that we have available to us are guaranteed to a negotiated settlement," Labor Secretary Marshall says. "But we believe that all of these options are preferable to a prolonged stalemate."

The Taft-Hartley "Two-Step"

Indeed, one senior government official says that "the beautiful thing about Taft-Hartley is that it's a two-day process." The President first appoints a "board of inquiry" to study the issues in the negotiations, only moving for a back-to-work injunction after receiving the board's report. While awaiting for the board's report, which can be delayed indefinitely, negotiations continue under greatly heightened pressure for a settlement.

All the possible choices, however, have serious weaknesses. "There are concerns about all three options—Taft-Hartley, arbitration and seizure," concedes presidential spokesman Jody Powell. "There is in every decision paper that I have seen a much longer list of cons than pros for each one of them."

The seizure possibility may seem particularly controversial. It's true Presidents Roosevelt and Truman seized the mines in the 1940s, but under special legislation. Today, "nationalization of the mines would set a dangerous precedent," says John Higgins, vice president, productions, Eastern Associated Coal Corp., a unit of Eastern Gas & Fuel Associates. "We'd be heading down the road toward socialism," he adds. Coal stockpiles could disappear altogether before Congress adopted a needed measure.

A Constitutional Issue

Not only might Congress be wary about setting a precedent of taking over by government takeover but there is also a constitutional issue: The government can't take private property without providing "just compensation." Almost any compensation the government suggests is likely to strike some mine operators as unjust. "There are certain to be suits," says one government lawyer.

If the government operated the mines, it could end up spending over the profits to operators. The miners could then run over private payroll without agreeing to work. At least the government would be free to set the miners' pay, to force them to abide by its orders, and to return them to work for an eventual permanent settlement, meaning the offer's sure to displace one side or the other.

Nevertheless, some state and federal officials, union leaders and even a few coal-company executives think seizure might be a way to get mines operating again. Asked what he would do if he were President Carter, George Meany, the head of the AFL-CIO, said seizing the mines

Please Turn to Page 38, Column 1

side, California. An *Asian Wall Street Journal* (circulation about 11,000) is also published in Hong Kong with its own staff, making it the fifth *Journal* edition.[3]

The *Wall Street Journal* accounts for more than 80 percent of the earnings of its parent company, Dow Jones & Co., which was established in 1882 by Charles H. Dow and Edward T. Jones. In addition to the *Journal*, the Company has a high-speed, coast-to-coast Dow Jones news ticker service, and publishes *Barron's National Business and Financial Weekly*. Also there is the AP-Dow Jones wire, an international business-financial news service having subscribers in 35 countries.

Throughout the years the emphasis of the paper has been on the gathering of economic news from around the world, and presenting it and analyzing it in a concise, clear, and interesting manner. It has also stressed in-depth reporting and thoughtful, well-researched editorials and analytical essays. Until about 1930 the paper saw itself specifically as an "economic" paper and its pages were filled with financial articles in a rather narrow sense. With the coming of World War II, however, the scope began to expand and more "general" news increased, and in-depth feature articles began to be commonly found in its pages. Today it is quite usual to find long features about the entertainment industry, about travel, about politics, and about science in the newspaper. Certainly it can still be considered a "financially oriented newspaper," but has taken a giant step beyond that.

The *WSJ* is constantly improving itself. Warren H. Phillips, president of Dow Jones & Co., said in 1977 that the paper during that one year had (1) added a Monday back page column called "Your Money Matters," (2) increased type size to make the paper more readable, and (3) strengthened foreign economic news coverage.[4] And, in 1978, an "Op-Ed" page was started, and general cultural coverage was greatly expanded.

To whom does *The Wall Street Journal* in the main appeal? A readership survey[5] in 1975 showed that of the paper's readers, 52 percent were top corporate management; 94 percent were male, and the average income of subscribers was $43,634. It can be said that the appeal of the paper is to those mainly earning their living in industry and commerce and in the field of finance, but sizable numbers of copies go to educators, students, housewives, professional persons, and workers in Government. About 50 copies of the paper go to the White House every day. Although the total circulation of the paper abroad is not large (in spite of the Asian edition), there are subscribers in nearly 100 countries including the Soviet Union.

[3] *The Asian Wall Street Journal* first appeared on September 1, 1976. It became the fifth separate edition of the *WSJ*, supplementing the four in the United States. It was started as a joint venture of Dow Jones & Co. and four prestigious Asian publishing firms: Japan's *Nihon Keizai Shimbun*, Singapore's *Straits Times*, *The New Straits Times* of Malaysia, and the *South China Post* of Hong Kong. The paper resembles its parent paper in basic format, but its small but experienced staff tailors its news to Asians, no matter its origin, putting it into its proper regional perspective.

[4] Speech by Warren H. Phillips at Goldman Sachs Institutional Investor Dinner Meeting, New York, October 26, 1977.

[5] Erdos and Morgan Study, 1975, included with a questionnaire sent the authors by David Kemp, manager of Public Relations for the *WSJ*, dated April 6, 1978. Henceforth cited as: Kemp Questionnaire.

Today the *Journal* has a staff of 4,100 (including the Asian edition), about 200 of whom are writers and editors. There are 31 correspondents in Washington, D.C. and 32 full-time reporters working for the *Journal* abroad. Main bureaus of the paper are in London, Hong Kong, Cyprus, Singapore, Tokyo, Montreal, Ottawa, Toronto, and Vancouver. The newspaper takes four news wire services—the AP, UPI, PR Newswire, and the Commodity Wire. The paper is printed by phototype process and uses no color and no photographs (except in advertisements); however, it does make use of many graphs and charts.[6]

The Wall Street Journal has won many prizes and awards. For example, in 1972 the paper won a Pulitzer Prize for distinguished international reporting (Peter Kann); in 1974 the Overseas Press Club Award for reporting on Latin America, and the Drew Pearson Award for investigative reporting (both to Jerry Landauer); in 1975 the Marquette University By-Line Award for coverage of the recession and the nation's future economic prospects (to James Gannon); in 1976 the National Headliner Award for foreign payoff stories; and in 1977 the Sigma Delta Chi Award for Public Service for coverage of corporate payoffs in the U.S. and abroad.

Editors of the paper make regular trips to more than 50 colleges and universities across the country recruiting reporters. In addition, the *Journal* also hires experienced newsmen, but it likes to bring young recent college graduates onto the staff. The new staffers must be bright, curious, with a good general education, and good writers. The news aspects of the paper are in the hands of Laurence G. O'Donald, the managing editor, who insists on careful but interesting writing and error-free editing. The quality of writing and editing in the *Journal* is probably the best in American daily journalism.

What about the general journalistic philosophy of the *WSJ*? In 1951 an editorial by then editor William H. Grimes expressed it well; in part it said:

> We like to have our editors and reporters experts in just one field, which is the field of making a newspaper, of finding information and telling it. We insist that they know what they are writing about and that they tell their story in the simplest language possible. If they can't do that latter, it indicates to us that their own knowledge is incomplete and we send them back for the rest of the information.

And, as to the editorial page, Grimes wrote that the newspaper makes no pretense of "walking down the middle of the road." Rather he said, "our comments and interpretations are made from a definite point of view." What does the *WSJ* believe in? Answer: the individual, his wisdom and decency. What does the *WSJ* oppose? Answer: all infringements on individual rights.

"People will say we are conservative or even reactionary," wrote Grimes. "We are not much interested in labels but if we were to choose one, we would say we are radical. Just as radical as the Christian doctrine." The editorial's final words: "We have friends but they have not been made by silence or pussyfooting. If we have enemies, we do not placate them."[7]

[6] Kemp questionnaire, and analysis of newspaper copies.
[7] Information sent authors by David Kemp, March 22, 1978.

The giant organization which is the *WSJ* today started modestly on the afternoon of July 8, 1889, when Dow and Jones decided to convert their "Customers' Afternoon Letter" into a four-page afternoon daily newspaper in their small offices at 15 Wall Street. The company at that time employed 50 people, and the paper was printed on a Campbell flatbed press.

Two imposing personalities in the growth and qualitative development of the *Journal* (and it is difficult to single any small number out) have been Clarence W. Barron, an electric personality who took over the paper in 1902, and Bernard Kilgore, who became president of Dow Jones in 1945.[8] Three outstanding editors who should be mentioned are Thomas Woodstock, William Grimes, and Vermont Royster—the last named still writes a column for the *Journal* ("Thinking Things Over") from his professorial chair at the University of North Carolina School of Journalism.

The Wall Street Journal is, indeed, one of the world's great daily newspapers. Throughout its history it has prized accuracy and thoroughness; and it has endeavored to report and interpret the world (primarily the financial world) incisively and intelligently. Few persons would say that this objective has not been reached by this increasingly "general" newspaper which represents the best in articulate and serious journalism.

The Washington Post

(UNITED STATES)

IN RECENT DECADES, the *Washington Post* has become one of the two top quality newspapers in the United States. By its insistence on editorial excellence, its financial strength, its dedication to the people's right to know the truth and its appeal to the nation's decision-makers, the *Post* has, in many respects, pulled even with its arch-rival, the *New York Times*.

Particularly in the past ten to fifteen years and above all in Watergate days, the *Post* has put together a combination of qualities—editorial innovations, crusades against governmental excesses, tough investigative reportorial digging and commitment to news and public service—which have thrust it into national

[8] Barron sought constantly to improve the quality of the paper, nearly tripled its circulation from 1902–1920, and hired Kenneth C. Hogate, one of the paper's outstanding managing editors. Kilgore was an innovator, beginning such projects as the weekly quality *National Observer* (1962–1978) and the Newspaper Fund, Inc., launched in 1959 to "get more bright people into news careers," in the words of Paul Swensson, Fund executive director for many years. The Fund also sponsors summer seminars, workshops, makes grants to teachers and students, and has helped put candidates for jobs in touch with prospective employers.

The Weather

Today — Variably cloudy, high in mid 30s, low near 20. Chance of precipitation 20 percent today, near zero tonight. Thursday — Partly cloudy, high near 40. Yesterday 3 p.m. AQI: 33; temp. range: 41-36. Details, C2.

The Washington Post

FINAL

76 Pages—4 Sections

Amusements	B 8	Financial	D 8
Classified	C 8	Metro	C 1
Comics	B13	Obituaries	C 6
Crossword	B15	Sports	D 1
Editorials	A30	Style	B 8
Fed. Diary	C 2	TV-Radio	B12

101st Year ···· No. 79   © 1978 The Washington Post Co   **WEDNESDAY, FEBRUARY 22, 1978**   Phone (202) 223-6000   Classified 223-6200 Circulation 223-6100   Home Served Metropolitan area See Box A2   **15c**

Coal Firms Ask Binding Arbitration

A Return to Work By Monday Sought; Union Aides Silent

By Helen Dewar
Washington Post Staff Writer

The coal industry called on the striking United Mine Workers Union late last night to submit their intractable contract dispute to binding arbitration and return to work immediately.

There was no immediate reaction from UMW leaders to the surprise proposal from the Bituminous Coal Operators Association, which resumed indirect negotiations with the union yesterday under the threat of government intervention to end the strike later this week. However, sources said it was doubtful that the UMW would accept the proposal.

In addition to other options, the government is reportedly considering pronouncing an impasse in the negotiations, which would end national contract bargaining and leave the companies free to go their own way in dealing with the striking miners.

This was understood to have contributed to the BCOA's decision to call for arbitration.

In a hand-delivered letter to UMW President Arnold Miller, BCOA President Joseph P. Brennan Jr. said third-party arbitration would be the "fairest approach to settle the coal strike," and would "return mines to production, our employes to work and coal to the nation."

Brennan said the 160,000 strikers at the mines owned by the 130 BCOA companies would be returning to work with the understanding that arbitrated contract gains would be retroactive to the first day of resumed work.

Under the BCOA's proposal, the union and the industry group would each appoint one arbitrator and jointly choose a third as chairman, with the secretary of labor to make the choice of chairman in case of a deadlock.

The three - member panel, which would be chosen by Feb. 24, would begin hearings March 6 to receive recommendations on points still at issue in the contract dispute. Its eventual decision would be binding on both sides and would take effect within five days of being handed down.

The proposal envisions a reopening of the mines by next Monday, when all the miners would be expected to return to work.

The BCOA proposal appeared aimed at seizing the initiative and putting the union in the position of inviting governmental seizure of the mines or court action to order the strikers back to work for 80 days—two options the White House has been considering to end the strike. A third option has been

See COAL, A5, Col. 1

Redskins quarterback Billy Kilmer smiles as his bride, the former Sandy Scott of Atlanta, receives a kiss

from Los Angeles Rams coach George Allen Monday in Las Vegas. The Kilmers will honeymoon in Hawaii.

United Press International

New York, New Jersey, Delaware Coastal Sites

High Court Upholds Drilling

By Morton Mintz
Washington Post Staff Writer

Clearing the way for possible discovery of billions of dollars worth of oil and natural gas, the Supreme Court yesterday let stand a decision to permit the first offshore exploratory drilling off New York, New Jersey and Delaware.

The action was among the most important taken by the justices in their first public sitting since they recessed Jan. 24.

Acting on a far-ranging list of appraisals of 450 cases, the court disposed of litigation as diverse as taxation and freedom of religion. The justices:

• Let stand a ruling requiring major universities—but only in certain states—to open campus meeting places to organizations seeking to promote "dialogue" about homosexuality. (Story, Page A8.)

• Agreed to decide whether anti-

fraud provisions in the federal securities laws apply to certain pension plans. (Story, Page A8.)

• Agreed to decide whether countervailing duties must be imposed on Japanese color television sets that Japan exempted from a certain tax. (Story, Page D8.)

In the offshore drilling case, the 2d U.S. Circuit Court of Appeals held that the secretary of the interior had prepared an adequate environmental impact statement and that exploration in the so-called Baltimore Canyon consequently could proceed.

The adequacy of the impact statement had been challenged—successfully in a trial court in Brooklyn—by Suffolk County, N.Y., and environmental groups.

Interior accepted bids of more than $1 billion in August for lease of 93 tracts occupying more than 500,000 acres. More sales are now expected.

Frank Ikard, president of the Amer-

ican Petroleum Institute, emphasized in a statement that "no one knows how much oil and natural gas may be found."

In addition, he said, there will be "a considerable time lag from the start of drilling operations until the country sees its first drop of oil or cubic foot of natural gas."

Delaware Gov. Pierre S. du Pont IV said of the court action, "That's super."

In briefs filed with the court, objectors contended that the circuit court ruling created "a major risk" of pollution in the Atlantic fishing grounds and on beaches.

The National Ocean Industries Association, composed of drilling companies and other firms with stakes in offshore exploration, argued that the delay caused by the trial court "resulted in losses running to several million dollars per week . . ."

See COURT, A6, Col. 1

Senate Informed Torrijos Probably Knew of Narcotics

By Robert G. Kaiser
Washington Post Staff Writer

The Senate Intelligence Committee believes Gen. Omar Torrijos of Panama probably knew that high officials of his government and his own brother were engaged in illegal narcotics trafficking, Sen. Birch Bayh (D-Ind.) told a secret Senate session yesterday.

But, the Intelligence Committee concluded after a long investigation, no reliable evidence linked Torrijos personally to this illicit activity. A sanitized version of the Intelligence Committee's report to the Senate was released to reporters during the locked-door debate on drug trafficking and its possible relevance to the Panama Canal treaties.

Several senators said there was no major new revelations during yesterday's debate. Nevertheless, public release of the Intelligence Committee's conclusion that Panama's "maximum chief" turned a blind eye to illegal activities is expected to strain Panamanian-American relations, and may encourage opponents of the controversial canal treaties.

However, Carter administration officials and treaty proponents expressed hope that the drug issue would not play a significant role in the debate over approval of the treaties. Sen. George McGovern (D-S.D.), who supports the treaties, said yesterday's secret session "may have been the biggest waste of time during the 15 years I have served in the Senate," and said it proved that opponents of the treaties "have run out of arguments."

Reliable sources said the White House overrode other government agencies in agreeing to public release of the Intelligence Committee's conclusions about Torrijos personally. The agencies, presumably including the State Department, feared that naming him in this context would complicate negotiations going on right now intended to persuade Torrijos to accept some Senate-imposed modifications to the treaties.

But the White House concluded that the committee's view of Torrijos' role would have to be stated publicly to avoid continued public debate and private innuendo from treaty opponents.

This is the relevant section of the Intelligence Committee report released yesterday:

"Some sources have provided intelligence which we view as reliable and which we believe suggests that Gen. Torrijos knew about narcotics trafficking by government officials and did not take sufficient action to stop his brother's activities."

The committee said it had been accusations that Torrijos too was personally involved, but "no conclusive evidence that could be used in a court of law" confirmed this.

See CANAL, A14, Col. 1

ORLANDO LETELIER
. . . slain former ambassador

U.S. Asks Chile To Produce 2 for Slayings Probe

By Timothy S. Robinson
Washington Post Staff Writer

The U.S. government has officially asked the Chilean government to produce for questioning two members of its military—who also are believed to be Chileans secret police agents—who have been linked by American investigators to the car-bombing murder of former Chilean ambassador Orlando Letelier here.

Yesterday's extraordinary public disclosure of the request was seen by diplomatic and legal sources as an indication that the federal government has reached the point in its sensitive, and so far highly secret, investigation that it wants to bring public pressure to bear against the Chilean government to force it to cooperate.

"This is obviously a situation where other diplomatic and investigative channels were thoroughly utilized before taking this route of public disclosure," one person familiar with the 17-month-old investigation said. "We want these men produced and these questions answered and we are aware of the possible diplomatic ramifications."

According to the documents filed yesterday, the two men entered the U.S. a month before the murders of Letelier and an aide at the Institute for Policy Studies, Ronni Moffitt, who were killed when a bomb blew up their car as they drove to work in

See LETELIER, A13, Col. 1

Va. Police Bias Trial Ends

Red Comma Denotes Race

By Bill McAllister
Washington Post Staff Writer

RICHMOND—Whenever a black applies for a job on Virginia's 1,320-member state police force, recruiters are careful not to list the applicant's race on their reports. Instead they add a small red comma after each black's name.

To many black Virginians and the Justice Department, the red commas are symbolic of a lingering streak of Southern racism that they claim still secretly guides the employment policies of the Virginia State Police Department - despite official proclamations to the contrary.

Yesterday, as Justice concluded an exhaustive 11-day trial into charges that the force systematically discriminates against blacks and women, lawyers for the state did not dispute the

RAMCHANDRA MALEKAR
. . . "a great happy life"

use of "red commas" or the hostile image that many blacks have of the force. But these, said Assistant State Attorney General Henry M. Massie Jr. do not amount to "one ounce of prejudice."

During the trial before D. Dortch Warriner, a conservative federal judge from Southside Virginia, the department has produced what one Justice lawyer yesterday characterized as evidence of "gross instances of discrimination." White investigators would pry into the sexual habits of black applicants and subject them to unwritten "vague standards" that white applicants seemed to avoid, said William White, a Justice lawyer.

See POLICE, A13, Col. 1

The U.S. is apparently at an impasse in its police bias suit against Prince George's County.

Page C1.

The Strike Hits Home

By T. R. Reid
Washington Post Staff Writer

NOBLESVILLE, Ind.—It was one thing when they blacked out the street lights. It was one thing when they turned off the heat and hot water in the schools. It was one thing when they cut out overtime at the Firestone plant.

But when they canceled the basketball game—that was something else. That's when the power shortage came home to the people of Noblesville.

Like most Indiana communities, this bustling county seat at the state's geographic center loves its high school basketball team with a passion that would shame the most devout Redskins or Bronco fans—with a devotedness that has come to be called "Hoosier Hysteria."

More than 2,000 people—a third of the town—turn out to see each week's game. This week, though, there won't be a game, because there's not enough electricity to light the gym.

The court clash between Noblesville High and arch rival Brownsburg is just one of the local casualties of the nationwide coal strike, Indiana's electric utilities, which rely almost entirely on coal to fire the boilers that drive their generators, have taken steps to conserve their declining fuel stocks. With the supply of electricity suddenly limited, the coal strike has suddenly become something more here than just another news item.

On Monday, the stockpiles at the power plants serving this town dropped

See NOBLESVILLE, A5, Col. 1

Vance Insists Mideast Jet Sales Are a Package

By John M. Goshko
Washington Post Staff Writer

Secretary of State Cyrus R. Vance strongly suggested yesterday that, if Congress blocks plans to sell jet fighters to Saudi Arabia or Egypt, the Carter administration will pull back its companion offer of planes for Israel.

The administration, Vance told Congress, will not accept any attempt to dismantle the proposed $4.8 billion package of advanced jet sales to the three Middle Eastern countries.

He sidestepped congressional questions about what the administration would do if Congress bars the sales to either of the Arab countries. But, in an impromptu chat with reporters, Vance hinted strongly that the administration would respond by canceling the Israeli part of the deal.

When a reporter asked if the administration's proposal is "all or nothing," Vance shot back "I said it's a package. That's what a package is, isn't it?"

This exchange occurred after Vance appeared before the House International Relations Committee to outline the administration's proposals for foreign aid programs totaling $9.4 billion during fiscal 1979.

However, members quickly turned instead to the plan, announced last week, to sell 60 F5E fighters to Egypt, 60 F15 fighters to Saudi Arabia and 75 F16 fighter-bombers and 15 F16s to Israel.

All or parts of this sale can be blocked if both chambers of Congress vote against them. Several members sympathetic to Israel have said they will introduce resolutions calling for a

See VANCE, A14, Col. 3

Lee Pardons Jailed Indian

By Elisabeth Becker
and Judith Valente
Washington Post Staff Writers

Acting Maryland Gov. Blair Lee III yesterday pardoned Ramchandra Malekar for his crime of manslaughter, giving the Indian a far greater chance to defeat a deportation order and stay in this country to serve the Hagerstown woman he loves.

Lee said he took this extraordinary measure to help salvage the life of Malekar who "was obviously rehabilitated in the fullest sense of the word." The governor said he feared that with deportation to his

See MALEKAR, A12, Col. 1

Retains Md. Tax Break

Burning Tree Can Stay All-Male

By Vernon C. Thompson
Washington Post Staff Writer

Maryland's attorney general ruled yesterday that Bethesda's Burning Tree Club, one of the most prestigious in the nation, can legally continue to bar women from its membership even though it receives special tax breaks from the state.

The tax breaks, in the form of reduced property tax assessments, are being withdrawn by the state from clubs that are found to discriminate against blacks and other minorities. Under Maryland law, however, "the club's policy of excluding women as members or guests" is acceptable if the club is operated "primarily" for men.

An evidence of that intent, Attorney General Francis B. Burch cited the fact that the men's locker room facilities occupy two thirds of the Burning

Tree's clubhouse and a "substantial addition" would have to be built to serve both sexes.

The attorney general also observes that the Burning Tree Club, unlike other clubs, "does not play host to women at any other time or any other function."

In fact, the attorney general notes: "The tax breaks, in the form of reduced property tax assessments, are being withdrawn by the state from clubs that are found to discriminate against blacks and other minorities. Non-members' wives only by appointment on specific December days prior to Christmas."

Jon F. Oster, deputy attorney general, said the ruling yesterday also found that the country club does not discriminate race because the 547 male members include two blacks as well as "members of Spanish, Indian and Oriental origin."

See CLUB, A6, Col. 1

Witnesses Say Elite Unit Fought

PLO Role Cited in Cyprus Battle

By Joseph Fitchett
Special to The Washington Post

NICOSIA, Cyprus—An elite squad of armed Palestinian guerrillas fought alongside Greek Cypriot National Guard forces in Sunday night's gun battle in which an Egyptian commando force was decimated at Larnaca airport, well informed sources said yesterday.

Wearing civilian clothes and carrying Soviet-made AK47 automatic rifles, members of the 12-man crack unit of the Palestine Liberation Organization were on the tarmac and took part in the 45-minute firefight that followed an attempt by the Egyptian commandos to storm a terrorist-held jetliner.

Despite official Cypriot evasiveness on this point, the Palestinians' participation in the Larnaca airport battle is

likely to further increase tension between Cyprus and Egypt.

Egypt suspended diplomatic relations with Cyprus Monday, angered by the incident in which 15 Egyptian soldiers were killed, and 16 others wounded. Two Egyptian commandos were reported missing, possibly having burned to death when a Cypriot shell set ablaze their C130 aircraft.

The Egyptians had mounted the Entebbe-style raid in an effort to capture two Arab gunmen who assassinated a prominent Egyptian editor in Nicosia, then took 11 hostages and commandeered a Cypriot jetliner with a crew of five.

The Palestinians' exact role at Larnaca airport and the number of casualties they may have inflicted on the Egyptians were not immediately clear.

See CYPRUS, A16, Col. 1

Ethiopia's government chief assures President Carter that his country does not intend to invade Somalia. Page A14.

prominence. Professor Lewis Wolfson calls the past decade one of "crusade and innovation that has made the *Washington Post* a great newspaper."[1] What took place to transform an ordinary paper into a leading newspaper could only happen because of the talents, leadership, brilliance and performance of a staff dedicated to the ideas of truth and to a free and responsible press. Their efforts have produced one of the world's most respected news organizations.

At least part of the *Post*'s status comes from its reader clientele. Early in the paper's history, British publisher Lord Northcliffe once remarked: "Of all the American newspapers, I would prefer to own the *Washington Post,* because it reaches the breakfast tables of the members of Congress."[2] Today, it not only reaches 98 percent of the principal government executives in Washington, including virtually all U.S. senators and congressmen, but an overwhelming majority of the executive-level decision-makers in business, labor and lower levels of government both in the capital and elsewhere. In that influence, there is power, as the events of the 1970's have shown. Chalmers Roberts, for 23 years a *Post* reporter, describes that strength thus:

> Today, a *Post* editor, reporter, or editorial writer can move a President or the Congress, influence the courts, cleanse a regulatory agency, affect elections, protect the public interest in myriad ways—or, as Katharine Graham (the publisher) has cautioned, the paper can "distort events, destroy reputations and influence public opinion recklessly."[3]

The *Post* has not always known the heady acclaim in which it revels today. In fact, for its first 90 years, it was never much better than a good newspaper.[4] It started humbly—as a four-page party paper on December 6, 1877, selling at three cents a copy to some 6,000 readers in the then muddy and somewhat drab capital. But it began hopefully, thanks to the visions and perseverance of its founder, Stilson Hutchins, who vowed his paper would be "a thorough-going newspaper, always abreast of the times . . . Democratic in politics and modern in style."[5] And it grew quickly—at the time of its first anniversary, it was already claiming a circulation of 11,875.

The early *Post* was bright, hard-hitting, bold, attention-getting and well-produced. Despite Hutchins' unabashed drive to furnish Washington with a party paper, he maintained strict independence on non-political matters. Foreign, congressional and New York news all regularly claimed front-page columns, and there was plenty of local news, too. While Hutchins' paper was unsympathetic towards blacks, Indians and Chinese, it was a bold advocate of civic improvements. It was unafraid to tackle the excesses of big business. When it was just a year old, it dared to hire a woman reporter. The *Post* owes much credit for its early success to the untiring, selfless dedication of its reporters,

[1] Lewis Wolfson, "Not Just Watergate Made this Paper Great," *The Quill* (January, 1978).
[2] Chalmers M. Roberts, *The Washington Post: The First 100 Years* (Boston: Houghton Mifflin Company, 1977), p. 76.
[3] *Ibid.*, p. 468.
[4] Wolfson, *op. cit.*
[5] Roberts, *op. cit.*, p. 5.
[6] Paper, "A Centennial History of the *Washington Post*," (Washington Post Company, 1977), p. 2.

who "built for themselves and the *Post* an excellent reputation by digging up enormous amounts of news, including exclusive reports that escaped the attention of competitors."[6] In January, 1889, when Hutchins sold the *Post* for $210,000, and retired, the paper's editors paid tribute to his accomplishments by writing:

> . . . he first gave to morning journalism at the national capital its modern and progressive stamp. It was his untiring enterprise and comprehensive sagacity that made an accomplished fact of what had come to be considered well nigh an impossibility—the establishment of a daily paper. . . .
>
> The paper became a paying investment from the start; its growth in circulation, influence and patronage was continuous . . . and Mr. Hutchins now leaves it one of the most valuable newspaper properties in the country, and an enduring monument to his ability.[7]

The *Post*'s new owners, Frank Hatton and Beriah Wilkins ended the paper's party affiliations. Upon their takeover, they promised a first-class "complete" paper, news without bias, with emphasis on the improvement and advancement of the city of Washington. Under their direction, the paper slowly changed and progressed, benefitting from Wilkins' ambition, foresight and capital and Hatton's inspiring genius. Their managing editor was the highly competent Scott Bone. While the size of the paper and its coverage grew in the Hatton-Wilkins era, it lacked the touch of greatness beause it was too conservative, prudish and unimaginative. After Wilkins' death in 1905 (Hatton had died earlier), his heirs sold nearly half of the *Post* to John R. McLean, publisher of the Cincinnati *Enquirer,* and the *Post* entered a low period in its history.

Within a decade McLean, who loved power, had associated the *Post* with sensationalism, Democratic Party politics, wealth, sex and social fluff and had turned it into "a second-rate newspaper."[8] McLean was more interested in making money than in serious journalism and he quickly re-created the *Post* "in his own image."[9] Although under his leadership the *Post* increased its circulation and its profits, it lost much of the objectivity and editorial independence his predecessors had given it. Journalistically, McLean was influenced by his friend, William Hearst, and sensationalism—crime, social gossip, rumors of war, sex—filled the *Post*'s pages. His loyalty to the Democratic Party biased his news judgments. He left major news decisions to a mediocre staff with limited vision and understanding of the fourth estate role of a newspaper. When, at 67, he died in 1916 from cancer, the paper had lost much of its credibility and influence as his son took over the paper's reins.

Edward (Ned) McLean took the *Post* from bad to worse in his 16 years as editor and publisher. Ned was a pleasure-loving lavish spender who was more interested in becoming a crony of President Warren Harding than in producing a good newspaper. He pushed personal journalism, switched the paper's allegiance to the Republican Pary (thus lowering its credibility still further), paid little attention to the news columns, and pursued the sensational story. Under

[7] Roberts, *op. cit.,* p. 41.
[8] Roberts, *op. cit.,* p. 132.
[9] *Ibid.,* p. 86.

Ned, the *Post* acted as if blacks did not exist, and it played the women's suffrage and prohibition movements for all the sensation value it could milk from such developments. Ned unfairly castigated President Wilson and closely associated himself with Warren Harding and his "Ohio gang." Finally, deeply in debt because of lavish spending, he sold the *Post* for $825,000 in 1933 to Eugene Meyer, a former New York banker who had recently been a governor of the Federal Reserve Board.

With the arrival of Meyer came rescue and renewal for the *Post*. Because of Ned McLean's partisan politics and sensationalism, the paper's circulation had fallen to about 54,000 and its credibility was at an all-time low. Meyer turned the trend around and pledged to make the *Post* vigorous, independent and serious again. In his first edition editorial, he promised "steadily to improve the *Post* and to make it an even better paper than it has been in the past. It will be conducted as an independent paper devoted to the best interests of the people of Washington and vicinity."[10] In his determination to improve the paper's service to the public, he drew up a set of seven principles to steer his new paper's commitment to the public's right to know:

> The first mission of a newspaper is to tell the truth as nearly as the truth can be ascertained.
> The newspaper shall tell ALL the truth so far as it can learn it, concerning the important affairs of America and the world.
> As a disseminator of news, the paper shall observe the decencies that are obligatory upon a private gentleman.
> What it prints shall be fit reading for the young as well as for the old.
> The newspaper's duty is to its readers and to the public at large, and not to the private interests of its owners.
> In the pursuit of truth, the newspaper shall be prepared to make sacrifices of its material fortunes, if such a course be necessary for the public good.
> The newspaper shall not be the ally of any special interest, but shall be fair and free and wholesome in its outlook on public affairs and public men.[11]

Although Meyer had had no publishing experience, he did have a clear idea of what a good newspaper should be, and he quickly learned the trade. In contrast to McLean's absence from the paper, Meyer was often in the newsroom, got to know his staff on a personal basis, "rapped" with them and even occasionally went with reporters on assignments. They liked him and responded by nicknaming him "Butch," but only used the term when he was not present.

Within a year, the *Post* had become aggressively independent, accurate and objective. Even though the paper was suffering heavy financial losses during this turn-around period, Meyer never wavered from his goal of bringing back quality and respectability. Although he made some mistakes, Meyer's moves largely were positive: he rebuilt his staff (Alexander "Casey" Jones became managing editor), improved national and international coverage, fought Franklin Roosevelt's attempt to "pack" the Supreme Court and, in general, ran a "tight ship." With crisp, non-partisan editorials, a new op-ed page, well-edited

---

[10] Roberts, *op. cit.*, p. 198.
[11] *Ibid.*, p. 214.

news and better production, the *Post* began winning awards. Within five years, circulation had doubled to 100,000. Soon Meyer began carrying articles by distinguished columnists Walter Lippmann, Dorothy Thompson, Ernest Lindley, Westbrook Pegler, book reviewer Lewis Gannett and theater critic Richard Watts.

By 1943, the *Post* was out of debt, circulation had climbed to 165,000 and advertising had risen from 4 million to 12 million lines annually. The paper's prestige soared, and shortly *Time* magazine was calling it "one of the world's ten greatest newspapers" and *Fortune* had placed it among the first half-dozen papers in the United States. Later, Meyer took on Drew Pearson's "Washington Merry-Go-Round" column. Under Meyer, the paper distinguished itself in World War II coverage and tackled local issues, such as greater fairness to Washington's blacks. The editorial page became a thunderer for social justice and equality. As one well-informed observer notes, during his 12 years Meyer not only made the paper solvent, "he also made it responsible, a paper that was read, and, what's more important, watched by government leaders and other journalists."[12] Another source observes that Meyer had given the *Post* "the priceless ingredients of success: integrity, decency and powerful idealism."[13]

In 1946, Meyer's son-in-law, Philip Graham returned from the Air Force to become the paper's associate publisher. When, five months later, Meyer took a World Bank assignment from President Harry Truman, Graham became the publisher. Like his father-in-law, Graham, formerly a brilliant president of the *Harvard Law Review,* had to learn newspapering. He vowed to follow the course already laid out and set to work to maintain and improve the *Post*'s objectivity, fairness in reporting, liberal outlook, independence and economic bases. In 1948, Meyer transferred his interest in the *Post* to Phil and Katharine Graham. Even though Katharine was his daughter, Meyer insisted that Phil should hold the bulk of the stock. The paper was then incorporated under The Washington Post Company, with a five-person board of directors, and Eugene Meyer as chairman.

Phil Graham built well on the solid foundations his father-in-law had laid. He acquired Russ Wiggins as his managing editor, John Sweeterman first as business manager and later as general manager and publisher, and Harry Gladstein as circulation boss. For the next two decades, their steadiness, loyal service and insights were to provide the backbone for the *Post*'s steady rise to increasing greatness.

Graham also moved swiftly to improve the *Post*'s economic base. He acquired radio and television stations WTOP in Washington and other stations in Florida and Connecticut. To improve the efficiency of his growing communications industry, he built a new plant on L Street. Financially, he turned the corner when he bought out the rival *Times-Herald* in 1954. From that point, the *Post* both had a monopoly of the Washington morning market and became the nation's ninth largest morning paper. Almost overnight, circulation zoomed

[12] Wolfson, *op. cit.*
[13] Roberts, *op. cit.,* p. 254.

from 200,000 daily to 380,000. Later, in 1961, he added *Newsweek* magazine to the *Post* empire.

Graham's boundless energy sparked the *Post* to new heights. He furnished a constant flow of news tips to reporters, worked to enlarge the news hole, used his contacts to increase advertising. He encouraged investigative digging and fought a courageous battle against Senator Joseph McCarthy's smear campaign. He hired the paper's first diplomatic reporter and added others to cover suburban news. He eliminated page three, the traditional "blood, guts and semen page." Up to 1957, the *Post* had had no foreign bureau, but Graham plugged that hole, too, first by setting up a London bureau, later another in New Delhi. Perhaps most important of all he was loved by those who worked for him and he constantly inspired and goaded them with his ideas and energy. But he became subject to spells of depression which made his behavior and performance oscillate with increasing rapidity between brilliance and despair. At 48, his brilliant career was cut short by suicide and his wife Katharine was left in control of the *Post*.

When Katharine Graham, at 46, assumed control of the *Post* and its related communication enterprises in 1963, she had had some editorial experience, but none in business management. She had worked at the San Francisco *News* and later had performed in a number of roles at the *Post*, including editorial writing. At first, she wisely left the paper's management in the capable hands of Wiggins and Sweeterman. On the editorial side, she brought Benjamin Bradlee over from his Washington bureau chief position at *Newsweek* in 1965, first to be her deputy managing editor, then managing editor, and later, when Wiggins went to the United Nations, executive editor. Mrs. Graham learned the business side of the *Post* quickly and well and her twin goals became editorial excellence and profitability. As one source notes, in the Kay Graham-Ben Bradlee era, "the *Post* has become a great newspaper, recognized as that by the best journalists in the country, by publishers who respect good business sense. by politicians. . . ."[14]

Bradlee has proven to be a "driver," an energetic, no-nonsense, self-confident, tough leader who demands excellence both in writing and reporting. He has added more and better "horseflesh" as he calls editorial personnel: Ward Just, Hobart Rowen, Stanley Karnow, Richard Harwood, Nicholas von Hoffman and David Broder, to mention a few. In fact, Bradlee has brought an entirely new journalistic environment to the *Post*. He has introduced a fresh, more attractive layout, especially on page one. He added the "Style" section, a sprightly section profiling people and their activities, culture and life-styles, entertainment, the performing arts, literature and art. He brought in talented Art Buchwald to enhance the op-ed page. He introduced a lively sports section. Above all, he has insisted on quality and has come down hard on "tilt," which abandons fairness, in the interest of giving the *Post* a liberal image. Despite his excellence, Bradlee could never have propelled the *Post* into rising greatness by himself. He was surrounded by talented people dedicated to responsibility, integrity and public service.

[14] Wolfson, *op. cit.*

During the past decade in particular, the *Post* has set numerous precedents that have earned it a reputation for honesty and courage. It dug into the secrets of U.S. involvement in the Vietnam War and, along with the *New York Times* and a few other papers, courageously published portions of the Pentagon Papers. But the activity for which the *Post* is best remembered is the exhaustive digging of two comparatively untried reporters, Bob Woodward and Carl Bernstein which led to the uncovering of the Watergate burglary scandal and the eventual fall of Richard Nixon from the Presidency. Later, two other *Post* reporters, Richard Cohen and Edward Walsh, uncovered Vice-President Spiro Agnew's involvement in bribery, a revelation that also led to his downfall. Nor has the paper's muckraking ended there. In 1976, it exposed Ohio Representative Wayne Hays' use of federal funds to hire his mistress as a secretary. Later, it unmasked the South Korean Government's attempt to "buy" certain members of Congress. With each new investigative "coup," the *Post* has gained public respect for its responsible role in keeping the institutions of democracy functioning honestly.

In the 'sixties and 'seventies, the *Post* has grown and expanded physically in several significant ways. In 1961, Phil Graham bought *Newsweek* magazine. A year later, with Otis Chandler, publisher of the *Los Angeles Times,* he established the joint *Washington Post-Los Angeles Times* national news service, which now has some 350 domestic and foreign clients. Shortly before his death, Graham added, for $8.4 million, a 49 percent interest in the Bowater Mersey Paper Company, which supplies most of the *Post*'s newsprint.

To serve the community, the *Post* extends itself beyond mere publication of a daily newspaper. It reaches its readers in personal ways through community programs, such as clinics, sports leagues, book and author luncheons. It has a School Service program which provides various classroom teaching aids free of charge to over 400 area schools. It has a summer in-service internship program for hopeful young journalists, a program so popular that some 1,500 apply each year for its 15 positions with the paper.

Once Katharine Graham gained confidence in her business acumen, she began adding to the Washington Post Company. In 1966, the Company gained a 45 percent interest in the New York *Herald-Tribune*'s Paris edition, later renamed the *International Herald-Tribune.* Then it built, and, in 1972, dedicated a new and modern *Post* building on 15th Street, N.W., which doubled the paper's work space. In 1974, the Company added WFSB-TV in Hartford and the *Trenton Times* and *Sunday Times-Advertiser* newspapers in New Jersey. In the same year, the Washington Post Writers' Group for syndication of newspaper feature stories and book publishing activities was formed.

The *Post*'s rise to ever-increasing credibility and greatness would have been impossible without Katharine Graham's determination, courage and insight. She overcame her initial "shakes" over being an uninitiated woman in the big business world to become the successful and shrewd president of the nation's 452nd largest company. She had the courage to publish the Pentagon Papers—the decision to print was ultimately hers—and the stamina to endure all the pressures of Watergate. Above all, she struggled to make the *Post* the responsible informer and servant of freedom in a democratic society for, as one of her colleagues has observed, "She has constantly sought to make the public understand that newspapers are the messengers, not the originators, of bad news, that freedom of the press means not special privilege for journalists but knowledge for the public."[15] Today, Kay Graham is considered one of America's top publishers, a recognition affirmed by her election as the first woman director of both the American Newspaper Publishers' Association and the Associated Press. However, it is not her "power to make or break Presidents, but the courage to trust her staff's best news instincts that has put Graham a peg above most publishers."[16]

In its earlier days, the *Post*'s foreign coverage was weak. It failed to enter seriously into foreign correspondence until Phil Graham established two overseas bureaus late in the 1950's. Not until the 1960's, with its reporting of the Bay of Pigs, Vietnam and the Middle East, did it begin to distinguish itself in this area. Today, it has eleven full-time correspondents in bureaus in Tokyo, Buenos Aires, Bonn, Jerusalem, Lusaka, Moscow, Paris, Cario, Hong Kong, London and Central America. Another 23 part-timers are distributed at key news-breaking points around the world. In addition to the foreign input from the AP and UPI wires, it now receives the internationally-recognized world coverage of Reuters and AFP, plus overseas items from the London *Sunday Times* and its own *Los Angeles Times—Washington Post* organization.[17] Its numerous international stories usually appear scattered throughout the first section or in special features.

The *Post* has always taken advantage of its proximity to national decision-making and has generally covered federal government in fair depth. Today, 33 reporters keep a watchful eye on all aspects of federal government. In the past, coverage of metropolitan Washington has been spotty and inadequate at times, but that, too, has changed under Kay Graham until the "Metro" section is now one of the paper's best. In 1975, the *Washington Monthly* found in the "Metro" pages "more creative thinking and innovative thinking . . . than in the big leagues of the national section."[18] Today, the "Metro" reporting corps is three times the size of that covering national developments.

The Washington Post Company employs more than 2,300 persons full time and another 500 part-time to work on the *Post*. The paper has a total editorial staff of 416, of which 119 are technical, 15 administrative and 296 directly related to the paper's writing and editorial functions. As of early 1978, total circulation of the weekday editions stood at 568,700 copies, with the Sunday edition selling about 800,000 copies. About 83 percent of the circulation is distributed to readers by some 5,000 newspaper carriers who work for almost 350 distribution dealers and agents. That, in itself, is no small task, as a typical daily averages over 100 pages and Sunday editions typically run between 200 and

[15] Roberts, *op. cit.*, p. 465.
[16] Wolfson, *op. cit.*
[17] Benjamin Bradlee, executive editor, Washington *Post*, in response to questionnaire, dated January 16, 1978.
[18] Roberts, *op. cit.*, pm 424.

over 300 pages. In 1976, the *Post* was consuming nearly 3,000 tons of news-print each week.[19] In circulation, it far outstrips its evening Washington com-petitor, the *Star,* which circulates about 375,000 copies.

The *Post* also leads all area publications in advertising linage. Whereas in 1933, it claimed only 14 percent of the advertising space in five Washington papers and less than one-fourth of the linage in 1953, today it displays over two-thirds of all the city's newspaper advertising. By 1966, it had already advanced to third nationally in total advertising, behind only the *Los Angeles Times* and the *New York Times* and 85 percent of its income was coming from advertising and only 15 percent from circulation. Each year its advertising linage—and the profits from it—mount. The 1977 total, for example, was about 16 percent greater than that for 1976. In 1976, the paper switched from a conventional eight-page column format to a new one of six news and nine advertising col-umns per page, thus making much-needed room for one-eighth more advertis-ing space while saving costs on the escalating price of newsprint.

The *Post* is economically sound. Each year, profits have increased, even in 1975 when the paper was under a crippling Guild strike and some of the presses were sabotaged. Overall revenues were $376 million in 1976, with profits run-ning at $24.5 million. Net income again increased significantly in 1977 and 1978. The paper is one of metropolitan Washington's largest businesses.

The economic health of the *Post* has allowed it to adopt the latest technical innovations. The paper's foreign correspondents now cable their stories to its London Communications Center, from where they are transmitted electronically across the Atlantic at 1,300 words per minute. A high-speed teleprinter converts them to copy at the *Post.* The newsroom began its conversion to the Harris com-puter composition system employing video display terminal input in 1976. At present, 35 Harris terminals set all early-run copy, plus the editorial and op-ed pages. Early in 1979, the paper went all cold type with a unique system devel-oped by the *Post* and Raytheon.

The *Post* and its editorial staff have won some 900 local and national awards for excellence in reporting, writing and photography. At least 15 have been newspapering's most prestigious award, Pulitzer Prizes, two of them in 1977. The year of Watergate marked a peak period for awards, when the paper won the Pulitzer Prize for public service and Woodward and Bernstein received numerous major reporting awards. Many of the *Post*'s editorial staff members have become well-known to the public through their by-lines, a device that also encourages excellence in writing and reporting.

Like all newspapers, the *Post* has had—and still has—weaknesses. At times in its history, it has gone after the sensational, has served pet projects and per-sonal interests of its publishers, has been snobbish and has neglected minorities and lower class coverage and readership. It was late in developing a network of foreign correspondents and did not introduce a high quality business and fi-nance section until 1977. But all that is in the past. Today, however, despite its

[19] Katharine Graham, in report to Washington Post Company Board of Directors, "Interim Report," April 3, 1977.

on-the-spot location, it still does not cover Congress and national events as thoroughly as the *New York Times*.[20] At least one critic has noted that its continuing rigid adherence to regular publication of certain columnists, even when their materials are poor, makes for a spotty op-ed page.[21] The editorial page frequently seems bland, too interested in remaining above the issues rather than wrestling forcefully with them. Some feel the *Post*'s recent reporting on remarks by Hamilton Jordan have bordered on gossip and have reflected poor editing. And others have questioned, perhaps partly out of jealousy, the ethics employed by the *Post* as it undercut the *New York Times'* and *Newsweek*'s rights to H. R. Haldeman's book, *The Ends of Power*, by publishing a front-page account of the book before its official release.[22]

In no way do such weaknesses undermine the *Post*'s greatness. Today, nearly every informed critic and journalist ranks the *Post* as one of America's two greatest newspapers alongside its arch-rival, the *New York Times*. In the minds of most, both tower, like twin skyscrapers, well above the nation's other quality papers.

The *Post* draws its claim to such heady greatness—and its right to be the nation's journalistic trend-setter—primarily from three sources. Its first strength is the individual brilliance of its numerous able, dedicated staff, beginning with Kay Graham and Ben Bradlee—people who have to be "tops" to remain at the *Post*. Then there is the paper's financial strength—"profitability" as Kay Graham calls it. And finally there is the *Post*'s commitment to editorial excellence, "to tell the truth as nearly as the truth may be ascertained" as former publisher Eugene Meyer once described it. This pledge to excellence, according to publisher Kay Graham, is "long term," one that "in an information-hungry world . . . has been and remains ultimately the bedrock of the Company's success."[23] These three marks of excellence, coupled with the *Post*'s strategic location, give it a critically important journalistic role, that of, in the words of Ben Bradlee, "a unique commitment to excellence as the morning monopoly in the capital of the free world."[24]

[20] Wolfson, *op. cit.*

[21] Henry Fairlie, "The Harlot's Perspective," *New Republic* (April 30, 1977), p. 24.

[22] Thomas Griffith, "Kay Graham and the Haldeman Snafu," *Time* (March 20, 1978), p. 70; "The Case of the Purloined Pages," *Time* (February 27, 1978), pp. 20–21; and "Does the End Justify the Means?" *Time* (March 6, 1978), p. 90.

[23] Kay Graham, quoted in "A Centennial History of the Washington *Post*," *op. cit.*, p. 14.

[24] Bradlee questionnaire.

Die Welt

(WEST GERMANY)

OF WEST GERMANY'S SEVERAL national newspapers, only *Die Welt* can claim to come directly from the nation's capital city of Bonn. *Die Welt* also has the more dubious distinction of being the country's most controversial national newspaper. In comparison to the Federal Republic's other two national papers, it lacks the size of *Süddeutsche Zeitung* and the ultraseriousness of *Frankfurter Allgemeine Zeitung*. However, it does manage to combine dignified and serious quality journalism with a modern dress and a lively demeanor.

Die Welt's move to Bonn from Hamburg in May, 1975—an operation that was spectacular in itself—was prompted partly by a desire for prestige and partly for pragmatic reasons. At the time of the move, the paper's owner, the Axel Springer Publishing Concern, pointed out that the world's great newspapers were produced at the political centers of their respective countries and *Die Welt* was joining the club.[1] Bonn was also envisioned as an ideal location because *Die Welt*'s main interests are coverage of political events and financial developments. And Bonn was seen as a location where the paper's financial problems could be more easily met.

Like West Germany's other current national dailies, *Die Welt* was a product of the post-World War II Western Occupation armies. Occupation forces established a total of 13 four-page papers called "Heeresgruppen Zeitung" which kept the German people informed about war results and the task of reconstruction. The most successful of this group was *Die Welt*, established in the British zone by Colonel H. B. Garland of the British army. The paper began on April 2, 1946, on a twice-weekly basis, and quickly gained a reputation for objective and comprehensive news coverage. Within a few months, it claimed a total circulation of a half million in two editions, one of 325,000 issued in Hamburg and the other of 175,000 published in Essen. Garland, who later became a professor of German at the University of Exeter, took Hans Zehrer, a highly respected German journalist and novelist, as his managing editor. Zehrer became the paper's editor for a short period until he felt impelled to resign because of political differences with the paper's philosophy. The position then went to Rudolf Küstermeier, who had more impact on the paper while it was in British hands than any other person. For a time, Alastair Hetherington, who later became editor of En-

[1] "World Press: *Die Welt*," Dispatch of the London *Times* (October, 1975).

gland's *Guardian,* was on the staff.[2] On September 17, 1953, the British sold
the paper to Axel Springer and Zehrer returned as chief editor.

A Berlin edition of *Die Welt* commenced publication from the old Ullstein
Publishing House in 1947 and total circulation surged to 600,000 almost at
once. By 1949, when the paper began appearing daily, over a million copies of
each issue were being sold. Foreign bureaus were established in London, Paris,
Amsterdam, Vienna, Salzburg, Stockholm, Copenhagen, Zurich, Rome and Madrid. It became a true national newspaper, but lost considerable circulation
when it went daily, partly because of political problems. In 1950, the British
authorities stepped down and *Die Welt* became a German-operated and controlled company.

In 1953, Axel C. Springer, a Hamburg publisher, bought 75 percent of the
company's shares for a reported sum of one million dollars. The purchase made
Springer, then only a 41-year-old businessman-journalist, the biggest publisher
of newspapers and periodicals in the Federal Republic.[3] Prior to buying *Die
Welt,* Springer had started a weekly broadcasting magazine called *Hör Zu* (Listen) in 1946 and the highly successful *Hamburger Abendblatt* two years later.
Hans Zehrer edited *Die Welt* for the first ten years Springer owned it. But his
editorials caused dissension and Springer had to intervene. From about 1957, as
Springer took more and more active control of his paper, the staff became increasingly disgruntled and began to leave in large numbers, a condition that
continued until a major policy change in 1965.

Die Welt has set extremely difficult goals for itself—goals towards which
the paper has worked consistently. They include provision of news from all parts
of life from all over the world comprehensively, precisely and quickly told,
organizing of those news so readers can find their own way in the paper, and
helping the reader to form his own opinions by providing comments, criticism
and other interpretation. One *Die Welt* official enlarged on the paper's motiva-
tions towards such high goals in this way:

> In the world of newspapers we want *Die Welt* to be a prestige symbol standing for
> intelligence and culture, for responsible thinking, initiative and success. We
> want *Die Welt* to be considered as a paper of unparalleled integrity, of compre-
> hensive, fast and reliable news reporting, of courageous and responsible com-
> mentary. Its voice must be authoritative and disciplined, its style lively yet timely
> and serious and trustworthy.[4]

Germany's history as a divided country caught on the front lines between
Communism and the free world gives *Die Welt* a special set of purposes. They
include the desire to reunite Germany in peace and freedom, rejection of extreme political views and intent to follow a middle-of-the-road path, peace between Germans and Jews and recognition of the rights of Israel, a free world
market and free trade, a democratic parliamentary government based squarely
on the West German Constitution, international cooperation under the aegis of

[2] John Sandford, *The Mass Media of the German-Speaking Countries* (London: Oswald Wolf Publishers, Litd., 1976), p. 22.
[3] "I've Got a Sixth Sense," *Newsweek* (Arpil 11, 1966) and London *Times* (September 18, 1953), p. 6.
[4] W. J. Freyburg, *Die Welt* in letter to J. Merrill, November 3, 1965.

DIE ● WELT

UNABHÄNGIGE TAGESZEITUNG FÜR DEUTSCHLAND

Belgien 20,00 bfr, Dänemark 3,70 dkr, Frankreich 2,70 F, Griechenland 25 Dr, Großbritannien 32 p, Italien 500 L, Jugoslawien 13,00 Din, Luxemburg 14,00 lfr, Niederlande 1,40 hfl, Norwegen 3,30 nkr, Österreich 10 öS, Portugal 30 Esc, Schweden 3,25 skr, Schweiz 1,20 sfr, Spanien 35 Pts, Kanarische Inseln 65 Pts

Mittwoch, 22. Februar 1978 · D**

Nr. 45 / 8. W. · Preis 80 Pf · 1 H 7109 A

Die Rentner sollen in vier Jahren 33 Milliarden weniger erhalten

Bonner Regierung will die Renten noch weiter beschneiden

HEINZ HECK, Bonn

Die geplanten Eingriffe der Bundesregierung in das Rentenversicherungsrecht sollen noch weiter reichen, als bisher bekannt. Dies geht aus dem Entwurf des Bundesarbeits-Ministeriums für das 21. Rentenanpassungsgesetz hervor, den das Kabinett am 8. März verabschieden will. Am 10. März tagt der Sozialbeirat, der den Regierungsvorschlägen den Vernehmen nach in seiner Mehrheit kritisch bis ablehnend gegenübersteht.

Während bisher der Eindruck vermittelt worden war, als handele es sich bei der für den 1. Januar 1981 geplanten Erhöhung der Beitragssätze auf 18,5 Prozent eher um eine unabwendbare Maßnahme, die man sogar noch – falls entsprechende vorrichtig wieder aufgebaut Kraft setzen könnte, sagt die Begründung zum Gesetzentwurf etwas anderes...

KOMMENTAR SEITE 6:
Rentenschwindel, neues Kapitel

...

Bundesbank-Pöhl: Amerika will den Dollar stützen

dpa, Frankfurt

Die Spitze der Deutschen Bundesbank hat in den Vereinigten Staaten wachsendes Verständnis für die Notwendigkeit einer Stabilisierung des Dollars entdeckt...

FDP-Minister fordert Lohnstopp wegen Dollar-Schwäche

Reuter, Wiesbaden

Der hessische Wirtschaftsminister Karry (FDP) hat an die Tarifpartner appelliert, angesichts der Dollar-Schwäche und der daraus resultierenden Verteuerung deutscher Exporte die Arbeitskosten einzufrieren...

Föderalismus steht hoch im Kurs

AP, Bonn

Die meisten und vor allem jüngere Bundesbürger stehen dem föderativen System der Bundesrepublik positiv gegenüber...

Die FDP sagt zur Neutronenwaffe doch nicht ja

RÜDIGER MONIAC, Bonn

Überraschend hat die FDP-Bundestagsfraktion gestern davon Abstand genommen, ein bedingtes Ja zur Neutronenwaffe zu beschließen...

Geiger: Abgeordnete umgehen das Karlsruher Diäten-Urteil

PETER SCHMALZ, München

Der ehemalige Bundesverfassungsrichter Professor Willi Geiger hat den Abgeordneten wegen ihrer Art der Umsetzung des Diätenurteils vorgeworfen...

Hunderte von Offizieren, Beamten und Journalisten sowie das ägyptische Kabinett begrüßten in Kairo die Kämpfer von Larnaka.
FOTO: AP

„Jene, die als Märtyrer fielen, sind für Ägypten gestorben"

DW, Nikosia

Der zyprische Präsident Spyros Kyprianou hat den Ägyptischen Präsidenten Anwar el-Sadat aufgefordert, sich in seiner Reaktion auf die Kreismme von Larnaka zu mäßigen...

Hochschul-Service der WELT

Alternative zum Studium: Immer mehr Abiturienten bemühen sich um einen Ausbildungsplatz in der Wirtschaft. Seit begehrt sind die kurzen Ausbildungsgänge mit qualifizierten Abschlüssen, die inzwischen von 200 Unternehmen angeboten werden...
Seite 9

Und weiter lesen Sie:
● SPD-Politiker Hansen greift die Bundesregierung an — **Seite 2**
● „Die Beamten sollen abnehmen" — **Seite 3**
● In Belgrad schwindet die Hoffnung auf ein Schlußdokument — **Seite 3**
● Die Red Wenns politischer vergeblich — **Wirtschaft**
● Fernseh-Krimis: Kein Gift durch den die Träume sind — **Fernseh-Seite**
● Ohne Sauerstoffgerät auf dem Everest — **Aus aller Welt**

TAGESSCHAU

IG Bau fordert 7,7 Prozent
...

West-Touristen erwünscht
...

Zypern in Cinemascope
...

Wohlfahrtsstaat Nr. 1
...

„Selbstdreher"-Rekord
...

Lösegeld liegt bereit
...

Trainer beurlaubt
...

Personalie
...

Kurse behauptet
...

Es wird wärmer
Die Temperaturen um 4 Grad stark werden bei einzelnen Regenschauern. Nur in östlichen Gebieten und in Berlin weiterhin kalt (0 bis –3 Grad), doch weitgehend trocken.

Unser Sohn und Sie befanden sich am Tage der Zustellung der WELT, 8 Uhr morgens.

Hirschkalbmützen für russische Dandys

DIETRICH MUMMENDEY, Moskau

Den sowjetischen Wirtschaftsfunktionären packt es mit dem Schwarzmarkt wie Herkules mit der vielköpfigen schlimmen Hydra: Kaum haben sie einen „Kopf" abgeschlagen, wachsen gleich mehrere neue nach...

SCHÖNHEIT VON BLEIBENDER DAUER

EIN ZEUGNIS kultivierten Wohnens von unvergänglichem Wert

BELEUCHTUNGSHAUS Remagen
EXKLUSIVE LAMPEN UND WOHNKULTUR
Neumarkt 35–37 · 5000 Köln 1
Telefon 0221/21 13 67

the United Nations, independence from political party or special interest groups and freedom to criticize all political views.[5]

Partly because of its firm adherence to these goals and partly for other reasons, *Die Welt*, according to at least one informed source, "has had a troubled history, and has long been a financial loss-maker."[6] Owner Axel Springer and his editors are conservative in their views, strong supporters of the Federal Republic and bitterly opposed to Communism and its policies. This stand made Springer a strong backer of United States' intervention in Indo-China and an aggressive opponent of Willy Brandt's attempts to establish greater rapport with the Soviet Union. Many have questioned the reactionary tactics of Springer papers; for example, in 1972 Springer's publications implied the Brandt government had promised millions of marks to the Soviet Union as reparation for World War II atrocities—a report the West German government labelled as "pure fabrication." And when radical students tried to destroy his papers as they were being delivered, Springer countered with a strongly worded response headlined "Criminal Terrorists."[7]

Springer has been the target of other criticism. Many have accused him of empire building. One source notes that Springer has created in West Germany "a concentration of newspaper ownership unequalled anywhere else in the world."[8] In addition to *Die Welt*, which has always been his quality showpiece and flagship, *Hör Zu* (circulation, 3.8 million in 1976) and *Hamburger Arbendblatt* (West Germany's biggest evening daily), Springer owns a lion's share of the remainder of the German media. In 1976, he owned 27 percent of the total West German daily newspaper market; for Hamburg and West Berlin, Springer's share of ownership totalled around 65 percent.[9] He has a monopoly of the nation's two Sunday papers, *Bild am Sonntag* and *Welt am Sonntag*. In 1952, he began publishing *Bild-Zeitung*, a garish mass appeal daily with a sex and violence formula. By 1966, it was printing an astounding 5 million copies daily, but its actual readership was triple that because an average of three Germans read each publication. Springer also publishes numerous magazines.

Springer's critics appear to be less concerned with his amassing of publications than with the power and influence he wields. One critic notes: "West German politicians have always been wary of criticizing him, and the reluctance of the Federal Government to face up to the problems of press concentration must be ascribed in part at least to the politicians' fear of having opinion mobilized against them by a campaign in the Springer press."[10]

Others are even more concerned over the influence Springer has through his publications, especially in *Bild-Zeitung*, on the attitudes and political opinions of the West Germany citizens. German leftists are constantly complaining that his strong conservatism leads to desire for unity within the nation at the expense of better relations with the U.S.S.R. and especially the German Demo-

[5] Brochure: "Ein Weltblatt stellt sich vor Die Welt," (Bonn: Axel Springer Verlag AG, 1977), p. 3.
[6] Sandford, *op. cit.,* p. 212.
[7] Adolph Schalk, "Putting the Starch in the German Press," *Saturday Review* (March 25, 1972), p. 81.
[8] Sandford, *op. cit.,* p. 32.
[9] *Ibid.,* p. 31.
[10] *Ibid.,* p. 33.

cratic Republic. Such critics point to the lavish skyscraper headquarters he built next to the Berlin wall as a gesture of defiance to Communism. In some of his publications, Springer also has aroused considerable opinion against dissident students and intellectuals. Some critics in Germany go so far as to accuse Springer publications, among them *Die Welt*, of manipulating headlines and stories to give false impressions.[11]

Axel Springer and his publications are controversial partly because of his staunch, conservative stand on the principles on which the Federal Republic is founded, partly because of his abhorrence of political Communism and partly because of his hyper-sensitivity to the evils of Fascism which makes him a rigid opponent of social change. He stated his own stance in this last respect clearly in a 1969 London *Times* advertisement: "The Axel Springer publications stand for progress but oppose all attempts to destroy or subvert our society . . . (and) reject any kind of political extremism."

Reduced advertising revenue, sharp rises in the costs of newsprint, wage increases, inflation and even a recession have combined in recent years to put many German newspapers into financial trouble, *Die Welt* among them. Although Springer has been propping it up with infusions from his popular *Bild-Zeitung* and other profit-earning publications, *Die Welt* has been losing money for years. *Die Welt* guards its financial status closely, but one 1975 estimate put its annual loss at $10 billion.[12] The recurring loss helped prompt Springer to move *Die Welt* to Bonn, where experts predicted the paper could save $5 million annually in production costs.

Since it peaked at over a million copies daily in 1949, *Die Welt*'s circulation has dropped slowly to where it has stabilized at today's level of about 230,000 copies each day and 295,000 on Saturdays. The decline partly results from a decreased number of daily editions. About 80 percent of the copies are sold by subscription, with the remainder distributed via street sales.[13] In 1975, that balance was more nearly two-thirds to one-third, with 174,467 subscriptions and 99,340 kiosk sales. A market survey taken the same year profiled the typical readers to be 30–39 year old employed men with a monthly income of 2,000 or more German marks and at least a high school education. Most reside in cities of 500,000 or more population in Hamburg and the heavily populated North Rhine/Westphalia "landers." The survey also showed readers to be distributed over a wide range of age and professional groups.[14] The paper's expressed aim is to reach decision-makers.

A serious, yet lively newspaper, *Die Welt* seeks to give concise, yet comprehensive information for dynamic, active readers in four main areas. The first section or "book" of the paper (six or more pages) features national and international news, on-the-spot reports, commentary and analyses of a political nature. Its political views lean towards the conservative side, reject extremism and sup-

[11] Schalk, *op. cit.*
[12] "World Press: *Die Welt*," *op. cit.*
[13] Arnd Pötter, vice-publishing manager, *Die Welt* in response to questionnaire, dated February 6, 1978.
[14] Brochure, "Your Way into the German Market," *Die Welt* (Bonn, 1976).

port parliamentary democracy and international cooperation. It claims to be politically independent under its sub-title, "An Independent Newspaper for Germany." The second section, an area in which the paper excels, provides
comprehensive business and economic information. This portion covers news of
about 4,800 leading companies in Germany and other major industrial nations.
Die Welt frequently reprints articles from London's *Economist* in this section
and in 1976 it began collaboration with the *Wall Street Journal* in the field of financial news. This section on economics is usually combined with the paper's
third emphasis area, cultural affairs, into the second "book." The third section
provides a wide range of material covering the arts, music, theater, film, radio
and television. Special consideration is also given science and technology in this
section; *Die Welt* has the only German journalist who reports regularly on
American scientific activity. The fourth area of emphasis covers sports and miscellany. *Die Welt* editors take pride in the fact that as much play is given to the
background of a sports event as the event itself. The daily miscellany feature
"Aus aller Welt" occupies the back page (the second most important place in
German papers) and contains news of well-known personalities, sensational
events, court cases and human interest stories.

   Die Welt provides numerous supplements and special pages. A third "book"
or supplement is offered almost daily. "Advertising and Marketing" is alternated
with "Business and Careers" on Mondays, "Travel–Automobiles" every Thursday, "Homes" on Fridays, and "Welt Report" on world and cultural affairs and
literature on Saturdays. There is also a weekend travel section. The paper joins
with London's *Times,* France's *Le Monde* and Italy's *La Stampa* in the publication of European Joint Special Reports, called "Europa und Die Welt," which
cover all aspects of industry, trade and finance, as well as sociological questions
appropriate to these topics. *Die Welt's* version in German always appears on the
first Tuesday of each month. Together, the four papers reach a total Western
European audience of some 5 million readers. From time to time, *Die Welt* also
publishes supplements on foreign countries jointly with Austria's *Die Presse*. In
addition, *Die Welt* often gives special reports and features on subjects related to
industry, urban life, careers, investments and leisure. For example, there is a
special "Transport and Shipping" supplement the second Tuesday of every
month.

   The editors thoughtfully group news, special feature materials and other
sidebar stories on a single topic for the convenience of *Die Welt* readers. Because of this tendency, the order of the sections if sometimes disrupted. According to the paper's publishers, the contents of the paper, by percentage of the
total "news hole" space volume they occupy could be categorized as follows: international news, 14 percent; national, 20; analysis and editorials, 6; features
and entertainment, 14; sports, 7; business, 25; travel, 3; home, 6; and public
service, 5 percent. Advertising takes up 48 percent of the paper's total volume.[15]

   Much is done to make *Die Welt* an interesting, highly readable paper. It
uses clear, "zingy" language. Paragraphs are frequently given a headline in

[15] Pötter questionnaire.

darker and larger type. There are numerous informative illustrations and except for the front page, where a single picture is the norm, photographs are used quite liberally. The paper is designed so it can be read rapidly. Under the blue border underscoring the paper's name on the first page are brief synopses of articles located inside. A digest of the key events of the day, "Tagesschau," fills the right-hand column. About a dozen of the day's principal national and international stories plus one advertisement in the lower left corner complete the initial page.

Die Welt has always paid especial attention to foreign news, and today it has a large overseas staff. Thirty-four full time correspondents are located in 17 strategic news-making capitals of the world: Athens, Beirut, Bogota, Brussels, Jerusalem, Johannesburg, London, Los Angeles, Madrid, Moscow, New York, Paris, Peking, Rome, Stockholm, Tokyo and Washington. Eleven part-timers are also posted in five centers—Vienna, Milan, London, Washington and Paris. In addition, the paper sends special correspondents to crisis spots. On top of all this, foreign news comes to *Die Welt* from four news wire agencies (AP, AFP, Reuters and DPA) and Springer's own foreign syndicated service, Springer Auslandsdienst (SAD). Coverage of international events and backgrounding of them must be considered excellent, though there is a definite pro-West bias. Distinguished foreign correspondents who have served *Die Welt* include George Vine, George Bailey, Bernhard H. Levy, James Buckley and Aldo Rizzo.[16]

Now that *Die Welt* has located in Bonn, its coverage of the Federal Republic's national affairs is without peer. With 25 senior journalists at the capital, the paper is "in a position to soak up all the news available in a town of only 250,000 people."[17] While the paper concentrates on national news, with offices in Berlin, Hamburg, Frankfurt and Munich as well as Bonn, it covers the country thoroughly. It has placed 50 correspondents in Germany's six leading cities and keeps 19 in other locations about the nation.

Die Welt is served by a total staff of 940, divided as follows: technical, 440; managerial, 240; and editorial, 220. It seeks highly qualified and experienced staff where possible. Editors must have finished university study and the commercial staff must be well trained in advertisement policy and procedures. Reporters are allowed by-lines on many of the paper's stories.

Die Welt's chief editor from 1953 through the 'sixties was Dr. H. F. Gerhard Starke, a conservative, hard-line anti-Communist. In 1966, the paper hired two further conservative columnists, William Schlamm and Winifred Martini. Starke's managing editors were two noted journalists, Hans-Wilhelm Meidinger and Dr. Heinz Pentzlin. In the 'seventies, there have been several experiments with top personnel. The paper is now jointly edited by topflight journalistic technician Klaus Jacobi and Dr. Herbert Krema. The latter is a right-wing ideologist and has been one of Springer's top political lieutenants.[18]

Two additional men have made significant contributions to *Die Welt*. Ernst Cramer formerly served as a managing editor of the paper, but in more recent

[16] Pötter questionnaire.
[17] "World Press: *Die Welt*," op. cit.
[18] *Ibid.*

times has headed the central planning bureau for the entire Springer organization and is one of Springer's most trusted advisers. And W. Joachim Freyburg, formerly a staff member of the paper, now heads its Information Department. Herr Freyburg publishes an excellent 16-page monthly house organ for *Die Welt* called *Verlagshaus Die Welt: Nachrichten fur unserer Mitarbeiter* and directs an elaborate public relations program.

Since 1954, *Die Welt* has been a member of the Top European Advertising Media (TEAM) group of 16 quality newspapers in eleven countries. These papers are all characterized by their stand for democratic principles, their intellectual readerships and their international reputations. The papers assist each other with international advertising and introduce international outlets to advertisers in their own countries. *Die Welt* was, for some time, the only German national newspaper to belong to this group. It is conscious of its advertising and uses some color for advertising purposes.

Die Welt has received many honors and special recognitions for its general excellence. In 1967, the University of Missouri School of Journalism awarded its Honor Medal to *Die Welt* for "distinguished service in journalism." Earlier, a group of 26 American professors ranked it one of the 20 best newspapers in the world.

Although *Die Welt* has proven to be a controversial paper inside West Germany , it has a well-known and respected image abroad. In recent years, it has taken on a more streamlined look and has toned down its strong rightwing political views, action which makes it less controversial to many Germans. But, as one source observes, "it still remains *Die Welt*," even to the point of refusing to refer to East Germany except by the initials "DDR" (for its German name) in quotation marks.[19] However, abroad, *Die Welt* has been and continues to rank as a newspaper of international standing, one described by some as "the voice of Germany in the world." Disagreement does continue over the man who makes *Die Welt* possible, Axel Springer. Some outside Germany regard him highly, even as a protector of freedom of expression in the traditions of Peter Zenger and Thomas Paine. But some Germans take strong exception to such views and to them Springer remains a controversial figure.

However, informed sources both within and outside Germany are in full agreement on one point—the impressive range of *Die Welt*'s news coverage, a value its editors believe sets it apart as a unique and distinctive paper. A 1965 German study found it gives widest coverage among German national dailies of political, economic and cultural affairs. And, in 1975, a London *Times* study called *Die Welt*'s general news coverage "still unrivaled."[20] So, despite its problems and the disagreements it fosters, *Die Welt* must be considered one of the world's quality papers.

[19] "World Press: *Die Welt*," *op. cit.*
[20] *Ibid.*

Winnipeg Free Press

(CANADA)

THE *Winnipeg Free Press*, nicknamed "Canada's Gadfly" by one of its own distinguished foreign correspondents, manifests a spirit of criticism and independence indicative of the "quality" press at its best.[1] The *Free Press* maintains that spirit because of its Independent Liberal political stance, its financial solvency, its sound ideology and its care to stay aloof from situations which would limit its editorial freedom.

Throughout its 108-year history, despite its own rich Liberal background, the *Free Press* has remained mildly conservative and has often admonished the Liberal government in Canada. Peter McLintock, the editor, considers his paper's political outlook to be "liberal, but more or less of the center."[2] Owned by F. P. Publications, Ltd., it has the financial stability to advocate "freedom of trade, liberty of religion and equality of rights" boldly and to encourage intensive investigative reporting.[3]

Of all Canadian newspapers, the *Free Press* is perhaps most serious, both in its sober dress and restrained writing. It takes itself and its readers seriously. It seeks to reach a wide spectrum of the public. Its primary interest is "to serve the public good."[4] For these reasons alone, it places high among North America's elite papers.

The *Free Press* is not a large paper: at least a half-dozen Canadian dailies are larger in both circulation and number of pages. Its present circulation is only about 143,000. But it is powerful, respected, feared, sometimes even hated. No paper in the country has topped it as a champion of minority causes and as a leader of informed and progressive national opinion. And no other paper is so consistently controversial or, as one well-informed writer has put it, "rough and cranky but always educated, fearless and unrepentant."[5]

The *Winnipeg Free Press* was begun as the *Manitoba Free Press* by William F. Luxton and John A. Kenny in 1872.[6] It struggled along until the 1880s, when it took new life while the Canadian westward movement was at its peak.[7] Dur-

---

[1] Bruce Hutchinson, "Canada's Gadfly: The *Winnipeg Free Press*," *Harper's Magazine* (April, 1963).
[2] Quoted in questionnaire completed by R. H. Shelford, general manager of the *Free Press* and mailed to Harold Fisher, February 27, 1978. (Hereafter called Shelford Questionnaire.)
[3] *Ibid.*
[4] Shelford questionnaire.
[5] Hutchinson, *loc. cit.*
[6] Shelford questionnaire.
[7] Shane MacKay, former executive editor, in letter to John Merrill, September 29, 1966.

ing this same period, John Wesley Dafoe came to Winnipeg as an Ontario farm boy. He was to become the great editor who would direct with great brilliance the "Old Lady of Carleton Street," as the paper became known, from 1901 until his death in 1944. Regarded generally as the finest editor Canada ever produced, Dafoe built the paper into what became "the Bible of Canadian prairies and the nation's thunderer."[8]

Dafoe edited the *Free Press* for 40 years, infusing into the paper a respect for thorough coverage combined with biting editorials.[9] He, more than anyone before or possibly since, gave the *Free Press* its special "personality" of brashness overlying a deep layer of serious and thoughtful calmness. He certainly gave the paper a character which made it a national newspaper, one which was essential reading for opinion leaders throughout the country.

When Dafoe died in 1944, Grant Dexter and George Ferguson jointly edited the paper for a short time. Ferguson left for Montreal to become editor of the *Star,* and Dexter returned to Ottawa and his main interest, reporting on Parliament. Tom Kent, a young Englishman trained at Oxford and on the *Manchester Guardian,* was brought in to edit the paper. He made some changes (such as reducing headline size on the front page) but did not essentially alter the character of the paper. After five years, he left the paper to enter politics in Ottawa.[10]

Although the *Free Press* has changed somewhat since the days of Dafoe, it retains the essential character of what is sometimes called its Golden Age. It still influences public opinion, at least in Cabinet offices and diplomatic circles. Its editorials still pull no punches and deal with vital issues on a day-to-day basis. Its circulation, a high percentage of which is delivered to homes, is rising steadily. Richard C. Malone, today's publisher, fearing outside pressures, desires to keep the paper financially independent and sound. He has succeeded on both counts.

Although the *Free Press* is probably best known for its local and national news, its policy is to seek balance in its coverage: "We stress international and national news as much as we do local."[11] It maintains a four-man bureau in Ottawa which provides especially strong parliamentary coverage. Although it carries a small staff of full-time foreign correspondents—it keeps its own men only in London and Washington—the *Free Press* considers international news important and gives it special play. Several specialists are always ready to take foreign assignments when and where the paper feels there is a need, and the paper also uses 15 expert part-time correspondents (stringers) throughout the world.[12]

[8] Hutchinson, *loc. cit.*
[9] Although most critics have nothing but praise for Dafoe's editorials, there have been dissenting voices. Grattan O'Leary, a Canadian journalist who was very familiar with the work of Dafoe, wrote in 1966: "I thought some of Dafoe's editorials during the election of 1917 were irresponsible, lacked measure and perspective. At the same time, I must add this: I think the two finest pieces of journalism I have ever read in my day were the last two pages of Dafoe's 'Laurier' and his obituary tribute to his friend, Harry Sifton." ("A Century of Journalism" in *The Gazette,* Montreal, September 15, 1966—a special edition on Canadian journalism.)
[10] "Newspapers of the World—XX," London *Times* (April 14, 1965).
[11] Shelford questionnaire.
[12] As of this writing, the *Free Press* had stringers in London, Paris, Munich, Madrid, Rome, Tel Aviv, Tokyo, Lusaka, Nairobi, Tehran, Melbourne and at U.N. Headquarters in New York.

Ottawa meet full of hot air — Broadbent —Page 3

China's Gang of Four to be 're-educated'

—Page 37

Personal bankruptcies increase —Page 9

Municipalities suspected of cheating UIC on jobs —Page 13

Rich man begs for fish freezer —Page 21

Joe Clark at Day 730 —Page 68

INSIDE

Anytime	7
Bio-dex, Horoscope	33
Bridge	24
Comics	67
Crossword	24
Deaths	5, 51
Finance	47-50
For People	21-33
Jumble	53
Letters	77
Movies	31
Television	28
Weather	5

WEATHER REPORT FROM *Advance*
Cloudy; low -15, high -5
SUN: Rises 7:28 a.m.; Sets 5:58 p.m.
MOON: Rises 5:56 p.m.; Sets 6:58 a.m.

Winnipeg Free Press

VOL. 85 — No. 122 | WEDNESDAY, FEBRUARY 22, 1978 | 15 CENTS 25¢ WITH COLORED COMICS

FINAL EDITION ★ ★

Whiteway says he'll prove fishy tales

By BILL HOLDEN

Manitoba Progressive Conservative MP Dean Whiteway said Tuesday he will release sworn affidavits in the House of Commons Thursday naming senior executives in the Freshwater Fish Marketing Corp. in connection with misappropriation of public funds.

Whiteway (PC-Selkirk) said the disclosures involve thousands of dollars, and implicate higher management in the firm.

"Specific charges will be levelled against people in the corporation," Whiteway said.

The MP said the documents would be signed under oath by two former employees who volunteered the information after The Free Press revealed mismanagement.

"They will outline specific things that happened in the corporation that are absolutely wrong morally and ethically," he said.

The affidavits, probably complete today, implicate "management in high places" but "it's hard to put a dollar figure" on the amount involved, he said. "It's thousands of dollars but I don't know the top figure."

Whiteway said he is confident the disclosures will force Federal Fisheries Minister Romeo LeBlanc to launch a full inquiry into the fish firm, which he has resisted on grounds of lack of evidence. Whiteway said he has been pressing LeBlanc for a full-scale audit for almost two years.

He said chances for an investigation now are "excellent."

"When I come forward with specifics, I will find it hard to believe that in light of that, he would say everything in the corporation is okay," Whiteway said.

Whiteway said he has not received a reply to a letter he sent LeBlanc including a call for the dismissal of Peter Moss, chairman of the corporation's board of directors.

Whiteway would not name the employees accusing senior management, but said one was a former accountant responsible for accounts receivable and the other was a receptionist and stenographer. Both are no longer employed by the corporation, he said.

The firm, a federal Crown corporation responsible for marketing fish caught in the Prairies, the Northwest Territories and some parts of northwestern Ontario, was criticized recently after it was disclosed that up to 15 million pounds of fish is being held in cold storage when demand for the product is high.

Manitoba Northern Affairs Minister Ken MacMaster urged the federal government last week to initiate an inquiry into the firm's marketing practices following published reports that tens of thousands of pounds of fish were destroyed or sold to pet food companies and fish-rendering plants after being held in cold storage too long and developing freezer burn.

It was also disclosed that employees forged a rabbi's initials on fish shipments.

Dollar shoots back up

The Canadian dollar gained nearly half-a-cent in opening trading on New York money markets today in apparent reaction to an announcement by the Canadian government that it plans to borrow funds abroad to support the dollar.

After trading started in the interbank currency markets, the dollar shot up to 89.90 U.S. cents from Tuesday's close of 89.49 U.S. cents.

However, the dollar started to decline soon after its initial spurt.

The U.S. dollar in terms of Canadian funds at noon Wednesday was down 13-50 at $1.1148. In New York, the Canadian dollar was up 21-100 at $0.8970.

A trader for the Bank Canadian National said there was still "substantial" demand for U.S. currency on the market and added it may take some time before the full effects of the government announcement are felt.

"Nothing has really changed — the negative sentiment towards the Canadian dollar is still with us," he said, although he added that the dollar could be trading above 90 U.S. cents this week in reaction to the govern-

—Continued

See CANADIAN page 4

—AP photo

Gesturing people attend the funeral in Cairo Wednesday of 15 Egyptian commandos killed in Sunday's attempt to storm a plane at Larnach, Cyprus where hostages were being held. People in the crowd shouted "no Palestine after today" and "down with Cyprus." Cypriot authorities fired on the Egyptian troops after they began an apparently unauthorized attempt to free the hostages.

Spending plans unveiled today

OTTAWA (CP) — The government reveals its spending intentions today for the year beginning April 1, hemmed in by its promise to hold the line on expenditure and the need to spend to support a troubled economy.

The main spending estimates, which set out in detail government outlays for the coming fiscal year, are expected to exceed $46 billion. In the current year ending March 31, the government hopes to keep its spending to $44.45 billion.

The estimates come a week after a federal-provincial premiers' conference in which the various governments agreed to restrain their spending.

After the premiers' meeting, the governments issued a statement saying growth of spending by government should be held — on average — to less than the increase in real economic growth.

In recent years, following much criticism by business, opposition politicians and others, the federal government has reduced its rate of increase in spending. But despite the downward trend, expenditures this year will still be about five times the level they were when Prime Minister Trudeau assumed office about 10 years ago.

The rate of increase brought criticism just over a year ago from Auditor-General J. J. Macdonell, who said the government had lost — or was close to losing — control over its spending.

Macdonell's recommendation that the government appoint a comptroller-general as its chief financial officer to help hold down spending was acted upon on Monday when the government appointed Harry Rogers, a Xerox of Canada Limited vice-president, to the post.

The estimates will reflect government attempts to balance inducements to economic growth against its commitment to restraint.

While avowing a tough line on spending, the government has piled up a record $9 billion debt this year.

While today's estimates suggest how the government will spend its money, plans for raising government funds will not be revealed until the next budget. Chretien has said that will be after mid-April.

Withdraws recognition

Cairo snubs Cypriot head

CAIRO (CP) — Egypt no longer recognizes Cypros Kyprianou as president of Cyprus, Egyptian President Anwar Sadat said today while speaking after the funeral of the 15 Egyptian commandos killed in Cyprus last Sunday.

"As of today, we withdraw our recognition" of Kyprianou, Sadat said in a speech to Egyptian troops.

Commando chief blames Cypriots for bloodshed —See page 43

He rejected any idea of meeting with the Cypriot leader — "we have nothing to say to each other."

"Egypt demands that Cyprus turn over the two murderers of Youssef Sebaei," Sadat said.

Sadat was referring to the two Palestinians who shot el-Sebaei, editor-in-chief of the semi-official newspaper Al-Ahram, in Nicosia at a conference of the Afro-Asian People's Solidarity Organization, of which he was the secretary-general.

The Palestinians then seized hostages at the conference, whom the Egyptian commandos were attempting to rescue the folllowing day at the airport when fired on by Cypriot security forces.

"The Palestinians should know better than other Arabs that Egypt will reposte 10 times harder to each blow against it," Sadat said.

"Egypt is defending Palestine everywhere yet, at the same time, some Palestinians are hiring themselves out as killers. Egypt will trample on these dwarfs no matter what the price."

Sadat made the speech after leading about 10,000 mourners at an emotional state funeral for the slain commandos.

"No more Palestine after today!" the crowd screamed as Sadat and his entire cabinet walked behind three closed ambulances carrying coffins.

Official announcers said the soldiers were "martyrs of treachery and the victims of Cypriot collusion."

—Continued

See CAIRO page 4

Keable RCMP inquiry closed by Quebec high court order

MONTREAL (CP) — After four successive defeats, the Trudeau government succeeded Tuesday in closing Quebec's inquiry into RCMP wrongdoing with a court order unlikely to be lifted for many months, if at all.

A three-man appeals tribunal of the Quebec Court of Appeal ordered commissioner Jean Keable to halt all proceedings and to give all documentation to Quebec Superior Court within 15 days.

Solicitor-General Jean-Jacques Blais, who inherited the fight from Francis Fox this month, said in Ottawa, "That's exactly what we wanted . . . I'm elated."

Quebec Justice Minister Marc-Andre Bedard, acting on Keable's recommendation, announced he would take the case before the Supreme Court of Canada.

Blais, Bedard said in Quebec City, "has succeeded for the moment in paralysing the work of an inquiry commission into certain criminal acts and into the actions and behavior of policemen which have imperilled, and probably still do, the individual rights and freedoms of Quebec citizens.

—Continued

See COURT page 4

Spying ignored, MP says

OTTAWA (CP) — The government has known for at least seven years that nearly half of the staff at the Soviet Union's embassy in Ottawa have been employed as intelligence agents but has chosen to ignore the situation, Progressive Conservative MP Tom Cossitt said Tuesday.

Cossitt condemned the government in the Commons for not acting on the information he says was compiled by the RCMP security service. He later released figures he said were taken from the top-secret file.

Solicitor-General Jean-Jacques Blais attacked Cossitt for his statements but did not deny their validity. Blais said only that Cossitt was working against the interests of national security.

The figures show that as of January, 1976, there were 28 persons working for the

—Continued

See SOVIET page 4

33% fee rise for ambulance?

By STEVE PONA

Winnipeg's civic finance committee has recommended the city assume direct control of its deficit-ridden ambulance operation from United Health Services Corporation, which has run it for the past three years.

Committee also agreed during an all-day budget session Tuesday to recommend general user fees be increased by 33 per cent on April 1 to inject an additional $186,000 into its revenue-starved coffers during the remainder of 1978, and $250,000 each year thereafter.

If approved by council on March 1, users of the ambulance service will have to pay $40 a trip instead of the present $30. But even with the increase, councillors said fees for service would not even begin to approach the break-even level of $100.

It is the second time in as many years that committee has come out in favor of the $10 hike and the first user fee increase to be recommended by a council committee since the civic board of commissioners unveiled its record$227 million spending estimates earlier this month.

Councillors warned then that user fees for a variety of services, including ambulance, transit, water and parking, could be increased to bring their revenues more into line with expenditures.

Council narrowly voted down the recommended $10 fee hike in 1977 when it decided instead to ask the provincial government to assume full responsibility for the operation, which it refused to do.

While the level of ambulance service will not be re-

—Continued

See 33% page 4

U.S. to consider reductions in children's television ads

WASHINGTON (AP) — The U.S. Federal Trade Commission is about to consider several proposals to cut severely television advertising aimed at children, an FTC official says.

Tracy Westen, who headed the team of FTC employees that spent months developing the proposals, outlined them in an interview Tuesday.

They include:

- Banning advertising on television programs with substantial audiences of children aged six years old or under.
- Prohibiting television ads for highly sugared foods aimed at older children, perhaps seven to 12 years old, by limiting such ads to after 9 p.m.
- Requiring advertisers of other products designed to appeal to seven- to 12-year-olds to buy extra time for "counter-advertising" to present health, safety or nutritional information about such products.

—Continued

See U.S. page 4

Tom-and-Jerry thief baffles police

By BRIAN COLE

Winnipeg police are waging a 'Tom and Jerry' battle against a new brand of break and enter artist.

For today's thief is a master of planning — and particular, to boot.

He'll rob, perhaps, some 50 houses and apartments over a two-month period, but always pick his spots over a wide area. And he'll often pass up perfectly reasonable booty such as appliances, jewels and other household goods for hard cash to avoid direct connection.

And he's on the increase, if statistics are any guide. In 1977, there were 7,334 break and enters in the city — an increase of 357 over the previous year.

How are police tracking down their elusive prey?

"A lot of our work in catching thieves is just slogging," says superintendent of detectives Ken Johnston.

In one case, police spent months investigating a string of break-ins without clues.

They were virtually stymied.

Johnston said the real cat-and-mouse begins when police think they are dealing with a group of persons.

If they feel a trend developing, they might put up to 10 extra men in the area, combing streets and back lanes . . . keeping an eye open for anything suspicious.

Recently, police were staked-out in Fort Garry for a few days hunting for a thief they thought responsible for about 30 break-ins, Johnston said.

But while they were there, a spate of thefts broke out in St. Vital, putting the police in the embarrassing situation of being at the right place at the wrong time.

The department faced a dilemma

Should it pull the extra men out of Fort Garry and "chase the thief like a chicken with its head cut off,"

—Continued

See MODERN page 4

Know the scores

HOCKEY

WHA

Quebec 6 New England 5

NHL

Los Angeles 4 Washington 1
Pittsburgh 5 St. Louis 4
Boston 3 Colorado 2

Central Senior

Transcona 7 St. Boniface 6

Western Canada

Lethbridge 6 Calgary 4
Portland 8 Regina 4
Victoria 7 Saskatoon 2
Seattle 4 Flin Flon 1

Details in Sports Pages 61-66

The editorial page is usually considered the best part of the paper. It is heavy reading: the manager notes, "We do not 'write down' to our readers, particularly in the editorial page."[13] Some even consider the page too argumentative, even to the point of weariness. Two columns of editorials, and six others of assorted serious material, fill the page. "The Page," as it is called, is packed with items written exclusively for the paper. Only a few syndicated articles are permitted in this "sacred" area. About three-fourths of the page's contents is written by staff writers, the other one-fourth by outsiders expressing a wide variety of views, many antagonistic to the paper's positions. The carefully written and well-researched editorials ("leaders") are perhaps the most articulate and literate editorial expressions in North American journalism.

The top of the editorial page bears a three-phrase slogan which spells out the key principles for which the *Free Press* stands: "Freedom of Trade—Liberty of Religion—Equality of Civil Rights." A page of news analysis and another containing Letters to the Editor usually follow the leader page. This section normally also carries a page or two of death and funeral notices (often with pictures of the deceased) and a dozen or more pages of classified advertisements.

Another unique public service oriented section is entitled "For People," a 12-to-16 page treatment of helpful human interest articles related to gracious living and the good life. This section features an amazing range of cultural, arts, entertainment and human interest materials. The spectrum of subjects treated may include topics as varied as recipes, painting, television, dance, restaurant reviews, cinema critic's comments and rock band groups.

The high quality of the *Free Press* is reflected in two additional sections—"Sports" and "Business and Finance." Sports coverage is thorough and the accompanying photography excellent, with large action shots. The Business section, usually extending to 6 to 8 pages, contains a wide array of business and financial news and features, plus stock market quotations.

The front page must be rated one of the world's elite dailies' more attractive and imaginative. Vivid color pictures and borders give it "class." The layout is so variegated one is hardly aware the paper's basic format is eight vertical columns. Some stories are run vertically in narrow columns; others are spread horizontally across four or five column widths. White space is used judiciously and generously; wide spacing between lines both makes for easy reading and emphasizes the importance of the stories. The reader gets the impression that the *Free Press* is interested in him and does not spare space and expense in the interest of serving him. Type is bold, black and larger than in most newspapers. The one or two large front-page photographs are usually action shots. All pictures are clear, meaningful and related to critically important events or people. Frequently, there are helpful drawings or maps. Several reader "teasers"—headlines, occasionally accompanied with small pictures or cartoon drawings, set off in boxes outlined in color borders—are spread across the front page above the nameplate. A brief up-to-date weather report appears to the left of the nameplate and the name of the edition on the right.

The initial section of the paper carries a mixture of local, Canadian and in-

---

[13] Shelford questionnaire.

ternational news and features and a commentary column by Alice Krueger. This section—and the entire paper—takes an analytical approach to news, events, and situations. Consequently, there are numerous articles which look behind surface events or analyze and interpret trends or complex problems. But this serious, almost scientific approach does not blight the paper's clear writing style. There is something of interest in the *Free Press* for a wide range of readers, and even complicated stories and complex situations and problems are made clear and easy to understand—an example of the paper's concern to communicate with its audience. This variety and easy readability makes the *Free Press* enticing and attractive to its readers.

The simple, straightforward and attractive appearance of the *Free Press* comes in part from employment of up-to-date technology. Video display terminals are used by reporters and editors for composing stories and for gathering copy from the paper's four wire service suppliers. Cold computer-controlled composition is employed. Color is used with such effectiveness for editorial and advertising purposes that twice in recent years—in 1972 and again in 1978—the paper won the Editor and Publisher Color Award.[14] Along with the St. Louis *Post-Dispatch,* the *Winnipeg Free Press* probably carries more weekday color photographs than any of the quality North American newspapers—another indicator of its interest in producing an attractive product for its readers. When it comes to production, it could be said of the *Free Press:* "It cares!"

In international affairs, the *Free Press* supports the United Nations and NATO. It early sought Canada's recognition of the People's Republic of China and has carried numerous news items and feature stories about the people and development of that vast nation. It calls for Canada to assume a more cosmopolitan viewpoint and lashes out at any attitude of neutralism or isolationism. As would be expected, it severely criticizes racism wherever it may be found and champions the causes of minorities everywhere. In many ways, it is like the St. Louis *Post-Dispatch* of the United States or *The Guardian* of Great Britain.

The *Winnipeg Free Press* is a good example of a paper which has managed to develop a cosmopolitan outlook without abdicating its local and regional emphasis. It certainly keeps its fingers on the pulse of the nation, not only providing its readers with a clear view of what is happening in Canada, but also stinging the national leadership in Ottawa with some of the most pointed and intelligent criticism provided by an elite newspaper anywhere in the world. If it is anything, it is a "rational" paper, leading its educated readership through complicated arguments often resembling forensic exercises but in simpler language and rousing itself from time to time to roar and thunder in deep-felt indignation at man's inhumanity to man. And all this is packed into one of the most attractive, readable newspapers in the world, a testimony to the excellence of its writing and makeup. Although in sparsely-populated Canada, the *Winnipeg Free Press* may reach less readers than many of the world's leading dailies, it unquestionably represents the best in quality journalism and therefore a justly deserved place among the world's great newspapers.

[14] Shelford questionnaire.

The Yorkshire Post

(ENGLAND)

CONSIDERED ON THE BASIS OF size and impact, the British newspaper industry may be divided into three tiers. At the top are the gigantic London Fleet Street quality and popular papers whose circulation usually run into the hundreds of thousands and in some cases exceeds a million readers. These papers, such as *The Times, The Daily Telegraph, The Guardian, The Observer, The Daily Mirror* and *News of the World* circulate outside the Isles and are generally known, at least in name, to even casual observers. At the bottom level are Britain's numerous local dailies and weeklies which provide coverage and advertising for the nation's many towns and villages.

Between these two tiers are a number of provincial dailies which are "influential and strong in their territories . . . and with great attention to local and regional news they carry weight in their areas."[1] Some have sizeable circulation running up as high as 450,000, especially evening papers such as the Glasgow *Evening Citizen,* Newcastle *Evening Telegraph,* Manchester *Evening News and Chronicle* and the Sheffield *Star.* Important among the morning provincial dailies are Birmingham's *Post,* Glasgow's *Daily Record,* Belfast's *Telegram* and Dublin's *Irish Independent.* Three papers dominate this classification of provincial dailies—Edinburgh's *Scotsman,* Manchester's *Guardian* (also in London), and Leeds' *Yorkshire Post*—in general quality and national prestige.

The Yorkshire Post, founded in 1754 by Griffith Wright as *The Leeds Intelligencer,* has made its influence felt throughout Britain as a quality newspaper which has always determined to be an excellent regional organ. A counterpart to the liberal *Guardian* of Manchester in politics, *The Post* has been satisfied to serve its locality well, to be read by serious opinion leaders outside its own county, and to have a substantial number of influential readers in London.

When *The Leeds Intelligencer* began, it was a modest weekly paper in four-page folio containing four columns to the page.[2] Like most early provincial papers its pages were filled largely with news from the London journals and with advertisements. From the start, although mildly at first, the paper was a Tory paper, and its local competition with the *Mercury,* a paper of vigor in its own right, forced the *Intelligencer* constantly to improve. From the first the

[1] Kenneth E. Olson, *The History Makers: The Press of Europe from Its Beginnings through 1965* (Baton Rouge, Louisiana State University Press, 1966), p. 27.
[2] Mildred A. Gibb and Frank Beckwith, *The Yorkshire Post: Two Centuries* (Leeds, The Yorshire Conservative Newspaper Co., Ltd., 1954), p. 3.

Gambol with Grenfell
in the wind or rain — either in coats, golfers, climbers or shooting jackets. This is a superb cloth for such occasions.
Allens
PROSPECT CRESCENT, HARROGATE.

YORKSHIRE POST

ESTAB. 1754 No. 40,639 LEEDS WEDNESDAY FEBRUARY 22 1978 PRICE 10p. Tel. LEEDS 32701

Ansafone
LET ANSAFONE ANSWER YOUR PHONE
From only £1.50 per week
57 New York Road, Leeds, LS2 7PJ
Leeds 39688

Where do racehorses go when there is no racing?

FROST and snow are forcing trainers and their racehorses to take to the beaches because inland gallops are impossible to ride on.

Each morning, trainers have been travelling up to 50 miles with their horses to Yorkshire beaches. The Malton trainer, Mr. Ted Carter, has been taking his string to Filey, where the jockeys have up to five miles of smooth, sandy, frost-free gallops to exercise their mounts.

His local training ground has been snow-covered and out of action for the past fortnight.

He said: "The gallops are useless for giving the horses a regular run and a trip to the beach is the only way they can get any speed up.

"They have about six miles of trotting and cantering exercise every outing and they thoroughly enjoy it. It makes a change for them.

One of Mr. Carter's horses is put through its paces (right) yesterday.

The last race meetings to be held in Britain were at Fontwell and Haydock on February 8. Tomorrow's Wincanton fixture, which was called off early yesterday, became the 56th card to be lost this season, which began last August, and the 49th programme to be lost since January 12.

Tomorrow's other scheduled meeting, at Warwick, looks likely to be abandoned today, but there is brighter news concerning Friday's meetings.

Council threat to stop police pay

A POWER struggle between a Labour-controlled council and a chief constable over how the county's police force should be run will reach a climax today.

The excuse is a dispute over the appointment of a crossing patrol warden, but South Yorkshire County Council has not seen eye-to-eye with Mr. Stanley Barratt since he became Chief Constable two years ago.

Now the council is threatening to withhold finance for the police force, which could mean there would not be enough money to pay policemen.

If today's meeting of the county council fails to approve a £12m. budget to finance the force, the only other cash would be from a Government grant of roughly the same amount.

The police committee chairman, Coun. George Moores, said: "We hope this will persuade the chief constable to review his attitude towards the council."

Some Labour councillors are talking in terms of troops being called in to stand in for unpaid policemen, but it seems inevitable that the Home Office would step in if there was any question of police being withdrawn from duty.

Under Home Office regulations, the Chief Constable is personally responsible to the Home Secretary for the deployment of manpower and resources within his force, but the councillors believe that as elected members they should have more say in the way the police force is run.

The councillors have decided to force the issue over an application for a crossing patrol in Market Street, Barnsley, directly outside the county council headquarters.

The councillors wanted a traffic warden assigned to the crossing but Mr. Barratt told them that the crossing did not warrant an attendant.

There were urgent cases in other parts of the county and, until sufficient manpower was available to cater for all desirable cases, the Market Street crossing would have to remain a low priority.

Now the Labour group is proposing that all Police Committee business, including bedgetary matters but with the exception of the item on the Market Street crossing, should be withdrawn from today's council meeting.

Mr. Barratt declined to comment yesterday but Coun. Danny George, a member of the Police Committee and Parliamentary candidate for Sheffield's Heeley division, said: "This political decision is both frightening and dictatorial.

Steel warns Healey on tax cuts

THE Liberal leader, Mr. David Steel, said yesterday that unless Liberal measures were included in the Budget, the Party would not support it.

His warning reflects a hardening of Liberal attitudes on the Budget and a determination to see that long-term reductions in income-tax are started.

The Liberal economic spokesman Mr. John Pardoe is to have a meeting with the Chancellor of the Exchequer today to discuss the matter.

Mr. Steel's remarks came in a speech to the London Society of Chartered Accountants in the City.

He said the "cry for tax reforms is one which our half of the Lib-Lab partnership intends to keep in the public ear."

He also said: "It is too early to say whether or not the Budget and Finance Bill will be an agreed measure between us under the Lib-Lab agreement.

"But, if it is to be, we will expect at least a beginning of a shift in the burden of taxation away from incomes as agreed between the Prime Minister and myself last July."

The Liberal MP for Colne Valley, Mr. Richard Wainwright, in a more outspoken speech to Cambridge University Liberal Club said the Party was certainly not going to support a Budget concocted more to reunite Labour for an election than to prepare the economy for years ahead.

"Liberal MPs have no intention of spending the summer putting into law a 'silly billy' Budget resembling Mr. Healey's 1974 vintage.

"If the Chancellor disappoints Liberal hopes severely, a June General Election becomes more likely," he said

In a Commons debate on taxation, initiated by the Tories, Conservative MPs also urged Mr. Healey to reduce income-tax.

Meanwhile, the Confederation of British Industry, in its Budget advice to Mr. Healey said North Sea oil income should be used to cut personal taxation by up to 30 per cent. over the next three years.

Commons debate — P.3.

Mrs Thatcher defies Labour 'bullies' on race

By JOHN FISHER, Political Correspondent

THE CONSERVATIVE leader, Mrs. Margaret Thatcher, yesterday warned opponents that she would not be "bullied or intimidated" over immigration.

"I shall stick clearly and staunchly to my views," she said during a tour of Ilford North, where by-election voting takes place next week.

She said that the claim by the Home Secretary, Mr. Merlyn Rees, on Monday that she was making racial hatred respectable was "absolute nonsense."

Other leading Tories also strongly criticised Mr. Rees' views in speeches yesterday.

But it was Mrs. Thatcher who led the attack.

"I have my views," she said. "I have noted that I have been bullied and intimidated in the House and outside."

She had only spoken on immigration three times, but since then she had been "vilified and treated to malicious attacks."

The Tories' deputy leader, Mr. William Whitelaw, commenting during a by-election meeting on the remarks by Mr. Rees said: "I deeply resent his manufactured artificial and thoroughly unjustified charge.

"I believe that he has made a grave error in lending the authority of his great office to make respectable the chorus of misleading abuse we have lately been hearing on this subject.

"Perhaps he is using a speech of this sort as a smokescreen for his own failures in office. For the truth is that his actions reveal a damaging lack of initiative based on almost shattering complacency, whether over crime, immigration or child pornography."

He urged Mr. Rees to "stop making silly speeches" and do something about the decline in the number of police, otherwise when people were mugged or their area wrecked by hooligans, they would know where the real blame lay.

The Prime Minister sent a message to Mrs. Tessa Sowell, the Labour candidate in the by-election as the inter-party exchanges grew more heated, predicting that "conflict and confrontation will result from the present doctrine being preached by some Tory leaders on immigration."

In an answer to Conservative charges of Government indifference to growing crime and lawlessness, Mr. Callaghan said:

"We are working to preserve our tolerant society which is just and fair towards all people regardless of creed or colour. But we shall not allow that tolerance to be taken advantage of by vandals and thugs.

"Hooliganism in the streets or elsewhere will be firmly dealt with by the courts in the interests of us all."

Outside Ilford, the Tory counter-attack was pressed home by Mr. William Shelton, MP for Streatham, speaking to Brent South Conservative supper club.

He said the Home Secretary's "disgraceful speech" was unworthy of his high office.

"I question whether he remains fit to be Home Secretary. He can no longer have the confidence of people of this country.

"He has presided over the relaxation of immigration rules which he must know is a contributory factor to racial tension, yet he now uses violent language to stifle discussion."

Mr. Shelton urged four steps "to allay fears once and for all.

"Firstly, we must introduce urgently a new British Nationality Law. There have been some 40 changes in the 1948 Nationality Act which confirmed the status for United Kingdom and Commonwealth citizens — some 950 millions of them.

"Their status has been changed by both Conservative and Labour Governments, so that, again to quote from the Government's own document, the law is now 'complicated and obscure.'

"If we define, once and for

Continued on page 3.
Editorial comment — P.8.

Lady in the iron mask

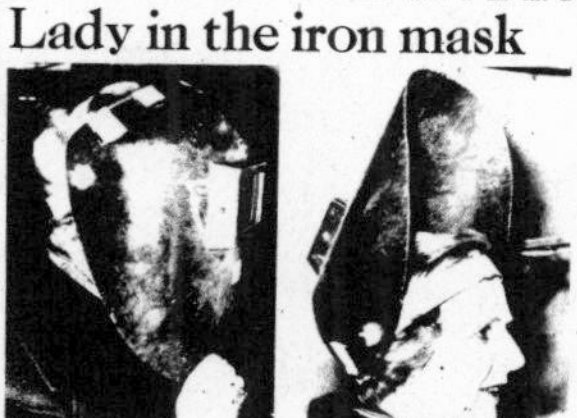

IT is a moment for opponents who have nicknamed Mrs. Thatcher "The Iron Maiden" to cherish . . . the Opposition leader puts on a welding mask as she watches work at an engineering company during her by-election tour of the marginal Ilford North constituency yesterday.

INSIDE TODAY

THE CHALLENGE FOR SALVATION ARMY
This year marks the centenary of the Salvation Army in its present form. After six months as its head, Gen. Arnold Brown talks to MICHAEL BROWN, Churches Correspondent, about the movement's challenge in the Seventies — P.8.

WOMEN'S POST
A campaigner for Soviet Jewry who is leaving England for Israel, choosing colour co-ordinates in your own home, the problems of rogue hairdressers and the latest fashions are featured in Women's Post — P.11.

TOMORROW
THE POPULATION TIME-BOMB
Can the population time-bomb be defused and if so what must be the first priorities to safeguard the world's peoples?

RALLY SPECIAL
A special 12-page feature on the three-day Mintex International Rally which starts in Harrogate on Friday morning.

Wall Street

On the New York Stock Exchange yesterday, the Dow Jones industrial average fell 3.38 points, to close at 749.31. —UPI.

Today's weather

Dull, some rain. Widespread mist.

Full forecast — Back Page.
Ski Report — P.9.

Snow baby Nicholas weighs in – at the right time

A GYNAECOLOGIST arrived on a farmer's tractor in snowbound Dorset yesterday — just in time for the birth of Nicholas Grist.

Attempts to airlift his mother, 28-year-old Angela Grist, to hospital from Piddlehinton had failed.

The helicopter crew with the gynaecologist on board were unable to get to the village because of fog. A local doctor managed to reach the house and villagers dug a path through the snow for the gynaecologist.

Nicholas' father, Mr. Colin Grist, said: "The doctors were alarmed about the safety of the baby and he was born as the consultant arrived. The flying squad team that came with him revived the baby."

Mr. Grist, a veterinary surgeon who has delivered domestic animals but never babies, said: "Both are as well as can be expected. They are very tired but sleeping it off."

Nicholas, who weighed in at 91/2lb., will be a brother for two-year-old Amanda.

The arrival of snow baby Nicholas was one of scores of human dramas in the West Country, still practically sealed off by huge drifts although a slow thaw started.

And yesterday there were new hazards — dense fog and fears of flooding.

In Taunton, Somerset, a premature baby boy, weighing 1lb. 13oz., was struggling for life after a four-hour Land-Rover journey through snow to hospital.

Graham Wilcox had to be driven to hospital when fog prevented a naval helicopter from making the trip.

The army sent emergency supplies to a snowbound public school in the tiny Dorset village of Milton Abbas where the 300 pupils and teachers are down to their last 12 hours food supply. They have been cut off since Saturday.

A crew from the Navy air station at Yeovilton, Somerset, flew through dense fog to airlift an 11-week-old baby boy in urgent need of hospital treatment from North Cadbury, Somerset.

Weather conditions were so bad that the helicopter had to fly at 50ft. over rooftops before landing at Yeovil where Wayne Woof was taken to hospital with a chest infection.

A helicopter from RAF Chivenor reached Okehampton to lift three casualties and a doctor to the North Devon Infirmary at Barnstaple.

The first patient was a boy with an eye injury taken from Shillstone Farm, Throwleigh, on the edge of Dartmoor.

A doctor from Okehampton had already reached the boy when the helicopter was diverted to lift a woman from near Okehampton who was threatening miscarriage.

Darkness had fallen when the helicopter was diverted for a third time to Symonds Park, Okehampton, to lift a man with serious internal injuries following an operation.

In the same area, two skiers

Continued on Page 3

Rail chief faces clash on jobs

A MAJOR clash is expected at talks today between the leader of Britain's biggest rail union and Mr. Peter Parker, the chairman of British Rail.

Mr. Sidney Weighell, general secretary of the 180,000-strong National Union of Railwaymen, will tell Mr. Parker that unless British Rail starts to fill some of the 9,000 vacancies on the railways, his members will stop co-operating on cost saving.

His ultimatum follows a speech by Mr. Parker in London yesterday in which he boasted of cutting 10,000 jobs in the last 18 months.

But Mr. Weighell said later: "We want new guidelines which will eliminate overtime and fill vacancies. We want guidelines to make it more attractive for men to come and work for the railways."

The union wants an end to a semi-official ban on recruitment, which has been in force for more than a year.

It says "good housekeeping" deals have resulted in NUR members averaging more than 12 hours overtime a week and savings of more than £10m. to British Rail.

Mr. Parker talked of the cuts in British Rail staff during a speech at London's Savoy Hotel, in which he gave a warning that further fare increases could be on the way.

"Our choice is either lower fares and higher taxes or higher fares and less Government support," he said.

"It's no fun raising the fares. Last year we had them steady for the whole year, but we still have to meet our annual target of contracts."

Mr. Weighell's end-of-month deadline coincides with the 24-hour strike threat issued by the train drivers' union, ASLEF.

The ASLEF executive has voted to stop work on March 1 in protest against bonus payments being offered to train guards — members of the NUR — but not drivers.

The Transport Secretary, Mr. William Rodgers, said: "I hope there will be no industrial stoppage. It will cause a great inconvenience to the public. It will be a setback of a kind I don't want."

Liberal leader visits Yorkshire

The Liberal leader, Mr. David Steel, will visit Yorkshire at the weekend to speak at the rally and annual meeting of the Yorkshire Liberal Federation at Aireville School, Skipton.

Mr. Steel will begin his visit to Yorkshire on Friday by meeting Liberal Party workers at Bradford City Hall, and on Saturday, he will call at a spring fair in Otley

Oil go-ahead

Extensive oil and natural gas drilling in the Atlantic will go ahead off the states of New York, New Jersey and Delaware, following a decision yesterday by the U.S. Supreme Court.

Pressure stepped up for ban on Front march

THE Metropolitan Police Commissioner, Sir David McNee, may call for a total ban on Saturday's National Front march through Ilford, Essex, rather than mount one of the biggest anti-riot control operations in Britain.

A four-man delegation from Redbridge Community Relations Council at Ilford, who went to Scotland Yard last night, said the Commissioner had told them he would make the decision within the next 48 hours.

Mr. Ian Haig, Redbridge Community Relations Officer, said: "If the march goes ahead, I understand the police will be using almost a quarter of the Metropolitan force — 5,000 out of 22,000 men. This is totally absurd."

Another of the delegation, Coun. John Hogben, leader of the Labour group on Conservative-controlled Redbridge Council, said: "I believe that there will be large-scale disorder if the march goes ahead.

"Sir David emphasised that a decision has still to be taken. He told us it would be taken within the next 24 or 48 hours."

This action by Sir David confirmed by Scotland Yard, came as a day of warnings on the danger to public order increased the pressure on the Home Secretary, Mr. Merlyn Rees, to ban the march.

The Socialist Workers Party has already called on "anti-Nazis" in London to gather in Ilford on Saturday to stop the march.

The Anti-Nazi League has predicted an "explosive mixture" of Right and Left-wing street demonstrations.

Post classified advertisements talk to thousands of people for you. Dial LEEDS
41234
For display advertising and Special Feature inquiries dial LEEDS
32701
Ext. 319

Latest news

NEW ZEALAND 126 BEHIND
New Zealand under-23s were 126 runs behind England, with seven second-innings wickets left at lunch, on the last day of their three-day match.

Callaghan fears slump ahead

THE Prime Minister fears that Britain could be heading for another economic slump.

Mr. Callaghan's recurring nightmare, as he confided to Labour party and TUC leaders at a meeting of the Liaison Committee between the two groups yesterday, is that, unless the world's richer nations do what they promised last year and reflate, the outlook for countries like Britain is bleak.

Mr. Callaghan is so pessimistic about the prospects that he is seeking an emergency summit meeting with President Carter.

He is particularly gloomy because of the prospect that a Left-wing victory in next month's French elections could lead to France putting up trade barriers against the rest of the world. This could be followed by protectionist moves by the United States, leading quickly to a major slump of 1930s proportions.

The British Government's hopes of reaching at least 3.5 per cent. growth would be shattered and there would be an inevitable increase in unemployment and a lowering of living standards, Mr. Callaghan told his colleagues.

Mr. Callaghan was speaking on the day the latest unemployment figures were published, showing 1,508,674 out of work in February, a drop of 39,870 on last month.

But Mrs. Thatcher said last night that the Tories could create a million more jobs in the next few years.

"It could happen by raising profits, cutting taxes and bureaucracy, freeing the labour market, encouraging managers, raising investment, and getting more value out of existing investment."

Mrs. Thatcher, speaking to the Engineering Employers Federation in London, said that most European countries already enjoyed better pensions, better housing, better hospitals and high living standards.

"On present trends the gap will soon become a chasm, and we will have difficulty in maintaining even our present standards.

"That is the danger if we do not rectify our basic and persistent weakness

Editorial comment — P.8.
Jobless figures — P.3.

Why the Leicester?

150,000 new accounts have been opened with the Leicester Building Society during the last twelve months.

Why?

Because there's such a good range of investment and savings schemes.

Because it's one of the very big, very experienced building societies, whose assets are now over £1,000 million.

Because it is convenient — there are 1,400 branch offices and local agencies throughout the UK.

Join the Leicester investors

119 ALBION STREET, LEEDS
Manager: Norman R Woodhead. Telephone: 36721.
BRADFORD 34 Sunbridge Road.
HARROGATE 49 Station Parade. KEIGHLEY 4/6 North St
MIDDLESBROUGH 111 Albert Road

paper was never a mere parochial newssheet, and it very soon gained a reputation as a paper interested in the events and problems of surrounding counties and of London. Under the title of *The Intelligencer*, the paper became well written and energetic, flourishing through the years of swift scientific progress and economic development.

In 1866, *The Intelligencer* became a daily and its name was changed to *The Yorkshire Post*, indicating an appeal to a wider area but bringing no change in its long-established literary and political traditions. The title change made no break in continuity of thought and purpose, and it is quite common to think of the paper, despite its change of name on becoming a daily, as having been founded in 1754.[3]

Following the example set by *The Times*, the makeup of the new daily was austere and made use of every inch of space. On some days the front page was given over to advertisements and public announcements, but often three or four of its columns contained some news—often dispatches from the foreign correspondents of *The Times* or *The Daily Telegraph* of London. The Saturday issue contained a supplement of literary articles, book reviews, and dramatic and music criticism, all packed neatly into only four pages.

One of the paper's most outstanding early editors was Charles Pebody, who took over the paper in 1882 and led *The Post* to seek a wider circle of readers by expanding the range of the paper's contents. For the next 20 years this was the objective of the journal: "To reflect the genius of the people among whom it circulated, and to represent and identify itself with what was distinctive in the Yorkshire character."[4] Under Pebody, *The Post* prospered in every way and an evening edition, *The Yorkshire Evening Post*, was begun. Pebody died in 1890, whereupon Henry John Palmer, who had been an editor in Birmingham, became editor.

Palmer had little use for the new journalism of the cheaply sensational kind which was becoming popular in England; he believed in the dignity of the press in all of its manifestations. Palmer thought of his paper as a moral force and always determined to "write nothing and say nothing that was not for the good of his fellowman."[5] He improved *The Post*'s makeup; its page was enlarged to eight columns, and by the end of the century it was printing an average of ten pages per issue, with twelve pages on Saturdays. Palmer died in 1903, after thirteen years of great accomplishment with *The Post*.

Under John Phillips, his successor, the paper continued to grow and prosper. The assistant editor was James Sykes, a modest and unassuming man, who was considered one of the best-rounded journalists in Britain. During this period, the editorial columns of *The Post* were distinctive and attracted attention throughout the country. Many of the editorials were contributed by Phillips himself. The paper's news and commentary on foreign affairs and important national issues, such as free trade, were much admired and discussed. Phillips died in 1919, and was succeeded by Arthur Mann, who left a key post on the

[3] Harold Herd, *The March of Journalism* (London, Allen & Unwin, 1952), p. 183.

[4] Gibb and Beckwith, *op. cit.*, p. 44.

[5] Gibb and Beckwith, *op. cit.*, p. 54 and information supplied by Denis B. Wylie of *The Yorkshire Post*.

London *Evening Standard* to take the new position. Mann distinguished himself in many ways with *The Post*, but he perhaps is best remembered for his long and determined stand on British foreign policy during the 1930's.

During the critical years prior to World War II, *The Yorkshire Post*, by its forceful expression of opinion, became one of the most generally respected journals of the day, even gaining considerable foreign readership. The paper insisted that it was only by means of collective action, through the machinery of the League of Nations, that European peace could be secured. In many cases *The Post* editorially rebuked Conservative leaders, an indication of the independence that characterized Mann's editorship. In fact, *The Post* criticized the Prime Minister repeatedly for the Government's casual attitude toward the ever more-threatening activities of Hitler and Mussolini on the continent. Its anti-appeasement policy in the pre-war period is one of its proudest stands, and one which, in retrospect, showed considerable understanding of the situation.

Even the *Manchester Guardian*, certainly not a paper to praise *The Post* without good reason, wrote in November, 1939:

> Soundness in judgement, tenacity of purpose, loyalty to principle, the courage to be unpopular . . . and even to offend the Party if the Party were not right; these qualities, which are the more precious for being rare, have marked *The Yorkshire Post* throughout the long controversy about British foreign policy which began with Mr. Chamberlain's Premiership. They represent something deep in the characteristic North, tough, earnest, individual. The country owes a debt for them to the old *Yorkshire Post*.[6]

In 1939, *The Post* absorbed its old rival, the *Leeds Mercury*, and early the next year Arthur Mann retired from his editor's chair and was replaced by William Linton Andrews who had edited the *Mercury* for several years previously. A man with a distinguished journalistic background, Andrews made the paper into one of the most critical British journals of the Second World War, one which offered constructive suggestions which were often adopted by Government departments. An example was the editor's proposal that men from the battle areas visit the war factories to tell them of their contributions to the fighting men.

In the post-war period, under the able editorship of Sir Linton Andrews, *The Post* continued to print its forceful commentary on foreign affairs and to provide its readers with a variety of well-written foreign and domestic news. At the same time, the vitality and sophistication of its coverage and evaluation of music, art and literature captured the respect of Britain's intellectual community. During his 21-year editorship until he retired in 1960, Andrews undoubtedly was one of the paper's most highly respected editors and one of Britain's more eminent newspapermen.[7]

During the 'sixties, *The Post* was edited by J. E. Crossley and reached a circulation of about 122,000. Today, the paper thrives under the editorship of John Edwards. Inflation and rising costs have contributed to a lowered circula-

---

[6] Gibb and Beckwith, *op. cit.*, p. 88.
[7] John Edwards, editor, *The Yorkshire Post*, in response to questionnaire and in accompanying letter to H. Fisher, dated January 26, 1978.

tion of about 102,000 currently, but the paper's tradition of high quality and conservative, but non-party stance continue. About 70 percent of today's *Post* customers represent street sales, and the remainder are subscribers.

Under Edwards, at least eight *Post* staffers have distinguished themselves since 1971. In that year, Victor Green won an award for his work in racing news and Derek Hudson received the Social Service Press Award for investigating excessive prescription of amphetamines and barbituarates. The following years Geoffrey Lean won several awards for his campaigning articles on the pollution of Yorkshire rivers. Robert Benson, Angus King and Angela Singer won recognition in 1975, Benson for his interpretation of agriculture to the public, King for his contributions as a medical correspondent and Singer for investigating the problems of child adoption. In 1976, Roger Cross received an award as Crime Reporter of the Year, and in 1977 Terry Brindle was highly commended and honored with the Astroturf British Sports Journalism Award.

In 1970, after a century in its old home in the center of Leeds, Yorkshire Post Newspapers moved to new, modern, well-equipped staff and production quarters about a half mile from its original site. The £6 million building, which had been planned by *The Post*'s managing director and publisher, Mr. J. G. S. Linacre, won an architectural award. It was officially opened by His Royal Highness, the Prince of Wales. At the time of its opening, the equipment the new edifice housed represented the world's largest hybrid press plant, printing by letter press and offset—either, or both in the same newspaper.[8]

Ownership of *The Post* is vested in a local Leeds-based corporation called Yorkshire Post Newspapers, Ltd. A staff of nearly 1,250 personnel working in the new building publishes the morning *Yorkshire Post,* an afternoon daily counterpart and some weeklies. Of that number, 120 writers and editors, 180 technical personnel and 58 in administrative and management positions directly serve *The Post.* They produce a daily which typically has 24 well-packed pages—*The Post* continues to use space as efficiently as in its earliest days—in length. *The Post* does not run a Sunday edition; consequently the Saturaday paper is usually larger and contains special weekend features, such as a larger Radio and TV Guide to cover the period.

The Post is a serious, dignified, somewhat "gray" appearing broadsheet, with its title offset in bold, black lettering, that typically runs nine vertical columns on all pages except for the six-columned editorial page. Some of the stories, particularly at the bottom of the pages, are blocked horizontally. One large picture usually dominates the upper right quartile of the front page, which may contain one or more additional photographs. Pictures with cut-lines are used quite liberally throughout the paper, often accompanied by a related story. The front page contains a column of directions called "Inside—Today and Tomorrow" and there is a "Latest News" column. Two small advertisements are placed on either side of the paper's title and one larger one appears in the lower right-hand corner of the front page.

Recent Royal Commission of the Press statistics reflect *The Post*'s deter-

[8] *Ibid.*

mined intent to provide excellent provincial and national coverage. The Commission's breakdown of *The Post*'s contents by categories showed about 15 percent of the paper is devoted to national news (including sports), and 12.5 percent to regional and local news, including local sports. The figures also reflect the paper's strong emphasis on features, showing 14 percent in that category, of which 4 percent is art, reviews and entertainment. Business news, another *Post* strength, took up 6 percent of space, and international news occupied 4.5 percent. Advertisements took up 35 percent, indicating a healthy income balance between advertising and sales. Editorial comment and other features, such as crosswords, letters and competitions, take up the balance of the daily space.

A review of a randomly-selected week's issues reveals a fairly consistent pattern of subject matter in *The Post*. The front page features top national and regional stories. The second page supplies radio, TV, theater and cinema guides. "Home News" takes up part of page three plus two to three additional pages. Page three also contains columns on Parliament. The "Business Post," offering latest developments in the regional and national business communities, regularly occupies pages four and five. There is a page given to editorial commentary, letters to the editor and a special guest column, and another page to foreign news. Two pages of sports news take up the last two pages just prior to the back side, which features local stories, the weather and an occasional carry-over from the front pages.

To keep its readers, who are largely "up-and-coming" middle class citizens, well informed about national government, *The Post* keeps a full-time staff of five at the seat of government in London. A large staff of correspondents cover regional and local news. Reporters frequently are allowed to by-line their stories in *The Post*. In general, except for a few with top high school qualifications, *Post* editorial staffers have a university degree. All have received *Post* on-the-job training before assuming regular positions.[9]

Because most Britons take several dailies, one of which is a large national paper with good international coverage, and because *The Post* is primarily a provincial newspaper, international news usually takes up only slightly more than half of one page. *The Post* has just two foreign correspondents, located in Brussels/Luxembourg for Common Market coverage, which is of especial concern to its middle-class businessmen. Five part-time staffers furnish further news from New York, Bonn, Paris, Sydney and Madrid. Much of *The Post*'s foreign input comes from the five wire services it takes—Reuters, AP, UPI, Extel and PA. At least one *Post* foreign correspondent, Harold King—formerly with Reuters and doyen of Paris correspondents—has distinguished himself.[10]

Two of *The Post*'s greatest strengths are its thorough investigative reporting and its presentation of feature materials. One indicator of its excellence in the former is the number of awards staff members have received for digging in recent years under Edwards' editorship. As for the latter, there are regular fea-

[9] Edwards questionnaire.
[10] Edwards questionnaire.

ture pages or columns, such as "People and Places" and "Farming," plus numerous special and background pieces each day.

The Post appears to possess most of those characteristics which are the trademarks of high quality elite journalism. It is serious, but does not forget the human interest and entertainment needs of its middle-class readers. Although its international news coverage is limited, it is acutely aware of its primarily provincial readers' needs for thorough coverage of local, regional and national news. To that end, it keeps "careful watch of the main local, regional and national issues of the day, plus an eye for the public good."[11] Its information on the national scene excels because it keeps good representation in the capital so it "can take a dispassionate look at affairs outside the Whitehall/Westminster hothouse"[12]—a unique quality for a regional paper. It is obsessed with a desire to be objective, to be responsible, lawful and decent. It stands firmly for freedom—free enterprise, free speech and all freedoms within the law. Its editors conscientiously seek to provide what is best for the readers. For at least these reasons, *The Yorkshire Post* enjoys a national and an increasingly international reputation and deserves to be considered one of the world's finest high-quality provincial dailies.

[11] *Ibid.*
[12] Edwards questionnaire.

Postscript

RATHER ABRUPTLY, with the *Yorkshire Post*'s place in the alphabet, this book of profiles ends. A few concluding remarks may be in order to soften the book's termination. As the year 1979 comes to a close, we find the worldwide state of the "great" newspapers virtually the same as when the authors collected data and wrote the profiles in 1977 and 1978.

Most of the dailies discussed in the preceding pages are experiencing formidable problems of one kind or another—not the least of which are labor disputes with their disruptive consequences, soaring production costs with their toll on editorial quality, and inflationary trends generally which constantly eat away at operating and expansion funds.

Others of the great dailies are finding within their audiences a deepening suspicion, even antagonism and cynicism vis-à-vis the press generally for what is rather commonly termed its "irresponsibilities." This growing anti-press attitude affects even the "great" dailies—especially these papers because they are *trying* to be responsible.

Others of the great dailies are plagued with growing hostility from government, ever anxious to influence and control free journalistic expression. Even in the United States, long secure in its tradition of press autonomy, government through the judiciary is applying more and more control. And, citizens of activist inclinations, together with minority and special interest groups are increasingly using various tactics to impose their wills, values, and policies on the great dailies. The "great" dailies, because of their prestige and social impact, are naturally the prime targets of the various power-grabbers-and-players.

The so-called Cold War of the 1950's–60's may be dormant today, but other international frictions—such as the Third World's constant criticism of the Western "developed" nations and their communication policies—have risen to become a new kind of war, fought vigorously by communications people and government officials (often the same people) in the battle arenas of UNESCO and other international groups.

Ideological differences in newspapering throughout the world persist—in fact, it may be said they appear to grow stronger. Homogenization of newspaper "greatness" is still a long way off—in spite of efforts in that direction by journalistic and communications "One-Worlders." From a U.S. perspective—at least from the perspective of the authors—this heterogeneous nature of newspaper greatness is not only natural but desirable.

Let *Pravda* speak with its voice, the *New York Times* with its, both being responsible to their respective societies. Let *Le Monde* and *Die Welt,* from their quite different worlds in Western Europe present their news and opinion for their constituents. And in the shadows of Brazilian press control, let *O Estado de S. Paulo* continue to provide its encyclopedic news picture to its readers—with certain domestic "political" gaps notwithstanding. And let *El Pais* and other vigorous dailies of Spain relish their new-found freedom and profit from the heady exercise of determining the boundaries of their own responsibility.

All of this is good. Pluralism is not only valuable within a country's journalism, but also when projected onto the giant journalistic screen of the world.

After our long and arduous attempt to understand and illustrate newspaper greatness in an international context, the authors are not certain we know exactly what it is. Greatness in newspapers, like greatness in people, eludes precise definition. But we do feel that the fifty dailies profiled in this book represent this elusive quality of greatness from a number of perspectives.

We do know that each of these dailies is seriously interested in "good"—socially-helpful—journalism, however the societal needs might be conceived. They all *want* to be great papers; they want to have an impact on the serious dimensions of society, on thinking, values, and policy. They all aspire to greatness—to serious and relevant social impact—and this may well be their only common denominator. If so, it is one well worth cherishing in the journalism of today and tomorrow.

Selected Bibliography

BOOKS AND PAMPHLETS

Alles über die Zeitung: "Frankfurter Allgemeine." Munich: Frankfurter Allgemeine, 1976.

Altbach, Philip G. *Publishing in India: An Analysis.* New York: Oxford University Press, 1975.

Asahi Shimbun: Facts and Figures. Tokyo: Asahi Shimbun Publishing Company, 1977.

Asahi Shimbun: The Foremost Newspaper in Japan. Tokyo: Asahi Shimbun Publishing Company, 1974.

Babb, L. L. and Washington Post Writers Group (eds.). *Of the Press, by the Press, for the Press, and Others, Too.* Boston: Houghton Mifflin, 1976. (About the *Washington Post*).

Banks, Arthur S., ed. *Political Handbook of the World: 1976.* New York: McGraw-Hill, 1976.

Beitrage Zur Zeitgeschichte. Bonn: *Die Welt,* 1976.

Berger, Meyer. *The Story of The New York Times, 1851–1951.* New York: Simon & Schuster, 1951.

Berlin Kochstrasse. Berlin: Verlag Ullstein, 1966.

Berrigan, F. J. *A Manual on Mass Media in Population and Development.* Paris, Unesco, 1977.

Brief History of The Statesman. Calcutta: Statesman Ltd., 1947.

Between Editions. Baltimore: The Baltimore Sunpapers, 1977.

Bhattacharjee, A. *The Indian Press: Profession to Industry.* New Delhi: Vika's Publications, 1972.

Bitter, Georg. *Zur Typologie des Deutschen Zeitungswesens in der Bundesrepublik Deutschland.* Munich: Eduard Pohl & Co., 1951.

Bowman, William D. *The Story of "The London Times."* London: Routledge, 1931.

Brodzky, Vivian, ed. *Fleet Street: The Inside Story of Journalism.* London: Macdonald, 1966.

Burnham, Edward F. L. *Peterborough Court: The Story of the Daily Telegraph.* London: Cassell & Co., Ltd., 1955.

Burr, Trevor. *Reflections of Reality: The Media in Australia.* Adelaide: Rigby, 1977.

Buzek, Antony. *How the Communist Press Works.* New York: Praeger, 1964.

Canham, Erwin D. *Commitment to Freedom.* New York: Houghton Mifflin, 1958. (about The Christian Science Monitor)

Centennial History of the 'Washington Post.' Washington, D.C.: The Washington Post Company, 1977.

Chu, Godwin C. *Radical Change Through Communication in Mao's China.* Honolulu: University Press of Hawaii, 1977.

Cleverley, Graham. *The Fleet Street Disaster: British National Newspapers as a Case Study in Mismanagement.* Beverly Hills: Sage, 1976.

Comparative Treatment of the U.S. and the U.S.S.R. in the Yugoslav Press. Washington, D.C.: USIA, 1978.

Creason, Joe. *Mirror of a Century.* Louisville: Courier-Journal, 1968.

Davis, Elmer. *History of the New York Times 1851–1921.* New York: The New York Times, 1921.

Davis, Morris. *Interpreters for Nigeria: The Third World and International Public Relations.* Urbana: University of Illinois Press, 1977.

De Jessen, Franz. *Two Hundred Years "Berlingske Tidende."* Copenhagen: Det Berlingske Bogtrykkeri, 1948.

Derieux, Emmanuel and Jean C. Texier. *Le Presse Quotidienne Francasie.* Paris: Armand Colin, 1974.

Desai, M. V. *Communication Policies in India.* Paris: Unesco, 1977.

Desmond, Robert W. *The Information Process: World News Reporting to the Twentieth Century.* Iowa City: University of Iowa Press, 1978.

————. *The Press and World Affairs.* New York: Appleton-Century-Crofts, 1937.

Desvois, J. M. *La Prensa en España, 1900–1931.* Madrid: Siglo, 1977.

Dinsmore, Herman H. *All the News That Fits: A Critical Analysis of the News and Editorial Contents of The New York Times.* New Rochelle, N.Y.: Arlington House, 1969.

Ein Weltblatt Stellt Sich Vor. Bonn: Die Welt, 1976.

Facts About the 'Los Angeles Times.' Los Angeles: Los Angeles Times, 1978.

Facts About the Washington Post Company. Washington, D.C.: The Washington Post Company, 1977.

Fischer, Heinz-Dietrich. *Die Grossen Zeitungen: Portraets der Weltpresse.* Munich: Deutscher Taschenbuch Verlag, 1966.

Fischer, H.-D. and J. C. Merrill, eds. *International and Intercultural Communication* (2nd ed.). New York: Hastings House, 1976.

Galliner, Peter. *Annual Review of World Press Freedom.* London: International Press Institute, 1977.

Ghose, H. P. *The Newspaper in India.* Calcutta: University of Calcutta, 1952.

Gibb, Midred A. and Frank Beckwith. *The Yorkshire Post: Two Centuries.* Leeds: The Yorkshire Conservative Newspaper Co., Ltd., 1954.

The 'Guardian' in London and Manchester. London: The Guardian, n.d.

Gustafsson, Karl Erik and Stig Hadenius. *Swedish Press Policy.* Stockholm: The Swedish Institute, 1976.

Gwynn, Denis. *The Vatican and the War in Europe.* London: Burns, Oates & Washbourne, Ltd., 1940.

Hachten, William A. *Muffled Drums: The News Media in Africa.* Ames: The Iowa State University Press, 1971.

Hammond, J. C. C. P. *Scott of the Manchester Guardian.* New York: Harcourt, Brace and World, 1934.

Harasymiw, Bohdan, ed. *Education and the Mass Media in the Soviet Union and Eastern Europe.* New York: Praeger, 1976.

Heikal, Mohamed. *The Road to Ramadan.* New York: Ballantine Books, 1975. (about *Al Ahram* and the Egyptian press)

Herd, Harold. *The March of Journalism.* London: Allen & Unwin, 1952.

The 'Hindu' Centenary. Madras: The Hindu, 1978.

History of the London Times, 1785–1948. London: The Times; New York: Macmillan, 1935–1948. 4 vols.

Hohenberg, John. *Foreign Correspondence: The Great Reporters and Their Times.* New York: Columbia Universtiy Press, 1964.

Holden, W. Sprague. *Australia Goes to Press.* Detroit: Wayne State University Press, 1961.

Horlamus, Sepp, ed. *Mass Media in C.M.E.A. Countries.* Prague: International Organization of Journalists, 1976.

Horton, Philip C. *The Third World and Press Freedom.* New York: Praeger Publishers, 1978.

Hudson, D. *British Journalists and Newspapers.* London: Collins, 1945.

Izvestia. Moscow: Izvestia, 1976.

Johnson, Gerald, Frank Kent, H. L. Mencken and Hamilton Owens. *The Sunpapers of Baltimore.* New York: Alfred A. Knopf, 1937.

Kaplan, Frank. *Winter into Spring: The Czechoslovak Press and the Reform Movement, 1963–1977.* Boulder, Colo.: East European Quarterly, 1975.

Kato, Hidetoshi. *Communication Policies in Japan.* Paris: Unesco, 1977.

Katz, Elihu and Michael Guerevitch. *The Secularization of Leisure: Culture and Communication in Israel.* Cambridge: Harvard University Press, 1976.

Kayser, Jacques. *One Week's News: Comparative Study of 17 Major Dailies for a Seven-Day Period.* Paris: Unesco, 1953.

Kesterton, Wilfred H. *A History of Journalism in Canada.* Toronto: McCleland and Stewart, 1976.

La Prensa, editors of. *Defense of Freedom.* New York: John Day Co., 1952.

Leifer, Walter, et al. *Man and the Press.* Munich: Max Hueber Verlag, 1970.

Lekovic, Zdravko and Mihalo Bjelica. *Communication Policies in Yugoslavia.* Paris: Unesco, 1976.

Lent, John A. *The Asian Newspapers' Reluctant Revolution.* Ames: The Iowa State University Press, 1971.

————. *Third World Mass Media and Their Search for Modernity.* Lewisburg: Bucknell University Press, 1977.

Levine, Irving R. *Main Street: Italy.* New York: Doubleday, 1963.

Magnusson, Magnus, et al. *The Glorious Privilege: The History of The Scotsman.* London: Thomas Nelson and Sons, 1967.

Markham, James W. *Voices of the Red Giants.* Ames: Iowa State University Press, 1967.

Matthews, T. S. *The Sugar Pill: An Eassay on Newspapers.* London: Victor Gollancz, Ltd., 1958.

Mayer, Henry. *The Press in Australia.* Melbourne: Lansdowne Press, 1968.

McKay, Ron and Brian Barr. *The Story of the Scottish Daily News.* Edinburgh: Cannongate, 1976.

Merrill, John C. *The Elite Press: Great Newspapers of the World.* New York: Pitman Publishing Corp., 1968.

————. *The Imperative of Freedom.* New York: Hastings House, Publishers, 1974.

Merrill, J. C., C. Bryan, and M. Alisky. *The Foreign Press.* Baton Rouge, LSU Press, 1970.

Mills, William H. *The Manchester Guardian: A Century of History.* London: Chatto and Windus, 1921.

Le Monde. Paris: Le Monde, 1977.

Mori, Arturo. *La Prensa Española de Nuestro Tiempo.* Mexico City: Ediciones Mensaje, 1943.

Murthy, Nadig Krishna. *Indian Journalism.* Mysore: "Prasaranga" of the University of Mysore, 1966.

Nayar, Kuldip. *The Judgement: Inside Story of the Emergency in India.* New Delhi: Vikas Publishing House, Ltd., 1977.

Neue Zürcher Zeitung und Schweigerisches Handelsblatt. Zurich: Neue Zürcher Zeitung, 1975.

The Newspaper in Society: A Short History of 'The Age'. Melbourne: The Age, n.d.

The New York Times Company: 1977 Financial Report. New York: The New York Times Company, 1977.

Olson, Kenneth E. *The History Makers: The Press in Europe from Its Beginnings Through 1965*. Baton Rouge: LSU Press, 1966.

Pool, Ithiel de Sola. *The Influence of International Communication on Development*. Cambridge: MIT, 1976.

——. *The "Prestige Papers": A Survey of Their Editorials*. Palo Alto: Stanford University Press, 1952.

Potter, Elaine. *The Press as Opposition: The Political Role of South African Newspapers*. Totowa, N.J.: Rowman & Littlefield, 1975.

Publishing in Africa in the Seventies. Ife Ife, Nigeria: University of Nigeria, 1975.

Rammelkamp, J. S. *Pulitzer's Post-Dispatch 1878–1883*. Princeton: Princeton University Press, 1967.

Read, William H. *Rethinking International Communication*. Cambridge: Harvard University Press, 1978.

Redaktionsstatut für die Süddeutsche Zeitung. Munich: Süddeutscher Verlag GMBH, 1971.

Remembered Joys. Washington, D.C.: The Washington Post Co., 1977.

Roberts, Chalmers M. *The Washington Post: The First 100 Years*. Boston: Houghton Mifflin Co., 1977.

Robinson, Gertrude Joch. *Tito's Maverick Media: The Politics of Mass Communications in Yugoslavia*. Urbana: University of Illinois Press, 1977.

Roett, Riordan. *Brazil: Politics in a Patrimonial Society*. New York: Praeger, 1978.

Ruben, Bent D. *Communication Yearbook*. New Brunswick, N.J.: Transaction Books, 1977.

Rogers, Everett M., ed. *Communication and Development: Critical Perspectives*. Beverly Hills: Sage, 1976.

Sandford, John. *The Mass Media of the German-Speaking Countries*. London: Oswald Wolff Publishers, Ltd., 1976.

Sanoma Publishing Company. Helsinki: Sanoma Publishing Co., 1976.

Schiller, Herbert I. *Communication and Cultural Domination*. White Plains, N.Y.: International Arts and Sciences Press, 1976.

Schmitter, Philippe C. *Interest Conflict and Political Change in Brazil*. Stanford: Stanford University Press, 1971.

Schramm, Wilbur. *Big Media, Little Media: Tools and Technologies for Institutions*. Beverly Hills: Sage, 1977.

—— *One Day in the World's Press*. Palo Alto: Stanford University Press, 1959.

Schulte, Henry F. *The Spanish Press 1470–1966*. Urbana: University of Illinois Press, 1968.

The Scotsman, 1817–1955: Scotland's National Newspaper. Edinburgh: The Scotsman Publications, Ltd., 1955.

Sharkey, Don. *White Smoke Over the Vatican*. Milwaukee: Bureau Publishing Co., 1943.

Signitzer, Benno, et al. *Massenmedien in Österreich*. Vienna: Internationale Publikationen Gesellschaft, 1977.

Singer, Benjamin D., ed. *Communication in Candian Society*. Toronto: Copp Clark, 1975.

Sitaram, K. S. and R. T. Cogell. *Foundations of Intercultural Communication*. Columbus, Ohio: Charles E. Merrill, 1976.

Smiley, Nixon. *Knights of the Fourth Estate: The Story of The Mimi Herald*. Miami: E. A. Seemann Pub. Co., 1974.

Smith, Anthony. *The British Press Since the War*. Plymouth: Latimer Trend & Co., Ltd., 1974.

Sommerlad, E. Lloyd. *National Communications Systems: Some Policy Issues and Options*. Paris: Unesco, 1975.

Sterling, Christopher and Timothy Haight. *The Mass Media: Aspen Institute Guide to Communications Industry Trends.* Aspen Institute, Colo., 1978.

The Story of the St. Louis Post-Dispatch. St. Louis: The Pulitzer Pub. Co., 1973.

Study of the International News Content of the Domestic Media of Mainland China. Washington, D.C.: USIA Office of Research, 1977.

Sussman, Leonard D. *Mass Media and The Third World Challenge.* Beverly Hills: Sage, 1977.

Thorsen, Svend. *Newspapers in Denmark.* Copenhagen: Det Danske Selskab, 1953.

The Times Organisation and the Daily Best Seller. Singapore: Times Publishing Co., 1978. (about *The Straits Times*)

Turnstall, Jeremy. *The Media are American: Anglo-American Media in the World.* New York: Columbia University Press, 1977.

Vaticana e Roma Cristiana. Vitican City: Typografia Poliglotta Vaticana, 1975.

Washington Post Company Annual Report: 1976. Washington, D.C.: The Washington Post Co., 1976.

Wells, Alan, ed. *Mass Communications: a World View.* Palo Alto: National Press Books, 1974.

Wilcox, Dennis. *Mass Media in Black Africa: Philosophy and Control.* New York: Praeger, 1975.

Wiskermann, Elizabeth. *A Great Swiss Newspaper.* London: Oxford University Press, 1959. (about the *Neue Zürcher Zeitung*)

Wolseley, Roland. *Journalism in Modern India.* New York: Asia Publishing House, 1964.

World-Famous Newspaper and its Publishers. Munich: Süeddeutscher Verlag, GMBH, 1972.

Year of Scandal: How the 'Washington Post' Covered Watergate and the Agnew Crisis. Washington, D.C. The Washington Post Co., 1973.

Index